Organization

NATIONAL UNIVERSITY
LIBRARY   SAN DIEGO

**Edited by
Arndt Sorge**

THOMSON
™
LEARNING

Australia • Canada • Mexico • Singapore • Spain • United Kingdom • United States

Organization

Copyright © Thomson Learning 2002

The Thomson Learning logo is a registered trademark used herein under licence.

For more information, contact Thomson Learning, Berkshire House, 168–173 High Holborn, London, WC1V 7AA or visit us on the World Wide Web at: http://www.thomsonlearning.co.uk

British Library Cataloguing-in-Publication Data
A catalogue record for this book is available from the British Library

ISBN 1-86152-627-X

Typeset by HWA Text and Data Management, Tunbridge Wells

Printed in Great Britain by TJ International, Padstow, Cornwall

Contents

Contents

Preface

It is much easier to write novels or poetry alone, whilst composing more comprehensive academic texts invariably requires comradeship, collegiality and at times friendship. In this sense, the value of the present volume, for what it is worth, is very much due to the authors and the understanding they brought about for this project. Next to them, I am particularly indebted to Maggie Smith, formerly of Thomson Learning, for giving the book and the underlying format the space it now has. So-Shan Au, also of Thomson, has become a collegial companion with great dedication, reliability and a penchant for keeping out of mischief through hard work. She had let it be known that penguins (not the publisher of that name!) are her favourites, which is why we show them on the cover. But there is also a substantive reason which is explained in the first chapter. The book would not have come about without the collegial friendship with Malcolm Warner, editor-in-chief of the *International Encyclopedia of Business Management* (IEBM), over twenty-five years.

Beyond the more personal collegiality, publishing efforts and services in Thomson linked to the IEBM, out of which this book also emerged, have generally been a model of efficiency, for which I am indebted to everyone in Thomson. Last but not least, the many students I had to teach in universities or business schools in five countries, have exerted invisible control over this volume, as a community which one is trying to serve.

Arndt Sorge
October 2001

List of contributors

Professor David M. Boje
Professor of Management
College of Business Administration
and Economics
New Mexico State University
USA

Professor Gibson Burrell
Industrial Relations and Organization
Behaviour Group
Warwick Business School
University of Warwick
Coventry, England

Professor Dr André Büssing
Chair of Psychology
Technical University of München
Munich, Germany

Professor Richard Butler
Management Centre
University of Bradford
England

Professor John Child
International Management and
Organization
Birmingham Business School
University of Birmingham
England

Professor Peter A. Clark
Professor of Organizational
Management
Birmingham Business School
University of Birmingham
England

Professor Stewart R. Clegg
Professor of Management
University of Technology, Sydney
Australia

Professsor Barbara Czarniawska
Professor of Management
Gothenburg Research Institute
Gothenburg University
Sweden

Kevin Dooley
Departments of Industrial
Engineering & Management
Arizona State University
USA

Professor Dr Diether Gebert
Technische Universität Berlin
Germany

Professor Silvia Gherardi
Department of Sociology and Social
Research
University of Trento, Italy

Dr Jacques Girin
Centre National de la Recherche
Scientifique
École Polytechnic
Paris, France

Samantha K. Graff
Graduate School of Business
Administration
Harvard University
Boston, Massachusetts, USA

Professor Anna Grandori
Universita di Modena and Universita
Bocconi, Milano
Italy

Dr Armand Hatchuel
Professor of Industrial Management
École des Mines de Paris
France

Dr Frank Heller
The Tavistock Institute
London, England

Professor Dr Friso den Hertog
Professor of Innovation Management
Maastricht Economic Research Insti-
tute on Innovation and Technology
University of Maastricht
The Netherlands

Professor Dr Geert Hofstede
Senior Research Associate
Institute for Research on Intercultural
Cooperation (IRIC)
Maastricht and Tilburg
The Netherlands
and Professor Emeritus
University of Maastricht
The Netherlands

Benoit Journé
Université de Nantes
France

Professor Kenneth Laudon
Leonard N. Stern School of Business
New York University
USA

Professor Jay W. Lorsch
Senior Associate Dean for Executive
Education
Louis E. Kirstein Professor of Human
Relations
Graduate School of Business
Administration, Harvard University
Boston, Massachusetts, USA

Professor Ray Loveridge
Leverhulme Research Fellow
Saïd Business School
University of Oxford
England

Professor Arndt Sorge
Professor of Organization Structuring
University of Groningen
The Netherlands

Professor William H. Starbuck
Leonard N. Stern School of Business
New York University, USA

Professor Dr Jörg Sydow
Professor of Business Administration
Institut für Allgemeine
Betriebswirtschaftslehre
Freie Universität Berlin
Germany

Thera Tolner
Research Fellow
Maastricht Economic Research Insti-
tute on Innovation and Technology
University of Maastricht
The Netherlands

Dr Cas Vroom
University of Maastricht
The Netherlands

Professor Richard D. Whitley
Professor of Organizational
Sociology
Manchester Business School
England

Professor Arjen van Witteloostuijn
Faculty of Economics
University of Groningen
The Netherlands

Professor Rolf Ziegler
Institute of Sociology
Ludwig-Maximilians-Universität
München
Munich, Germany

Introduction

'Organization' is a fundamental subject in business or management studies, in economics and social sciences, and also in engineering, social work or similar applied studies. In a world encumbered with increasing complexity and uncertainty, 'organizing' – as a practice – and Organization, as a body of knowledge, to some extent help to increase this complexity and uncertainty. But their ambition and ethos are different. They strive to help conceptualize manageable solutions on the basis of a more systematic knowledge, which reflects a realistic understanding of human nature and social, economic and technical matters. Properly understood, organizing people and the things they are concerned with, is a key to addressing burdensome complexity and uncertainty. Organization does not pretend to have well understood solutions to all our problems. But it unpretentiously claims to have viable indirect solutions to many of our problems. Such indirect solutions imply that you will do a better job when you organize the inter-relations of people, tasks and tools in such a way that knowledge is unearthed or found when it appeared to be absent, motivation arises where it seemed deficient, and co-operation comes about between self-interested actors.

The present book is certainly not an introductory text for beginners. Further Readings at the end of chapter 1 indicate which texts are more suitable for that, notably the eminent textbook by Richard Daft (*Organization Theory and Design*, South Western College 2001). The present volume is intended to help students at an intermediate level enter into specific areas of organization studies and sciences. It may also be used in conjunction with a good basic textbook. It helps curious students switch from the neat and glossy treatment of many textbooks, rich with tidy and colourful diagrams and slides, nice pictures, clear-cut cases and unambiguous recommendations, to a posture which is more mature. In an uncertain and complex world, the self-assurance and certainty that many textbooks exude or bring about is childish. It is therefore not something inherently bad, but something one should go beyond.

But what is the alternative? Where to turn to? At the other end of the spectrum, we have highly intellectualized treatments of the field. These tend to abandon any self-assurance and conviction within the larger field of Organization. They confer on them competing approaches, strands of research and theorizing, that have manifested and established themselves. In this way, self-assurance is exuded by each competing individual approach. Such treatments are adored by scholars and they may be highly fruitful for very specialized or slightly esoteric research purposes. Their draw-back is that Organization tends to evaporate, as a coherent body of knowledge, being decomposed as it is into an unending array of many conflicting perspectives or approaches, each of them mainly locked into self-explanation and self-inspection. It is not the intention of this book to compete on this terrain. For the opposite of childishness, at the other end of the spectrum, is not maturity but senility.

Maturity is probably somewhere in the middle, where Organization is posited as a subject which blends the substantive coherence (of basic texts) with the pluralism of different approaches (in sophisticated handbooks). Such a collection is therefore a precarious and difficult balance. But it has to be tried out, and this is what the present volume did. It tries to instil the attitude that any useful organization knowledge requires judicious blending and critical treatment of available theory. Handled in this way, theory will prove to be of more lasting value than any of the most recent management hypes at whichever point in time.

The contributions in this book were written by well-known authors, initially for the *International Encyclopedia of Business and Management* (London: Thomson Learning), in precisely this spirit. Their selection and combination is to ensure that students with a good grounding (such as having worked through Daft) can on this basis advance into the core specialities of Organization. These can be defined along some some main divisions of the Academy of Management, as the largest world-wide association in our field: Organization and Management Theory, Organizational Behaviour, Organization Development and Change, Managerial and Organizational Cognition, and Organizational Communication and Information Systems. The first two divisions are also those from which all the others more or less emerged. Whilst for more specific courses more specialized literature would be called for, the present volume seeks to maintain the coherence of the larger field and prevent the reader from losing sight of the wood, with all these trees standing about. This, after all, should be one of the main concerns of both the mature theorist and the mature practitioner. For without a sense of coherence, organization turns into disorganization. But those interested in more specific articles and keywords are also invited to consult any edition of the *International Encyclopedia of Business and Management* or its many spin-off products.

The overall structure of this book is to introduce, first, the traditional core concepts and epistomological foundations of organization theory. Then comes a second part to set the organizational scene within the wider landscape of institutions and factors that matter for organizing. The third part enters right into organizational life, to deal with its elementary processes, structuring and tools. The fourth part extends this by going into the human and social foundations of organizing and organized action. The fifth part digs deeper into the organizational microcosm, bringing in acting individuals and small groups. The sixth part returns to broader perspectives, explaining main concepts of organization change and development, as well as the implications of what most people expect from organizations: specific sorts of performance.

Arndt Sorge
Groningen, The Netherlands, October 2001

Fundamentals and the organizational core

Organization

Arndt Sorge

Overview

This entry provides conceptual and methodological pointers and a guide through the field of organization. It is an extremely complex and broad-ranging area, and there are references to other organization entries and an attempt to show how they all fit into a larger concept.

Organization has to be seen as both a practical and an academic field. A discipline in itself, it is also a cross-disciplinary endeavour. Essentially the word 'organization' has two different meanings: one refers to a particular social collectivity and the other to organizational properties of collectivities. The field of organization is subdivided into specialist topics according to various criteria. The main ones are: the level of aggregation and analysis; specific aspects of organizational life; goal-, product- or service-related specificities; criteria of performance in organizational domains; particular approaches to theory-building; synchronic or diachronic perspectives.

Subdivisions cannot be broken up into separate compartments. A satisfactory treatment of one specific topic usually requires reference to other fields. This requirement can be described by reciprocal 'predication', whereby a specific organizational insight emerges on the basis of different insights from other sub-fields.

Despite the co-existence of different theoretical and research traditions, a coherent body of organization theory can be summarized. Dominant explanatory factors are utilitarian, culturalist and institutionalist approaches. There are also different types of theory distinguished by their epistemological foundations: nomothetic, idiographic and dialectic approaches. Such approaches compete with one another, but they can also be intertwined. Academic advance and innovation in organization proceeds through the mutual competition and cross-fertilization of distinct approaches. It can be argued that more satisfactory accounts and explanations result when students are competent in different approaches and in combining these to create new fields.

This is also the basis for an effective cross-fertilization between theory, research and practice. A pragmatic, undogmatic handling of theoretical approaches leads to more useful practical recipes, and organization theory and research thrive where practical organizational experience is systematically integrated into a more properly academic treatment.

1 The differing meanings of organization

Although most people think that they have an idea of what 'organization' means, in the more rigorous field of scientific terminology things are much less simple (Morgan 1986). Essentially the word is used in two different ways which must be carefully distinguished. The distinction is important in order to understand further notions and propositions of organization theory. Also, it is important to distinguish the more scholarly usage of 'organization' (in its two meanings) from the more everyday usage. For instance, in shops you may see a notice which reads: 'Closed during reorganization'. You are likely to see that the shop is empty, that there are ladders standing about and workmen painting the walls and the ceiling or doing the floor. Evidently the shop owners have used the term 're-organization' to glorify the more mundane activities of redecoration. Similarly, people say that they have to 'get organized', which means they want to have more order in their working or private life.

Likewise, natural scientists have become accustomed to discussing the organization of things like molecular structures. This is not so far removed in meaning from the shop being reorganized, and it is arguably further from the meanings of the word that are implied here because human action is more visible in the shop than in most molecular structures. However, they obviously have something in common because they are all metaphorically related to each other, metaphorical relations making the understanding of meanings much easier. But metaphor is also a danger because it can make meanings exchangeable which, under rigorous scrutiny, should not be so.

The first meaning of organization, within the body of theory and findings covered here, is a particular *social unit* or *collectivity*. Not all social units and collectivities are organizations; neither a tribe, nor a family, nor a complete society can be depicted as such. What defines an organization in this particular sense will be discussed below but, for the moment, it is important to remember that organizations are social units which can be demarcated on the basis of the people who belong to them. Thus, with this approach organizations may include the Methodist Church, a multinational enterprise, a local construction firm, a hospital and a tank battalion.

The second meaning of the word refers to *organizational properties*, both structures and processes, within a social unit or collectivity. Units and collectivities are, in this sense, 'organized' in specific ways. They have types of management, authority relationships, numbers of supervisors per worker, definitions of rights and obligations, modes of decision making and other aspects which are used to characterize them.

An organization in the first sense – a social collectivity – not only is an organization but also has an organization in the second sense. This is not sophistry. The literature discusses organizational properties of collectivities which are not typified as organizations. For example, complete societies are described as organized in particular ways; but, although they have organizational properties, they are not in themselves organizations! For the purposes here, however, we will largely disregard the organization of entities that are not organizations. This is something for the wider disciplines of sociology and social anthropology. Here, it is crucial to be precise: the organization as a collectivity or the organizational properties which it has.

The difference between the two meanings is best realized when we acknowledge that organizations (in the first sense) not only have organizational properties but many other things in addition. They have goals: specific targets towards which action in the organization is orientated. The Methodist Church aims at the spiritual and religious well-being of people that belong to the Church; a multinational enterprise like General Motors has as its goal the manufacture of cars; a construction firm aims to build houses; a hospital has the aim of curing people of illnesses; and a tank battalion has the goal of exerting physical force and violence against enemies, with the aid of battle tanks. Organizational goals immediately imply specific products such as motor cars, but products can also be services, including church services, medical treatment and military services.

The picture on the cover of this book leads to the question: Are grouped penguins, or penguin societies, organizations? The straight answer, on the basis of this definition of organizations as implying functionally specific goals and involvement of members, would be an unqualified no. As far as we know, or we think we know, pengiuns do form societies and have intricate group and team patterns, but they do not appear to involve members of groups in functionally specific activities on a stable basis, diffentiating between marital and working life and between occupations or professions. On a second thought, they just might qualify for what Scott (1981) called 'open systems', i.e. organized functionally specific entities with fluctuating and temporal attachment of members. Furthermore, it is perfectly sensible to discuss the organizational properties of penguin societies and groupings as truly organizational variables or constructs. And it may very well be that we can learn a lot from the way that penguins organize themselves in their groups. It is not beneath human dignity to learn from animals; a friend who used to be an engineer once said that engineers can learn from anything for their job of constructing machines or whatever, including 'the way monkeys peel bananas in Penang'. Despite all this, penguin groupings are for the greater part not what we call organizational collectivities. Still, they do deserve to be put on the cover, following the suggestion of So-Shan Au of our publishers, as a challenge to our received wisdom and understanding.

Organizations – as collectivities – also have techniques, technologies, physical capital (buildings, machines, offices), knowledge and strategies to achieve their goals. Whereas the techniques and technologies of a motor manufacturer consist of things such as transfer lines, robots and metal-working machines, the technique of a church includes sermons, prayer, singing, confession, holy communion and group meetings. The technique of the tank battalion is rooted in the design and operating principles of battle tanks. There are also specific techniques for accounting and control, such as double-entry book-keeping, budgeting systems, hospital management systems, military administration, tactics, strategy and command principles. Furthermore, organizations make use of typical inputs like human resources, raw materials and information to achieve their goals. Having members that help to achieve these goals, organization size is also a feature – members are necessary to help attain goals, thus numbers are important. Then there are the stakeholders, with a more or less controlling interest in the organization. These include shareholders, governments, employees and public action groups.

Such properties can be extremely important, although they are not necessarily counted as part of the organizational properties of the collectivity. In organization theory, they are grouped under the notion of *organizational context*. In terms of our two notions of organization, context embraces precisely those properties of the organization (the collectivity) which are not properly organizational, i.e. which do not directly include organization structures and processes. Context is, at least in part, integral to the organization, situated on the side of the fence which separates everything that belongs to the organization from that which does not belong to it. In this sense all assets and liabilities – whether financial, human or technical – stakeholder structures and organization size are the central ingredients of the context of an organization.

Human resources and personnel management practices naturally are very important elements of the organizational context. The skills and knowledge of employees, their professional competence, posture and attitudes, their obligations, performance and aspirations, the socialization and career they follow in an organization and beyond, and the employment relation and industrial relations in which they are engaged, are all very much related to organizational structures and practices. Hence, the relations between human resource theory and research and organization have been intense, and there has been substantial overlap between these fields. Organizational phenomena usually can only be explained if human resources are included in the explanation, and vice versa.

Organizational environment is also important. This lies outside the organization itself, situated on the opposite side of the fence to context. It includes banks and financial institutions, and all kinds of other organizations (suppliers, clients, governmental authorities, industrial federations, trade unions) and persons. For the Methodist Church it would include other Christian denominations, agnostics, Jews, Muslims, Buddhists and other spiritual world views, depending on the country in which it is situated. For the tank battalion it would include all other units and levels of command in the army and, of course, enemy and allied forces, plus the local environment in which it is located. The environment of General Motors meanwhile includes all competitors, clients and suppliers, plus many institutions that provide it with all kinds of personnel, regulations and information.

It is customary to make a distinction between the *task environment* and the *general environment*. The task environment relates to everything that bears on the immediate achievement of the organizational goal, for example state-of-the-art technology, competitors, market structures, sales networks and sources of finance. The general environment, however, is less specific with regard to the task or goal of the organization; it includes the law of the land, general governmental policies, public attitudes, education systems, political affairs, social stratification and everything else which may indirectly affect organizational life. For instance, national holidays have been instituted without a direct regard for what they imply for a motor car manufacturer but they do affect its operations in that they are part of a general scheme to structure the rhythm and pace of working activities in the society at large.

Human resources are also a powerful environmental factor. They have to be apprehended as governed by societally specific institutions, disposition, preferences, values and other endowments. As such, they cannot simply be governed by enterprise personnel management, or even top management for that matter. Societally specific types of socialization into roles, careers, labour markets and occupations are interdependent with organizational structures and practices. This interdependence very much gives organizing a societal, and therefore also environmental, flavour.

The difference between contexts and environments is better understood if the difference between the two meanings of organization is borne in mind. Contexts are located on the inside of organizations as collectivities, or on their boundaries, but outside the ambit of organizational properties. Environments, however, are located outside the organization as a collectivity.

The essence of organization theories lies primarily in the relationships between organization structures and processes on the one hand and contexts and environments on the other. Certain structures and processes thrive in specific contexts and environments, and others in different ones. Specifically, well-matched contexts, environments and organizational properties are often considered to be a prime condition of success (Mintzberg 1983). The selection of specific contexts and environments basically constitutes an enterprise *strategy*.

Whether you reduce or increase the size of an organization appreciably, or change its products, technology or controlling interests (contextual changes), or enter new markets, or create subsidiaries elsewhere (environmental changes), you do in most of these cases make strategic moves. To a large extent, the literature on strategy is an outgrowth of the organizational literature. Basically, strategy making and implementation has come to be identified as the central link between the organization, its organizational properties and contexts and environments.

After these clarifications, it is easier to explain what is particular about organizations and what distinguishes them from entities like families and complete societies. First, organizations, as collectivities, have reasonably clear boundaries; one can distinguish non-members from members and things within the domain of the organization from those without. They distinguish internal forms of capital, machines, buildings, information and types of behaviour from external forms. Where blurred boundaries occur, as in the 'open systems' mentioned by Scott (1981: 22–3), it may be that the membership role is poorly defined: membership fluctuates and it is not always clear which types of behaviour belong within the organizational domain. Civic action groups are an example of this.

Nevertheless, where boundaries are drawn too generously, there is a strong sensitivity. Members of such characteristically open and ambiguous organizations do not mind the openness as long as the organization does not encroach on the rest of their life. In modern societies with pluralist political systems, most of the time and with regard to most of their members, organizations only care about what happens inside their domain. They do not care about their members' leisure, family life and political persuasion. However, the contrary may apply in societies with pre-modern or totalitarian patterns.

Sensitivity with regard to organizational boundaries is related to another characteristic of modern organizations: their goals and purposes. The domain that is defined in this way usually is specific rather than encompassing. Neither an employee of General Motors, nor a minister in the Methodist Church, nor a nurse in a hospital, nor a corporal in a tank battalion has to ask their superior's permission before marrying, for example. In past centuries, however, the contrary was evident in most societies. On the other hand, many organizations do provide marriage counselling, help against drug abuse, kindergartens, sporting or other facilities that are not directly related to the organization's goal. Asian firms are often styled as 'family firms'. Yet, even there, when the employee is encouraged to consider the firm as a type of family and relations at work are very much personalized, it is still true that working life is separated from private life, maybe precisely because the family acts as a cushion for the demands of working life.

Where enterprises, or armies or hospitals, in whichever modern society, take on wider responsibilities, these are usually organized in functionally specific forms. Counselling in the case of alcohol abuse is offered by specialized social workers rather than supervisors regardless of whether it is offered by the firm or the community. Childcare is provided by a kindergarten rather than directly in the office or the factory, and so on. The fact that something is organized overwhelmingly implies that it is imposed on functions and people that become specialized through the very act of organizing. Of course, not everything happens in organizations in the societies we live in, but a very great deal does. Sometimes organizations imply a more encompassing, rather than specific, involvement. Owner-manager families, for example, may be involved in the enterprise to such an extent that the difference between working and family life is minimal. Religious ministers' and battalion commanders' partners are often still expected to furnish services for the community or the battalion free of charge. The social closure of some milieux often goes against the grain of modern organization.

The clear demarcation of an organizational domain is linked to the definition of membership in organizations. This is embodied in personnel rosters, identity cards or similar documents. Members are all those who are officially acknowledged as employed or who are contributing towards the purpose of the organization. Clubs have members that are not employed, but most of the time members contribute work for a wage and are involved in the labour process. Hospitals and educational institutions have patients or students who are not members but are part of the 'throughput', which is 'processed' to become more healthy, sane or educated, and who leave the organization as a 'product'. Likewise, inmates in prisons should not be counted as members but as throughput and final products, leaving the organization equipped with improved civic virtues or criminal skills.

(The latter illustrates that the declared goal of an organization may radically diverge from its factual, or latent, result.)

Our notion of modern organization is very much an 'ideal type' which is found in reality to a limited extent. The partners of many managers, ministers of religion, military officers, or nurses and doctors, may become jealous of the organizational involvement of the partner. Companies may examine the private life of managers before giving them promotion or a foreign posting. Unsupportive partners are often considered a career obstacle. Methodist ministers with changing sexual partners arouse conflict in most church communities. But note that such conflict is overwhelmingly due to the expectation that some people ought to define a specific organizational goal as their central interest in life. Even where there are strong drives to accommodate non-work roles in the organization, there are also strong drives to eliminate sexual harassment and preferential treatment. Watchdogs are increasingly appointed to counteract such tendencies which were the rule in pre-modern or early modern enterprises or other institutions.

As an ideal, but also in reality, organizations have specific goals, members that help achieve them and are most of the time only partially involved, and a reasonably clear demarcation of their own physical, human and financial resources. Specificity of goals is linked to the deployment of overt, visible and formalized organization structures, all of which are linked to the spread of rationality. In principle, rational organization is only possible where a goal is clearly and specifically defined, and other goals are, within the organizational domain, subordinated to it or relegated to other organizations or to other spheres of life. There are, of course, different types of organizations.

Scott (1981) has conceptualized organizations as implying three kinds of systemic properties. Systems are, generally speaking, integrated sets of elements that are both differentiated and linked by strong interrelationships. They are, therefore, reasonably complex internally and demarcated from their environment. But they also sustain themselves through the interrelationships which they have with their environment. Systems are found in nature, technology and human life. There are economic, social and political systems. In organizational life, specific and stable goals imply 'rational systems'; specific and shifting or changeable goals imply 'natural systems'; ambiguous goals and membership involvement imply 'open systems'. These tend to have different sets of organization structures and processes.

2 Characteristics of organization

Let us now turn to organization as an academic subject and a field of study. This mainly consists of organization structuring and behaviour of the people in organizations. Behaviour includes mental behaviour, such as thinking, feeling or imagining.

Organization looks at the following manifestations of behaviour:

- the mental attitudes, values, preferences and inclinations of individuals;

- the behaviour of individuals in the way they handle physical objects, information and social encounters;
- groups, teams and other face-to-face groupings such as cliques of friends;
- organized units such as departments, divisions, firms or larger concerns;
- networks of sets of organizations;
- organizational contexts and environments, for example, the evolution of technology, markets, competition, governmental regulation, etc.

We cannot simply reduce organization phenomena to individual human behaviour. The outcome of conflict between individuals in organizations, for example, may be decided by distributions of power, information or other resources, or by contextual or environmental structures. Such factors are not reducible to individual behaviour. They refer to arrangements and processes at a supra-individual level which may, naturally, have implications at the level of individuals. To some extent seemingly objective arrangements or distributions depend on subjective and inter-subjective 'enactment'. But even in this case individual behaviour implies structures at supra-individual levels (Giddens 1986).

Organization as an academic field came into existence in the beginning of the 1960s when several sub-disciplines that were relevant for the explanation of what happens in and between organizations and between organizations and their contexts and environments were grouped together. A historical treatment of the field makes it abundantly clear that organization has been derived from disciplines such as industrial engineering, the sociology of work and organization, social psychology, business studies, administrative science and law. In addition, some of these disciplines have arisen in different forms under specific national constellations. The resulting complexity of organization as an international field is daunting. Some pioneers, who are defined more by their practical experience and autodidactic insights, are hard to slot into an academic discipline.

Using this historical approach, the subject unusually appears as cross-, trans- or multidisciplinary. It is marked by human and social sciences, engineering, economics, business studies and law, all wrapped into one. Such a basis makes one wonder whether it is at all possible to provide a fairly coherent treatment of the field. The answer is 'yes', despite many impressions to the contrary. Conceptually, and in comparison to most other specialities in human and social sciences, organization is probably one of the most integrated subjects, having a strong empirical foundation. This was probably helped by the fact that pioneers of the field, such as Max Weber, Henri Fayol, Frederick W. Taylor and Chester Barnard, or of the sociotechnical school, such as Fred Emery, Eric Trist, E.J. Miller and A.K. Rice, were very keen systematizers (Pugh and Hickson 1989: 210–17). In addition, the orientation of the problem and the focus which this provided helped to erase the disciplinary differences which earlier academic training and specialization tended to bring about. The writings of Hofstede, Mintzberg (1983), Tannenbaum or Heller, for example, do not suggest immediately that they are engineers by training and, in part, job experience.

As might be expected in any field that is concerned with evolving, living and – worst of all – human phenomena, there is no absence of controversy and conflicting approaches. Organization is certainly under tension from the pull that is being exerted in different directions. Yet there is increasing agreement regarding the legitimacy of some countervailing forces and conceptual differences. The subject has moved beyond the point where proponents of countervailing approaches have thought it desirable to attack the opposition.

Organization is a subject which branches out in many different directions. On the one hand, through its psychological and sociological foundations, it is keen to explain organizational phenomena, as is any other 'basic' discipline. As such, it is concerned with the way in which the organizational world actually is, rather than the way it ought to be. On the other hand, the subject is, through inspiration both from practising engineers and managers and from humanistically concerned scholars, decidedly normative, or keen to pronounce on the way organization ought to be fashioned and improved. However, criteria for evaluating what is best or better may differ. Efficiency, effectiveness, profits, added value, market growth, employee satisfaction and use and development of human capacities (personal growth) are all used in different combinations and accentuations. Add to this the differences between organization paradigms, and the result is a fairly complex set of approaches.

The way such different approaches relate to each other, and the ways in which they may even be intertwined despite conceptual differences, is now understood better and may be debated without acrimony. Despite the differences which will always exist between scholarly theory and everyday practice, it is fair to say that a good level of applicability of theory has been maintained despite the increasing academicization. This conflicts with the image that is frequently projected by many practitioners. Businessmen scoffed for decades at concepts like work in groups and job enrichment until they started to be sold by consultants under a new trend called 'lean production'. They earlier derided discussion of organization culture, but adopted the theories when consultants started selling 'organizational excellence'.

It is a frequent experience in the history of organization that practitioners may be particularly gullible victims of organizational fashions, to the extent that they have not previously read or understood sound organization theory and research. For instance, the enthusiasm about 'excellent organizations' largely meant that people had not bothered to grasp and apply standard organization concepts which had been known for up to thirty years. To learn from this experience requires a continuous two-way dialogue between theory/research and practice.

3 Subdivisions of organization

The overall field of organization is often broken down into two parts: organization theory and organization. The latter refers to the behaviour of people in organizations. Organization theory refers to theory and findings about the behaviour of complete organizations. This distinction indicates that the level of analysis can be used to subdivide the whole field. Theories and findings can be specialized according to the analytical level, which is a level of aggregation. Throughout organizational life there is this vertical dimension which stretches from the single individual to aggregations of complete organizations. Somewhere in the middle we have what is called the 'focal organization': a more or less self-contained organized unit with a reasonable measure of autonomy and a collective identity which makes it a primary reference point for all its members.

To give an example, a tank battalion, a medium-sized owner-managed firm or a local hospital may be salient focal organizations. Their members may conceive themselves, in the first instance, as belonging to this unit, and they will expect the unit to maintain its identity, boundaries and autonomy in the face of its environment. The matter is much less clear in the case of a larger concern like General Motors. This larger industrial group has big local sub-organizations in countries outside the USA, such as Vauxhall in the UK and Opel in Germany. The latter operate under their own company and brand names and have different plants with individual identities. These are all tied into the international group via a complex hierarchy of subdivisions. In this case there is no immediately visible focal organization. There are competing sets of boundaries and identities in the shape of the brand name, the locality or a national subsidiary. The larger an organization is, the more there is a tendency for the focal organization to be blurred.

Sometimes management tries to shift the focus and identity of organizations. It may try to get hospitals to see themselves as more independent and responsible, rather than as dependent units of a larger health service (a tendency which can be seen in Europe). Or it may try to unite the identities of car workers in the bigger concern, by emphasizing the 'GM' label next to divisional (Oldsmobile, Chevrolet, etc.) and subsidiary (Vauxhall, Opel) labels. Sometimes both tendencies occur parallel with one other. Military forces in many countries have seen a proliferation of unit or service badges, berets, caps, etc., after the onslaught of standardization of rules and dress. This adds to the difficulty of defining empirically exactly what is the focal organization identity.

In many cases it is better to speak of complex sets of organizations that are hierarchically and laterally intertwined (Aldrich and Whetten 1981). In such an arrangement most organizational units have different measures of autonomy, self-containment and a collective sense of identity. A discussion of the vertical or hierarchical dimensions of such organizational sets helps to demonstrate the implications of such interlocking for organization analysis.

At the lowest level, that of the working individual, we find that organization is the study and explanation of work attitudes, motivation and satisfaction, cognition or perception in work roles and beyond. To some extent individuals bring such properties with them when entering the organization, but they also evolve with the experience of working in, or contributing to, the organization. Individual factors interact with the situation in which individuals find themselves, in which they become socialized and try to adapt the situation to suit personal tastes and requirements. Matching individual and work context is one of the primary concerns of personnel/human resource management.

The next analytical level is that of face-to-face groups. In groups and teams organization members meet, cooperate, quarrel and build personal friendships or allegiances. They have a dynamic of their own and evolve properties that are not simply the average of individual properties. Individuals influence group and team life but they themselves also become modified by the dynamics that develop in face-to-face groupings. Groups and teams are central ingredients in the coordination and control of organization processes. They are important both in informal and formal organization structures. Management both encourages and obstructs the formation of groups and teams, depending on different contexts, perceptions and policies.

Above the aggregation and analytical level of face-to-face groups things are more complicated. A small hospital may consist of a few interlocking groups, above which a clearly identifiable focal organization is the next and most important unit. However, in a company like General Motors or in a large military service there is instead a complicated web of sub-components which is hard to typify according to a generally applicable scheme. Terms like department, shop, site, establishment, battalion, regiment, brigade, division, business unit, faculty or others are used depending on the line of activity an organization is in and the level of aggregation.

Sometimes it is hard to say whether we are dealing with inter-organizational relations or organization networks, or with sub-components of a self-contained organization. As suggested above, this is due to the difficulty in identifying a truly focal organization. Where the focal organization evaporates, it is appropriate to analyse organizational sets, inter-organizational relations and networks. Sometimes these are controlled from a centre and, where this happens, a common organizational goal and identity can be said to exist. But, even in industrial groups, business units or divisions or subsidiaries may compete with each other rather than cooperate.

Some subdivisions include various levels of aggregation and specialize in thematic aspects of organizational life. Managerial behaviour, leadership, labour process, cognition, organizational learning and decision making are clear examples. For some purposes such a distinction is impractical.

Organizational sets may feature different amounts of common goal orientation, coordination and control of activities and different identities. 'Industrial districts' are an example of interlinked firms that are formally independent of one another but which may share a number of pooled functions, such as research and development, marketing, education, training or maintenance; or they are interlinked firms in the industrial chain. The linkages between organizations in the set may be strongly competitive, cooperative or quasi-absent. Where focal organizations share at least a product market, the term 'organizational populations' increasingly has come to be used: societies and economies become populated by organizations and types of organizations in the same way that the earth becomes populated by biological species. Note, however, that different focal organizations may well compete fiercely in their task environment (in the same market) while cooperating in their general environment, for example by setting up a common training scheme. But they may also cooperate in their task environment; oil companies that compete nevertheless tend to set up and operate common pipeline systems.

Organizations tend to spawn other organizations. Part of this phenomenon is the formation of interest associations by various firms and public corporations. Examples are employers' associations, industry and professional organizations, chambers of industry and commerce, guilds and other more specific organizations dedicated to particular missions and purposes. Private individuals also set up organizations. These do not produce or sell anything but are intimately involved in economic organizational life and constitute an important part of the environment for industrial and service firms. Trade unions are the most obvious example. Furthermore, organizations set up 'daughter' organizations. Ours are organizational societies where, even if you want to work against organizations, you are likely to set up another organization. More recently, some people have tried to counteract this trend by setting up social movements, more 'open systems' with more ambiguous goals, less demarcated boundaries, unhierarchical structures, more free-floating coordination and less formally circumscribed responsibilities. Even these tend to be subject to modern organizational drift.

The high organization of organizational environments leads us to the phenomenon of institutionalization. Organizational sets and populations are part of, and embedded in, institutionalized relationships with other organized actors. For the purposes of economic life, the world of such institutionalized relationships and sets is captured by the literature on business systems. Organizing, in the sense of endowing social behaviour with organizational properties, implies institutionalization. Sellers encounter organized customers and organized patterns of demand. Recruiting firms face institutionalized producers of skills and knowledge such as schools and colleges. Product and service markets are often highly regulated. Even deregulated airlines have to succumb to safety regulations and air traffic control.

This demonstrates that, as well as vertically integrated organization sets, at each level of aggregation, there are institutions which are part of the task and the general environment of units. They extend right into the context of organization. For example, work safety regulations imposed by governments have to be internalized and implemented. This has led to the visualization of organization itself as institutionalized. It is filled with institutions that are specific not to focal organizations but to local, regional or societal entities. Institutionalization is a highly salient concept in the literature on the process of organizing. This sets a counterpoint to theories that have been highlighted above. The idea is that goals, structures, boundaries and other patterns are not as fixed as mainstream organization theory pretends. They are modified and developed in an unending process whereby individuals and systems interact to bring forth fluctuating and evolving patterns.

Institutionalization therefore is not only linked with rigidity of patterns but with their ambiguity and constant modification. Where the literature on structure emphasizes neat systems and predictable actors, the literature on the process of organizing stresses unpredictable actors and unruly systems. Institutionalization brings in conflict, contradictions, power, ideology and politics as very important traits of organizational life. Blurred, fluctuating goals imply power, conflict and politics. Again, this applies to analyses at all the levels of aggregation. Essentially this means that organizations are only imperfectly explained as 'systems'. The systems aspect of organizations emphasizes that behaviour is informed by clear system goals. This is only partially true. Actors in organizations have, in addition, goals such as furthering their own well-being or career, or those of friends and specific colleagues, or the well-being of interests outside the organization. Hence, actors are not simply like wheels in an organizational machine; they are also to some extent likely to 'throw a spanner in the works'. This is why organizations have to be considered as entities in which opposing parties wrangle for power and influence and strike compromises. This aspect indicates that organizational life may be orientated by goals different from the systemic goals.

The political character of organizational life extends across all levels of analysis. Individuals operate politically in groups and other face-to-face contacts, to accommodate their interests and further their personal aims. Groups wrangle and form coalitions with other groups. Departmentally, divisionally or professionally specific segments do likewise. Organizational units, in addition, have reference points in the organizational context or environment. They are dedicated or opposed to specific strategies, stakeholders, customers and markets. They maintain certain professional, industrial or industrial relations standards. They may be linked to interests in the governmental sphere. The analytically sharp boundary between the organizational unit and its environment is, in everyday life, more like a revolving door than a wall and many transfers and transactions occur across this boundary; of people with their preferences and values, of various sorts of information and of behavioural and institutional routines. Such routines are anchored in collectivities which cross-cut the organized unit in question. However, such units do not passively absorb influences from outside the organization but interact with actors and systems within their own environment, helping to fashion it in a more active way.

Interaction between contexts, environments and organization structure and process is endemic to subdivisions such as business systems, organization culture, organization development, innovation and change, managerial behaviour, decision making, cognition, agency, markets and hierarchies, organization types, technology, labour process, information and knowledge and organizational learning. Current research in organization theory can be described as imbued with a drive to identify and analyse intense interaction and correspondence between contextual, environmental and organizational properties.

Whichever way organizational units are demarcated (large or small), and whichever side of organizational life is considered, analysis of such *correspondences* is a widespread and powerful tool. Theories elaborating on this are usually called contingency theories. A lot may be learned about the functioning of groups by looking at their tasks, technology, product range and variation, size, and control and management systems. There are also contingency theories for leadership and decision making. Focal organizations are shown to be designed in conjunction with contingencies such as size, task structures, technology and environmental variables (Mintzberg 1983). One of the most important series of research studies has brought forth a theory on general relationships between organization structure, its context and environment (Pugh and Hickson 1989: 16–23). Contingency arguments are also applicable to the design of conglomerates or networks but the importance attached to market structures and external institutions tends to be greater if the analytical focus is moved from the individual to sets of organizations.

On the other hand, correspondences of these types are not uncontroversial. There is a great deal of empirical proof for the opposing principle, functional *equivalence* or *equifinality* (Child 1972). This quite simply means that different sorts of internal arrangements are perfectly compatible with identical contextual or environmental states. This principle goes against the idea of a quasi-ideal 'match', which is inherent to the principle of correspondence. Whereas correspondence theory suggests that rigid and bureaucratic structures are not a good match for volatile and shifting product markets, equifinality theorists claim that it may very well turn out to be a good match, but only if the level and diversity of competence in the workforce is large and organization culture produces motivated and flexible actors.

The diligent reader, scholar and practitioner is well advised to make judicious and eclectic use of both, opposed, perspectives. To some extent and in specific situations correspondence works well, and for other problems and questions, equifinality is the better one. The literature on performance emphasizes correspondence theory, explaining performance by tight matching, or the 'fit', of environments, contexts, structures and processes. Against that, the consideration of poor performance shows that organizations survive very well, notwithstanding poor fit.

A subdivision of increasing importance, that of organizational populations, is concerned with the way environmental 'niches' get populated by organization types. This terminology has been transferred from population ecology, a speciality within biology. At the centre of this field of study are larger sets of organizations, the focal organization being more peripheral. Furthermore, it is often assumed, in line with the literature on decline and failure, that organizations are typically inelastic, not really capable of achieving fit by their own actions, whether this is proactive or reactive. However, to date there is not much organizational population research of sufficient depth in matters of organization forms and processes. Yet, this approach rightly highlights the role played by environmental 'selection', whereby 'fit' between environmental and organizational characteristics may indeed emerge.

Again, two perspectives have to be combined. On the one hand, all organizations are inelastic, clinging to established ways of doing things. Their identity would be blurred if everything was in flux all the time. Organizations need stable routines, otherwise goal-directed coordination would be impossible. But they can achieve good performance despite this inelasticity, and for a very simple reason: according to the equifinality principle one can make do, under varying circumstances, with basically similar organizational tools. On the other hand, there is, in organizational as in biological life, a persistent random variation of the genetic – in our case socio-economic – heritage. Thus the environment can be imagined to select those variations that show acceptable or good fit and weed out those that do not.

Such considerations get us involved at levels of analysis above the focal organization. Subdivisions in organization cannot only be divided up on the basis of criteria like the level of aggregation or the substance of organizational life covered. In addition, there are subdivisions of the field due to the type of theoretical approach put forward.

Another criterion for demarcating subdivisions relates to the specific goals or products of organizations. Much of current general organization theory has been derived from evidence from industrial, service, financial or commercial organizations. Such organizations are often exposed to competition and particular criteria of performance. The latter usually consist of profitability, efficiency, productiveness, effectiveness, product quality, added value, market share, growth and returns on invested capital in various combinations. Alongside such criteria and their consequences for theory and findings are fields with different or quasi-absent performance criteria. A notable field is that of public sector organization, which has differing mixes of performance criteria.

Such organizations often hold protected monopolies and are instruments of the body politic. Therefore, criteria like political conformity, predictability, standardization of behaviour and transparency may be more important than performance in the commercial and economic sense. However, it has also become clear that the ossification of larger enterprises has reduced the difference with regard to public organization practice; more recently, there has also been a drive in many countries to make public organizations operate according to competitive and commercial criteria and to change their structures and behaviour accordingly. Thus, there is a lot of to-and-fro between the different domains, which increases the salience of organization theory in the public administration domain.

A classic theorist, Max Weber, underlined the importance of military and bureaucratic patterns in setting the organizational tone for commerce, finance and industry. This has taken place to an extent which is often unknown. For example, the doctrine of 'management by objectives', which became a buzzword in industrial and commercial management in the 1960s, dates back to the principle of *Auftragstaktik* (tactical operations by objectives) that was introduced into the Prussian Army in the first half of the nineteenth century. In return, evidence shows that officers in the military are encouraged by their education and training to adopt methods and postures from management and organizational experiences outside the military.

Some fields emphasize the investigation of different organizations at one point in time whereas others emphasize the study of organization over time. This latter view is very much concentrated in fields such as organizational populations, organizational evolution, organization development, innovation and change, the process of organizing, decision making and organizational learning. Other fields are more likely to feature the former view, but the distinction is far from clear-cut.

Taking an overview of the topic, it can be seen that the entire field of organization is subdivided by criteria stressing:

- the level of aggregation and analysis;
- specific aspects of organizational life;
- goal-, product- or service-related specificities;
- criteria of performance in organizational domains;
- particular approaches to theory-building;
- synchronic or diachronic perspectives.

Chapter headings of standard textbooks are mostly rather untidy combinations of such criteria. However, it is impossible to arrange organization in a fashion which is as tidy as the organizational chart of a tank battalion. Here, we have tried to make the systematization as tidy as possible but, in reality, the picture of the discipline is more akin to that of a software consultancy, with a messy division of labour. There still exist ambiguities, overlaps and inconsistencies but this has made it possible to preserve the closeness of organization to real organizational life.

4 Types of theory

The paradoxical nature of organization has already been mentioned. Attempts to augment the logical consistency of a theory which is endemic to all scientific activity leads to a reduction, or covering up, of paradox. Hence, a counter-theory to any existing theory is a logical necessity in any regime which simultaneously has to come to grips with paradox and to expel it. This conflict may even be described as the methodologically necessary climax to paradox.

The simple but important consequence is that knowledge and mastery of different organization paradigms are central. Paradigms are one-sided views of the real world. The necessity for conflicting paradigms to exist is a consequence of simultaneous attempts to take account of and to expel – under the ruling norms of scholarly discourse – the pervasive phenomenon of paradoxicality. However, even conflicting paradigms can be predicated upon another in a novel form, such that new paradigms emerge that displace older ones. Seen in this way the co-existence of paradigms is not as bewildering as it may appear at first sight. It is a normal ingredient of reasonable discourse, research and theory-building.

In different paradigms different types of theory are represented and combined. Types of organization theory can be distinguished according to two criteria. The first criterion is the *substantive foundation of explanations*. Theories aim to explain reasons for events, forms and developments. They can be distinguished according to the kinds of reasons they provide; that is, which groups of substantive factors they refer to. According to this first criterion, the first class of theories in organization consists of *utilitarian theories* (Mintzberg 1983). These explain organizational life with reference to the usefulness of events, forms and developments. This is the case where organization is explained through its potential to meet requirements or opportunities in the organizational context or in the environment. Every time that organizational properties are explained by their match with goals, contexts, environments, and strategies, and by their profitability, efficiency or effectiveness under such contexts and environments, this is utilitarian theory. Such a theory is invariably founded upon a type of behaviour that rationally (by the conscious evaluation of different outcomes and courses of action) or by trial and error is geared to maximize or satisfy utilitarian ambitions. The type of utility may differ however. Such conflict is underlined by the *behavioural theory of the firm* (Cyert and March 1963), which is one of the cornerstones of organization.

The second class of theories are *institutional theories*. Institutions are relatively stable and typified patterns in the social fabric of society or in networks of social interaction. With institutional theories the usefulness of organizational arrangements is secondary. Things are done a certain way because institutionalized norms or rules suggest courses of action, either explicitly or implicitly. The legitimacy of a specific institution, including all institutionalized patterns of behaviour, may be separate from its relative utilitarian value (Meyer and Rowan 1977). To paraphrase Abraham Lincoln: some people manage to be utilitarian all of the time, most people are utilitarian some of the time, but not all people can be utilitarian all of the time. Usually, utilitarian orientations can survive to the extent that they are embedded in a context which is thick with institutions.

Third is *culturalist theory*. This is concerned with values, preferences, meaningful symbols and mental programmes in the widest sense. It is the mental programming of acting individuals that matters. Under such an approach usefulness is also secondary, but it crops up as a function of the mentioned preferences and values. Culturalist theorists stress the fact that utilities differ according to classes of actors and that such classes of actors are differentiated by different processes of socialization. Culturalists also tend to look at institutions as reducible to individual mental programmes. While they do not go against notions of utility and institutionalization in principle, they do reiterate their cultural relativity.

Utilitarian theories tend to have a strong economic or business administration element. Institutionalist theories have strong sociological, social anthropological or political science roots. Culturalist theories are bound up with psychology or anthropology. However, such distinctions are far from clear-cut. organization theorizing tends to combine foundations of the utilitarian, institutionalist and culturalist kinds. Accents are placed differently in each theoretical approach. Theories which explain organizational life with reference to the characteristics of a capitalist or socialist order feature a blend of utilitarian and institutionalist approaches. There may also be a blend of institutionalist and culturalist arguments, such as in the explanation for the commitment of employees in Japanese organizations (Lincoln and Kalleberg 1992). Last but not least, there is a blend of utilitarian and culturalist approaches, for instance in the links established between Calvinist or Buddhist beliefs, entrepreneurship and economic success.

Note that utilitarian, institutionalist and culturalist theories are not simply alternatives. They do not compete only with one another but are systematically intertwined – or can be. All human behaviour, including organization, is impossible to imagine as guided by utilitarian, institutionalist or culturalist considerations only. Economic research and theory show that utilitarian considerations are shaped by mentalities and social institutions. This was the basic idea behind the ground-breaking contribution of Cyert and March (1963) when they conceived the behavioural theory of the firm. Sociological research and theory has shown that institutions, although at least partly autonomous with regard to utilitarian criteria, are also legitimated or created because of their utility in maintaining the coherence and survival of larger collectivities. This is the essence of the structural–functionalist school in the social sciences. Such reflections essentially tell us that these three theory types are predicated upon one another.

In simple terms this means the following. Institutions and mentalities are very utilitarian (useful) things. A specific institution may exist without being concerned about its utility, but utility cannot be achieved without institutions. Unbridled and one-sided emphasis of utilitarian motives is ruinous for the achievement of a utility as it leads to disorientation and anarchy. Utilitarian considerations themselves need institutions and mentalities to be cultivated. Cultural mentalities interact with institutions, and they are similarly useful in guiding human action through an overly complex world. An artificial behavioural repertoire of cultural attitudes and institutions limits purely utilitarian behavioural choice, but the restriction of behavioural choice which is thereby achieved also makes utilitarian action possible. We try to arrive at 'satisficing' solutions which, although not necessarily the best, are satisfactory within cultural and institutional bounds, and such bounds are not only restrictive but also 'enabling'. In the wake of the classic work by March and Simon (1958) the emergent idea was that rationality is always 'bounded', that is, confined to a more narrowly circumscribed area; unbounded rationality would quite simply amount to irrationality.

There is another class of theory types based on epistemological criteria. *Epistemology* is concerned with the theory of knowledge, providing an explanation of the background from which systems of knowledge, particularly scientific systems, emerge. One school has argued that the highlight of science is the construction of *nomothetic theories*. Such theories posit generally valid statements about relations between independent phenomena. The logic of such statements implies propositions in the form: 'if A happens, this will be associated with B', or 'if A happens, this will lead to B'. Mainstream organization theory, for example, argues that environmental and contextual properties, such as the variability of the task environment, and organizational characteristics, are interdependent. Another central finding is that the increasing size of an organization is associated with greater hierarchical, departmental and professional differentiation. Such nomothetic theories, usually conceived according to the epistemology of natural sciences, are easier to construct if the emphasis is placed on a specific class of substantive factors, whether utilitarian, institutional or cultural.

There also exists a tradition of *idiographic theory*. Idiography means the depiction of what is specific to individual things or people, and it illuminates phenomena that deviate from generally established theories. It focuses on phenomena that are specific to industrial sectors, products, societies or enterprises. Note that idiographic treatments may again construct arguments that are utilitarian, institutionalist or culturalist. All these perspectives may provide reasons for deviations from generally established patterns. High organizational simplicity in a large organizational unit, as an exemplary deviant phenomenon, can be explained by the attitudes of ruling elites in the organization (culture), professional roles rooted in training systems and labour markets (institutions), or overhead cost-cutting (utilitarian considerations).

Both of these theory types aim at statements which are, ideally, free from contradictions. This kind of logical streamlining and empirical corroboration are the idealistic goals of what is often called 'positivistic' theory-building. Positivism has come to be a word with a derogatory meaning through its usage by opponents of such methodological currents but, unfortunately, there is no other convenient neutral word available for use.

Lammers (1978) put forward nomothetic and idiographic theory as the two basic variants of theory-building in comparative organization theory. Other scholars argue that this classification is not exhaustive or complete. Reality usually discounts a single-minded reference to one class of substantive factors only and forces theorists to employ approaches that at least partly contradict each other. Thus, nomothetic theories with the same epistemological foundation, but stressing different explanations, cannot be reconciled under a theory programme which stresses logical consistency. In addition, the tension between nomothetic and idiographic accounts of reality generates inconsistencies in the larger body of theory.

There is a necessity for a third epistemological type, *dialectical theory*. Essentially this is the acknowledgement, rather than avoidance, of conflicting and contradictory statements. In a positivistic statement a phenomenon may only be classed as A or non-A: a third possibility is ruled out. In dialectical theory, the opposite applies: a phenomenon may be classed as both A and non-A.

Consider a simple example. There are different approaches to explaining Japanese organization and employment practices (Lincoln and Kalleberg 1992). One school argues that these have grown out of societally specific values and institutions that predate the modernization and industrialization of Japan and that such practices cannot be explained by the task environment, only by the cultural and institutional environment of organizing, entrepreneurship and industrial relations.

Other scholars argue that such practices are, in fact, perfectly rational and utilitarian responses to the industrial and labour market situation of that country. They represent solutions which can also be found elsewhere and which increasingly are being propagated in many countries. These conflicting views can be simplified as one of the importance of task environmental versus cultural and institutional factors. It can be seen how such a conflict is linked to the prevalence of positivistic theory-building. Within a dialectical approach it would be possible to argue that organization and employment practices are, in fact, the conjoint result of task, cultural and institutional factors: although such environments must be looked at independently of each other, the effect of a particular environment has to be explained by its predication upon another type of environment. Thus, the admission that both non-A (independence) and A (reciprocal interdependence) apply. Dialectic theorists would be particularly prevalent in fields such as the process of organizing, power, symbolism, conflict and politics, and cognition.

Positivistic theorists, however, would counter this view by arguing that logical contradictions are impossible to sustain, and they would try to find out under which conditions precisely factors are independent and under which other conditions they are interdependent. This would be an attempt to suspend contradictions by advancing nomothetic theory-building. Stalwarts of both nomothetic and dialectical theory-building would look at such an attempt by the 'opposite' side to extend its domain with strong misgivings. The sharpness of some academic debates can only be explained by feelings of being threatened, on your own substantive 'patch', by the encroachment of people who lay claim to this patch or part of it: academics are able to live with the plurality of epistemological approaches only if no-one trespasses.

Students should remember that competition between different organization paradigms and approaches is the central ingredient of academic innovation. There is no harm in trying to 'dialecticize' a nomothetic theory or in trying to 'nomotheticize' a theory framed in dialectical terms. Where there is no one single valid dogma students should be prepared to live with different paradigms and epistemological foundations. Besides, in the last instance the reconciliation of opposing approaches happens pragmatically rather than dogmatically, research, instruction and discourse in actual practice being a very pragmatic affair. This works because we operate without one single and lasting epistemological foundation. In the same way that people in organizations have 'tacit' (not formally and coherently expressed) knowledge, so does the coherence of academic discourse arise from a tacit understanding rather than the application of a formally laid-down and logically consistent theory of scientific activity.

As a consequence, students and practitioners are not well advised to absorb and try to apply theory as if it were a dogma. Organizational practice is not a technocratic affair where a received wisdom can be monopolized by specialists in the field. organization practitioners will have to select, specify, recombine and modify theories which they find in the literature in an active way. The evaluation of organizational experimentation bears out the fact that practice has always been to a large extent autonomous with regard to organization theory. There is an important element of trial and error and adaptation to locally specific ambitions and perceived requirements involved (Warner 1981). This means that practitioners who demand intellectual grounding and the refinement of what they do will have to be theory-builders and researchers themselves, at least to some extent, if they are to expound a rationale.

Some of the leading theorists and researchers in organization have been eminent practitioners themselves. Obvious examples are Frederick W. Taylor, Henri Fayol and Chester Barnard, to name some pioneers. In return, parts of organizational practice such as organization development, team or group work, quality circles and lean production, which have become available in very practical easy to follow forms, rest on eminent theoretical and research foundations, such as the social psychology of Kurt Lewin or the sociotechnical school.

Most organization authors and practitioners will not realistically see themselves as a business leader and pioneering scholar rolled into one. But they may all realistically aspire to a tentative emulation, on a more modest scale, of an ideal: an ideal that aspires to the closest possible integration of practice, theory and research. However, this must be followed in a way which does not confuse and compromise business and academic goals: scholarly rectitude is not the only thing that makes organization theories useful. The practical value of theories may be founded not on their factual corroboration and logical consistency, but on their ideology, short-sightedness and manipulative character. A differentiation between practical and scholarly roles is, therefore, a necessity.

Further reading

(References cited in the text marked *)

* Aldrich, H. and Whetten, D.A. (1981) 'Organization-sets, action-sets, and networks: making the most of simplicity', in P.C. Nystrom and W.H. Starbuck (eds), *Handbook of Organizational Design*, vol. 1, Oxford: Oxford University Press. (Fundamental conceptualization of sets of organizations and their interrelations.)

* Child, J. (1972) 'Organizational structure, environment and performance: the role of strategic choice', *Sociology* 6 (1): 1–22. (Important article about the difference between contingency theory and functional equivalence principles linked with strategic choice.)

Clegg, S.R., Hardy, C. and Nord, W.R. (eds) (1996) *Handbook of Organization Studies*, London: Sage. (Concerned with the critical, non-managerialist accounts of organizational life, which challenge presumed certainties and models of good management practice.)

Crozier, M. and Friedberg, E. (1977) *L'acteur et le système* (Actors and Systems), Paris: Editions du Seuil. (A central conceptualization of organization theory, with reciprocal interaction of actor and system constructions as an important ingredient.)

* Cyert, R.M. and March, J.G. (1963) *A Behavioral Theory of the Firm*, Englewood Cliffs, NJ: Prentice Hall. (A classic and still informative work that argues that business behaviour is governed by the normal principles of human behaviour.)

Daft, R.L. (2001) *Organization Theory and Design*, 7th edn, Cincinatti: South Western: Thomson Learning. (Probably the best basic textbook in the field, with an emphasis on structure and design and featuring many examples and exercises.)

* Giddens, A. (1986) *The Constitution of Society*, Berkeley, CA: University of California Press. (A general social theory text which intertwines individualistic and structuralist perspectives under 'structuration theory'.)

Hackman, J.R., Lawler, E.E. and Porter, L.W. (eds) (1983) *Perspectives on Behavior in Organizations*, 2nd edn, New York: McGraw-Hill. (A volume with fifty-seven important readings from the whole field of organization. Probably the best edited volume of its kind; very useful at intermediate levels of instruction.)

Hellriegel, D., Slocum, J.W. and Woodman, R.W. (1992) *Organizational Behaviour*, 6th edn, St Paul, MN: West Publishing Co. (A well-known introductory text which is particularly strong on the psychological and socio-psychological aspects of organization. Includes cases and exercises.)

* Lammers, C. (1978) 'The comparative sociology of organizations', *Annual Review of Sociology* 4: 458–510. (Derives nomothetic and idiographic approaches in organization from the philosophy of the social sciences.)

* Lincoln, J.A. and Kalleberg, A.L. (1992) *Culture, Control and Commitment: A Study of Work Organization and Work Attitudes in the United States and Japan*, Cambridge: Cambridge University Press. (A methodologically intriguing comparison which goes against stereotypes of how and why attitudes and behaviour are different between Japan and other countries.)

* March, J.G. and Simon, H.A. (1958) *Organizations*, New York: Wiley. (A classic conceptualization of organization.)

* Meyer, J.W. and Rowan, B. (1977) 'Institutionalized organizations: formal structure as myth and ceremony', *American Journal of Sociology* 83: 340–63. (Sketches an institutionalist programme as opposed to systemic and contingency approaches.)

* Mintzberg, H. (1983) *Structure in Fives: Designing Effective Organizations*, Englewood Cliffs, NJ: Prentice Hall. (An original statement of contingency theory in structure and design.)

* Morgan, G. (1986) *Images of Organization*, Newbury Park, CA: Sage Publications. (Presents a whole range of different perspectives on organizations, stressing paradigmatic and conceptual pluralism, and is eminently readable.)

Mullins, L.J. (1989) *Management and Organisational Behaviour*, 2nd edn, London: Pitman. (A good basic textbook with an emphasis on the management and 'behaviour within organizations' aspects of organization.)

Nystrom, P.C. and Starbuck, W.H. (1981) *Handbook of Organizational Design*, 2 vols, Oxford: Oxford University Press. (A classic advanced-level handbook in organization theory.)

Perrow, C. (1986) *Complex Organizations: A Critical Essay*, 3rd edn, New York: McGraw-Hill. (A well-written and vivid overview, with an emphasis on the presentation and critique of different approaches in organization structure and design; theoretically committed but balanced, and rich in facts.)

* Pugh, D.S. and Hickson, D.J. (1989) *Writers on Organizations*, 4th edn, Newbury Park, CA: Sage Publications. (Contains the biographies and the main ideas, findings and publications of thirty-six important authors in organization.)

* Scott, W.R. (1981) *Organizations: Rational, Natural and Open Systems*, Englewood Cliffs, NJ: Prentice Hall. (An important conceptualization of organization theory, stressing the plurality of organization models.)

Thompson, J.D. (1976) *Organization in Action*, New York: McGraw-Hill. (A pioneering statement of organization and administration theory which has been influential and can suggest even today new insights and hypotheses.)

* Warner, M. (1981) 'Organizational experiments and social innovations', in P.C. Nystrom and W.H. Starbuck (eds), *Handbook of Organizational Design*, vol. 1, Oxford: Oxford University Press. (Summarizes the lessons from experiments in the history of organizational design and experimentation.)

Organization paradigms

Gibson Burrell

1 **Introduction**
2 **The origins of paradigm thinking**
3 **Paradigms in sociology**
4 **Paradigms in organization theory**
5 **The current state of organization theory**
6 **The future state of organization theory**
7 **Paradigms as narratives**

Overview

On both sides of the Atlantic, the notion of 'paradigms' in organizational analysis has received much attention since the early 1980s. While by no means invented by the US philosopher of science, Thomas Kuhn, the term has become associated with his work on the development of the physical sciences and how old ideas and frameworks for carrying out science become overthrown by the new. The term revolves around the idea of 'classic laws' and 'modes of community life'. This is to say that the paradigm marks out, in an agreed and deep-seated sense, a way of seeing the world and how it should be studied and that this view is shared by a group of scientists who live in a community marked by a common conceptual language and a very defensive political posture to outsiders.

Social scientists alighted on the Kuhnian approach with great enthusiasm in the late 1960s and early 1970s and began to see their own disciplines in this 'paradigmatic' way. The articulation of paradigms which were alternative to the ruling one of structural functionalism began in sociology and then spread to organization theory in the decade of the 1970s. For those opposed to the dominant orthodoxy, the concept of alternative paradigms was very liberating for it established their revolutionary credentials and legitimated them as the progressives to whom the future belonged. As a meta-narrative – a story which explained their place in intellectual development – Kuhnianism was a very powerful tool for the younger generation of organization scholars.

Links between organization studies and social theory were laid out, although not using Kuhnianism in anything like a faithful way. The four 'paradigms of social theory' were identified as being constructed from meta-theoretical assumptions about the nature of society and the nature of science. Since organizational analysis was a social science, it was argued, it *must* make these sorts of assumptions irrespective of whether individual authors were aware of them.

Paradigm analysis became the battlefield upon which strategies of an intellectual and power-seeking kind could be worked out, often between young and old. Those who engaged in it were seen as challenging the right of functionalism and functionalists of whatever age to dominate the field. Those who denigrated the very concept of paradigm itself often did so in order to undermine the right of others to have an alternative voice. The debate became acrimonious and hostilities often broke out.

The situation in the mid-1990s was characterized by a decline in interest in the concept of paradigms. The debate moved on to issues of postmodernism in Europe where theoretical and methodological alternatives might still be attempted, and to the excesses of population ecology in the USA where the scientization of organization theory reached a new high-water mark. Conservatism once again stalks the land and the next generation of organization scholars are still looking for ways of revolutionizing the discipline and escaping from the dead hand of aged scholars.

1 Introduction

When the term 'paradigm' is used in organizational analysis it can mean many things. For some it seems to mean a 'theory' or an approach or a general orientation towards some academic issue. The dictionary definition simply states, '*paradigm* 1. the set of all the inflected forms of a word or a systematic arrangement displaying these forms. 2. a pattern or model (C15: via French and Latin from Greek)'. This definition emphasizes the term's Greek origins and stresses the 'patterning' notion. However, as this entry will show, 'paradigm' became a word which was thought to be so powerful that it had to be weakened by dilution and dissembling.

The pivotal notion in Thomas Kuhn's *The Structure of Scientific Revolutions* (1962; 1970) was that of 'paradigm'. Kuhn takes the word to mean 'universally recognized scientific achievements that for a time provide model problems and solutions to a community of practitioners' (Kuhn 1970: x). From this came models which give rise to 'coherent traditions of scientific research' (Kuhn 1970: 10). However, paradigm means more than this. It also refers to a global theoretical structure within which one finds 'the network of commitments – conceptual, theoretical, instrumental and methodological' within a research tradition. Paradigms give us the source of our 'methods, problem field, and standards of solution accepted by the mature scientific community at any given time' (Kuhn 1970: 103).

Masterman (1970) showed that this conceptualization was one which contained many ambiguities and uncertainties. Kuhn was later to distinguish two different meanings of 'paradigm'. On one hand it was 'a constellation of beliefs, values, techniques' while on the other it was a 'shared exemplar'. He goes on to refer to these as 'disciplinary matrix' and 'exemplar' respectively (Kuhn 1977).

However, this bifurcation in the meaning that the author attributed to the one concept is nothing as compared to the later fissuring of the notion which took place. A major fault line that has to be recognized is one based around politics, for in the Kuhnian description of scientific progress there is a real sense of the importance of power and political infighting for dominance of knowledge. 'Normal science' is based upon past scientific achievements but is punctuated by periods of 'revolutionary science' when the ruling paradigm is replaced by an incompatible new one. Paradigm thinking then, from the first publication of Kuhn's work, involved writers thinking about the political position in which they, themselves, were placed in their own discipline's pecking order. Thus, there was a struggle for mastery of the Kuhnian paradigm concept from the outset in order to give the protagonists political advantage over their opposition. Control of the concept was to come to have strong implications for a number of disciplines.

The concept of paradigm is used today in two very distinct, possibly oppositional, ways. On one hand it has come to mean a single unifying approach in which theory, method, the interpretation of findings and the way research should develop are all laid out and agreed by a community of scholars. The key figures that one might wish to identify in this approach to paradigms are those who act as mind police – guardians of the integrity and cohesion of the paradigm – whose task is to ensure that boundaries are not transgressed and the power of the paradigm in the scientific community is not diminished. Perhaps these might be termed 'paradigm Walsinghams' after Sir Francis Walsingham, who acted as Queen Elizabeth I's Secretary of State in charge of internal and external espionage. In the period 1573–90, Walsingham uncovered several plots against Elizabeth through these methods of surveillance. The sovereignty of the monarch and the defence of her territory were his key concerns. And thus it is with paradigms.

On the other hand, there are members of another group who see things very differently where paradigms are concerned. They do not see before them a single unifying paradigm but many – or at least several – paradigms lying alongside each other in a relationship characterized by hostility and conflict. This type of grouping is sometimes referred to as consisting of 'paradigm warriors', for they see themselves as engaged in a struggle for survival. The membership of these types of social group are typically subordinate in political terms within any discipline and use conflict as an expression of their political inferiority. 'Paradigm Walsinghams', however, tend to be from elite groupings within a discipline and hold positions of power themselves. These are superordinate members of the profession or in some cases are those who, for services rendered to the elite, are looking for access into its upper ranks.

Thus, when the term 'paradigm' is seen being utilized in the contemporary setting, it may well be being used by those who are powerful within a discipline and seeking to control it further or by those relatively powerless members of small groups seeking to legitimate what they do and how they do it in order to create some space for themselves. Examples of paradigm warriors and paradigm Walsinghams will be illustrated in the course of this entry.

2 The origins of paradigm thinking

What Kuhn achieved in *The Structure of Scientific Revolutions* (1962) did not sit well with the then contemporary views on scientific progress and how this was to be explained. Kuhn argued that the evidence on progress in the physical sciences, particularly in the grand works of synthesis by Newton and then Einstein, did not fit with the inductivist or falsificationist views of science. Science does not proceed by the facts revealing themselves to clever thinkers nor by scientists attempting to falsify their hypotheses in each and every experiment. For Kuhn, science develops through political tensions being resolved in the scientific community in a cycle beginning with the challenge of youth, resistance from the powerful, death of the powerful, their replacement by the rapidly ageing young who then dominate, and the challenge yet again of new youth. Thus, the life cycle of individuals and the path of scientific progress are heavily intertwined.

Science is not a linear pathway of falsifiable hypotheses. Rather, for Kuhn, it is a series of discontinuous periods of normative and revolutionary change. Old ways of seeing the world are replaced, throughout history, by tremendous upheavals in thought. So great are these changes that the old ways of thinking are totally incompatible with the new. To embrace the new is to undertake a conversion experience – which by no means all scientists in the field are willing to contemplate. The new view of the world – an Einsteinian one rather than a Newtonian one, for example – creates a new structure, a revolutionary new set of social arrangements, a new set of community agendas, a new paradigm which revolutionizes our understanding. To see the full enormity of this requires the scientist to undergo a 'gestalt switch'.

As we have already seen, 'paradigm' as used in Kuhn (1962) is a word which excited many commentators, some in the philosophy of science but others, many others, from elsewhere. Masterman (1970), in a widely quoted but little read article, shows that Kuhn uses the term in very many different ways in *The Structure of Scientific Revolutions*. In a postscript to the second edition written in 1970, Kuhn maintains, in a much watered-down version of the radicalism of the first, that he now prefers the term 'disciplinary matrix' to that of the much besieged notion of 'paradigm'. The term 'besieged' is not used lightly here, for Kuhn's work enjoyed the time-honoured status of all important work. It was subjected to hostile and prolonged attack! A conference at Cambridge organized by Imre Lakatos, the leading sophisticated falsificationist of the period, went through the Kuhnian position with an extremely fine tooth comb and, unsurprisingly, found it had weaknesses. In the face of this, or possibly because he was getting older and as we have seen age is a factor in his conceptualization of revolutionary science, Kuhn retreated to a less radical position. Since 1970, this retreat has continued and reached the stage where he could say in 1982 that 'paradigms' did not preclude full communication across the revolutionary divide and in 1990 that understanding across barriers could not be ruled out.

Howard Sankey (1993), in a very full discussion of Kuhn's changing position on paradigms, articulates the view that Kuhn's work may be divided into three phases: the 'early position'; the 'transitional phase'; and the 'later position'. In the first stage, paradigm incommensurability – the inability of paradigms ever to be anything but at cross purposes – comes about because of a failure in communication. They will not agree on the problems to be addressed, their definitions of science will be different, they will see different things when they look from the same point in the same direction (Sankey 1993: 761–2). Paradigms cannot agree because they use different observational terms which are based upon different theories which in turn are based upon different meta-theoretical assumptions. There is, in debate, little if any exchange of ideas because there is a wholesale change in what is referred to by those who speak.

In the intermediate phase in Kuhn's thinking, the emphasis begins to focus on language and translation of terms. The concern is to show that translation always involves compromise and inscrutability. Terms of debate and analysis used by a theory within the dominant paradigm cannot be expressed fully with terms originating from within another rival paradigm, for 'languages cut up the world in different ways' (Kuhn 1970: 268). There can only be translation failure.

In the later standpoint adopted by Kuhn and identified by Sankey (1993), there is a retreat to a position of saying that only in localized cases does intranslatability function. In other words, significant parts of theories can be translated so that both sides fully understand what is being said with regard to what is held in common. While Kuhn retains the notion that certain parts of paradigm work is incommensurable with that of another paradigm, now it is stated that these are localized issues only.

From the point of view of the present entry, what is crucial about this is the extent to which organizational researchers lay claim to a Kuhnian understanding (whatever that may be) of the term 'paradigm' in their work. Have they any right to use the notion if they do not quote the full range and nature of the Kuhnian retreat? Is it legitimate for them to manipulate a concept designed for use in the natural sciences exclusively, as if it contained no problems for what some see as the rapacious social scientists trying to steal the concepts of others who hail from the more mature and respectable natural sciences? If Kuhn is the authorial source of the concept and one is concerned to be hagiographically true to the author, then organization analysis is almost sure to be lost. However, so too would be any form of paradigm thinking which did not match the most recent of Kuhn's publicly available thoughts on the topic! If, on the other hand, Kuhn happened to produce a book in 1962 which even today stimulates thought and encourages the development of a concept which he would now disown (or would have disowned then), is it of great consequence?

What may have been Kuhn's ideas in 1962 (but not today) became transmogrified into a relatively potent notion which possibly came to bear little resemblance to Kuhn's views of three decades ago. His work thus became *our* work. If we are content to think thus, we can reject the supposed authority of the author and embrace what we have forced his original ideas into – namely a framework of our own! If we take the risk and do not worry about the intellectual movements of a single human in the course of their career but concern ourselves instead with a particular intellectual artefact which is no longer (if it ever was) Kuhn's property then there is iconoclastic hope for us.

As the late, great Michel Foucault said of being 'true' to a writer:

The only valid tribute to thought such as Nietzsche's is precisely to use it, to deform it, to make it groan and protest. And if the commentators say that I am being unfaithful to Nietzsche that is of absolutely no interest.

(Sheridan 1980: 116–7)

Thus, it may be for some that what Kuhn said then or what Kuhn says now is not of the greatest significance. We have a book, *The Structure of Scientific Revolutions*, which we can translate from within our own 'paradigms'. If (and it is a big if) the ideas locked deep within Kuhn's book are translatable into social science concerns and issues, then perhaps it is possible for us to develop multiple forms of localized translation rules and, therefore, produce several versions of its significance. If Kuhn is not the final arbiter of his work then a plurality of perspectives open up. At first sight this wide range of interpretation does appear to have been the case – in one interpretation at least!

3 Paradigms in sociology

'Paradigms' came from Kuhn to the study of organizations via sociology, where paradigm thinking proved to be very popular in addressing the power, role and fate of the school of thought called 'functionalism'. In the 1970s, the sociology of sociology became an active and, some would say, interesting area of study. In the same year as Kuhn began his reatreat from the radical high-water mark of the original 1962 position, two important sociology books were published which have a direct bearing on this exposition. The first was Alvin Gouldner's *The Coming Crisis in Western Sociology* (1970). In this revealing class-based analysis, the dominance of Parsonian sociology is attacked and the various strands of anti-functionalist thinking, to a greater or lesser extent, are elaborated and defended. The functionalist hegemony is seen as deeply problematic and in need of replacement. The links with Kuhn are not explicit but the call for some revolutionary stance with regard to Parsonianism had far from distant echoes of Kuhn.

Much more explicitly Kuhnian was Friedrich's *A Sociology of Sociology* (1970). Here sociology was seen as a multi-paradigm science in which functionalism, having dominated for twenty years, by the late 1960s had become a science in crisis. Sociology, argues Friedrich, has a history which can also be explained in paradigm terms. In the 1930s, sociology was pre-paradigmatic, but between 1945 and 1963 the systems approach achieved paradigmatic status and gained hegemonic control over the discipline. After 1964, according to Friedrich, sociology had entered a revolutionary period in that functionalist systems theory was in decline and a struggle for supremacy had begun. Which new paradigm was to succeed to pre-eminence was still unclear in 1970. His candidate for success was the then high profile 'conflict theory'.

However, as the 1970s wore on, who or what was to be the success story of the paradigm wars was by no means clear. Ethnomethodology's high point was probably the American Sociological Association meeting in 1975, but it went into decline thereafter. Conflict theory, too, never reached the status Friedrich has envisaged for it. And while the nominations for paradigmatic status kept coming in, there were those who argued that Parsonian functionalism had never, ever been of the overarching status of Newtonian physics in the natural science disciplines and that, therefore, in Kuhnian terms, sociology was pre-paradigmatic and immature. Hassard (1993) outlines the debates around this time in sociology and highlights the contribution of Ritzer (1975), who argued that there are four elements which form constituent parts of a paradigm; namely, exemplars, theories, methods and, most importantly, 'images of the subject matter'. Ritzer argues that the great names in sociology are thought to have this high status by the very nature of their ability to act as paradigm bridgers who can span the chasm between one set of apparently opposing ideas and another. Irrespective of the validity of this claim, by the late 1970s the idea that sociology was a multi-paradigm science and was not possessed of a hegemonic domination had gained a hold.

4 Paradigms in organization theory

In organization theory, similar developments had been taking place. David Silverman's important book *The Theory of Organizations* (1970) had some comments on the breakdown of the functionalist orthodoxy but it was only in the late 1970s that 'paradigmatic' thinking came into organization theory (see Hassard 1993). Pondy and Boje (1981), for example, use Ritzer (1975) in ways which helped clarify some confusion by classifying different theoretical and methodological approaches to the analysis of organizations. Similarly, methodological issues dominated Evered and Louis (1981) who argued that there are two distinct paradigms for research techniques and that organizational science confronts this multi-paradigmatic situation every day.

The present author has an obvious vested interest in saying that the appearance of *Sociological Paradigms and Organizational Analysis* (Burrell and Morgan 1979), where 'paradigms' meant certain assumptions of a meta-theoretical kind about the nature of science and the nature of society, respectively, marked the beginning of a period of increase in interest in paradigms in the sociology of organizations. The length and strength of the conclusions of this book are, however, partially explained by rigorous editing. After much deliberation the authors opted to use the concept of 'paradigm' in the title but on publication one of the authors quickly decided that it had been an error of judgement in the sense that the book became seen as predicated upon Kuhnianism in one form or another. The same author also abandoned his strong commitment to the idea that the paradigms identified could not be seen as commensurable with each other.

The other author remains convinced by the utility of the framework first laid out in 1977. Despite the deep criticisms levelled against both the notion of paradigm incommensurability and the prescription that progress for organization theory lay in rejecting functionalism and speaking only to convince those who were already in no need of convincing, he continued to argue for many years that the relevance of organization paradigms, conceived of in a meta-theoretical way, remained undamaged. Until, that is, the arrival of postmodernism.

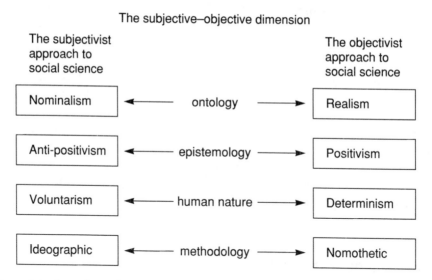

Figure 1 A scheme for analysing assumptions about the nature of social science

Burrell and Morgan (1979) argue that all of organizational science contains work in which two sets of assumptions have, perforce, to be made. One set of assumptions concerns the nature of science; the other set concerns the nature of society. These assumptions can be expressed as a binary opposition between 'subjectivist/objectivist' conceptions of science on one hand and 'radical change/regulation' theories of society on the other. In *Sociological Paradigms and Organisational Analysis* it is stated, 'Our proposition is that social theory can usefully be conceived in terms of four key paradigms based upon different sets of metatheoretical assumptions about the nature of social science and the nature of society' (Burrell and Morgan 1979: x). Figures 1–3 show the way in which the argument was constructed.

From this 'geographical' representation the four paradigms come to be seen as founded upon mutually exclusive views of the social world. Each stands in its own right and generates its own distinctive analyses of social life. With regard to the study of organizations, for example, each paradigm generates theories and perspectives which are in fundamental opposition to those generated in other

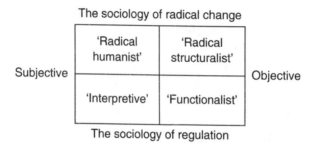

Figure 2 Four paradigms for the analysis of social theory

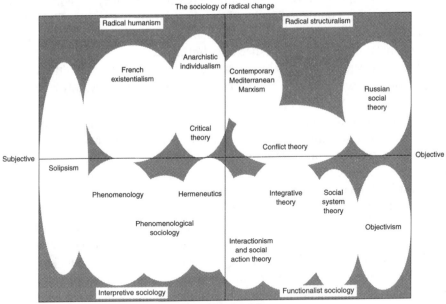

The sociology of radical change

| Radical humanism | Radical structuralism |

French existentialism

Anarchistic individualism

Critical theory

Contemporary Mediterranean Marxism

Russian social theory

Conflict theory

Subjective ———————————————————————— Objective

Solipsism

Phenomenology   Hermeneutics

Integrative theory

Social system theory

Objectivism

Phenomenological sociology

Interactionism and social action theory

| Interpretive sociology | Functionalist sociology |

The sociology of regulation

Figure 3 The four sociological paradigms

paradigms (Burrell and Morgan 1979). Note that this is the preface to the book and here in stark form is an apparent willingness to march under the Kuhnian banner. Or is there?

Burrell and Morgan (1979: 37) clearly state that they are using the term 'paradigm' in a way which is not consonant with that of Kuhn. They say that they are utilizing the term in a 'broader' way than that found in *The Structure of Scientific Revolutions*. Yet Donaldson (1985: 38–9) and others before and since seem to miss this note. As Willmott (1993b: 686) has recently noted, key arguments of the book depart from Kuhn's thesis. He notes that the complaint of divergence from Kuhn does not take us very far but goes to show that there are some marked differences in the position taken.

As suggested above, this divergence might be seen by some as a betrayal of the Kuhnian position but it is often the self-same critics who feel that the Kuhnian position, variously defined in time, is itself indefensible. Thus, one is condemned if one speaks supportively of Kuhn, yet condemned if one diverges from his (highly mobile) position. Perhaps it would be better not to speak of Thomas Kuhn at all.

Yet this criticism is but a small fragment of that heaped upon Burrell and Morgan (1979). Critics have concentrated variously upon the use of the classic functionalist technique of drawing a 2 × 2 matrix in what is purportedly a non-functionalist text, upon the neglect of feminist theory, on the difficulties in placing Freud, or Weber or Foucault in any one of the paradigms, on the question of how the term ontology is used, on the oversimplifications in the schema and in the way it was expressed. While all of these are true in one way or another, by far and away the major burden of critique has focused upon the notion of 'paradigm incommensurability'. This is the dimension which really irritates the functionalists in the area most especially, but it also tends to concern all those who believe in the values of debate, argument and compromise. In other words, the notion of incommensurability hits at the very centre of the widely held belief in rational academic debate and discourse.

Commensurability as a concept articulates a belief in the idea that 'translation rules' exist for discussing the findings, methods, theories and assumptions of all positions in the academic world and if we were able to find these then nation could speak unto nation, school of thought could speak unto school of thought and hostilities based on different assumptions between groups within the academic community would soon be sorted out if only translation rules were possible. Here a question springs to mind. Is this not the search for the unifying language which Carnap *et al*. and the logical empiricists undertook? Would not commensurability come from this magic language which all would speak and hear? Would not all difficulties, misunderstandings and tensions virtually disappear if such translation devices came into being?

What the proponents of the thesis of paradigm commensurability fail to understand is that one of the lessons of history, in things epistemological, is that despite the best endeavours of many able minds the dream of translation remains just that. It is clear that culture does have consequences, making language not only difficult to learn but implying that its nuances are rarely, if ever, to be understood by a non-native. Wittgenstein said much the same in the famous aphorism 'meaning is use'. Here is that most eloquent yet enigmatic assertion that if you do not use it on a regular basis then you cannot fully understand how it is used by natives.

Paradigm incommensurability revolves around the notion that inhabitants of a scientific community – let us call it a paradigm – use words, phrases and statements in ways which are familiar, shared and speak far beyond the simple message carried within the phonemes themselves. They are part of a language game in which what is not said is as important as that which is articulated. Translation rules allow us to understand, albeit in partial ways, what is noisily said. They do not allow us to comprehend what is unsaid, what is missed out, what is taken for granted. The believers in paradigm commensurability think that language is all words. How wrong they are. Language is much more signified by those deeply meaningful silences punctuated by noise. It is not the noise which signifies so much as those happy breaks for silence and the blissful need not to speak. Those who write of paradigm incommensurability recognize this and while they speak of it, knowing that it needs not to be spoken of to those who share its intimacy, they take pleasure in the terror of those who understand silence so little. The comparative absence of the defence of paradigm incommensurability in the literature should be taken not as a lack of will nor still less of argument but as a concern not to fill the void with idle prattle in some mistaken belief that noise signifies importance of contribution. Silence can be the greatest signifier of all.

The problem of the incommensurability of paradigms remains at the very core of the issue of organization paradigms. If the approaches of the smaller, less politically strong, groups can be so easily incorporated into the language of the dominant orthodoxy then their language, their culture, their very existence is unlikely to be secure. For those who argue for paradigm incommensurability there is a real tendency to think that any course of action predicated upon a belief in translation rules will result, sooner or later, in the takeover – the overrunning – of their position by hostile forces.

For this reason, the 'paradigm warriors' which, as discussed above, is the name by which they are sometimes called, continue to advocate the notion of incommensurability. The separation of the approaches taken within the paradigm, from those without, is of crucial importance for the membership because what this isolationism (Reed 1985) does is to ensure in the short term at least the survival of that approach and more importantly perhaps of the ideological standpoint from which it is made. The belief in incommensurability then has its origins in politics as well as in epistemology. The attacks upon 'paradigm warriors' which depend for their force on issues based upon logic, linguistic theory and discourse analysis, fail to recognize this. These criticisms fail to appreciate that not only is discourse about power but that concomitantly power without discourse is much weaker. Dialogue is a weapon of the powerful.

Much of what one reads is concerned with some Habermasian injunction to engage in speech and to talk through one's problems. Much of what one reads is predicated upon the university culture of debate, argumentation and dialogue. The presentation of ideas is seen as separate from the intellectual force of one's argument yet the latter is heavily dependent upon convincing the audience of the utility of the thought contained in the presentation. It is almost impossible to escape from these conventions. Universities rely upon the goodwill of those who try to speak to others in convincing terms. Yet Burrell and Morgan (1979) 'advance a very pure and hermetic form of sociological relativism, one which brings into question the very basis for scientific communication and progress' (Hassard 1993: 69). Indeed, *Sociological Paradigms and Organizational Analysis* does advocate a form of paradigm closure whereby paradigm should not speak unto paradigm and it is further argued that the resulting heterogeneity will enrich the study of organizations tremendously by allowing a thousand flowers to bloom.

The most virulent attack upon the concept of paradigm closure in organization theory has come from Lex Donaldson (1985) whose aptly named text, *In Defence of Organization Theory*, attempts to refute the arguments contained, *inter alia*, in Burrell and Morgan (1979). Donaldson argues that structural functionalism has not been in a state of crisis between the 1960s and the 1980s and in fact has been very well able to deal with new issues (and old ones) when they arise. He maintains that the functionalist concepts like 'goals' and 'system' are very sound ones both conceptually and philosophically. He believes that a revamped contingency theory would carry the field in the face of the paltry work carried out by the critics of functionalism. In 1988, the editors of the journal *Organization Studies* devoted an issue to the Donaldson piece and invited a number of scholars to talk about 'offence or defence' (see Hassard 1993: 71). To some, the debate high-lighted the existence of paradigms and their potency. To Donaldson, it showed the opposite.

Confronted in this work is a precise case of a 'paradigm Walsingham' who has set himself up as the mind guard of the discipline, developing surveillance tech-niques to assess whether what is said is organization theory which is acceptable or is the sociology of organizations which is decidedly not. Pfeffer (1993) has 'Walsinghamed' into view more recently.

Reed (1985) also discusses these issues, by no means from the same position as Donaldson but nor should it be assumed that he is close to accepting the argu-ments for paradigm closure. Reed's book *Redirections in Organizational Analy-sis* ends with a discussion of what these redirections might actually look like. He outlines four possibilities: integrationism, isolationism, imperialism and plural-ism. The first refers to the hope for eclectic reconciliation; the second to the strat-egy of paradigm separatism; the third to the success of one theoretical position over another (in this case, Marxism); and the fourth to that which Reed person-ally advocates which involves the rejection of premature closure to debate and conversation. According to Hassard (1993: 72), 'In Reed's book we find histori-cal interpretations similar to those of Burrell and Morgan (1979) and Clegg and Dunkerley (1980) but coupled with an eschewing of paradigm apartheid and incommensurable positions'.

Reed has gone on to debate these issues directly with Donaldson, who he claims presents an image of 'an intellectual orthodoxy which has been violated in various ways by heretical counter movements' (Reed 1985: 258).

The language here is very telling, for in this little phrase Reed uses the highly charged terms of rape and heresy in attempting to make the point that Donaldson seems to treat these issues as personally made and personally taken. Hassard opines that we now face a crisis:

> The crisis is deepened by the fact that the notion of paradigm heterodoxy is often joined by one of paradigm closure. Writers who specify a range of para-digm candidates often add that these various communities are incommensur-able with one another. Professional practice in different traditions is based on philosophies which are antithetical; scientists from different paradigms do not debate, they talk through one another. This is a problem in that paradigm incommensurability seems to infer (sic) an extreme form of sociological rela-tivism. If scientists cannot debate how can progress be signalled?
>
> (Hassard 1993: 74–5)

This set of questions leads us to ask how the current state of organization theory stands in relation to the notion of paradigm. Where are the paradigm warriors and where are the paradigm Walsinghams?

5 The current state of organization theory

Notwithstanding the purpose and aims of this volume, any overview of the field which claims to be anything but personal is misleading. One might wish to argue that the 'two p's' have dominated either side of the Atlantic in recent years. In Europe predominantly, there has been a concomitant concern to understand the relevance of Derrida, Lyotard, Habermas and more importantly Foucault for the study of organizations, and the links between social theory and organization theory have become closer. In the US context, population ecology has come to dominate certain arenas and still makes a good showing despite claims that it is faltering. Here the world of science predominates and the metaphor of survival with its roots in biology is the basis on which much is discussed.

Thus, on one side of the Atlantic the dominance of art and literature and the visual arts is faced; on the other the natural sciences hold sway. However, the simple notion that the *Geisteswissenschaften* face the *Naturwissenschaften* across 3,000 miles of ocean is to miss much of the complexity. In the USA there are those who focus on gender from a wide variety of perspectives which matches the European interest in the topic and although one cannot say that there is an identity of interest there are many things which are held in common. Postmodernism has also come to influence some US writing and the importance of the topic is now recognized on both sides of the ocean.

In Europe there has been little interest in carrying out work in the population ecology area although it is read with interest. So the kind of impact that writers such as Aldrich have needs to be contextualised very carefully indeed. Howard Aldrich (1992: 17) tells his audience of his attempts to understand 'two fairly new approaches to the understanding of organizational change – the ecological and institutional approaches – as well as a third which is enjoying continued vitality – an interpretive approach'. He informs the reader that two possible titles for the paper had been 'Confessions of a disillusioned positivist' and 'Pursued by the postmodernist panic' but instead he decided to focus upon 'Incommensurable paradigms'. He describes these relatively new approaches in some detail and outlines how they differ from each other and what they have to contribute in certain particular areas of study. What he seeks to do is to show that each perspective can illuminate the analysis of organizations. He says that:

All the perspectives I have reviewed have achieved significant standing today because, at their core, they have groups of dedicated researchers working on empirical research to test hypotheses derived from the perspectives. They read one another's papers, hold conferences and issue edited volumes collecting recent empirical work...In the process of constructing theory groups they have bounded themselves and organizational boundaries can be extremely difficult to surmount. The groups work very hard at emphasizing how they differ from one another, and investigators have a stake in stressing their incompatibilities.

(Aldrich 1992: 37)

One of the interesting things to emerge from Aldrich's article is the very different images of what is important to organization theory from the standpoint of writers in the USA and the UK. As Aldrich comments in the footnotes, Reed makes no mention whatsoever of any of these three perspectives 'of significant standing' in *Redirections in Organizational Analysis* (1985). Clearly, he says, they must 'have different conceptions of what constitutes modern organization theory' (Aldrich 1992: 38).

This recognition of difference has to be seen alongside what is deemed to be valuable in the US context with its emphasis on conferences, teams of researchers and the like. If the non-anglophone world is added to even this level of heterogeneity what is begun to be contemplated is an absence of shared understandings. If much of what has been learnt is not the product of the 'unequal cognitive power' of researchers but is in fact the produce of 'dead white males' then perhaps we should begin to contemplate the work on organizing in the Hispanic world, in the part of the globe which from the point of view of the occidental is the Far East, and in the continent of Africa. If Americans and Britons are separated by a common language how can we hope to incorporate the world views of non-western thinkers? Paradigm thinking assumes that the membership of individual nation states, who supposedly speak the same mother tongue, cannot understand each other at the finest level of detail. How much more is paradigm thinking likely to lead to incommensurability if there are truly global differences between the theorists?

6 The future state of organization theory

Jeffrey Pfeffer (1993), one of the leading 'paradigm Walsinghams', has recently argued that the concept of paradigm is important for the discipline as he perceives it, because a Kuhnian approach emphasizes the importance of consensus as a necessary but not sufficient condition for the systematic advancement of knowledge. Organization theory has to become more paradigmatic because 'the organizational sciences are severely fragmented and ... this fragmentation presents a serious obstacle to scientific growth of the field' (Zammuto and Connolly 1984: 30). Pfeffer begins by developing measures of the level of paradigm development and thence of the degree of consensus found. Once this quantification is complete the author asks where organization studies stands. The answer, should we be unsure, is that organization studies are not well developed in terms either of consensus or paradigm development. Pfeffer says:

> Proponents of functionalism, post-modernism, critical theory, realism and many other theoretical approaches contend vigorously in the study of organizations. Whatever else one might think of this state of affairs, it is, by definition, a state that signifies a field that is fragmented and that does not share the consensus characterizing more paradigmatically developed disciplines.
>
> (1993: 608)

The consequences of this low level of development are mainly political in the sense that the resources required by organizational scholars to carry out their work are scarce and are also bid for competitively by representatives from other more developed disciplines. In the competition, says Pfeffer, organizational science is likely to lose out. What is required in the face of this is more consensus. Quoting form Stephen Cole, Pfeffer maintains that consensus should be developed in the face of what is new to and contradictory to the established position, for these innovations often prove to be of little value. To develop in this way there needs to be an elite, a set of stars, who create and impose order on the field. Consensus should be enforced by 'a comparatively small elite' with power concentrated in their hands if we wish to see our 'paradigm rating' increase. Pfeffer bemoans the fact that the field encourages the development and advancement of differences rather than attempts integration or resolution. Compared to political science, he argues, we have not put our house in order and the current state of affairs is 'downright dangerous' for what it does is leave organization studies 'ripe for either a hostile takeover from within or without' (Pfeffer 1993: 618).

As a piece from a leading US theorist of organizations this article should not be ignored. Consider first the language in which the piece is couched. What could possible be meant by a hostile takeover from within? Which direction does he see this threat as emanating from and why should this be seen as hostile? Why is his consensus the best one to seek out when he articulates the possibility – no more – that other forms of consensus are possible and therefore presumably positively good for the discipline? Within the penultimate sentence of the article the hidden threat of internal takeover lies there awaiting a full discussion.

Furthermore, Pfeffer's notion of a paradigm as the dominant approach towards becoming a 'science' and the methods employed to uncover the present situation in organization studies clearly indicates his penchant for things positivistic. In Reed's terms the strategy adopted by Pfeffer is clearly imperialistic. The language is the rhetoric of imperialists everywhere. We face an internal or external threat – actually if it is both, so much the better. We need living space in order to do our thing properly. To achieve distinction we need a powerful elite who will impose order and bring law to the territory. Without them, what we value as distinctive – our way of life – will be irretrievably lost. Rhetoric like this often frightens the local populace but surely we are too sophisticated to swallow this whole?

The editors of the journal *Organization* have articulated a position which dissents from that of Pfeffer by advocating a strategy of integration rather than imperialism. They speak of a journey towards something they term 'neo-disciplinarity' in which there is evident an 'integrative impetus which is both ambitious and unusual'. The aim is to escape from the limitations of being paradigm warriors in which there is hostility expressed to other visions of the discipline, but also not to fall into the trap of becoming paradigm Walsinghams who seek to dominate, police and discipline the land in the interests of the 'monarchy'. A neo-disciplinary approach based on honouring the work of others yet trying to forge links between disparate language communities is the ultimate goal.

However, whether such a new journal can establish a readership for itself with such a manifesto and then go on to achieve anything like 'neo-disciplinarity' remains a moot question.

7 Paradigms as narratives

Hugh Willmott (1993) has argued that the issue of paradigm commensurability in organization studies needs to be rethought. He develops a critique of Burrell and Morgan (1979) and claims that the paradigm walls which they identified, particularly between the objective and subjective views of the nature of science, could be transcended by labour process theory.

This view of the need to transcend the boundaries which supposedly exist between paradigms thus described drew a hostile response from the self-confessed 'paradigm warriors' Norman Jackson and Pippa Carter. The language they use is a military one. It contains the metaphors and phrases of 'wars', 'sustained attack', 'one side to subordinate the other' and so on (Jackson and Carter 1993: 721). However, even if one thinks the language to be excessive there can be no doubt that there is passion here. There is the strong sense that they are agitating politically in order to survive and to allow the 'anti-Functionalist constituency' some chance of prospering. Willmott's response to this battlefield rhetoric is much more couched at the level of technical debate and the philosophical niceties. These are very important, but in this case they only serve to mask the passions that arise from one's political standing within a highly politicized field.

Returning at this point to Kuhn and the notion of paradigms as symbolic of and constitutive of power, for Jackson and Carter the concept of paradigm is a liberating one. It shows that they have a place for their work which cannot be denied them, since what they do and where they come from intellectually has a long tradition and a great heritage. It gives them a narrative in which they play a role, have a mission and set of objectives and there is a stage upon which all this might be played out. It allows them to see that the future may belong to them and it offers hope in a world where particular frameworks dominate despite the rhetoric of pluralism. The narrative of revolution and the decline of the orthodoxy is a well-established one which Kuhn was by no means the first to provide.

However, Kuhn also provided another parallel narrative. In the same way as it has been said that Marx forewarned the bourgeoisie of the dynamics of capitalism in *Das Kapital* and thereby prevented revolutions from being successful, so too Kuhn forewarned the paradigm paragons of the very processes that would come to threaten them. Forewarned of the danger of revolutionary science, normal science is much better prepared to stave it off. Forewarned of the dangers of revolutionary science in organization theory, functionalism, by the same token, is better prepared to stave it off.

It should, however, be questioned to what extent the notion of paradigms as a narrative can be maintained at a time when the very existence of narratives of this all-embracing kind has come into question. In other words, can the paradigm concept survive the ravages of postmodernist introspection? For within postmodernism there is a concern (Eagleton 1994: 12–3) to transgress bound-aries, to refuse to accept the walls which are put around us and our ideas, to speak in a babble of idioms and not in only one voice. The aim is to question the very conceptualization of the Enlightenment itself with its view of the unity of the self, the idea of progress, the concern for law and civilization and the whole monolith of western Reason. Postmodernist thinkers are against the notion of fixed binary oppositions, of us/them thinking. Instead, they celebrate the mar-ginal, the nomadic, the transitional and the indeterminate. They detest unity, fixity, progress, stability in and of the self and consensus. Postmodernism relies upon transgressors and their search for an elusive in-betweenness. Thus, it (or should we say 'they') rejects holistic explanations. It turns its back upon con-cepts which are deemed to be *passé*. Things like emancipation, political exploita-tion and justice are no longer fashionable. Political liberation, too, is no longer worth talking about within a postmodern landscape.

If this is correct then the concept of 'paradigm' has had its day. Born into that all too solid world of the early 1960s, when the young seemed about to have their day, the concept of paradigm fell sparkingly into a world ripe for its vitality. Today, notions of politics, fixed walls, barriers to communications, the Tower of Babel and the language of liberation can be found, certainly, but they are not the force they once were. Paradigm thinking and the paradigm warriors are going out of fashion – despite a flurry of writing in the area. It is almost as if, in the last rays of the dying light, some last reflections become trapped in a small prism and blind us to its imminent decline.

Some would have hoped, along with Jackson and Carter for example, that this were not so and the 'paradigm' concept would continue to provide us with our narrative. With its military metaphor and the scent, so to speak, of battle in our nostrils it was hoped that the struggle against US functionalism could continue. Marching perhaps under the banner of a loose European federation of ideas and perspectives the opportunity to attain distinction was seen. This cannot, how-ever, be a realistic scenario in the contemporary epoch.

For reasons discussed earlier, the globalization process has created an atmo-sphere in which difference and diversity are supposedly tolerated, where cultural differences are welcomed and celebrated, where non-European languages and traditions are emphasized for their powers of vitality. Barriers are down. Whether in the form of those pulled down by GATT (General Agreement on Tar-iffs and Trade) or by the East Germans or by opening up trade to Vietnam or in the decline of feminist separatism, the concept of muralification – building walls – is no longer fashionable.

For all our optimism, paradigms are dying. Because of our optimism, para-digms are dying. But the light may not have gone completely, for it may well be that the concept of paradigm or something very like it will be rekindled again and come once more into organization theory to haunt both the militant young whom we always, always need and the Walsinghams whom we almost certainly do not.

Further reading

(References cited in the text marked *)

* Aldrich, H. (1992) 'Incommensurable paradigms', in M. Reed and M. Hughes (eds), *Rethinking Organization*, London: Sage Publications. (Considers the major theoretical, methodological and substantive developments that have occurred in the field of organization studies between 1970 and 1990).

* Burrell, G. and Morgan, G. (1979) *Sociological Paradigms and Organisational Analysis*, Oxford: Heinemann.

* Donaldson, L. (1985) *In Defence of Organization Theory*, Cambridge: Cambridge University Press.

* Eagleton, T. (1994) Review of 'The location of culture' by H. Bhabha, *Guardian* 8 February: 12–13.

* Evered, R. and Louis, M. (1981) 'Alternative perspectives in the organizational sciences', *Academy of Management Review* 6 (3): 385–95.

* Friedrich, R. (1970) *A Sociology of Sociology*, New York: The Free Press.

* Gouldner, A. (1970) *The Coming Crisis in Western Sociology*, Cambridge: Cambridge University Press.

* Hassard, J. (1993) *Sociology and Organization Theory*, Cambridge: Cambridge University Press. (Traces the history of the orthodox systems theory paradigm in organization studies.)

* Hoyningen-Huene, P. (1992) 'The interrelations between the philosophy, history and sociology of science in Thomas Kuhn's theory of scientific development', *British Journal for the Philosophy of Science* 43 (4).

* Jackson, N. and Carter, P. (1993) 'Paradigm wars: a response to Hugh Willmott', *Organization Studies* 14 (5): 727–30.

* Kuhn, T. S. (1962) *The Structure of Scientific Revolutions*, Chicago, IL: University of Chicago Press.

* Kuhn, T.S. (1970) *The Structure of Scientific Revolutions*, 2nd edn, Chicago, IL: University of Chicago Press.

* Kuhn, T.S. (1977) 'Second thoughts on paradigms', in *The Essential Tension*, Chicago, IL: University of Chicago Press.

* Masterman, H. (1970) 'The nature of a paradigm', in I. Lakatos and A. Musgrove (eds), *Criticism and the Growth of Knowledge*, Cambridge: Cambridge University Press.

* *Organization* (1994) 'Editorial statement' 1 (1): 1–12.

* Pfeffer, J. (1993) 'Barriers to the advance of organizational science: paradigm development as a dependent variable', *Academy of Management Review* 18 (4): 599–620.

* Pondy, L. and Boje, D. (1981) 'Bringing mind back in', in W. Evan (ed.), *Frontiers in Organization and Management*, New York: Praeger.

* Reed, M. (1985) *Redirections in Organizational Analysis*, London: Routledge.

* Ritzer, G. (1975) *Sociology: A Multiple Paradigm Science*, Needham Heights, MA: Allyn & Bacon.

* Sankey, H. (1993) 'Kuhn's changing concept of incommensurability', *British Journal of the Philosophy of Science* 44: 759–74.

* Sheridan, A. (1980) *Michel Foucault: The Will to Truth,* London: Routledge.

* Silverman, D. (1970) *The Theory of Organizations*, Oxford: Heinemann

* Willmott, H. (1993a) 'Paradigm gridlock: a reply', *Organization Studies* 14(5): 727–30.

* Willmott, H. (1993b) 'Breaking the paradigm mentality', *Organization Studies* 14(5): 681–719.

* Zammuto, R.F. and Connolly, T. (1984) 'Coping with disciplinary fragmentation', *Organizational Behaviour Teaching Review* 9: 30–7.

Organization types

Richard Butler

Overview

An organization type defines the general characteristics of a class of organization. A major purpose in defining an organization type is to be able to distinguish one class of organization from another. A typology provides a system of types whereby classes of organization can be distinguished according to their relative position on a number of predetermined variables.

Other terms which are used almost synonymously with 'typology' are categorization, classification, configuration and taxonomy. The term cluster, especially since the widespread use of the statistical technique of cluster analysis, may also be used to refer to empirically derived typologies.

Typologies have been extensively developed in the life sciences as a means of categorizing plants or animals. The social sciences, such as organization theory, have also been active in developing typologies. A major argument for the use of a typology in the management and organizational fields is to move away from reductionist theory, with its emphasis upon bi-variate relationships and fragmentation, towards a more holistic perspective. The case for using a typology rests upon the notion that organizations have discrete interdependent structural and environmental elements which tend to coalesce into recognizable patterns making it difficult for just one of these elements to change on its own. An effective typology therefore should have the capacity to provide an economical explanatory theory of why particular features are found.

Two main problems often become apparent with typologies which suggest that a heavy reliance upon typologies in a subject indicates a pre-theoretical stage of development. First, is obtaining agreement among scholars concerning the basis for categorization. This has led to a proliferation of typologies each with its own set of advocates. Second, is the problem of choosing the category within the typology to which a particular member of a population of organizations belongs. For instance, a well-established simple typology makes the distinction between bureaucratic/mechanistic and flexible/organic organizations. To categorize an organization as bureaucratic is to imply that it cannot have some characteristics of the organic category; in practice, however, organizations will exhibit some aspects of both categories.

I Ideal types

Bureaucracy, as identified by the German sociologist, Max Weber (1968), is often taken as a starting point for organizational theory. For Weber, bureaucracy formed part of a wider system of types of authority, with bureaucracy itself seen as based upon rational–legal authority, in contrast to traditional and charismatic authority types. These types were not to be seen as ends in their own right but are called 'ideal types', meaning that they provide analytical anchorage points against which the real world can be measured. Weber's purpose in identifying these types was to carry out a historical analysis of Western societies in order to understand the processes of change, particularly the relentless march of bureaucratic organization, and the routinization of charisma into rational–legal authority. Weber's use of the ideal type provides a lesson for those interested in developing typologies: a typology is most useful when it is used to help understand a wider issue or process of change during which one type becomes transformed into another.

The US sociologist James Thompson (1967) provided an elaborate system of types relating to various aspects of organization. There are types of interdependence, coordination, technology, decision making and performance standards, but a particular contribution of Thompson's system of types is to allow them to interact with one another to provide a dynamic view of organization. Thompson does not therefore provide an overall organization type, but uses typologies to provide a contingency theory of organization which has become extremely influential. In this sense it could be argued that almost the entire edifice of organizational theory is built upon the two-by-two table giving four ideal types of some characteristic of organization.

In order to make sense out of the myriad of existing typologies in the field it is useful to categorize the major typologies found in the organizational literature into those which are based predominantly upon institutional factors, strategy, technology, managerial ideology, national culture or internal structure. Another aspect of typologies concerns whether they are deductive or empirically derived. Deductive typologies tend to be based upon a wider theory of organization and upon the expectation that if we look at the world in this way this is what we will see. Empirical typologies, or taxonomies, derive from analysis of a database whereby scores on a number of variables form a pattern which can then be given a theoretical meaning.

A summary of the types to be covered in this article is given in Table 1. This is by no means a complete coverage of the range of types to be found but a selection of those which are particularly influential, either because of their long-standing influence or some particular theoretical or empirical interest.

Table 1 A typology of organizational types

Category	Criterion	
	Deductively derived	*Empirically derived*
Institutional factors	Societal functions (Parsons 1960)	
	Prime beneficiary (Blau and Scott 1963)	
	Norms of performance (Butler 1991)	
	Markets versus hierarchy (Williamson 1975)	
Task environment	Causal textures (Emery and Trist 1965)	
Strategy	Analyser, defender, prospector and reactor (Miles and Snow 1978)	
Technology		Unit, batch and process production (Woodward 1980)
	Variability and analysis level (Perrow 1970)	
Managerial ideology	Authority (Weber 1968)	
	Power and compliance (Etzioni 1964)	
Structure		Mechanistic–organic (Burns and Stalker 1962)
		Structuring and the concentration of authority (Pugh and Hickson 1989)
	Five functions, five coordination types (Mintzberg 1983)	

2 Institutional factors

Perhaps the oldest form of organization typology is what may be called a typology based upon institutional factors. By this method organizations are given a name describing some significant aspect of how the socio-legal framework defines them. Organizations may be described as profit or non-profit, or as military, business, educational, governmental, voluntary, multinational, functional, divisional and so forth. These categories form a 'common sense' view of the world and are generally terms embedded within everyday language. Underlying them, however, is usually a distinction as to the way in which these organizations are treated and measured in the institutional environment.

Parsons (1960) derived a typology of organizations based upon their function within a wider social system. His four types include organizations with economic goals or political goals, integrative organizations (such as government agencies) and pattern maintenance organizations (such as churches and schools).

As with Weber, Parsons was a 'grand theorist' of sociology whose greater concern was to derive a theory of society rather than of the structures of organizations.

Blau and Scott (1963) developed a typology based upon the notion of the 'prime and beneficiary' of an organization. Four types result from this typology: (1) mutual benefit associations, where the prime beneficiary is the membership; (2) business concerns, where the prime beneficiaries are the owners; (3) service organizations, where clients are the prime beneficiaries; and (4) commonweal organizations, where the public at large is the prime beneficiary.

Butler (1991) developed a typology based upon the performance norms that are used by dominant regulators to assess an organization. This typology, therefore, takes a regulator's eye view of how to devise suitable regulatory instruments for organizations under their surveillance. Two dimensions of the environment are seen as particularly significant in this task. First, is the uniqueness versus comparability dimension; if there are readily available comparable organizations the regulator's task is much easier than if an organization is unique. Second, is the clarity–ambiguity dimension; when there is a clear measure of performance a regulator's task is easier than when performance is difficult to measure.

Combining these two dimensions gives us four types of organization. When performance is clear and comparable is the easiest form of regulation and regulators tend therefore to apply economic norms; the type of organization corresponding to this situation is a *market* or *business organization*. When performance is clear but unique instrumental norms tend to be applied which means that regulators tend to set targets but have no means of knowing whether those targets are realistic; the type of organization corresponding to this is an *agency*, typified by government agencies such as tax collecting where there is a well-defined target but only one such agency carrying out the work. When performance is ambiguous but comparable referent norms tend to apply; these involve a high degree of self-regulation through the use of practitioners' associations, as is typically found in *professional* organizations. When performance is ambiguous and unique is the most difficult case for regulators and they tend to apply moral norms, as are typically found in *religious* movements, *charities* or *voluntary* organizations. The basis for regulation in this situation becomes trust which, in practice, means appointing highly trustworthy people to run the organization.

This typology of performance norms allows us to see the regulation of organizations in the institutional environment as a dynamic process involving an interaction between an organization and its regulator. Regulators will tend to emphasize comparability and clarity; organizations will tend to emphasize uniqueness and ambiguity. The typology also allows us to translate the impact of external regulation into the internal ideological needs of the organization. For example, an organization under a strong regulatory regime of market norms will tend to emphasize these norms in its internal structures and decision-making practices.

Another institutionally based typology identifies the market and hierarchy as two distinct forms of organization (Williamson 1975). This distinction revived a long-standing question as to the boundary between economics and organizational theory with regard to the point at which it becomes more efficient for transactions conducted in a marketplace to come under the umbrella of hierarchical organization. This argument has been further extended to a third type of organization, the clan or the collective type (Butler 1983), where the main governing mechanism is trust, rather than competition as in a market, or obedience to rules in the hierarchy.

3 Task environment

Other external criteria upon which organizations may be classified concern the task environment; that part of the environment with which exchanges of resources take place. Emery and Trist (1965) introduced the notion of the causal texture of organizational environments based upon the interconnectedness of organizations within it.

Four environmental types were distinguished in terms of their dynamic processes (placid, disturbed or turbulent), and their connectedness (random, clustered, reactive or mutually causal), each with an associated coping or adaptive mechanism on the part of the focal organization.

1 With a placid and random causal texture coping involves tactical decision making, with relatively short time horizons since there is little change taking place.
2 With a placid but clustered environment a strategic coping mechanism becomes possible. Due to the interconnectedness of the environment, it becomes necessary to plan relationships more carefully.
3 With a disturbed, reactive environment 'operations' are required as a coping mechanism. This means that a series of planned tactical initiatives are needed to manage the complex set of relationships, for example, through horizontal integration.
4 With a turbulent, mutually causal environment an organization has to be aware of the complexity of two-way relationships in the environment and hence has to adopt a series of multilateral agreements, for example, joint ventures or other forms of cooperative strategies.

The Emery and Trist typology has been influential and has the advantage of focusing our attention upon the importance of environmental factors in determining how organizations act. It also makes the vital link between environmental characteristics and internal structure.

4 Strategy

Heavily influenced by the business policy and strategic management literature, typologies have also been based upon the strategies that organizations adopt in their environments. Prominent amongst these typologies is that of Miles and

Snow (1978), a classification of organizations into four generic strategic types: (1) the defender emphasizes price competition and internal efficiency; (2) the prospector actively seeks innovation and new markets; (3) the analyser is a hybrid combining features of both prospector and defender; and (4) the reactor is seen as an ineffective type who simply waits and responds to events.

These types are based upon three underlying problems that organizations have to contend with in developing a successful strategy: the entrepreneurial problem, the engineering problem and the administrative problem. Each type develops its own pattern of solutions to these problems. For example, the prospector's answer to the entrepreneurial problem is to locate and exploit market opportunities, to the engineering problem to avoid long-term commitments to a single technology, and to the administrative problem to facilitate and coordinate numerous and diverse operations.

The Miles and Snow typology has attracted attention but also controversy. Intuitively appealing and allowing some precise prescriptions to be made, it highlights some significant problems when applying a typological approach to the study of organizations. It is difficult to make these categories mutually exclusive, especially when dealing with large organizations. What was meant to be a classification system, therefore, becomes a number of variables whereby one can perceive degrees of defending, prospecting and so forth, within any one organization. To overcome this problem, Miles and Snow found it necessary to introduce the hybrid analyser type.

5 Technology

Typologies of organization based upon technology classify organizations in terms of their core work and outline a number of structural characteristics that are affected. Woodward (1980) was able, from an overall scale consisting of 13 points, to identify three broad types of technology: (1) unit and small batch production (output made to customer's orders); (2) large batch and mass production (output made for stock); and (3) process production (near continuous making of a uniform product).

Perrow (1970) outlined four types of technology based upon the two major dimensions of technology: (1) analysability of task, which goes from being very difficult to break down into identifiable steps (low analysability) to easily broken down into identifiable steps (high analysability); and (2) variability of stimulus, which goes from operators who are continuously presented with new tasks (high variability) to tasks that are monotonous and unchanging (low variability). *Routine technology* occurs when the task is easily analysed and the stimulus non-variable; the organizational problem here is to maintain efficient control of the operators. *Engineering technology* occurs when the task is still analysable but the stimulus varies, such as when standard products and procedures are modified or put together in different ways to meet varying customer requirements; the organizational problem here is to keep efficient control while allowing sufficient variability. *Craft technology* occurs when the task cannot be analysed but the stimulus is non-variable, such as for a performing artist who is repeatedly performing the same show but whose show is difficult to analyse or reproduce; the organizational problem here is to develop the skill contained within the expertise of the operators which cannot be easily managed by outsiders. *Non-routine technology* occurs when analysability is low and variability high; the organizational problem here is to get teams working together who are not quite sure what they are doing or how to do it.

This typology is useful for tracing the consequences for an organization of a change in the two underlying dimensions of technology. Hence, an increase in the degree of analysability and a decrease in the variability of tasks would indicate an increase in formal structures, centralization and standardization of procedures.

6 Managerial ideology

The belief systems that underlie the structures used in organization also provide a basis for classification. Weber's (1968) three types of authority (discussed above) provide one such classification. Although the rational–legal authority, corresponding to bureaucratic organization, has dominated organizational theory it should not be forgotten that the other two types also have an important part to play in organizational theory. Charismatic authority emphasizes a highly personal style of management and is related to Weber's notion of patrimonial organization, while traditional authority is related to feudal organization.

Not unrelated to Weber's typology is a classification based upon managerial power and the associated compliance of subordinates. Etzioni (1964) proposed that the way in which lower participants in an organization respond to managerial power is a critical factor in considering an organization's mode of operation. Three types of the power–compliance combination are proposed as representing a stable position: (1) coercive–alienative, whereby management uses force and punishments with a consequent alienation of participants from the objectives of the organization (typified by a prison); (2) remunerative–calculative, whereby management uses economic exchange with a consequent response by participants who see the degree of their involvement in terms of a cost–benefit balance (typified by a business organization); and (3) normative–moral, whereby the process of management is more a case of reaching common understandings and trusting participants to adhere to these (typified by a commune or other form of collective organization).

An essential aspect of Etzioni's typology is that the power compliance and systems need to be congruent; incongruent matches, such as coercive authority with moral compliance would be considered unstable and a shift in authority or compliance would be expected in order to restore congruence. There is obviously a similarity between Etzioni's typology and the market, bureaucracy and collective distinctions discussed above.

7 Structure

Internal structure, the pattern of rules and relationships in an organization, has probably provided the most common base for organization typologies, some prominent examples of which are given below.

Mechanistic versus organic organizations

One of the most enduring classifications of organizations is the distinction between the bureaucratic or mechanistic structure, which is suitable for routine standardized tasks, and the organic structure which is more flexible, suitable for changing technology and market conditions. The terms originated from a classic study by Burns and Stalker (1962), who observed in the post-Second World War British electronics industry that the companies most successfully adopting and developing the new technology were those using an organic structure which allowed for greater horizontal and informal communication, and in which employees had a sense of mission for the whole company; this was in contrast to a mechanistic–bureaucratic structure relying upon hierarchical authority.

Structuring and the concentration of authority

While the mechanistic–organic distinction has provided an enduring typology, it lacks the distinctions needed to capture the diversity of organizations. Another typology, which is empirically based but covers a broader sample of organizations, is derived from the work of the Aston research programme (Pugh and Hickson 1989). Forty-six organizations from the public, private and service-manufacturing sectors offered a broad base to develop this typology. The organizations were measured on a series of scales to capture five variable groups of bureaucratic structure. Two salient dimensions of structure stood out from analysis of the data. First, was the structuring of activities; a highly structured organization tends to have many standard procedures formalized into documents and breaks tasks down into precise specialties. The second dimension, concentration of authority, signifies an organization in which authority is highly concentrated, centralizing decision making within the top management or even outside the organization within a parent or owner organization.

From these two dimensions four types of organization can be identified:

1 full bureaucracy (seen when both structuring of activities and concentration of authority is high);
2 workflow bureaucracy (seen when structuring is high but concentration of authority is low, leading to precisely programmed work with written instructions so that little direct managerial intervention is needed);
3 personnel bureaucracy (seen when structuring is low but authority is concentrated and formal procedures are replaced by direct managerial action);
4 non-bureaucracy (a rather undefined type using neither direct authority nor structuring but relying upon informal relationships (Pugh and Hickson 1989)).

The advantage of this empirically derived taxonomy is that it makes explicit the basis upon which organizations are placed in one category or another. In practice, however, it is the constituent variables and dimensions of these studies that are cited more than the taxonomy.

Five-by-five design configuration

Building upon the argument for a configurational approach to organizational design Mintzberg (1983) has proposed five types of organizational design. Each design has a dominant characteristic and is suitable for different conditions (Mintzberg 1983). The typology is built up from the need of organizations to carry out five internal functions and for these functions to cohere with each other in a particular way:

1 the *strategic function* involves the making of strategic decisions at the apex of the organization;
2 the *technostructure* is where technical activities such as research and development take place;
3 the *operating core* is where the central work and production activities of the organization take place;
4 the *middle line* consists of middle management, such as plant managers;
5 the *support staff* who provide services such as payroll administration.

The five design types are derived from various patterns of key functions and associated coordinating mechanisms. These are as follows:

1 The *simple structure*, where the strategic apex is dominant and direct supervision is the prime coordinating mechanism; this is most suitable for the young, small company in a dynamic environment.
2 The *machine bureaucracy*, where the technostructure is the prime function and the organization is ruled by technocrats whose main job is to provide standardized procedures for the operating core; this is most suitable for older, larger, semi-monopolistic organizations in stable conditions.
3 The *professional bureaucracy*, where the operating core is dominant, is based upon coordination by standardization of skills; this organization is most suitable for complex but relatively stable environments.
4 The *divisionalized form*, where the middle line is the primary function, is coordinated by standardization of outputs; this is most suitable for diversified markets.
5 The *adhocracy*, where it is more difficult to identify a single dominant function since, by definition, it is a type of organization in which there are shifting patterns of power. None the less the support staff, it is suggested, would tend to be dominant and the conditions under which this comparatively anarchic form would be most appropriate would be in a highly complex and unstable environment where prediction and planning is difficult.

8 Conclusion

Many researchers see fit to produce their own typology of whatever is being studied and the taxonomic method of producing types ensures a systematic and explicit basis for forming a typology. Typologies represent an essentially pre-theoretical stage of development but provide useful summarizing concepts when considering issues of organization design. Types are also useful when examining the dynamics of change from one type to another and, consequently, reference to a type often leads to its decomposition into component variables and a search for an explanation of why these variables should, at a particular time, cohere into a recognizable configuration. It is when thinking along these lines that a typology can help towards building a more general theory of what is being studied.

Further reading

(References cited in the text marked *)

* Blau, P.M. and Scott, W.R. (1963) *Formal Organizations: A Comparative Approach*, London: Routledge & Kegan Paul. (Contains a typology based upon the prime beneficiaries of organizations placed within a broader framework.)
* Burns, T. and Stalker, G.M. (1962) *The Management of Innovation*, London: Tavistock Publications. (The highly influential organic– mechanistic dualism survives.)
* Butler, R.J. (1983) 'A transactional approach to organizing efficiency: perspectives from markets, hierarchies and collectives', *Administration and Society* 15 (3): 323–62. (Suggests three underlying modes of organization, ordered along the two dimensions of collaboration and feedback but with an intermediate form.)
* Butler, R.J. (1991) *Designing Organizations: A Decision Making Perspective*, London: Routledge. (Contains a typology based upon norms of performance. A source of references.)
* Dawson, S. (1998) 'Woodward, Joan, (1916–71)', in *The IEBM Handbook of Management and Thinking*, London: Thomson Learning. (Detailed biography of the life and works of Woodward.)
* Emery, F.E. and Trist, E.L. (1965) 'The causal texture of organizational environments', *Human Relations* 18: 21–32. (A sophisticated and still relevant treatment of types of organizational environments.)
* Etzioni, A. (1964) *Modern Organizations*, Englewood Cliffs, NJ: Prentice Hall. (Compliance of participants is the basis for a typology in this early book on the sociology of organizations.)
* Miles, R.E. and Snow, C.C. (1978) *Organizational Strategy, Structure and Process*, New York: McGraw-Hill. (A typology linking strategy to technical and structural characteristics.)
  Miller, D., Friesen, P.H. and Mintzberg, H. (1984) *Organizations: A Quantum View*, London: Prentice Hall. (Argues that each type within an organization typology will display a unique pattern of characteristics.)
* Mintzberg, H. (1983) *Structures in Fives: Designing Effective Organizations*, Englewood Cliffs, NJ: Prentice Hall. (Five useful types based upon patterns in five organizational functions.)
* Parsons, T. (1960) *Structure and Process in Modern Society*, Glencoe. IL: The Free Press. (An early statement of the importance of institutional factors for the patterning of organization structures.)

* Perrow, C. (1970) *Organizational Analysis: A Sociological View*, London: Tavistock Publications. (Particularly useful for a typology connecting technology and structural features of organizations.)
* Pugh, D.S. and Hickson, D.J. (1989) *Writers on Organizations*, 4th edn, Newbury Park, CA: Sage Publications. (Outlines the Aston typology and is a useful source of references.)
* Thompson, J.D. (1967) *Organizations in Action*, New York: McGraw-Hill. (A high level of understanding about organizations is achieved through a unique combining of types of technology, interdependence, coordination, decision making and standards of assessment.)
* Weber, M. (1968) *Economy and Society: An Outline of Interpretive Sociology*, G. Roth and G. Wittick (eds), New York: Bedminster Press. (Famous for the ideal type of bureaucracy which needs to be put within the wider perspective of this great classic.)
* Williamson, O.E. (1975) *Markets and Hierarchies: Analysis and Anti-trust Implications*, New York: The Free Press. (Re-introduced an old debate as to the nature of the firm and its distinction from the marketplace.)
* Woodward, J. (1980) *Industrial Organization: Theory and Practice*, 2nd edn, intro. S. Dawson and D. Wedderburn, Oxford: Oxford University Press. (A typology of manufacturing technology first published in 1965.)

Organization structure

Cas Vroom

Overview

Organization structure has been one of the central issues in organization theory over the last century. This entry presents the historical development of the term and the related theory formation from a particular point of view: the sociology of knowledge. Three main parts will be distinguished: the archetypical bureaucracy; the stakeholder model; newer ways of thinking, especially the reflexive theories. It will be argued that both organization theory and organizational practice are to benefit from a critical reflection on the significance and use of the concept of structure. The sociology of knowledge, concerning itself with questioning the way knowledge is produced and used, provides an excellent starting point for such reflection.

1 The analysis of organization structure

This entry will look at the development of a central object of research in organizational analysis: structure. A provisional definition of structure is: the way in which an organization is built up, the way in which relations and relationships between people in an organization are more or less regulated. Structure formation could be seen as a process of generating and recreating meaning, one in which organizational members wish to secure their 'provinces of meanings' (Berger and Luckmann 1967) within the very structure and working of the organization. Research and the construction of theories surrounding this concept have always had a prominent place in organizational theory, especially when seen from the sociological perspective. It is here that sociology distinguishes itself from psychology, economy, law and other sciences which are concerned with human behaviour. The focus on the development of inter-human relationships, the different forms these take, the way in which people learn to adjust to each other's behaviour and at the same time realize innovations and changes, in short the growth and decline of social institutions, constitutes the domain of sociology.

54

Structure and structure formation: a two-track approach

Who are the people so interested in structure and the creation of structures? The sociology of knowledge addresses this type of question. There are, provisionally, at least two types of people to consider. First, sociologists and other social scientists of organization have a self-evident professional interest in the forms that people develop to coordinate the way they live and work together. The structure of an organization is a highly instructive field of research because it usually involves a deliberate and normally fairly powerful level of formal regulation. Second, for those who are involved in the actual functioning of an organization, the structure and the accompanying rules are, to say the least, interesting. After all, structure forms the battlefield in which those actors endeavour to keep each other under control.

The structure of an organization and the accompanying coordination problems can thus be approached from two angles:

1 the theoretical domain – as a scientific field of research, which is one of the central domains of organizational theorists (and sociologists in particular), especially those concerning themselves with institutional explanation;
2 the empirical-practical domain – as a practical management problem for the internal and external parties involved in an organization because they endeavour, via the creation of structures, to safeguard their interests, and therefore concern themselves with action-orientated explanations.

The premise here is that both domains are not linked to one another in the rather traditional relationship between science and practice. Theorists usually see the world of everyday life and work as the empirical domain, the so-called material object of scientific research, of which they can make use in order to test their theoretical hypotheses. These hypotheses, in their turn, are based on their formal object, their perspective on or approach to reality – in German their *Erkenntnisinteresse* ('knowledge interest'). The world of day-to-day practice is just the domain of non-scientific considerations and decisions, meaning that the average practitioner is acting on principles which differ from those of the scientist. The case may be pleaded of an ongoing, dynamic interaction in which social theorists and managers are continually learning from each other. To put it even more forcefully: it is precisely the learning process that makes it worth while to enter into both domains in conjunction.

The sociology of knowledge: a fruitful vantage point

It will be demonstrated that in social research, especially in research into organizational phenomena, one is not only concerned with an empirically correct description and explanation of the facts. There are also other matters at stake; notably, the questions of why we want to acquire certain knowledge, why we are interested in certain phenomena and, as has been mentioned above, who is interested. As discussed, that is the core of the sociology of knowledge. If the history of research teaches us one thing, it is that our material object can be looked at in different ways. Many diverse cross-sections have been made through the facts, and the facts have been in turn coloured by theoretical notions. This building upon one another's work produced the accusation that no stable formulation of a theory could be arrived at.

In considering the important question of the nature of the research object, it is worth referring to the distinction that Burrell and Morgan (1979) made between a subjective and an objective approach to the social sciences. Do we see the social world as a hard reality which exists outside ourselves, or rather as a social construction of and by individual people, who manage to firmly convince each other of the worth of such a construction? Both authors have explored the roots of that difference thoroughly and with reason, but unfortunately they have confined themselves to the field of the development of the science itself and paid no attention to the interaction between the formulation of theories and the practical use of theoretical insights.

Scientific and organizational dynamism: an assignment

It is important to realize that the dynamics of scientific analysis are tied to the dynamics of the organizational processes themselves. Both the organizational processes and our thinking about them are subject to ongoing development. Any attempt to lend them apparent permanence by looking for empirically valid, and therefore perhaps 'definitive' theories, is a waste of time. It is the continuous learning which is important, both for the theoreticians and for those who are actually involved in the organizational processes. This entry will seek to demonstrate that a sound understanding of these reciprocally dynamic forces is providing a powerful contribution to organizational practice and to the development of organization theory. It is precisely through an understanding of this that we can come a step closer to what may be regarded as the central theoretical and practical assignment for the social sciences and thus also for organizational theory: how to explain movement? If one objection can be made to the results of organization theory research to date, it is that there are few terms and theories, if any at all, with which change can be described. The effects of this on the thinking and actions of people in organizations are unmistakable. Practically everyone still thinks in terms of Archimedes' fixed points as a way of understanding change. Organization structure, too, would seem to offer such stability. This entry will attempt to go a step further towards dynamic analyses. The practical importance of this can be endorsed by every management consultant.

Having founded our perspective in the sociology of knowledge, the discussion below will concentrate on an analysis of the main streams of thought on organizational structure. The archetypal bureaucracy, the stakeholder model and some newer theories, especially those concerning learning, will be discussed.

2 The archetypal bureaucracy: structure as the steering mechanism in the hands of the leader

This section begins with a description of Weber's thesis (1947) before briefly outlining the classic description of the bureaucratic organization. The archetypal bureaucracy (rationality, task specialization, hierarchy, regularity) arose with the modernization of social relations. Social issues were becoming ever more complex and the organizational density was thought to be increasing continually. A solution to such problems was required. The giving of such answers or, expressed in a different way, social and organizational management, could only be accomplished with the help of large-scale bureaucratic organizations based on specialist knowledge and regularity. Through this, moreover, ongoing further rationalization of social and organizational relationships arose, which in its turn generated new complexities, one reason being because of differences in phases of development. This is the core of Weber's ideas.

Leaders are given the opportunity of carrying out two major activities by means of bureaucratic organizational structures. Further suggestions can be made for objectives and policy on the basis of expert analyses by the bureaucratic staff. Senior management in the organization determines the main direction of policy and indicates the parameters within which the policy makers should operate. In addition, management is able to implement the chosen policies by means of those bureaucrats who keep to the rules and guidelines imposed from above. One barely needs to argue that in such a situation the question of the structure's best design plays a vital role. After all, it is by structuring tasks, competencies and responsibilities that the leadership of the organization is able to convert its ideas and wishes with reference to policy and policy implementation, and to convert results into deeds in a relatively accurate fashion (Barnard 1938). It can do so on a relatively large scale and on a reasonably efficient basis.

Theoretical and empirical research into variants on the bureaucratic organization

Many have contributed in the past to enhancing theoretical knowledge on organizational structures (by empirically verifying theoretical statements). Initiatives have been taken to explain the formation of structures. Attempts have been made to draw up comprehensive classifications. This state of affairs can be described using some parallel and sometimes intersecting lines. The first line can be described as an attempt to devise, as it were, a biological identification system which would allow people to classify types of organizational structures. Major representatives of this line are Blau and Scott (1962) with their *cui bono* principle (who has an interest in the results of the organization?), Etzioni (1961) with 'compliance' (questioning the way people subordinate themselves to the organization), the Aston Group (Pugh *et al.* 1969) with an empirical taxonomy of organizations, and more recently, Mintzberg (1979) with the way in which coordination comes about within organizations. In addition, in a second line, an attempt was made to relate types of organizational structure to all kinds of internal and external influences linked to the environment, technology and information. Thus, gradually a fairly diverse collection of insights, empirically verified statements and methods of approach arose. What they all have in common is a relatively objective view of organizations: relatively objective statements can be made on the class of empirical phenomena called 'organization'.

The concept of structure

The student of business and management should have a clear understanding of the basic foundations of the structure debate before entering into the more subtle discussions and criticisms. Hence a summary is presented here, in the form of an intermezzo, of some more or less common connotations of the concept of structure. One source is the so-called Aston School (Pugh *et al.* 1969), the other is the influential work of Mintzberg (1979).

The concept of structure could first be explored in a more analytical way. Structure as such could be unravelled into distinct elements or dimensions, which in turn are logically connected. Researchers have used this approach for distinguishing between types of organization structure and for comparing these in terms of effectiveness and efficiency. One could describe this effort as a kind of flora and fauna determination of the variety of the organizational species. The following list of structural dimensions is generally accepted:

1 *Specialization* refers to the division of work within the organization. First, one could point to the level of the individual employee: the total number of specialisms in a given organization and the degree of role specialization (the number of different tasks or actions which are brought together in one single function). Second, one could speak of specialization on the level of organization units. This refers to the way in which the various individual functions are grouped into organizational units. The logical counterpart to specialization is coordination: specialized tasks, functions or units should be lined up in a way that facilitates reaching the organizational goals.

2 *Standardization* refers to the way the organization has structured its processes according to standards or routines. Two subdimensions could be distinguished in this respect. Firstly, one has the standardization of procedures, the rules according to which decision-making processes, work implementation processes or external contacts should take place. Secondly, one could speak about the standardization of roles, the way people have to behave in the organization in a variety of aspects, for example the possession of standard qualifications and the implementation of standard job evaluations.

3 *Formalization* has to do with the level of writing down information and procedures. This is a rather traditional dimension, formulated already by Weber, who emphasized that written information could be used as a safeguard against the arbitrariness of the rulers. This dimension furthered the rationalization of organizational processes because only then was a critical and comprehensive analysis of written documentation on the organizational processes possible.

4 *Centralization* refers to the level on which legitimate decisions with regard to the organization can be made. The level of centralization can easily be

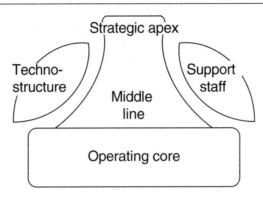

Figure 1 Mintzberg's model

determined by asking the question: who is the last person in the organization who has to give approval before a planned activity could be implemented in a legitimate way?

5 *Configuration* concerns the super- and subordination of tasks, functions and positions. In this respect the concept of configuration could be matched with *hierarchy*. One speaks of long hierarchical lines when the organization is characterized by many layers of authority. The classic example of hierarchy is the armed forces, although the term itself is first mentioned in the Bible, referring to the hierarchy of angels.

The last element of these analytical distinctions (configuration) has been worked out by Mintzberg (1979). His contribution is especially interesting, because it could be connected to the discussion of the stakeholder model of organizations in section 3 of this chapter. The visual representation of his model is well known (Figure 1).

According to Mintzberg, every organization is made up of five component parts and the people within it. The strategic apex consists of the top management people; the operating core executes the daily work of the organization; the middle line is by definition in the middle, translating downwards the goals of the apex and upwards the information emerging from the operational processes. The technostructure people are responsible for the standardization of work processes, the support staff for the people in the organization and all other types of staff advice.

Mintzberg distinguishes at least five configurations which it is useful to present here. In each of his configurations he gives structural preponderance to each of these five 'groups' in the organization. In his *simple structure* the strategic apex is responsible for the direct supervision of the day-to-day work processes and is therefore the most important group. An example is a relatively small independent supplier to a larger enterprise. In the *machine bureaucracy* the technostructure deals with the standardization of the work in order to improve the efficiency of the various activities. If successful, it contributes most to the overall result of the organization, and is therefore the most powerful. Mass assembly industries illustrate this type of configuration. In the *professional bureaucracy* the operating core consists of professional workers, normally highly trained and with a strong inclination to autonomy. They are the most valuable asset in the organization and they tend to defend that position against the other groups. Universities and hospitals are good examples. The *divisionalized form*, as is the case in many larger multinational enterprises, is characterized by the fact that the middle line is carrying out the actual business. The strategic apex often acts as a kind of investment banker, while the operating core implements their product–market combination. The middle line is responsible for the development of new business and the control of operations. Finally, the *adhocracy* refers to the type of configuration in which the operating core and the support staff work together to achieve their goals. They tend to do this by way of mutual adjustment because the nature of the work is rather variable and the necessary knowledge to deal with this kind of work is not readily available.

Mintzberg's collection of insights, in relatively systematically ordered manuals, was subsequently passed on to the next generation of students interested in studying the phenomenon of organization. The advent of business, public administration and organization studies (and even military business studies) is partly based on the notion that such insights are useful for those who will become future leaders in all kinds of social organizations. After all, future generations could benefit from the knowledge which has been collected in the course of time. They can build on the progressive rationalization and thus proceed along the intellectual path already being pursued.

This would seem to be a rather optimistic view of the status quo. Looking back over the past 100 years, it is astonishing that there has been no systematic synthesis of the research into all these different organizational structure variants. Jokingly it might be said that a small guide on organization (for example, *The Prince* by Machiavelli), offering definitive solutions to organizational problems, could be guaranteed to be a commercial success. Now it has to be observed that the different theoretical and empirical findings exist alongside each other in relative peace. This prompts some (for example, Lammers and Hickson 1979) to make the reproach that so little replication research has been done in order to verify relationships, discovered earlier, in a different context. They plead, therefore, for more vigorous activities in the field of inter-institutional and international comparative research. However, it is dubious whether by doing so, anything essential could be contributed to solving this problem of the lack of a definitive synthesis.

3 The stakeholder model of organizations: structure as a weapon

Since the approach described above did not produce the desired results, some researchers pursued different avenues. Further scrutiny of the human organization provided the insight that an organization can also be analysed as a collection of parties or factions with less or more power, each of which has its own view of the different events occurring in and around organizations (for example, Crozier 1964). The managers or leaders are then seen as one of the many parties in and around the organization. Sometimes they are the ones who have taken the initiative to create an organization. In any event, they believe themselves to have a special claim on giving direction to the aims, processes and results of the organization. This insight into the stakeholder structure within and around organizations partly emerged from research findings that the different parties involved valued the same items in different ways.

Basically this is a perfectly normal sociological notion: one tends to view the matters differently depending on one's position and role. This line of thinking led at least to people beginning to question the rationality of the earlier bureaucracy model. What was earlier regarded as an automatic claim of leaders to authority now came to be seen as an ideologically determined division of power. A comprehensive idea of rationality is abandoned for the sub-rationalities of the various parties.

Each stakeholder strives to achieve its own interests:

1 *leaders*, by developing an ideology of solidarity and focusing on common goals;
2 *internal parties with little power*, by combining forces to be able to negotiate with more powerful parties;
3 *internal parties with a lot of power*, by forming coalitions with the leaders;
4 *external parties*, by direct attempts at influencing (mainly addressed at the leadership of an organization), sometimes also by using more powerful third parties (for example, the government).

Each of these variants can be found in empirical research: the first, in terms of 'getting all noses pointing in the same direction' which is popular in some companies and which can be found in a lot of naïve research into organizational culture; the second, in all kinds of analyses of labour relations; the third, for example, in Pettigrew's (1973) analysis of the power of automation specialists; the last, in Greenpeace campaigns for the conservation of the natural environment. An interesting theoretical alternative for solving the stakeholder problem lies in what is now called economic organizational theory; the question of the forms of contract and transaction costs between parties within and outside organizations.

Structure as an instrument in the stakeholders' struggle

The growing complexity of organizational relationships and their interplay with social developments poses major problems for powerful stakeholders in organizations. They consider themselves responsible for managing the essential processes inside and outside the organization. They have to look for simplifications if they are to be able to keep the matter in a manageable form. Traditional organizational structures (line staff, functional, geographical or product-orientated, matrix and unit structures, single-head and polycentric management, and also Mintzberg's classification) are basically attempts by powerful parties to reduce organizational complexity as much as possible.

Structures and rules are no longer more or less objective features of the way in which organizations are set up and managed but equally well constitute instruments for disciplining in the hands of the parties in question. Rules are the outcome of negotiations between people rather than the product of an objective and rational system that is comparable to a machine. This idea should lead to the fundamental insight that organizational rules can be changed. In the next section this idea will be explored in greater detail.

If researchers were to confine themselves, as observed in a preceding section, to drawing up an academically sound system of identifying structures and accompanying phenomena and thus opt for an exclusively objective approach to organizations, then they would be denying the relevance of the stakeholder approach to organizations for the sociology of knowledge. They would then be incapable of seeing that their own contribution to the development of this type of instrument of control also plays an essential role in its design, colouring, uses, and so on. There is no longer any point in looking for an objective flora and fauna of structures. Making statements about their chances of survival would equally be a waste of time.

The main question, now, is to acquire insight into the causes, processes and significance of the somewhat deliberate moves which are made by organizational players in the humanly determined design and evolution process of these organization structures. It is especially important to bear in mind the fact that the theoretical reflections and the results of empirical research by the researchers themselves exercise an influence on this process of creating structures. As a result, the objective nature of the structure debate becomes highly dubious. The researcher is a stakeholder too, whether he or she wants to be or not. Ideas on organizational structures in publications and teaching (for example, in business study courses or encyclopedias) exercise an influence on the way in which people devise and use structures in organizations.

The above line of thought is nicely illustrated in the exchange of ideas between Western organizational theorists and consultants and their Central and Eastern European colleagues after the fall of the Berlin Wall. In this light the dynamic interaction between theory and practice becomes easy to perceive. Thinking about organizations for more than forty years on the basis of different points of departure also produces different structures. The point in this debate is that it is these different points of departure and ways of solving concrete organizational problems that are being addressed, rather than the solutions themselves. The 'updating' of colleagues in the East does not take place so much at the level of a so-called first-order learning process (that is, the level of the solutions that have been devised in the West), but at the level of a second order (that is, how and why such solutions were arrived at). The transfer of meaning is at stake, not the transfer of knowledge. Others have called this the distinction between *langue* and *parole*. This should be kept in mind in carrying out intercultural research or engaging in intercultural management. The following section will consider in detail the differences between these two forms of learning.

It may be said that both this line of thinking on organizations as parties and the implications of this for the sociology of knowledge have their roots in Weber. He has gained in influence considerably through (neo-)Marxist thinkers and re-searchers, for example Perrow (1979) in the 1970s. People asked themselves whether the relatively objective way in which organizational phenomena were approached did not impede the analysis of the really interesting issues. It also led people to devote more and more attention to the language in which organizations and organizational processes are discussed. The observation that the parties in-volved in an organization can have different interests in its survival or termina-tion has had impressive repercussions on current thinking about social policy, organizational processes of change, communication, co-participation, environ-mental policy, and so on.

4 New ways of thinking on organizations

As it should have become clear in the preceding section, there is no simple, straightforward relationship between scientific theory and practice. Even the much used distinction between the inductive (moving from the facts to theoreti-cal statements) and the deductive (vice versa) approaches is no solution. The cir-cular relationship between research and practice itself now constitutes the point of departure for developing a way of thinking which offers new opportunities for the evolution of academic thought and the enrichment of organizational practice.

The preceding section touched on the distinction between learning of the first order and of the second order. In organizations all kinds of situations occur which can be characterized as being first-order learning. This is what research into the archetypal bureaucracy was based on. First-order thinking centres around the question, put in simple programming language (BASIC), 'if, then' – What hap-pens if I do this? It is concerned with simple chains of cause and effect, based on research into past situations. In the chaos of daily life, the drawing up of rules can have a salutary, ordering effect. Hence people (and especially management) in organizations think that they will be able to act on new and more complex prob-lems by drawing up new rules.

It is a way of thinking in which existing solutions to problems are expected to be suitable for solving new problems. The bureaucratic organization enhances the predictability of human behaviour. The chance of unreasonable deviations from the set rules is smaller; conflicts between people are less intense because such rules after all apply to everyone (Gouldner 1954). And yet we are dealing here with relatively mechanical thinking. A machine is expected to do the things for which it was constructed. This assumes a relative stability in input, output and method of processing. However, as soon as different questions are posed, in other words as soon as things are no longer predictable, first-order thinking can-not fail to lead to major conflicts. A frozen fear of life then becomes the standard pattern of thinking of the bureaucrat.

Of course, there will follow reactions to this line of thought. People have their own interests and organize themselves in all kinds of internal and external interest groups. They themselves start thinking about the way in which the organization is put together and they begin searching for new solutions. The ensuing fragmentation does not make it any easier either to manage or to carry out research. The metaphor of the political arena (Morgan 1986) describes not only the struggle for power in the organization but also the changing vision of organizing (read also structuring) as such. This is a reason for underlining the importance of second-order thinking about organizations.

Second-order thinking always poses the question of what would happen if one were to react in a certain way to an earlier stimulus – in BASIC: 'if (if, then) then'. This means that first-order thinking is included within a second loop. At the second-order level one asks oneself what is going on and what would happen if one were to use instruments of the first order in a particular way. This results in a certain flexibility in thinking up, designing and using first-order instruments. In daily language second-order thinking represents a willingness to learn to learn.

The structure concept in organizational theory has long been understood as a variable of the first order. Organizations are characterized by certain structures; it is in the interests of the development of the discipline to describe and explain these structures. Through the analysis of parties, the instrumental rationality of these variant structures became less absolute. Equally, the manageability of complex organizations is diminished. The contribution of organizational theory could well become stuck at the simple observation that things are rather complex. However, the stakeholder approach, in terms of the sociology of knowledge, should be related to the development of organizational theory itself and to the influence of this on practical organizing endeavours. The debate becomes then elevated to a higher plan, that is of thinking in terms of a second order or meta-level.

This places in a new light a lot of theoretical and empirical research in recent years into culture (Hofstede 1984), into metaphors (Morgan 1986), into learning forms (Argyris and Schön 1978), into dynamic organizational variants and into fields such as total quality management and the related paradigm shift. Such research is not merely the next theoretical initiative, to the dismay of the more traditional researcher. It is the necessary strengthening, from the point of view of the sociology of knowledge, of the relationship in which the theory and practice of organization have ended up. The search for more dynamic organization theories cannot terminate with one of the many new structure variants. Instead, a quantum leap has been made. The scientific and managerial interest in culture has to do with the search for new foundations for organizational theory, which can only be found at a higher level. The accusation that organizational theory only offers fashionable explanations is consequently much too easy. If some kind of order is wanted in the chaos and dynamics of organizing, it is certainly not going to be found in a bureaucratic regression. It can only be found in the insight that people can learn to think and can learn to learn in rapidly changing situations. That is the only stability which can be considered. People should be put in a position to develop these skills. Only then can they and will they contribute to the aims of an organization. That is the assignment for the theoreticians as well as for the practitioners.

5 The end of the structure debate?

Will there now be an end to the structure debate in organizational theory? The answer is both yes and no. As demonstrated in the previous sections, it all depends on how one looks at organizations. Different views offer different insights. There are all kinds of target groups which have an interest in a different and fresh look at what organizing is really about. For the organizational scientist it is important to map out as many of such perspectives and distortions as possible. By doing so one learns to analyse from new angles. This is learning at the level of the first order. If all is going well, one will learn more. One will also learn that such analyses depend on the problems confronting people in organizations in the course of time. This type of learning is of the second level. The cross-sections made by analysts are in themselves a reason for the practitioners (managers, members of staff, consultants) to look again at their problems. This may perhaps again lead to new solutions. The road that has to be pursued is becoming clear. In the historical phase of the stakeholder model, organizational parties demonstrated that they can think and do think, above all, in terms of their own interests. Now they have to be taught to think with others. This requires forms of polycentric management, not a one-sided emphasis on decentralization and self-management, for instance, which allows management to get rid of its problems. Attention should be paid to circular and dynamic thinking. The biggest chance of tackling current social problems lies in jointly developing learning strategies, both for that which we wish to achieve and for the way in which we wish to achieve it.

It is thus that the circle between theorizing at the first and second levels and practice can be closed. Both types of stakeholders must know their limitations. Theoreticians are not automatically good consultants, let alone good practitioners, merely because they can speak intelligently about organizations. The practitioner is not the one who puts theories into practice on the one hand, and thus corroborates these, while being, on the other hand, the one who submits material for explanation to the theoretician. The Weberian dilemma of choosing between science and politics as a career continues to exist. This does not make the dialogue between the two professions pointless, however. Dialogue assumes that the stakeholders at least try to understand each other's language in order to learn from each other. The social responsibility of intellectuals for the development of work, organization and society is the final foundation for such efforts.

Further reading

(References cited in the text marked *)

* Argyris, C. and Schön, D.A. (1978) *Organisational Learning: A Theory of Action Perspective*, Reading: Addison-Wesley. (A classic in changing the perspective from a structuralist to a more interpretative way of thinking on organizations.)
* Barnard, C. (1938) *The Functions of the Executive*, Cambridge, MA: Harvard University Press. (A classic with a definite pre-war elitist perspective.)

* Berger, P. and Luckmann, T. (1967) *The Social Construction of Reality: A Treatise in the Sociology of Knowledge*, Harmondsworth: Penguin. (An influential publication taking up the thoughts of Weber, W.I. Thomas and Mead and ending with a strong stand for interpretative sociology.)

* Blau, P.M. and Scott, W.R. (1962) *Formal Organisations: A Comparative Approach*, London: Routledge & Kegan Paul. (One of the first comparative studies; based on a theoretical distinction of types of stakeholders.)

* Burrell, G. and Morgan, G. (1979) *Sociological Paradigms and Organisational Analysis: Elements of the Sociology of Corporate Life*, London: Heinemann. (A history of organizational analysis cross-bred with various sociological paradigms.)

* Crozier, M. (1964) *The Bureaucratic Phenomenon*, Chicago, IL: University of Chicago Press. (One of the most influential organization theory studies from France, discussing the typical bureaucratic aspects of the French Tobacco Monopoly and a large Paris administrative agency.)

* Etzioni, A. (1961) *A Comparative Analysis of Complex Organisations*, New York: The Free Press. (Published as a contribution to comparative studies; based on a theoretical distinction of compliance structures.)

Gay, P. du (2000) *In Praise of Bureaucracy*, London: Sage. (An interesting work in which bureaucracy is analysed not as something out-of-date, but as a guarantee of organizational ethos [doing the right thing on the right moment for the right person, including the accountability for its deeds] which is a fundamental principle for every well-functioning democracy).

* Gouldner, A. (1954) *Patterns of Industrial Bureaucracy*, New York: The Free Press. (Written in the theory of functionalism; still one of the most interesting and provocative empirical studies of organizational behaviour.)

Hall, R.H. (1987) *Organisations, Structures, Processes and Outcomes*, 4th edn, Englewood Cliffs, NJ: Prentice-Hall. (A classic handbook for the student of organizational (mostly structural) phenomena, especially useful because of the vast number of references.)

* Hofstede, G. (1984) *Culture's Consequences, International Differences in Work-related Values*, Beverly Hills, CA: Sage Publications. (A report on the famous IBM culture studies of Hofstede, conceptualizing culture as the software of the mind.)

* Lammers, C.J. and Hickson, D.J. (1979) *Organisations Alike and Unlike*, London: Routledge & Kegan Paul. (Taking up the original ideas of Etzioni and Blau and Scott and giving a strong impetus to the methodology of comparative studies.)

* Mintzberg, H. (1979) *The Structuring of Organisations*, Englewood Cliffs, NJ: Prentice-Hall. (The first, now famous, book by Mintzberg.)

* Morgan, G. (1986) *Images of Organisation*, Beverly Hills, CA: Sage Publications. (Succeeds in presenting the history of organizational theory from an interpretative point of view.)

* Perrow, C. (1979) *Complex Organisations: A Critical Essay*, Dallas, TX: Scott, Foresman and Co. (Interesting to read sentence for sentence; Perrow is ready to analyse critically the US organizational system.)

* Pettigrew, A.M. (1973) *The Politics of Organisational Decision-making*, London: Tavistock Publications. (One of the few older empirical and historical case studies of real-life organizations.)

Pfeffer, J. (1981) *Power in Organizations*, Boston, MA: Pitman. (An insightful book on the sources and uses of organizational power in a variety of aspects.)

* Pugh, D., Hickson, D.J. and Hinings, C.R. (1969) 'An empirical taxonomy', *Administrative Science Quarterly* 14: 115–26. (The famous founding article of the Aston School.)

Senge, P. (1990) *The Fifth Discipline*, New York: Doubleday. (One of the most influential books on organizational learning, including a separately sold Fieldbook with thoughts and exercises.)

Senge, P. (1999) *The Dance of Change, The Challenges of Sustaining Momentum in Learning Organisations*, London: Nicholas Brealy. (As often happens, a second book by an author on the same subject is interesting for the freshman, but not for the professional. Some parts are insightful, but not new; the others are simply repetitions of Senge's viewpoint. The only really interesting things are the tricks of the trade of an experienced consultant).

* Weber, M. (1947) *The Theory of Social and Economic Organisation*, New York: The Free Press. (Although Weber is referring to the problems of his day, the way he thinks and writes is still among the most outstanding.)

Williamson, W. and Ouchi, W. (1981) 'The market and hierarchies program of research', in *Perspectives on Organisational Design and Behavior*, New York: Wiley. (Now well known as the distinction between two types of coordination, at the time it was an eye-opener.)

Woodward, J. (1965) *Industrial Organisation, Theory and Practice*, London: Oxford University Press. (Still worthwhile to read because of the inclusion of technology as an important organizational factor.)

Organization culture

Geert Hofstede

Overview

The concept of 'organization culture' has become popular since the early 1980s. There is no consensus about its definition but most authors will agree that it is something holistic, historically determined, related to the things anthropologists study, socially constructed, soft and difficult to change. It is something an organization *has*, but can also be seen as something an organization *is*.

Organization cultures should be distinguished from national cultures. Cultures manifest themselves, from superficial to deep, in symbols, heroes, rituals and values. National cultures differ mostly on the values level; organization cultures at the levels of symbols, heroes and rituals, together labelled 'practices'.

Differences in national cultures have been studied for over fifty countries. They show five independent dimensions of values: power distance, individualism versus collectivism, masculinity versus femininity, uncertainty avoidance and long-term versus short-term orientation. National culture differences are reflected in solutions to organization problems in different countries, but also in the validity of management theories in these countries. Different national cultures have different preferred ways of structuring organizations and different patterns of employee motivation. National culture differences limit the options for, for example, performance appraisal, management by objectives, strategic management and humanization of work.

Research into organization cultures identified six independent dimensions of practices: process-oriented versus results-oriented, job-oriented versus employee-oriented, professional versus parochial, open systems versus closed systems, tightly versus loosely controlled, and pragmatic versus normative. The position of an organization on these dimensions is partly determined by the business or industry the organization is in. Scores on the dimensions are also related to a number of other 'hard' characteristics of the organizations. These lead to conclusions about how organization cultures can be and cannot be managed.

Managing international business means handling both national and organization culture differences at the same time. Organization cultures are somewhat manageable while national cultures are given facts for management; common organization cultures across borders are what keeps multinationals together.

I The concept of organization culture

The term 'organization culture', in the US generally 'organizatio*nal* culture', became popular in the English language around 1980 (Pettigrew 1979; Schein 1985). In the management literature the term '*corporate* culture' is common (Deal and Kennedy 1982). An earlier concept, in use since the 1950s, is 'organization climate'. The difference between 'culture' and 'climate' is a matter of definition; there is no consensus in the literature. 'Culture' tends to be treated as a long range, stable characteristic of an organization and 'climate' as a shorter range, more changeable characteristic.

Since the early 1980s an extensive literature has developed on organization culture which has also spread to other language areas. 'Culture' has become a fad, among managers, among consultants, and among academics, with somewhat different concerns. An important role in its popularization was played by a book by Peters and Waterman (1982), *In Search of Excellence*. The authors claimed that excellent American companies were characterized by strong, dominant, coherent cultures, in which 'people way down the line know what they are supposed to do in most situations because the handful of guiding values is crystal clear' (1982: 76).

Because of the faddish nature of the concept, the literature on organization culture consists of a remarkable collection of pep talks, war stories, and some insightful in-depth case studies. Systematic research is rare; Peters and Waterman's study of 'excellent companies', for example, does not meet academic standards.

Nevertheless, organization culture has proven to be more than just a fad. It has gained its place in organization theory. Organization(al)/corporate culture has acquired a status similar to structure, strategy and control.

There is no consensus about its definition, but most authors will probably agree that the organization(al)/corporate culture concept refers to something that is:

1 holistic (describing a whole which is more than the sum of its parts);
2 historically determined (reflecting the history of the organization);
3 related to the things anthropologists study (like rituals and symbols);
4 socially constructed (created and preserved by the group of people who together form the organization);
5 soft (although Peters and Waterman assure their readers that 'soft is hard');
6 difficult to change (although authors disagree on how difficult).

All of these characteristics of organizations had been separately recognized in the literature of the previous decades; what is new about organization culture is their integration into one single concept.

A distinction can be made between authors who see organization culture as something an organization *has*, and those who see it as something an organization *is* (Smircich 1983). The former leads to an analytic approach and a concern with change. It predominates among managers and management consultants. The latter supports a synthetic approach and a concern with understanding and is almost exclusively found among pure academics. Discussion here is from the first perspective (has), while accepting some insights from the second – especially that culture should be treated as an integrated whole.

2 Organization cultures and national cultures

The organization culture literature has been influenced by reports of differences among national cultures that affect organizations and management, sometimes labelled 'comparative management' (Farmer and Richman 1965; Haire *et al.* 1966; Negandhi and Prasad 1971; Lammers and Hickson 1979; Hofstede 1980). The evident competitive success of Japanese organizations in the 1960s and 1970s led to a recognition that national culture mattered (Ouchi 1981; Pascale and Athos 1981).

'Culture' in general has been defined as 'the collective programming of the mind which distinguishes the members of one group or category of people from another' (Hofstede 1991: 5). Consequently 'organization culture' can be defined as 'the collective programming of the mind which distinguishes the members of one organization from another'. Next to organization and national cultures, one can distinguish occupational cultures, business cultures, gender cultures, age group cultures (like youth culture), and so on. However, the use of the word 'culture' for all these categories does not mean that they are identical phenomena. For different kinds of social systems, their 'cultures' may well be of a different nature. This is particularly the case for organization cultures versus national cultures, if only because membership of an organization is usually partial and voluntary, while the 'membership' of a nation is permanent and involuntary.

Culture as collective programming of the mind manifests itself in several ways. From the many terms used to describe manifestations of culture the following four together cover the total concept rather neatly: symbols, heroes, rituals and values. These can be imagined as the skins of an onion, symbols representing the most superficial and values the deepest manifestations of culture, with heroes and rituals in between.

Symbols are words, gestures, pictures or objects which carry a particular meaning only recognized as such by those who share the culture. The words in a language or jargon belong to this category, as do dress, hair-do, Coca-Cola, flags and status symbols. New symbols are easily developed and old ones disappear; symbols from one cultural group are regularly copied by others. This is why symbols represent the outer, most superficial layer of culture.

Heroes are persons, alive or dead, real or imaginary, who possess characteristics which are highly prized in a culture, and thus serve as models for behaviour. Founders of companies often become cultural heroes. In this age of television, outward appearances have become more important in the choice of heroes than they were before.

Rituals are collective activities, technically superfluous to reach desired ends, but which within a culture are considered as socially essential: they are therefore carried out for their own sake. Ways of greeting and paying respect to others, social and religious ceremonies are examples. Business and political meetings organized for seemingly rational reasons often serve mainly ritual purposes, like allowing the leaders to assert themselves.

Symbols, heroes and rituals together can be labelled *'practices'*. As such they are visible to an outside observer; their cultural meaning, however, is invisible and lies precisely and only in the way these practices are interpreted by the insiders.

The core of culture is formed by *values*. Values are broad tendencies to prefer certain states of affairs over others. Values are feelings with an arrow to it: a plus and a minus side. They deal with:

- evil versus good
- dirty versus clean
- dangerous versus safe
- decent versus indecent
- ugly versus beautiful
- unnatural versus natural
- abnormal versus normal
- paradoxical versus logical
- irrational versus rational
- moral versus immoral

Values are among the first things children learn – not consciously, but implicitly. Development psychologists believe that by the age of ten, most children have their basic value system firmly in place, and after that age, changes are difficult to obtain. Because they were acquired so early in our lives, many values remain unconscious to those who hold them. Therefore they cannot be discussed, nor can they be directly observed by outsiders. They can only be inferred from the way people act under various circumstances.

Two large research projects, one into national (Hofstede 1991) and one into organization culture differences (Hofstede *et al.* 1990) showed that national cultures differ mostly at the level of values, while organization cultures differ mostly at the level of the more superficial practices: symbols, heroes, and rituals.

Figure 1 illustrates the different mixes of values and practices for the national and the organization levels of culture, as well as for gender, (social) class, occupation and business. These differences can be explained by the different places of socialization (learning) for values and for practices; these have been listed at the

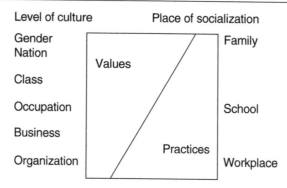

Level of culture   Place of socialization

Gender   Family
Nation
                    Values
Class

Occupation   School

Business
                                Practices
Organization   Workplace

Figure 1 The mix of values and practices in culture for different social systems

right side of the diagram. Values are acquired in one's early youth, mainly in the family and in the neighbourhood, and later at school. The two characteristics present at birth are gender and nationality. By the time a child is ten years old, most of its basic values have been programmed into its mind. The school as a socializing place relates to the student's future occupation. Organization cultures are only learned through socialization at the work place, which most people enter as adults – that is, with the bulk of their values firmly in place. A business culture level (like the culture of banking or of tourism) is placed somewhere between occupation and organization.

Figure 1 illustrates that national cultures and organization cultures are phenomena of a different order. Using the same term 'cultures' for both can be misleading.

In the popular management literature organization cultures have often been presented as a matter of values (see for example Peters and Waterman 1982). The confusion arises because this literature does not distinguish between the values of the founders and leaders and those of the ordinary employees. Founders and leaders create the symbols, the heroes and the rituals that constitute the daily practices of the organization's members. Members do not have to adapt their personal values to the organization's needs. A work organization, as a rule, is not a 'total institution' like a prison or a mental hospital.

Members' values depend primarily on criteria other than membership in the organization, like their gender, nationality, class and occupation. The way these values enter the organization is through the hiring process: an organization recruits people of a certain gender, nationality, class, education, age. Their subsequent socialization in the organization is a matter of learning the practices: symbols, heroes and rituals. Personnel officers who pre-select the people to be hired play an important role in maintaining an organization's values (for better or for worse).

The fact that organization cultures are composed of practices rather than values makes them *somewhat* manageable: they can be managed by changing the practices. The values of employees, once hired, can hardly be changed by an employer, because they were acquired when the employees were children. Sometimes an employer can activate latent values which employees possess but were not allowed to show earlier: like a desire for initiative and creativity, by allowing practices which before were forbidden.

3 Dimensions of national cultures

The large research project into national culture differences referred to took place across subsidiaries of a multinational corporation (IBM) in 64 countries. Subsequent studies covered students in 10 and 23 countries, respectively (Hofstede 1991; Hofstede and Bond 1988); elites in 19 countries (Hoppe 1990); commercial airline pilots in 23 countries (Helmreich and Merritt 1998) and upmarket consumers (De Mooij 1998). These studies together identified and validated five independent dimensions of national culture differences:

1 *Power distance*, that is the extent to which the less powerful members of organizations and institutions (like the family) accept and expect that power is distributed unequally. This represents inequality (more versus less), but defined from below, not from above. It suggests that a society's level of inequality is endorsed by the followers as much as by the leaders. Power and inequality, of course, are extremely fundamental facts of any society and anybody with some international experience will be aware that 'all societies are unequal, but some are more unequal than others'.

   Figure 2 lists some of the differences in the work place between small and large power distance cultures. The statements refer to extremes; actual situations may be found anywhere in between the extremes. People's behaviour in the work situation is strongly affected by their previous experiences in the family and in the school: the expectations and fears about the boss are projections of the experiences with the father – or mother – and the teachers. In order to understand superiors, colleagues and subordinates in another country we have to know something about families and schools in that country.

2 *Individualism* on the one side versus its opposite, *collectivism*, that is the degree to which individuals are integrated into groups. On the individualist side we find societies in which the ties between individuals are loose: everyone is expected to look after him/herself and his/her immediate family. On the collectivist side, we find societies in which people from birth onwards are integrated into strong, cohesive in-groups, often extended families (with uncles, aunts and grandparents) which continue protecting them in exchange for unquestioning loyalty. The word 'collectivism' in this sense has no political meaning: it refers to the group, not to the state. Again, the issue addressed by this dimension is an extremely fundamental one, regarding all societies in the world.

   Figure 2 also shows some differences in the work place between collectivist and individualist cultures; most real cultures will be somewhere in between these extremes. The words 'particularism' and 'universalism' are common sociological categories. Particularism is a way of thinking in which the standards for the way a person should be treated depend on the group or category to which this person belongs. Universalism is a way of thinking in which the standards for the way a person should be treated are the same for everybody.

3 *Masculinity* versus its opposite, *femininity*, refers to the distribution of roles between the sexes which is another fundamental issue for any society to which a range of solutions are found. The IBM studies revealed that (a) women's values differ less among societies than men's values; (b) men's values from one country to another contain a dimension from very assertive and competitive and maximally different from women's values on the one side, to modest and caring and similar to women's values on the other. The assertive pole has been called 'masculine' and the modest, caring pole 'feminine'. The women in feminine countries have the same modest, caring values as the men; in the masculine countries they are somewhat assertive and competitive, but not as much as the men, so that these countries show a gap between men's values and

Small power distance societies	Large power distance societies
Hierarchy means an inequality of roles, established for convenience	Hierarchy means existential inequality
Subordinates expect to be consulted	Subordinates expect to be told what to do
Ideal boss is resourceful democrat	Ideal boss is benevolent autocrat (good father)
Collectivist societies	**Individualist societies**
Value standards differ for in-group and out-groups: *particularism*	Same value standards apply to all: *universalism*
Other people are seen as members of their group	Other people seen as potential resources
Relationship prevails over task	Task prevails over relationship
Moral model of employer–employee relationship	Calculative model of employer–employee relationship
Feminine societies	**Masculine societies**
Assertiveness ridiculed	Assertiveness appreciated
Undersell yourself	Oversell yourself
Stress on life quality	Stress on careers
Intuition	Decisiveness
Weak uncertainty avoidance societies	**Strong uncertainty avoidance societies**
Dislike of rules – written or unwritten	Emotional need for rules – written or unwritten
Less formalization and standardization	More formalization and standardization
Tolerance of deviant persons and ideas	Intolerance of deviant persons and ideas
Short-term oriented societies	**Long-term oriented societies**
Immediate need gratification expected	Deferred need gratification accepted
Traditions are sacrosanct	Traditions adaptable to changed circumstances
Social spending	Saving, investing
The bottom line	Future market position
Analytical thinking	Synthetic thinking

Figure 2 Consequences in the workplace of differences in national culture

women's values. Figure 2 also lists some of the differences in the work place between feminine and masculine cultures.

4 *Uncertainty avoidance* deals with a society's tolerance for uncertainty and ambiguity; it ultimately refers to man's search for Truth. It indicates to what extent a culture programmes its members to feel either uncomfortable or comfortable in unstructured situations. Unstructured situations are novel, unknown, surprising, different from usual. Uncertainty avoiding cultures try to minimize the possibility of such situations by strict laws and rules, safety and security measures, and on the philosophical and religious level by a belief in absolute Truth; 'there can only be one Truth and we have it'. People in uncertainty avoiding countries are also more emotional, and motivated by inner nervous energy. The opposite type, uncertainty accepting cultures, are more tolerant of opinions different from what they are used to; they try to have as few rules as possible, and on the philosophical and religious level they are relativist and allow many currents to flow side by side. People within these cultures are more phlegmatic and contemplative, and not expected by their environment to express emotions. Figure 2 lists some of the differences in the work place between weak and strong uncertainty avoidance cultures.

5 *Long-term* versus *short-term orientation*: this fifth dimension was found in a study among students in 23 countries around the world, using a questionnaire designed by Chinese scholars (Hofstede and Bond 1988). It can be said to deal with Virtue regardless of Truth. Values associated with long-term orientation are thrift and perseverance; values associated with short-term orientation are respect for tradition, fulfilling social obligations, and protecting one's 'face'. Both the positively and the negatively rated values of this dimension are found in the teachings of Confucius, the most influential Chinese philosopher who lived around 500BC; however, the dimension also applies to countries without a Confucian heritage. Figure 2 concludes with some of the differences in the work place between long-term and short-term oriented cultures.

Scores on the first four dimensions were obtained for 50 countries and 3 regions on the basis of the IBM study, and on the fifth dimension for 23 countries on the basis of student data collected by Bond. For score values see Hofstede (1991). Power distance scores are high for Latin, Asian and African countries and smaller for Germanic countries. Individualism prevails in developed and Western countries, while collectivism prevails in less developed and Eastern countries; Japan takes a middle position on this dimension. Masculinity is high in Japan, in some European countries like Germany, Austria and Switzerland, and moderately high in Anglo countries; it is low in Nordic countries and in the Netherlands and moderately low in some Latin and Asian countries like France, Spain and Thailand. Uncertainty avoidance scores are higher in Latin countries, in Japan, and in German speaking countries, lower in Anglo, Nordic, and Chinese culture countries. A long-term orientation is mostly found in East Asian countries, in particular in China, Hong Kong, Taiwan, Japan, and South Korea.

The grouping of country scores points to some of the roots of cultural differences. These should be sought in the common history of similarly scoring countries. All Latin countries, for example, score relatively high on both power distance and uncertainty avoidance. Latin countries (those today speaking a Romance language i.e. Spanish, Portuguese, French or Italian) have inherited at least part of their civilization from the Roman empire. The Roman empire in its days was characterized by the existence of a central authority in Rome, and a system of law applicable to citizens anywhere. This established in its citizens' minds the value complex which we still recognize today: centralization fostered large power distance and a stress on laws fostered strong uncertainty avoidance. The Chinese empire also knew centralization, but it lacked a fixed system of laws: it was governed by men rather than by laws. In the present-day countries once under Chinese rule, the mindset fostered by the empire is reflected in large power distance but medium to weak uncertainty avoidance. The Germanic part of Europe, including Great Britain, never succeeded in establishing an enduring common central authority and countries which inherited its civilizations show smaller power distance. Assumptions about historical roots of cultural differences always remain speculative but in the given examples they are quite plausible. In other cases they remain hidden in the course of history.

The country scores on the five dimensions are statistically correlated with a multitude of other data about the countries. For example, power distance is correlated with the use of violence in domestic politics and with income inequality in a country. Individualism is correlated with national wealth (per capita gross national product [GNP]) and with mobility between social classes from one generation to the next. Masculinity is correlated negatively with the share of their GNP that governments of the wealthy countries spend on development assistance to the Third World. Uncertainty avoidance is associated with Roman Catholicism and with the legal obligation in developed countries for citizens to carry identity cards. Long-term orientation is correlated with national economic growth during the past 25 years, showing that what led to the economic success of the East Asian economies in this period is their populations' cultural stress on the future-oriented values of thrift and perseverance.

4 National cultures and the functioning of organizations

Organization structure

The national culture of a country affects its parents and its children, teachers and students, labour union leaders and members, politicians and citizens, journalists and readers, managers and subordinates. Therefore management practices in a country are culturally dependent, and what works in one country does not necessarily work in another. However, not only the managers and subordinates are human and children of their culture: the management teachers, the people who wrote and still write theories and create management concepts, are human and constrained by the cultural environment in which they grew up and which they know. Such theories and concepts cannot without further proof be applied in another country; if they are applicable at all, it is often only after considerable adaptation.

The structuring of organizations is primarily influenced by the two dimensions of power distance and uncertainty avoidance. This is because organizing always demands the answering of two questions: (1) who should have the power to decide what? and (2) what rules or procedures will be followed to attain the desired ends? The answer to the first question is influenced by cultural norms of power distance; the answer to the second question, by cultural norms about uncertainty avoidance. Individualism and masculinity affect primarily the functioning of the people within the organizations. Long-term orientation affects the economic performance of organizations.

Research into the *formal* structures of organizations carried out by British researchers from the University of Aston in Birmingham in the 1960s and early 1970s (the 'Aston studies': Pugh and Hickson 1976) already concluded that the two major dimensions along which structures of organizations differ are 'concentration of authority' and 'structuring of activities'. The first is affected by power distance, the second by uncertainty avoidance. Power distance and uncertainty avoidance indices measure the *informal,* subjective mental programming of the people within a country. The fact that these vary systematically between countries explains why the formal structures of organizations also vary between countries: formal structures serve to meet informal cultural needs.

Differences in implicit models of organizations were proven for the case of France, Germany and Great Britain by a study among INSEAD business students in Fontainebleau, France (Hofstede 1991: 140–3). In dealing with a case study of organizational conflict, French students, coming from a country with large power distance and strong uncertainty avoidance, treated the organization like a *pyramid of people* and advocated measures to concentrate the authority and also structure the activities. Germans, coming from a country with strong uncertainty avoidance but small power distance, treated the organization as a *well-oiled machine* and wanted to structure the activities without concentrating the authority. British students with a national culture characterized by small power distance and weak uncertainty avoidance treated the organization as a *village market* and advocated neither concentrating authority nor structuring activities but developing the managers' negotiation skills – and all of them were dealing with the same case study. Other things being equal, French organizations *do* concentrate authority more, German ones *do* need more structure, and people in British ones *do* believe more in resolving problems *ad hoc* (Maurice *et al.* 1980). A fourth combination, large power distance with weak uncertainty avoidance, is found in Asia and Africa and leads to an implicit model of an organization as an (extended) *family*, in which the owner-manager is the omnipotent (grand)father.

Mintzberg (1983) has provided a well-known typology of organization structures. Organizations in general contain up to five distinct parts: operating core, strategic apex, middle line, technostructure and support staff, and they use one or more of five mechanisms for coordinating activities: mutual adjustment, direct supervision, standardization of work processes, standardization of outputs and standardization of skills. Most organizations show one of five typical configurations: (1) the simple structure, in which the key part is the strategic apex and the coordinating mechanism is direct supervision; (2) the machine bureaucracy, in which the key part is the technostructure, and the coordinating mechanism is standardization of work processes; (3) the professional bureaucracy, in which the key part is the operating core, and the coordinating mechanism is standardization of skills; (4) the divisionalized form, in which the key part is the middle line, and the coordinating mechanism is standardization of outputs; and finally (5) the adhocracy, in which the key part is the support staff and the coordinating mechanism is mutual adjustment.

Mintzberg did not count with national culture in his typology, but the link between the five configurations and the quadrants of the power distance × uncertainty avoidance matrix is easy to make. The adhocracy corresponds with the 'village market' implicit organization model; the professional bureaucracy with the 'well-oiled machine' model; the full (machine) bureaucracy with the 'pyramid' model; the simple structure with the 'family' model, while the divisionalized form takes a middle position on both culture dimensions, containing elements of all four models. Other things being equal, organizers in a particular country will favour a particular configuration because it fits their implicit mental model of what an organization should be.

Motivation

The power distance × uncertainty avoidance mix also affects the motivation of employees within organization. Herzberg *et al.* (1959) argued that the work situation contains elements with a positive motivation potential (the real motivators), and elements with a negative potential (the hygiene factors). The motivators were the work itself, achievement, recognition, responsibility and advancement. These are often labelled 'intrinsic' elements of the job. The hygiene factors, which had to be present in order to prevent *de*motivation but could not motivate by themselves, were company policy and administration, supervision, salary and working conditions: 'extrinsic' elements of the job. Herzberg assumed this distinction to be a universal characteristic of human motivation. According to him it is the *job content* which makes people act, not the job context.

Long before Herzberg the issue of human motivation was raised by Sigmund Freud (1856–1939), one of the founding fathers of present-day psychology. According to Freud we are impelled to act by unconscious forces inside us which he calls our 'id'. Our conscious conception of ourselves, our 'ego', tries to control these forces. The ego in its turn is influenced by an inner pilot, again unconscious, our '*superego*'. The superego criticizes the thoughts and acts of the ego and causes feelings of guilt and anxiety when the ego is felt to be giving in to the id. The superego is developed in the young child, mainly by the influence of the parents.

Freud was an Austrian and he conceived his ideas in the Austrian intellectual environment of his days. Austria in the PD × UA matrix takes an extreme position: small power distance but strong uncertainty avoidance. The latter stands for a strong psychological need for rules; the former for psychological independence from a flesh-and-blood boss to enforce these rules. The superego can be interpreted as an interiorized boss/father, who controls the individual through self-imposed guilt feelings. In Austria and other small PD, strong UA countries, like Germany, rules as part of what Herzberg called 'company policy and administration' should not be seen as 'hygiene'; they can be real motivators.

In a similar way, when power distances are large supervision should not be seen as a hygienic factor. In large PD countries, dependence on more powerful people is a basic need which can be a real motivator. When in addition uncertainty avoidance is strong, as in most Latin countries, the motivator is the *boss* in the sense of the formally appointed superior. When UA is weaker, as in Asian and African countries, the motivator should rather be labelled the *master*. The 'master' differs from the 'boss' in that the power of the former is based on tradition and charisma more than on formal position.

A cultural analysis thus shows that Herzberg's theory of motivation is culturally constrained; like all management theories it reflects the culture of the environment in which its author grew up and did research. The same holds for another US theory of motivation: Maslow's (1970) 'hierarchy of human needs'. In Maslow's hierarchy 'self-actualization' is seen as the supreme need. However, this assumes an individualist culture, in which the self prevails over the group. In collectivist cultures, harmony with the group will rather be the supreme need. Maslow also puts 'esteem' over 'belongingness'. This assumes a masculine culture; in feminine cultures, belongingness will prevail over esteem as a motivator.

A third culturally constrained motivation theory is McClelland's (1961) 'achievement motive'. McClelland predicted that countries for which he found a stronger achievement motive would show faster economic growth. This prediction did not come true. Hofstede (1980: 170–1) showed that McClelland's achievement motive corresponds to weak uncertainty avoidance plus strong masculinity; a combination found in all Anglo countries. However, in the years following McClelland's study some stronger uncertainty avoidance countries like Japan and Germany grew faster economically than the Anglo countries. McClelland presented a culture pattern specific to his home society (the USA) as a universal norm.

Performance appraisal and MBO

Performance appraisal systems are recommended in the North American and West European management literature. They assume that employees' performance will be improved if the employees receive direct feedback about what their superior thinks of them, which may well be the case in individualist cultures. However, in collectivist countries such direct feedback destroys the harmony which is expected to govern interpersonal relationships. It may cause irreparable damage to the employee's 'face' and ruin his or her loyalty to the organization. In such cultures, including all East-Asian and Third World countries, feedback should rather be given indirectly, for example through the withdrawing of a favour, or via an intermediary person trusted by both superior and employee.

Management by objectives as a management technique was developed in the USA. Under a system of management by objectives subordinates have to negotiate about their objectives with their superiors. The system therefore assumes a cultural environment in which issues can be settled by negotiation rather than by authority and rules, which means a medium to low power distance and a not too high uncertainty avoidance. In a large power distance (PD) environment subordinates and superiors will be unable to function in the ways the system prescribes. In a stronger uncertainty avoidance environment the system needs a more elaborate formal structure with norms and examples; this is the case in Germany.

Strategic management

Strategic management as a concept has also been developed in the USA. It assumes a weak uncertainty avoidance environment, in which deviant strategic ideas are encouraged. Although it is taught in countries with a stronger uncertainty avoidance, like Germany or France, its recommendations are rarely followed there, because in these cultures it is seen as top managers' role to remain involved in daily operations (Horovitz 1980).

Humanization of work

This is a general term for a number of approaches in different countries trying to make work more interesting and rewarding for the people who do it. In the USA which is a masculine and individualist society, the prevailing form of humanization of work has been 'job enrichment': giving individual tasks more intrinsic content. In Sweden which is feminine and less individualist, the prevailing form has been the forming of *semi*-autonomous work groups, in which members exchange tasks and help each other. In Germany and German speaking Switzerland the introduction *of flexible working hours* has been a popular way of adapting the job to the worker. Flexible working hours have never become as common in other countries; their popularity in German-speaking countries can be understood by the combination of a small power distance (acceptance of responsibility by the worker) with a relatively strong uncertainty avoidance (internalization of rules).

5 National cultures: convergence or divergence?

Do national cultures in the modern world become more similar? The evidence cited is usually taken from the level of practices: people dress the same, buy the same products, and use the same fashionable words (symbols), they see the same TV shows and motion pictures (heroes), they perform the same sports and leisure activities (rituals). These rather superficial manifestations of culture are sometimes mistaken for all there is; the deeper, underlying level of values, which moreover determine the meaning to people of their practices, is overlooked.

Value differences between nations described by authors centuries ago are still present today, in spite of continued close contacts. Studies at the values level continue to show impressive differences among nations; after the IBM studies from around 1970 (Hofstede 1980) this was also the case for the 1990–93 World Values Survey across 43 societies (Inglehart *et al.* 1998). The only convergence is on the individualism dimension: countries that became richer are moving towards greater individualism, but even here pre-existing differences between countries survive. Japanese on average have become richer than Americans and there is evidence of an increase of individualism in Japan, but traditional elements of Japanese collectivism survive as well. As the process of organizing is affected by national cultural *values*, the nationality component in the structure and functioning of organizations is unlikely to disappear for the decades or even centuries to come. International organizations will continue to have to take this component into account.

6 Dimensions of organization cultures

A research project similar to the IBM studies but focussing on organization rather than national cultures was carried out by IRIC (the Institute for Research on Intercultural Cooperation, the Netherlands) in the 1980s (Hofstede *et al.* 1990). Qualitative and quantitative data were collected in twenty work organizations or parts of organizations in the Netherlands and Denmark. The units studied varied from a toy manufacturing company to two municipal police corps. As mentioned above, this study found large differences among units in practices (symbols, heroes, rituals) but only modest differences in values, beyond those due to such basic facts as nationality, education, gender and age group.

Six independent dimensions allowed to describe the larger part of the variety in organization practices. These six dimensions can be used as a framework to describe organization cultures, but their research base in twenty units from two countries is too narrow to consider them as universally valid. For describing organization cultures in other countries and/or in other types of organizations, additional dimensions may be necessary or some of the six may be less useful. The dimensions of organization cultures found are listed in Figure 3, together with some of the ways in which they manifest themselves.

1 *Process-oriented versus results-oriented cultures*. The former are dominated by technical and bureaucratic routines, the latter by a common concern for outcomes. This dimension was associated with the culture's degree of homogeneity: in results-oriented units, everybody perceived their practices in about the same way; in process-oriented units, there were vast differences in perception among different levels and parts of the unit. The degree of homogeneity of a culture is a measure of its 'strength': the study confirmed that strong cultures are more results oriented than weak ones, and vice versa (Peters and Waterman 1982).

1 Process-oriented	Results-oriented
People avoid taking risks	Comfortable in unfamiliar situations
People spend little effort	People spend maximal effort
Each day is the same	Each day presents new challenges
2 Job-oriented	**Employee-oriented**
Pressure for getting job done	Attention to personal problems
Important decisions by individuals	Important decisions by groups
Organization only interested in work people do	Organization concerned with welfare of employees and their families
3 Professional	**Parochial**
Think years ahead	Do not think far ahead
Employees' private life is considered their business	Norms of organization cover behaviour on job and at home
Only competence plays a role in recruiting	Family, social class and school play a role in recruiting
4 Open system	**Closed system**
Organization and people transparent to newcomers and outsiders	Organization and people closed and secretive, even to insiders
Almost anyone fits into the organization	Only very special people fit into the organization
New employees need only a few days to feel at home	New employees need more than a year to feel at home
5 Tight control	**Loose control**
Everybody cost-conscious	Nobody cost-conscious
Meeting times kept punctually	Meeting times only kept approximately
Lots of jokes about job and organization	Always serious about job and organization
6 Pragmatic	**Normative**
Emphasis on meeting needs of customers	Emphasis on correctly following procedures
Results more important than procedures	Correct procedures more important than results
Pragmatic not dogmatic in matters of ethics	High standard of ethics, even at expense of results

Figure 3 Manifestations in the workplace of differences in organization culture

2 *Job-oriented versus employee-oriented cultures.* The former assume responsibility for the employees' job performance only, and nothing more; employee-oriented cultures assume a broad responsibility for their members' well-being. At the level of individual managers, the distinction between job orientation and employee orientation has been popularized by Blake and Mouton's Managerial Grid (1964). The IRIC study shows that job versus employee orientation is part of a culture and not (only) a choice for an individual manager. A unit's position on this dimension seems to be largely the result of historical factors, like the philosophy of its founder(s) and the presence or absence in its recent history of economic crises with collective layoffs.

3 *Professional versus parochial cultures*. In the former, the (usually highly educated) members identify primarily with their profession; in the latter, the members derive their identity from the organization for which they work. Sociology has long known this dimension as 'local' versus 'cosmopolitan', the contrast between an internal and an external frame of reference.

4 *Open systems versus closed systems cultures*. This dimension refers to the common style of internal and external communication, and to the ease with which outsiders and newcomers are admitted. This dimension is the only one of the six for which there is a systematic difference between Danish and Dutch units. It seems that organizational openness is a societal characteristic of Denmark more than of the Netherlands. This shows that organization cultures also contain elements that reflect national culture differences.

5 *Tightly versus loosely controlled cultures*. This dimension deals with the degree of formality and punctuality within the organization; it is partly a function of the unit's technology: banks and pharmaceutical companies can be expected to show tight control, research laboratories and advertising agencies loose control; but even with the same technology, units still differ on this dimension.

6 *Pragmatic versus normative cultures*. The last dimension describes the prevailing way (flexible or rigid) of dealing with the environment, in particular with customers. Units selling services are likely to be found towards the pragmatic (flexible) side, units involved in the application of legal rules towards the normative (rigid) side. This dimension measures the degree of 'customer orientation', which is a highly popular topic in the management literature.

7 Determinants of organization cultures

Inspection of the scoring profiles of the twenty units on the six dimensions shows that dimensions 1, 3, 5 and 6 (process versus results, parochial versus professional, loose versus tight and normative versus pragmatic) are affected by the type of work the organization does, and by the type of market in which it operates. In fact, these four dimensions partly reflect the *business or industry culture*. In Figure 1 it was located in between the occupational and the organizational level, because a given industry employs specific occupations and it also maintains specific organizational practices, for logical or traditional reasons. On dimension 1 most manufacturing and large office units scored process-oriented; research/development and service units scored more results-oriented. On dimension 3 units with a traditional technology scored parochial; high-tech units scored professional. On dimension 5 units delivering precision or risky products or services (such as pharmaceuticals or money transactions) scored tight, those with innovative or unpredictable activities scored loose. Surprisingly the two city police corps studied scored on the loose side: the work of a policeman is unpredictable, and police personnel have considerable discretion in the way they carry out their task. On dimension 6 service units and those operating in competitive markets scored pragmatic while units involved in the implementation of laws and those operating under a monopoly scored normative.

While the task and market environment thus affect the dimension scores, the IRIC study also identified distinctive elements in each organization's culture, even compared to other organizations in the same industry. These represent competitive advantages or disadvantages.

The remaining two dimensions, 2 and 4 (employee versus job and open versus closed) seem to be less constrained by task and market but rather based on historical factors like the philosophy of the founder(s) and recent crises. In the case of dimension 4, open versus closed system, the national cultural environment was shown above to play an important role.

Although organization cultures are *mainly* composed of practices, they do have a modest values component. The organizations in the IRIC study differed somewhat on three clusters of values. The first resembles the cross-national dimension of uncertainty avoidance. A cross-organizational uncertainty avoidance measure is correlated with dimension 4 (open versus closed), with weak uncertainty avoidance obviously on the side of an open communication climate. A second cluster of cross-organizational values bears some resemblance to power distance. It is correlated with dimension 1 (process- versus results-oriented): larger power distances are associated with process orientation and smaller ones with results orientation.

Clusters of cross-organizational value differences associated with individualism and masculinity were not found in the IRIC study. Questions which in the cross-national study composed the individualism and masculinity dimensions formed a different configuration in the cross-organizational study labelled 'Work Centrality' (strong or weak): the importance of work in one's total life pattern. It was correlated with dimension 3: parochial versus professional. Obviously work centrality is stronger in professional organization cultures. In parochial cultures, people do not take their work problems home with them.

For the other three dimensions: 2, 5 and 6, no link with values was found at all. These dimensions just describe practices to which people have been socialized without their basic values being involved.

In the cross-national IBM study the country scores on the five dimensions were statistically correlated with a multitude of other data about the countries. The IRIC cross-organizational study has included a similar 'validation' of the dimensions against external data. This time, of course, the data used consisted of information about the organizational units obtained in other ways and from other sources.

Besides interviews and an employee survey the IRIC study included the collection of quantifiable data about the units as wholes. Examples of such information (labelled 'structural data') are total employee strength, budget composition, economic results, and the ages of key managers.

There was a strong correlation between the scores on practice dimension 1, process versus results orientation, and the balance of labour versus material cost in the operating budget. Labour-intensive organizations (holding number of employees constant) scored more results-oriented, while material-intensive organizations scored more process-oriented. Results-oriented units had lower absenteeism. They also had flatter structures (larger spans of control) and less specialization and formalization. Also, in results-oriented units union membership tended to be lower.

The strongest correlation with dimension 2 (employee versus job orientation) was with the way the organizational unit was controlled from above. If the top manager was evaluated on profits and other financial performance measures, the members scored the unit culture as job-oriented. If the top manager was evaluated on performance versus a budget, members scored the unit culture as employee-oriented. Where the top manager stated he allowed controversial news to be published in the employee journal, members felt the unit to be more employee-oriented. Job orientation was also correlated with the employees' average seniority and age and negatively with the education level of the top management team.

On dimension 3 (parochial versus professional), organizational units with a traditional technology tended to score parochial; high-tech units professional. The strongest correlations of this dimension were with various measures of size: larger organizations fostered more professional cultures. Professional cultures had less labour union membership. Their managers had a higher average education level and age. Their organization structures showed more specialization. An interesting correlation was with the way the top managers claimed to spend their time. In the units with a professional culture the top managers spent a larger share of their time in meetings and person-to-person discussions. Finally, the privately owned organizations studied tended to score more professional than the public ones.

Dimension 4 (open versus closed system) was responsible for the single strongest correlation with external data, i.e. between the percentage of women among the employees and the openness of the communication climate. The percentage of women among *managers* and the presence of at least one woman in the top management team were also correlated with openness. Openness was negatively associated with formalization and positively with higher average seniority of employees.

The strongest correlation of dimension 5 (loose versus tight control) was with an item in the self-reported time budget of the top managers: where they spent a relatively large part of their time reading and writing reports and memos from inside the organization, control was tighter. Also, material-intensive units had more tightly controlled cultures. In units in which the number of employees had recently increased, control was felt to be looser; where the number of employees had been reduced, control was perceived as tighter. Finally, absenteeism among employees was lower where control was perceived to be less tight. Absenteeism is evidently one way of escaping from the pressure of a tight control system.

For dimension 6 (normative versus pragmatic) only one meaningful correlation with external data was found. Privately owned organizations in the sample were more pragmatic, public units (such as the police corps) more normative.

Missing from the list of external data correlated with culture are measures of the organizations' performance. This does not mean that culture is not related to performance; only that it is extremely difficult to find valid yardsticks for comparing performance across different organizations.

8 Individual perceptions of organizational culture

Different individuals within the same organization will not necessarily perceive the culture of their organization in the same way. Hofstede, Bond and Luk (1993) re-analysed the data of Hofstede *et al.*'s (1990) Organization Culture study. This time, they focused on the variance of answers within the organizations studied. They did this by deducting from every individual's answer on a question the mean score on that question for the organizational unit. Thus, they only retained the within-unit variance, eliminating the between-unit variance that had been the basis of the dimensions of organizational culture found. After elimination of the between-unit variance, the data from the individuals within the twenty units were combined into one matrix of within-unit variance.

Study of this matrix revealed that individuals within units showed large differences in values, but smaller differences in (perceptions of) organizational practices. This is the opposite of what was found at the between-organization level. It is obvious, because value differences rest in individual personalities, whereas perceptions of practices are based on a shared organizational context.

A further (factor-)analysis of the individual answers showed these to vary along six dimensions:

1 Integration (in the organization)
2 Active involvement
3 Orderliness
4 Need for achievement
5 Machismo
6 Authoritarianism

The first five correspond closely to the five basic dimensions of personality ('the big five') recognized by modern personality theory: neuroticism (with a negative sign), extra-version, conscientiousness, openness and agreeableness (again with a negative sign). The sixth reminds us of the 'Authoritarian Personality' studied by Adorno *et al.* (1950).

In conclusion, differences among individuals in their perceptions of the culture of their organizations were shown to be a matter of the individuals' personality. Agreeable individuals perceive the organization as agreeable, conscientious individuals perceive the organization as conscientious, etc.

9 Managing (with) organization culture

In spite of their relatively superficial nature organization cultures are hard to change because they have developed into collective habits. Changing them is a top management task which cannot be delegated. Some kind of culture assessment by an independent party is usually necessary, which includes the identification of different subcultures which may need quite different approaches. The top management's major strategic choice is either to accept and optimally use the existing culture or to try to change it. If an attempt at change is made it should be preceded by a cost-benefit analysis. A particular concern is whether the manpower necessary for a culture change is available.

Turning around an organization culture demands visible leadership which appeals to the employees' feelings as much as to their intellect. The leader or leaders should assure themselves of sufficient support from key persons at different levels in the organization. Subsequently, they can change the practices by adapting the organization's structure: its functions, departments, locations, and tasks – matching tasks with employee talents. After the structure, the controls may have to be changed, based on a decision on what aspects of the work have to be coordinated – how and by whom at what level. At the same time it is usually necessary to change certain personnel policies related to recruitment, training and promotion. Finally, turning around a culture is not a one-shot process. It takes sustained attention from top management, persistence for several years, and new culture assessments to see whether the intended changes have, indeed, been attained, as well as what other changes occurred in the meantime.

In the case of mergers and acquisitions a diagnosis is needed for identifying the potential areas of culture conflict between the partners. Decisions on mergers are traditionally made from a financial point of view only: mergers are part of a big money power game and seen as a defence against (real or imaginary) threats by competitors. Those making the decision rarely imagine the operating problems which arise inside the newly formed hybrid organizations. An important consideration for deciding whether or not to merge should be a diagnosis of the cultures involved. After the merger has been concluded this diagnosis should become an input to a post-merger integration plan, so as to minimize friction losses and preserve unique cultural capital.

The six dimensions describe the culture of an organization but they are not prescriptive: no position on one of the six dimensions is intrinsically good or bad. Peters and Waterman (1982) have presented eight maxims as norms for excellence. The results of the IRIC study suggest that what is good or bad depends in each case on where one wants the organization to go, and a cultural feature that is an asset for one purpose is unavoidably a liability for another. Labelling positions on the dimension scales as more or less desirable is a matter of strategic choice, and this will vary from one organization to another. In particular the popular stress on customer orientation (becoming more pragmatic on dimension 6) is highly relevant for organizations engaged in services and the manufacturing of custom made quality products, but may be unnecessary or even harmful for, for example, the manufacturing of standard products in a competitive price market.

10 Managing culture differences in multinationals

Most multinational corporations do not only operate in different countries but also in different lines of business or at least in different product/market divisions.

Different business lines and/or divisions often have different organization cultures. By offering common practices strong cross-national organization cultures within a business line or division can bridge national differences in values among organization members. Common practices, not common values are what keep multinationals together.

Like all organizations multinationals are held together by people. The best structure at a given moment depends primarily on the availability of suitable people. Two roles are particularly crucial: (a) country business unit managers who form the link between the culture of the business unit, and the corporate culture which is usually heavily affected by the nationality of origin of the corporation, and (b) 'corporate diplomats', i.e. home country or other nationals impregnated with the corporate culture, multilingual, from various occupational backgrounds, and experienced in living and functioning in various foreign cultures. They are essential to make multinational structures work, as liaison persons in the various head offices or as temporary managers for new ventures.

The availability of suitable people at the right moment is the main task of multinational personnel management. This means timely recruiting of future managerial talent from different nationalities, and career moves through planned transfers where these people will absorb the corporate culture. Multinational personnel departments have to find their way between uniformity and diversity in personnel policies. Too much uniformity is unwarranted because people's mental programmes are not uniform. It leads to corporate-wide policies being imposed on subsidiaries where they will not work (or only receive lip service from obedient but puzzled locals). On the other side, the assumption that everybody is different and that people in subsidiaries therefore always should know best and be allowed to go their own ways, is unwarranted too. In this case an opportunity is lost to build a corporate culture with unique features which keep the organization together and provide it with a distinctive and competitive psychological advantage.

Mergers and takeovers within countries have a dubious success record, but cross-national ventures are even less likely to succeed. They have to bridge both national and organization culture gaps. Even more than in the case of national ventures, they call for a cultural map of the prospective partner as an input into the decision making on whether to merge or not.

Structure should follow culture: the purpose of an organization structure is the coordination of activities. For the design of the structure of a multinational, multi-business corporation, three questions have to be answered for each business unit (a business unit represents one business line in one country). The three questions are: (1) which of the unit's in- and outputs should be coordinated from elsewhere in the corporation? (2) where and at what level should the coordination take place? and (3) how tight or loose should the coordination be? In every case there is a basic choice between coordination along geographical lines and along business lines. The decisive factor is whether business know-how or national cultural know-how is more crucial for the success of the operation.

Matrix structures are a possible solution but they are costly, often meaning a doubling of the management ranks, and their actual functioning may raise more problems than it resolves. A single structural principle (geographic or business) is unlikely to fit for an entire corporation. Joint ventures further complicate the structuring problem. The optimal solution is nearly always a patchwork structure that in some cases follows business and in others geographical lines. This may lack beauty, but it does follow the needs of markets and business unit cultures. Variety within the environment in which a corporation operates should be matched with appropriate internal variety. Optimal solutions will also change over time, so that the periodic reshufflings which any large organization knows should be seen as functional.

Further reading

(References marked in the text marked *)

* Adorno, T.W., Frenkel-Brunswick, E., Levinson, D.J. and Sanford, R.N. (1950) *The Authoritarian Personality*, New York: Harper and Row. (One of the classics of US psychology, inspired by the horrors of Nazism. Based on a survey of 2,000 US respondents from various parts of society.)

* Blake, R.R. and Mouton, J.S. (1964) *The Managerial Grid*, Houston, TX: Gulf. (A classic US management theory arguing that the behaviour of individual managers can be classified along two independent dimensions: concern for people and concern for production.)

Czarniawska-Joerges, B. and Guillet de Monthoux, P. (1994) *Good Novels: Better Management: Reading Organizational Realities*, Chur: Harwood Academic Publishers. (Descriptions and analyses of famous nineteenth- and early twentieth-century novels from nine countries, considered as case studies of management.)

* Deal, T.E. and Kennedy, A.A. (1992) *Corporate Cultures: The Rites and Rituals of Corporate Life*, Reading, MA: Addison-Wesley. (An introduction to the subject, demonstrating how anthropological concepts can be used in the study of organizations.)

* De Mooij, M. (1998) *Global Marketing and Advertising: Understanding Cultural Paradoxes*, Thousand Oaks CA: Sage. (Application of Hofstede's national culture dimensions to the field of marketing and advertising.)

* Farmer, R.N. and Richman, B.M. (1965) *Comparative Management and Economic Progress*, Homewood, IL: Irwin. (A pioneer book on comparative management, now dated.)

* Haire, M., Ghiselli, E.E. and Porter, L.W. (1966) *Managerial Thinking: An International Study*, New York: Wiley. (First international survey study of values in organizations.)

* Helmreich, R.L. and Merritt, A.C. (1998) *Culture at Work in Aviation and Medicine: National, Organizational and Professional Influences*, Aldershot, UK: Ashgate. (Contains data from a replication of Hofstede's national cultures study among airline pilots from 23 countries.)

* Herzberg, F., Mausner, B. and Snyderman, B.B. (1959) *The Motivation to Work*, New York, NY: Wiley. (A well known American management theory distinguishing 'motivators' from 'hygiene factors'.)

* Hofstede, G. (1980) *Culture's Consequences: International Differences in Work-Related Values*, Beverly Hills CA: Sage. (The first and comprehensive presentation of the first four dimensions of national culture across 40 countries, written for a scholarly readership and with extensive validation against data from other sources. An entirely re-written second edition should appear in 2001.)

Hofstede, G. (ed.) (1986) 'Organizational culture and control', special issue of the *Journal of Management Studies*, 23 (3). (Links two central concepts in management; five papers on the relationship of culture with information, control and meaning; two on empirical studies of organization culture.)

* Hofstede, G. (1991) *Cultures and Organizations: Software of the Mind*, London: McGraw-Hill; (1994) London: Harper Collins; (1997) New York: McGraw-Hill. (A popular overview of the author's and related research; deals with national as well as organization cultures. Translated into Chinese, Czech, Danish, Dutch, Finnish, French, German, Japanese, Korean, Norwegian, Polish, Portuguese, Romanian, Spanish, Swedish.)

Hofstede, G. (1994) *Uncommon Sense about Organizations: Cases, Studies and Field Observations*, Thousand Oaks, CA: Sage. (Seventeen studies revealing unexpected truths about organizational life.)

* Hofstede, G. and Bond, M.H. (1988) 'The Confucius connection: from cultural roots to economic growth', *Organizational Dynamics* 16 (4): 4–21. (Using the results of the Chinese Values Survey, introduces the fifth dimension of national culture differences and argues that it explains national economic growth in the past 25 years.)

* Hofstede, G., Bond, M.H. and Luk, C.L. (1993) 'Individual perceptions of organizational cultures: a methodological treatise on levels of analysis', *Organization Studies* 14: 483–503.

* Hofstede, G., Neuijen, B., Ohayv, D.D. and Sanders, G. (1990) 'Measuring organizational cultures', *Administrative Science Quarterly* 35: 286–316. (The account of the results of the IRIC survey of organization cultures across 20 units in Denmark and Holland.)

Hofstede, G. and Associates (1998) *Masculinity and Femininity: The Taboo Dimension of National Cultures*, Thousand Oaks, CA: Sage. (Validations of this dimension in studies of subjective well-being, consumer behaviour, gender, sexuality and religion.)

* Hoppe, M.H. (1990) *A Comparative Study of Country Elites*, PhD thesis, University of North Carolina at Chapel Hill. (A replication of the Hofstede survey with elites from 19 countries.)

* Horovitz, J.H. (1980) *Top Management Control in Europe*, London: Macmillan. (A comparison between Great Britain, France and Germany.)

* Inglehart, R., Basañez, M. and Moreno, A. (1998) *Human Values and Beliefs: A Cross-Cultural Sourcebook*, Ann Arbor, MI: University of Michigan Press.

* Jaques, E. (1951) *The Changing Culture of a Factory*, London: Tavistock. (A classic: the story of social change at the Glacier Metal Company in London.)

* Lammers, C.J. and Hickson, D.J. (1979) *Organizations Alike andUnlike: International and InterInstitutional Studies in the Sociology of Organizations*, London: Routledge & Kegan Paul. (A sociological overview of the relationship between societies and their institutions.)

* Maslow, A.H. (1970) *Motivation and Personality*, 2nd edn, New York: Harper & Row. (The popular American theory of motivation, arguing that needs can be ordered in a pyramid.)

* Maurice, M., Sorge, A. and Warner, M. (1980) 'Societal differences in organizing manufacturing units: a comparison of France, West Germany and Great Britain', *Organization Studies* 1, 59–86. (A three-nation study showing the relationship between the larger society and the way work is organized.)

* McClelland, D.C. (1961) *The Achieving Society*, Princeton, NJ: Van Nostrand Reinhold. (An American theory arguing that the strength of the Need for Achievement is the determining factor in the economic development of societies.)

* Mintzberg, H. (1983) *Structure in Fives: Designing Effective Organizations*, Englewood Cliffs, NJ: Prentice-Hall. (A well-known North American theory distinguishing five typical ways of structuring organizations.)

* Negandhi, A.R. and Prasad, S.B. (1971) *Comparative Management*, New York: Appleton-Century-Crofts. (An early introduction into the field.)

* Ouchi, W.G. (1981) *Theory Z*, Reading, MA: Addison-Wesley. (Describes how American management can use Japanese methods.)

* Pascale, R.T. and Athos, A.G. (1981) *The Art of Japanese Management*, New York: Simon & Schuster. (Japanese management described for American readers.)

* Peters, T.J. and Waterman, R.H. (1982) *In Search of Excellence: Lessons from America's Best-Run Companies*, New York: Harper & Row. (Bestselling missionary document prescribing eight maxims for companies to become excellent.)

* Pettigrew, A.M. (1979) 'On studying organizational cultures', *Administrative Science Quarterly* 24: 570–81. (Early introduction to the 'organization culture' concept.)

* Pugh, D.S. and Hickson, D.J. (1976) *Organizational Structurein its Context: The Aston Programme I*, London: Saxon House. (An overview of the 'Aston Studies' on organization structure.)

* Schein, E.H. (1985) *Organizational Culture and Leadership*, San Francisco, CA: Jossey-Bass. (A boardroom consultant's view of organization culture and change; thorough discussion of the concept of organization culture but surprisingly blind to the influences of nationality and industry.)

* Smircich, L. (1983) 'Concepts of culture and organizational analysis', *Administrative Science Quarterly* special issue on 'Organizational Culture', 28, 339–58. (A clear guide in the conceptual jungle; the whole issue is recommended as an overview of the state of the art at that time.)

Perspectives beyond the focal organization

Internal contexts and external environments

Arjen van Witteloostuijn

1 **An organization in its context and environment**
2 **Environmental scanning and organization sciences**
3 **The inside and outside world: a definition-driven classification**
4 **Environmental scanning: an issue-driven classification**
5 **An interdisciplinary perspective: a theory-driven framework**
6 **Environmental scanning in practice**
7 **Are organizations flexible or inert?**

Overview

An organization does not operate in isolation. On the contrary, an organization continuously interacts with its environment. In a way, the search for a fit between the features of the internal organization on the one hand and the characteristics of the external environment on the other is the key issue that is implicit (or explicit, as in contingency theory) in much organization science. The bottom line is that an organization has to understand (the dynamics of) its environment in order to be able to adapt to the changing demands of the outside (and inside) world. There are many different ways of scanning the organizational environment. A useful distinction can be made between three differently orientated, although overlapping, taxonomies of the environment: definition-driven classification, issue-driven classification and theory-driven classification. These may structure the way that an environment is scanned.

1 An organization in its context and environment

Stories of organizations in trouble abound in the financial press. This is true not only in times of economic recession, as in the early 1990s, but also in relatively prosperous years such as the late 1990s. For example, news reports on the disappointing performances of the US automobile industry (Chrysler, alone or with Daimler, Ford and GM) and European electronic multinationals (Philips, Olivetti, Siemens and Thompson) reflect a continuing story. Within The Netherlands, a quick reference to newspaper cover stories on DAF, Fokker and Philips throughout the 1990s should suffice to underline this point. One reason for this unremitting attention is of course the fact that organizational decline is not only a serious matter for immediate stakeholders, but also for (regions in) societies as a whole. Insights that can help to understand, and perhaps even to prevent or restore, organizational decline are, therefore, wanted. An increasing amount of literature in the organization sciences deals with this issue.

The central tenet in the organization sciences literature is that firms should change their strategies and structures so as to adopt organizational 'blueprints' (Hannan and Freeman 1977) which enhance performance and, ultimately, survival chances. For instance, firms should replace their 'bureaucratic blueprint' with a 'network blueprint'. An illustrative case in point is the result in studies on organizational decline suggesting that 'strategic paralysis' (d'Aveni 1989), which is a manifestation of inert strategic behaviour, foreshadows organizational failure. Broadly speaking, two important assumptions are (implicitly) made by adherents of the adaptation (or strategic choice) model of organizational change: first, organizations are able to implement such incremental or radical transformations with success; and second, flexibility increases profitability and, ultimately, survival chances. These assumptions are typical of standard textbooks in strategic management such as Johnson and Scholes (1998).

The key to effective and timely organizational adaptation – if possible at all – is an understanding of what drives competition and selection in the outside world. Environmental scanning serves this purpose by deepening an organization's understanding of which environmental opportunities and threats require a proactive move or a reactive response (strategy) in a specific (industrial, market or societal) setting. This entry provides an introduction to the concepts, frameworks and theories that may guide such an undertaking and provides a number of illustrative examples, such as global competition, national and industrial culture, industry and market dynamics, and governmental regulation. But first the issue of environmental scanning is put into the broader perspective of the organization sciences and the functioning of organizations.

2 Environmental scanning and organization sciences

The ideal form of the stepwise strategic decision-making process in Figure 1 serves to locate the environmental scanning issue within the broader context of the overall functioning of an organization.

The literature on strategic management (Johnson and Scholes 1998) provides an overview of the ideal stepwise strategic decision-making procedure. Environmental scanning focuses on steps 3 and 4, whereas the well-known areas of organization theory (Daft 1998) and organizational behaviour (Robbins 2001) deal with steps 1, 2, 7 and 8. Here, the investigation of internal strengths and weaknesses – the so-called capability analysis (step 2) – deals with the 'internal' context, and the scanning of opportunities and threats – the so-called environmental (step 3) and competitor (step 4) analysis – focuses on the 'external' environment. The key point is that a well-argued strategy formulation requires an investigation of the trends – that is, the strengths and weaknesses as well as the opportunities and threats – in the context and environment that the organization faces. This entry focuses on step 3, as the issues of capability analysis (step 2 in particular) and competitor analysis (step 4) deserve separate treatment.

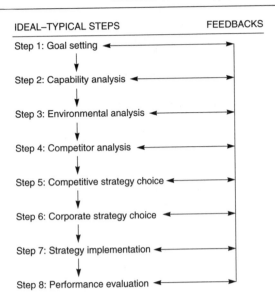

IDEAL–TYPICAL STEPS   FEEDBACKS

Step 1: Goal setting

Step 2: Capability analysis

Step 3: Environmental analysis

Step 4: Competitor analysis

Step 5: Competitive strategy choice

Step 6: Corporate strategy choice

Step 7: Strategy implementation

Step 8: Performance evaluation

Figure 1 The ideal stepwise strategic decision-making procedure

3 The inside and outside world: a definition-driven classification

In a way, the notion of the environment is a 'dustbin' concept: that is, all issues not internal to the organization are captured by the concept of the environment. As such a definition is not manageable, a number of classification schemes have been proposed in the literature to sharpen the environmental scanning issue. A first distinction focuses on internal versus external dimensions. On the one hand, context is defined as the set of outside variables that are internalized by the organization. That is, context variables operate within the organization while being largely outside the organization's sphere of influence. In a way, context is the internal environment of the organization. On the other hand, the environment relates to the large number of variables located outside the organization. Put in this way, it is the organization's external environment.

Two well-known examples of key context variables are organizational size and processing technology. As far as size is concerned, a number of theories on organizational evolution predict a specific development of internal organization features over time if the organization under consideration grows larger. For instance, with growing size the need for delegation and departmentalization – and thus coordination and integration – increases. As far as technology is concerned, the classic contribution of Woodward (1965) is still worth citing. Her message is that on the basis of a typology of processing technologies – particularly continuous-process, mass-production and unit-production technologies – hypotheses relating to organization design characteristics can be formulated. For example, the argument is that mass production goes hand in hand with centralization and formalized procedures.

Two clear examples of the impact of the environment are demographic trends and government policies. First, demographic trends have an effect on both

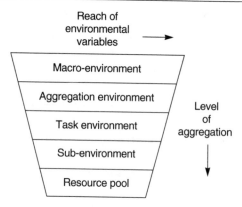

Figure 2 A definition-driven classification

demand and supply variables. For instance, the development of a society's birth rate influences both the future demand for goods (output) and the future composition of the resource pool of potential employees (input). Second, government policies have a direct and an indirect impact on the functioning of industries and organizations through, for instance, tax rates and antitrust laws. Antitrust laws determine the extent to which inter-organizational relations and organization networks are allowed to operate.

Additionally, within the context and environment dimension several sub-classifications are widespread in the literature. This is reflected in Figure 2, which is adapted from Castrogiovanni (1991).

The classification in Figure 2 is definition-driven. Five different types of environment are defined, which vary in terms of their reach of environmental variables. That is, a higher level is more encompassing (or, in other words, less specific) than a lower environmental type.

1 The *resource pool* concerns the specific input variables that the organization needs for its functioning. For example, an environmental scan may focus on a particular category of labour (such as chemical process engineers) or raw material (such as oil).
2 The *sub-environment* relates to the outside variables that influence a specific organizational sub-unit. For instance, a research and development (R&D) department is interested in developments in the scientific community, whereas a marketing unit scans the trends in customer needs.
3 The *task environment* is composed of the set of organizations with which the focal organization has to interact directly in order to grow and survive. Hence, immediate stakeholders – such as customers, finance providers, suppliers and competitors – are all part of the task environment.
4 The *aggregation environment* captures the parties outside the task environment (that is, outside the group of direct contacts) that have an impact on the functioning of the focal group of organizations (for example, an industry) at hand. Examples are interest groups, trade unions and governmental bodies.
5 The *macro-environment* refers to the broader societal forces that influence the functioning of (groups of) organizations as a whole. This includes, for

example, a country's educational system, political constitution, industrial re-lations and national culture.

Note that the context–environment distinction cuts across the five environ-mental definitions. For example, technology as a context variable may be part of the sub-environment, whereas technology in the form of an environmental factor may refer to the macro-environment (see the examples above).

Many studies in the organization sciences use the research strategy of charac-terizing the environment (of any of the above types) in terms of a discrete (gener-ally two-scale) dimension. Here, the three most widely used dimensions are complexity, dynamism and uncertainty (Mintzberg 1983). That is, an environ-ment may be assessed to be complex or simple, dynamic or stable, and/or certain or uncertain. In contingency theories, the next step is to reveal the features of the internal organization that fit the identified environmental characteristic. For ex-ample, Lawrence and Lorsch (1967) established the well-known hypothesis that environmental uncertainty requires organizational differentiation through such things as fine-grained departmentalization and integration devices.

A final remark relates to the manoeuvring opportunities associated with con-text and environment variables. That is, a context or environment variable may be either exogenous or endogenous to the organizations under consideration. Two examples – one on the level of an individual organization and one referring to a group of related organizations – may illustrate this point. First, an individual organization has, of course, influence on its own size through the (growth) strate-gies it pursues – for example, in the form of an active acquisition policy. This means that the context variable of size is then at least partly endogenous to the in-dividual organization. Second, a set of organizations (such as an industry) may establish an interest group that lobbies for favourable governmental policies, such as import restrictions to limit foreign competition. Thus, one environmental factor – government regulation – is then partially endogenized.

4 Environmental scanning: an issue-driven classification

Within the field of environmental scanning, capability analysis (step 2 in Figure 1), environmental analysis (step 3) and competitor analysis (step 4) can be con-sidered as the three key elements. Here, context variables are included in the capability analysis and competitor analysis is part of a broader environmental investigation (see Figure 3). Environmental analysis focuses on overall trends outside the organization that can influence the future functioning of the organiza-tion. These trends can be macroeconomic (for example, fluctuations in interest rates or business climates) or industry-specific (for example, trends in produc-tion technologies or prices of raw materials). In Figure 3, an overview is given of factors that can play a central role in an environmental analysis (see e.g. Johnson and Scholes 1998). Figure 3 reveals that competitor analysis is part of a broader approach to environmental scanning.

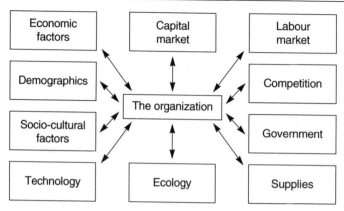

Figure 3 An issue-driven classification

Many (sub-)disciplines outside the organization sciences deal with the analysis of specific environmental elements, examples being the bodies of knowledge relating to capital and labour markets in the domains of finance and macroeconomics, respectively. It goes without saying that organizations have to select those factors which are, from their point of view, most important. The very notion of the environment – an umbrella concept that captures the whole world outside the organization – implies that the danger of an infinitely regressive selection cannot be ignored. However, the long experiences of 'professional observers' within companies facilitate the well-argued selection of the environmental elements that deserve in-depth analysis. Otherwise an environmental scan would be a never-ending story. In the chemical industry, for example, the development of the oil market is vital (will the Organization of Petroleum Exporting Countries cartel be able to push up prices in the near future?), whereas in the airline industry companies have to carefully watch the deregulation of their market within the European Union (when will national governments stop protecting their major airlines?). A labour-intensive company is more interested in changes in supply and demand in the labour market than a capital-intensive firm. An international company, in contrast with a domestic (and non-exporting and non-importing) firm, is vulnerable to exchange rate fluctuations.

The context–environment distinction cuts across the issue-driven classification as well. For example, technology may be a manifestation of both the context (for example, new computer technologies applicable within the organization) and the environment (for instance, increasing productivity of the transport infrastructure outside the organization). Similarly, the five definition-orientated types of environment (Figure 2) are related to the issue-driven framework (Figure 3). For instance, many labour market issues have an effect on the resource pool and sub-environment (for example, scarcity in professional segments of the labour market), whereas economic factors are part of the macro-environment (for example, the overall growth rate of the economy).

5 An interdisciplinary perspective: a theory-driven framework

Figure 3 is issue-driven: that is, the framework is organized by categories of specific environmental elements that may affect organizational functioning. From the point of view of theory, the field of organization sciences in general and environmental scanning in particular can be structured along two dimensions: first, level of aggregation; and second, disciplinary perspective. On the one hand, the level of aggregation can vary from 'macro–macro' – society as a whole – to 'micro–micro' – the organizational member as an individual. On the other hand, the disciplinary orientation is basically threefold: economics, psychology and sociology. A broad theoretical classification of organization sciences is depicted in Table 1.

The level of aggregation dimension in Table 1 partly overlaps with the definition-driven framework in Figure 2. Therefore, the associated labels in Figure 2 are reproduced between brackets in Table 1. In addition, a number of related entries are indicated in both Table 1 and Table 2.

The classification of theories in Table 1 again indicates how a part of the organization sciences is structured. Table 2 disaggregates the broad theoretical categories of Table 1 into specific theories within economics, psychology and sociology. However, it should be noted that the list of specific theories in Tables 1 and 2 is illustrative only and does not pretend to be exhaustive.

Of course, many theories are multifaceted: for example, the behavioural theory of the firm is economic and psychological, and deals with the organization, organizational group and organizational member level of analysis. However, a theory generally emphasizes a specific level of aggregation and a specific disciplinary perspective. Broadly speaking, for the purpose of this entry the classification along the level of aggregation dimension can be split into two clusters, as indicated in Table 3: first, the society, multi-industry and single-industry aggregation levels (above the line in Tables 1 and 2) focus on the external environment of the organization (henceforth indicated by the adjective 'inter-organizational'); second, the organization, organizational group and organizational

Table 1 A broad theory-driven classification

Level of aggregation	Disciplinary perspective		
	Economics	Psychology	Sociology
Society (macro-environment)	Macroeconomics	Macropsychology	Macrosociology (business systems)
Multi-industry (aggregation environment)	Industrial organization and strategic management (competitor analysis)		Organizational (or meso) sociology (organizational populations)
Single-industry (task environment)		Mesopsychology (Organization culture)	

Table 2 A specific theory-driven classification

Level of aggregation	Disciplinary perspective		
	Economics	Psychology	Sociology
Society (macro-environment)	• National economies • International economics	• National attitude and perception studies • National culture theory	• Social fit theory • Institutional theory (power) • Business system framework (business systems)
Multi-industry (aggregation environment)	• Multimarket competition theory (industrial organization) • Corporate strategy theory (diversification)		• Organizational ecology (organizational populations) • Resource dependence theory (inter-organizational relations)
Single industry (task environment)	• Theory of isolated market competition (industrial organization) • Competitive strategy theory (competitor analysis)	• Industry culture studies	• Organizational ecology (organizational populations)
Organization	• The theory of the firm • Transaction cost economics (agency, markets and hierarchies)	• Organizational culture theory (organization culture) • Strategy process studies (decision making)	• Contingency theory (organization types)
Organizational group (sub-environment)	• Agency theory (agency markets and hierarchies) • Behavioural theory of the firm (managerial behaviour)	• Social psychology of organizing (process of organizing) • Top management team studies (decision making)	• Contingency theory (organization structure)

member levels of aggregation (below the line in Tables 2 and 3) deal primarily with the internal context of the organization (henceforth indicated by the adjective 'intra-organizational').

Below, the resulting six sets of theories are briefly introduced. By way of illustration, only a few theories are discussed in more detail.

1 *Inter-organizational economics.* The majority of economic sub-disciplines focus on the world outside organizations. This is clear from the standard

Table 3 Six sets of theories in the organization sciences

Level of aggregation	Disciplinary perspective		
	Economics	*Psychology*	*Sociology*
Inter-organizational (Society, multi-industry and/or single industry)	Inter-organizational economics	Inter-organizational psychology	Inter-organizational sociology

assumption in much of economics that a firm operates as an entity that maximizes a unitary objective, particularly profit. The hard core of the economic study of inter-organizational competition is industrial organization, particularly the structure–conduct–performance paradigm (Scherer and Ross 1990). This paradigm inspired Porter (1980) to develop his 'five competitive forces' model as a benchmark for a competitor analysis in the context of strategic choice.

2 *Intra-organizational economics*. A limited number of economic theories deal with the internal functioning of organizations. Although Coase analysed aspects of the internal organization of firms in the 1930s, the development of so-called organizational economics did not gain momentum until the 1970s and 1980s. The textbooks by Douma and Schreuder (1991) and Milgrom and Roberts (1992) introduce the current state of the art.

3 *Inter-organizational psychology*. By virtue of its object of study – the behaviour and cognition of individual human beings – psychology rarely analyses industries or societies. However, in the field of economic psychology issues related to inter-organizational behaviour do pass under review – notably in the form of studies of buying, entrepreneurship, saving and tax-paying behaviour (Lea *et al.* 1987). Moreover, the importance of interorganizational psychology is underlined by studies on national and industrial culture.

4 *Intra-organizational psychology*. The behaviour of (groups of) organizational members is the central concern of labour and organizational psychology. Within this sub-discipline a large number of specific issues are studied, which are usually captured by the umbrella term 'organizational behaviour'. Issues vary from motivation and perception to conflict and leadership (Robbins 2001).

5 *Inter-organizational sociology*. In a way, sociology – with its focus on the aggregate functioning of human systems – is the mirror image of psychology. The sub-discipline of inter-organizational sociology has produced a large number of theories. Broadly speaking, two types of theory can be distinguished, by their focal level of aggregation: (a) societal (or macro) theories; and (b) populational (or meso) theories. The former relate to the societal embeddedness of organizations in general, whereas the latter relate to the (multi- or single-) industry environment.

6 *Intra-organizational sociology*. An organization may be considered as a micro-society. This is probably why sociology has contributed to the study of the internal organization as well. The *pièce de résistance* of intra-organizational sociology is contingency theory, which is part of a broader organization theory. Basically, this theory is a search for external

environment–internal organization situations that facilitate organizational performance. Broadly speaking, this tradition focuses mainly upon organization design issues – such as organization structure, hierarchies and (de)centralization – as determined by contingencies such as age, size and technology (Daft 1998).

6 Environmental scanning in practice

If environmental scanning is to be applicable in practice, an organization has to be able to take three steps: (1) *selection* of key environmental issues; (2) *collection* of relevant information; and (3) *analysis* of the available data. The issue of selection is largely a matter of experience and intuition; an organization may not only benefit from in-house knowledge, but also from expertise present outside the organization. For example, the London-based consultancy firm Chemsystems first collects data on the chemical industry (largely from chemical companies) and then sells the data to firms in that industry. The second step, collection of data, is prone to the (costly) pitfall of information overkill. To be manageable, the information provided per selected environmental item has to be restricted to essentials. Regarding the third step, the analysis of the available data should not be limited to a search for one best way. Rather, a scenario analysis is needed to investigate the robustness of the environmental scanning outcomes.

The literature on the functioning of organizational participants in general and top management team members in particular reveals that successful implementation of an environmental scan may not be as straightforward a process as that outlined above. Not only may decision makers misperceive environmental trends, but also disagreement among key decision makers may block the successful execution of an environmental scan. Moreover, subsequent steps (see Figure 1) have of course to deal with strategic decision making and the implementation of actions.

7 Are organizations flexible or inert?

The key debate underlying many of the organization sciences relates to the determinism versus voluntarism issue. Here the strategic choice perspective is opposed to the organizational ecology view. On the one hand, the strategic choice argument is that an organization is capable of adapting on time to changes in the environment. On the other hand, organizational ecology argues that organizations are hard pressed to alter their 'blueprints', as they suffer from relative inertia; that is, they lag behind changes in the environment (Hannan and Freeman 1984). Environmental scanning research is able to determine the conditions under which either the strategic choice or the organizational ecology perspective will be closer to reality. Without an understanding of its environment an organization will certainly make the predictions of organizational ecology come true; such an organization will be unlikely to even attempt to adapt to changing environmental conditions.

Further reading

(References cited in the text marked *)

* d'Aveni, R.A. (1989) 'The aftermath of organizational decline: a longitudinal study of the strategic and managerial characteristics of declining firms', *Academy of Management Journal* 32: 577–605. (An empirical study into patterns, consequences and explanations of organizational decline.)

Boone, C.A.J.J. and van Witteloostuijn, A. (1995) 'Industrial organization and organizational ecology: the potentials for cross-fertilization', *Organization Studies* 16: 265–98. (In this paper, two important theories of the organizational environment – economics' industrial organization and sociology's organizational ecology – are systematically compared as to their complementarity.)

* Castrogiovanni, G.J. (1991) 'Environmental munificence: a theoretical assessment', *Academy of Management Review* 16: 542–65. (An integrative perspective on the prevailing definitions and theories of the environment with an emphasis on the underlying concept of munificence.)

Coase, R.H. (1937) 'The nature of the firm', *Economica* 4: 386–405. (Classic pioneering article setting the scene for what later became known as transaction cost economics.)

Connor, K.R. (1991) 'A historical comparison of resource-based theory and five schools of thought within industrial organization economics: do we have a new theory of the firm?', *Journal of Management* 17: 121–54. (Extensive overview of five schools of thought within industrial organization, which is economics' theory of competition.)

Daft, R.L. (1998) *Organization Theory and Design*, Cincinnati: South-Western Publishing. (An illuminating introduction to organization theory with contingency theory as the central theme.)

DiMaggio, P.J. and Powell, W.W. (1983) 'The iron cage revisited: institutional isomorphism and collective rationality in organizational fields', *American Sociological Review* 48: 147–60, reprinted in Powell, W.W. and DiMaggio, P.J. (1991) (eds), *The New Institutionalism in Organizational Analysis*, Chicago: University of Chicago Press, pp. 63–82. (Seminal paper that introduces an institutional perspective on the organization–environment linkage.)

* Douma, S. and Schreuder, H. (1991) *Economic Approaches to Organizations*, Englewood Cliffs, NJ: Prentice Hall. (A lucid, undergraduate-level introduction to economic theories of organization.)

* Hannan, M.T. and Freeman, J. (1977) 'The population ecology of organizations', *American Journal of Sociology* 82: 929–64. (Classic introduction to the sociological theory of selection (organizational ecology) outlining the basic assumptions and arguments.)

* Hannan, M.T. and Freeman, J. (1984) 'Structural inertia and organizational change', *American Sociological Review* 49: 149–64. (Key contribution to the organizational ecology perspective explaining in depth the crucial assumption that organizations are considered to be relatively inert.)

Hrebiniak, L.G. and Joyce, W.F. (1995) 'Organizational adaptation: strategic choice and environmental determinism', *Administrative Science Quarterly* 30: 336–49. (An admirable attempt to classify and compare many theories along the lines of environmental determinism and organizational voluntarism.)

* Johnson, G. and Scholes, K. (1998) *Exploring Corporate Strategy: Text and Cases*, 5th edn, Englewood Cliffs, NJ: Prentice Hall. (Advanced textbook on strategic management providing an overview of the content and process of strategy making as a whole.)

* Lawrence, P.R. and Lorsch, J.W. (1967) *Organization and Environment*, Cambridge, MA: Harvard University Press. (Contribution to the development of contingency theory; reports the results of a study of organizations in three environments.)

* Lea, S.E.G., Tarpy, R.M. and Webley, P. (1987) *The Individual in the Economy: A Survey of Economic Psychology*, Cambridge: Cambridge University Press. (An extensive survey of the psychology of economic behaviour.)

* Milgrom, P. and Roberts, J. (1992) *Economics, Organization and Management*, Englewood Cliffs, NJ: Prentice Hall. (An advanced textbook on economic theories of organization.)

* Mintzberg, H. (1983) *Structure in Fives*, Englewood Cliffs, NJ: Prentice Hall. (Synthesis of the contributions to organization theory in the 1960s and 1970s providing a typology of organization structures in relation to internal and environmental features.)

Pfeffer, J. and Salancik, G.R. (1978) 'The design and management of externally controlled organizations', reprinted in Pugh, D.S. (ed.) (1990) *Organization Theory: Selected Readings* (3rd edn), pp. 146–77. (Classic introduction into the resource dependency theory.)

* Porter, M.E. (1980) *Competitive Strategy: Techniques for Analyzing Industries and Competitors*, New York: The Free Press. (One of Porter's most famous works which outlines his 'five forces'.)

* Robbins, S.P. (2001) *Organizational Behavior*, Englewood Cliffs, NJ: Prentice Hall. (Broad account of the findings of organizational behaviour research.)

* Scherer, F.M. and Ross, D. (1990) *Industrial Market Structure and Economic Performance*, Boston, MA: Houghton Mifflin. (This wellknown textbook introduces a well-argued mixture of insights from the structure–conduct–performance paradigm and game-theoretic modelling traditions.)

Wernerfelt, B. (1984) 'A resource-based view of the firm', *Strategic Management Journal* 5: 171–80. (This paper introduces the resource-based view of the firm, aiming at integrating external and internal theories of the organization.)

Witteloostuijn, A. van and Wegberg, M.J.A.M. van (1992) 'Multimarket competition: theory and evidence', *Journal of Economic Behavior and Organization* 18: 273–82. (Extension of Porter's force of potential entry by reviewing the literature on multipoint contact.)

* Woodward, J. (1965) *Industrial Organization: Theory and Practice*, London: Oxford University Press. (Introduces the technology context variable, along with production system typology and associated contingencies.)

Zajac, E.J. and Bazerman, M.H. (1991) 'Blind spots in industry and competitor analysis: implications of interfirm (mis)perceptions for strategic decisions', *Academy of Management Review* 16: 37–56. (Lucid illustration of what the consequences may be of psychological filtering in the context of environmental scanning and market competition.)

Strategic choice

John Child

1 **The origins of strategic choice analysis**
2 **Analysis of the 1972 model**
3 **Three key issues in strategic choice analysis**
4 **The role of strategic choice in contemporary organization studies**
5 **Conclusion**

Overview

The 'strategic choice' perspective was originally advanced as a corrective to the view that the way in which organizations are designed and structured has to be determined largely by their operational contingencies. This view overlooked the ways in which the leaders of organizations, whether private or public, were in practice able to influence organizational forms to suit their own preferences. Strategic choice drew attention to the active role of leading groups who had the power to influence the structures of their organizations through an essentially *political* process. It led to a substantial re-orientation of organizational analysis and stimulated debate on three key issues: the role of agency and choice in organizational analysis; the nature of organizational environment; and the relationship between organizational agents and the environment.

Since the intention was to redress an imbalance in organization theory, the exposition of strategic choice the time contributed to the diversity of perspectives on the subject, along with other emerging approaches such as radical organization theory. Over twenty years later, the situation has changed considerably, in that the field is now extremely diversified with a wide range of competing perspectives.

While different theoretical perspectives or paradigms may be irreconcilable in their own philosophical terms, when applied to the study of organizational phenomena they are not necessarily 'incommensurable'. It does not follow from the attachment of different meanings to the same concept that reference is being made to wholly different phenomena. Without an attempt to draw upon, and even to reconcile, the insights offered by its various perspectives, organization studies will run a serious risk of becoming little more than an arena of 'clashing cymbals' (or indeed symbols), making little real theoretical advance and having nothing useful to say for practice either.

A major contribution of strategic choice analysis today derives from its potential to integrate some of these different perspectives. This integrative potential derives from the fact that strategic choice articulates a political process, which brings agency and structure into a dynamic tension and locates them within a significant context. In so doing, it not only bridges a number of competing perspectives but also adopts a dynamic, non-deterministic position. Strategic choice analysis has been from its inception critical of determinism within organizational analysis, which derives from the adoption of an essentially mechanistic paradigm. The model of strategic choice points to the possibility of a continuing adaptive learning cycle, but within a theoretical framework that locates 'organizational learning' within the context of organizations as sociopolitical systems. Strategic choice is thus consistent with a more *evolutionary* model of organizations, in which organizational learning and adaptation proceed towards not wholly predictable outcomes within the shifting forces of organizational politics. This model finds a parallel in the new evolutionary political economy that bids to revitalize microeconomics.

The following two sections summarize the key features of the original strategic choice analysis. The third section then considers the key issues arising from this analysis and how they have been interpreted. The fourth section examines the integrative potential of strategic choice analysis within the contemporary study of organizations, with particular reference to organizational change and learning.

I The origins of strategic choice analysis

Organization studies had by the early 1970s seen the completion of several major research programmes which investigated the components of organizational structure and their relationships with situational variables ('context') on a systematic comparative basis (for example, Blau and Schoenherr 1971; Pugh *et al.* 1968). The mode of research was cross-sectional and positivistic, involving the statistical examination of associations between phenomena which were regarded as objective in nature. The processes accounting for any statistical correlation were left to be inferred. The inferences which were being drawn reflected the predominant theoretical orientation at the time, which was one of structural determinism. This assumed that the contextual factors of environment, technology and size imposed certain constraints upon the structural choices managers could make, especially in the case of work organizations which had to achieve certain levels of performance in order to survive. The general argument was that: 'if organizational structure is not adapted to its context, then opportunities are lost, costs rise, and the maintenance of the organization is threatened' (Child 1972: 8).

Burrell and Morgan (1979) placed this theoretical orientation squarely within the 'functionalist' paradigm and there are continuities with it in several contemporary approaches, namely *the structural contingencies* perspective (Donaldson 1985, 1995), the *ecological* approach (Hannan and Freeman 1989) and the *institutional* perspective (Powell and DiMaggio 1991). The first stresses the importance for organizational performance of matching internal organizational capabilities to external conditions. The second considers that units which do not have organizational forms characteristic of their sector or 'niche' have a poorer chance of survival; its focus is primarily on organizational populations and it gives little attention to how decision makers might endeavour to adapt to the environment. The institutional perspective is a rather 'broader church', but most of its adherents find common ground in the assumption that the structural forms (as well as the identities and values sustaining these) of relevant external institutions map themselves onto organizations which depend on them for legitimacy, resourcing or staffing. All of these contemporary approaches therefore regard environmental conditions as ultimately determining organizational characteristics. *They stress environmental selection rather than selection of the environment.*

Consideration of strategic choice led to the conclusion that this deterministic view was inadequate because of its failure: 'to give due attention to the agency of choice by whoever have the power to direct the organization' (Child 1972: 2). 'Strategic choice' was defined as the process whereby power holders within organizations decide upon courses of strategic action. (Such action could be directed towards different targets, although the 1972 paper focused on the design of an organization's structure.) 'Strategic choice extends to the environment within which the organization is operating, to the standards of performance against which the pressure of economic constraints has to be evaluated, and to the design of the organization's structure itself' (Child 1972: 2). Strategic choices were seen to be made through initiatives within the network of internal and external organizational relationships – through *proaction* as well as *reaction*. It was assumed that effective strategic choice required the exercise of power and was therefore an essentially *political* phenomenon:

> Incorporation of the process whereby strategic decisions are made directs attention onto the degree of choice which can be exercised ..., whereas many available models direct attention exclusively onto the constraints involved. They imply in this way that organizational behaviour can only be understood by reference to functional imperatives rather to political action.
>
> (Child 1972: 2)

This identified the need for a corrective to, rather than an outright rejection of, the prevailing paradigm. Indeed, it implied a potential synthesis between the political process and functionalist perspectives. For the power available to decision makers was seen to be accountable in terms of the consequences for organizational performance that flowed from its exercise. It was assumed that some assessment of those consequences (albeit not necessarily well-informed or rational) would enter along with actors' prior preferences into their decisions. The model towards which strategic choice analysis led would therefore:

> direct our attention towards those who possess the power to decide upon an organization's structural rationale, towards the limits upon that power imposed by the operational context, and towards the process of assessing constraints and opportunities against values in deciding organizational strategies.
>
> (Child 1972: 13)

The 1972 paper offered the outline of a processual model under the title of 'The role of strategic choice in a theory of organization'. This model is repro-

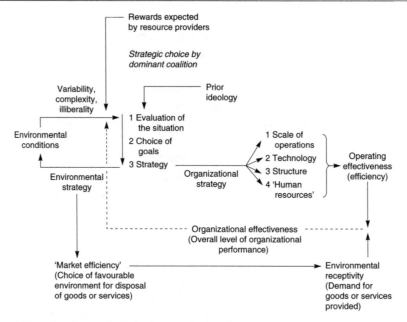

Figure 1 The role of strategic choice in organization theory

duced as Figure 1. It locates strategic choice within the organizational context, and through the feedback of information to decision makers, depicts the conditions for what today some would call an *organizational learning process*. Since much of the discussion in the third section of this article will refer to the model, a brief explanation now follows.

2 Analysis of the 1972 model

In the model, the exercise of strategic choice by organizational decision makers refers to a process in which the first stage is their evaluation of the organization's position – the expectations placed on it by external resource providers, the trend of relevant external events, the organization's recent performance, how comfortable the decision makers are with its internal configuration, and so on. Their prior values, experience and training are assumed to colour this evaluation in some degree. A choice of objectives for the organization is assumed to follow on from this evaluation, and to be reflected in the strategic actions on which they decide. This process is, in practice, often formalized into an annual planning round and/or procedure for making capital expenditure, which appears usually to be accompanied by considerable informal lobbying and negotiation.

Externally-oriented actions may include a move into or out of given markets or areas of activity in order to try and secure a favourable demand or response that will be expressed by a high consumer valuation of the organization's products or services. They could also include attempts to negotiate the terms of acceptable organizational performance with external resource-providers or institutions holding sanction over the organization, although this possibility was not considered in the 1972 paper. Rather common examples occur when companies go to banks for a substantial loan and when they seek permission to erect a new processing facility that has an environmental impact. Internally-oriented actions may involve an attempt, within the limits of resource availability and indivisibility, to establish a configuration of personnel, technologies and work organization which is both internally consistent and compatible with the scale and nature of the operations planned. The 'goodness of fit' that is in the event achieved is seen to determine the level of efficiency expressed by output in relation to costs. The conjunction of efficiency with external demand will determine the organization's overall level of performance. Performance achieved becomes in turn a significant informational input to the organization's decision makers when they next make an evaluation of the organization's position. Thus, a *circular, evolutionary* process is established.

3 Three key issues in strategic choice analysis

The earlier exposition of strategic choice gave some attention to the choice of internal organization with reference to the 'contextual' parameters of size and technology; how, for example, formalization could be a response to increasing scale. It was, however, more fundamentally concerned with the relationship between agency and environment. The ability of decision makers ('agents') to make a 'choice' between policies was seen to depend ultimately upon how far they could preserve autonomy within the environment, through achieving the levels of performance expected of them. The term 'strategic' was used to signify matters of importance to an organization as a whole, particularly those bearing upon its ability to prosper within an environment where it faces competition or the need to maintain its credibility. It is closely related to the idea of 'stratagem', which is a way of attempting to accomplish an objective in interaction with, or against, others. The three key issues arising from strategic choice analysis therefore concern: (1) the nature of agency and choice; (2) the nature of environment; and (3) the nature of the relationship between organizational agents and the environment.

Agency and choice

'The problem of human agency' has had a continuing intellectual significance in the social sciences. Human beings have succeeded during the course of their history in creating socially organized systems which then limit further exercise of human agency, even to the point of determining human action. Such organized constraint acts both upon individuals and organizations. The forms it takes include culture, institutionalized norms for socially approved action (often prescribed in laws), and the constricting bureaucracies of government and big business. While the derivation of each of these forms is external to any one person or group of people, cultural values and institutional norms can become internalized so that they act to constrain choice primarily through the social actor's own interpretative mechanisms rather than through constraints which are ostensibly imposed from outside. For example, the management of many organizations have banned smoking within their buildings although there is no law obliging them to do so.

Whittington (1988) developed the distinction between external and internal forms of constraint, with the intention of thereby refining strategic choice analysis. He pointed out that the initial impact of the strategic choice concept had been to encourage analysts to dichotomize perspectives on organization between those which focus on agency (the 'voluntaristic' approach) and those which emphasize determinism. The dichotomous approach tended to ignore the preconditions for exercising agency, and the possibility that actors themselves may not have sufficient capacities for exercising choice could also be overlooked. This reasoning led Whittington, following Estler (1984), to distinguish between 'environmental determinism' and 'action determinism'.

Action determinism qualifies the simple assumption that organizational actors can exercise choice once external constraints are removed. It draws attention to the mechanisms used by actors in deciding what to do. Action determinism holds that, given certain types of drive, such as an overriding intention to maximize a firm's profits, a decision maker will only select one kind of action such as keeping costs to the bare minimum. This formulation is clearly problematic as it stands, since it assumes that actors can perceive only one way of realizing their intentions. Nevertheless, the concept of action determinism does draw attention to the relevance of predetermined mind-sets for the interpretative process which takes place when strategic choice is exercised, and it accounts for how they could limit the range of choices recognized and considered. It points to the significance of managerial beliefs, and of the factors shaping them, for an understanding of the strategic choice process in organizations, a subject which has attracted a growing body of research in recent years. Spender (1989), for example, showed how managers in particular industries tend to share a common set of strategic 'recipes' – beliefs as to the priorities and actions appropriate for performing well in their industry – which can become embedded, to the extend of inhibiting an innovative response to changing competitive conditions. The latter phenomenon is illustrated by the difficulties which the managers of the British clothing firm, Foster Brothers, had in adjusting to a new competitive situation at the beginning of the 1980s (Johnson 1987).

The original analysis of strategic choice identified 'prior ideology' as exercising an influence over how decision makers would evaluate their organization's situation. The concept of ideology draws attention to the ways that class, occupational and national socialization may shape managerial beliefs about action choices. While its relevance has been supported by subsequent research, we are now able to understand how other factors, such as age and educational level, can also exert an influence. Age and education, although they locate people within social categories which can generate common identities and beliefs, are likely to affect action determination not only through the medium of ideology but also through competence.

The introduction of action determinism enriches the analysis of strategic choice because it focuses attention onto the characteristics of key organizational actors themselves which may foreclose the degree of choice that they exercise, even in the absence of external constraints. It complements the political process perspective, present in the original exposition of strategic choice, which assumes that limitations on action choices not arising from outside the organization derived from its internal politics. The political process perspective draws attention to what would be collectively acceptable within the 'dominant' decision making group, or acceptable to the organization's wider body of employees or members, and it allows for an internal negotiation process though which there can be a coalescence of diverse initial action preferences into an agreed policy. The notion of action determinism draws attention to the prior factors which shape the mind-sets of key actors. Its application in research promises to shed light on how firmly beliefs are held by actors as they enter into discussions and negotiations with others in the organization, and how flexible they will be in modifying their beliefs in the light of the pressures of contrary opinion and evidence.

While action determinism can lead to an unwillingness to consider information that does not fit preconceived ideas, the scarcity of information as a resource can also inhibit the range of choices considered. There are two issues to note here. The first concerns the problem of securing relevant information that is timely, in an analysable form and not prohibitively expensive. The second concerns the problem of coping with information that is ambiguous, of questionable reliability and incomplete. Decision making, especially of the non-routine kind considered within strategic choice analysis, is thus liable to be conducted with uncertainty. The degree of choice will therefore be limited not only by action determinism and the constraints of intra-organizational political process; it will also be inhibited by limited and/or ambiguous information. The three phenomena – action determinism, political process and imperfect information – are likely to react upon each other. The foreclosing of options through action determinism is one way of coping with uncertainty – the actor 'enacts' the situation in his or her terms instead and is not troubled by externalities. If this behaviour predominates, it is likely to heighten the political process, either between key actors themselves if they hold divergent beliefs and/or between closed-minded actors and the rest of the organization. A lively political process around the making of strategic organizational decisions will of itself generate greater uncertainty, at least as to how information should be interpreted.

In short, limitations to agency and choice may arise from action determinism and intra-organizational political process, and also from informational deficiencies. The identification of these limitations carries the original concept of strategic choice forward, since they highlight the constraints upon choice additional to those which are imposed by an organization's environment.

Environment

It is not possible to abstract from the environment when considering the strategic choices available to organizational actors. This is partly because the environment presents threats and opportunities for the organization which establish the parameters of choice. It is also because the ways in which organizational actors understand the environment affect the extent to which they believe they enjoy an autonomy of choice between alternatives.

Strategic choice analysis recognizes both a pro-active and a reactive aspect in organizational decision making *vis-à-vis* the environment. Organizational agents are seen to enjoy a kind of 'bounded' autonomy. They can take external initiatives, including the choice to enter and exit environments, and also make adaptive internal arrangements. At the same time, the environment within which they are operating is seen to limit their scope for action because it imposes certain conditions for their organization to perform well. It is assumed that organizational actors will themselves have a similar understanding of the environment, because this is what experience teaches them.

Weick (1969) maintains that people in organizations 'enact' their environments. This can be interpreted in two ways. The first is that people can only be aware of a literally all-embracing concept like 'the environment' in terms of how they enact it in their minds. Organizational actors therefore necessarily respond to their own subjective definitions of the environment. This interpretation is fundamental to strategic choice analysis and indeed to any view of organizations that admits of human agency. The second interpretation is that people in organizations can enact the environment in the sense of 'making it happen as they wish'.

A very qualified form of this second interpretation informed the original description of strategic choice that could be exercised by organizational decision makers:

> To an important extent, their decisions as to where the organization's operations shall be located, the clientele it shall serve, or the types of employees it shall recruit determine the limits to its environment – that is, to the environment significant for the functions which the organization performs.
>
> (Child 1972: 10)

The possibility of environmental enactment is here limited to the selection of environments in which to operate, and even this decision cannot necessarily be entered into lightly or frequently since it many incur large entry and exit costs. Enactment in strategic choice analysis thus refers mainly to actions which bring certain environments into relevance – which introduce them onto the organizational stage. Once entered, the conditions of an environment assume an object reality which is consequential for an organization, however much they are filtered by a subjective interpretation. That interpretation will shape the actions taken within the environment, which will amount to further enactment insofar as they are able to effect intended changes in it. The level of change which the managers of an organization can effect within its environment is always liable to be limited by the countervailing powers of institutions, as telecommunication companies found under previously regulatory regimes, and/or by the possibility of new competition, as former market leaders like IBM have experienced.

This interpretative view sees the decision maker entering into interaction with people outside the organization, but it does not necessarily conceive of the two forming an identity either objectively or in the minds of organizational actors. What they are interpreting, albeit within the cognitive and informational limits discussed earlier, can exist apart from them. A person or organization does not constitute its environment; the environment consists of other actors in other organizations, and it cannot be reduced to the subjective interpretations of any one group of organizational players. Some writers, however, have pursued Weick's argument to the point of maintaining that environments are wholly enacted through the social construction of actors (for example, Smircich and Stubbart 1985). This is to apply an extreme form of voluntarism to the concept of strategic choice. Rather, the emphasis on human agency and subjective interpretation contained in strategic choice analysis was intended to counteract the theoretical shallowness and inherent pessimism of environmental determinism, *not* to reduce either organization or environment to being simply the products of a subjective understanding. Strategic choice analysis recognizes that environments have real and consequential properties distinct from the perceptions and understandings of organizational actors, but it maintains that those perceptions and constructions are also of consequence in their own right if they contribute to determining the actions of organizations.

Strategic choice analysis thus incorporates both subjectivist and objectivist perspectives on organizational environment. This dualism does not result only from identifying organizational decision makers' subjective evaluations of the environment as a critical link between its objective features and organizational action, although that is an important element in it. It also reflects a recognition that organizational actors do not necessarily, or even typically, deal with an 'environment' at arm's length through the impersonal transactions of classical market analysis but, on the contrary, often engage in relationships with external parties that are sufficiently close and long-standing as to lend a mutually pervasive character to organization and environment. This indicates that the environment of organizations has an institutional character and, indeed, that people inside and outside the formal limits of an organization may share institutionalized norms and relationships. Examples include the members of occupational unions and professional associations. The 'environment' contains cultural and relational dimensions in addition to the 'task' and market variables identified respectively by structural contingencies and economic theories. This conception of the organizational environment as a social entity has provided useful additional insights into how companies have developed over time (for example, Smith *et al.* 1990). It also helps to clarify two long-standing issues in the relationship between organizational agents and the environment which arise from strategic choice analysis, namely: (1) whether or not the environment is constraining or enabling; and (2) how externalized the environment actually is.

Organizational agents and the environment

Whittington (1988) criticizes environmental determinism in which exogenous structural constraints are assumed necessarily to limit and regulate the actions that can be taken by organizational decision makers. This point is consistent with the strategic choice argument, which drew attention to various possibilities allowing for choice on the part of organizational actors without their incurring intolerable penalties. Whittington conceives of environment in terms of how it is socially structured and argues that this structuring can be enabling as well as constraining for strategic choice. Thus, organizational actors who are members of a professional occupation and bound by norms of appropriate conduct may thereby be externally constrained in their actions, whereas owner-managers supported by entrepreneurial ideologies and the rights of capitalist ownership may thereby be externally enabled to consider a wider range of action alternatives.

A more extended consideration of the enabling and constraining features of the environment is similarly encouraged by the sectoral concept of environment just described. This indicates how, for instance, long-standing relationships between the members of the same sector, structured within industry associations, can furnish a basis for concerted action on matters of common interest such as political lobbying. Or it may show how the sharing of sector-specific strategic recipes (Spender 1989) can facilitate the interpretation of the environment by a firm's managers. At the same time, the cultural and relational norms shared by members of a sector are likely to constrain organizational actors who seek to diverge from them. For example, divergence from normal strategic recipes may be perceived as risk by members of the capital market familiar with the sector, with the result that they impose a premium on the cost of raising external funds. Thus, while the social nature of an organization's environment will under some circumstances act as a constraint upon action, even to the point of determining it, it can also enable action and widen the range of available strategic alternatives. It is a misleading oversimplification to treat the environment simply as an external determinant of organizational action.

The concept of an organizational environment as a social network also raises doubts about how externalized it really is from its constituent organizations. The distinction between organization and environment contained in the original strategic choice article (Child 1972) has to be softened by a recognition that organizational actors often create choice possibilities through their relationships with people who are formally outside the organization. They may, for example, be able to secure from officials with whom a good relationship has been developed a rather more liberal interpretation of environmental controls, especially in countries like China where the application of regulations is open to a flexible interpretation. Organization and environment are becoming interpenetrated through collaboration between actors in such a way as to diffuse the distinction between the two entities and, incidentally, to blur the distinction between 'firm' and 'market'. With the rapid growth of collaborative relationships between organizations, in the forms of joint ventures and other strategic alliances, this interpenetration assumes a fully operational form. It is, of course, qualified by the terms on which the parties can agree to cooperate and by how far they can identify mutual complementarities. Such alliances can indeed be unstable, and many survive for only a limited period. Nevertheless, they constitute an increasingly important arrangement through which part of the relevant environment is internalized, often with the motive of affording greater control over, or access to, other areas of the environment (such as markets) in a bid to extend strategic choice. The recent spate of alliances between telecommunications companies, for example, has facilitated entry into markets otherwise protected by governments and they may also restore a degree of market control following the implementation of deregulation policies.

Strategic choice analysis therefore allows for the objective presence of environments, while at the same time it recognizes that organizations and environments are mutually pervasive. This pervasiveness occurs in two main ways. The first is through the interpretation of environments as being consequential for organizational action. The second is through the relationships that extend across an organization's 'boundaries'. It takes the very definition of those boundaries to be in large part the consequence of: 'the kinds of relationships which its decision makers choose to enter upon with their equivalents in other organizations, or ... the constraints which more dominant counterparts impose upon them' (Child 1972: 10). Organization and environment therefore permeate one another both cognitively and relationally – that is, both in the minds of actors and in the process of conducting relationships between the two.

The concept of strategic choice was for some time interpreted as justifying a sharp distinction between organizational agency and organizational environment, with the former emphasized by voluntaristic perspectives and the latter by deterministic approaches (see the comprehensive review by Astley and Van de Ven 1983). Strategic choice was associated with an absence of external determination, a procedure maintained even in later analyses which explored the possibility of different combinations of choice and determinism (for example, Hrebiniak and Joyce 1985). This is understandable, given the intention of the 1972 article to criticize the then prevailing dominance of determinism, but it overlooked that article's statement that organizational decision makers are in a position of response to feedback from the environment. This feedback may in turn provide them with a learning opportunity which brings to light new action choices, but the process overall was seen as an *interactive* one between organizational agents and the environment, and in effect between choice and constraint.

This interactive view is one which writers on strategic management have generally adopted, exemplified by the influential study of US firms and hospitals conducted in the 1970s by Miles and Snow (1978). They recognized how strategic choice analysis identified the ongoing relationship between organizational agents and the environment, giving rise to what they termed 'the adaptive cycle':

> The strategic-choice approach essentially argues that the effectiveness of organizational adaptation hinges on the dominant coalition's perceptions of environmental conditions and the decisions it makes concerning how the organization will cope with these conditions.
>
> (Miles and Snow 1978: 21)

From their investigation, Miles and Snow concluded that the policies which organizational agents adopted towards the environment could be placed into the four generic categories of 'defender', 'prospector', 'analyser' and 'reactor'. This categorization was an important refinement of the strategic choice concept.

Bourgeois, in similar vein, argued for a view of strategic management as a creative activity which is intrinsic to a dialectic between choice and constraint: 'So, though environmental and internal forces act as constraints, strategy making often selects and later modifies the sets of constraints' (1984: 593). Hambrick and Finkelstein (1987) developed and explored the concept of chief executive discretion, defined as 'latitude of action'. They argued that this concept reconciled popular views of organizations as either inertial or highly adaptive. Their premise was that chief executives vary in how much discretion they possess, and that variation is due to a combination of: (1) factors in the environment; (2) organizational characteristics which promote inertia (such as size, age and culture); and (3) the chief executive's own attributes. While Hambrick and Finkelstein in this way identify discrete factors rather than the processes and relationships through which choice and constraint work themselves out, they identify the influences which might enter interactively into the process.

More recently, Neergaard (1992) has developed a 'partial contingency model'. This recognizes that the nature of the environment, such as its levels of dynamism and complexity, can impact upon the internal controls systems which it is functional for an organization to adopt. At the same time, the model also recognizes that environmental management is possible through two main strategies which Neergaard (borrowing from previous writers) calls 'buffering' and 'bridging'. Through buffering, managers aim to protect their core activities from external influences – examples include stockpiling, attempts to reduce input and output fluctuations such as marketing campaigns, and public relations activities. With bridging, managers endeavour to manage their environments through various forms of negotiation, cooperation, exchange of information and other forms of reciprocity. Neergaard illustrates how environmental management has a direct bearing on the type and degree of organizational control that it is necessary to adopt. His conclusion in effect reiterates the basic strategic choice argument: 'Only by studying the interplay between environment and environmental management is it possible to gain a more full understanding of different controls [that is, internal organization]' (Neergaard 1992: 29).

Strategic choice is recognized and realized through a process whereby those with the power to make decisions for the organization interact among themselves (so constituting a shifting 'dominant coalition'), with other organizational members and with external parties. Analytical centrality is given to organizational agents' interpretations (their goals and views of the possibilities for realizing them) as they engage in these relationships. This is to say that organization, as a social order, is the subject of adjustment through negotiation on a continuing, although not necessarily continual, basis. The possibilities for this negotiation are at any one point in time framed by existing structures, both within and without the organization. The use of 'framing' here is intended to convey a sense that the issues and options open to negotiation by actors have some structured limits, although it may be possible to change the limits themselves over time through the negotiation process. Structures within the organization include the channels through which relevant information is obtained and processed, and formalized policies which define action priorities for the organization. External structures include the configuration of competitor organizations within the organization's operating domain, that of its suppliers and customers, and the system of regulations relevant to its activities.

Strategic choice in organizational analysis thus furnishes an example of 'structuration' (Giddens 1984). That is, action is bounded by existing structures but at the same time acts upon those structures. Through their actions, agents endeavour to modify and redefine structures in ways that will admit of different possibilities for future action. The process is a continuing one. Strategic choice thus presents a dynamic rather than a static perspective on organizations and their environments. In keeping with structuration theory, it also addresses the so-called problem of levels of analysis. For, while the actions taken in the name of organizations may be individually driven, and some of this drive may be explicable at the level of the individual, they are organizational both in their representation and in the resources, relationships or other features which are activated. When these actions become a constituent element in the relations between organization and external bodies, they move into an even higher level of social process. The consequences of this process for the organization, which strategic choice analysis depicts as being transmitted to it through a feedback of information on its performance, are social in origin but may be interpreted in some circumstances by individual actors primarily in terms of their own personal values or priorities. Strategic choice analysis admits of a role for the individual organizational actor (as an entrepreneur), assumes that actors will more often constitute a collective (as in a dominant coalition), and treats the cycle of action and response as one that is environmentally and therefore socially contextualized. It does not regard the wider social arena simply as a constraining or defining context for the narrower, lower-order unit of analysis, as did, for instance, the founders of the influential Aston Programme of organizational research in their original 'conceptual framework' (Pugh *et al.* 1963). Nor does it do the opposite and simply treat action as explicable in individual terms or, for that matter, as interpretable solely in terms of any one individual's understanding. Rather, its conception of agency entering into a cycle of organizational development within the environment cuts across analytical levels and in this sense helps to bridge what has sometimes been a source of division among theorists of organization.

The following section examines how these characteristics of strategic choice analysis – the interaction between agency and structure, and the cyclical nature of organizational development – can contribute to the challenge of constructively reconciling different paradigms. In so doing, the consistency of this integrative interpretation with an evolutionary learning perspective will become apparent.

4 The role of strategic choice in contemporary organization studies

It is significant that the classification of paradigms within organization studies which has attracted the most attention (Burrell and Morgan 1979) did not attempt to allocate strategic choice analysis to any of its categories. Its authors claimed that the paradigms they identified were mutually exclusive, a claim which has contributed substantially to present divisions in the subject area. Strategic choice analysis, by contrast, cannot be contained within any one of these paradigms. Indeed, it bridges and potentially integrates them.

Burrell and Morgan placed different perspectives within four main paradigms which were defined in terms of two dimensions. The first dimension was whether the perspective regarded organizational phenomena as subjective constructs or as objective in nature. The second was whether the perspective was concerned with the possibilities, or process, of radical change or with the maintenance of the existing order ('regulation'). Burrell and Morgan argued that the four paradigms 'offer alternative views of social reality' and cannot therefore be synthesized. Hence the claim of 'paradigm incommensurability' in organization studies.

Strategic choice analysis would actually be impossible if an assumption of paradigm incommensurability was maintained. It bridges the four paradigms identified by Burrell and Morgan. First, it is concerned *both* with the ways in which subjective constructions have objective consequences through the actions they inform, *and* with how those consequences subsequently impinge upon future actions through the subjective interpretations which are given to them. *Cash flow* would be one objective indicator of such action consequences, which is open to divergent subjective interpretations as to its sufficiency and implications. Neither a wholly subjectivist paradigm nor a wholly objectivist one could of itself provide a sufficient theoretical foundation for this process. The argument here is, in effect, that process of agency in organizations cannot be treated adequately by a perspective that does not incorporate both the subjective and objective features inherent in structuration.

Second, it is also impossible to consign strategic choice analysis to either the Burrell/Morgan paradigm of the sociology of regulation or that of radical change. For, while the original exposition of strategic choice analysis did tend to assume that dominant members of the organization would act in ways that preserve their privileged positions (an aspect of 'regulation'), it does not assume they will necessarily succeed in so doing. It therefore allows for situations in which organizational change can occur and this change could possibly be quite radical. For example, conditions of crisis occasioned by the failure of an organization to achieve a level of performance in its environment that can meet the expectations of its member groups are likely, according to strategic choice analysis, to give rise to a radical change in the composition of the 'dominant coalition' (for example, through takeover, employee buyout or election of new leaders in an association or union) with a probable consequent change in the policies and practices instituted for the organization. Strategic choice analysis draws attention to conditions under which change is likely to be activated, either by the established decision makers or by new ones. In the former case, the change will be motivated by the desire to preserve certain continuities and thus be conservative, if not regulatory, in character. In the latter case, the change may be motivated by a desire to introduce relatively radical reformulations. The mutual dependence between different groups in an organization implies, according to strategic choice analysis, that even a dominant group will have to preserve certain features valued by the others when it is endeavouring to introduce change, thus giving rise to the paradox of continuity and change in organizational life. Studies of organizational transformation have in fact noted how even apparently radical developments usually incorporate elements of continuity, at least of an ideological nature, in order to increase the acceptability of the changes among those who have to work with them (Pettigrew 1985; Child and Smith 1987).

The strategic choice perspective on organizational process thus brings agency and structure into a dynamic tension along the subjective–objective dimension. It locates this relationship within a social context which is significant to the *subjective* aspect as the source of agents' values and perceived interests towards the organization (referred to as 'ideology' in Child's article). It also locates the relationship within an economic or institutional context which is relevant to how an organization performs *objectively*; for example, in terms of its capacity to attract further resources. The level and type of performance that is achieved in relation to the expectations of those with power over an organization in turn bear upon the question of whether that organization's status quo can be maintained or not. This form of analysis draws from insights provided by each of Burrell and Morgan's four paradigms and offers a bridge between them. It is not, as the role accorded to performance might suggest, a pseudo-functionalist analysis, since it admits that the conditions for organizational survival are open to negotiation between organizational agents and external resource-holders and that the evaluation of performance can be the subject of claim and counter-claim. For example, the employees of a company may claim that the lack of opportunities for further training are a mark of poor managerial performance, even though the cost savings boost profits in the short term. Like functionalism, strategic choice analysis adopts a position of contextual relativism, but it differs from it in not admitting of incontestable and overriding situational determinants.

The continuing relevance of the strategic choice perspective derives to a large extent from the way it identifies possibilities for integration between different paradigms. Its rejection of paradigm incommensurability is not intended to open the door to imperialistic claims from any particular theoretical quarter and, indeed, one should recall that the approach grew out of a critique of a then dominant paradigm in organizational analysis. In fact, its position is quite the opposite. The integrative potential of strategic choice analysis stems from the way it is conducive towards a recognition of the fundamental paradoxes in organizational life, which both paradigm incommensurability and paradigm imperialism fail to take into account. There is a tension between apparently contradictory aspects of organizational life – the subjective and objective, the conservative and innovative – that establishes a dynamic which transcends them.

This dynamic contributes to an evolutionary adaptive or 'learning' cycle. There is a parallel here between the strategic choice adaptive cycle and the analysis of knowledge formation advanced by Boisot (1986). Both analyses regard new circumstances as posing a potential challenge to knowledge which has been previously codified into formalized/structured organizational practices. If adaptation is to take place (which of course does not necessarily happen), this challenge will initiate a process of enquiry and search which initially brings ill-defined information specific to the new situation within the purview of organizational factors (uncodified/undiffused knowledge in Boisot's terminology). From the process of evaluating this new knowledge, proposals emerge for the definition and formalization of new actions and structures, which if acceptable and successful become standardized and hence widely applied ('diffused'). The contribution that this adaptive cycle model can offer stems largely from the fact that it bridges the subjective/objective and change/continuity dichotomies in the study of organizations. It begins to unpack the concept of structuration through suggesting how interpretation becomes objectified into structures and individual learning becomes translated into organizational practice, while it indicates that structure and practice are themselves always liable to become deconstructed in the face of external and internal changes with which they are inconsistent. Recognition that the interplay between organization and environment is mediated by the interpretation and evaluation of actors operating within the arena of organizational micropolitics also helps to resolve the paradox that change and continuity co-exist and may even by symbiotic.

Apart from the attractiveness of its integrative potential, further development of the strategic choice approach along the lines just indicated promises to offer insights into what has come to be called 'organizational learning'. This is a prominent topic within the study of organizations which, however, exhibits considerable theoretical disarray despite attracting much attention over the past twenty years. The term 'organizational learning' appears to be quite beguiling, even contradictory, in the light of the Burrell and Morgan scheme. Does it reflect a subjective or objective view of organization? Individuals can learn through a process of internalization, but what about organizations? Organizational learning implies the acquisition of new understanding and competence, but does this lead to a radical change or to new ways of maintaining the status quo in the light of different circumstances? Some of the confusion about organizational learning stems from a failure to apply to it an analysis that can incorporate these apparent contradictions within the framework of a dynamic adaptive cycle.

A great deal of the thinking about organizational learning has modelled itself on studies of individual learning, borrowing terms such as 'organizational memory'. Both cognitive and behaviourist theories of individual learning have been imported into discussions of organizational learning. A cognitive orientation is reflected in terms such as 'organizational intelligence', and a behavioural orientation in a concept such as 'organizational routines', which are regarded as codifications of understanding and competence that the organization has acquired. A subjective–objective distinction is also present here, in that cognition is by definition subjective whereas behaviour can in principle be externally observed. Although frequently attempted, the application of individual learning models to organizations is deeply problematic. It reifies the organization into a mechanism or organism and wholly avoids the politics of agency which are integral to strategic choice analysis.

Much of the organizational learning literature fails to locate the prime movers of the process, the relevant actors – managers or other staff – within the political systems of organizations. In recognizing that there are barriers to learning, this literature explores defensiveness as a personal attribute, but usually fails to enquire into its non-psychological sources such as the organizational micro-politics which lead to much learning and innovation being contested between groups (Child and Loveridge 1990). For the actors involved in organizational learning and adaptation often belong to several groups which have different views about the desirable future path for their organization to follow. They may, for instance, be a mix of top managers, technical experts, functional managers and external consultants. Strategic choice analysis, by focusing upon a leading or initiating group operating within a political context that is both internal and external to the organization, draws attention not just to the capacity of individuals or groups to learn but equally to those people who are controlling and managing the learning process 'on behalf of' the organization. It admits the possibility that existing structures may limit learning because of the way they can close off certain options, through, for example, the absence of procedures or staff that can access certain areas of information, or because the options are too politically sensitive to consider in the light of the hierarchical privilege embedded in a organization's structure. At the same time, strategic choice analysis also allows for the possibility that such structures may offer some resources for the achievement of change.

Strategic choice analysis thus recognizes that it may be necessary to sustain certain paradoxes for learning to take place as a collective phenomenon in organizations, such as the need to achieve consensus from a diversity of views and the preservation of some continuities within the process of introducing change. In particular, it can bring an appreciation of the politics of change to bear upon the understanding of the organizational learning process. The relevance of these considerations may be illustrated by quoting just three of the conclusions drawn from a detailed study of organizational transformation in the Cadbury chocolate company.

1 A lengthy process of recognition preceded transformation. This involved a combination of symbolic and power-relevant activities, namely: (a) re-framing the definition of relevant contextual conditions and appropriate internal arrangements with (b) the ascension into powerful positions of those advocating new interpretations and solutions.

2 Competing frames of meaning and recipes for improvement were advanced by actors whose views were conditioned by their training, speciality and previous experience in the company.
3 The traditional and hitherto dominant corporate ideology was not simply a barrier to transformation. Its wide acceptance and cohesion provided a clear position against which the case for change had to be developed. This was easier because the ideology itself was malleable, stressing receptivity to new techniques and intellectual enquiry, and management had been encouraged to proceed in that mode. (Child and Smith 1987: 590).

The strategic choice perspective places the agency–structure relationship within a context. The evaluation by organizational agents of information feedback on the organization's performance in its environment, if it identifies either problems or new opportunities, encourages a learning process and provides a trigger for further action. The cycle is thus:

choice→action→outcome→feedback→evaluation→choice

In this way, a structuration dynamic is established in which previously codified policies and practices become targets for reformulation but where elements from the old structure are normally incorporated into the new. Hence the paradox of change and continuity.

5 Conclusion

This chapter has highlighted the key points of strategic choice analysis within a theory of organizations. It has traced the issues which arose from the introduction of this perspective and it has considered some of the refinements of the original analysis which were indicated by subsequent criticism and deliberation.

An important corrective to some of the interpretations which others have made of strategic choice is the affirmation that it is neither a pseudo-functionalist perspective (showing organizational leaders how to run the show in a politically more sensitive manner) nor an outright rejection of the contingency strand of functionalism which it originally criticized. The strategic choice perspective transcends these distinctions which some have built up into formidable barriers within the study of organizations and it is precisely this which gives it the potential to assist future integration within the subject.

Strategic choice analysis therefore opens a door to future progress in organization studies by drawing together insights from different paradigms and locating these within a dynamic process of interplay between agency and structure, and organizations and environment.

Note

This chapter has benefited greatly from editorial advice kindly offered by Sally Heavens and Malcolm Warner.

Further reading

(References cited in the text marked *)

* Astley, W.G. and Ven, A. Van de (1983) 'Central perspectives and debates in organizational theory', *Administrative Science Quarterly* 28: 245–73. (Classifies perspectives according to levels of organizational analysis, and deterministic versus voluntaristic assumptions.)

* Blau, P.M. and Schoenherr, R.A. (1971) *The Structure of Organizations*, New York: Basic Books. (Reports on comparative research examining organization structure and its predictors.)

* Boisot, M. (1986) 'Markets and hierarchies in a cultural perspective', *Organization Studies* 7: 135–58. (An early exposition of an influential model of the 'knowledge cycle' which is consistent with the strategic choice process.)

* Bourgeois, L.J. (1984) 'Strategic management and determinism', *Academy of Management Review* 9: 586–96. (Suggests a dialectic between free will and determinism in conceptualizations of strategic behaviour.)

* Burrell, G. and Morgan, G. (1979) *Sociological Paradigms and Organizational Analysis*, London: Heinemann. (Extremely influential division of organizational sociology into four discrete paradigms.)

* Child, J. (1972) 'Organizational structure, environment and performance: the role of strategic choice', *Sociology* 6: 1–22. (Classic exposition of the strategic choice perspective.)

* Child, J. and Loveridge, R. (1990) *Information Technology in European Services*, Oxford: Blackwell. (Considers political versus technologically-deterministic perspectives in the light of detailed cases of information technology introduction into services in six European countries.)

* Child, J. and Smith, C. (1987) 'The context and process of organizational transformation – Cadbury Limited in its sector', *Journal of Management Studies* 24: 565–93. (Application of 'firm-in-sector' analysis which incorporates the paradoxical combinations of action with constraint, and continuity with change.)

* Donaldson, L. (1985) *In Defence of Organization Theory*, Cambridge: Cambridge University Press. (Criticizes strategic choice analysis because it does not adopt a normative approach towards organizational design.)

* Donaldson, L. (1995) *American Anti-Management Theories of Organization*, Cambridge: Cambridge University Press. (Criticizes organization theories which, the author claims, do not admit the role of managers as designers of organization structure in the light of operational contingencies.)

* Estler, J. (1984) *Ulysses and the Sirens: Studies in Rationality and Irrationality*, Cambridge: Cambridge University Press. (Proposes a two-step model of human action which recognizes both exogenous constraints and those inherent in the action selection mechanisms of actors themselves.)

* Giddens, A. (1984) *The Constitution of Society*, Cambridge: Polity Press. (One of many works in which Giddens articulates 'structuration' theory.)

* Hambrick, D.C. and Finkelstein, S. (1987) 'Managerial discretion: a bridge between polar views of organizational outcomes', *Research in Organizational Behavior* 9: 369–406. (Develops and explores the concept of chief executive discretion.)

* Hannan, M.T. and Freeman, J.H. (1989) *Organizational Ecology*, Cambridge, MA: Harvard University Press. (The main source on this perspective, collecting together these authors' previous work.)

* Hrebiniak, L.G. and Joyce, W.F. (1985) 'Organizational adaptation: strategic choice and environmental determinism', *Administrative Science Quarterly* 30: 336–49. (Develops a typology of organizational adaptation based on the assumption that choice and determinism are independent variables.)

* Johnson, G. (1987) *Strategic Change and the Management Process*, Oxford: Blackwell. (Presents research exploring how managers' understandings affect their action in respect of environmental changes.)

* Miles, R.E. and Snow, C.C. (1978) *Organizational Strategy, Structure and Process*, New York: McGraw-Hill. (Develops the strategic choice perspective into an 'adaptive cycle' which identifies four generic policies adopted by managements towards their environments.)

* Neergaard, P. (1992) 'Environment, strategy and management accounting', in D. Otley and H. Lebac (eds), *Proceedings of the Second European Symposium on Information Systems*, Versailles: HEC. (Explores and illustrates the need to modify contingency approaches to management accounting through cognizance of the interplay between environment and its management. Available from the Copenhagen Business School.)

* Pettigrew, A.M. (1985) *The Awakening Giant: Continuity and Change in ICI*, Oxford: Blackwell. (Major study which traces the impact of its top management on a major UK corporation.)

* Powell, W.W. and DiMaggio, P.J. (1991) *The New Institutionalism in Organizational Analysis*, Chicago, IL: University of Chicago Press. (Exposition of the new institutionalism and a collection of the significant contributions to that approach.)

* Pugh, D.S., Hickson, D.J., Hinings, C.R., Macdonald, K.M., Turner, C. and Lupton, T. (1963) 'A conceptual scheme for organizational analysis', *Administrative Science Quarterly* 8: 289–315. (Sets out the framework for the Aston Programme of organizational studies which strategic choice analysis later critiqued.)

* Pugh, D.S., Hickson, D.J., Hinings, C.R. and Turner, C. (1968) 'Dimensions of organization structure', *Administrative Science Quarterly* 13: 65–105. (One of many publications reporting on the findings of the first study in the Aston Programme.)

* Sklair, L. (2000) *The Transnational Capitalist Class*, Oxford: Blackwell. (This book links strategy and globalization to offer a new perspective.)

* Smircich, L. and Stubbart, C. (1985) 'Strategic management in an enacted world', *Academy of Management Review* 10: 724–36. (Takes an interpretative worldview and claims that environments are enacted.)

* Smith, C., Child, J. and Rowlinson, M. (1990) *Reshaping Work: The Cadbury Experience*, Cambridge: Cambridge University Press. (Traces in detail how the senior management of a large confectionery company articulated the requirements for changes in its organization.)

* Spender, J.-C. (1989) *Industry Recipes*, Oxford: Blackwell. (Pioneering study of senior managers' mental maps for guiding their businesses.)

* Weick, K.E. (1969) *The Social Psychology of Organizing*, Reading, MA: Addison-Wesley. (Influential book which stresses the enactment of the organizing process by those involved.)

* Whittington, R. (1988) 'Environmental structure and theories of strategic choice', *Journal of Management Studies* 25: 521–36. (Argues for a more sophisticated analysis of choice and determinism, recognizing how 'action determinism' may limit the perception of choice and how the environment may enhance actors' capacities for strategic choice.)

Inter-organizational relations

Jörg Sydow

1 Inter-organizational relations in practice and theory
2 Content and form of inter-organizational relations
3 Market-like relations: the theme of economic theory
4 Organization-like relations: the theme of inter-organization theory
5 Interrelating organizations: the agenda of research
6 Managing inter-organizational relations
7 Conclusions

Overview

In a 'society of organizations' the economic success and survival of profit-making organizations, as much as for non-profit organizations, increasingly depends on the quality of the relations they maintain with other organizations. These inter-organizational relationships, which above all provide access to external resources, can be of two sorts: a rather market-like nature may prevail, or, increasingly evident, they may resemble relations within organizations, in terms of the intensity of communication, exchange of personnel or level of trust. These two types of relationships, although they often coincide in practice, are of a very different nature, and hence have been analysed within the traditions of two different lines of theoretical thought: economics and inter-organization theory. However, both lines of thought lack a processual understanding of the formation and management of inter-organizational relations. This is why the development of future inter-organization theory should focus upon the processes of interrelating and coordinating organizations, yet without ignoring the enabling and restraining effects of existing inter-organizational structures on inter-organizational interaction.

1 Inter-organizational relations in practice and theory

Inter-organizational relationships – that is, the often patterned relations *between* two or more organizations which result from inter-organizational action or behaviour – have always been a management concern. This is because via these relations both profit-making and non-profit organizations acquire know-how, material, services, personnel, capital and other resources they require for transforming input into output and marketing this output, thereby satisfying the interests of external and internal stakeholders. For this reason alone inter-organizational relations are considered the most valuable resource an organization may have, whether they be with suppliers, customers or even competitors (Håkansson 1987). Their importance increases in direct proportion to the value of the resources which may be sourced and the better the access to them.

Since the early 1980s, the significance of inter-organizational relations for the survival of profit- and non-profit-making organizations has been on the increase. This is in part because of the increasingly complex nature of business. The purchasing, development, production and marketing of varied products and services requires more intensive collaboration with customers and suppliers while globalization and the growing demand for universal technical standards provide additional impetus for inter-organizational cooperation. Relations have, however, also become more problematic. The effective organization of such collaboration has become more difficult with the introduction of complex systems technologies, rapid technological innovation, shortened product life cycles and rising capital requirements. Often those relations that do exist cut across different industries; the multimedia industry is a particularly good example of this. Start-ups, which are thought of as being essential for economic development, rely heavily on intense inter-organizational relations and thus are particularly troubled by the issue (Larson 1992). Difficulties are compounded by the fact that they usually lack the capability (that is, the relations) to set up such relations.

Emerging strategic alliances and networks, which have contributed much to the increased economic importance of inter-organizational relations, however, are not only entered into in order to manage increasingly varied and complex products and services but also result from the continued attraction to outsourcing which leaves hardly any of the aforementioned functional areas untouched. This necessarily dramatizes the dependence of organizations on effective inter-organizational relations.

In face of their increased significance, the management of inter-organizational relations often becomes a strategic capability. In some cases, when it cannot easily be imitated, it even acts as a barrier to market entry by potential competitors and results in a core-competence of organizations. Moreover, existing inter-organizational linkages provide specific opportunities for strategic action while excluding others. For instance, trustee and tightly coupled relations which may emerge from close collaboration over research and development (R&D) may restrict future choices (for example, exclude some potential partners) and simultaneously enable strategic moves which would not have been possible otherwise (for example, developing a complex technology).

While relations *within* organizations have been subject to organizational and managerial analysis from the very beginning of what is now called 'organization science', relations *between* organizations were not analysed from an organizational perspective until the early 1960s (Levine and White 1961). In those days inter-organizational research relied heavily on social exchange theory and concentrated almost exclusively on relations among non-profit organizations in the public sector. Today, the increased significance of inter-organizational relations for profit-making enterprises is reflected in research undertaken from multiple perspectives, and sometimes even from multiple paradigms.

Only since the mid-1980s has empirical research on inter-organizational relations been conducted in the private sector. However, much of this research is relevant for non-profit organizations also because these are increasingly being linked with enterprises (in public–private partnerships, for example) and, more importantly, because of comprehensive deregulation and marketization increasingly face a competitive, profit-making environment. This development may not only lead to a convergence of public and private sector inter-organizational relations but also to a higher relevance of research on inter-organizational relations for managing organizations of any kind.

In contrast to organization science, inter-organizational relations have, in principle, always been within the focus of economics – at least if such relations exhibit market-like properties. Economic approaches assume, however, that organizations are surrounded by a faceless environment rather than by the organized environment which inter-organizational research conceptualizes, for example, as 'interorganizational fields' (Warren 1967), 'interorganizational collectivities' (Van de Ven *et al.* 1974) or 'inter-organizational networks' (Nohria 1992). In ignorance of these concepts, economic approaches have for the most part disregarded the organization of organizational environments in general and the institutional character of most inter-organizational relations in particular.

For this reason, and despite advances in (institutional) economics, the study of inter-organizational relations, which includes dyadic linkages, organization sets, action sets and networks (Aldrich 1979; Whetten 1987), can profit much from organization theory, or more precisely, from inter-organization theory. Presumably only research on inter-organizational relations informed by inter-organization theory will be of practical value for managers and other interested practitioners who must act in institutionalized rather than atomistic inter-organizational contexts.

2 Content and form of inter-organizational relations

Inter-organizational relations, which have gained in significance for organizational success and survival, yet at the same time are difficult to manage, may be analysed in terms of content and form, both of which are of course dependent on each other. Due to this interdependence some types of relations are more likely to emerge than others.

In terms of content, inter-organizational relations may serve as a way to exchange goods and services, to raise capital and to source labour, to give advice or to transmit information and emotion. Typically, organizations exchange different kinds of content via the same linkages. Therefore, many inter-organizational relations exhibit at least some degree of multiplexity. Japanese *keiretsu* and other business groups are a good case in point in this respect (Gerlach 1992).

Turning to the form of inter-organizational relations, these may be either voluntary or mandated, formal or informal, hierarchical or heterarchical, cooperative or competitive, vertical or horizontal, deliberate or emergent, tightly or loosely coupled, functional or dysfunctional, national or cross-national, stable or fragile, and so forth. Moreover, as far as their legal form is concerned, inter-organizational relations may be found under one corporate legal structure (a 'hierarchy' in the sense of Williamson) as in the case of trusts, conglomerates and holding companies, or they may transcend a single corporation and instead form the basis of inter-corporate networks and business groups (a 'hybrid'). In practice, inter-organizational relations are often characterized by several of these attributes which vary by degree and, hence, should not be considered dichotomic.

In this respect inter-organizational relations may be *more or less* institutionalized. Typically the more they are infused with norms and values, the more institutionalized they are. In the end such relations are taken for granted by their users. When inter-organizational relations are institutionalized, informal personal relationships supplement formal inter-organizational relations, psychological contracts substitute for or at least add to legal contracts, and formal agreements sometimes even mirror informal understandings and commitments. This intricate balance of formal and informal characteristics seems to be largely responsible for the emergence, evolution and dissolution of inter-organizational relations (Ring and Van de Ven 1994).

Past research on inter-organizational relations has produced several useful typologies, two of which will be looked at in some detail here. These typologies are useful since they represent more or less distinct modes of collective action within inter-organizational fields, evolve in different contexts, require different management capabilities and may be better analysed from one theoretical perspective than from another.

The first typology, developed by Astley and Fombrun (1983) and much referred to in organization science literature, is based upon a social ecology framework. This typology begins with the insight that collective action can produce two forms of interdependence: commensalistic, where actors of the same species compete or cooperate, and symbiotic, where actors of different species interrelate. In addition, this typology differentiates between two types of associations: direct and indirect. The resulting four ideal types of inter-organizational collectives are: agglomerate, confederate, conjugate and organic.

Agglomerate collectives consist of organizations of the same species that are only indirectly linked through competition for a limited supply of similar resources. Respective kinds of inter-organizational relations are found less in ideal than in cartelized markets. Moreover, this type includes relations among organizations which compete within markets but which may cooperate within trade and professional associations. *Confederate collectives* are clusters of organizations from the same species that directly associate with each other in order to achieve common ends. Pertinent examples are collusion, informal industry leadership, franchising networks and (horizontal) strategic alliances built among competitors and aiming at joint R&D. *Conjugate collectives*, in contrast, are comprised of organizations from different species (possibly even different industries) whose interactions are directly and tightly coupled because of the complementary functions they fulfil for each other. Such symbiotic relations typically emerge with suppliers and customers tied to a focal organization by means of subcontracting, licence agreement, joint venture or interlocking directorates. *Organic collectives*, finally, consist of organizations from different species that are – despite their membership in an over-arching system – only indirectly related. A case in point are organizations that form informal 'multiorganizational systems' (Chisholm 1989) or very loosely coupled inter-organizational networks. One drawback with such a typology is that, independent of the real existence of these types of inter-organizational relations, a theoretical network perspective (for examples see Warren 1967; Aldrich 1979; Håkansson 1987) will certainly make almost any industry or inter-industry population appear as a network of direct and indirect inter-organizational relations.

A second typology has been proposed by Macneil (1985) and is much referred to in economic literature. This typology proposes a relatively simply contractual continuum which is anchored by the transactional contract at one end and by the relational contract at the other. A *transactional contract* is thought of as emphasizing extrinsic, mainly economic rewards, a narrow scope and specific duration of collaboration, and rather tangible results. A *relational contract*, in contrast, also considers intrinsic rewards of different kinds, embraces a more comprehensive scope and indefinite duration, and includes not only tangible but also less observable results. In view of this contractual typology, inter-organizational relations may be seen as market-*like* relations in the first case and as organization-*like* relations in the second. The latter refers more to the need for a sophisticated relationship management, whose task is to develop and maintain inter-organizational linkages, than to the hierarchical or organizational character of this kind of linkage. Although seemingly abstract from concrete inter-organizational interaction, this contractual typology constitutes a continuum that embraces most of the inter-organizational relations distinguished by other typologies.

In accordance with the organized character of real markets, many if not most inter-organizational ties should be classified as organization-like rather than as market-like relations. Possible examples are inter-organizational relations constituted by interlocking directorates (Mizruchi and Schwartz 1987), joint ventures and programmes or consortia (Harrigan 1985), inter-organizational information systems (Johnston and Vitale 1988), knowledge linkages (Badaracco 1991) or personnel exchange relations (Pfeffer and Leblebici 1973), which at the very least take a middle position on the continuum. However, those organizations linked by means of trade and professional associations, forming cartels or informally colluding (Astley and Fombrun 1983) have less organized relations and may qualify as market-like relations.

3 Market-like relations: the theme of economic theory

Inter-organizational relations are not very important in ideal markets, in which transactions are assumed to be short-lived, social bonds virtually non-existent and the structure of suppliers and customers, which are coordinated via the invisible hand of the price mechanism, rather atomistic. Real markets, however, depart substantially from this ideal, for they exhibit a richness of different forms, reflecting intended as much as unintended consequences of corporate strategy and inter-organizational action, embrace at least some strategically interdependent organizations and are, in a sense, 'domesticated' (Arndt 1979). Nevertheless, market-like inter-organizational relations retain their mainly competitive character.

Microeconomic theory and theoretical approaches within the range of industrial or organizational economics have tried to model these kinds of inter-organizational relations appropriately. While many of these models cope reasonably well with a structure of demand or supply which deviates from the ideal (for example, oligopolistic market structures), they all do not grasp the 'social embeddedness' of economic action. The notion of social embeddedness, expounded by Granovetter (1985), refers to the fact that even in rather ideal-type markets agents are tied by social bonds, share certain beliefs and ideologies and act according to established rules. All this very much affects the course and outcome of real market processes. The neglect of the social embeddedness of economic action by economic models is particularly severe since even transactions in spot markets (like stock or options exchanges), usually considered to resemble closely the model of the ideal market, are in fact socially structured (Baker 1984). And how much more important is this embeddedness in markets which are subject to competitive strategies of organizations (market differentiation, building market entry barriers), in which competition co-exists with cooperation (in the case of long-term business relations, for instance), and in which organizations try to construct environments to their needs, not least by means of collaboration?

Industrial economics, similar to microeconomic theory and population ecology (Aldrich 1979), focuses on competitive relations among organizations. Inter-organizational behaviour from this perspective is essentially understood as a function of market structures. The effects of possibly unique resources and strategic capabilities remain largely unnoticed by this perspective, although modern game theory has somewhat cured this deficiency. None the less, cooperative, or at least more socially organized, relations are not considered as important by industrial economics, and if they are, they are often interpreted as collusion reducing the level of (desirable) competition.

Organizational economics, including agency theory and transaction cost economics, offers a more comprehensive framework for the analysis which applies not only to competitive but also to cooperative relations among organizations. Although providing useful insights, these approaches do not grasp the social embeddedness of economic action even if they refer to organized business relations. Moreover, they overlook how power which is not based on economic structures (high asset specificity, for instance) impacts on the formation and management of inter-organizational relations. Finally, these approaches have no concepts or tools to enhance our understanding of the underlying processes which make inter-organizational relations emerge, grow, adapt or dissolve, either incrementally or discontinuously. While this is not much of a problem in the case of rather ideal market-like relations, it is in the case of relations which resemble those within organizations.

4 Organization-like relations: the theme of inter-organization theory

Inter-organization theory, in contrast to economic approaches, is based upon concepts from organization science. From such a perspective relations between profit-making as much as between non-profit-making organizations result from inter-organizational interaction and, more importantly, are themselves considered as more or less socially organized. In fact, they are organized by the visible hand of boundary-spanning managers and workers, and may develop structural properties which make them closely resemble *intra-organizational relations*. However, *inter-organizational relations are not* identical to intra-organizational relations, even as it becomes harder to differentiate between an inside and an outside as more and more organizations are transformed into network organizations or are part of a single yet somewhat decentralized corporate structure, as in the case of some conglomerates or holding companies. In all these cases: 'a corporate interorganizational design closely approximates the control features (incentives, decision-making structure) of a single multi-unit organization' (Whetten 1987: 244). Nevertheless, an over-arching authority of a corporate structure will not dissolve all difficulties to coordinate organizations within an inter-organizational network or business group either.

Inter-organizational relations which closely resemble intra-organizational relations and exhibit more cooperative than competitive properties are a suitable candidate to be analysed from an inter-organization theory perspective. Traditionally, from this perspective, inter-organizational relations have been conceptualized as social exchanges (for example, Levine and White 1961). Later, resource dependence theory continued this research tradition before neo-institutional theory somewhat broke with this resource exchange-orientated tradition.

Resource dependence theory, which above all focuses on the function of inter-organizational relations to secure the procurement of critical resources (Pfeffer and Salancik 1978), was for some time the most popular approach to the analysis of inter-organizational relations. Among other things it hypothesizes that organizations will try to retain control over resource supply to absorb uncertainty, either by the internal strategy of adaptation or by the external strategy of managing (or even avoiding) commensalistic and symbiotic dependence. Suitable means for the latter are, among other things, the formation of either cooperative linkages or interlocks, or merger. Resource dependence theory has dominated much of empirical research on inter-organizational relations, however, most of this research has not utilized fully the potentials of this theoretical approach.

More recently, *neo-institutional theory* (DiMaggio and Powell 1983; Powell and DiMaggio 1991) has stressed that inter-organizational relations not only provide access to technical resources but also serve legitimacy needs. For instance, organizational actors prefer to maintain relations with highly respected organizations in order to ensure the necessary support and legitimacy from their institutional environment. Moreover, and again in contrast to resource dependence theory, this approach focuses on processes of interpreting, believing, routinizing, legitimizing and sanctioning occurring within and between organizations. In this way neo-institutional theory stresses the cultural and ideological aspects of organizational and inter-organizational behaviour. Rather than focusing on individual interaction this theory emphasizes the forces of the institutional environment which make organizations take one another's behaviour into account when planning their own actions. To explain this largely adaptive behaviour of individual and organizational actors the theory distinguishes three general types of institutional pressure: (1) coercive forces that stem from political influence and problems of legitimacy (for example, government mandate); (2) mimetic changes which have their roots in uncertainty (for example, imitation of the industry leader); and (3) normative influences resulting from growing professionalization (DiMaggio and Powell 1983). However, by concentrating on the rules of the institutional environment, neo-institutional theory somewhat downplays not only the agency and scope of choice in inter-organizational interaction but also the importance of technical resources for the survival of organizations. Therefore, a more integrative approach is needed which, in a balanced way, pays conceptual attention to both structure and action on the one hand, and institutional forces and technical dependence on critical resources on the other.

Apart from resource dependence and neo-institutional theory, a wide variety of theoretical approaches ranging from action theory through systems theory to structuralist and ecological approaches (see Sydow 1992 and Smith *et al.* 1995 for an enumeration of most, and Davis and Powell 1992 for a discussion of several relevant theories) is applied as inter-organization theory. At the turn of the century, inter-organizational analysis, almost as much as intra-organizational research, has evolved into a multi-theory or even multi-paradigm status. After all, these inter-organization theories conceptualize markets as complex networks or as social structures rather than as simple allocative mechanisms coordinated by prices. From such a perspective markets are socially constructed systems which serve to measure economic value, to generate norms for this kind of measurement and to provide institutional means for sustaining these norms (Abolafia and Biggart 1991). Most inter-organization theories not only share this view of 'markets as social structures' (Swedberg 1994) but also provide necessary information on the antecedents and/or consequences of inter-organizational relations in the face of particular contingencies.

Antecedents relevant to the constitution of inter-organizational relations in general and cooperative inter-organizational relations in particular are, among other things, common interests or asymmetric power, positive attitudes towards cooperation, including the readiness for relation-specific investments and collective action, industry-wide norms, some common history, trust and, not least, the organizational capabilities for interrelating and coordinating. Consequences of cooperative inter-organizational relations comprise efficiency, profitability, adaptive capacity, innovativeness, quality of products and services, among other things (Whetten 1987). The analysis of antecedents and consequences from the perspective of the theories discussed above results in distinguishing more or less among different types of relations, contingencies, and, above all, levels and units of analysis (Oliver 1990).

Inter-organization theories in most cases refer to organizations or even more macro levels of analysis when explaining the antecedents and effects of inter-organizational relations (rather than to the behaviour of individuals and groups). The most common units of analysis are thus either dyadic linkages, organization sets, action sets, networks or inter-organizational fields. *Dyadic linkages* form as a result of the interaction among only two organizations and are typically analysed from the perspective of either resource dependence theory or transaction cost economics. Organization sets and, even more so, action sets and networks, are more comprehensive units of analysis and mainly analysed from a network perspective (Aldrich 1979; Whetten 1987). An *organization set* consists of organizations with which a focal organization has direct links. In contrast to a 'strategic network' (Jarillo 1988; Sydow 1992) which constitutes a real network organization led by a hub firm, an organization set, however, is only an analytical construct of researchers. *Action sets* and *inter-organizational networks*, on the other hand, are real phenomena, refer to both temporary sets or stable networks of organizations, respectively, and include all the relations, direct and indirect, these organizations have formed, even though empirical research may typically cover only sections of these collectivities. The concept of *inter-organizational field* forms the unit of analysis of much neo-institutional theorizing (DiMaggio and Powell 1983; Powell and DiMaggio 1991; Scott 1994). This concept is similar to that of an action set or network in that it may include relations with key suppliers and customers, regulatory agencies and other organizations providing required resources; it differs, however, in that it highlights the impact of more encompassing social, historical and cultural structures of a societal sector or industry on the formation and management of inter-organizational relations. More specifically, it includes organizations that: 'participate in the same meaning systems, are defined by similar symbolic processes, and are subject to common regulatory processes' (Scott 1994: 71).

5 Interrelating organizations: the agenda of research

Both economic approaches and conventional inter-organization theory have contributed to a better understanding of the emergence, maintenance and dissolution of inter-organizational relations, of their antecedents and their consequences. However, both lines of theorizing are rather static and have focused mainly on dyadic relations. The need for a more processual and comprehensive understanding of the formation and management of inter-organizational relations – the interrelating and coordinating of organizations – has meant that further theories, concepts and frameworks have been developed, some of which conceive (cooperative) inter-organizational relations as: 'socially contrived mechanisms for collective action, which are continually shaped and restructured by actions and symbolic interpretations of the parties involved' (Ring and Van de Ven 1994: 96). Others emphasize that: 'networks are constantly being socially constructed, reproduced and altered as the result of the actions of actors' (Nohria 1992: 7).

Of these, the *structuration theory* developed by Anthony Giddens (1984) as a social theory seems most promising. This theory provides a framework which is not very different from the conceptual–developmental path that neo-institutional theory has taken most recently (see Scott 1994). In short, structuration theory considers economic relations as social relations stemming from social practices; focuses on process without disregarding structure; and conceptualizes action and structure as a duality rather than a dualism. Thus structures do not exist outside of action but are chronically implicated in its reproduction.

Applied to the analysis of inter-organizational relations, this means that these relations result from inter-organizational practices in which organizations as corporate actors act with reference to other organizations and draw not only on allocative and authoritative resources (structures of domination) but also on signifying and normative rules (structures of signification and legitimation). In this respect at least, referring equally to all three structural dimensions, structuration theory offers a more integrative approach to the analysis of inter-organizational relations than either resource dependence or neo-institutional theory.

These structures of domination, signification and legitimation, to which actors refer via facilities, interpretive schemes and norms, both enable and restrain inter-organizational interaction (see Sydow and Windeler 1998 for details). Moreover, they are themselves the recursive product of inter-organizational practices. These practices reflect neither the simple causation nor the state of equilibrium often assumed by economic approaches and many inter-organization theories. Rather, the reproduction of inter-organizational relations via these practices is considered to be a complex and dialectical process in which knowledgeable organizational actors who pursue their own interests refer to structural properties of organizations and their environments via the duality of structure. In this way, structuration theory leads researchers (and practising managers) to analyse the practical constitution of market-like and organization-like relations via structured and structuring action (structuration), whereby this action is both constrained and enabled by sets of – usually inter-organizational – rules and resources.

Signifying and normative rules, which are prevalent in or across a specific industry (industry mind-sets) and on which interrelating organizations agree, influence inter-organizational practices the more such practices have been institutionalized in the process of reproduction. Institutionalized rules then allow for a certain stability and predictability of inter-organizational interaction (Leblebici and Salancik 1982). Although they may acquire the status of structural constraints, they do not determine inter-organizational interaction because both the individual and organizational actors who refer to these rules may always act otherwise. This is in line with the structurationist 'dialectic of control' (Giddens 1984).

For structuration theory, as much as for resource dependence theory (Pfeffer and Salancik 1978) and the inter-organizational dialectics framework (Zeitz

1980), allocative and authoritative resources are a potential source of environmental dependency and a potential means of domination and active environment control. For 'organizations construct major portions of their environment through the production of resources and through their control of interaction networks; organizational actions and interactions are channelled and constrained through structured resources and through networks of relationships' (Zeitz 1980: 73).

From a structurationist perspective inter-organizational relations, as much as the organizations which form these relations, are an outcome of structuration processes in which managerial and other agents intervene in interaction sequences via the duality of structure. These relations, then, are not necessarily a product only of purposeful inter-organizational interaction but also of unintended consequences of this interaction. They are, furthermore, the product of organizing and of self-organizing processes, of consensus and of conflict, of stability and of change. Although in some cases latent relations may be sufficient for procurement of technical resources and institutional legitimacy, most inter-organizational relations are in need of manifest and continuous reproduction by holders of boundary spanning roles.

Structuration theory, moreover, offers a multi-level approach to inter-organizational analysis urgently needed. For inter-organizational relationships should preferably not only be investigated by taking more comprehensive units of analysis such as organization sets and networks. Rather, they should also be investigated on different levels of analysis such as individual, group, organization, population/industry and society. On each of these levels the impact upon the formation and management of inter-organizational relations and their effects on the individual, the organization, the industry and the community should be studied. In this respect structuration theory would exclude neither the analysis of the influence of individual actors nor the impact of national cultures and business systems on the formation and management of interorganizational relations (and vice versa).

Research on inter-organizational relations has tended to focus on strategic issues and top management action at the level of organizations or interorganizational fields while neglecting operational issues that often plague interorganizational relations. More studies are urgently needed which consider the complementary micro-level part, analysing, for instance, concrete boundary-spanning activities and the managerial skills necessary for building cooperative relationships, or the interpersonal cross-organizational collaboration among professional experts. Such research could help to clarify the peculiarities of working in inter-organizational committees (if any) or to analyse the effects of established inter-organizational relations upon internal power structures and organizational politics. Such micro-level research paying attention to the dynamics of inter-organizational relations by adopting a processual approach, however, should, by all possible means, avoid ignoring the enabling and restraining impact of macro structures on micro behaviour. By doing so this kind of research could in turn stimulate meso- and macro-level research on inter-organizational relations (Smith *et al.* 1995).

Research on inter-organizational relations within a broad theoretical framework such as that provided by structuration theory, comprising on the one hand the whole spectrum between micro and macro levels of analysis and on the other a more processual perspective on the constitution of inter-organizational relations, may help to overcome the extensive fragmentation of the literature as well as the prevailing concentration on the antecedents and consequences of relationship formation. Such research may contribute towards overcoming the problem that: 'we no longer know what we know about the formation of inter-organizational relationships' (Oliver 1990: 241; see Van de Ven *et al.* 1974, for a similar conclusion fifteen years earlier).

6 Managing inter-organizational relations

The management of inter-organizational relations, which may be informed by academic research on the topic as much as by the 'in-house' research of organizational boundary spanners (Zeitz 1980: 84), has to take care of at least four management tasks: selection; regulation; allocation; and evaluation. All these tasks are densely interwoven, relate to the formation, maintenance and termination of inter-organizational relations, and may be first explored and then executed with respect to all three of the structural dimensions of inter-organizational practices discussed above.

The first management task includes the *selection* of appropriate organizations with which direct or indirect relations should be built up, maintained or dissolved. For this purpose it is necessary to establish criteria and methods as to how organizations should be selected when forming, extending or reducing a network of inter-organizational relations. Thus, selection aims directly at the concrete composition of a particular organization set or network.

The management task of *regulating* activities between organizations includes fixing the inter-organizational division of work, designing modes of exchange of goods, services, information and personnel, shaping methods of decision making, and the like. This task also embraces the definition of organizational boundaries within the inter-organizational system, and of the system's boundary with its environment (Ortmann and Sydow 1999). Wherever possible, both kinds of definition should be derived from a 'collective strategy' (Astley and Fombrun 1983) which is necessarily shaped by all three structural dimensions of inter-organizational practices. Nevertheless, the task of regulation focuses upon the setting up and reproduction of appropriate rules of signification and legitimation. For instance, organizations have to agree on boundary definitions or to accept each partner's more or less legitimate power over the establishment, maintenance and dissolution of particular inter-organizational relations. Usually only a fraction of these cognitive and normative regulations will be formalized by means of a legal contract.

The task of inter-organizational resource *allocation* goes hand in hand with that of regulation. Central to inter-organizational relations, this task implies, above all, deciding upon the nature and extent of resource control, including determining the type of interdependence being created among the organizations of a network. Recursively, the network relationships in most cases offer additional opportunities for resource control. Following the typology of technological interdependence as proposed by Thompson (1967), pooled, sequential or reciprocal interdependencies may thus be created, each of them having particular implications for the management of inter-organizational relations. For instance, in the case of pooled interdependence, in which all organizations linked together refer to a common pool of resources, partners have to agree on quantity, quality and price of resource usage. This again demonstrates the interwovenness of allocation with that of regulation.

Finally, the task of *evaluation* – in particular of inter-organizational relations – has to be of management concern. More than any of the other management tasks, evaluation integrates the other three under one common theme. The resulting evaluation practices are dominated by economic considerations, obviously in the case of profit-making organizations and increasingly in the case of non-profit-making organizations. Nevertheless, evaluation practices may be analysed with respect to the three structural dimensions of domination, signification and legitimation (Sydow and Windeler 1998). It will then become clear that economic evaluation is not so much a matter of technical as of institutional interest. Up to now, only a few instruments have been developed to assist the practical evaluation of inter-organizational relations with respect to profitability, flexibility or innovativeness, and virtually none have been critically analysed with respect to one or more of the three structural dimensions.

These four management tasks affect – and are affected by – the level of redundancy, strength of coupling and multiplexity of inter-organizational relations within an organization set, action set or inter-organizational network (Staber and Sydow 1995). Particularly in the case of organization-like relations, carrying out the four tasks is anything but simple, since it involves the balancing of tensions and contradictions between, for example, cooperation and competition, autonomy and dependence, trust and control, and stability and change. These along with other tensions, such as those between differentiation and integration, efficiency and innovation, rhetoric and action, are from a structurationist perspective as much a result of, as a medium for, the management of inter-organizational relations (Sydow and Windeler 1998).

As far as the tensions between *cooperation* and *competition* are concerned, cooperative inter-organizational relations are often under pressure from other, more competitive relations. Furthermore, cooperative relations themselves may incorporate elements of competition. This is particularly obvious in the case of 'multi-faceted relationships' (Dowling *et al.* 1996), where a supplier or customer is also a competitor. Finally, cooperative relations may turn into competitive ones – and vice versa. In both cases the past history of the inter-organizational relation affects the present task of managing the relation.

Forming a relationship with another organization often implies a loss and an increase of *autonomy* and *dependence*, respectively. However, the same inter-organizational relations may also serve to increase resource control and, thereby, to expand the scope of strategic choices in other respects. Managing inter-organizational relations with respect to autonomy and dependence has particular relevance for organizations like intermediaries or brokers which often rely on a certain degree of autonomy in order to be credible in their business.

Managing inter-organizational relations furthermore implies the balancing of *trust* and *control*. While trust is usually thought of as facilitating the formation and maintenance of inter-organizational relations, controls are suspected to threaten their existence. However, and particularly in the 'sphere of the economic' (Giddens 1984), relationship management will hardly live up to its potentials without any controls. But, if these controls are used in a trust-sensitive way they may well increase the level of inter-organizational trust (Sydow 1998).

Similar to relations within organizations, the effectiveness of inter-organizational relations requires both *stability* and *change*. Effective business operations assume a certain stability of the content and form of such relations as well as of the organizational actors concerned. On the other hand, the actors as well as the attributes of the relationship have to adapt to changing circumstances, either radically or incrementally. In addition, change may be needed in order to enhance the adaptive capacity of an organization or inter-organizational network (Staber and Sydow 1995). However, frequent or dramatic inter-organizational change may disturb effective inter-organizational interaction. Hence, managing inter-organizational relations implies the balancing of such tensions too.

In practice, the selection, regulation, allocation and evaluation of inter-organizational relations may profit from the concept of 'trans-organizational development' (Cummings 1984), which makes use of various methods grouped together under the heading of 'organizational development techniques'. Usually, at least two steps are distinguished, each of which requires different techniques: inter-organizational diagnosis and inter-organizational intervention.

Inter-organizational diagnosis concentrates primarily on the purposes and boundaries of the relation, network or 'transorganizational system' (Cummings 1984). It also focuses on the cognitive orientation and on the economic inducements and contributions offered to organizations to encourage interrelating. *Inter-organizational intervention* aims, for instance, at the strengthening of particular boundary-spanning roles, the creation of a cooperative climate between organizations, the transfer of know-how and/or personnel, or at coalition building in order to gain control of the organizing process. According to Cummings (1984), both steps may profit from the use of a change agent who has to have the political competence to understand and resolve conflicts of interest and value dilemmas in social systems which consist of multiple organizations striving not only for profit but also for organizational autonomy.

In contrast to organizational development, transorganizational development is not blind towards power, interests, coalition building and other political processes within and between organizations. However, until now this approach has had at least three deficiencies. First, it adheres to an ideology of feasibility, largely ignoring unintended consequences of action and self-organizing processes. Second, it supports only the organizing of under-organized relations or systems. Consequently, there exists no conceptual help for the marketization of hierarchical organizations via outsourcing and de-merger. Third, trans-organizational development fails to acknowledge that inter-organizational relations are not only formed and, from time to time, adapted to changing circumstances, but that organization-like relations are inter-organizational learning systems for which change is a common experience.

7 Conclusions

'The major factors that organizations must take into account are other organizations' (Aldrich 1979: 265) – and also, one might add, the relations these organizations maintain for the sake of technical resource supply and institutional legitimacy. These inter-organizational relations emerge as an intended or unintended consequence of purposeful inter-organizational interaction constrained and enabled by inter-organizational structures of domination, signification and legitimation. The management of these relations implies the tasks of selection, allocation, regulation and evaluation, all referring not only to the aforementioned three structural dimensions of inter-organizational practices, but also to specific tensions and contradictions in the inter-organizational field.

Three decades of inter-organizational research have taught us something about the antecedents and consequences of relations among profit-making and non-profit-making organizations, but little about the processes by which these relations are established and reproduced. Although many of the findings are only of a tentative nature and have hardly been integrated within one theoretical framework, scholars and managers alike should profit from this theoretical or empirical research on inter-organizational relations – relations which characterize the society of organizations almost as much as the organizations themselves.

Further reading

(References cited in the text marked *)

* Abolafia, M.Y. and Biggart, N.W. (1991) 'Competition and markets', in A. Etzioni and P.R. Lawrence (eds), *Socio-economics: Toward a New Synthesis*, Armonk, NY: M.E. Sharpe Inc. (Criticizes economic models of competition as asocial, provides a neo-institutional perspective on competition and illustrates this with reference to three empirical examples.)
* Aldrich, H.E. (1979) *Organizations and Environments*, Englewood Cliffs, NJ: Prentice Hall. (Important book promoting an ecological and, to some extent, a network perspective for the analysis of organizations.)
  Alter, C. and Hage, J. (1993) *Organizations Working Together*, Newbury Park, CA: Sage. (Excellent overview of research on collaborative inter-organizational relations.)
* Arndt, J. (1979) 'Toward a concept of domesticated markets', *Journal of Marketing* 47: 79–82. (One early article on inter-organizational relations from a marketing perspective.)
* Astley, W.G. and Fombrun, C.J. (1983) 'Collective strategy: social ecology of organizational environment', *Academy of Management Review* 8 (4): 576–87. (Classic paper discussing collective strategy making among organizations.)
* Badaracco, J. (1991) *The Knowledge Link*, Boston, MA: Harvard Business School Press. (One of the rare studies of inter-organizational knowledge transfer and learning.)

* Baker, W.E. (1984) 'Social structure of a securities market', *American Journal of Sociology* 89: 775–811. (Important sociological study of a type of market which is usually thought of as coming close to the neo-classical ideal.)

Buono, A.F. (1997) 'Managing strategic alliances: intervening in network organizations', *Journal of Organizational Change Management* 10 (3): 251–266. (One of the few articles with an emphasis on managerial issues, focusing on inter-organizational development.)

* Chisholm, D. (1989) *Coordination Without Hierarchy: Informal Structures in Multiorganizational Systems*, Berkeley, CA: University of California Press. (Detailed case study of the San Francisco Bay Area transport system which is coordinated effectively by informal mechanisms.)

* Cummings, T.G. (1984) 'Transorganizational development', in B.M. Staw and L.L. Cummings (eds), *Research in Organizational Behavior*, Greenwich, CT: JAI Press Inc. (Gives an overview of the specialities, methods and techniques of inter-organizational development.)

* Davis, G.F. and Powell, W.W. (1992) 'Organization–environment relations', in M. Dunnette (ed.), *Handbook of Industrial and Organizational Psychology*, 2nd edn, New York: Consulting Psychologist Press. (Excellent discussion of theories focusing upon dyadic inter-organizational relations, inter-organizational networks and the more embracing organization of environments.)

* DiMaggio, P.J. and Powell, W.W. (1983) 'The iron cage revisited: institutional isomorphism and collective rationality in organizational fields', *American Sociological Review* 48: 147–60. (One of the classic texts on neo-institutional theory, introducing the inter-organizational field as the decisive unit of analysis.)

* Dowling, M.J., Roering, W., Carlin, B. and Wisnieski, J. (1996) 'Multifaceted relationships under coopetition', *Journal of Management Inquiry* 5: 155–167.

Doz, Y. and Hamel, G. (1998) *Alliance Advantage*, Boston, MA: Harvard Business School Press. (Useful guide to managing alliances and networks of alliances.)

Ebers, M. (ed.) (1997) *The Formation of Inter-organizational Networks*, Oxford: Oxford University Press.

* Gerlach, M. (1992) *Alliance Capitalism – The Social Organization of Japanese Business*, Berkeley, CA: University of California Press. (Most comprehensive study to date of different kinds of inter-organizational relationships within Japanese *keiretsu*.)

* Giddens, A. (1984) *The Constitution of Society*, Cambridge: Polity Press. (Most comprehensive presentation of structuration theory as a social theory.)

* Granovetter, M. (1985) 'Economic action and social structure: the problem of embeddedness', *American Journal of Sociology* 91: 481–510. (Critique of economic analyses of markets emphasizing the influence of social bonds; first appearance of the notion of 'social embeddedness'.)

* Håkansson, H. (ed.) (1987) *Industrial Technological Development: A Network Approach*, London: Croom Helm. (One of the many books presenting and applying the Uppsala network approach which was originally developed for research in industrial marketing.)

* Harrigan, K.R. (1985) *Strategies for Joint Ventures*, Lexington, MA: Lexington Books. (Classic book on the evolution and management of joint ventures.)

* Jarillo, J.C. (1988) 'On strategic networks', *Strategic Management Journal* 9: 31–41. (Classic article on strategic networks as an organizational form; transaction costs and game theory.)

* Johnston, H.R. and Vitale, M.R. (1988) 'Creating competitive advantage with inter-organizational information systems', *MIS Quarterly* 12 (2): 153–65. (Deals with applications of inter-organizational information systems and their impact upon competitive advantage.)

* Larson, A. (1992) 'Network dyads in entrepreneurial settings: a study of the governance of exchange processes', *Administrative Science Quarterly* 37: 76–104. (Empirical study of the impact of external relations on the success of start-ups.)

* Leblebici, H. and Salancik, G.R. (1982) 'Stability in interorganizational exchanges: rulemaking processes of the Chicago Board of Trade', *Adminstrative Science Quarterly* 27: 227–42. (One of the few longitudinal studies of inter-organizational relations, focusing upon how the stability of relations within working rules is achieved and how these rules are changed.)

* Levine, S. and White, P.E. (1961) 'Exchange as a conceptual framework for the study of inter-organizational relationships', *Adminstrative Science Quarterly* 5: 583–601. (Classic article on inter-organizational relations based upon the then dominant social exchange theory.)

* Macneil, I.R. (1985) 'Relational contract: what we do and do not know', *Wisconsin Law Review*: 691–716. (Clarifies the concept which was introduced ten years earlier and has been well-received in organization economics.)

* Mizruchi, M.S. and Schwartz, M. (eds) (1987) *Intercorporate Relations: The Structural Analysis of Business*, Cambridge: Cambridge University Press. (Reader presenting empirical research on interlocking directorates, mainly from the perspective of resource dependence and social class analysis.)

* Nohria, N. (1992) 'Is a network perspective a useful way of studying organizations?', in N. Nohria and R.G. Eccles (eds), *Networks and Organizations*, Boston, MA: Harvard Business School Press. (Introductory chapter to the most comprehensive book on the network perspective on organizations to date.)

* Oliver, C. (1990) 'Determinants of inter-organizational relationships: integration and future directions', *Academy of Management Review* 15 (2): 241–65. (Distinguishes six types of inter-organizational relations and analyses them with respect to critical contingencies.)

* Ortmann, G. and Sydow, J. (1999) 'Grenzmanagement in Unternehmungsnetzwerken: theoretische Zugange', *Die Betriebswirtschaft* 59 (2): 205–20. (Uses structuration theory for analysing the management of organization and network boundaries.)

* Pfeffer, J. and Leblebici, H. (1973) 'Executive recruitment and the development of interfirm organization', *Administrative Science Quarterly* 21: 445–61. (One of the few studies on the exchange of personnel among organizations which is very common in Japanese *keiretsu*, for instance.)

* Pfeffer, J. and Salancik, G.R. (1978) *The External Control of Organizations*, New York: Harper & Row. (Classic book on the management of inter-organizational relations from a resource dependence perspective.)

* Powell, W.W. and DiMaggio, P.J. (eds) (1991) *The New Institutionalism in Organizational Analysis*, Chicago, IL: University of Chicago Press. (Reader presenting classic papers and up-to-date research on neo-institutional theory.)

Powell, W.W., Koput, K. and Smith–Doerr, L. (1996) 'Interorganizational collaborations and the locus on innovation: networks of learning in biotechnology', *Administrative Science Quarterly* 41: 116–45. (Excellent empirical study of inter-organizational learning processes in the field of biotechnology.)

* Ring, P.S. and Ven, A.H. van de (1994) 'Developmental processes of cooperative inter-organizational relationships', *Academy of Management Review* 19 (1): 90–118. (One of the few publications taking a processual perspective on the formation of inter-organizational relations.)

* Scott, W.R. (1994) 'Institutions and organizations: toward a theoretical synthesis', in W.R. Scott and J.W. Meyer (eds), *Institutional Environments and Organizations*, London: Sage Publications. (Provides an excellent overview reconciling different institutional theories without neglecting their differences; focuses on organizational fields.)

* Smith, K.G., Carroll, S.J. and Asford, S.J. (1995) 'Intra- and inter-organizational cooperation: toward a research agenda', *Academy of Management Journal* 38 (1): 7–23. (Introductory chapter to a special issue which highlights the importance of cooperative and trustee relations in and between organizations.)

* Staber, U. and Sydow, J. (1995) 'Adaptation and adaptive capacity: issues for organizations and interorganizational networks', in *Revitalising Organizations – The Academic Contribution*, Proceedings of the British Academy of Management Annual Conference, Sheffield, 11–13 September 1995. (Discusses redundancy, loose coupling and multiplexity as structural properties of organizations and networks; taken from a managerial perspective.)

Staber, U.H., Schaefer, N.V. and Sharma, B. (1996) (eds) *Business Networks: Prospects for Regional Development*, Berlin and New York: de Gruyter. (Edited volume on inter-organizational networks, emphasizing the spatial embeddedness of inter-organizational relationships.)

* Swedberg, R. (1994) 'Markets as social structures', in N.J. Smelser and R. Swedberg, (eds), *The Handbook of Economic Sociology*, Princeton, NJ: Princeton University Press. (Comprehensive overview of models of the market as viewed by economic and sociological theories.)

* Sydow, J. (1992) 'On the management of strategic networks', in H. Ernste and V. Meier (eds), *Regional Development and Contemporary Industrial Response*, London: Pinter. (Explores strategic inter-firm networks as an organizational form and highlights the implications of this form for management.)

* Sydow, J. (1998) 'Understanding the constitution of interorganizational trust', in C. Lane and R. Bachmann (eds), *Trust Within and Between Organizations*, Oxford: Oxford University Press: 31–63. (Based upon structuration theory, trust is considered as an element of network resources and network rules: particular reference is given to structural, trust-enhancing properties on the level of networks.)

* Sydow, J. and Windeler, A. (1998) 'Organizing and evaluating interfirm networks – a structurationist perspective on network processes and effectiveness' *Organization Science* 9 (3): 265–84. (Gives an overview of structuration theory and applies this theory to the analysis of inter-firm networks.)

* Thompson, J.D. (1967) *Organizations in Action*, New York: McGraw-Hill. (One of the classics in organization theory, paying much attention to resources and resource control.)

Uzzi, B. (1996) 'The sources and consequences of embeddedness for the economic performance of organizations: the network effect', *American Sociological Review* 61: 674–98. (Empirical study of inter-organizational relationships in the New York apparel industry; takes up Granovetter concept of social embeddedness and specifies it.)

* Van de Ven, A.H., Emmet, D.C. and Koenig, R., Jr (1974) 'Frameworks for inter-organizational analysis', *Organization and Adminstrative Science* 5 (1): 113–29. (Early article reviewing three frameworks for inter-organizational analysis and proposing the systemic concept of inter-organizational collectivity.)

* Warren, R.L. (1967) 'The interorganizational field as a focus of investigation', *Adminstrative Science Quarterly* 12: 396–419. (Classic paper conceptualizing the environment of organizations as inter-organizational fields.)

* Whetten, D.A. (1987) 'Interorganizational relations', in J.W. Lorsch (ed.), *Handbook of Organizational Design*, Englewood Cliffs, NJ: Prentice Hall. (One of the leading review articles on inter-organizational analysis.)

* Zeitz, G. (1980) 'Interorganizational dialectics', *Administrative Science Quarterly* 25: 72–88. (Early article anticipating core propositions of structuration theory in the analysis of interorganizational relations.)

Further resources

See also recent special issues on the topic of inter-organizational relations and networks by *Academy of Management Journal* (AMJ) 1997, *International Studies of Management and Organization* (ISMO) 1998, *Organization Science* (OSc) 1998, *Organization Studies* (OS) 1998 and *Strategic Management Journal* (SMJ) 1999. Also SMJ 2000 on strategic networks.

Corporate governance

Jay Lorsch and Samantha K. Graff

1 **Context of corporate governance**
2 **Structures and practices of corporate boards**
3 **Common constraints to board effectiveness**
4 **Boardroom innovations**
5 **Future convergence?**

Overview

Throughout the developed world, corporate boards play an important role in the governance of publicly owned corporations. In most developed countries, they are intended to oversee the conduct of management on behalf of shareholders and/or other stakeholders. The structures and practices of boards vary across national boundaries, as boards have evolved according to each country's history, culture, laws and economy. None the less, boards in the developed world share many of the same challenges in their efforts to monitor corporate performance. This entry explores the structures and practices of boards of publicly owned corporations in four developed countries: the USA, the UK, Germany and Japan. These countries represent a range along the spectrum of models for corporate boards in developed countries.

1 Context of corporate governance

Before examining corporate boards in the USA, the UK, Germany and Japan, it is important to have at least a cursory understanding of the broader corporate governance systems in which these boards are operating. Each nation has developed a system of corporate governance that can be characterized according to its decision-making methods (checks and balances versus networks), its ownership patterns (dispersed versus concentrated) and its chief goals (shareholder primacy versus multiple stakeholder welfare).

Checks and balances versus networks

In the USA and the UK, corporations are governed in the context of a national belief in economic and political checks and balances. Anglo-Americans are suspicious of concentrated authority, and their laws go to great lengths to hinder excessive consolidation of power in both government and business institutions. To ensure checks and balances, Anglo-American institutions are more inclined to use adversarial and litigious than cooperative approaches to conflict resolution. Corporations operate in a regulated environment that curbs consolidations of economic power and that favours competition on an even playing field. The

Anglo-American culture encourages self-reliance and individual wealth creation, so that investment in corporate stock is prevalent.

German and Japanese institutions are more concerned than their Anglo-American counterparts with promoting collective welfare. Germans are less wary of concentrated economic power, and they favour a cooperative approach to problem solving that includes various parties in the national economy. According to Charkham: 'The German ... way of operating quietly and effectively behind the scenes to influence company management would strike Americans as underhanded and wrong (and the lawsuits would start flying)' (Charkham 1994: 179). Germans believe that a less adversarial approach facilitates the consideration of a longer-term view and the sustenance of trusting and mutually advantageous relationships. The German government is often perceived by business as an ally rather than an adversary. Government entities even own the shares of various companies, and the government uses tax policy and other financial incentives to encourage research and development, to foster long-term investment in plant and machinery, and to attract jobs on a local level (Monks and Minnow 1995: 293).

The notion of family loyalty extends far beyond blood relations into Japanese companies. According to Charkham, common participation in an enterprise: 'envelopes one's life ... command[ing] the allegiance and prime attention of everyone from top to bottom' (Charkham 1994: 71). Companies, in turn, are expected to treat stakeholders as extended family members by promoting their long-term health and well-being. Immense efforts go into building consensus in every walk of life – even at the cost of arriving at a solution through a slow and cumbersome process. In Japan relations between business and government are tight, amiable and cooperative. Business and government align themselves to the national economic policy set by the Ministry of International Trade and Industry, sharing a mutual understanding that they will support one another in advancing the national good. Businesses use government as a chief source of information, and the Ministry of Finance commonly becomes involved in solving the difficulties of a troubled company.

Dispersed versus concentrated ownership

The public corporation in three of the four countries discussed in this entry has evolved so that ownership and control no longer fall under the jurisdiction of the same individual or small core group. Rather, there is a separation of those who own a company from those who oversee and manage it. This condition of 'ownership without appreciable control and control without appreciable ownership' (Berle and Means 1991: 112) is most evident in the USA, the UK and Germany. In Japan, cross-shareholdings among affiliated companies mean that owners are generally still closely involved in the activities of management.

According to the New York Stock Exchange: 'In no other country in the world [than the United States] does the general public involve itself so extensively and so directly in the ownership of business' (*NYSE Fact Book* 1990: 2). Over 51 million Americans own stock either directly or through institutional investors that manage the combined assets of many individual and corporate investors (*NYSE Fact Book* 1992: 3). Institutional investors hold approximately half of the equity market. The largest institutions are mutual funds, public and private pension funds, insurance companies and bank trust departments. Banks are prohibited by law from owning themselves more than 5 per cent of the voting stock in any non-bank company or from otherwise controlling an industrial firm, and the tax code encourages diversification of bank-managed trust holdings so that no more than 10 per cent of a bank's trust is invested in any corporation (Lightfoot and Kester 1992: 3). In fact, it is rare for any individual or institutional investor to hold a large block of stock in a particular company, so public companies are generally owned by hundreds or thousands of widely dispersed shareholders.

Ownership in the UK resembles that in the USA. There are over nine million individual shareholders in the UK, well over half of whom opt to invest indirectly through institutional investors (Charkham 1994: 283). In the UK, the largest institutional investors are pension funds and insurance companies.

Because they are so numerous, scattered and disengaged, individual US and British shareholders are relatively powerless to affect decisions about the companies in which they invest. They have to rely on boards of directors to represent their interests. Their only real source of control over their own risk is their ability to buy and sell their holdings at a moment's notice – for stock is almost as liquid as cash.

There are fewer than 700 quoted companies in Germany, as opposed to nearly 3000 in the UK (Monks and Minnow 1995: 289). Not only are there significantly fewer listed companies, but these companies are owned by much more concentrated groups of shareholders. Metallgesellschaft Aktiengesellschaft, one of Germany's largest industrial groups, is typical in its composition of owners. In 1994, approximately 75 per cent of its stock was owned by five institutions: Deutsche Bank AG and Dresdner Bank AG (which together own 25 per cent); Allegemeine Verwaltungsgesellschaft für Industriebeteiligungen mbH (General Administration Industrial Holding Company – which owns about 25 per cent); Kuwait Investment Authority (20 per cent); and Australian Mutual Provident Society (5 per cent). Banks and insurance companies are the major institutional investors in Germany. There are no pension funds as they exist in the USA and the UK because employee pensions are carried on company books as a contingent liability.

Banks play a particularly powerful role in German corporate governance. In contrast to the USA and the UK where shareholders vote their own proxies, German banks are custodians for individuals' shares. Furthermore, German banks can and do own large blocks of company stock in their own names. As of 1992, banks held about 5 per cent of all shares but they voted over 50 per cent (Monks and Minnow 1995: 292). German banks tend to hold on to their stocks for much longer time periods than Anglo-American investors. Germany's concentrated ownership pattern and cultural emphasis on collective welfare make for patient investors. According to one German executive:

In Germany, banks do not sell long-term shares. For example, at Daimler Benz, Herr Reuter is restructuring the company and profits are down, but Deutsche Bank is staying with them. They did financing for Mr Daimler and Mr Benz in the 1920s and they own 25 per cent of the shares today. It is an important part of their portfolio.

(Lorsch and MacIver 1991: 15)

Ownership in Japan is characterized by the extensive networks of cross-shareholdings referred to above that generally include banks, suppliers, subcontractors and customers. According to Kester: 'This corporate networking achieves its highest expression in the *keiretsu* – a group of companies federated around a major bank, trading company, or large industrial firm' (1991: 54). Companies belonging to *keiretsu* account for over half of all listed corporations. One-third of a typical Japanese corporation is owned by banks and one-third is owned by other related corporations (Kester 1991: 57–9). These shareholders comprise a stable core, and they are tied by a complex web of claims against one another. They abide by a strong tacit mutual agreement not to sell shares that are held reciprocally, meaning that over 70 per cent of shares are not for trading (Charkham 1994: 81). One of the most common safeguards in Japanese governance is the ability of one or more equity-owning stakeholders (typically banks) to intervene directly and explicitly in the affairs of another company. For example, when Kojin Corporation failed, its main bank voluntarily repaid all its debts and assumed responsibility for recovering its loans. In another instance, a Tokai Bank executive assumed the presidency of a client company, Okuma Machinery Works, in order to resolve a bitter dispute over presidential succession (Lightfoot and Kester 1992: 8).

Shareholder primacy versus multiple stakeholder welfare

In the USA and the UK, the chief aim of corporate governance is the creation and enhancement of shareholder wealth. Shareholders are generally viewed as the most important stakeholders in Anglo-American corporate governance.

In contrast, the German constitution states: 'Property imposes duties. Its use should also serve the public weal' (Charkham 1994: 10). German corporate governance focuses ultimately on the long-term health of a company while considering not only the owners but also any other stakeholders, such as suppliers, creditors, customers and especially employees. Thus, shareholder wealth could at times be a lower priority than the development of quality products, the growth of market share, or the protection of jobs.

In Japan, the goal of corporate governance is the preservation and prosperity of the 'family'. Kester explains: 'The Japanese company is a coalition of stakeholders ... holding a complex blend of senior and junior, short term and long term, conditional and unconditional, implicit and explicit claims against the company' (Kester 1991: 76). He proceeds to observe: 'Corporate growth tends to emerge as the common denominator among stakeholder groups – the one objective that nearly everyone can agree on as having a potential benefit' (Kester 1991: 77).

Although all stakeholders in Germany and Japan are given consideration, German and Japanese corporate governance pays more attention to employees than Anglo-American corporate governance. One reason is that Germany and Japan have had historic issues of maintaining high employment rates and stable industrial relations.

2 Structures and practices of corporate boards

Goals and duties

Since the goals of corporate governance vary among the USA, the UK, Germany and Japan, it follows that the goals of corporate boards also vary among the four countries. US and British boards are charged with promoting the financial interests of shareholders. Although over half of the US states have passed statutes allowing directors to consider the interests of constituents other than shareholders, shareholders none the less remain the pre-eminent concern of both US and British boards. (In the USA corporate laws pertaining to boards fall under the jurisdiction of individual states, but these laws tend to conform to a common pattern.) By national law, a German board must ensure the long-term health of its company, taking into account the diverse parties which hold a stake in the successful sustenance of the business. Japanese boards are basically ceremonial bodies that exercise minimal power, for real corporate governance takes place within the industrial group. To the extent that Japanese boards do have a function, it is to balance and further the interests of the extended family that comprises the Japanese corporation.

German law is much more specific than British or US law in delineating the structures and practices of corporate boards. In both the USA and the UK, sparse laws are supplemented by requirements established by their respective stock exchanges and by a tradition of corporate boards rooted in colonial enterprises to produce a common understanding of the structures and practices with which boards are meant to comply. Despite this difference, US, British and German boards share in practice the same three major functions: (1) to oversee the selection and succession of managers and directors; (2) to review financial performance, approve corporate strategy, and generally monitor the activities of management; and (3) to ensure that the officers and employees of their company are meeting legal and ethical standards.

Board models

Among the four countries, there are two board models: unitary and two-tiered. US, British and Japanese boards of directors are the only boards required by law and are composed of some combination of executive and outside directors. This unitary board structure is typical of most public companies around the world with the exception of Germany and certain northern European countries. By law, German boards have two tiers, the management board (*Vorstand*) and the supervisory board (*Aufsichtsrat*). The management board's membership and responsibilities are in many respects similar to those of US, British and Japanese executive committees. The supervisory board is made up entirely of directors who cannot be members of the management board, half of whom are elected by the owners and half of whom are elected by the employees. Because the German supervisory board's role is basically equivalent to that of US, British and Japanese unitary boards, this entry will hereafter focus only on this tier of the German system.

Composition

No legal requirement exists regarding the number or background of British and US directors. The average British board has twelve members, and the average US board has thirteen members (Pic 1995: 8). Many directors argue that the relatively small size of the average board allows its directors to form a cohesive working body and to act with greater agility than larger, more unwieldy boards (Lipton and Lorsch 1992: 65). Directors in the UK and the USA commonly sit on three or four boards. Although shareholders have the legal right to elect their directors, in practice they almost always ratify the nominations put forward by their boards on the proxy cards they receive annually. Chief executives in the English-speaking countries have traditionally used their personal and business networks to find colleagues with whom they feel familiar and comfortable, and boards have often rubber-stamped their chief executive's selections.

British and US boards differ greatly in their combination of inside and outside representation. In the UK, only about 40 per cent of all directors are outsiders, and nearly 10 per cent of the largest companies have no outsiders on their boards (Monks and Minnow 1995: 303). Of the outside directors, 62 per cent are chief executives of other companies and another 12 per cent are high-ranked professionals from the industrial, service and financial sectors (Charkham 1994: 269). US boards average nearly 80 per cent outsiders, and all listed companies must have outside directors (Monks and Minnow 1995: 180). Well over 60 per cent of these directors are Chief Executive Officers (CEOs) and other high-level executives (Lorsch and MacIver 1989: 18), and many boards also include lawyers, academics, or experts from the financial industry. Customarily, boards have consisted entirely of white males. Recent years have brought the beginnings of a movement to make US boards more diverse along race and gender lines.

German boards range from twelve to twenty-two members, depending by law on the size and the industry of their company. German law requires that one-half of every board be elected by employees and the other half by shareholders. The employee side of the board is composed of employees of the given company and, in some industries, must include one or two trade union representatives. The owners' side is usually drawn from the upper ranks of the major shareholding corporations, banks, and other financial institutions.

Directors from the owners' side often sit on up to ten boards, which is the upper limit set by law (Pic 1995: 11).

Boards of large Japanese companies consist of twenty to thirty members, over 90 per cent of whom are present or former inside senior managers. Approximately 80 per cent of Japanese corporations have no outside board members at all, and another 15 per cent have no more than two outside directors (Monks and Minnow 1995: 272). Directors are chosen by the company president, whose recommendations are rubber-stamped by the board and the shareholders. Because most directors of a particular company are in a direct-line relationship with one another, it is a rare occurrence that a lower-level board member will challenge the policies laid out by senior officers (Charkham 1994: 86).

Board leadership

In 80 per cent of US public companies, the same person is both the board chairman and the CEO. When these roles are separate, it is generally for temporary reasons, such as a top management transition. Therefore, in most companies, the American CEO is recognized as the pre-eminent leader of both management and the board. The position of an American CEO is accompanied by a cult of personality similar to that surrounding the president of the USA. Americans seem to place great value on strong leadership. The American CEO who is also the board chairman can dominate meetings, controlling the agenda and the flow of information to directors. While the CEO's traditional power may seem to defy the US tradition of checks and balances, at least in theory, the fact that a majority of outsiders must sit on the board is intended to curb the CEO's influence in the boardroom.

In the UK, 80 per cent of public companies have a non-executive chairman of the board (Pic 1995: 7). British law does not recognize the post of chairman, but most boards appoint a chairman to orchestrate their activities. Since British boards are dominated by insiders, the non-executive chairman is meant to act as an objective check on the activities of management.

German law requires that the chairman of the supervisory board and the chairman of the management board (the chief executive) should always be two different individuals. The chairman of the supervisory board is elected by the owners' side and is legally given two votes in case of a tie in a board vote – thus limiting somewhat the power of the employee half of the board.

In Japanese companies, authority is vested in the company president, who heads a small and close-knit management committee. The chairman of the board is often a retired company president or retired government official who serves the role of elder statesman, representing the company at public functions and nurturing relationships with key contacts in industry and government. The chairman generally wields little influence over the corporate decision-making process, particularly since the board is largely a ceremonial body.

Compensation

The average total director compensation is approximately $55,000 per year in the USA and about $25,000 in the UK (Pic 1995: 15). Some institutional investors in the USA argue that the stock component of many US compensation schemes is not significant enough to provide a financial incentive for directors to align their interests with shareholders, so they are agitating for an increase in stock options relative to cash. A survey of outside directors of Standard & Poor's 400 companies revealed, however, that US directors do not find financial rewards to be an important reason for serving on boards. Rather, they are motivated by such incentives as the opportunity to learn and to be challenged (Lorsch and MacIver 1989: 26).

Board remuneration in Germany and Japan is not a matter of major concern. Because their goals of governance are more broadly based than just promoting shareholder wealth, Germans do not favour linking pay directly to profits or share price. Moreover, German directors do not receive stock options for tax reasons. The average annual salary of a German director is $30,000. Since Japanese directors are virtually all insiders, director compensation is not an issue.

Meeting frequency

US and British boards generally meet between five and six times per year, whereas German and Japanese boards only congregate on average four times. The greater frequency of board meetings in the English-speaking countries allows directors to maintain more regular contact with one another and with management, thus facilitating communication and effective oversight.

Committees

Board committees are common only in the USA. Here, large corporations average five standing committees (Pic 1995: 10), all of which report to the entire board the results of their deliberations. The most common US board committees are: (1) audit (required by all major stock exchanges to monitor reports of the outside audit firm and to oversee internal audit and accounting procedures); (2) compensation (required by the Securities and Exchange Commission to set and report executive pay); (3) nominating (selects candidates for the board); (4) finance (oversees company's financial investments and reviews company's capital needs and allocations); and (5) executive (approves crucial decisions which must be made between full board meetings). Outside directors typically serve on two or more of these committees (Pic 1995: 10), but they must make up the entirety of the compensation committee and, depending upon on which stock exchange their company is listed, the majority or the entirety of the audit committee. US board committees provide an efficient way for directors to use their limited time together. Through committee work and reports, directors can obtain a more detailed understanding of a company than if they conducted all board business *en masse*.

3 Common constraints to board effectiveness

Boards in all four countries share certain common constraints on their ability to execute their duties. Probably the most obvious is the limited time that directors can devote to their board responsibilities. It takes a great deal of time even for a director with wisdom and experience to comprehend sufficiently the complicated workings of a company. US and British boards are the best situated, because they meet more frequently than their German and Japanese counterparts and because their directors serve on fewer boards than do German directors. US boards have the further benefit of the standing committees referred to above. None the less, directors around the world find their lack of time together to be one of the biggest hindrances to fulfilling their duties (Lorsch 1996).

A related problem is that of receiving and digesting the information necessary for directors to fulfil their obligations. In all countries, the individual in the chief executive role is the primary source of information for the board. Even if there is no deliberate attempt to distort information, top managers inevitably offer their own interpretations and biases. Furthermore, directors often receive hundreds of pages of material before each meeting. It is a challenge for directors to digest these data and to determine what is most relevant to an understanding of a company's situation.

Social norms are a less tangible but still significant obstacle to a board's ability to provide effective oversight and guidance. For instance, US directors in the 1980s observed a social norm against directors speaking to one another outside of board meetings and against criticizing their CEO in meetings. They were also reluctant to discuss among themselves the question of their accountability to stakeholders other than shareholders (Lorsch and MacIver 1989). In another example, many German top executives have suggested that German directors representing the owners' side are hesitant to raise certain strategic and financial issues in full board meetings because of the presence of employee and union representatives. Instead, delicate matters are frequently discussed either informally among the owners' representatives or in specially created *ad hoc* committees (Lorsch 1996).

4 Boardroom innovations

During the 1980s and 1990s, various stakeholders in each of the four countries have agitated for boardroom innovations to make directors more active, independent or accountable. In the USA and the UK, however, calls for reform in the boardroom have been more urgent and forceful than in Germany and Japan. US institutional investors are strong proponents of change, and in both the USA and the UK the press is influential in advocating reform.

The United States of America

Change in the US boardroom has been propelled not only by pressure from institutional investors but also by examples set by a few ground-breaking boards.

Cutting-edge boards – including those of Dayton Hudson, Medtronic, Stanhome and Lukens – have adopted a number of innovations. The momentum is growing for more boards to follow suit. A significant impetus to this momentum was provided by the board of General Motors, which established guidelines for itself that embraced a variety of innovative practices. Because it is a prominent company that struggled through many problems, General Motors lent great credibility to the idea of constructive reform in the boardroom.

One change that some leading-edge boards have enacted is a reduction in board size. Depending on a company's size and complexity, anywhere from eight to twelve directors is believed to be ideal (Lipton and Lorsch 1992: 65). A group of this number is large enough to allow for a suitable range of knowledge and experience, yet small enough to allow for free discussion and for the development of a cohesiveness that enhances the board's power.

A second shift in many boardrooms centres on how directors allocate their limited time together. Innovative boards have considered closely the question of how best to spend their time in order to monitor effectively company and management performance. The answer for many such boards involves: approving company strategy on an annual basis; reviewing company progress in executing that strategy; and explicitly and thoroughly reviewing the performance of both the chief executive and the board itself (Lorsch 1996). In order to facilitate this strategic approval and review, some companies have introduced an annual strategic retreat of one or two full days attended by the board and top managers. This retreat allows directors and managers to hold in-depth discussions of company plans and accomplishments, and it provides the board with an opportunity to understand the CEO's thinking.

Another increasingly prevalent practice is the performance review of the CEO. This review gives directors a formal venue in which to share with the CEO their assessment of his or her strengths and weaknesses and in which to explain the correlation between his or her compensation and the performance of the company and of him or herself. CEOs appreciate the feedback, because as their company's leader, this may be the only direct verification of their performance that they will receive.

The implementation of CEO performance reviews is linked to another emerging boardroom practice in the USA: executive sessions, in which the outside directors meet alone without any members of management present. These sessions are clearly necessary if directors are going to assess openly and reach consensus about the CEO's performance, but they often address subjects far broader than just an evaluation of the CEO. Many boards hold executive sessions on a regular basis, and some even hold them after every full board meeting.

To run executive sessions of a board on which the CEO and chairman are the same individual, the outside directors have to appoint a leader from among themselves. While a few US companies have adopted the British model of having non-executive chairmen, most CEOs frown upon this practice and it is very rare in the USA. CEOs are reluctant to lose the power and prestige associated with the title of chairman. Furthermore, in those companies that do split the roles of chairman and CEO, the chairman is often the current CEO's predecessor. The typical American CEO is bothered by the idea of a predecessor looking so closely over his or her shoulder. An alternative arrangement is the election of a lead director. This individual can preside over executive sessions and can lead the CEO performance review. The lead director can also consult with the CEO on matters such as: the selection of board committee members and chairpersons; board meeting agendas; the adequacy of information directors receive; and the effectiveness of the board meeting process. Moreover, if the independent directors should face a crisis because of the incapacity of the CEO or a failure in top management, they have a designated leader to help them act promptly (Lipton and Lorsch 1992: 71).

A final US boardroom innovation gaining wider use is an annual evaluation by the board of its own activities. In some cases, this entails a special meeting in which directors appraise their own policies and procedures. In others, directors respond to a written questionnaire that is compiled by a trusted third party and presented to the board. Certain boards even review the performance of individual directors. This can be a sensitive and controversial process, but the intent is to encourage directors to be self-critical, to consider ways to improve their participation, and to avoid renominating directors who are not making valuable contributions.

The United Kingdom

As in the USA, institutional investors in the UK are dedicated to augmenting the accountability of boards to shareholders. Thus far, however, the most powerful forces behind change in the British boardroom have arisen out of two groups established by confederations of London business organizations.

PRO NED (Promotion of Non-Executive Directors) was founded in 1980 by the Bank of England together with other banks, the Stock Exchange, the Confederation of British Industries and the British Institute of Management. It was charged with promoting the wider use of non-executive directors (Charkham 1994: 269) and has encouraged the trend towards greater outside representation on boards.

A committee chaired by Sir Adrian Cadbury was appointed in 1992 by the Financial Reporting Council, the London Stock Exchange and a group of accountancy professionals, who: 'were concerned at the perceived low level of confidence both in financial reporting and in the ability of auditors to provide the safeguards which the users of company reports sought and expected' (Charkham 1994: 249). In fact, the committee found itself probing deep into many aspects of the UK's corporate governance system, and its ultimate report served as a rallying cry for reforms in the boardroom.

The Cadbury Code presents an official code of best practices accompanied by a set of additional recommendations. The code includes the following dictates: (1) there should be a clear division of responsibilities at the head of a company that involves either a chairman who is separate from the chief executive or a strong independent element on the board; (2) the majority of the board should be outside directors; (3) a remuneration (compensation) committee composed of at least a majority of non-executive directors should recommend executive pay; and (4) the board should appoint an audit committee that includes at least three outside directors. The recommendations that accompany the code include suggestions about board policies and procedures, an articulation of the major duties of directors, and a detailed account of how audit committees should be organized to operate effectively.

The London Stock Exchange now requires listed companies to state in their annual reports to what extent they comply with the recommendations of the Cadbury report, and where they do not comply, they must explain why. There is no penalty for failing to adopt the recommendations, but there is confidence that good judgement and social pressure will prompt most companies to abide by the bulk of the recommendations.

Germany and Japan

German and Japanese boards have not yet been the subject of significant reforms. Perhaps, however, the seeds of change are being planted. Many Germans have begun to argue that banks wield too much power due to the quantity of shares and board seats they control. Some German stakeholders have suggested that the supervisory boards of companies like Daimler Benz and Metallgesellschaft failed to anticipate and avoid crisis because of their large and cumbersome size. Japanese insurance companies seeking higher dividends and greater return on equity have put pressure on top management to be more performance orientated. A 1993 change in the Japanese commercial code formally established the position of an independent board auditor; although most auditors are only nominally independent, the position none the less represents a symbolic step to greater board accountability.

5 Future convergence?

At least in the USA, the UK and Germany, corporate boards are all striving to perform the same tasks of oversight. Boards in these countries are grappling with some universal challenges and with some problems that are unique to their own national board structures and practices. As capital markets and corporations become more global, it may be that some board structures and practices will converge. Where directors across borders face common obstacles to carrying out their duties, they may learn from their counterparts abroad and may foster the development of a set of more similar cross-national structures and practices. It is unlikely, however, that corporate boards will ever look or act the same from country to country; boards represent only one component of each nation's complex system of corporate governance that is embedded in its unique history, culture, laws and economic environment.

Further reading

(References cited in the text marked *)

American Bar Association (1994) *Corporate Director's Guidebook*, Chicago, IL: American Bar Association. (An overview of the functions and responsibilities of US directors, an analysis of the structure and operations of the US board and a consideration of the applicable legal standards of conduct.)

* Berle, A.A. and Means, G.C. (1991) *The Modern Corporation and Private Property*, New Brunswick, NJ: Transaction Publishers. (An early look at the separation of ownership and control in the modern corporation.)

Cadbury, A. (1990) *The Company Chairman*, Cambridge: FitzWilliam Publishing. (An examination of the role of the non-executive chairman in British corporate boards.)

* Cadbury Committee (1992) *Cadbury Committee Report: Financial Aspects of Corporate Governance*, Basingstoke: Burgess Science Press. (An official code of best practices for governance in the UK accompanied by a set of additional recommendations.)

* Charkham, J. (1994) *Keeping Good Company: A Study of Corporate Governance in Five Countries*, Oxford: Oxford University Press. (An in-depth exploration of corporate governance in Germany, Japan, France, the USA and the UK.)

Demb, A. and Neubauer, F. (1992) *The Corporate Board: Confronting the Paradoxes*, New York: Oxford University Press. (An argument that boards in different countries are more similar than they are different.)

Gay, K. (2000) 'Moving centre stage: the changing role of the non-executive director', *Journal of General Management* 26 (1): 1–17. (A study of the changing role of the non-executive director.)

Harvard Business Review (2000) *Harvard Business Review on Corporate Governance*, Boston, MA: Harvard Business School Press. (Focuses on both policy and strategic matters of governance issues.)

* Kester, C.W. (1991) *Japanese Takeovers: The Global Contest for Corporate Control*, Boston, MA: Harvard Business School Press. (A detailed analysis of the recent increase in Japanese merger and acquisition activity. Includes a chapter on Japanese corporate governance.)

* Lightfoot, R.W. and Kester, C.W. (1992) *Note on Corporate Governance Systems: The United States, Germany, and Japan*, Harvard Business School Case no. 292–012, Boston, MA: Harvard Business School Press. (A description of the corporate governance systems of three countries.)

* Lipton, M. and Lorsch, J.W. (1992) 'A modest proposal for improved corporate governance', *The Business Lawyer* 48 (11): 59. (A critique of certain common US board practices accompanied by a list of recommendations to make boards more active and independent.)

Lorsch, J.W. (1995) 'Empowering the board', *Harvard Business Review* 73 (1): 107. (A discussion of why boards should be empowered and what makes for an empowered board. Uses examples of select innovative US boards.)

* Lorsch, J.W. (1996, forthcoming) 'German corporate governance management: an American's perspective', *Zeitschrift für Betriebswirtschaftliche Forschung*. (This paper compares German and US corporate governance and suggests that the two systems face similar challenges.)

* Lorsch, J.W. and MacIver, E. (1989) *Pawns or Potentates: The Reality of America's Corporate Boards*, Boston, MA: Harvard Business School Press. (A comprehensive study of US corporate governance informed by nearly 100 personal interviews and by over 2000 responses to a written questionnaire.)

* Lorsch, J.W. and MacIver, E.A. (1991) 'Corporate governance and investment time horizons', unpublished paper, Boston, MA: Harvard Business School. (A consideration of the relation between the characteristics of the corporate governance systems and the investment time horizons in the USA, Germany and Japan.)

McGregor, L. (2000) *The Human Face of Corporate Governance*, New York: Macmillan. (Corporate governance has become a crucial issue for many companies and organizations. Much has been written on the formal systems but this book uncovers the human element examining personal and interpersonal governance.)

* Monks, R.A.G. and Minnow, N. (1995) *Corporate Governance*, London: Blackwell. (A thorough textbook overview of the history and current status of US corporate governance. Includes a chapter on international corporate governance.)

* New York Stock Exchange (1990) *NYSE Fact Book*, New York: NYSE. (Contains data on over 2500 companies from around the world; includes statistics about bonds, options and stock prices, and historical information.)

* New York Stock Exchange (1992) *NYSE Fact Book*, New York: NYSE. (See New York Stock Exchange 1990.)

* Pic, J.-J. (1995) *Europe's Diverse Corporate Boards – How they Differ from Each Other & The U.S.*, San Francisco, CA: Spencer Stuart Executive Search Consultants. (A concise report comparing board practices and structures in various European countries and in the USA.)

Rosenbaum, E., Bonker, F. and Wagener, H. (eds) (2000) *Privatisation, Corporate Governance and the Emergence of Markets*, New York: Palgrave. (This volume focuses on privatization in transitional economies, addressing issues ranging from corporate governance to the relationship between privatization and the emergence of markets.)

Agency, markets and hierarchies

Anna Grandori

1 Introduction
2 Markets
3 Market failures
4 Variety of markets
5 Hierarchy
6 Types of hierarchy
7 Alternatives to markets, hierarchy and agency

Overview

The area of studies presented here is concerned with the analysis and comparison of alternative modes of coordination of economic activities. The relatively new branches of economics called information economics and organizational or neo-institutional economics offer major contributions on how to deal with this problem. These contributions are presented here with attention to integrating them with those branches of organization theory that are also pertinent and relevant for the problem at hand, especially the organizational theories of bureaucracy and incentive systems.

The entry is organized in two main parts, one devoted to markets and the other to hierarchies. Within each part, the main different types of market and hierarchies are examined. As to markets, the characteristics of a perfect market as a coordination mode are set out first; then the main sources of departure from that ideal type are reviewed in the section on market failure. Third, a section is devoted to two main varieties of 'modified markets' – oligopolistic markets and assisted markets. As to hierarchy, the reasons for the emergence of this mode of coordination, and the corresponding types of emerging hierarchies, are grouped into three classes: informational hierarchies in 'teams'; supervisory hierarchies; and agency-based hierarchies. The main tenets of agency relations and agency theory are explained in this last section. The final paragraph briefly connects agency, markets and hierarchies to other alternative effective modes of coordination of economic activities.

1 Introduction

In a developed economy, many differentiated organizational units take part in the transformation and consumption of good and services, because of the productivity advantages brought about by specialization and the division of labour. A high degree of differentiation among economic actors which depend on each other for exchanging valuable resources requires *coordination*.

As history teaches us, the most 'natural' and historically earliest system employed for coordinating economic action and exchanging resources was barter and, more generally, the direct joint decision making and negotiation among interested parties. Even now, there are important economic activities that are coordinated through direct informal agreement. They range from informal collaboration on research and development activities among a few firms, to the coordination on price decisions among a few oligopolists, to the simple cooperation among people in activities of common interest (for example, taking a joint legal action against a common adversary; or cooperating in carrying a weight, provided that all the contributors needed are interested in moving it).

A direct all-to-all communication mode of coordination becomes increasingly inefficient, however, if the number of interdependent parties grows large and so does the number of matters on which they are interdependent. It is difficult to think, and find an example of, a national or international economy or a large firm entirely governed through direct unstructured communication and joint decision making among parties.

What then are the main alternative modes of coordination capable of governing complex economic systems? In the most influential systematization of this problem, two main alternatives have been contemplated: a system based on a central coordinating agent, or *hierarchy*; and a system based on autonomous decisions of economic agents based on a common system of quantified information (prices), or *market* (Hayek 1945; Williamson 1975).

Both these coordination modes have the property of enormously reducing the costs of coordination of complex systems: costs of gathering and transmitting information, of devising a set of actions to be adopted by all relevant actors, of deciding who should do what, of ensuring that decisions are actually implemented. This is an interesting property indeed in a world characterized by limited capacity of processing information and fallible knowledge, as Simon has extensively argued through his seminal concept of 'bounded rationality' (1945), on which almost all the contributions examined here are built. Let us examine what are the principal mechanisms through which markets and hierarchies can achieve this result.

2 Markets

Under a market system the solution to the problem of the high costs involved by the coordination of large numbers of players is quite radical: economic actors do not entertain any direct relationships beyond those necessary to stipulate 'instantaneous' contracts and to transfer goods/services and money. All actors take their decisions unilaterally on the basis of their *local* information. The only kind of general information that they need to consider is *prices*; these should embody the information on all the other variables that are relevant for their decisions. More specifically, the local information of economic actors will include knowledge of their own preferences or utility and knowledge on what type and level of physical and financial resources are available to them. On the basis of this local knowledge, decision makers are able to formulate feasible production plans (in their producer roles) and feasible consumption plans (in their consumer roles)

(Milgrom and Roberts 1992). Prices should provide all other relevant information, and therefore it is said that they should be sufficient statistics of the relative quality of goods and services as well as of their relative scarcity (Hayek 1945).

Profits synthesize the results of the combinations between the 'states of nature' in terms of demand and the response moves of producers in terms of type and quantity of output offered, thereby measuring the correctness of the actions undertaken and rewarding them. Because of this measuring and signalling function, it is said that profits should be taken into account by actors playing under a market system and that if they pursue their own interest, then an 'invisible hand' would bring about a coordinated result. More precisely, economists have shown that this coordinated result has the properties of a general equilibrium. Core propositions describing this property of markets have been that, if the above-mentioned informational requirements are satisfied, a list of prices will exist for which the allocation of resources is Pareto-efficient, that is, such that no actor could improve its position with respect to it, without worsening the position of others.

If on one side the market mechanism can be thought of as being marvellously efficient, when it works (Hayek 1945), the domain in which this can be expected to happen is limited, especially in modern economies.

3 Market failures

The causes of market failure that have been highlighted initially by economists are generated by production processes and affect production costs. The existence of *economies of scale and scope*, that is, the circumstances under which the unitary total production cost decreases if larger lots are produced or if more than one type of product is produced using common equipment or know-how, is always considered in textbook treatments of market failure. In fact, these circumstances imply that output cannot be adapted economically in a continuous fashion to demand, and therefore a system of prices that satisfies the equilibrium condition may not exist.

A second source of market failure traditionally analysed is the presence of *externalities*. Markets are unable to regulate efficiently those exchanges in which important positive or negative consequences affect third parties (with respect to those who are partners in the exchange). Typical examples are those of industrial pollution (as a case of uncompensated external damage) and that of product or process innovation that can be easily imitated (as a case of uncompensated externally enjoyed benefit).

Organizational economists have analysed those causes of market failures stemming not only from production costs but also from transaction costs, that is, the information, decision, search, negotiation and control costs incurred for effectively transferring goods and services between two technically separable transformation units (Williamson 1981). Major sources of transaction costs in markets are information complexity and small numbers.

Information complexity

Any violation of the above-stated knowledge requirements of markets can be a source of a bad functioning of market exchanges. For example, consumers may find it difficult to ascertain what the utility of goods and services is to them, because they do not have the competencies to express this judgement (as often occurs, for example, in health and law services). This may be a source of *information asymmetries* (Akerlof 1970) between the two parties of an exchange that make the transaction unattractive for the uninformed party in the absence of safeguards and guarantees that the market itself cannot provide.

Another informational problem is that of missing markets and the incompleteness of preference orderings, that is, actors define preferences over different sets of alternatives so that, for example, consumers may like things that no producer offers.

Third, information-intensive goods and services are very difficult to exchange against compensation: the 'paradox of information' described by information economists consists of the fact that a potential buyer, in order to know how much information is worth, should know the information itself, but if this were the case then the information would have been transferred without being compensated.

Uncertainty in the conditions relevant to define the terms of exchange is a major cause of market failure (Williamson 1975). Imagine that a producer of a raw material such as glass fibre is interested in having some other specialized actor to transform this material into final or semi-final products, like tissues, through a process in which many conditions can vary unpredictably: the costs of raw materials, the quality of the materials, the time of processing and the degree of difficulties encountered. It may be either cognitively impossible or too costly to write complete contracts covering all the conceivable contingencies: it may be more effective and efficient to set up some coordinating system different from a market exchange.

Finally, both the economics of technological innovation and information processing-based organization theory have shown that the intrinsic information complexity of goods or services – that is, the extent to which they incorporate sophisticated and uncodifiable or tacit knowledge and a variety of interconnected elements – undermines the effectiveness of standardized coordination mechanisms in general and of those based on the formation of an exchange value in particular.

Small numbers

The formation of a market value of an item requires that many buyers and sellers exist so that exit is possible as a signal of the appropriateness of the undertaken action (Hirschman 1970). However, economic actors may become irreplaceable, not only because of natural monopoly reasons but also for the more endemic reason that economic actors easily develop competencies in and commit resources to their relationships that are specific to that relationship, that is, that would have less value in any other potential relationship. The specificity of relationships and exchanges between economic actors is obviously more and more relevant as goods and services become more 'differentiated', customized and subject to continuous innovation as has occurred in modern economies. In addition, it has been noticed that once a commercial relation is started with a given counterpart, even if it was originally a market exchange, it is likely that over time a repeated transaction will generate reciprocal learning and partner-specific knowledge so that the identity of the partner starts to matter, switching costs would be incurred in the case of exit and the market relationship undergoes a 'fundamental transformation' into something different (Williamson 1991).

What are the possible characteristics of these 'different' relationships? The study of market failures has shown that the use of markets is costly and the allocative results are likely to be biased under many conditions. However, all systems of coordination have their own costs and biases and, if there were no feasible and more effective alternative mode of coordination for those circumstances, what would be observed is a persistence of less than perfect markets. Yet, alternatives are available, and hierarchical coordination is one of the most important alternative candidates for the coordination of complex systems.

Hierarchy, however, as will be illustrated in the next section, is a very powerful and very costly system of coordination. It requires a significant commitment of resources to coordination activities. It entails its own internal transaction costs. It may therefore be justified in conditions of very strong interdependence and hazard in the relationship between economic actors.

When these conditions are not met, a variety of 'modified markets', different from the extreme model of perfect competition, may be more attractive than hierarchy and are in fact observed.

4 Variety of markets

As a critical response and an alternative to the restricted assumptions defining the ideal type of a 'perfect market', a theory of imperfect competition was developed in the 1930s. This framework referred to – and was meant to solve – the problem of what kind of market can regulate the exchange of differentiated goods. This form of market includes the following. If the sets of firms that compete include few actors, then the individual action of each one has a direct effect on the consequences (payoffs) for each of the others that can no longer be neglected. Prices become a decision variable rather than exogenous information. The relationship can be modelled as a game, and it has been a typical field of application of game theory. If overt communication and agreement on the actions to be taken (quantities offered and prices) is not allowed, however, this game can still be defined as a market.

On the other side, as information economists have noticed, the amount of information that decision makers must process in monopolistic or oligopolistic markets are radically different and radically higher with respect to the case of competitive markets, because they have to make predictions about both consumers' and competitors' behaviours. In addition, the lack of competitive conditions may also have consequences on firm objectives. It has been noticed that if firms can directly influence prices, then owners – especially if dispersed – may prefer lower prices (as consumers themselves) rather than higher profits; and that if firms are not subject to competitive selection forces, they can viably pursue a variety of other goals in addition to profit.

Therefore, in oligopolistic markets, both transaction costs for the firms involved and negative externalities for consumers are likely to be present. However, the alternative of creating integrated firms may turn out to be even more costly (Williamson 1975). In fact, the costs of communication and reciprocal control among 'conspiring oligopolists' can be reduced for the firms involved by setting up a central structure. On the other hand, the costs of this structure itself should be compared with the savings in transaction costs in a market relation; second, and more important, the advantages for the firms involved, if any, should be 'compared' with the losses of the increased concentration for consumers and other firms.

Other ways in which markets may be 'modified' in order to remain viable under conditions of perfect competition entail the 'reinforcement' of the institutional context in which exchanges take place. All markets, including the ideal type of perfect markets, do require an adequate institutional framework. In particular, a classical market requires a legal framework for the legitimacy and transferability of property rights.

It has been shown that the economic exchange of complex goods requires more institutional support. For example, it may require certification of competence and the formation of reputation (Karpik 1989) as well as deep knowledge of the individual characteristics of the trading counterpart in order to be able to forecast what performance is likely to be offered, or even for identifying promising trading partners (Granovetter 1985). These markets have been defined as *relational* or 'assisted' markets to stress the fact that they are supported by laws or norms, authorities or social control more extensively than the model of a 'complete and competitive' market would consider.

The development of a variety of models of imperfect, bounded and embedded markets is, however, only at a beginning. A lot of work is under way, especially at the interdisciplinary border between economics and sociology.

5 Hierarchy

The term hierarchy derives from the two Greek words 'hierai' – meaning sacred – and 'archein' – meaning govern. The etymology of the term indicates that the original meaning of hierarchy was the governance of sacred things, used in religious doctrine where all ultimate powers emanated from God.

The concept of hierarchy, in the technical meaning it has been assuming in organization science, maintains one core element of that original conception: a hierarchy is a mode of coordination in which the rights of access to information, of decision making and of controlling the implementation of decided actions are allocated to a central agent. In a simple hierarchy this principle is applied only at one level: there is one central agent and a number of controlled agents. In complex hierarchies the principle is applied recursively at multiple levels, thereby generating a pyramidal structure.

On the other hand, in the scientific rather than religious meaning of hierarchy, the origins of this order, the reasons why a collectivity of actors accepts to allocate decisions and control rights in that way, and the condition under which it is effective and efficient are in need of explanation.

Before addressing this issue, it should be said that the above-mentioned concept of hierarchy as a decisional order has been used for a long time in organizational thought until the relatively recent contributions of organizational economics (Williamson 1975; Alchian and Demsetz 1972) enlarged the concept to include the dimensions of the allocation of property rights and of the rights to the residual economic results of economic activities (that is, profits). In their definition, hierarchy is not only a mode of coordination of economic activities in which information, decision and control rights are centralized, but also one in which the ownership rights and rights to receive the residual rewards related to those activities are centralized. This idea that hierarchy and planning are connected to property rights derives from the elaborations of one of the economists who has been called the father of the new institutional economics, Ronald Coase (1937). He criticized, in fact, the opposition between economic systems organized through planning and through market, and set out a research programme aimed at studying the 'optimal amount of planning' in a liberal system, in which this planning function is chiefly performed by firms. Coase also established the connection between the need for designing property rights allocation and the presence of transaction costs in market exchange. A central result of his analysis has been that if all actors maximized expected value and parties could transact without attrition, they would find those transactions that 'internalize all externalities' independently from the initial allocation of property rights (Coase 1960). Inversely, if transaction costs are non-zero, then a theory of property rights allocation becomes necessary and possible. This theory has been developed both in transaction cost economics (Williamson 1975; Grossman and Hart 1986) and in agency theory (Jensen and Meckling 1976) – although with some internal differences.

Having included the issue of property rights, organizational economists have also distinguished between two classes of asset over which hierarchical control can be defined, that are fundamentally different in this respect: technical assets and human assets (Williamson 1981). In fact, property rights over technical assets can be transferred and centralized – and this can serve as a coordinating mechanism among all actors using those assets. By contrast, property rights over human assets are not transferable in a slavery-free society: therefore the most integrated or 'hierarchy-intensive' arrangement that is possible with respect to labour transactions is a 'nexus of treaties' by which the rights that are transferred to a central agent are the rights to residual rewards (profits) and the particularly crucial decision right to negotiate all the contracts or treaties regulating the contributions and rewards of all other parties (Alchian and Demsetz 1972; Jensen and Meckling 1976).

6 Types of hierarchy

The concept of hierarchy is closely linked to that of *authority*. In fact, for a hierarchical order to be feasible, a very special relationship should be constructed between a superordinate party and any one of its subordinate parties. This is an asymmetrical influence relationship requiring that one actor agrees to accept the decisions of another actor in a defined 'zone of acceptance' (Simon 1951). For example, people agreeing to work as subordinates in a mechanical engineering plant agree to be trained to use the tools available there and to conform to the indications issued by the owners of those tools or their delegates on how to use them.

Within this defined range of work behaviours – their 'zone of acceptance' – these people are said to accept an authority relation. On the other hand, people taking a flight can be said to accept the authority of the captain for behaviours related to flight safety and the well-being of other passengers; or patients can be said to accept the authority of physicians; or members of a trade union can be said to accept the authority of their leaders. What all these relationships have in common is that their governance system is authority; and a stable and formalized system of authority relationships is a hierarchy. However, whatever the bases of these authority relationships, the reasons why they are accepted are different. Max Weber was the initiator of a work aimed at discerning what the different types of authority that can regulate social and economic life are and what the conditions for their emergence and effectiveness could be. He contrasted authority relationships that were more typical of pre-modern societies – the 'traditional' and 'charismatic' types of authority – with the 'rational–legal' type of authority in which legitimation is founded on considerations of effectiveness and efficiency.

For the problem that we are considering here – the comparative assessments of the different coordination modes of market, hierarchy and agency in modern economies – the rational–legal type of authority is by and large the most important type. Within it, it will also be necessary to distinguish between different subtypes of 'rational' authority and, consequently, different types of hierarchy as stable systems of authority relationships. The criteria for distinction should be able to discriminate among different conditions in which hierarchies emerge. The *raisons d'être* for hierarchy, and the corresponding types of hierarchy, will be grouped into three classes, according to the configuration of actors' interests and the possibility of controlling behaviours. One of these classes is that of agency relationships and agency-based hierarchies.

The emergence of hierarchy in teams

A first type of hierarchy is based on authority relations exercised in the interest of a set of cooperating parties, under the assumption that these parties have common interests and objectives (such a system of actors is called a 'team' in organizational economics). For example, a group of people can accept as a common objective solving a problem or performing a common task – for example, choosing a profitable investment or assembling a complex output. In these conditions a simple hierarchy can emerge as a coordination system for reasons of effectiveness (quality of outcome) and efficiency (speed of process), provided that the relevant knowledge can be concentrated in one agent. Early laboratory studies on group behaviour have demonstrated that if information is structured, in the sense that it is easy to interpret and useful for solving a problem, then a centralized scheme in which all information is communicated to one actor who integrates them is more efficient and effective than an 'all-to-all' communication network (Bavelas 1951). If the system of cooperation is large, and one single actor cannot handle all the information because the task would be too complex for the limited capacities of information processing of the human mind, then a complex hierarchy can solve the coordination problem effectively by decomposing the complex problem into many manageable sub-problems (Simon 1945): each actor can deal only with a limited set of information and inferior levels of hierarchy can synthesize, codify or otherwise reduce and simplify the information conveyed at higher levels.

In all these situations, the emergence of hierarchy has been explained not only with respect to the market alternative (market failure conditions are obviously verified for joint problem solving activities) but also with respect to the group alternative (group failure conditions include, therefore, system size, competence concentration and structuring of information).

Supervisory hierarchies

The interests and objectives of a set of interdependent actors can easily diverge. All transactional or sequential interdependence situations in which one party is structurally in a supply position and the other in a supplied position generate conflicting objectives. Also, joint-action interdependence situations in which different actors pool and integrate their resources for reaching a joint output become structurally conflictive if actors perceive that their efforts are costly, so that an incentive to *free-ride* emerges. Why is hierarchy a relatively effective and efficient way of coordinating these conflictive relationships? Why should an actor agree to obey orders given by another actor who holds different objectives? An authority relation is sustainable in these conditions on the basis of an exchange.

Consider the authority relation on which most employment relations at the operational, non-managerial levels of firms are based. The theory of this important type of authority relation has been set out by Herbert Simon (1951). Why does an actor contributing work services not simply transfer them through a market contract? They could, if all the contingencies affecting the ways in which labour should be most effectively employed could be anticipated and written into a contract, and if the output of the individual worker could be measured. These conditions sometimes hold, for example in activities such as harvesting, cleaning or other standard services: there, labour services are bought on a spot market for defined and measurable activities.

For most labour transactions, however, these conditions are not met. In particular, because of the uncertainty of conditions affecting the best use of work, the employer is interested not only in having workforce contributions but also in having the right to decide what particular tasks to impose on the employee, that is, in having authority over the employee. On the other hand, it is not uncommon for the employee to have no strong preferences regarding the particular tasks that might be required of them, provided that they fall into their work-related 'zone of acceptance', that is, they may be *quasi-indifferent* over these alternatives (Simon 1951). By contrast, a highly valued item for labour conferrers is a stable risk-free compensation: in fact, these actors are often risk-averse because of the low differentiation of their investments and because variance in current income may affect their total wealth substantially. Under these conditions, an exchange-based authority relationship is likely to be a Pareto-efficient agreement: the risk-averse employees receive a risk-free reward, and transfer a decision right about their work-related behaviours on which they are quasi-indifferent; the risk-neutral employers bear the risk and get the decision rights about the employees' behaviour that matter to them.

An additional reason for the emergence of hierarchy in the regulation of economic interdependence relationships can be found in the influential explanation of the classical firm structure by Alchian and Demsetz (1972). They have argued that the impossibility of detecting the individual work contributions in a collective output is a major reason for setting up a hierarchy, in addition to that of uncertainty stressed by Simon. They called these conditions a *team production* situation, in which the output is greater than the sum of its parts and cannot be clearly attributed to the various inputs, so that their marginal productivity is undetectable. The typical examples are activities like discharging a truck or transporting a weight. If it is not possible to measure outputs, as the market would require, and if work efforts are costly for workers – it is argued – then the supervision of input behaviours can be a reasonable alternative for achieving a coordinated result. In fact, all the actors contributing to the common activity will be interested in insuring each other against the possibility that someone eludes their tasks (shirks). In small teams reciprocal monitoring is likely to be sufficient; but in large teams a failure of reciprocal control is likely. A central agent or supervisor is able to observe input behaviours so that free-riders cannot hope to go undiscovered.

But who will control the controllers? The answer to this question has been that the controller should be entitled to receive the residual rewards of the collective activities and to negotiate centrally the contracts with the other agents. In this way, the team production factor has led to a justification of hierarchy in its larger meaning, including a centralization not only of decision and control rights but also of residual rewards and property rights.

The emergence of supervisory hierarchies in this wide meaning of classical firms, in which one central actor owns the set of activities to be coordinated and has all decision and control rights over them, has also been explained by coupling conditions of *uncertainty* with conditions of *specificity* (Williamson 1975, 1981; Grossman and Hart 1986). The hypothesis is that if two separate partners of a market exchange make investments in technical or human assets that have more value in that relationship than in any alternative use (that is, are partner-specific); and if uncertainty makes complete contracts unfeasible; then parties will have an incentive to behave 'opportunistically' and will not be able to defend themselves against these hazards in front of any court. Then the centralization of property rights over those interdependent activities is prescribed as an efficient solution. Grossman and Hart (1986) and Hart and Moore (1990) have demonstrated the theorem that in the case of different degrees of specificity and irreplaceability of the assets conferred by different parties in a transaction, property rights should be allocated to those parties who make the specific commitments and whose contribution is indispensable and critical in the creation of a surplus.

A final interesting property of supervisory hierarchy as a mode of coordinating interdependence among actors with divergent interests is that a central agent can assume the role of an *arbitrator*. If parties are not easily replaceable, the contracts linking the cooperating parties are incomplete, and the relation is not otherwise regulated by the external law system, then market exchange is highly hazardous, because no court would hear the claims of the parties. Therefore, if parties are interested in having an exchange or entertaining a cooperative venture in those conditions they are also interested in setting up 'their own court of last resort' (Williamson 1991). Of course, arbitration authority must be legitimized (as any type of authority). Competence and identification with the interests of the whole system are the obvious 'rational–legal' bases of arbitration authority acceptability.

Supervisory hierarchies, however, are viable and can display their properties of effectiveness and efficiency under particular and limited circumstances. In fact, a basic requirement for their feasibility is that the behaviours of actors agreeing to be supervised is *observable* and that the supervisors have the relevant *knowledge* for indicating what the best behaviour is. Therefore, supervisory hierarchy is an effective way of coordinating activities that are subject to uncertainty, only in the sense of variability of circumstances that cannot be foreseen but that, once occurred, allow clear interpretation of what the best response actions are. Uncertainty in the stronger senses of lack of consolidated schemes for solving the problems that those activities present (Perrow 1967), and of lack of consolidated standards for evaluating performance (Alchian and Demsetz 1972), would undermine the effectiveness of supervisory hierarchy.

There is wide organizational literature documenting the biases and internal transaction costs of hierarchical coordination when applied in those informationally complex circumstances, that is, in describing '*hierarchical failures*' in the regulation of innovative activities; in conflict resolution when innovative solutions are required, in governing the cooperation of actors conferring complex and critical work competencies, such as professionals or researchers, and in controlling logistically dispersed and unobservable activities such as sale activities.

Agency-based hierarchies

Some of the problems that lead supervisory hierarchy to failure can be solved by an *agency* relationship. In this relation one actor or party (the principal) delegates to another (the agent) the discretionary power to act in its own interest (Jensen and Meckling 1976). For example, stockholders delegate to managers the power to make decisions in their interest, clients delegate to lawyers the power to act on their behalf, workers delegate to their union representative the power to negotiate in their name. Jensen and Meckling, two economists of organization who have become leading authors in the theory of agency relations, have in fact maintained that agency relations are very common in economic life.

An agency relation has some elements in common with rational–legal authority, but also differs in important respects. The basic common element is that in all cases one party accepts that its own actions are decided by another party. The basic difference is that in a classic authority relation, when one party agrees to take action in the interest of another, the decisions and control rights over that action rest with the 'interested' party (the 'principal' in agency theory language). By contrast, in an agency relation the party delegating action rights in its interest also delegates the discretionary power to choose among different possible sets of action, in a definite range or 'zone of acceptance'.

The difference is important because for many activities action rights cannot be separated from the decision rights over them: typically, all activities with a certain degree of informational complexity and all activities that must be performed in places and situations that make them unobservable for the 'principal' – for example, managerial activities (rather than operational), many service activities (rather than productive), professional activities (rather than bureaucratic). In fact, agency theory has been applied mostly as a theory of governance of these types of activities. Interestingly, these activities are exactly some of those for which a classical authority relation would fail, as explained above.

More precisely, agency theory treatments distinguish between situations in which agent behaviour is observable by the principal and situations in which it is not. Observable behaviour is defined as an action that can be discerned by the principal (they can tell which action has been performed) and can be evaluated by the principal (they can tell whether or not the action is in their best interest). In these conditions the delegation of discretion over a range of possible actions can still be efficient because the principal does not have the time or cognitive capacity to make all these decisions directly, or because the activities may require undelayed responses and adaptive action, thereby making the transmission of local information to a central agent and the feedback of orders slow and ineffective. Still, if the principal retains the right to control actions *ex post* and by exception, and can perfectly observe them, this relation can be seen as a more decentralized version of a classical exchange-based authority relation. In fact, for conditions of observable behaviour, agency theorists have reached the same contractual solution contemplated by Simon's model of authority and employment relation: supposing that the agent is risk-averse (because of their concentrated resource investments and the likelihood of wealth effects) and that the principal is risk-neutral (for the opposite reasons), the best solution is to offer the agent a fixed wage.

The amount of this wage should be exactly as much as is necessary to retain the contribution and to elicit the desired type of action. This problem is solved in agency theory by taking into account the possibility that the agent is not 'quasi-indifferent' (as in Simon's model) between the possible work behaviours, but that they have a defined preference ordering over them. The usual assumption is that the utility function of the agent can be divided into a utility function for money (concave because the agent is supposed to be risk-averse) and a disutility function for effort (convex, because the marginal cost of effort is supposed to be increasing).

The principal can then calculate what level of effort from the agent is optimal from their point of view and the amount of wage that it is necessary to offer to elicit that level of effort. Knowing the principal's total expected profits from each level of effort of the agent, the principal will give the agent the wage W* that satisfies the following relations:

1   the utility of wage minus the disutility of effort for the agent is non-negative;
2   it is at least as great as the net utility the agent can derive from the best alternative contract;
3   within those constraints, the optimal level of effort is that action for which the difference between profit-from-effort and the required wage for obtaining it is largest (Levinthal 1988; Douma and Schreuder 1992).

One can note, again, that this analytical solution includes the propositions of earlier organizational thinking on incentives in organizations (March and Simon 1958): incentives should be at least as great as contributions, and should be as great as those offered in alternative similar work positions.

The most interesting and distinctive contribution of the theory of agency concerns the governance of those situations in which agents' actions are not observable. If the principal can only observe the final results of an activity, the principal has a perfect signal of the action undertaken by the agent only if the outcome depends purely on the agent's action. For example, for a standard production task in which the relevant result is the number of finished units with a given technology, the level of output would be a sufficient signal of the level of effort chosen by a producer agent. Then, this contingency would bring us back to a condition of complete information. However, in many cases the observed outcomes depend on many other things in addition to the agents' actions. This generates a condition of incomplete information or non-observability of agent behaviour. The higher the uncertainty of an activity (that is, the higher the variance in outcomes that cannot be attributed to an agent's actions), the more the agent's behaviour is unobservable, and the more the agent has incentives to choose those actions which will bring the highest utility to them, rather than to the principal. A fixed wage contract would therefore be inefficient: for example, if the utility function of the agent is such that they value money positively and value effort negatively, the agent would be led to choose the minimum level of effort if they were to maximize their utility.

A solution to this problem is to make agent compensation contingent on outcomes: if results are superior according to the principal's interests, compensation should be higher; if results are inferior, compensation should be lower. This is, in fact, the contractual scheme that we find in the regulation of sale activities and in managerial compensation plans linking pay to performance. The problem with these contracts, however, stressed by agency theorists, is that they are always *second-best* contracts, if the agent is risk-averse: in order to provide incentives for superior performance they transfer risk from a risk-neutral to a risk-averse actor, who will demand a premium for that risk-bearing. This is the fundamental trade-off that should be solved by an agency contract (Levinthal 1988; Milgrom and Roberts 1992; Douma and Schreuder 1992).

The Pareto-optimal incentive structure, that is, the 'intensity of incentive' or 'risk-sharing rule' that maximizes utility with respect to the principal's interests, taking into account the fact that the agent chooses actions with regard to their own interest, depends on various factors. For example, Milgrom and Roberts (1992: 221) present an analytical solution in which the intensity of incentives β is a function of four fundamental variables:

1 the incremental profits that are generated by additional effort $P'(e)$ (first derivate of profits-from-effort);
2 the degree of agent's risk aversion (r);
3 the degree of unmeasurability of performance, expressed as the variance of non-performance factors affecting results $[\text{Var}(X)]$;
4 the rate at which the marginal cost of effort increases (C''/e) (second derivative of cost-of-effort).

$$\beta = P'(e) / [1 + r \, \text{Var}(X) \, C''(e)]$$

Various refinements have also been proposed in order to reduce the difference between first-best and second-best contracts, and therefore the magnitude of incentive needed. The most important element to be taken into account is that 'the degree of measurability of performance' is not a 'given' but depends on the investments in monitoring. What is meant by monitoring if agent actions are not observable? Monitoring, under these conditions, consists of observation of *signals* or predictors of agent performance. For example, the hours of presence at the workplace is a frequently monitored signal of the level of effort. The signal is informative 'if observing the signal provides information about effort that is not already reflected in the outcome itself' and 'if the conditional probability of observing any signal varies with the agent's effort level' (Levinthal 1988: 168). Given that monitoring is a costly activity, a trade-off is needed between the cost of incentives because of inefficient risk-bearing, and the cost of monitoring. Therefore, important conclusions, consistent with widely held qualitative principles of organization design, are that the intensity of incentives and the intensity of monitoring should be designed together; and, in addition, that incentive and monitoring systems should be designed together with jobs. In fact, assigning a mix of measurable and unmeasurable tasks to an agent, in this perspective, is likely to have the biasing consequence that the agent would be led to allocate effort only to measurable (and rewarded) tasks (Milgrom and Roberts 1992).

The study of agency relations has explained the nature and emergence of a particular type of non-supervisory, decentralized hierarchy. In fact, by definition, decision power is delegated from principals to agents and supervision is an unfeasible coordination and control mechanism if behaviour is unobservable. This type of hierarchy is coordinated much more through incentives than through control. This finding is associated with uncertainty and unobservability, thereby justifying the idea of decentralized organization forms in those conditions.

Agency theory has in fact provided an explanation and justification of decentralized hierarchy not only on the dimension of the allocation of decision and rewards rights – as illustrated so far – but also in the dimension of the allocation of property rights – a dimension which is typically part of the organizational economists' concept of hierarchy, as noted above. The seminal contribution of Jensen and Meckling (1976) is central in this respect. What are the consequences of the introduction of an agency costs hypothesis for the ownership structure of the firm?

Jensen and Meckling compare the behaviour of a manager who is also the owner of a firm to his behaviour when he sells off a portion of 'residual claims' on the firm's activities to outsiders. An owner-manager would make decisions in their own firm in order to maximize a complex utility function including not only residual monetary rewards but also a variety of other benefits which may include power, technical excellence, slack on the job or other things. As long as the owner-manager actor is unitary, the same actor would bear the full cost of the consumption of those items as well as enjoying the benefits. If, however, the manager only owns a fraction of a firm's shares, a free-riding incentive will emerge: they will in fact bear only a part of the costs of the managerial benefits they might assign to themselves. Agency costs can then be defined as the sum of the costs sustained for realigning the decisions taken in the agent's interest to those taken in the principal's interest, plus the costs generated by the residual divergence between these decisions that will in general remain.

But is there any particular reason why an owner-manager should sell part of his shares? Jensen and Meckling (1976: 349) maintain that 'a manager who invests all of his wealth in a single firm (his own) will generally bear a welfare loss (if he is risk averse) because he will bear more risk than necessary'. Low diversification of investments and wealth effects are sources of risk-aversion. Therefore, the fundamental trade-off between the requisites of risk-bearing and the need of providing incentives to management to act in the interest of ownership, is likely to lead to an optimal ownership structure that is a mixture of internal and external financing.

In addition, the main different sources of external financing, equity and debt, can also be evaluated in terms of agency costs. Both bring about divergence be-

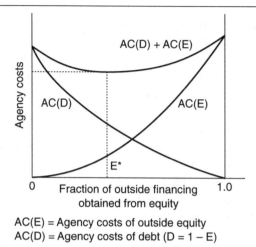

AC(E) = Agency costs of outside equity
AC(D) = Agency costs of debt (D = 1 – E)

Figure 1 Optimal structure of a firm's external financing
Source: Adapted from Jensen and Meckling (1976: 344)

tween the investors' interest and those who use the funds. Therefore, in order to reduce the potential divergence (and the fear of divergence) between these risk-taking decisions and those that would maximize the value of the firm, the bondholders incur monitoring costs (for example, auditing) and the manager-agents incur 'bonding' costs (for example, certifications, safeguards and commitments that guarantee to principals that their interests will not be eluded).

The problem of the optimal structure of external financing can therefore be stated as follows and as represented in Figure 1. As the fraction of outside financing obtained from equity increases (from 0 to 1) with respect to the fraction obtained from debt, the agency costs of outside equity increase and the agency costs of debt decreases. The sum of these two cost functions is likely to be in many circumstances (typically if both functions are convex) a U-shaped curve. That is, the point of minimum total cost is likely to be intermediate between 0 and 1, that is, to be a mixture of debt and equity.

Therefore, the somehow counter-intuitive implication of the presence of agency costs for the ownership structure of the firm is the following: rather than predicting the superiority of 'full hierarchies' in which ownership and control are centralized in the same agents, agency theory predicts that in many circumstances a decentralized hierarchy with decision rights and residual rewards rights allocated to managers, and property rights allocated to a mixture of equity holders and bondholders is likely to be an effective solution.

This presentation of agency-based hierarchies has emphasized that the domain of effectiveness of this coordination mode is contiguous but different from that of supervisory hierarchies. In particular, the latter imply that the principal in whose interest the agent action is selected has the right to decide over them (retain decision-making authority); while in agency relation those decision rights are allocated to the agent (who exerts decision-making authority). Therefore, supervisory hierarchies are suited to regulate relatively uncomplex activities, which a central agent can have the information and time to decide upon; while agency-based hierarchies are viable and efficient in the regulation of activities in which, because of lack of information, time or other resources, the delegation of discretion is necessary.

However, the problem of agency costs leads to a governance system characterized by a mixture of incentive and monitoring that, in turn, is of limited applicability. Specifically, for very uncertain and complex activities where the variance of exogenous variables is high – for example, research activities or professional activities – finding good signals of agent performance may be too costly or even methodologically impossible, and incentives would turn out to be uncorrelated with performance. In addition, for very complex activities the set of relevant actions that the agent might choose from may be undefinable, making all calculations of optimal contracts unfeasible. In fact, agency theory itself has been used to analyse the limits of agency contracts, and has led to predict that in complex activities the governance structure of firms will not be that of an agency-based hierarchy (nor of course that of a classic authority-based hierarchy) but will be close to that of a 'peer group' (such as a partnership or a cooperative firm) (Fama and Jensen 1983a, 1983b).

In conclusion, therefore, it is necessary to say that market, hierarchy and agency cannot solve all the problems of coordination of economic activities, and that alternative feasible governance systems are available.

7 Alternatives to markets, hierarchy and agency

At the end of our treatment of the governance forms of market and hierarchy (including agency-based hierarchy) we are left with one main puzzling question: what governance system may be feasible for coordinating very complex and uncertain activities, for which neither markets nor any sort of hierarchy are suitable? What is the solution, if there is no possibility of knowing the performance of interdependent actors, either through a central agent observing actions, action signals or action outcomes, or through market signals?

One main alternative is to use some form of *group* coordination. On the dimensions of the allocation of information and decision rights, various forms of group coordination through joint decision making have been modelled, ranging from normatively controlled groups or 'clans' (Ouchi 1980), to groups regulated by democracy (Arrow 1951) to groups regulated by negotiation and 'poliarchy' (Lindblom 1977). If we also consider the property rights and reward rights dimensions highlighted by organizational economists, we are led to consider discrete, ideal-type governance systems such as peer groups in which all rights are diffused (Williamson 1975). An illustration of the specific attributes and the comparative assessment of these group forms is beyond the purposes of this entry; but it can be said that among the variables affecting their relative advantage, problems of knowledge and information complexity, problems of conflict of interest and the nature of games and problems of group size play a fundamental role.

Another fundamental alternative mode of coordination – often 'embedding' the other mechanisms considered so far – is that of setting *rules and norms*

(Brennan and Buchanan 1985; North 1990); when the stability/repetitiveness of activities allow it and the size of system makes it cost efficient.

A final important qualification is that not only the polar types of markets, hierarchies and groups are viable and efficient. A wide stream of recent research has shown that a variety of 'hybrid' forms may be superior to those polar forms in many circumstances. For example, inter-firm interdependencies may be regulated through complex associational and contractual agreements such as joint ventures, consortia, franchising and sub-contracting. These hybrids can handle a number of trade-offs among organizational design parameters, by better combining rights of ownership, reward, decision and control in different ways with respect to those contemplated in markets, hierarchies or groups.

Further reading

(References cited in the text marked *)

* Akerlof, G.A. (1970) 'The markets for "lemons": qualitative uncertainty and the market mechanism', *Quarterly Journal of Economics* 84 (August): 488–500. (Key economic treatment of the implications of information asymmetries for the establishment of forms of market assisted by other coordination mechanisms.)

* Alchian, A.A. and Demsetz, H. (1972) 'Production, information costs and economic organization', *American Economic Review* 62 (December): 777–95. (Analysis of the implication of 'team production' for the internationalization of economic activities under the 'classic firm' governance structure.)

* Arrow, K.J. (1951) *Social Choice and Individual Values*, New York: Wiley. (Standard work of reference by one of the leading authors in this field.)

* Bavelas, A. (1951) 'Communication patterns in task-oriented groups', in D. Lerner and H.K. Lasswell (eds), *The Policy Sciences*, Stanford, CA: Stanford University Press. (Early experimental studies on the comparative effectiveness of hierarchical and decentralized communication patterns in the processing of structured and unstructured information.)

* Brennan, G.H. and Buchanan, J.M. (1985) *The Reasons of Rules*, Cambridge: Cambridge University Press. (Economic treatment of the issue of assessment and choice of laws and embedding institutional rules in the coordination of economic activities.)

* Coase, R. (1937) 'The nature of the firm', *Economica* 4: 386–405. (An early work on this subject.)

* Coase, R. (1960) 'The problem of social cost', *Journal of Law and Economics* 3 (October): 1–44. (Standard reference article.)

* Douma, S. and Schreuder, H. (1992) *Economic Approaches to Organizations*, Englewood Cliffs, NJ: Prentice Hall. (Textbook presentation of the main perspectives in the economic analysis of organizations.)

* Fama, E. and Jensen, M. (1983a) 'Agency problems and residual claims', *Journal of Law and Economics* 26 (June): 327–49. (Looks at the implications of agency theory for the explanation of non-hierarchical forms of enterprise.)

* Fama, E. and Jensen, M. (1983b) 'Separation of ownership and control', *Journal of Law and Economics* 26 (June): 301–25. (Looks at the implications of agency theory for the explanation of non-hierarchical forms of enterprise.)

* Granovetter, M. (1985) 'Economic action and social structure: the problem of embeddedness', *American Journal of Sociology*, 89: 481–510. (Often-quoted article on the social embeddedness of all governance systems of economic activities in webs of interpersonal ties.)

* Grossman, S. and Hart, O. (1986) 'The costs and benefits of ownership: a theory of vertical and lateral integration', *Journal of Political Economy* 94: 691–719. (Game theoretic extension and mathematical modelling of the Coase–Williamson property rights theory.)

* Hart, O. and Moore, J. (1990) 'Property rights and the nature of the firm', *Journal of Political Economy* 98 (December): 1119–58. (Game theoretic extension and mathematical modelling of the Coase–Williamson property rights theory.)

* Hayek, F. von (1945) 'The use of knowledge in society', *American Economic Review* 35 (September): 519–30. (Article by a leading post-war writer and economic theorist.)

* Hirschman, A.O. (1970) *Exit, Voice and Loyalty: Responses to Decline in Firms, Organizations and States*, Cambridge, MA: Harvard University Press. (Standard reference on this subject.)

* Jensen, M.C. and Meckling, W.H. (1976) 'Theory of the firm: managerial behaviour, agency costs and ownership structure', *Journal of Financial Economics* 3: 305–60. (Core statement of agency theory and its implications for firm boundaries and ownership structure.)

* Karpik, L. (1989) 'L'économie de la qualité', *Revue Française de Sociologie* 30 (2): 187–210. (Analysis of market failures and the formation of a market assisted by social networks in the law firms sector by a prominent sociologist.)

* Levinthal, D. (1988) 'A survey of agency models of organization', *Journal of Economic Behaviour and Organization* 9: 153–85. (Standard reference article.)

* Lindblom, C. (1977) *Politics and Markets*, New York: Basic Books. (Comparative analysis of the properties of markets, authority systems and poliarchic systems by a prominent political scientist.)

* March, J.G. and Simon, H.A. (1958) *Organizations*, New York: Wiley. (Major reference work on this subject by two of the best known analysts of organizations.)

* Milgrom, P. and Roberts, J. (1992) *Economics Organization and Management*, Englewood Cliffs, NJ: Prentice Hall. (Standard reference text.)

* North, D.C. (1990) *Institutions, Institutional Change, and Economics Performance*, Cambridge: Cambridge University Press. (Historical analysis of the role of property rights and of embedding institutions in the evolution of the organization of economic activities.)

* Ouchi, W.G. (1980) 'Markets, bureaucracies and clans', *Administrative Science Quarterly* 25: 129–41. (Comparative analysis of the properties of markets, bureaucracies and cohesive socially controlled groups in dealing with uncertainty and conflict.)

* Perrow, C. (1967) 'A framework for comparative organizational analysis', *American Sociological Review* 32 (April): 194–208. (Early influential analysis of the implications of different kinds of uncertainty for organizational structuring.)

* Simon, H.A. (1945) *Administrative Behaviour*, New York: The Free Press. (Historical analysis of the role of property rights and of embedding institutions in the evolution of the organization of economic activities.)

* Simon, H.A. (1951) 'A formal theory of the employment relationship', *Econometrica* 19: 293–305. (A study of employment relationship theory, follows on from Simon (1945), above.)

* Williamson, O.E. (1975) *Markets and Hierarchies: Analysis and Antitrust Implications*, New York: The Free Press. (Core exposition of the market and hierarchies comparative assessment.)

* Williamson, O.E. (1981) 'The economics of organization: the transaction cost approach', *American Journal of Sociology* 87: 548–77. (Exploration of the effects of asset specificity and uncertainty on efficient organizational boundaries and the nature of contracts distinguished for technical and human assets.)

* Williamson, O.E. (1991) 'Comparative economic organizations: the analysis of discrete structural alternatives', *Administrative Science Quarterly* 36 (June): 269–96; and in S. Lindenberg and H. Schreuder (eds), (1993) *Interdisciplinary Perspectives on Organization Study*, Oxford: Pergamon, 3–37. (Extension of the comparative assessment of organization forms to 'hybrid' forms between market and hierarchy.)

Business systems

Richard Whitley

1 **Characteristics and varieties of business systems**
2 **Characteristics of firms in different business systems**
3 **The institutional structuring of business systems and firms**

Overview

Business systems are distinctive ways of organizing economic activities that develop interdependently with dominant institutions in market economies. They vary in the extent to which, and primary means by which, economic activities are authoritatively coordinated and controlled, especially through ownership and alliances. Six major kinds of business systems in twentieth-century capitalism can be identified in terms of these characteristics. These are dominated by different types of firms with distinctive governance characteristics and organizational capabilities. These differences arise from variations in processes of industrialization and in key institutions governing economic activities. Major institutions that affect the sorts of business systems and firms that become established are the cultural conventions that govern trust relations between exchange partners and authority relations, state structures and policies, the organization of the financial system and the norms governing the development and availability of different kinds of skills in labour markets. Changes in business systems occur interdependently with changes in these institutions as well as from the increasing interdependence of, and competition between, market economies.

1 Characteristics and varieties of business systems

Business systems constitute relatively cohesive and integrated systems of economic coordination and control that develop interdependently with dominant institutions in industrial capitalist societies and reflect differences in those institutions. The more cohesive and mutually reinforcing are those institutions in a society, the more integrated and homogeneous is the business system that becomes established there. For example, in post-war Japan, the interdependencies between the state bureaucracy, the dominant political party, large banks, business associations, the educational system and the organization of labour markets were so strong that a distinct 'society of industry' (Clark 1979) became established. This institutionalized particular patterns of firm behaviour and managerial practices which constrained and guided growing enterprises across industrial sectors to the extent that most successful firms have followed its distinctive logic.

Individual countries may develop one single, dominant and homogeneous business system, or a number of different kinds of economic organization which overlap in some, but differ in other, characteristics, depending on the cohesion, integration and stability of key institutions governing economic activities. Thus, states and business systems are not necessarily coterminous. However, since the nation-state itself is one of the critical institutional sectors for any market economy, and often plays a major role in determining the structure and operation of the financial system and the educational and training system, it is the primary unit of analysis for studying business systems, particularly where state boundaries overlap with those of distinctive cultural conventions and ethnic groups, as in Japan and South Korea (Whitley 1992a).

Business systems differ significantly in the extent to which, and dominant ways through which, organizational routines, hierarchies and institutionalized expectations coordinate economic decisions and actors in various market economies (Whitley 1999). They also vary in the ways that differently constituted groupings of social actors control economic activities and resources. The organization of ownership and control of private property rights, for instance, varies across capitalist societies such that controllers of financial assets have different kinds of connections to salaried managers and the authority structures they dominate. Additionally, managerial elites vary in their ties to particular organizations and in their relations with technical staff and other employees. Put simply, owners and controllers of capital, salaried managers, skilled manual and non-manual workers, and other employees are organized differently across varieties of capitalism. They also compete and cooperate with each other in contrasting ways. These differences mean that the nature of economic actors and their interrelations vary significantly across market economies.

Ownership, for example, can be exercised directly over economic activities and resources as in the owner managed firm, or may be delegated to trusted agents with varying degrees of interdependence and commitment. It may also integrate whole production chains through formal authority systems or be much

Table 1 Characteristics of business systems

A Ownership relations

1   Primary means of owner control (direct, alliance, market contracting)

2   Extent of ownership integration of production chains

3   Extent of ownership integration across sectors

B Non-ownership coordination

1   Extent of alliance coordination of production chains

2   Extent of collaboration between competitors

3   Extent of alliance coordination across sectors

C Employment relations and work management

1   Employer–employee interdependence

2   Delegation to, and trust of, employees (Taylorism, task performance discretion, task organization discretion)

more narrowly specialized. Similarly, interfirm relations within production chains can be dominated by *ad hoc*, one-off, anonymous and adversarial bargains, as in much pure market contracting, or by more repeated, particularistic and cooperative connections. Competitor relations may likewise be almost entirely adversarial and zero-sum, or may in contrast encompass collaboration over a number of issues such as R&D, training and union negotiations. Finally, employer–employee relations can vary considerably between the sort of adversarial zero-sum conflicts typical of early industrialization in many societies and the more institutionalized forms of cooperation represented by Germany's Co-Determination Acts, and large firm–core workers interdependencies in post-war Japan.

The general characterization of market economies in terms of the degree and mode of organizational integration of economic activities, together with differences in the nature of controlling groups, suggest eight key dimensions for comparing business systems. These are listed in Table 1. Three of these eight dimensions deal with variations in the organization of ownership relations and the role of ownership in coordinating activities. A further three concern other forms of organizational integration in which authority does not depend on unified ownership. The last two summarize major differences in employment relations and work organization which reflect both the extent of integration within enterprises and the organization of interest groups in the wider society.

Ownership coordination

Considering first relations between owners and controllers of private property rights and controllers of economic resources and activities, i.e. salaried managers, an important dimension for distinguishing between economies concerns the extent of owners' direct involvement in managing businesses. Three major types can be distinguished here: (1) *direct* control of firms by owners; (2) *alliance* control in which owners delegate considerable strategic decision making to managers but remain committed to particular firms; and (3) *market* or arms' length portfolio control. Owner managers of family businesses – whether artisanal elements of industrial districts or the massive Korean conglomerates (*chaebol*) – typify direct control. Bank and allied companies' ownership of some shares in Germany and Japan exemplify alliance control, while the Anglo-Saxon pattern of institutional portfolio investment demonstrates the market type of owner control.

The scope of ownership integration of economic activities also varies greatly across market economies. Two further dimensions for comparing ownership relations across business systems, then, concern: (1) the extent of *ownership integration of production chains* in a number of sectors; and (2) the degree of *ownership integration of activities across sectors*. The largest *chaebol* in Korea are both vertically and horizontally diversified, but the smaller ones tend to focus on vertical integration rather than unrelated diversification (Fields 1995). In contrast, many large German firms are also quite vertically integrated but limit their horizontal diversification to technologically and/or market related fields (Feldenkirchen 1997; Herrigel 1996). Chinese family businesses have been characterized as pursuing opportunistic diversification which is typically horizontal, although backward integration from retailing and distribution to manufacturing in light consumer goods industries is also quite a common pattern of development (Hamilton 1997; Redding 1990).

These three characteristics of ownership relations are often interrelated, in that alliance forms of owner control tend to inhibit unrelated diversification while market ones encourage it as a way of spreading risks that cannot easily be shared with business partners. Where owners become locked into the fates of particular firms they tend to develop expertise and knowledge about their technologies and markets in order to manage their greater exposure to risk and uncertainty. Diversification into unknown fields increases owners' risks and so is unlikely to be encouraged by them. Portfolio holders in capital markets, on the other hand, can usually sell their assets on liquid secondary markets if diversification fails and so are unlikely to oppose it strongly.

Non-ownership coordination

The integration of activities through alliances, obligations and similar non-ownership linkages applies to three sets of inter-firm relationships. First, there are those between members of a production chain, this can be termed the extent of *alliance coordination of production chains*. Second, there are those between competitors which can be characterized as the extent of *collaboration between competitors*. Third, there are alliances between firms in different industries that can be summarized as the extent of *alliance coordination across sectors*. In each case, the key contrast is between zero-sum, adversarial contracting and competition, on the one hand, and more cooperative, long-term and mutually committed relationships between partners and competitors, on the other hand.

Production chains, for example, may be quite fragmented in ownership terms, but exhibit strong networks of obligational contracting between relatively stable suppliers and customers – sometimes with limited exchanges of shares as in Japan. Similarly, competitors may compete fiercely for customers and yet collaborate over the introduction of new technologies, employment policies and state lobbying through various formal associations and alliances. They may also form production and profit pooling federations and interest groups as in some European countries.

Thirdly, firms may develop alliances across sectors, of varying stability, scope and depth, to enter new markets, reduce the risks of specialization or acquire new technologies. Occasionally these may involve long-term exchanges of equity, as in the Japanese intermarket groups (Gerlach 1992) but more commonly they take the form of subsidiary joint ventures and partnerships focused on fairly specific activities. Inter-sectoral business networks therefore differ considerably in (1) the range of activities they carry out jointly; (2) the extent and longevity of their collaboration; and (3) the variety of linkages between members, with the Japanese *kigyo shudan* at one extreme and short-term, opportunistic, narrowly based alliances at the other.

These variations in non-ownership forms of economic coordination and control are linked to differences in ownership relations. For example, direct owner control of managerial decisions will often limit the scope and depth of collaboration with competitors because of the strong sense of personal identity with the enterprise and reluctance to share information or control, especially in cultures where trust in formal institutions is low. Similarly, market forms of owner control are unlikely to encourage inter-firm alliances and cooperation since they are typically associated with capital market based financial systems that develop strong markets in corporate control and hence unstable owner–firm connections. Establishing long-term and wide-ranging alliances with business partners is riskier and more difficult in this situation than in economies where owners are more committed to the future of particular enterprises. Furthermore, since alliance and ownership based modes of coordination and control are functionally equivalent in many circumstances, the dominance of large, diversified firms tends to prevent the development of alliances within and across production chains.

Employment and work management

Considering, finally, employer–employee relations and work systems, these vary in a considerable number of ways, as the extensive literature on Fordism, labour processes and industrial relations shows. The key contrast here, though, is between those societies encouraging reliance on external labour markets in managing the bulk of the labour force and those encouraging more commitment and mutual investment in organizational capabilities. This can be summarized as the degree of *employer–employee interdependence*.

Organization based employment systems, such as those institutionalized in many large Japanese firms in the 1960s and 1970s, represent perhaps the greatest extent of mutual dependence between employers and the bulk of the workforce. The Anglo-Saxon pattern of 'flexible' external labour markets and high rates of employment change, on the other hand, represents the other extreme of this dimension. Intermediate employment systems combine greater mobility among manual workers than is common in large Japanese firms with considerable employer and employee investment in skill development and improvement and *de facto*, if not formally agreed, long-term commitments by both parties. The post-war German and some Scandinavian business systems perhaps come closest to this combination.

Patterns of work organization and control can be distinguished primarily in terms of the discretion and trust employers grant to the bulk of the workforce in organizing and carrying out tasks, summarized here as the degree of managerial *delegation to, and trust of, employees*. The pure case of 'scientific management' removes all discretion from manual workers and fragments tasks to simplify them for unskilled and easily replaced employees. 'Responsible autonomy' strategies, on the other hand, trust manual workers to carry out tasks with more discretion and independence from managers.

This autonomy, though, need not extend to questions of work organization and task definition. Few Japanese companies, for example, and even fewer Korean or Taiwanese ones, delegate the allocation and organization of jobs to manual workers, while being keen to involve them in problem solving activities and grant many workers considerable discretion over task performance. In many Danish, German and firms in some other European countries, on the other hand, employees have substantial influence on work organization decisions, both formally and informally, particularly skilled workers (Whitley and Kristensen 1997).

These eight dimensions are general characteristics of business systems that exhibit particular interdependencies with each other to form quite distinct ways of organizing market economies. For example, both direct and market forms of owner control tend to limit inter-firm cooperation within industries and between them because of the strong connections between ownership based coordination and authoritative control in the societies where these control types are highly institutionalized. Typically, control over economic activities is difficult to share between ownership units on a stable, long-term basis in such societies and so collaboration within production chains and sectors and across them is restricted.

Alliance forms of ownership, on the other hand, presume risk sharing and mutual dependence between owners/controllers of financial assets and enterprises, which implies the development of an institutional framework for coordinating inter-firm relations in a non zero-sum manner. Such a framework encourages other forms of inter-firm risk sharing within production chains and collaboration between competitors. Similarly, it can lead to greater employer–employee interdependence as investors, managerial elites and employees become locked into particular sectors and each others' destinies. Market based ownership relations, conversely, are associated with limited commitment between business partners. The existence of liquid external markets in labour and capital enable owners, managers and workers to exit easily from organizational ties.

Varieties of business systems

These and other interconnections suggest a limited number of combinations of business system characteristics are likely to remain established over historical periods because contradictions between them can be expected to generate conflicts between social groupings and prevalent institutional arrangements. In particular, business systems combining adversarial competitor relations with alliance forms of ownership and long-term employment commitments are unlikely to be reproduced over long periods because owners and employees who are locked into the fate of particular firms will attempt to control market risks. Similarly, business systems based on market types of ownership relations are unlikely to be supportive of long-term risk sharing between suppliers and customers or employers and employees because portfolio owners usually prefer liquidity to lock-in.

At least six major ideal types of business system can be identified as a result of these linkages (Whitley 1999). Initially, four types can be distinguished in terms of: (1) their degree of ownership based coordination of economic activities; and (2) the extent of non-ownership or alliance forms of organizational integration. First, those where both forms of coordination are low so that the overall level of coordination is quite limited. These can be termed *fragmented* business systems. Second, *coordinated industrial districts* combine relatively low levels of ownership integration – and so are dominated by small firms – with more extensive inter-firm integration and cooperation. Third, *compartmentalized* business systems are dominated by large firms but exhibit low levels of cooperation between firms and business partners. Finally, *coordinated* or *collaborative* business systems combine relatively large units of ownership coordination with extensive alliances and collaboration between them. These last two types of market economy can be further differentiated by owner control type, size of firm and extent of alliance integration between firms and within them to generate a further two kinds of business system: *state organized* and *highly coordinated*.

Fragmented business systems are dominated by small owner controlled firms which engage in adversarial competition with each other and short-term market contracting with suppliers and customers. Typically, employment relations are also short-term and dominated by 'efficient' external labour markets. Thus, organizational integration of economic activities is low both across and within units of financial control in these economies. Such low risk sharing by firms with business partners and with employees is often associated with relatively short-term commitments to particular technologies, skills or markets. In the case of Hong Kong, firms have been known to move rapidly from making plastic flowers, to wigs, to toy manufacturing and then property development and financial services as market conditions have altered, representing perhaps the most exemplary low commitment economy in recent decades.

Coordinated industrial district business systems, in contrast, exhibit more organized integration of inputs and outputs within production chains as well as more sectoral cooperation. Ownership units remain small and owner controlled, but rely more on worker commitment and, especially, on employees' willingness to improve task performance and innovation. As the title suggests, these kinds of economies are exemplified by the post-war Italian industrial districts and similar European regional business systems.

Where ownership integration of economic activities is greater, so that leading firms are quite large in terms of the activities controlled, considerable variations in non-ownership forms of economic coordination, types of owner control and extent of ownership integration are both theoretically feasible and empirically observable. In *compartmentalized* business systems large unified ownership units integrate activities both within production chains and across sectors. However, they exhibit little commitment or collaboration between firms or between employers and employees. Usually, owner control is exercised at arms' length through financial markets. Firms are here islands of authoritative control and order amidst market disorder, as in the stereotypical Anglo-Saxon economy.

State organized business systems are similarly dominated by large firms that integrate production chains and activities in different sectors through a unified administrative apparatus. However, they differ in their ownership patterns. Families and partners in these economies are typically able to retain direct control over large firms because the state supports their growth through subsidized credit. They are termed state organized because the state dominates economic development and guides firm behaviour. As post-war South Korea demonstrates, horizontal linkages between economic actors and employer–employee interdependence are limited in these business systems by strong ties of vertical dependence, both between firms and the state and within enterprises dominated by owner managers (Fields 1995; Janelli 1993; Kang 1997).

Collaborative business systems, on the other hand, manifest more collective organization and cooperation within sectors, but less ownership integration of activities in technologically and market unrelated sectors. Owner control of these large firms is typically alliance in nature and they tend to focus on particular industries rather than diversify across quite different ones. They develop a greater degree of employer–employee interdependence and trust of skilled workers than employers in compartmentalized and state organized business systems. Many continental European economies come close to this kind of economic system, especially the more corporatist kind.

Highly coordinated business systems also are dominated by alliance forms of owner control but exhibit even more organizational coordination of economic activities throughout the economy. This is achieved through extensive intra- and inter-sectoral alliances and networks coordinating a large variety of activities, as in post-war Japan's 'alliance capitalism' (Gerlach 1992). Within ownership units, employers in these business systems additionally integrate the bulk of the workforce into the organization to a greater extent than in other kinds of market economy and so employer–employee interdependence is typically very high here.

2 Characteristics of firms in different business systems

These variations in the ownership coordination of economic activities across market economies highlight the significant differences in dominant firm types and behaviour in different forms of capitalism. How firms are constituted as ownership-based units of decision making and control, and in whose interests they are managed, vary considerably between business systems in ways that have significant consequences for economic coordination and competition. Two sets of characteristics are particularly important. First, there are those dealing with the nature of the groups controlling dominant firms and their interests. The relative importance of owners, managers, different kinds of employees, business partners and other groups in deciding on dominant firms' objectives varies greatly between market economies and significantly affects their behaviour. These characteristics can be summarized as those dealing with 'governance' issues. At least four distinct governance characteristics of firms arise from variations in the roles of owners, employees and business partners in deciding on firm policies and actions, and in the nature of dominant performance standards and goals.

Second, firms also differ in the nature of the organizational capabilities they develop and coordinate, as well as in the sorts of strategies they pursue with these capabilities. Capabilities are sets of organizationally specific experiences, knowledge and expertise that confer competitive advantages in carrying out particular economic activities, what are sometimes referred to as firms' competencies (Foss and Knudsen 1996). At least three distinct aspects of firms' capabilities and strategies can be identified that vary considerably between institutional contexts. These concern the role of workforce skills, the development of collective competencies concerned with efficiency or with innovation, and the extent of flexibility and responsiveness to customer demands.

Governance characteristics

The direction and management of firms can be analysed in terms of the relative influence of different economic interest groups and their dominant objectives. Considering initially the role of owners, this varies according to the concentration of ownership and how directly beneficial ownership is related to the control of financial assets. Four varieties of owner constraints on managerial actions can be distinguished. First, direct owner control implies highly concentrated ownership and managerial subservience to owner directors. Second, alliance owner control implies more segmented ownership with business partners, banks and other organizations having long-term shareholdings, typically combined with other forms of business cooperation such as credit provision. Here, top managers have some autonomy but are quite constrained by these commitments. Third, market forms of owner control grant managers more formal autonomy from owners because beneficial owners are usually fragmented and operate more as portfolio holders than controllers. However, nominee control over financial assets by fund managers and banks may be more concentrated than beneficial ownership and this can lead to strong capital market constraints upon managers' actions in liquid capital markets (Lazonick and O'Sullivan 1996). Finally, fragmented ownership of shares by individuals may be combined with relatively low levels of concentration of nominee shareholdings and/or regulatory constraints on the market for corporate control. This enables managers to exercise considerable autonomy over firms' strategies.

The second major aspect of governance relations to be considered here concerns the broad influence of employees' interests on firms' actions and priorities. This characteristic combines the general significance of employee interests for decision making and priorities, on the one hand, with the scope of those interests, on the other hand. In many companies in the USA (Lazonick and West 1998), white-collar employees are considered to be part of the firm in a way that manual workers are not, and are treated differently as a result. Their broad interests may be seen as consonant with the firms', and so be taken more notice of, than those of less educated and less committed manual employees. In such firms managerial integration is greater than organizational integration. For the purposes of comparing the general level of influence of different groups and interests on firm behaviour, the significance and scope of employee interests can be integrated into a single characteristic of the extent to which top managers are constrained by the interests and concerns of employees as a whole in determining firms' objectives, strategies and performance standards.

A high level of such constraint means that most employees are considered to be members of the enterprise with distinct rights and interests that have to be respected in making decisions. Whether these are formally enshrined in legislation such as the German Works Constitutions Acts is less important than managers' recognition that the firm depends greatly on the skills and commitment of its staff for its success and that developing these constitutes an important part of its performance. A medium degree signifies that such interests are restricted to managerial and technical employees, while a low degree implies that all employees below top management are regarded as disposable and readily traded resources which are unimportant for the strategic development of the business.

The third important characteristic of firms' governance structures to be considered here arises from the earlier distinction between firms as ownership based units of economic coordination and control and broader units of authoritative coordination, such as networks and alliances. As this point highlights, firms vary dramatically across market economies in the extent to which they share control and risks with other companies and agencies. The highly networked economy of post-war Japan is commonly contrasted with the USA in this respect, but other societies also manifest considerable differences in the scope, intensity and stability of cross-firm alliances and federations. Such authority sharing has major implications for the determination of firms' goals and strategies, as well as for the nature of their priorities and performance standards. This dimension can be termed the extent to which managers are constrained by the interests of business partners.

These characteristics of the governance structures of firms affect the sorts of dominant objectives pursued by the controllers of firms, and the criteria by which they judge success. Direct owner control can lead to a variety of dominant objectives being pursued depending on the context. Although many family owned and controlled businesses may seek growth as the means of achieving family wealth and social standing, others may limit it because of a reluctance to share control. Owner managers may concentrate on sectors where personal capital commitments are limited and direct personal control can be maintained. In Belgium, for example, differences between regions in state policies and patterns of owner control have encouraged the growth of low capital intensity industries in Flanders and more capital intensive ones in Wallonia (Iterson 1996).

In addition to growth, broadly understood, and profitability goals, some firms seek to develop strong reputations for technical excellence and the development of new knowledge and skills. While this is especially important for 'artisanal' type firms in the industrial districts of Italy, Jutland and elsewhere, it is also a feature of many firms in highly innovative industries. The need to make profits is of course a constraint in such firms, but often this is subordinated to the search for technical excellence and innovative success. Together with the different combinations of profitability and growth outlined above, this suggests four major kinds of dominant goals and performance standards pursued by firms can be usually distinguished: first, the pursuit of personal and family wealth accumulation; second, high returns to portfolio managers and shareholders; third, growth in assets, turnover and markets; fourth, increasing technical excellence and reputation. In practice of course, these are usually combined, but one tends to dominate as a result of different interest groups' control over firms' strategic priorities and the nature of the broader institutional environment.

Characteristics of firms' capabilities and strategies

Turning now to consider how firms vary across market economies in terms of the kinds of competitive capabilities they develop and how they do so, a crucial characteristic stems from their role as employers. Through employment agreements firms are able to develop idiosyncratic and flexible collective competencies by organizing people in a variety of ways to undertake a range of tasks. Authority based on labour market relationships enables managers to coordinate economic activities in more flexible ways than contractual arrangements do, and so in principle improves their ability to deal with productive and market uncertainties.

This characteristic of firms has two aspects. First, the extent to which they develop particular kinds of competencies as integrated administrative structures, in contrast to functioning as loosely coupled collections of individuals or small groups coordinated in quasi-contractual ways. The so-called 'virtual' firm which subcontracts almost all its operations to separate organizations represents an extreme instance of such loose coupling, while highly integrated Chandlerian and post-war Japanese firms represent the other end of this sub-dimension. The second aspect concerns the degree of involvement of employees in the organization and their contribution to the development and enhancement of its capabilities. It reflects both their skills and their inclusion as members of the firm. Together these aspects can be summarized as the contribution of employees to the development and improvement of organizational capabilities.

The next two characteristics of firms' capabilities concern the sorts of competitive advantages they concentrate on generating. We can distinguish between firms that focus on competing within existing industry 'rules of the game' from those that attempt to develop innovative capabilities for changing them. The former pursue essentially adaptive strategies aimed at reducing costs and/or improving quality incrementally, while the latter try to generate new knowledge and ways of doing things that result in radical innovations.

These more 'entrepreneurial' strategies concentrate on achieving strategic advantages by being continuously innovative in terms of products, processes and organizational abilities. They seek to destabilize current industry practices and competitive patterns by developing new ways of making products or delivering services, introducing new goods and services, and responding flexibly and quickly to customer demands on a continuing basis. Such firms focus on reducing process times and product development times in addition to the throughput times given priority by 'Fordist' firms. This reshaping of technologies and markets can be achieved as much through continuous improvement of existing competencies as by the development of different kinds of knowledge, but both capabilities are concerned to dominate markets by innovation rather than by price or incremental improvements in quality. This characteristic can be summarized as the extent to which firms develop innovative capabilities.

The third characteristic of organizational capabilities deals with the ability of firms to adapt quickly to changes in market demand and respond to customers' needs. As Storper and Salais (1997), among others, have emphasized, producers vary greatly in their differentiation of outputs to suit particular kinds of demand. On the one hand, the classic Fordist strategy produces highly standardized products for all customers, while in contrast artisanal producers make highly individual goods. This capacity of firms can be termed their responsiveness to changing demands and ability to produce differentiated outputs.

These characteristics of organizational capabilities are connected in particular ways to the dimensions of firm governance outlined above. Where firms rely extensively on the contribution of the bulk of their employees to the development of distinct organizational capabilities, they will obviously tend to pay more attention to their interests and concerns than if they pursue Fordist employment policies. Growth and technical excellence goals will likewise be given greater priority by such firms than portfolio returns. Similarly, highly innovative firms will pursue technical excellence and growth goals at the expense of short-term profitability as they invest resources for long-term dominance. Often relying heavily on the commitment and flexibility of employees, managers in these firms are quite constrained by their interests. The risks involved in this kind of strategy are unlikely to appeal to portfolio investors whose performance is evaluated every quarter and so firms subject to strong capital market constraints are less likely to develop such capabilities than those in other situations.

On the other hand, firms pursuing efficiency and adaptive strategies will typically not feel constrained by employee interests, and probably not develop strong interdependencies with business partners. Market domination through producing large volumes of standardized goods at relatively low prices is the dominant objective for these firms and this usually encourages adversarial, cost-based relationships with suppliers and limited cooperation with competitors. Flexibility and responsiveness, of course, are not associated with such firms.

3 The institutional structuring of business systems and firms

These characteristics of business systems reflect the nature of key institutions governing economic activities in different market economies (Whitley 1999). They include the set of cultural conventions regulating exchange relations between economic actors and those generating commitment and acceptance of particular superior–subordinate relations. These institutions can be summarized as the dominant norms governing trust relations and authority relations. Where these conventions differ between societies, the nature of economic actors, the organization of market relations, and the dominant pattern of work organization and control also vary.

For example, societies where trust is highly dependent on personal knowledge are unlikely to develop highly formal means of contracting or to rely greatly upon the legal system for settling disputes. Their economies are also unlikely to be dominated by firms which rely extensively on formal procedures for organizing and controlling work activities. Similarly, the prevailing pattern of authority relations and means of justifying subordination in a society structure the sorts of managerial authority that develop in firms, so that attempts to institutionalize 'deviant' forms of authority which contradict the dominant rules legitimating political authority are unlikely to succeed.

Additionally, market economies organize the generation of skills and other resources in a variety of ways as well as the means by which, and conditions under which, economic actors gain control over human and material resources. These variations affect the sorts of firms that become established and how they organize economic activities through, for example, structuring risks and encouraging certain combinations of resources at the expense of others. The key institutional sectors here are: the state, the financial system and the labour system. They govern the ways in which private economic interests are able to obtain, and control the use of, economic resources.

Two critical features of the state in market economies are: (1) the extent to which the state is cohesive and dominates the allocation of key resources so that private firms are highly dependent on it; and (2) the extent to which the political executive and the bureaucracy are committed to economic development and the state is willing to share economic risks with private economic actors. The greater is business dependence on the state, the more firms will concentrate on managing political risks and ensure that their activities do not deviate greatly from state policies. This encourages a centralization of strategic decision making within firms as top managers develop plans interdependently with state agencies.

State risk sharing is often associated with a strong state but need not always be so. It is possible, for example, for a strong, cohesive state controlling resource allocation to exist without it being committed to helping the private sector develop efficiently, or to sharing capital investment risks with private firms. Equally, states can perform a coordinating role which includes some risk sharing without necessarily dominating the economy or firms being highly dependent on it, as is arguably the case for post-war Japan (Whitley 1992a). In general, state involvement in coordinating plans and sharing risks with private economic actors means that firms do not have to manage uncertainty on their own and can take a longer term view of resources and markets than if they were forced to be self-sufficient. Thus, unrelated diversification as a way of hedging against risks and a reluctance to invest in large scale production facilities are less likely in economies where the state does become involved in risk sharing.

The ability of the state to coordinate and influence firms' decisions and industrial development is closely connected to the nature and functioning of the financial system in market economies. As Zysman (1983) has suggested, it is much easier for state agencies to direct investment and channel resources into export industries and particular sectors in credit-based financial systems than in capital market ones. In the former, firms raise funds primarily from banks and other financial intermediaries which are often dependent on the central bank to rediscount their loans, especially if interest rates are deliberately subsidized to direct investments to specific purposes. Where capital markets are more important in the financial system, on the other hand, the cost of capital is set more by market competition. In credit-based systems liquidity is often low because the secondary market in financial assets is weak. As a result, banks and firms become interdependent and 'locked in' to each others' destinies. Risk sharing and close links between them are thus more common than in capital market financial systems where shareholders can buy and sell shares much more easily. Furthermore, since banks are more dependent on their major clients' success and have to evaluate loans very carefully in credit-based systems, they develop considerable expertise in particular industries and knowledge of firms' businesses. This enables them to offer a range of services which, again, ensures their commitment to borrowers' growth and expansion. Banks in capital market systems, on the other hand, are more remote from borrowers and prefer to treat assets as components of portfolios to be bought and sold on short-term considerations.

The development and certification of skills and the organization of labour markets are important parts of the labour system which have strong consequences for work organization and employment practices (Lane 1989). Two major components here are: (1) the education and training system and (2) the strength and structure of the trades unions and similar occupational associations, including the importance of publicly standardized, certified skills. Dual systems of education and training in which practical skills are taught in school and colleges, have relatively high prestige and are jointly controlled and assessed by employers, unions and training institutions, produce a range of broadly based competencies which integrate theory and practice and are widely accepted by firms. Unitary systems, in contrast, progressively filter children through a hierarchy of academic examinations that have little connection with practical skills or with employers. Training is here largely left to employers and practical skills are devalued relative to the publicly attested and highly selected achievements in the academic system. Dual education and training systems thus generate relatively broad and flexible practical skills which employers can rely upon in organizing and controlling their workflow, as a result jobs are often broadly specified and task autonomy can be considerable. The relative prestige of practical skills and qualifications in these systems also encourages supervisors and managers to acquire them in addition to more academic credentials, thus integrating manual and non-manual expertise and formal authority with technical superiority.

Table 2 Institutional influences on business systems

A	*Cultural system*

Norms governing:

1   Trust relations

2   Authority relations

B	*Political system*

1   State integration and autonomy

2   State commitment to economic development and risk sharing with private enterprises

C	*Financial system*

1   Capital market or credit-based financial system

D	*Labour system*

1   Dual or unitary education and training system

2   Power and structure of trade unions and occupational associations

3   Formal regulation of labour markets

The overall strength of trades unions and similar representative organizations has considerable importance for employment policies and the exercise of authority. It obviously affects supervisor discretion and the ability of managers to treat labour as a short-term cost. When strong trades unions are additionally organized around specialist skills, which they partially or totally control, then the division of labour and dominant pattern of work organization become greatly influenced by their definitions of skills and have to adapt to them rather than the reverse. Work autonomy tends to be high in these circumstances and coordination is often achieved more through informal cooperation than through formal hierarchies, as appears to be the case in Denmark (Kristensen in Whitley, 1992b: 117–36). Relatedly, strong white collar professional associations and occupational identities based on publicly certified skills structure work organizations so that jobs become tied to particular specialist competencies and can be difficult to integrate cohesively, except in a formal sense.

These general features of institutions, summarized in Table 2, together help to explain significant differences between business systems. Additionally, where they are similar across market economies as in the case of the capital market based financial systems of the UK and USA, they lead to common characteristics of firms and markets. The institutional interdependence of business systems means that not only do their characteristics follow the dominant logic of the environment in which they become established but any major changes in these are also constrained and guided by dominant institutions. Significant alterations to the nature of economic actors in an economy, for example, are unlikely without related changes in the financial and political systems. Where, then, institutional inertia is high, it is unlikely that major changes to business systems will occur, especially in the characteristics most closely connected to central institutions in the society. Correlatively, when institutional change does take place, as in Germany and Japan after their defeat in the Second World War, it is likely to have significant effects on the dominant form of economic organization.

Two other major sources of change in business system characteristics are internal conflicts and contradictions between component parts, and external influences and competition. Although business systems are relatively cohesive configurations of particular characteristics of firms and markets that become established in different economies, the degree to which their features are mutually reinforcing and coherent does, of course, vary and different firms and sectors do develop alternative ways of organizing economic activities as they compete and cooperate over time. Also, ways of dealing with issues in one aspect of firms' operations, such as the management of financial risks, may conflict with common practices in other areas, such as employment policies and ways of managing employees when introducing technological changes. These alternatives and conflicting pressures can lead to significant changes in associated institutions over time resulting in the development of new forms of economic coordination and control developing, especially in areas which do not threaten central institutions and in economies where institutional sectors are not highly integrated and interdependent, such as the Anglo-Saxon ones.

Similarly, growing international interdependence and competition have both diffused alternative patterns of economic organization across market economies and intensified the direct comparison and contrast of business systems and institutional arrangements. Thus, the relative performance of firms, markets and institutions has become easier to assess internationally and different kinds of market economies increasingly compete as alternative ways of structuring economic activities. As a result, business system characteristics in some societies are changing, particularly those connected to relatively weak institutions – such as those controlling the allocation of labour in deregulated states – but these changes remain piecemeal and limited as long as dominant institutions do not alter significantly. Where institutions are highly integrated and mutually reinforcing, though, such international interdependence is unlikely to have a major impact on business system characteristics and, indeed, the dominant pattern of economic organization is more likely to structure the way in which internationalization occurs and to limit its effects, as seems to be the case in Japan.

Further reading

(References cited in the text marked *)

* Clark, R. (1979) *The Japanese Company*, New Haven: Yale University Press. (A good synthesis of research on Japanese firms and a useful case study of one company.)
* Feldenkirchen, W. (1997) 'Business groups in the German electrical industry', in T. Shiba and M. Shimotani (eds), *Beyond the Firm*, Oxford: Oxford University Press. (A useful summary account of the development of Siemens and AEG and their alliances.)

* Fields, K.J. (1995) *Enterprise and the State in Korea and Taiwan*, Ithaca, NY: Cornell University Press. (A comparison of the role of the state and business development in South Korea and Taiwan.)

* Foss, N.J. and C. Knudsen (eds) (1996) *Towards a Competence Theory of the Firm*, London: Routledge. (A good collection of papers on this approach to the theory of the firm.)

  Gerlach, M. (1992) *Alliance Capitalism: The Social Organization of Japanese Business*, Berkeley, CA: University of California Press. (An important empirical study of linkages between Japanese firms since the war.)

* Hamilton, G. (1997) 'Organization and market processes in Taiwan's capitalist economy', in Marco Orru, N. Biggart and G. Hamilton, *The Economic Organization of East Asian Capitalism*, Thousand Oaks: Sage. (A useful account of the nature of firms and markets in post-war Taiwan.)

* Herrigel, Gary (1996) *Industrial Constructions: The Sources of German Industrial Power*, Cambridge: Cambridge University Press. (An important historical account of the development of German firms and their interconnections as distinct industrial orders.)

* Iterson, Ad van (1996) 'Institutions and types of firm in Belgium: regional and sector variations', in R. Whitley and P.H. Kristensen (eds), *The Changing European Firm*, London: Routledge. (A useful comparison of firm types in different regions of Belgium.)

* Janelli, R.L. (1993) *Making Capitalism: the Social and Cultural Construction of a South Korean Conglomerate*, Stanford: Stanford University Press. (An ethnographic study of a major *chaebol*.)

* Kang, Chul-Kyu (1997) 'Diversification process and the ownership structure of Samsung Chaebol', in T. Shiba and M. Shimotani (eds), *Beyond the Firm*, Oxford: Oxford University Press. (A study of the development of Samsung and its ownership pattern in comparison with the Japanese *zaibatsu* and other groups.)

* Lane, C. (1989) *Management and Labour in Europe*, Aldershot: Edward Elgar. (A useful synthesis of research on firms and the management of labour in Britain, France and Germany.)

* Lazonick, W. and O'Sullivan, M. (1996) 'Organization, finance and international competition', *Industrial and Corporate Change* 5: 1–49. (An historical account of the changing relationships between investors and firms in the USA in the twentieth century.)

* Lazonick, W. and West, J (1998) 'Organizational integration and competitive advantage', in G. Dosi, D.J. Teece and J. Chytry (eds), *Technology, Organization and Competitiveness*, Oxford: Oxford University Press. (An analysis of variations in the degree and mode of organizational integration of economic activities and their effects on competitiveness.)

* Redding, S.G. (1990) *The Spirit of Chinese Capitalism*, Berlin: de Gruyter. (One of the few detailed studies of Chinese family businesses linking their structure and strategy to Chinese culture and the institutional environment.)

* Storper, M. and R. Salais (1997) *Worlds Of Production: The Action Frameworks of the Economy*, Cambridge, MA: Harvard University Press. (A significant attempt to analyse differences in economic organization across sectors in terms of the standardization of product qualities and inputs.)

* Whitley, R. (1992a) *Business Systems in East Asia: Firms, Markets and Societies*, London: Sage. (A comparative analysis of firms and markets in Japan, South Korea, Taiwan and Hong Kong which explains their differences in terms of variations in dominant institutions.)

* Whitley, R. (ed.) (1992b) *European Business Systems: Firms and Markets in their National Contexts*, London: Sage. (A collective volume of studies of national business systems in Europe, focusing on institutional influences on characteristics of firms and markets.)

* Whitley, R. (1999) *Divergent Capitalisms: The Social Structuring and Change of Business Systems*, Oxford: Oxford University Press. (A systematic outline of the comparative business systems framework and its application to Asian and European societies.)

Whitley, R. and Kristensen, P.H. (eds) (1996) *The Changing European Firm: Limits to Convergence*, London: Routledge. (A collection of papers analysing major differences in the nature of dominant firms in European economies.)

* Whitley, R. and Kristensen, P.H. (eds) (1997) *Governance at Work: The Social Regulation of Economic Relations*, Oxford: Oxford University Press. (A collective volume showing how institutional and historical factors have affected the organization and control of work in different societies.)

* Zysman, J. (1983) *Governments, Markets and Growth: Financial Systems and the Politics of Industrial Change*, Ithaca: Cornell University Press. (The classic study of financial systems in advanced market economies, and their relations to the state and firms.)

Organizational populations

Rolf Ziegler

Overview

The study of organizational populations is inspired by evolutionary and ecological thinking (Aldrich 1999). It considers the dynamic processes affecting the development of organizational populations over extended periods of time and, in contrast to the prevailing adaptive perspective, focuses on selection as the main mechanism of change. Organizational theory has long been preoccupied with the adaptation of single organizations to their environments (Aldrich 1979; Pfeffer and Salancik 1978). In their seminal paper, Hannan and Freeman (1977) shifted the level of analysis to populations of organizations and suggested selection instead of adaptation to play a major role in shaping the development and composition of organizational communities. The role of structural inertia of organizations is stressed, that is, strong limitations on organizational flexibility and speed of response to changing opportunities and constraints in the environment are assumed. The driving force of global change is postulated to be selection – the excess of births over deaths of organizations that possess certain relatively fixed strategies. Selection in organizational ecology is mainly based on differential advantage among organizational forms in competition for scarce resources. In studying the dynamics of processes that influence vital rates of entries and exits, the full histories of populations of organizations are covered.

The observed diversity of organizational forms and populations is postulated to be the outcome of variation, selection and retention. These evolutionary and ecological processes involve analysis at several levels of complexity. The first level concerns the demography of organizations. It considers variations in vital rates and life-cycle processes across individual organizations and tries to relate these variations to changes in environments. The second level deals with the population ecology of organizations. It analyses population growth and decline as the dynamic outcome of localized sets of populations occupying partially overlapping niches. The third level refers to the community ecology of organizations. A community of organizations, sometimes referred to as an organizational field, is a set of interacting populations, linked by ties of competition, commensalism and symbiosis, like an industrial setting composed of populations of firms, populations of labour unions and employers associations and populations of regulatory agencies. Studies at this level focus on the evolution of patterns of interaction among these populations and the emergence and disappearance of organizational forms. So far most attention has been devoted to demographic and ecological processes, while studies at the community level have been rare.

1 Basic conceptual framework

An *organizational population* is defined as a set of organizations of the same organizational form within a bounded system. They have a unitary character due to their common dependence on the material and social environment. There are several theoretical approaches to define *organizational forms*. One approach looks for an analogue to the genetic structure that reproduces a biological species. Organizational forms are conceptualized as 'blueprints' (like the DNA molecules) for building organizations and conducting collective action. McKelvey (1982: 195ff) defines organizational species as 'a set of highly probable combinations of dominant competence elements that are temporarily housed at any given time among the members of an organizational population'. The disadvantage of this approach is that blueprints for organizational action (or 'Comps' as McKelvey calls them) are not directly observable. Hannan and Freeman (1977; 1989) suggest that they should be inferred from formal structure, repetitive patterns of activity and the normative order. However, these observable features sometimes overlap considerably among organizations with different blueprints. There is also no analogue to the process of biological reproduction in which genetic material is passed from parent to offspring in a single event. There exists neither a clear-cut parent–offspring relation defining species as common lines of descent nor an analogue to 'reproductive isolation' of biological species, for example by the boundaries of 'cross-breeding'.

Another possibility of defining organizational forms is based on the notion of structural or (more generally) regular equivalence. The idea is to obtain data on flows of resources among organizations, like input–output matrices, and to identify structurally equivalent sets of organizations, that is, sets of organizations which are similarly dependent on each other, by using block-modelling techniques.

These approaches emphasizing content and pair-wise relations have been supplemented by others that look at the dynamics of boundaries in organizational space (Hannan and Freeman 1989). Boundaries are created and eroded by technological factors, transaction costs, closure of social networks, mobility of persons, and processes of institutionalization. An organizational form is institutionalized to the extent that it is considered to be a taken-for-granted solution to problems of collective action and that other powerful actors in the system endorse its claims in disputes. For example, after a long historical struggle unions have finally become the institutionalized organizational form of workers' representation, while political parties are now increasingly being challenged by social movements as the taken-for-granted organizational form for representing citizens' interests. According to this definition an organizational form is an abstract code-like specification of organizational identities. If an organization violates these persisting cultural rules to which it is expected to conform, then the valuation of the organization by outsiders drops sharply (Carroll and Hannan 2000).

Empirical research has relied on a very pragmatic approach. 'Native' classifications, usually based on similarity of products and services supplied, have been used in operationalizing the concept of organizational form and organizational population: banks and credit unions, newspapers, breweries, wineries, telephone companies, semi-conductor and microcomputer manufacturers, automobile industries, railroad companies, airlines, restaurants, hotels, labour unions, trade associations, religious denominations, bar associations, mutual benefit life insurance societies, voluntary associations, consumer cooperatives, day care centres, social movement organizations, etc. have been studied at local, regional or national levels (Carroll 1988; Singh 1990; Baum 1996; Carroll and Hannan 2000). Of course, the main reason for this inductive approach has been availability of data, but from a theoretical point of view it may also be argued that these 'native' classifications based on conventional wisdom influence the behaviour of relevant actors.

A fundamental concept in organizational ecology is the notion of an *organizational niche*. It is defined as the set of environmental conditions within which a population can grow or at least sustain its numbers, that is, where its growth rate (defined as the difference between the birth and death rates) can be non-negative. The classical competition theory of population bioecology assumes both birth and death rates to be linearly dependent on population size. These assumptions result in the well-known model of logistic population growth. The steady state of the population is called the carrying capacity of the environment for the population in question. If two (or more) populations interact, that is, if their niches overlap, the size of each population influences the carrying capacity of the other as postulated in the famous Lotka–Volterra model. If both populations compete, this influence is mutually negative, that is, growth of one population lowers the carrying capacity of the other and vice versa. The relationship is called commensalistic or symbiotic if the influence is mutually positive, that is, if the growth of one population stimulates growth of the other and vice versa. The predator–prey case has one positive and one negative link. This kind of pattern is found, for example, among craft and industrial unionism. Growth of the population of craft unions stimulated the founding rate of industrial unions, while the spread of industrial unions decreased the founding rate of craft unionism.

Although some efforts have been made to measure central aspects of organizational niches directly – like carrying capacity or niche overlap – a more indirect strategy is usually followed. As will be shown below, additional assumptions about specific properties of organizational niches are formulated, from which testable hypotheses are then derived.

As already noted, *structural inertia* is a central factor in explaining the dynamics of organizational populations. In contrast to the adaptive perspective that stresses flexibility and innovativeness of individual organizations, it is argued that structural inertia due to internal and external constraints gives a selective advantage. Pressures towards inertia arise especially from several internal factors.

Asset specificity and sunk costs constrain adaptation; the organization's invest-ment in plants, equipment and specialized personnel make these assets less eas-ily transferable. Altering structures always implies a shift of resources that challenges vested interests and upsets internal political coalitions. Established organizational routines become 'legitimate' in at least two ways: they are taken for granted, precluding serious consideration of other alternatives, and they are normatively justified beyond self-interest as the 'natural' way to do things. Un-der high environmental uncertainty 'bounded rationality' (limits on informa-tional and decisional capabilities) favours incremental instead of radical change. As individuals tend to give greater weight to potential losses than to equally large gains, and since losses from giving up established routines are subjectively more certain than gains recovered from new strategies, opposition against change is usually stronger than a push for reorganization.

External factors also contribute to structural inertia, sometimes paralleling in-ternal constraints. Specialization of boundary spanning units limits the range of information available about the environment. Barriers to entry into and exit from realms of activity, as well as legitimacy constraints, often restrict the breadth of organizational activities and structural variations too. For example, in many countries only pharmacies, not general drugstores, are permitted to prepare and dispense drugs and medicines. There are of course many other examples of state-licensed monopolies.

To claim that organizations are subject to strong inertial forces is not the same as claiming that organizations never change. Therefore structural inertia must be defined in relative and dynamic terms (Hannan and Freeman 1984; 1989). Orga-nizations are characterized by *relative* inertia in structure, that is, the typical rates of organizational change are much lower than the rate at which environmental conditions change.

Why do structurally inert organizations have a selective advantage? Because they are more reliable and accountable. Compared with other types of social col-lectivities (inert) organizations are capable of generating collective action and producing results with relatively small variance in quality: higher reliability. Or-ganizations have a second property that gives them an advantage in the modern world, where general norms of procedural rationality are widespread. As institu-tional theories of organization have pointed out, they are able to account 'ratio-nally' for their actions. This does not necessarily mean that they are telling the truth, but they are able to produce internally consistent reports about the se-quence of decisions made and action taken, and to demonstrate that appropriate rules and procedures have been applied. It is postulated that selection in modern societies favours organizational forms with high reliability of performance and high levels of accountability. However, reliability and accountability require that an organization continually reproduces its structure. Yet the very factors that lead to high reproducibility – standardized routines and institutionalization – make the system resistant to change, that is, structurally inert.

2 Vital processes

In human demography birth and death (besides migration) are the two fundamental processes determining population growth and decline. In organizational
demography there are multiple types of entry events: foundings, mergers,
spin-offs, takeovers, or entering, *de alio*, from another population or industry,
and of ending events: disbandings, exits to another industry, mergers or acquisitions (Hannan and Carroll 1992; Singh 1990; Baum 1996; Carroll and Hannan
2000). Research has concentrated on the processes of founding and disbanding.
However, there is a crucial difference. While 'mortality' can meaningfully be
studied both at the organizational and at the population level, it is obvious that
existing organizations can 'die' only. There is no analogue to the 'naturally'
defined risk-set of women of childbearing age. (Should all gainfully employed
people or even all adults be included in the risk-set of 'potential founders';
should all organizations form another risk-set of 'potential parents' liable to set
up subsidiaries, joint ventures or spin-offs?) Therefore variations in the *rate of
founding* are exclusively modelled at the population level. Five groups of factors
affecting founding activity are mentioned most often in the literature:

1 type and amount of resources required to set up an organization;
2 availability of these start-up resources;
3 prior failures and foundings;
4 institutional rules;
5 facilitating conditions.

Simplicity, smallness, short periods of gestation and widely disseminated
knowledge reduce the costs of organizing and increase founding rates. Relevant
knowledge of how to set up and operate an organization may even be codified,
like franchised restaurants. The amount of resources that could potentially be
mobilized and the degree to which they are fixed to other social units are relevant: the size of capital and labour markets, the number of potential suppliers and
consumers, but also barriers to the free flow of resources, like contracts prohibit-
ing employees to start a business in the same industry after leaving their
employer. Social changes that destroy monopolies over resources speed up the
founding process; especially in periods of social revolution and political crises
resources are freed, increasing the amount and diversity of new organizational
forms. Previous patterns of organizational founding and failure in a population
can influence current rates of foundings. A curvilinear relationship is predicted
as, initially, prior foundings signal a fertile niche to potential entrepreneurs. But
as foundings increase further they indicate stronger competition, discouraging
potential founders. Failures, at first, increase the likelihood of foundings as they
release resources that can be reassembled, but further failures signal a hostile
environment to potential founders.

Concentration of institutional control and degree of licensing is another important factor influencing both barriers to entry and the length of the start-up
phase. Strategic organizational forms reducing transaction costs (stock markets),

spreading risks (venture capital firms) or facilitating the creation and dissemination of new technologies (research and technology parks) may have important multiplier effects on founding rates.

Some of the factors mentioned influence *mortality rates* as well. However, the most systematically studied determinants of the chances of survival are size and ageing. Larger organizations have lower death rates irrespective of how size is measured: by number of employees, total assets, volume of sales, etc. While 'liability of smallness' is a fairly stable empirical phenomenon, the pattern of age dependence in failure rates is somewhat more intricate. In general it is true that organizations face a 'liability of newness': new organizations fail at higher rates than old ones because it takes time to create roles and routines, to socialize new participants, to establish and stabilize external relations and to build up trust among members and with clients who are strangers. At a closer look the relationship with age turns out to be non-monotonic with an inverted U-shape. Immediately after founding the mortality rate is low, rising quickly to a maximum and declining continuously afterwards. This pattern has been labelled 'liability of adolescence'. The location of the maximum depends on the size of the initial stock of resources and endurance in the face of decreasing success. The declining failure rate with increasing age is not an artefact due to (observed or unobserved) heterogeneity: the same pattern would occur if a cohort of newly founded organizations differed in certain aspects determining longevity, like size. The most fragile organizations would be the first to disband, leaving a more resistant population. In the aggregate this would result in a declining mortality rate. However, careful analysis has shown that liability of newness cannot be explained as a spurious phenomenon.

While liability of newness and adolescence arguments both agree that rates of failure decline monotonically with later age, the 'liability of senescence or obsolescence' hypotheses predict an increasing failure rate for older organizations as internal frictions accumulate or the original fit with the environment erodes (Hannan 1998). However, if age coincides with the amount of environmental change experienced by an organization, then the probability of failure will increase, spuriously, with age, if accumulated environmental change is uncontrolled in the analysis. Some studies treat age dependence not as a universal tendency among a homogenous population, but as a performance outcome that is contingent on other factors, e.g. a firm's technology strategy. Proprietary strategists offering products whose key technologies are internally developed and firm-specific exhibit a liability of obsolescence in their failure rates while standards-based strategists selling products whose key technologies conform with open and publicly available specifications exhibit a liability of adolescence. However, without a carefully designed study addressing left-censoring, right-censoring, and specification bias issues it will not be possible to disentangle these various influences on the age dependence of failure rates.

Something like setting the liability-of-newness clock back happens when an organization is restructured. The process of dismantling an old structure and building a new one makes an organization temporarily more vulnerable. This leads to a short-run increase of the mortality rate even if in the long run the disbanding rate of a restructured organization is lower. The effects of age on the 'liability of reorganization' are complex. First, older organizations are less prone to reorganization than younger ones. Second, if they restructure themselves they experience a higher increase in the risk of failure. Third, even though the effect of a structural change is more severe for older organizations (there is a larger jump in the mortality rate), the total rate of mortality of younger organizations after change is higher, because due to liability of newness they are less robust than older ones (the lower jump in the mortality rate starts from a higher base rate). Because of these complex interdependencies the global outcome of exogenously induced changes, for example through technical innovations, on the development of a heterogenous organizational population, is hard to predict.

3 Dimensions of niches and organizational strategies

There is a duality of niche and organizational form; both concepts are defined in relative terms, as are niche width and organizational strategies, like specialism versus generalism (Hannan and Freeman 1989). A population's *niche width* is defined as the variance of its resource utilization and can vary differently along multiple dimensions. A set of insurance companies offering only policies against damage or loss of property has a lower variance of resource utilization: it has a narrow niche; a population of companies that in addition insure against damage or loss of life has a broad niche. Organizations that are able to survive in a broad niche are called *generalists* while those concentrating on a narrow niche are named *specialists*. Their niches may overlap, like those of savings banks and universal banks. The latter not only take deposits and offer short- and long-term credit or mortgages, but are also engaged in underwriting and trading securities, financing foreign trade, and providing other services like investment consulting.

Some of the efficiency of specialist organizations derives from their restricting themselves to a few tactics for dealing with the environment which requires less excess capacity or organizational 'slack'. The relative evolutionary advantages of specialism versus generalism, however, depend on two other features of the niche they jointly occupy. One is the *uncertainty and variability* of environmental conditions, that is, the variance of a spatial or temporal series about its mean; the second is the pattern of variation or *grain*. For example, populations facing frequent changes of extremely high and low demand have a high level of environmental variability. This holds for urban public transportation systems, but also for restaurants at typical winter resorts. However, the pattern of variability of public transportation is fine-grained; the temporal distribution is composed of small patches of extremely high (rush-hours) or low traffic, while that of the restaurants is coarse-grained; large runs of the same type (high winter and low summer seasons) occur. It must be stressed that grain is defined in relative terms. A patch is small and the niche is fine-grained for a population if typical duration in the patch is short, relative to average life expectancy of an individual organization. Except for the extreme case of complete stability (for which grain is undefined), variability and grain can vary independently. A third dimension is the adaptation demand which different 'environmental patches' impose on a population. If environmental variations are small, relative to the adaptive capacities of organizations, they form a so-called *convex fitness set*, if they are large the fitness set is *concave*.

Ecological theory makes the following predictions regarding the evolutionary optimal strategy. First, stable environmental conditions favour populations of specialists regardless of environmental grain and shape of the fitness set. Changes are simply so infrequent that it does not pay to build up organizational slack. Second, under high variability and if adaptation demands do not differ too much (that is, in convex fitness sets) generalists are superior to specialists. The higher tolerance of generalists of frequently varying but not too dissimilar conditions gives them better life chances than the capacity of specialists for high performance in any particular situation. Third, if adaptation demands differ very much (in concave fitness sets), and under high variability, the relative evolutionary advantage of the two strategies depends on the grain of the environment. If the patches are short, that is, if the environment is fine-grained, specialists are superior. They are able to endure the relatively short runs of unfavourable environmental conditions while generalists are required to build up large excess capacities to meet these highly different adaptation demands. However, if the environment is coarse-grained specialists are unable to bear the long runs of unfavourable conditions and turn out to be less fit than generalists. An empirical example is given by restaurants which seem to operate close to the margin, suggesting that even small variations in demand are straining their adaptive capacities; they are located in concave fitness sets. In a coarse-grained environment, where demand has a strong seasonal component, and with high variability of total demand, generalists have much lower mortality rates than specialist restaurants that offer a limited menu or specialize in ethnic cuisine. A polymorphous population, that is a mixture of specialists, seems to fit this particular combination of environmental conditions even better.

A different theory of niche width, the resource-partitioning model, applies to concentrated markets with strong economies of scale (Hannan and Carroll 1992). Under these conditions only a few generalists, who move towards the centre of the market, survive. This opens up small pockets of resources at the periphery and enhances the life chances of specialists. It has been pointed out that this is only a special case of a dual market structure which can be the result of both lateral migration towards the fringe of the market, as resource partitioning theory postulates, and also of exit and replacement due to increased competition (Boone and van Witteloostuijn 1995).

Another classification is based on different life history strategies. First mover strategies that rely on the capacity to move quickly and with little investment into markets opened by technical innovation or other social changes are contrasted with efficient production strategies that maximize the ability to expand even in the face of dense competition, but require larger resources and are more difficult to build up. These conditions prevail when the population is operating close to its carrying capacity, usually denoted by K in ecological models. Therefore organizations relying on efficient production strategies are called *K-strategists*. First movers are named *r-strategists* because they typically flourish in situations when the intrinsic growth rate r determines population growth, that is, far away from the limits imposed by the carrying capacity. Highly volatile environments providing ephemeral opportunities are exploited by r-strategists, and their high mortality rate is more than balanced by high founding rates. This approach to considering organizational strategies as being suited to different environmental conditions clearly illustrates the logic of population analysis. While r-strategists are not said to be individually more flexible or less vulnerable than K-strategists, their higher death rate is more than compensated by their extremely high birth rate, due to the ease with which they are set up. If competition intensifies, barriers of entry rise and mortality increases, shifting the balance of vital rates in favour of K-strategists. This situation characterizes the middle phases of the total evolution of an industry or market. Then K-strategists dominate.

4 Dynamics of organizational populations

Empirical studies covering the whole history of a variety of organizational populations have revealed a remarkably similar pattern of development of population *density*, that is, the number of organizations existing at any given point in time. In somewhat stylized fashion four phases may qualitatively be distinguished. After the introduction of a new organizational form a more or less extended period of very low density is usually observed, followed by a very rapid S-shaped growth in population size. The third phase of maturity is characterized by a levelling off at carrying capacity, sometimes after 'over-shooting' this plateau. If the development is covered at full length, a fourth phase of decline in density (but not necessarily of 'mass' – aggregated size) concludes the history of a population.

Population ecologists have tried to account for this pattern by a very general and simple model of endogenous change: the *density dependence model* (Hannan and Carroll 1992). The two vital processes, birth and death, are postulated to be dependent on population density. However, the relationship is not assumed to be linear, as in the Lotka–Volterra model, but non-monotonic, due to the peculiar functioning of two intervening social processes: *competition* and *legitimation*. First, if members are few, adding one organization to the population increases frequency and strength of competition only slightly. However, if density is high, the addition of an organization notably increases the scarcity of resources on which the organizations jointly depend. Density therefore intensifies competition at an *increasing* rate. Second, density also increases legitimacy but at a *decreasing* rate. If there are very few organizations, adding another strengthens the taken-for-grantedness and appropriateness of an organizational form, while the addition of a single organization to an already numerous population does not significantly enhance its legitimacy. Third, founding rates are increased by legitimacy of the population and depressed by competition within the population. Fourth, disbanding rates, on the contrary, are depressed by legitimacy of the population and increased by competition within the population. These four assumptions together imply non-monotonic relationships between density and vital rates. Founding rates tend to increase and then decline with rises in density, and disbanding rates tend to fall and then increase as density rises.

Competition also shows delayed effects on mortality rates. Stinchcombe (1965) has argued that organizations are 'imprinted' with the social, cultural and technical features prevalent at the time they were founded. Intense competition creates a 'liability of resource scarcity' by pushing new entrants to the margins and leaving them little time and resources to build up efficient reproducible structures. Therefore high density at the time of founding produces a permanent increase in mortality rates even of 'mature' organizations. The past also impinges on the present in a more indirect way: because mortality rates are age-dependent, the historically developed age-structure of a population exerts an influence on the actual global rate of disbandings.

The general model of density dependence has stood up rather well under empirical testing (Singh and Lumsden 1990; Baum 1996), even when: (1) affected by several exogeneous factors (for example, political and economic crises, wars, technical innovations, different political and economic regimes, changes in legal regulations); (2) taking into account general trends (for example, economic or demographic development); and (3) applied to different populations (for example, labour unions, newspapers, breweries, banks and life insurance companies). There are indications that density by itself, that is, the number of organizations in a population, raises the level of competition and that its effects do not simply reflect the mass of the population – the aggregate size of all organizations in the population.

However, there is still another question as to whether the model of density dependence is able to produce growth paths of density that resemble the empirical histories of real populations. In many well-documented cases, organizational densities decline sharply after an extended period of early proliferation; and they sometimes rise again later. So far it is not possible to specify an analytically tractable model in which the two underlying processes of founding and mortality have been coupled. The results of simulation studies suggest three general conclusions (Hannan and Carroll 1992).

1 The basic processes of contemporaneous density dependence of foundings and disbandings yield a fairly stable pattern of S-shaped growth, to an approximate ceiling of carrying capacity as observed empirically.
2 The effects of density delay, that is, density at founding, on mortality rates can generate declines of density from the carrying capacity and even cyclical variations – the stronger the effect, the bigger the declines and cycles.
3 The models imply great stochastic variation in the timing of the explosive growth or take-off period, that is, the same generic social processes can produce very different historical realizations of organizational population growth.

Logical formalization of population dynamics has shown that the assumption of a ceiling on the relationship between density and legitimation is needed for the conclusions of the theory of density dependence to hold. This has lead to a revision of the original model (Hannan 1997; Carroll and Hannan 2000). It is no longer assumed that legitimation and competition have the property of *strict reversibility* – they react symmetrically to growth and decline in density. Instead it is now argued that density strongly shapes legitimation during a population's youth and becomes increasingly irrelevant at older ages. The relationship between intensity of competition and a population's longevity is more intricate and depends on the development of population structure. Competition may be more intense among regional units leading to location dependence while legitimation effects may even cut across national boundaries. A multilevel analysis of entry rates to the automobile industries of five European countries supports this revised hypothesis. However, we still do not know whether the decline and resurgence of populations mainly reflects a single process or some combination. Nor is it clear whether density matters, or whether the empirical regularities reflect the consequences of density delay, concentration, the mix of specialists and generalists, the shape of the size distribution, resource partitioning, localized competition or the distribution of ages within the population (Hannan 1997).

5 Critique, misunderstandings and open questions

The use of biological terminology has tended to produce some confusion about the main intentions of the ecological approach to organizational populations. Although population theories in biology obviously have been, and continue to be, a considerable source of inspiration, organizational ecologists do not seek to use biological theory to explain organizational change. Even when formal models are taken from bioecology their successful application to organizational phenomena depends upon reinterpretation in terms of social science theories. The heuristic power of biological analogies should therefore not be overestimated, leading to a blind search for an organizational analogue to each biological concept. Efforts to conceptualize 'organizational form' in strictly analogous terms to its biological counterpart of 'species' have not been successful. A very fundamental critique has been raised by Winter (1990): the objects of evolutionary selection should be considered as organizational routines, but not whole organizations which are more or less coherent and unitary packages of competence. The claim that generalization of empirical findings presupposes a systematic and empirically validated taxonomy of organizational forms and carefully delineated populations has also been challenged. However, despite the 'fuzziness' of some of its concepts the research programme has proved to be productive and has contributed to our understanding of long-term and large-scale organizational change (Carroll and Hannan 2000). Suggestions for a fruitful exchange of ideas with other theoretical approaches like industrial organization or strategic management have been made (Boone and van Witteloostuijn 1995) but criticism has also been voiced (Singh 1990; Singh and Lumsden 1990; Baum 1996).

A central issue in the discussion has been the role of structural inertia in constraining adaptation, which is replaced by environmental selection as the main vehicle of change. Structural reorganization, intentionally planned and implemented by managerial action, is not precluded, but adaptation is assumed to be relatively slow compared with environmental rates of change and selection derives from the consequences of action, not the intentions of actors. Further research is required into the specific conditions determining the rate of undertaking fundamental reorganization, and the probability of succeeding in implementing change given an attempt. Little effort has been made towards the study of the speciation process, that is, the initial creation of a new organizational form, where almost by definition strategic choice and entrepreneurship play an important role.

However, some progress reconciling the adaptive and selective view has been made (Barnett and Carroll 1995; Baum 1996). Two questions have been addressed: Which factors determine *organizational change*? and What are its consequences? The originally hypothesized negative effects of age and size on rates of organizational change have received ambiguous empirical support. A more complete understanding requires consideration of an organization's history of change: experience with change of a particular type increases the likelihood that the change will be repeated in the future. Organizations may even be able to develop routines for change giving them an evolutionary advantage. Among external factors changes in the institutional environment, for example new legal mandates or regulations, market volatility but also technological innovations, play a decisive role. The outcome is different if change affects core or peripheral structural elements. Organizational change is riskier if it involves core features, including an organization's mission, its authority structure, its technology and its marketing strategy (Hannan and Freeman 1984). Changes affecting the periphery may even lead to a lower risk of death.

Some critics have pointed out that the natural selection model fits small, powerless organizations operating in environments with dispersed resources better than large, politically well-connected organizations that operate with concentrated resources and can exercise control (for example by advertising and lobbying) over their environment. This is of course an empirical question not to be decided *a priori*, because in the long run even giant organizations are not completely immune to selective pressure. To study how (sub)populations are able to control their environments shifts the analysis to the community level where several populations interact, each constituting part of 'the environment' of the other. An interesting answer has been proposed to the question of whether the strongest organizations will survive by distinguishing between an organization's viability, on the one hand, and its competitive intensity –defined as the magnitude of effect that an organization has on its rivals' life chances – on the other. While small organizations become both more likely to survive and to be stronger competitors, for large organizations viability does not require competitive success, because they can buffer their weak units from selection pressures. The model accounts for the persistent tendency of organizational populations to become concentrated (Barnett 1997).

Several criticisms have been raised against the density model and its claim to account for the observed relationship between density and vital rates by the mechanism of competition and legitimation.

1 Both variables have seldom been operationalized to allow for a direct test of the hypothesis; but even granted their logical status as hypothetical constructs some of the implications of the theoretical argument may be questioned, for example, that legitimacy should automatically decrease if density declines although the total mass of population may remain constant or even increase. Logical formalization, a tool developed in the early 1990s, has helped to find and repair logical flaws in the theoretical structure, to resolve ambiguity, to clarify the mechanisms at work, and to derive new conclusions. It has been applied to various theory fragments in organizational ecology dealing with inertia (Péli *et al.* 1994), niche theory or age dependence in organizational mortality (Hannan 1998).

2 The assumption that density is the sole determinant of 'diffuse' competition is also criticized. The amount of resource overlap, that is, competition between any two organizations for their targeted resource bases, may vary between organizations of different size, degree of specialization or geographical location. The social network approach stresses the pattern of 'direct' competition among organizations, and economic theory suggests that the level of concentration in the population (the shape of the size distribution of individual organizations) is relevant. However, to study populations dynamically with level of concentration endogenously taken into account would require an explanation of shifts in size distributions which are not only the result of size-dependent founding and mortality processes, but are also due to the (internal or external) growth and decline of individual organizations.

3 Besides legitimacy and competition, other mechanisms have been suggested, for example, time- and density-dependent learning and diffusion processes that result in an accumulation of competence. Some scholars argue that processes of learning and innovation among already existing organizations are at least as important as the founding of new organizations for producing variation on which the evolutionary selective process can operate.

4 The composition of organizational populations is not only changed by foundings and disbandings but also by mergers and divestitures, acquisitions and joint ventures. Some of these types of events have been studied but with inconclusive evidence.

5 The density model does not account for the generally observed decline and disappearance of populations. Therefore, it seems necessary to shift the analysis to the community level and to include the study of the speciation process: older populations may be out-competed by newly created, more efficient organizational forms or new technologies.

The ecological study of organizational populations is decidedly a macro approach. This kind of explanation posits that changes in vital rates alter the composition of populations and thereby change features of the social structures based on these populations. But it is silent on the role of individual action. While there are good reasons to look at relationships at the macro level first and investigate the microfoundations only 'if necessary', this task cannot be avoided. Without an explicit microbehavioural theory it seems impossible to understand in a deeper sense how variations in their environments affect the actions of organizations and their members and to explain under which conditions relationships at the macro level hold or break down.

Further reading

(References cited in the text marked *)

* Aldrich, H.E. (1979) *Organizations and Environments*, Englewood Cliffs, NJ: Prentice Hall. (Introduction to organizational sociology from an evolutionary, ecological perspective.)

* Aldrich, H.E. (1999) *Organizations Evolving*, London: Sage Publications. (The general evolutionary approach is put in the context of other approaches: the ecological, institutional, interpretive, organizational learning, resource dependence and transaction cost approaches. It is used to explain the genesis of organizations, populations and communities in modern industrial societies.)

* Barnett, W.P. (1997) 'The dynamics of competitive intensity', *Administrative Science Quarterly* 42: 128–60. (By distinguishing between two aspects of organizational strength, viability and competitive effects on the life chances of its rivals, the persistent tendency of organizational populations to become concentrated is explained.)

* Barnett, W.P. and Carroll, G.R. (1995) 'Modelling internal organizational change', *Annual Review of Sociology* 21: 217–36. (Review and comment of research on organizational change and its outcomes from an organizational ecology perspective.)

* Baum, J.A.C. (1996) 'Organizational ecology', in Clegg, S.R., Hardy, C. and Nord, W.R. (eds), *Handbook of Organizational Studies*, London: Sage. (Assessment and consolidation of the state-of-the-art in organizational ecology; presents in summary form the results of empirical studies.)

Baum, J.A.C. and Singh, J.V. (eds) (1994) *Evolutionary Dynamics of Organizations*, New York and Oxford: Oxford University Press. (Collection of theoretical and empirical articles dealing with evolutionary dynamics at the intra-organizational, organizational, population and community level.)

* Boone, Ch. and van Witteloostuijn, A. (1995) 'Industrial organization and organizational ecology: the potentials for cross-fertilization', *Organization Studies* 16: 265–98. (The authors argue that considerable progress can be made by adding insights from industrial organization and strategic management to organizational ecology.)

* Carroll, G.R. (ed.) (1988) *Ecological Models of Organizations*, Cambridge, MA: Ballinger. (Collection of empirical studies applying ecological models to a wide range of organizational populations.)

* Carroll. G.R. and Hannan, M.T. (eds) (1995) *Organizations in Industry. Strategy, Structure, and Selection.* New York and Oxford: Oxford University Press. (Empirical studies of a dozen different industries from the perspective of organizational ecology.)

* Carroll. G.R. and Hannan, M.T. (eds) (2000) *The Demography of Corporations and Industries*, Princeton, NJ: Princeton University Press. (The most comprehensive and up-to-date presentation of theory, models, methods and data used in the demographic approach to organizational studies. The authors review and synthesize the major theoretical mechanisms of corporate demography and explore some implications for public policy.)

* Hannan, M.T. (1997) 'Inertia, density and the structure of organizational populations: entries in European automobile industries, 1886–1981', *Organization Studies* 18: 193–228. (Re-

vised theory of density dependence specifying that the effects of density on legitimation and competition change systematically as populations age.)

* Hannan, M.T. (1998) 'Rethinking age dependence in organizational mortality: logical formalizations', *American Journal of Sociology* 104: 126–64. (The article uses logical formalization to clarify the mechanisms at work in the relation between organization age and the hazards of mortality. It provides guidance for empirical research to discriminate between the competing theories.)

* Hannan, M.T. and Carroll, G.R. (1992) *Dynamics of Organizational Populations: Density, Legitimation, and Competition*, New York and Oxford: Oxford University Press. (Elaboration, empirical test and simulation studies of the density dependence model; the links between theoretical arguments and statistical models are carefully explicated.)

* Hannan, M.T. and Freeman, J. (1977) 'The population ecology of organizations', *American Journal of Sociology* 82 (5): 929–64. (First major essay on the topic outlining the basic theoretical framework and suggesting lines of empirical research.)

* Hannan, M.T. and Freeman, J. (1984) 'Structural inertia and organizational change', *American Sociological Review* 49: 149–64. (Clarifying the meaning of structural inertia and deriving propositions about structural inertia from an explicit evolutionary model.)

* Hannan, M.T. and Freeman, J. (1989) *Organizational Ecology*, Cambridge, MA: Harvard University Press. (Comprehensive theoretical, methodological and empirical presentation of the population-ecology approach.)

* McKelvey, B. (1982) *Organizational Systematics: Taxonomy, Evolution, Classification*, Berkeley, CA: University of California Press. (Synoptic presentation of theoretical and methodological problems in constructing a 'natural' organizational classification.)

* Péli, G., Bruggeman, J., Masuch, M. and Nualláin, B.O. (1994) 'A logical approach to formalizing organizational ecology', *American Sociological Review* 59: 571–91. (By use of first-order logic the theory of organizational inertia is formalized to evaluate its consistency and to suggest previously unrecognized implications.)

* Pfeffer, J. and Salancik, G.R. (1978) *The External Control of Organizations: A Resource Dependence Perspective*, New York: Harper & Row. (Overview of organizational adaptations and responses to environmental resource dependence from the perspective of a single 'focal' organization.)

* Singh, J.V. (ed.) (1990) *Organizational Evolution. New Directions*, Newbury Park, CA: Sage. (Collection of articles focusing on founding and mortality processes and organizational evolution.)

* Singh, J.V. and Lumsden, C.J. (1990) 'Theory and research in organizational ecology', *Annual Review of Sociology* 16: 161–95. (Comprehensive review of ecological studies on foundings, mortality and organizational change, convergence of ecological and institutional research, and criticism of organizational ecology.)

* Stinchcombe, A.L. (1965) 'Social structure and organizations', in J.G. March (ed.), *Handbook of Organizations*, Chicago, IL: Rand McNally. (Classic article about the influence of society on the founding of organizations and their characteristics.)

* Winter, S. (1990) 'Survival, selection, and inheritance in evolutionary theories of organization', in J.V. Singh (ed.), *Organizational Evolution. New Directions*, Newbury Park, CA: Sage. (Critical article discussing the relationship between evolutionary economics and population ecology.)

Essential processes and tools

Organizational complexity

Kevin Dooley

1 **Organizational complexity defined**
2 **Antecedents of organizational complexity**
3 **Consequences of organizational complexity**
4 **Organizational complexity and complexity science**

Overview

Organizational complexity is defined as the amount of differentiation that exists within different elements constituting the organization. This is often operationalized as the number of different professional specializations that exist within the organization. For example, a school would be considered a less complex organization than a hospital, since a hospital requires a large diversity of professional specialties in order to function. Organizational complexity can also be observed via differentiation in structure, authority and locus of control, and attributes of personnel, products and technologies.

Contingency theory states that an organization structures itself and behaves in a particular manner as an attempt to fit with its environment. Thus organizations are more or less complex as a reaction to environmental complexity. An organization's environment may be complex because it is turbulent, hostile, diverse, technologically complex or restrictive. An organization may also be complex as a result of the complexity of its underlying technological core. For example, a nuclear power plant is likely to have a more complex organization than a standard power plant because the underlying technology is more difficult to understand and control.

There are numerous consequences of environmental and organizational complexity. Organizational members, faced with overwhelming and/or complex decisions, omit, tolerate errors, queue, filter, abstract, use multiple channels, escape and chunk in order to deal effectively with the complexity. At an organizational level, an organization will respond to complexity by building barriers around its technical core; by smoothing input and output transactions; by planning and predicting; by segmenting itself and/or becoming decentralized; and by adopting rules.

Complexity science offers a broader view of organizational complexity – it maintains that all organizations are relatively complex, and that complex behaviour is not necessarily the result of complex action on behalf of a single individual's effort; rather, complex behaviour of the whole can be the result of loosely coupled organizational members behaving in simple ways, acting on local information. Complexity science posits that most organizational behaviour is the result of numerous events occurring over extended periods of time, rather than the result of some smaller number of critical incidents.

1 Organizational complexity defined

The concept of 'organizational complexity' is defined in a variety of different ways by different authors, and these different definitions lead to various operationalizations of the term. In discussing the general concept of complexity, Luhmann states 'we will call an interconnected collection of elements complex when, because of imminent constraints in the elements' connective capacity, it is no longer possible at any moment to connect every element with every other element. … Complexity in this sense means being forced to select; being forced to select means contingency; and contingency means risk' (Luhmann 1995: 25).

The ability or inability for organizational entities to 'connect' depends on the number of entities, and their diversity – it is easier to make connections between similar as opposed to dissimilar elements. The number of entities also in part drives the diversity of organizational entities; as size increases, then administrative functions must be added for the purpose of communication and coordination. Thus we can define organizational complexity as *the amount of differentiation that exists within different elements constituting the organization.* In this manner, complexity is roughly equivalent to variety. Since organizations are about making sense and taking action, complexity impacts how easy it is for organizational members to make sense of their current perceptions, and the type of effort that is needed to determine and implement effective action.

Many studies operationalize organizational complexity in two ways: professional specialization and the associated level of required professional qualifications, typically measured by actual qualifications of the job holder, as opposed to the qualifications required by the job. For example, a restaurant would be considered to be rather low in complexity, since there are few job specialties (waiter/waitress, cook, dish cleaner), and each job requires minimal qualification, with perhaps the exception of the cook. A hospital would be considered to have quite great complexity, as there are numerous specialties (nurse, surgeon, family practitioner, radiologist, etc.), and many of those specialties require significant training and interned experience.

These two dimensions are not necessarily correlated. For example, a consulting firm may have workers representing few functional specialties (consultant, secretary, marketing), but the professional qualifications required for those specialties can be quite significant. The converse is not generally true however; organizations that have many functional specialties tend to have jobs that have distinct qualifications. Note also that organizations can, to some extent, choose where to distribute complexity. One firm may choose an organizational structure with high variety between groups and low variety within groups; while another firm may choose an organizational design with loosely differentiated groups containing high diversity.

Professional specialization is not the only organizational characteristic that indicates organizational complexity, although it is one of the more indicative. Organizational complexity could also be defined as the amount of variety, or differentiation, in the organization's: core processes and technologies; customers and markets; products and product lines; distribution networks; suppliers; or geographical locations. For example, an organization such as a religious group may have little professional specialization and require few professional qualifications of its members, but could be considered complex because its membership stretches across geography and thus cultures and environment. Organizational complexity may also represent other types of variation in the workforce not necessarily associated with professional specialization. For example, gender difference is typically considered significant when examining the differences in beliefs and norms between doctors and nurses. Finally, diversity could exist in the causal processes underlying the work of the organization, leading to organizational complexity.

A simple way to quantitatively measure organizational complexity is to count the number of different categories that exist for the variable in question. In measuring the organizational complexity associated with job categories, one could refer to the formal organizational titles as embodied in job descriptions and records of the human resource department and count the number of job titles. This type of measure calls for clear articulation concerning the 'level of detail' that one associates with the job title; for example, should 'rank' be considered something that differentiates two otherwise relatively similar positions? A raw count of the number of categories present does not take into account the fact that the distribution of these counts amongst the various categories may differ. For example, an organization with twenty accountants and one salesperson is probably not as complex as an organization with twenty accountants and twenty salespeople. Various entropy-based measures can take these distributional characteristics into account. The more uniformly spread the variation is amongst the different categories, the greater the measured complexity will be.

2 Antecedents of organizational complexity

At the simplest level, organizations are complex because the people constituting organizations are complex. This perspective leads us not to attempt to differentiate organizations as more or less complex than one another, but rather accept the fact that all organizations, regardless of their internal diversity, are complex. Schein (1980) points out that individuals vary tremendously in their age, gender, their histories and experiences and their beliefs and desires. Even within a homogenous group of people who have the same professional qualifications and represent the same professional specialty, the diversity and thus complexity of the group must not be ignored. As Bateson said, there are many 'differences that can make a difference', and job function is only one of them.

Besides the obvious interpersonal differences, Schein points out that people are capable of wearing many 'hats' within the organization, playing out various roles at different times. For example, an administrator may play the role of a bureaucrat, an accountant, a leader, a coach, a friend, and a team member, switching between these roles with little apparent effort. People are often 'matrixed' into both a functional and project team category, and most are fully capable of enacting the beliefs and norms associated with the given role at an appropriate time, even though the roles may actually conflict with one another – most people are capable of dealing effectively with such role conflict and, for the most part, do not give it a second thought.

Therefore, in attempting to develop programmes aimed at, for example, employee motivation, we know that different people will be motivated by different things, and that a single individual is likely to be motivated by different things at different times. Thus, the complexity of human nature demands that managers be flexible, adaptive, experimenting and learning.

More typically, organizational complexity is considered a response to complexity within the internal or external environment. The internal environment consists of the processes and technologies that constitute the core operations of the organization. The external environment includes customers, markets, suppliers, competitors and institutions that shape what the organization must respond to. The complexity of the internal and external environment can be described along three dimensions: its differentiation or variety, its dynamic properties, and the complexity of its underlying causal mechanisms.

Consider the external environment first. Organizational scholars such as Thompson, March, Simon, Lawrence and Lorsch have contributed theory and empirical evidence that states that organizations arrange themselves in such a way to react to environmental contingencies – thus a complex environment requires a complex organization. This follows the general principle within systems theory called 'requisite variety', which states that the complexity of a control system must be at least as great as the complexity of the system that is being controlled. In reality, of course, this can never be completely true – the organization's environment will always be more complex than the organization itself. Nevertheless, an organization attempts to match its own complexity with that of the environment through differentiation: 'differentiation into similar units (segmentation), the differentiation of center/periphery, the differentiation conforming/deviant (official/unofficial, formal/informal), hierarchical differentiation, and functional differentiation' (Luhmann 1995: 190). Khandwalla (1977) reports some of the attributes that may lead to environmental complexity: turbulence, hostility, diversity, technical complexity and restrictiveness.

A movie theatre is an example of an organization with low complexity, because its environment is characterized by low complexity. First, in terms of differentiation, the theatre's customers may be very diverse, but when it comes to sitting and watching a movie, all customers can essentially be treated the same. The only differentiation that exists is children versus adult, as enacted by the movie's rating. The theatre reduces any possible environmental variation in terms of the types of movies that people would like to see, or the type of food and beverages that they would like to purchase, by restricting variety in those components. Typically, only movies produced by one of the few major studios are ever even considered for showing.

The movie theatre is also low in complexity because elements of its environment are slow to change over time. The desires of people relative to movies have remained relatively unchanged for decades, and even the narrative structure of movies has changed little since the advent of talking films. What works today for a movie theatre will likely work next year – in fact, innovations that theatres have taken on, such as a wider selection of food or video arcades, have not for the most part been successful. Finally, complexity in such an organization is low because the causal mechanisms that drive the organization's markets are simple – if people show up to the theatre, other people are likely to show up, and vice versa. Movie reviewers give theatre managers yet another way to estimate the potential market of the film.

An organization making computer peripherals is likely to be complex as a reaction to the complex environment it is a part of. First, the market needs are multiple and varied, and always dynamically changing. Second, the supply chain is also varied and dynamic; standards may not be adopted quickly enough to maintain pace with the markets and technologies, therefore compatibility is always an issue. Finally, causal mechanisms related to the external market are not simple, because adoption and diffusion processes are complex and unpredictable in the industry.

Organizations can also differ in complexity due to complexity in their internal environment – as Thompson (1967) refers to it, the organization's technologies. By technology, Thompson included the physical artifacts as well as the procedures, methods and processes that constitute organizational action. As the organization's technologies become more complex, more specialists are required to understand the underlying causal mechanisms, and this subsequently requires greater effort at integration and coordination, again adding to the variety of tasks that the organization must do in order to function effectively. The movie theatre has relatively low complexity because the showing of the movie, including the technology that projects the film's images, is automated, and the business processes associated with selling tickets and food are straightforward. The computer peripherals firm is likely to be significantly more complex, because the technology it is dealing with (micro-electronics) is often complex, especially when products are pushing the existing technological envelope.

Perrow (1984) differentiates the technologies within an organization as being either linear or complex. Linear systems are denoted by: spatial segregation, dedicated connections, segregated subsystems, easy substitutions, few feedback loops, single purpose controls, direct information, and extensive understanding. Examples would include dams, rail transport, assembly-line production, most manufacturing, and single-goal agencies (e.g. motor vehicles, post office). Complex systems are denoted by: proximity, common-mode connections, interconnected subsystems, limited substitutions, feedback loops, multiple and interacting controls, indirect information, and limited understanding. Examples would include nuclear plants, aircraft, chemical plants, space missions, military events, research and development, multi-goal agencies (e.g. welfare, department of energy), and universities. One would expect structural complexity and differentiation in such organizations with embedded technological complexity.

Finally, organizations may be complex as a response to their institutional environment – this is especially true for public sector organizations. Powell (1988) reports that public organizations 'located in environments in which conflicting demands are made upon them will be especially likely to generate complex organizational structures with disproportionately large administrative components and boundary spanning units' (Powell 1988: 126).

3 Consequences of organizational complexity

There are numerous consequences of environmental, and thus organizational, complexity. For example, the amount of learning that goes on inside an organization is affected by environmental complexity. When environmental complexity is low, organizational members can succeed in their daily routines by maintaining the status quo, and there is little incentive or need for learning. When environmental complexity is very high, organizational members are constantly barraged with demands for their attention, solving existing problems and scanning for new ones. This taxes the information processing capacity of the organization, and individuals tend to shut down, saving their energy for emergency needs that may arise. The opportunity for organizational learning is maximized when environmental complexity is moderate, pushing organizational members to learn new skills and solve problems, within the limitations of their ability to process information. For example, 'learning' about new products and processes has been reported as low in the steel industry, where the environment is relatively simple, and in the Internet products industry, where the environment is very complex; conversely, learning is reported as significant in the automotive and semiconductor industries, two industries with middling levels of environmental complexity.

Environments can be complex simply because they are voluminous in their nature and demands, thus overwhelming organizational members with information. Organizational members respond in a variety of ways in order to reduce the stress of the information overload situation: individuals 'begin with omission, and then move to greater tolerance of error, queuing, filtering, abstracting, using multiple channels, escape, and end with chunking' (Weick 1995: 87).

In addition to being voluminous and thus overwhelming, the environment may also be complex because of its inherent nature. People deal with complex problems and decisions in several different ways (March 1994). First, decisions can be broken down into their constituent parts and treated sequentially. Second, secondary and tertiary features of the decision may be ignored, allowing people to focus on only a few select issues. Third, people may draw from their experience, seeking solutions from previous problems, and minimizing their effort searching for entirely new solutions. Fourth, solutions can be chosen which satisfy, rather than optimize, the given situation, thus reducing the search effort. Fifth, people make assumptions about data that is not present, rather than going through the effort of questioning those assumptions, and/or seeking confirmation of their assumptions. Finally, people use stories and narrative procedures to convey information about complex situations that could not be readily assimilated via other modes of communication.

Thompson (1967) discusses theory concerning how an organization will respond to environmental complexity. First, following the norms of rationality, an organization is more likely to build barriers around its 'technical core' if the environment is complex, surrounding it with input and output components. For example, engineers in a high technology firm rarely directly deal with customers, marketing or sales representatives do. Second, an organization will attempt to reduce the complexity of its environment by smoothing input and output transactions. For example, a school often requires its students (customers) to attend a fixed programme of classes, rather than allowing them to select from a broader array of offerings. Third, an organization will attempt to predict the amount of uncertainty and fluctuation in a complex environment. For example, hospital emergency rooms know there are peak times for medical emergencies and staff accordingly.

Fourth, an organization will segment itself in order to make its sub-environments relatively homogenous. For example, divisionalization along product lines enables the marketing function to focus on a reduced set of demographic groups. Fifth, organizations will adopt rules as a means to coordinate the less-complex aspects of their internal and external environments. For example, the military is a highly complex organization with many contingencies in its internal operations and external environment; however it operates with strict rules regarding (e.g.) communication protocol and behaviour between members of different rank, in an attempt to minimize the uncertainty associated with at least part of its world.

Weick points out that as an organization operates under these 'norms of rationality', it can lead to 'a potentially incoherent assortment of issues to be managed by people at the top. … This is precisely what we see in military command and control systems that are designed starting with the field and ending with people at headquarters. The issues left over for judgment, the portions most likely affected by deep decision premises of social class, ethnic origins, social networks, or national culture, are precisely those portions that defy order' (Weick 1995: 116).

Mintzberg (1993) builds from Thompson's ideas and suggests that the more complex the environment, the more decentralized the organizational structure. He suggests that as the environment moves from simple to complex, the organization will move from direct supervision to standardization of work processes, of outputs, of skills and, finally, to mutual adjustment. Mintzberg separates the concept of complexity, having to do with comprehensibility, from that of stability or turbulence. His model states that in a complex but stable environment, the organization will choose standardization of its work processes and outputs. We can see this, for example, in the automotive industry, where interrelationships in the supply and distribution chain make operating very difficult to comprehend, but a stable environment allows for standardization, for example, of an organization's quality system according to ISO 9000 guidelines. Further still, an organization may simply standardize work skills; for example, the manner in which tenure is decided at major research universities represents such a decentralized bureau-cracy. In a complex and turbulent environment, the organization will resort to mutual adjustment. For example, firms in the Internet industry mutually co-evolve standards (e.g. Java language) in order to maintain compatibility with one another. There are losers and winners in such mutual adjustments, but it is the only means by which to move forward at all.

4 Organizational complexity and complexity science

Significant new scientific advancements in the area of complexity science (e.g. Anderson 1999; McKelvey 1997) highlight new ways in which we may think about and operationalize organizational complexity. Complexity science makes the assumption that all organizations are more or less 'complex', and that complex behaviour is not necessarily the result of complex action on behalf of a single individual's effort; rather, complex behaviour of the whole can be the result of loosely coupled organizational members behaving in simple ways, acting on local information. Complexity science is a haven for positivists and constructivists, and has served as a common meeting place for the different research paradigms.

With roots in numerous disciplines, modern theories and models of complex systems, or more specifically, complex adaptive systems (CAS) focus on the interplay between a system and its environment and the co-evolution of both. CAS models extend traditional systems theory by explicitly representing the dimension of 'time' and its related concepts. Internal to a CAS are agents. Depending on the scale of analysis, an agent may represent an individual, a project team, a division or an entire organization. Agents have varying degrees of connectivity with other agents through which information and resources can flow. Agents possess schema that are both interpretive and behavioural. Schema may be shared amongst the collective (e.g. shared norms, values, beliefs and assumptions) that make up an organization's culture, or may be highly individualistic. Agents behave so as to increase the 'fitness' of the system that they belong to either locally or globally. Fitness is typically a complex aggregate of both global and local states within the system.

Behaviour in a CAS is induced not by a single entity but rather by the simultaneous and parallel actions of agents within the system itself. Thus, we refer to a system as self-organizing if it undergoes 'a process ... whereby new emergent structures, patterns, and properties arise without being externally imposed on the system. Not controlled by a central, hierarchical command-and-control center, self-organization is usually distributed throughout the system' (Goldstein 1998: 270). In other words, the behaviour of a CAS is emergent. Emergence is 'the arising of new, unexpected structures, patterns, properties, or processes in a self-organizing system. These emergent phenomena can be understood as existing on a higher level than the lower level components from which [emergence took place]. Emergent phenomena seem to have a life of their own with their own rules, laws and possibilities unlike the lower level components' (Goldstein 1998:

265). Self-organization and emergence has been used to describe numerous social phenomena such as social movements, group dynamics, and open market
economics.

What is intriguing is that such emergent behaviour can be quite complex –
highly varied and differentiated – having evolved from rules that are really quite
simple. For example, the clustering behaviour that one sees in spatial configurations of groups, whether it be birds in a flock or cars on a highway, is the result of
a few simple rules (e.g. go the speed of your neighbour) acted upon locally. It is
thus the nature of interaction between components of a system, and the number
of components, that determines whether the resulting behaviour is complex or
not, and if so, what type of complex pattern emerges.

Complexity theory highlights that most organizational behaviour is the result
of numerous events occurring over extended periods of time, rather than the result of some smaller number of 'critical incidents'. This represents a change in
the manner in which organizations should be studied, because most existing
methods emphasize (post hoc) identification of key 'turning points' in an organization's history in order to understand where it came from and what it's about.
For example, the Minnesota Innovation Research Program (MIRP) studies (Van
de Ven *et al.* 1999) found that innovations were not initiated on the spur of the
moment, or by a single dramatic incident or by a single entrepreneur. An extended gestation period, often lasting several years, of seemingly random events
occurred before concentrated efforts were launched to develop an innovation.
Many of these divergent events were not intentionally directed toward starting an
innovation. Some events triggered recognition of the need for change. Other
events generated awareness of the technological feasibility of an innovation.
Events such as these often 'shocked' entrepreneurs into courses of action that, by
chance, intersected with the independent actions of others. These intersections
provided occasions for people to recognize and access new opportunities and potential resources. Where these occasions were exploited, people modified and
adapted their independent courses of action into convergent interdependent actions to mobilize efforts to initiate an innovation. Thus complex organizational
behaviour can be generated by the simultaneous and parallel actions of organizational members, sometimes resulting in a process that is relatively divergent, and
sometimes by processes that are similar to one another and convergent in nature.

Another useful complexity theory concept is that of Kauffman's rugged landscapes (1995). Complex adaptive systems evolve in such a manner as to maximize some measure of 'goodness' or fitness in a dynamic environment. The
potential states that a system can attain can be represented by a 'landscape',
where the coordinates on the terrain represent the organizational configuration,
and the height of the terrain represents fitness. The highest point in this landscape
and its associated fitness value could be considered the optimal state for the system. When the organization's fitness landscape is simple – e.g. single-peaked – it
is relatively simple to optimize organizational performance. Managers must determine which factors are important, and how those factors should be configured

so that an overall organizational configuration best matches the contingencies of the environment.

If, however, the landscape is multi-peaked, with many local optima, then organizational optimization becomes difficult. Such complex or 'rugged landscapes' exist in problems where optimality of the organizational system is determined by tightly coupled components. When elements of the organization can be optimized individually without regard for one another, and this leads to global, systemic optimality, the landscape is simple (single-peaked). When individual components of the organization contribute to overall organizational fitness in different ways, depending on the value/state of other organizational components in a contingent manner, the optimal organizational configuration becomes difficult to find, as many configurations that 'satisfice' exist. Thus, similar to Perrow's formulation, an organization (or its environment) is considered complex to the extent that its constituent elements are interdependent upon one another. For example, the successful production of engine turbines requires deep knowledge of metal alloys, but also knowledge of how to interact successfully with suppliers. These two dimensions may well not be independent – an ability to leverage supplier knowledge may in fact counteract lack of local engineering expertise – so the two can be viewed as composing a complex landscape, where different configurations of 'goodness' on the two dimensions correspond to different levels of 'successful production'.

Further reading

(References cited in the text marked *)

* Anderson, P. (1999) 'Complexity theory and organization science', *Organization Science* 10: 216–32. (An overview of complexity theory and its implications for organizational researchers and practitioners.)
* Goldstein, J. (1998) 'Glossary', in Zimmerman, B., Lindberg, C. and Plsek, P. *Edgeware*, Irving, TX: VHA. (Presents a glossary of terms in complexity science.)
* Khandwalla, P. (1977) *The Design of Organizations*, New York: Harcourt Brace Jovanovich. (Discusses the most common definitions of organizational complexity.)
* Lawrence, P.R. and Lorsch, J.W. (1967) *Organization and Environment: Differentiation and Integration*, Cambridge, MA: Harvard University Press. (Presents the idea that organizations attempt to match their structure and behaviour to that of their environment.)
* Luhmann, N. (1995) *Social Systems*, translated by J. Bednarz and D. Baecker, Stanford, CA: Stanford Press. (Presents theory pertaining to open, social systems.)
* March, J.G. (1994) *A Primer on Decision-Making*, New York: Free Press. (How people react to complexity while making decisions.)
* McKelvey, B. (1997) 'Quasi-natural organization science', *Organization Science* 8: 351–80. (Presents an argument for the study of micro-processes and an emphasis on living systems theory.)
* Mintzberg, H. (1993) *Structure in Fives: Designing Effective Organizations*, Englewood Cliffs, NJ: Prentice-Hall. (Demonstrates how different organizational structures react to different organizational environments.)
* Perrow, C. (1984) *Normal Accidents*, Normal Books. (Discusses how complexity arises from the core technologies of the organization.)

* Powell, W. (1988) 'Institutional effects on organizational structure and performance', in L. Zucker (ed.), *Institutional Patterns and Organizations: Culture and Environment*, Cambridge, MA: Ballinger. (Discusses the role of institutions in terms of how they influence organizational complexity.)

* Schein, E. (1980) *Organizational Psychology*, Englewood Cliffs, NJ: Prentice Hall. (Presents the theory that organizations are complex because people are complex.)

* Thompson, J.D. (1967) *Organizations in Action*, New York: McGraw-Hill. (Discusses what an organization does to deal with complexity.)

* Van de Ven, A.H., Polley, D., Garud, R. and Venkataraman, S. (1999) *The Innovation Journey*, Oxford: Oxford University Press. (Presents the findings of extended field studies of innovation processes.)

* Weick, K. (1995) *Sensemaking in Organizations*, Thousand Oaks, CA: Sage. (How individuals think in complex situations.)

Decision making

Richard Butler

Overview

Decision making has long been seen as a central managerial activity. At the centre of this activity is the problem of choosing a course of action under conditions of uncertainty and ambiguity. A number of different strategies for making a choice are outlined. Underlying these strategies is a dualism between programmed, routine decisions which, given intendedly rational decision makers, would use a computational strategy, and unprogrammed, non-routine decisions which would use an iterative process involving interaction and mutual adjustment between decision makers.

Decision making takes place within an organizational context, setting a timeframe for the definition of problems, solutions and participants. Within this timeframe preceding decisions have already set constraints for choices made in the present which will, in turn, affect succeeding decisions. Concurrent decisions also compete for the attention of decision makers.

Coping with uncertainty forms the nub of decision making. Without uncertainty as to which course of action to take there would be no decision to be made. The dominant paradigm of organizational decision making assumes that decision makers are intendedly rational but that rationality is 'bounded' by lack of knowledge about preferences and any associated instrumentalitites.

Uncertainty involves the interpretation of problems and possible solutions through an interplay between a number of psychological and sociological processes. Psychological approaches to decision making tend to emphasize the inherent biases resulting from information assymetry and framing effects. Sociological approaches tend to be more descriptive and to emphasize the use of power and the interplay between different interests.

Much of the empirical research into organizational decision making has been concerned with finding patterns between variables that attempt to describe the processes found in real-life situations. This research, more by implication than by empirical measurement, has been concerned with discovering appropriate decision patterns for particular situations and types of decision. The general conclusion is that what has been called a 'sporadic' or 'muddling through' process is effective under conditions of high uncertainty while the more orderly 'constricted' process is appropriate for routine, relatively clear-cut decisions. In this respect, the general well-established thesis of the distinction between routine and non-routine decision making is supported.

There is increasing interest in finding linkages between decision-making processes and aspects of the general organizational culture and institutional framework within which an organization exists. According to this approach managerial decision making is seen as being severely constrained both by the cultural limitations upon the way in which problems and solutions are defined and by the external institutional forces acting on an organization, requiring it to demonstrate its worthiness for support through adopting certain structures and procedures.

I Understanding decision making

The study of decision making has attracted continual interest in the literature on business and management. This is so especially since the publication in 1938 of *The Functions of the Executive* by Chester Barnard, a book which put decision making and the associated processes of communication and cooperation at the centre of managerial work.

Prior to Barnard's book, writing on business and management emphasized the rational processes of decision making: the good manager was a 'rational economic man' (March and Simon 1958) who carefully planned and organized. Barnard, however, observed that the practice of management is very different to this, a point developed further by Simon (1947). In Simon's theory decision making under uncertainty is seen to be far removed from utility maximization because decision makers do not possess enough information about end preferences and the means to reach them. The reality for decision makers is scarcity of information and lack of ability to determine all possible outcomes. In this condition of 'bounded rationality' decision makers tend to 'satisfice' by using simple rules of thumb, selecting the first satisfactory solution to a problem.

This emphasis upon how decision makers behave opened up the idea that the highly rational image of business decision makers presented by classic economic theory is limited to a quite restricted set of conditions. As conditions get more complex a different type of decision process begins to take over. A behavioural view pushed consideration of decision beyond simply examining the outcomes of decisions to examining the processes by which decisions are made.

The Behavioral Theory of the Firm (Cyert and March 1963) was another landmark book linking a psychological theory of the decision maker to an economic and organizational theory of how organizations, as opposed to individuals, learn and adapt to changing conditions. Although only partially achieved, the ambition of linking individual utilities to organizational needs for cooperative behaviour remains a vital item on the research agenda through cultural or institutional perspectives (Douglas 1987).

More recent writings investigating the nature of managerial work (Mintzberg 1975; Hickson *et al.* 1986; Butler *et al.* 1993) have emphasized the centrality of decision making and how managers take action upon intuitive and political factors in addition to using computational procedures while Hickson (1995) surveys a number of classical papers.

The decision maker: visions of rationality

Any theory of decision making must include consideration of human nature and how people make choices. Personality, risk-taking propensity and the need for achievement are all factors which have been proposed as having an effect upon decision making, as have Jung's psychological types (Nutt 1993). Any number of human characteristics exist but we limit our discussion to those characteristics which are related to human problem solving and, in particular, the notion of rationality.

Rationality has long formed the backbone of managerial decision making (Jennings and Wattan 1998). Rationality is the reason for doing something and to judge a behaviour as reasonable is to be able to say that the behaviour is understandable within a given frame of reference. That behaviour may, however, appear as rational to the actors in a situation but irrational to an observer. Behaviour inconsistent with the actor's frame of reference may be deemed irrational, as may behaviour for which an observer can find no explanation. Even 'abnormal' behaviour may be explicable as, for instance, when Freud sought explanations for neuroses and psychoses.

Two terms that are also at the centre of a behavioural theory of decision making are risk and uncertainty. Although closely related a distinction can usefully be made. When utilities and probabilities can be attached to a number of different outcomes decision making can be said to take place under risk whereas decision making under uncertainty does not even allow complete knowledge of all possible outcomes and their associated probabilities and pay-offs (March and Simon 1958: 137). Most theories of risk assume that decision makers prefer smaller risks to larger ones although there are exceptions to this.

There are many ways in which the term rationality has been used in the decision-making literature. Classic economic theory assumes a perfectly informed decision maker and a rational decision maker would successfully optimize outcomes. The ability to map out a complete decision tree was called by Lindblom (1959) 'synoptic' decision making. However, other than as a point of reference, such a notion does not get us far in considering decision making under uncertainty in complex organizations.

Intended rationality is the most useful starting point for thinking about the decision maker since we must assume that: a choice is to be made, even if it means doing nothing; there are decision makers who are aware of the possibility of choice; and their behaviour will be orientated towards the achievement of a goal or an improvement in their condition, but without necessarily achieving that goal. Intended rationality may be seen as consisting of two component rationalities to which the literature sometimes refers: (1) substantive rationality, which describes the primary orientation of economics whereby decision makers use the available information to increase their position on a given utility function; and (2) procedural rationality, which refers to an acceptance on the part of decision makers that their computational power is limited and that they are not in possession of complete information about options.

Bounded rationality is a general term refering to the limits of both substantive and procedural rationality. When there is uncertainty as to what is wanted and how to achieve it we can say that bounded rationality exists. *Cognitive limits to rationality* refers to the idea that bounded rationality is a result of the cognitive constraints of decision makers to understand their utility function and their powers of computation. *Local rationality* takes into account the notion that behaviour in decision making, which might appear irrational from an organizational perspective, can be explicable in terms of the interests of individuals, groups or organizational sub-units.

Studying decision making

Decision making has attracted the attention of a wide spectrum of social scientists, particularly since the Second World War when it was seemingly given an impetus by the needs of the US Military searching for ways to manage large complex organizations. March's *The Handbook of Organizations* (1965) with its two articles on decision theory also shows the importance of the topic at this time. The term 'behavioural decision theory' was coined at this time to distinguish a broader social science approach from economic theories of decision making which traditionally emphasized the goal of utility maximization.

This article concentrates upon theories of decision making that are especially relevant to the understanding of organizational and managerial problems. It is useful to summarize the many key approaches, concerns and orientations that have been used to study organizational decision making as follows.

Case studies have been used to investigate particularly complex or difficult decisions such as the purchase of a new computer. Case studies aim to give richness of detail especially about the political problems of making and implementing a decision (Pettigrew 1973).

Laboratory experimentation has typically attracted psychologists concentrating upon issues such as the extent to which bias occurs in the way in which information is used in decision making (Hogarth 1980).

Game theory came to prominence during the Cold War due to a particular interest in military application (the notion of 'winning' and 'losing' providing an attractive analogy). It remains a useful way of thinking about decision making.

Simulation can be used in decision-making research using computers (Kleindorfer *et al.* 1993) or other techniques, such as case vignettes upon which participants pronounce a choice, or 'synthetic' investment decisions where scores on a limited number of variables are provided and decision makers have to decide whether to accept or reject a proposal (Butler *et al.* 1993).

Comparative field studies have become an increasingly common way of investigating organizational decision making as a way of overcoming the lack of generalizability of single cases, and the lack of a real-life feel associated with laboratory experiments and game theory. Typically, these studies create types of decision out of patterns in the associated processes and draw conclusions as to the likely conditions under which each type is best suited (Mintzberg *et al.* 1976; Hickson *et al.* 1986; Butler *et al.* 1993).

Descriptive, normative and *prescriptive orientations*. Research on decision making either aims to describe what happens in particular situations (descriptive), to develop a more explanatory theory whereby propositions can be tested with a view to defining norms as to how certain aspects of decision making can be changed (normative) or to develop heuristics (Bazerman 1998) to act as simplifying strategies to guide judgement (prescriptive).

Psychological and *sociological orientations*. Decision making may be studied in terms of the psychological characteristics of individuals through, for instance, variables concerned with Jung's personality types (Kleindorfer *et al.* 1993) or as sociological studies where the aim is to identify key powerful individuals in an organization and to discover interrelationships between them to explain how they manage to influence the outcomes of major decisions (Pettigrew 1973).

Information and its use is a major concept in decision theory: an information processing approach to decision making sees information as central to the process of coping with uncertainty and hence many studies of decision making have investigated the use of information.

Studies of power and politics help mitigate the problem of a sole reliance upon information processing by focusing on the strategic use of information; it can be withheld, used opportunistically or distorted, while the use of power opens up a political dimension to decision making (Hickson *et al.* 1986).

Programmed and unprogrammed decisions

Programmed decisions are those which are routine, repetitive and have clearly defined ends and means. Unprogrammed decisions are those which are non-routine, one-off and badly structured. As already implied, the bounded rational model is appropriate for unprogrammed decisions whereas the computational rational model is appropriate for programmed decisions.

The processes involved in each type of decision differ (Simon 1960). The computational rationality of the programmed decisions leads to the use of extensive search procedures to explore all possible options and, after application of appropriate algorithms, an optimal choice can be made. The bounded rationality of unprogrammed decisions will tend to involve problematic searches, with the need for alternatives prompted by a crisis or the availability of a solution and the

Table 1 Programmed and unprogrammed decisions compared

Decision type	Programmed	Unprogrammed
	Routine, repetitive	Novel, badly structured
Rationality	Intended, synoptic	Intended, bounded
Process	Computational methods	Heuristic
	Extensive search	Problemistic search
	Optimizing	Satisficing
		Disjointed and incremental

use of satisficing to make a choice. Implementation will tend to be disjointed and incremental (see Table 1).

Conceptual framework

The great diversity of approaches to the study of organizational decision making makes it necessary here to delimit the subject by means of a conceptual framework.

The core of the framework draws upon the 'garbage can' model of decision making (March 1988) by proposing that decision making involves streams of activities which serve to cope with uncertainty over time, specifically, problem definition, solution building, choosing, influencing and implementing.

Essentially, a decision is constrained by the performance of preceding decisions and will, in turn, affect succeeding decisions by its own performance. A decision can also involve sub-decisions, and concurrent decisions taking place elsewhere in the organization may also affect a decision. This network of decisions exists within an organization which, in turn, exists within a task and institutional environment (see Figure 1).

2 Strategies for choosing

The activity of choosing is central to decision making. Thompson (1967) notes that decision making involves two kinds of uncertainty. There can be uncertainty over outcome preferences (the ends) due to disagreements among managers, or there can be uncertainty concerning the means to reach the ends. Combining these two dimensions gives four decision strategies – computation, judgement, negotiation, inspiration (Figure 2) – each of which can be associated with a particular organizational type – bureaucratic, collegiate, political, charismatic.

When there is agreement over ends and clear means to reach those ends the appropriate choice strategy is computation, implying the existence of an algorithm into which the appropriate data can be fed and a number of known steps followed to calculate the optimal choice. Providing participants see the procedure as legitimate, the answer comes out of the calculations, even though those calculations

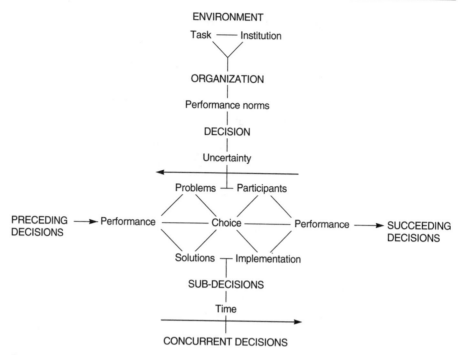

Figure 1

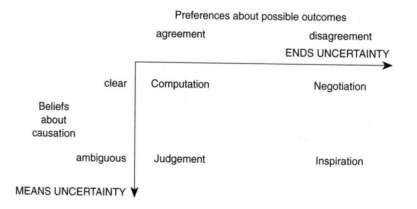

Figure 2

may be complex. This is the kind of rational-legal authority identified by Weber as belonging to bureaucracy.

If there is a high degree of means uncertainty due to ambiguous beliefs about causation, decision makers will no longer have faith in their algorithms to give an optimal choice. Bounded rationality rules and the decision strategy needs to accommodate this by satisficing methods. This does not mean that computations are not needed; they may provide a useful heuristic or a symbolic function to show that procedural rationality is being adhered to. This strategy rests upon a collegial view of organization whereby a self-governing college group will talk, opinionate and strive to reach a view on a solution. At the minimum, sufficient agreement over a step forward would be made to allow action to be taken.

If there is a high degree of ends uncertainty due to disagreements over preferences about possible outcomes decision makers will have to negotiate and bargain to clarify their objectives. This strategy rests upon the notion of decision making as a political process in which trade-offs and deals are made, and coalitions built. The outcome of this political process, if a decision is to be made, will at the minimum be a sufficient agreement on ends to allow action to be taken (Cyert and March 1963).

When ends and means uncertainty is high, decision makers would seem to have an almost impossible task of choosing any course of action. Inspiration is the only way forward with individual decision makers acting on hunches and, in extreme cases, on a belief in divine intervention. Under these conditions errors would be accepted as a possibility and the problem becomes one of correcting those errors in further decisions. This image of decision making puts an emphasis on decision making as a stream of choices whereas the computational strategy emphasizes the independence of each decision. The notion of inspiration connects with theories of leadership and charisma since under conditions of very high uncertainty trust in the characteristics of an individual replaces trust in procedures. The charismatic leader is seen by the followers to have solutions, or at least to possess the wisdom to find solutions, and may offer a new set of preferences to shift attention away from old conflicts.

The kind of organization surrounding this process is obviously the most difficult to define having been described as organized anarchy, as pertaining to chaos theory, or as a garbage can, into which various odds and ends are thrown and sorted.

Patterns of decision making

In practice, mixtures of processes are used and various comparative studies have attempted to discover patterns in these decision-making processes.

From a study of 17 investment decisions and 55 participating managers Butler *et al.* (1993) found that computation provides a necessary but not sufficient condition for effective decision making. Those decisions which manage to achieve an interaction between computation, bargaining, judgement and inspiration are the most effective in terms of objectives attainment and learning.

Mintzberg *et al.* (1976) examined the processes of decision making used in a range of decisions by comparing 25 decision cases in a variety of organizations. Data were collected concerning the extent to which various phases of decision making were used and concerning other factors such as the duration of each decision, the extent to which interruptions occurred and the number of branches and recycles in the sequence suggested by the model. From analysis of the data six generalized types of decision were identifiable.

1 *Simple interrupt*. Stimulus by problem, solution given, recognition and diagnosis stages used with a lot of interruptions. These were the non-complex decisions with given solutions which got blocked.
2 *Political design process*. Given solutions or modifications to ready-made solutions were used in these decisions but interruptions were more extensive due to intensive political activity.
3 *Basic search*. This type of decision would appear to come nearest to the rational type in that there were few interruptions and the emphasis was upon rational search processes and finding solutions in accordance with organizational procedure.
4 *Modified search*. Represents a rather more complex basic search type in which ready-made solutions are modified to a particular decision.
5, 6 *Basic* and *dynamic designs*. These two decision types appear to move towards the bounded rational type in that custom-made solutions are found following considerable design and evaluation effort.

Hickson *et al.* (1986) also provided a systematic attempt to observe the processes of strategic decision making across a large number of decision issues in many different types of organization. These studies examined 150 strategic decisions in 30 organizations of many different types ranging across a spectrum of manufacturing and service, and public and private organizations. Detailed observations and interviews were carried out concerning the processes used in a range of decisions within each organization and covering a range of topics. Generally these were high-level or 'top decisions', involving the long-term strategy of the organization and covering a range of issues dealing with matters such as the introduction of new products, closing down facilities and factories, reorganizations, mergers or acquisitions, personnel matters or investment in new equipment. Observations were made concerning a number of specific variables of the processes. *Scrutiny* is the basic process of searching, designing and evaluating solutions using various information sources. Also included in scrutiny is the degree of effort that goes into preparing reports, such as test markets or engineering development tests. *Interaction* is the degree of social interaction between participants, which may be formal, whereby a decision is processed through committees and procedures, or informal involving discussions over lunch, in corridors or elsewhere. *Negotiation* is the degree of bargaining over preferences ranging from the decision being not open to negotiation, through negotiation occurring only in the final stages, to negotiation resulting in limited consensus. *Delays* are the number of impediments and interruptions in the smooth flow of a decision which may occur for a number of reasons ranging from problems of sequencing, through awaiting priority in the order of attention, solving and awaiting further investigations, to wait to overcome resistance to change. *Duration* is measured by the time between an issue being deliberately considered in the organization to final authorization. *Centrality*, or the extent to which a decision is centralized or decentralized, is usually considered to be a major variable of decision making in an organization.

Data were subjected to a cluster analysis to establish patterns of decision making. Three distinct patterns or clusters emerged. The first, the sporadic cluster, consisted of a group of 53 decisions with above average delays, impediments, scrutiny (on all sub-variables), informal interaction and duration, and were authorized at the highest level in the organization following some negotiation. Overall these decisions may be described as informally spasmodic and protracted.

As a means of making decisions, in a wide range of British organizations, the sporadic method was used in about one-third of the decisions studied. This sporadic cluster may be contrasted to the fluid cluster, which also accounted for about one-third of the decisions. With these, there were less delays, impediments, scrutiny and duration, some negotiation and more formal interaction, but all decisions were still authorized at the highest level. Overall, these decisions may be described as steadily paced, quick and formally channelled.

The third group, the constricted decision cluster, is characterized by less scrutiny, negotiation and formal interaction than the other decision types. Decisions were authorized below the highest level but, paradoxically, used more sources of information during scrutiny than did the fluid decisions. Overall these may be seen as narrowly channelled decisions.

The complexity and political nature of the various decision issues were also assessed and, in general, the most complex and politically sensitive decisions were treated in a sporadic way; hence, sporadic issues were found to be those involving many diverse interests, were serious in their potential consequences, contentious and externally influenced.

Those decisions which scored slightly less on complexity and least of all on political sensitivity tended to be treated in a fluid manner. The distinguishing feature here with regard to the sporadically-treated issues was that the fluid issues were less serious but rarer (more unusual). It appears that top management wanted direct control over these decisions and permitted only that degree of delegation that could be formally managed.

Decision issues with the least complexity and political sensitivity were handled by the constricted process, the distinguishing feature being that the issues were familiar (programmed), involving internal interests only and were non-contentious.

3 Performance

The question of the performance and effectiveness of organizational decision making has been somewhat neglected but is obviously of concern to managers. The problem is, however, to find appropriate dimensions upon which to assess performance.

A field study of investment decisions indicated two dimensions of decision effectiveness (Butler *et al.* 1993). The first, objectives attainment, is the extent to which prior objectives, financial and non-financial, are reached. One feature found to have a strong effect upon increasing objectives attainment involved clarity over who was providing leadership for the decision. The second is the extent to which a decision and its associated processes lead to learning. Decision processes that involved a high degree of negotiation taking place over time, and a high degree of inspiration, tended to have high levels of learning. The distinction between the two views of performance pinpoints two different but pervasive aspects of organizational decision making; decision making as a rational process of meeting objectives or as an adaptive process.

Bias in information use

Much of the research carried out within a psychological paradigm has concerned itself with possible sources of bias in the way in which information gets used in decision making (Tversky and Kahneman 1981; Hogarth 1980; Bazerman 1998).

Following are some key biases which have been noted:

- *Availability of information.* There is a tendency for people to pay attention to information that is readily available in the immediate environment, for example, by drawing upon well-publicized or frequently occurring events.
- *Selective perception.* People will come to a problem with a bias according to existing group organizational or cultural memberships. Information is then sought which is consistent with prior ideas or first impressions, rather than to falsify a hypothesis.
- *Concrete information.* A view which is supported by received, statistical or verifiable information tends to get more weight than a view about which there is scant, ambiguous or more subjective information.
- *Illusory correlation.* A belief that two variables co-vary when they are, in fact, unrelated in any causal connection, can lead to a spurious analysis of a situation.
- *Inconsistency of judgements.* There may be an inability to apply a given set of criteria consistently, such as when selecting students for admission to a university.
- *Conservatism.* There can be a failure to revise opinions if new information comes to light. This is discussed below under Bayes' theorem.
- *Order effects of data presentation.* Sometimes the first items in a presentation can assume undue importance – primacy – sometimes the last items can be considered more important – recency.
- *Incorrect extrapolations.* Past trends are often used to estimate the future by assuming a linear growth. In practice growths can be exponential, like the growth of an epidemic, as can declines.
- *Use of heuristics to reduce mental effort.* Habit and rules of thumb are part of a satisficing approach to decision making. They can be a source of bias and lead to lazy decision making when, in fact, more complete information is available.
- *Apparent representativeness.* Judging the likelihood of an event by estimating the degree of similarity to a class of event, for example selecting a manager for

a job because he exhibits characteristics typical of a good manager in terms of dress, speech, etc.

- *Law of small numbers*. A small sample is taken as representative of a population.
- *Justifiability*. Data are selected to support a preconceived argument. The converse would be falsifiability whereby decision makers deliberately set out to find data to refute an argument.

In order to help overcome some of these biases Neustadt and May (1986: 37) recommend that decision makers should identify clearly the historical analogues they are using, suggesting that an elementary procedure is to break these analogues down into information which is known, presumed or unclear. Positive action can be taken on known information whereas further search or cautious action only should be taken on the presumed or clear.

Error coping

The notion of bias suggests that there is a correct answer to a problem and that a decision process can be subjected to the same kind of analysis as statistical hypothesis testing, which identifies two types of error. A Type I error leads to rejection of a true hypothesis: an example of this would be management neglecting to use basic cost accounting methods to assess the worthiness of a cost-reduction proposal where the information and techniques are available with great precision. This kind of error is an error of lack of precision in the process. A Type II error leads to acceptance of a false hypothesis: an example of this would be management making a major investment decision based entirely upon a rate of return calculation but where the data fed into that calculation are highly dubious with regard to what is meant. This kind of error is an error of spurious precision. The garbage can model suggests that sometimes accepting errors can be rational since the costs of making a possible mistake can be outweighed by the possible advantages to be gained from making an inspirational type of decision.

Risk and disasters

Another approach to decision effectiveness comes from the burgeoning literature on disaster and risk management given impetus by a number of well-publicized incidents such as the Chernobyl reactor failure (Royal Society 1992).

This literature points to a difference between an engineering and a social science view of risk. The engineering definition follows a computational approach to decision making and defines risk in terms of the probability of an adverse event, whereas the social science definition follows a judgemental perspective and emphasizes the perception and interpretation of the risk by participants in a given social situation. A kind of 'institutional blindness' can be used to explain how signals of forthcoming problems can be ignored, sometimes through a process of 'defensive avoidance' (Janis and Mann 1977). The literature serves to reinforce the idea that both what is perceived as a disaster and what are then perceived as the causes of that disaster are socially as well as technically induced.

On a less dramatic scale investigations of the management of large projects (Morris and Haugh 1987) show that cost overruns between 40 and 200 per cent are the norm, with higher levels in defence. It is particularly at the early stages of a project that the incubation of later disasters can be laid through a combination of internal and external management problems.

4 Defining problems

Literature on decision making emphasizes that a problem is perceived when there is a gap between the expectation and the reality of performance. There is also an assumption that problems tend to start as ill-defined but get less uncertain with the process, which may be generally true although many problems which initially appear simple may become more complex as the decision proceeds.

The problem stream

Problems are constantly being recognized, defined and labelled by organizational participants. Labels can get attached to these problems or topics according to their relevance for organizational subsystems. Hickson *et al.* (1986) identified ten such problems or topics: technology, reorganizations, control, domain, services, products, personnel, boundary, inputs and location. Topic type was found to affect some aspects of decision processes; for example, reorganization decisions are the most rare and are amongst the most contentious.

Psychological research uses the term 'framing' to describe the parameters by which problems become defined, especially through the way in which information about choices and their possible effects is interpreted (Tversky and Kahneman 1981). For example, in public policy issues the manner in which information about the possible risks of a disease, diet or not wearing seatbelts in cars is presented can make a vital difference to how people respond.

Interest

Problems can involve the interests of a wide range of diverse organizational groups each with their different motivations for getting involved in decisions. Organizations can provide financial incentives for managers to raise new capital investment project proposals although it has been found that managers do not generally admit to any great amount of career interest in raising such proposals (Butler *et al.* 1993). More usually the rewards for involvement in decisions is less clear cut and may range from a simple desire to be 'in on things', or to gain information that may be of use, or at a later stage be identified as the champion of a successful project (Butler *et al.* 1993: ch. 6). People sometimes fight for the right to participate without necessarily pursuing that right (March 1988: 396).

The ability of individuals to set the agenda of discussions about a topic has an important part to play in defining a problem. A distinction needs to be made between power exerted by someone directly taking part in decision making and the power exerted by someone who manages to suppress the discussion of certain issues while surreptitiously allowing discussion of other issues; this is the power of non-decision making (Hickson *et al.* 1986).

Chairing committees and other formal bodies in an organization gives an ability to control admission of topics on an agenda and to control the order in which topics are discussed; topics which are placed at the end of a long agenda tend to get less attention (Pfeffer 1981).

Avoidance of problems

Rather than actively seeking to identify possible problems, decision makers can indulge in defensive avoidance, a process whereby decision makers filter out information which does not conform to an existing point of view. This condition is encouraged by 'groupthink' whereby strong group norms can give group members an illusion of invulnerability, make it difficult for individual dissent to emerge, or top management can filter out information which does not fit existing policy (Janis and Mann 1977).

If information systems are too precisely engineered to current organizational needs, organizational problems will be defined more and more within the same parameters. Ambiguity will, therefore, be weeded out when the need is to increase ambiguity (March 1988).

Aspects of problem definition

Comparative research into organizational decision making generally assesses the nature of the problem that is being considered, many of the ideas being related to the concept of decision framing used in the psychological paradigm of decision research. Sociological studies of decision making tend to search for one or two summarizing descriptors of the overall process of decision making. For example, the nature of the problem under consideration can be described in terms of the associated technical complexity and political sensitivity (Hickson *et al.* 1986).

Consequentiality captures an aspect of complexity, giving the idea of decision makers looking forward to assess the future impact of a decision, such as the seriousness for the organization if things go wrong. Certain problems can also be seen to set precedents or to be particularly radical for the organization and therefore need to be considered more carefully. These aspects tend to be related to the comparative rarity of a decision within an organization. The greater the rarity the less likely there will be well-established procedures for solution building. Reorganization decisions were found to be the most rare, whereas decisions about products and supplies (inputs) were the least rare. Although such measures vary according to conditions there appears to be little doubt that reorganization decisions are one of the most difficult for an organization to cope with due to their rule-setting nature.

5 Solution building

The computational model of decision making requires that solutions are designed and evaluated in response to a problem. The inspirational model suggests that solutions form a stream of action relatively independent from problems, that solutions are more abundant than problems and can provide the impetus to a choice rather than vice versa (March 1988).

Professionals and members of skill groups have an in-built bias towards producing solutions in accordance with the ideology of that profession; engineers may suggest a product design solution to a problem of declining sales while a marketing person may see a solution more in terms of improvement in service.

Capital budgeting theory and practice provides an example of the tension between the computational and inspirational ways of building solutions. The theory is particularly concerned with methods of appraising the worthiness of projects, with the concept of risk playing a key role. Surveys have shown how techniques such as discounted cash flow (DCF), internal rate of return (IRR) and net present value (NPV) are increasingly being used in industry. Case studies of actual decisions, however, show how frequently such techniques are abused, either by figures being manipulated to support a particular interest or by calculations being conducted after a choice has been made. Managers consistently show a satisficing behaviour by preferring 'naive' methods of appraisal, such as payback period, to more sophisticated and theoretically more rational methods, such as DCF (Butler *et al.* 1993).

Assimilating new information

The computational strategy relies upon the ability of decision makers to scan the environment for as many alternative solutions as possible and to evaluate their likely outcomes. One problem with formal methods of appraisal is that new information may come to light as a decision proceeds through the implementation phase, thus providing decision makers with the chance to alter their original prediction.

Bayes' theorem provides an analytical method to take into account the effect of new information upon an initial probability estimate of a particular outcome. Assume fairly rational decision makers in a company wish to assess the national market success of a new product line and they have an initial probability estimate of product success based upon the best available information at that time. They decide to carry out a test market before a full-scale launch (a sub-decision in terms of the organizational model of decision making) but they know that test markets are not infallible and can only be relied upon with a limited degree of confidence.

There are two aspects to the confidence that can be placed in a test market: (1) the likelihood that the test market will indicate a success and that the product will be successful nationwide; (2) the likelihood that the test market will indicate a success and that the product will be unsuccessful nationwide. The question is: How can an original estimate of a successful national product launch be amended in the light of a subsequent test market? Bayes' theorem gives a method for computing the answer based upon the assumption of rational decision makers. An original estimate of the probability of success is increased by a test market indicating a success given that the product has been successful but is decreased by an estimate that the test market will indicate a success even if the product has not been successful in the market. Put in more formal terms, Bayes' theorem states that when two hypotheses are being considered the posterior odds (the ratio of the two probabilities after the information) are proportional to the product of the prior odds and the likelihood ratio.

The significant aspect of Bayes' theorem for a theory of organizational decision making is that it represents a move away from a pure computational strategy by recognizing the importance of subjective probabilities. Investigations of the actual information processing behaviour of decision makers shows a tendency towards conservatism, meaning that individuals do not make as much revision to initial probability estimates as the theorem suggests they should. Explanations for this have been sought in terms of how the new information may be misperceived or misused; the discovery of a conservative bias accords with case studies of decision making whereby, once a decision is being implemented, it requires a large body of contrary evidence to alter that action.

Intuition

The trend is increasingly to challenge the overly rational view of organizational decision making and to see the process more as a matter of making sense of situations (March 1999). Case studies of managerial decision making generally support the idea that decision makers are prepared to act on what they see as incomplete information (Hickson *et al.* 1986). Intuition and judgement are central to the process of solution building, a topic that has been attracting an increasing amount of research. Isenberg (1984) found a number of key characteristics concerning the thought processes of senior managers:

- a feel for inconsistencies in information;
- ability to build upon well-learned patterns of behaviour;
- synthesis of isolated pieces of information;
- intuition to check on formal analysis;
- an understanding of the importance of interpersonal and organizational processes.

At the individual level techniques are suggested to develop lateral thinking and improve intuition but these characteristics should not be ignored. Managers need to develop a 'map' or framework for linking together the myriad problems with which they have to cope. Such a framework may offer a number of specific suggestions:

- bolster intuition with rational thinking;
- offset tendencies to be overly rational by imagination and learning to act with incomplete information;

- learn to 'map' unfamiliar territory;
- use 'rules of thumb';
- spend time understanding a problem;
- look for connections between diverse problems;
- recognize thinking as a critical asset.

Most models of judgement and intuition can be seen as ways of trying to push the process as far as possible towards the computational strategy by systematizing the intuitive processes of judgement and bargaining.

Hogarth (1980) identified a number of models for the improvement of judgement which go beyond the linear model of giving each outcome a weight according to the product of an outcome and its probability. One way is to use a conjunctive model whereby cut-off points are selected such that any alternative falling below this point is rejected; this can be seen as a systematized form of satisficing.

Janis and Mann (1977) present a method for resolving psychological conflicts in decision making involving a 'decisional balance sheet'. The process encourages vigilance (but not hypervigilance) and overtly develops alternatives in order to ensure that groupthink does not force decision makers into agreeing to a choice which they are against.

The architecture of complexity

Simon (1962) argues that the processes of intuition can be analysed in terms of a hierarchical arrangement of assemblies and sub-assemblies, illustrating this point by the parable of two watchmakers, Hora and Tempus.

Hora learned to assemble watches by building a series of sub-assemblies and then assembling the sub-assemblies. If Hora was interrupted during assembly, work already put into a partly finished sub-assembly could be lost, but this would be the limit of the loss. The other sub-assemblies would remain intact and, providing there was a set of rules for assembling the sub-assemblies, the watch could be completed. Tempus, on the other hand, assembled watches in one big leap which meant simultaneously holding many parts in a state of suspension. If everything meshed the watch could be assembled very quickly. If there was an interruption, however, all the work done to that point on a particular watch could be lost and Tempus would have to start again.

The two methods of assembling complex bits of machinery can be compared to different methods of learning. Simon argues that mystical processes called intuition or experience can be decomposed into architectures of sub-assemblies. In this way experienced practitioners in many fields, such as chess, can hold in their heads the solutions to many standard moves to be fitted together into a pattern during a match.

Formal planning systems lay down procedures for strategic decision making. Such procedures attempt to identify systematic ways of defining problems and building solutions. If, however, they do not sufficiently reflect the reality of decision making within an organization such procedures may come to be carried out primarily for symbolic reasons (Langley 1989).

6 Participating and influencing

The way in which power and influence are exerted in decision making is a major feature of most descriptions of decision making. One approach to the measurement of influence has been through the use of a 'control graph' (Tannenbaum 1968). By dividing an organization into different levels (lower, middle and upper) of management it is possible to map the extent to which each level has influence over decisions, the slope and the shape of the graph portraying the distribution of influence. A straight line sloping upwards from left to right (that is, influence increases as levels are ascended) gives a 'normal' bureaucratic type of organization whereby higher management has more influence than lower management.

Some organizations, notably democratic ones in which a total membership can vote on an issue, tend to show a horizontal graph. It is also possible to have an inverted graph whereby influence decreases as the hierarchy is ascended, a situation approximated by some professional organizations whereby the higher levels are mainly administrators for autonomous professional workers. However, the 'iron law' of oligarchy suggests that this could be an unstable situation and that higher echelons would tend to accumulate power by virtue of being at the centre of an information network.

Other studies (Butler *et al.* 1993; Hickson *et al.* 1986) have assessed the extent to which participants from different functional groups and external organizations get involved and exert influence over decisions. In general, the involvement and influence of external participants is much less than for internal participants. Liaison positions, followed closely by marketing and sales departments, were found to exert the most influence in decision making, the least influential internal departments being purchasing departments, and the least influential of all participants to be trades unions.

Power

The degree of influence exerted by participants will vary according to their power in the organization. The strategic contingencies theory of power predicts that the influence exerted by managers over a range of decision topics is a result of the strategic position of the particular department to which they belong.

The strategic position of a department with regard to exerting influence is increased by its centrality in the workflow and by the extent to which it is non-substitutable by other departments or outsiders. In particular, managers' power is increased if their departments can show that they are able to cope with critical uncertainties for the organization.

The strategic contingencies theory of power gives us a useful way of thinking about connections between problems and solutions. Making the connection requires action by participants in the organization and relies upon the ability of that participant to activate both a problem and a solution.

Other approaches to power emphasize the ability of powerful people to make the rules concerning who can participate in decision making and the kinds of procedures that have to be followed. It is this rule-making ability that is at the heart of the institutional effects upon decision making.

Individual versus group decision making

An important question underlying the issue of participation in decision making concerns the question of whether groups are more effective decision makers than individuals. A number of factors are likely to favour groups over individuals:

1 as the need for acceptance increases it becomes more necessary to involve those affected by the decision to enable implementation and legitimate outcomes;
2 as complexity increases it becomes necessary to include other individuals for reasons of expertise;
3 defining, solving and choosing are likely to be slower, but implementing to be quicker, in groups;
4 where creating ideas or remembering information is needed a group increases the probability of task success;
5 when the task gains from duplication of effort and/or the division of labour groups gain over individuals; no one individual can comprehend the entirety of the task and there needs to be selection of individuals according to ability.

Brainstorming is a technique to facilitate the generation of creative alternatives by encouraging free expression and by avoiding the evaluation of options until all ideas are assembled. The following three rules are generally used: (1) ideas are freely expressed without considering their quality; (2) group members are encouraged to modify and combine previously stated ideas; and (3) there is a moratorium upon evaluation until all ideas have been stated. The Delphi technique (developed at the Rand Corporation) is a similar but rather more formalized technique involving physically separating participants during idea generation and then collating judgements on topics (Kleindorfer *et al.* 1993).

Devil's advocates are one way in which new ideas can be injected and conflict deliberately engendered to counteract the effects of groupthink. This necessitates someone deliberately presenting an opposite viewpoint to any prevailing or emerging consensus. The process works by getting people to think again before committing themselves to a course of action (Schwenk 1984).

Risky shift deals with a question that has long been a focus of controversy: whether groups are more likely to take risky decisions than individuals. Under certain conditions there is a shift towards riskier decisions when an individual rather than a group makes a decision, although if a group shows particularly innovative values it can show more risk than the individuals (Kleindorfer *et al.* 1993).

Centralization/decentralization

A major dimension of organizational decision making concerns the extent to which the process is centralized or decentralized. Some decisions require authorization at a level above the highest internal level (usually chief executive or board) by being authorized outside the organization, at a headquarters or some equivalent location (Butler *et al.* 1993).

Centralized decision making is generally associated with low levels of innovation but helps implementation when minimal commitment is required from other organizational participants. As decisions get more complex centralization becomes a less effective method since high-level decision makers do not have enough information to make effective choices and are liable to be overloaded with decision making. Centralization can occur either by top management directly making a decision or by laying down some general parameters and policies but delegating actual operating decisions to a lower-level authority.

Leadership

Leadership is a feature of decision making that is often noted. 'Great man' theories of politics, business and organization tend to explain decisions in terms of the individual characteristics of someone who is particularly adept at guiding the processes. The four choice strategies suggest four types of leadership ability: for the computational strategy a good administrator would be needed; for the judgemental strategy a person who can build consensus; for the negotiation strategy an organizational politician is needed; and for the inspirational strategy a charismatic leader. If during the decision process ends and/or means uncertainty shifts, the nature of the required leadership may change. For instance, a decision may start off as highly uncertain on both dimensions and be driven by a charismatic leader but as it shifts towards implementation a good administrator is needed.

Transactional and transformational leadership

Two types of leadership, the transactional and the transformational have been referred to by Burns (Butler 1991). The transactional leader is comparable to the administrator or bureaucrat who sets up a system intervening only on a management by exception basis and providing rewards proportional to effect. Transformational leadership, related to inspirational decision making, is characterized by charisma (exuding enthusiasm, encouraging expression of opinions, exciting a vision), individual attention to subordinates and intellectual stimulation.

Game theory

Game theory is a method for analysing decision making under conditions of conflict when the pay-off to a participant depends upon the behaviour of others in the game. A game requires: (1) participants or players; (2) rules; (3) pay-offs and associated values; (4) controllable moves which each player can make; and

(5) information availability. Early writings emphasized two-player, zero-sum competitive games but developments have led to a theory of *n*-person cooperative games holding promise of greater validity for the theory of organizational decision making (Kreps 1990; Kleindorfer *et al.* 1993). The essence of the cooperative game is the need for equal pay-offs to players if they cooperate but large punishments for betrayal of trust. Games can also be strategic, laying out possible moves in a matrix of pay-offs, or games can be extensive, laying out a decision tree of moves giving pay-offs based upon previous moves made, thereby introducing time as a variable (Kreps 1990: 9).

As the available moves and associated pay-offs are predetermined by the rules of the game the essence of game theory is to determine the extent to which players choose the most rational route. It provides a way of thinking forward in a series of 'what if' thought experiments but in so doing makes simplifications as to how the rules of the game and pay-offs are set. The past is compressed into these rules and pay-offs which represent experience of past behaviour.

Decision makers do not necessarily behave as in the crisp moves of game theory, as shown by the much analysed Cuban Missile Crisis (Allison 1971) during which the USA and the former Soviet Union stood face to face on the brink of nuclear war. In setting up missile bases in Cuba the Soviet leadership assumed that the Americans would not seriously challenge their move; game theory predicted a step-by-step military escalation whereas President Kennedy threatened a 'complete one-shot annihilation' of the Soviet Union.

7 Time

Speed in managerial decision making is often thought to be a virtue but evidence indicates that the speed of analysing and choosing is less important than getting commitment so that implementation can proceed quickly. Evidence also shows that the duration of strategic decision making as assessed by the time from the inception of an issue to its authorization varies greatly, ranging from three weeks to nine years with a mean of one to two years (Hickson *et al.* 1986; Butler *et al.* 1993). The image of managerial decisiveness is further eroded when it is also seen that various forms of discontinuities are normal.

Discontinuities in the process is one of the most troublesome aspects for decision makers. Two of the most common reasons for delays concern awaiting further investigation and awaiting the outcome of external resistance to a proposal. The least common cause of delay concerns searching for further information, followed by sequencing delays due to awaiting priority in the order of attention (Hickson *et al.* 1986). Another aspect of time found to concern managers is if the decision is perceived to be of too slow a pace. Nevertheless there is evidence to show that slow, deliberate decision making increases learning (Butler *et al.* 1993).

Preceding the more overt problem-defining and solution-building phases of decision making may be an extensive gestation period during which an idea is conceived. Gestation times have been found to vary widely, from a matter of days to 15 years, with a mean approximating to two years. Gestation time is found to be uncorrelated with duration (Hickson *et al.* 1986).

The value of time

Cultures valuing individualism (the English-speaking nations) could be expected to value quick decisions, whereas a culture valuing collectivism (Japan) could be expected to value a more deliberate participative process especially during problem defining and solution building (Hofstede 1980).

Organizations inevitably put a money value on time and the kinds of rules an organization uses for appraising capital projects can be critical in determining the way in which time is conceived. Using the more popular payback period rather than the more sophisticated DCF calculation tends to encourage a shorter time horizon (Marsh 1990), with attendant concerns over the propensity for managers to take an overly short-term view of business strategy. Capital appraisal methods generally ignore the managerial cost of making the decision – the managerial time spent on the process. Managerial time comprises the sum of the time spent by participants over the decision and an organization 'spends' this in anticipation of a future return (Butler *et al.* 1993).

The timeframe

Decision making is located within a time-frame of preceding, succeeding and concurrent other decisions. Topics arise in part out of preceding decisions which set constraints for a current decision. The more frequently a given topic occurs the greater the ability to develop routines and procedures, these procedures in turn setting constraints for succeeding decisions.

If decision makers' attention is involved with concurrent decisions their attention may be drawn away from a focal decision. Hence the greater the degree of interdependence between other decisions in an organization the greater the urgency and pacing of decision making. The Bay of Pigs débâcle that haunted President Kennedy in the 1960s, when American troops were forced to make a hasty exit from Cuba after mounting an invasion, has been attributed to the idea that the President and his advisors were never able to spend more than 45 minutes together at a time prior to making the decision to invade (Neustadt and May 1986).

As decision making proceeds sub-decisions are often made on the way; for example, a sub-decision for an investment decision might be to set up a project team. The membership of such a team and its terms of reference can critically affect the progress of the focal decision issue. Thus, sub-decisions also set constraints (Simon 1947; Butler *et al.* 1993).

Timeframes are useful for thinking about the question of timing in decision making. For example, the ability of an aspiring chief executive to bring himself to the attention of the board of directors by appropriately timing the raising of the particular issue of electricity generation in a chemical company was critical to the achievement of that ambition (Hickson *et al.* 1986). To be too early or too late in raising problems or proposing solutions can lose or fail to gain support for an issue. Bringing people in, or leaving them out, or choosing a decision strategy at the right moment can make the difference to a solution's acceptance and implementation.

8 Implementation

We can identify two opposing ideas as to how choices are implemented. First, planned implementation is a dominant idea in the strategic planning literature and clearly related to the computational choice strategy whereby the process of choosing by policy makers is largely separated from the process of implementation which is carried out by different people.

Incremental implementation is a different process and clearly more related to inspirationally produced decisions. The emphasis now turns upon the process of feedback between policy makers and implementers during implementation. At the extreme, the distinction between the two sets of people disappears and in extreme cases implementation can be initiated prior to completion of other decision activities (Butler *et al.* 1993).

Much has been written about how to formulate formal strategic planning but assessment of whether these systems improve the effectiveness of strategic decisions is inconclusive. However, planning systems are usually seen to: increase problem awareness; identify organizational strengths and weaknesses; provide information and communications; allocate resources; provide quantification of objectives and resources; and provide a moral framework for decision making. Research has also shown that well-developed formal planning systems increase lateral communications in an organization (Bazzaz and Grinyer 1981).

Knee-deep in the big muddy

As implementation of a choice proceeds, commitment to that choice grows, making it difficult to withdraw, a phenomenom called 'knee-deep in the big muddy'. Experiments show how decision makers who have made an initial investment in phase one of a project are more likely to spend larger amounts in a subsequent phase two investment when phase one shows signs of going wrong than when phase one is showing signs of success. This escalating commitment is amplified if the decision makers are held personally responsible for the consequences of a decision (Bazerman 1998).

This phenomenon is alarming from a managerial perspective but is illustrated by cases as varied as a government sinking more troops into a war that cannot be won, to individuals sinking more money into repairing an unrepairable used car. The implication is that decision makers need to gather strength as evidence accumulates to indicate that a mistake has been made and to quickly withdraw.

Project implementation

There is a well-established literature on project management which gives us an opportunity to investigate the relationships between different decision-making activities in order to achieve success. It is an axiom of project management that implementation can be eased if a number of factors are present, in particular thorough early planning involving the client.

There is also evidence to show that when efficiency is the measure of project success planning factors are emphasized in the early stages but give way to political factors as the implementation proceeds. When, however, external success measures, such as client satisfaction, are more important planning factors dominate throughout the life of a project (Pinto and Prescott 1990).

9 Organization and decision making

Central to the model of organizational decision making presented here is the notion of norms as applied to the performance of organizations and of decisions made therein. To understand the source of these norms we need to see an organization as a technical system, as a natural system and as an institutionalized system.

The ideal for the technical system perspective is to remove uncertainty by perfecting ideologies and structures aimed at fulfilling instrumental objectives. Decision making thereby becomes more routinized and computational as internal structures are developed. A natural system perspective sees an organization as open to an inherently uncertain task environment. Decision making involves steering a course between the efficiency logic of improving technical methods and the adaptability logic of responding to competitive changes and demands in the task environment. This established perspective is well summarized in prescriptions about the need for fuzzy organizational structures and satisficing/inspirational decision making as environmental and technical uncertainty increases (Thompson 1967; Butler 1991). Managerial ideology also needs to match structure and context; in a stable task environment with well-defined technology ideology tends to focus upon efficiency but as the environment gets more uncertain a 'robust' ideology becomes necessary, meaning that decision makers need to hold among themselves a broad set of beliefs about aims and methods and that most importantly there should be an over-arching understanding of what the organization as a whole stands for and is trying to achieve. Structures to enhance robustness include the use of group rather than individual decision making and organizational mission statements.

The institutional environment

A criticism of the natural system perspective is that it presents a too intentionally rational view of decision making. An essential aspect of the institutional approach to organizational decision making emphasizes the limitations upon choice for both individuals and organizations imposed by social norms (Douglas

1987). Four types of norm constraining action have been suggested: economic; instrumental; referent (or social) and moral (Butler 1991). Norms are carried into an organization, forming individual and group preferences as regards particular decisions. For example, strong economic norms as a result of a competitive environment will tend to filter through to the evaluation of investments as an emphasis upon financial measures such as IRR.

Whatever typology may be suggested, norms act as standards of desirability and vary across different sectors of the environment and over time, and in this respect an organization has to make choices as to which norms are most important (Butler 1991; Thompson 1967). Here the notion of sector (or industry) helps us to identify the set of interrelated organizations to which a focal organization belongs and provides norms concerning appropriate technologies and structures (Butler 1991). For example, if funding decisions are centralized within an institutional sector, funding decisions within an organization also tend to be more centralized, whereas a more complex fragmented sector will involve organizations in complex linkages. It is under these more complex conditions that organizations anxious to demonstrate conformity with institutional procedures tend to stress symbolic aspects in their decision making (Meyer and Scott 1983).

As organizations have become increasingly international, national cultures have gathered great significance in theories of decision making (Hofstede 1980). For example, a comparison of Brazilian and UK managers finds that UK managers tend towards more individualistic, methodical and slow decision making (Oliveira and Hickson 1991).

One way in which the institutional environment defines organizations is by ownership (private versus public); whether they are commercial in the degree to which revenues are raised by selling a product direct to customers or whether they are service rather than manufacturing organizations. Hickson *et al.* (1986) found that there was a slight tendency for public organizations to display more sporadic processes, while the degree of commercialism made little difference to the decision processes, but it was found that manufacturing organizations had a slightly greater tendency towards sporadic decision making.

The classification of external interest units by Hickson *et al.* (1986: 63) further illuminates the importance of institutional forces upon organizational decision making. Transactions with suppliers, customers and clients take place in the task environment and these units were the most involved and the most influential of all external units. However, units concerned with private institutional norms, such as auditors, trade associates and shareholders were also quite involved and influential in decision making. Units concerned with public institutional norms such as government departments and agencies (for example, health and safety regulators) were also quite highly involved. Both public and private standards enforcement is a factor that is taken into account in strategic decisions but these enforcers do not exert much direct influence.

Decision topics over which private standard units had most influence concerned topics about inputs, location and personnel, whereas public standard units had most influence over domain and location topics. Public standard units exhibited a very high degree of influence over decisions concerning mergers, alliances and various forms of cooperative ventures where the need for public regulation necessarily appears very high. There is also evidence to indicate that a high number and diversity of external interest units over decision making leads to the sporadic type of decision process. Regulations create their own uncertainties and dependencies. The extent to which there is agreement or disparity over the impact of regulation upon a particular issue can therefore be important to the effectiveness of a decision. There is evidence that disparity about the impact of regulations upon an organization increases learning during decision making (Butler *et al.* 1993).

10 Conclusions

This article has approached the examination of managerial decision making using an organizational model of decision making which sees decisions as involving a number of activities, with participants in the process acting with intentional rationality but constrained by a number of factors. It is well established within the literature on organizational decision making that uncertainty poses a major constraint due to lack of information about the means to achieve certain ends and lack of agreement over outcome preferences.

More recent theorizing about organizational decision making is emphasizing the importance of institutional factors, which also impose constraints upon decision makers. These institutional factors are historically determined and set performance norms for organizations which are then translated into norms to assess the performance of decisions and also the means by which decisions are made.

Further reading

(References cited in the text marked *)

* Allison, G.T. (1971) *The Essence of Decision: Explaining the Cuban Missile Crisis*, Boston, MA: Little Brown & Co. (A classic case highlighting the importance of political factors in decision making.)
* Barnard, C.I. (1938) *The Functions of the Executive*, Cambridge, MA: Harvard University Press. (A foundation book in modern management theory, written by a practising manager, which indicates the importance of decision making.)
* Bazerman, M. (1998) *Judgment in Managerial Decision Making*, 4th edn, New York: Wiley. (A practical book from a psychological perspective; includes exercises.)
* Bazzaz, S. and Grinyer, P.H. (1981) 'Corporate planning in the U.K.: the state of the art in the 70's', *Strategic Management Journal* 2: 151–68. (Helps to link the strategic planning and decision-making literatures.)
* Butler, R.J. (1991) *Designing Organizations: A Decision Making Perspective*, London: Routledge. (Sees organizational design in terms of the need to provide structures that enable effective decision making.)
* Butler, R.J., Davies, L., Pike, R. and Sharp, J. (1993) *Strategic Investment Decisions: Theory, Practice and Process*, London: Routledge. (A study of 55 managers making 17 strategic investments. Uses case studies and a survey.)

* Cyert, R. and March, J.G. (1963) *The Behavioural Theory of the Firm*, Englewood Cliffs, NJ: Prentice Hall. (A pathbreaking book indicating the need to see the actions taken by firms in terms of the limits to rationality in managerial decision making.)

* Douglas, M. (1987) *How Institutions Think*, London: Routledge & Kegan Paul. (Introduces us to the neglected anthropological view of decision making in institutions.)

* Hickson, D.J. (ed.) (1995) *Managerial Decision Making*, Aldershot: Dartmouth. (A collection of classic papers on decision making.)

* Hickson, D., Butler, R.J., Cray, D., Mallory, G. and Wilson, D.C. (1986) *Top Decisions: Strategic Decision Making in Organizations*, Oxford: Basil Blackwell. (The theory of organizational decision making based upon an extensive study of 150 decisions in 30 highly varied organizations.)

* Hofstede, G. (1980) *Culture's Consequences: International Differences in Work-related Values*, Beverly Hills, CA: Sage Publications. (Study across 40 countries, introducing the four dimensions of national culture.)

* Hogarth, R.M. (1980) *Judgment and Choice: The Psychology of Decision*, Chichester: Wiley. (An extensive discussion of the psychological perspective on decision making.)

* Isenberg, D.J. (1984) 'How senior managers think', *Harvard Business Review* 62 (November–December): 80–90. (A practical introduction to intuition.)

* Janis, I.L. and Mann, L. (1977) *Decision Making: A Psychological Anaylsis of Conflict: Choice and Commitment*, New York: The Free Press. (Incorporates the influential notions of 'groupthink' and 'defensive avoidance' into an overall framework.)

* Jennings, D. and Wattam, S. (1998) *Decision Making: An Integrated Approach*, London: Financial Times Pitman Publishing. (Provides useful but different perspectives from the rational perspective of decision making.)

* Kleindorfer, P.R., Kunreuther, H.C. and Schoemaker, P.J.H. (1993) *Decision Sciences: An Integrative Perspective*, Cambridge: Cambridge University Press. (Integrates the managerial science and psychological perspectives on decision making.)

* Kreps, D. (1990) *Game Theory and Economic Modelling*, Oxford: Clarendon Press. (An introduction to game theory.)

* Langley, A. (1989) 'In search of rationality: the purposes behind the use of formal analysis in organizations', *Administrative Science Quarterly* 34 (4): 598–631. (Emphasizes the symbolic nature of formal analysis.)

* Lindblom, C. (1959) 'The science of muddling through', *Public Administration Review* 19: 79–88. (Colourfully points to the limits of rationality in decision making.)

* March, J.G. (1965) *The Handbook of Organizations*, Chicago, IL: Rand McNally. (Gives the 'state of the art' in the 1960s. Many things have not changed.)

* March, J.G. (1988) *Decisions and Organizations*, London: Blackwell. (Contains a number of papers on the anarchic theme of decision making.)

* March, J.G. (1999) *The Pursuit of Organizational Intelligence*, Oxford: Blackwell. (A compilation of many years of writing in the field.)

* March, J.G. and Simon, H.A. (1958) *Organizations*, New York: Wiley. (A classic book in part concerned with building a model of organizations from the microprocesses of decision making.)

* Marsh, P. (1990) *Short Termism*, London: Institutional Fund Managers Association. (Introduces us to the importance of time horizons with special reference to financial decisions.)

* Meyer, J.W. and Scott, W.R. (1983) *Organizational Environments: Ritual and Rationality*, Beverly Hills, CA: Sage Publications. (A view on the effect of institutional environments upon organizational decision making.)

* Mintzberg, H. (1975) *The Nature of Managerial Work*, New York: Harper Row. (Emphasizes the interrupted nature of managerial decision making.)

* Mintzberg, H., Raisinghai, D. and Theoret, A. (1976) 'The structure of unstructured decision processes', *Administrative Science Quarterly* 21 (2): 246–75. (A study of 25 decisions in

terms of a number of basic routines. Most decisions illustrate a discontinuous circular process.)

* Morris, P.W.G. and Haugh, G. H. (1987) *The Anatomy of Major Projects: A Study of the Reality of Project Management*, Chichester: Wiley. (Illustrates the implementation aspect of decision making.)

* Neustadt, R.E. and May, E.R. (1986) *Thinking in Time: The Uses of History for Decision Makers*, New York: The Free Press. (Emphasizes the importance of time.)

* Nutt, P. (1993) 'Flexible decision styles and the choices of top executives', *Journal of Management Studies* 30 (5): 695–721. (Looks at the effect of Jung's personality types upon decision making.)

* Oliveira, B. and Hickson, D.J. (1991) 'Cultural bases of strategic decision making: a Brazilian and English comparison', paper presented at the European Group for Organization Studies (EGOS) 10th colloquium, Vienna, July 15–17. (A cross-cultural study of decision making.)

* Pettigrew, A. (1973) *The Politics of Organizational Decision Making*, London: Tavistock Publications. (The case that injected the vital political dimension into the study of decision making.)

* Pfeffer, J. (1981) *Power in Organizations*, Marshfield, MA: Pittman Co. (A useful treatment of organizational power with implications for decision making.)

* Pinto, J.K. and Prescott, J.E. (1990) 'Planning and tactical factors in the project implementation process', *Journal of Management Studies* 27 (3): 305–27. (An investigation of the balance between planning and political factors.)

* Royal Society (1992) *Risk: Analysis, Perception and Management*, London: Royal Society. (A presentation of the differences between an engineering and a social science perspective on risk.)

* Schwenk, C.R. (1984) 'Devil's advocacy in managerial decision making', *Journal of Management Studies* 21 (2): 153–68. (Argues that an organization needs someone to speak out against prevailing assumptions.)

* Simon, H.A. (1960) *The New Science of Management Decision*, New York: Harper Row. (A presentation of the bounded rational critique of the rational model of decision making.)

* Simon, H.A. (1962) 'The architecture of complexity', *Proceedings of the American Philosophical Society* 106: 467–82. (A stalwart attempt to reduce the processes of intuition and judgement to a hierarchy of learned routines.)

* Simon, H.A. (1976) *Administrative Behaviour: A Study of Decision Making Process in Administrative Organizations*, 3rd edn, New York: The Free Press. (First published in 1947, this book built upon Barnard's *The Functions of the Executive* to emphasize the shift from classic to modern management theory.)

* Tannenbaum, A.S. (1968) *Control in Organizations*, New York: McGraw-Hill. (Provides a simple and effective way of mapping the influence of different organizational functions on decision making.)

* Thompson, J.D. (1967) *Organizations in Action*, New York: McGraw-Hill. (This enduring classic allows us to put decision making in an organizational context.)

* Tversky, A. and Kahneman, A. (1981) 'The framing of decisions and the psychology of choice', *Science* 211: 453–8. Also in G. Wright (ed.) *Behavioural Decision Making*, London: Plenum Press, ch. 2. (A sample paper from these key authors writing within the psychological paradigm.)

Coordination and control

Armand Hatchuel

1 **Concepts and connections**
2 **Coordination models: some traditional approaches**
3 **Cognition and relation: the double nature of coordination**
4 **Towards a dynamic view of coordination: projects, collective design and managerial innovation**

Overview

Coordination is a central concept in business studies that is shared by economists, sociologists and management scientists. This entry first examines the concept from the perspectives of the entrepreneur's role, bureaucratic apparatus and informal adjustments. New perspectives are then arrived at by connecting cognitive and relational approaches. The resulting framework highlights the coordination mechanisms that are adapted to dynamic and uncertain contexts and which correspond to collective design processes within a competitive environment.

1 Concepts and connections

In management or other social sciences, coordination is a very common word, yet it is not an easy concept for systematic analysis. A consideration of the problems of such an analysis will help us to define the scope of this entry.

First, coordination is almost a synonym for the word 'organization'. Classical definitions of organization often refer directly to 'coordination', as in the following definition proposed by Chester Barnard: 'Organization is a system of consciously coordinated activities or forces of two or more persons' (1938: 67). The two words are so close, that we could interchange them in Barnard's proposition and define coordination as 'a consciously organized relation between activities or forces'. The second problem is more academic. The concept of coordination is so broad, that one could review all management and organization theories investigating its potential meanings. While it is widely accepted that coordination requires instruments of several kinds, there are still too few attempts to build a complete theory of coordination mechanisms, and so each discipline in the management and social sciences develops distinct approaches to the concept.

Hence, this entry cannot pretend to offer a comprehensive and unified theory. However, it attempts to (1) revisit some of these academic trends; and (2) indicate how new perspectives are opened by connecting cognitive and relational approaches in the analysis of coordination mechanisms, and how this framework enlightens both static and dynamic approaches of coordination, the latter aspect being too rarely mentioned.

Before coming to these points, clarification is needed regarding connections between coordination and two other related concepts: control and cooperation.

Control

Control is a central concept of two different theories. One is the *systems control theory*, whose developments mostly belong to engineering science. It describes such concepts as open-loop and closed-loop controls, feedback or automatic controls. The other theory deals with *social control*, an important trend in sociology which is mainly devoted to the study of how societies regulate the tensions beween conformity and deviance. It was recognized early on that coordination and control were narrowly linked and we can find in coordination models elements coming from the two types of control theory. As management is mainly focused on the control of human individuals or groups, coordination is often referred to, in this field, as some form of open-loop control. The pattern is classic: goals are settled (quantitative and qualitative), while periodic reports or evaluations will indicate achievements or discrepancies, and therefore suggest some corrective actions. From the point of view of social control theory, it is easy to recognize that any coordination scheme requires that participants share some basic values or social norms: at least common language and non-violent behaviour.

Cooperation

Cooperation is also related to coordination without bearing the same meaning. Cooperation is a class of human relations where mutual interests are stressed in opposition to competition or rivalry. Thus, coordination is more likely to be intentional and formally designed when cooperative behaviour is dominant. Nevertheless, it is now widely recognized that economic competition also needs coordination mechanisms even if they are reduced to fairness and loyalty rules (although they have given birth to a complex set of laws).

In summary, if control is part of any form of coordination, coordination will depend on the nature and degree of existing cooperation or competition. Now, briefly revisiting the main academic traditions will lead us to focus on some classical coordination models, and to introduce a more general framework.

2 Coordination models: some traditional approaches

The invisible hand and the visible entrepreneur

Since its early steps, political economy has distinguished between two different coordination models. Adam Smith's seminal quest analysed both the work division inside the factory and the market mechanisms between producers through competition, exchange and price setting.

However, mainstream economics focused mainly on market mechanisms which have received extensive attention and mathematical analysis since the beginning of the twentieth century. The 'invisible hand' is indeed a coordination mechanism, but somehow an unconscious one, as it is based on the aggregation of different local preferences. In contrast, the conscious activities which design, guide and regulate the work division inside a factory or a firm were not studied in detail by economists. Indeed, if many authors in the field recognized the necessity of such coordination mechanisms, they praised the figure of the entrepreneur, the leader who invented and implemented these necessary coordination mechanisms. In the words of Charles Gide (a leading French economist at the beginning of the twentieth century), work division could also be renamed complex cooperation, and be seen as the result of the entrepreneur's endeavours: '*L'entrepreneur est donc tout à la fois le grand metteur en oeuvre et le grand répartiteur*' (the entrepreneur is both the great system builder and the great dispatcher of revenues: author's translation) (Gide 1911: 141). This view is largely shared by most economists.

Since the 1970s, through the renewal of *institutional economics* and the development of *dynamic games theory*, economists have paid new attention to coordination mechanisms which are different from usual market ones. Agency theory, assymmetric information or transaction costs are popular concepts in these trends (Williamson 1975). Most modelled situations are games where the outputs for each player are dependent on some external and uncertain event or on some hidden information possessed by one of the players. The mathematics of these new economics often show that players do not easily adopt some coordination schemes even if these could be rewarding (prisoner's dilemma). Being more qualitative in its approach, institutional economics offers new insights into market failures or investigates social regulations needed by markets. Job markets or wage formation are typical problems where many economists consider that coordination is achieved more by contingent rules and contracts than by price formation as in classical market theory.

From the entrepreneur to the bureaucratic apparatus

Early in the twentieth century, the sociological tradition which was investigated more than others by economists was the qualitative conditions of effective coordination in groups. It was obvious that in the big organizations emerging at the end of the nineteenth century, the entrepreneur was not the demi-god of the economic tradition, and that regulation of tasks and people was obtained through various mechanisms, some of which were already familiar to state or military institutions. These include:

1 organized authorities: boards and executive committees, command lines, scalar chains or hierarchies;
2 horizontal specialization of middle managers and white collar employees;
3 extensive statistical reporting and recording about tasks, personnel and accounts;
4 wage and career rules, rewards and sanction systems at individual or group level.

In 1922, Max Weber had synthesized all these mechanisms by introducing the concept of 'bureaucracy'. However, of deeper theoretical importance was his idea that coordination rules could be derived from different principles of rationality and legitimacy. Bureaucracy corresponded to a *rational–legal* model of coordination where hierarchical authority required a necessary legal support, while functional specialization was based on the rationality of skills differentiation or work division. The rational–legal model was thus clearly distinguished from the traditional or charismatic models where coordination rules are supported respectively by cultural inheritance or by the influence of a leader. The rational–legal model offered a frame for the development of several coordination devices, like careful resource allocation and control (budget, personnel), strategic and planning analysis, product and task design, quality control, etc. Chandler (1977) has described in detail the history of this apparatus in the case of the US business.

In 1925, Henri Fayol's pioneering work advocated the idea that these coordination mechanisms, which he described independently from Weber's work, were universal principles of administrative science deserving methodical study and implementation. However, in Fayol's theory coordination was restricted to a narrow sense. This can be seen in his famous definition of administration in five elements:

- planning
- organization
- command
- coordination
- control

Coordination appears in this list as a day-to-day activity of the administrative units, a regulation intervening after the great strategic and structural orientations had been decided. Thus, Fayol's model is an explicit top-down model of coordination. Nevertheless, the model could be more bottom-up if planning and even organization were considered as coordinating mechanisms, allowing different members of a firm to share the basic visions and choices of their collective action. These two perspectives correspond to an important conceptual and practical choice: is coordination restricted to creating harmony between different means and players when the goals are already defined? Or is goal setting also a matter of coordination? In the theoretical landscape and social context of Fayol the first perspective seemed natural, but in many situations, if uncertainty and risk are prevalent, coordination must be extended to goal setting if effective commitment and appropriate action has to be obtained.

Invisible hands in organizations

The Weberian and Fayolian bureaucracy offered the main theoretical reference for coordination and control, but many empirical studies have shown that these formal coordination mechanisms were neither peaceful nor free from backlashes or dysfunctions. Specifically, (1) clear-cut functional specialization is never perfect and interface problems are permanent; (2) legal hierarchy and functional units are subject to the well described 'staff and line' conflicts (Dalton 1950); and (3) controlling the efficency of each department or each task separately, in spite of several interdependencies all along the production process, creates 'local' optimization and overconformity which may endanger the overall performance. The viability of the bureaucracy was thus often related to less visible regulations: the multiple 'slacks' allowed to each actor (Cyert and March 1963), the informal network of relations and initiatives that compensate the rigidity of the formal bureaucratic apparatus (Selznick 1948), the flow of 'political' negotiations around the formal structure (Crozier and Friedberg 1977).

All these mechanisms appear as equivalents to Adam Smith's 'invisible hand' inside organizations: a different set of coordination mechanisms completing the bureaucratic ones, which can also be favoured by managers once their importance is recognized and when they seem appropriate. Budget and work autonomy, horizontal and vertical communications, task forces and project groups can be developed to allow and enhance the efficency of informal or invisible adjustments. These informal regulations often seem more humanistic as they largely rely on goodwill, self-organization or personal commitment. However, it would be misleading to consider that effective coordination stands only in these interpersonal processes: formal and informal mechanisms are two faces of the same coin, and efficient coordination may be more realistically viewed as a difficult and unstable balance between these two types of regulation.

Numerous critics, however, have been claiming that the pendulum has swung too far in favour of formal coordination; current trends advocate flexible coordination rules by reducing the length of the scalar chain, allowing more individual autonomy and strongly rewarding team cooperation or new skills acquisition (Peters and Waterman 1982). It is also claimed that even if coordination schemes, linked to proper incentives, influence decisions and shape behaviours, they do not entirely determine them. They cannot create the commitment needed when uncertainty, anxiety, pressures and conflicts require initiative, self-organization or temerity. As many firms in Western countries faced such contexts during the 1980s, many authors stressed the importance of embedding coordination mechanisms in cultural or community values: visions, symbols, meanings, heroes or ceremonies. Even if these aspects have a favourable influence on coordination, it is unlikely that they will compensate in the long run for inconsistent formal coordinations, biased controls and knowledge gaps. Furthermore, coordination mechanisms are not outside the organizational culture, they contribute by themselves to the evolution of values and relations, and participate in the creation of cultural trends in firms.

Most of these classical debates were too focused on structures and power mechanisms, and they left in the dark the cognitive and knowledge regulations existing in both formal and informal coordination. This perspective is deeply rooted in the engineer's tradition, which now deserves a different interpretation.

Taylorism and the knowledge problem

Usually, Taylorism is viewed as the ideological impetus to mass production and extreme work division. This is a widespread but strongly biased interpretation of Taylor's work. This view is also very different from the perception of Taylor's texts by Japanese engineers who have contributed to the manufacturing breakthrough in their country in the last few decades (Shingo 1987). The roots of Taylor's thought can be better understood by recalling the coordination problem that mechanical industries had to solve, which was a wage problem (Taylor 1895). Monetary incentives and price formation are usual coordination mechanisms in markets, but in the factories where Taylor obtained his first industrial experience, skilled workers on machine-tools were still paid through a piece rate system. Thus two coordinating and often conflicting mechanisms were in action: professional hierarchy and price setting. At that time, piece rates were calculated on the basis of the workers' average per hour wages (regulated by the job market) and through estimates of the required machining and work times (internal rules).

In a Weber–Fayolian model, these time estimates should be fixed by the technical departments of the bureaucratic apparatus. The same attitude was advocated by Taylor, but his main merit was to insist on a simple and important consequence of this idea: the necessity of developing a suitable and accurate knowledge of the machine and human work to obtain valid and acceptable estimates. In Taylor's view, bureaucracies were efficient not only because they established legal regulations or clear separation of tasks, but because they offered the opportunity to develop a 'scientific' approach towards tasks and duties, and maintain a research and learning attitude towards work. Taylor, first celebrated as an innovative engineer, thus attempted to build a management theory whereby knowledge could be seen both as an input and as an ouput of coordination between technical departments, managers and workers. This explains why leading French scientists like Henri Le Châtelier saw in Taylor's philosophy a defence plea on behalf of industrial research. In most cases, the 'entry', say 'technocratic' model of knowledge, became popular in Western bureaucracies leading to a strong separation between design and operations.

By stressing the dynamics of knowledge, Taylor was reviving the engineer's view of collective action where scientific progress is the main factor of social transformation and a permanent spur for new coordination and control schemes. Two messages of present value are implicit in this tradition, although too often neglected:

1 Experts are an essential part of many coordination mechanisms; moreover, experts and expertise have to be considered as coordination and control devices *per se*.
2 Bureaucracies find both a support and a threat in the dynamics of knowledge, and flexible coordination is strongly linked to the ability to recognize knowledge distribution and renewal as a crucial goal for survival.

These points will play an important role in the following presentation of a more general approach to coordination.

3 Cognition and relation: the double nature of coordination

During the 1960s and 1970s, contingency theory was a keyword in organization theory. Universal principles of good management were rejected; structures and coordination mechanisms were seen as context-dependent. Supported by empirical studies, this approach stimulated the elaboration of Weberian-style typologies of observed coordination mechanisms. Joan Woodward (1965) first offered a categorization of industrial firms. Later, Henry Mintzberg (1979) suggested that a general classification of organizations could be derived from five basic principles of coordination:

- direct supervision
- standards and methods
- performance output
- skills
- mutual adjustment

In Mintzberg's approach each of these principles was dominant in five different organizational types: 'the simple enterprise, the mechanistic bureaucracy, the divisional firm, the professional bureaucracy, and the ad-hocracy'. This classification fitted correctly a great number of the cases described in the literature before 1975, but it could not pretend to be valid for all instances. However, the formulation of the five coordination principles reveals an underlying structure that is common to all coordination schemes: a combination of either relational or cognitive rationalities.

It is easy to see that the first and last coordination principles proposed by Mintzberg are exclusively defined using a *relation-based rationality*. Hierarchy, power and leadership are the social basis for direct supervision; promises, contracts, associations or bargains are the elements of mutual adjustment. Symmetrically, the three other principles do not refer explicitly to any relational model and are only supported by different *cognition-based rationalities*: the ability to transfer know-how through standards and methods, the ability to evaluate expected effects through performance output, the ability to assess professional skills.

These two rationalities are different in nature, but one can better understand the substance and variety of coordination mechanisms by stressing such a dual nature: a specific arrangement of devices coming from both types of rationalities. In other words, coordination can be effective only if some coherence between a specific system of relations (such as legal, informal, interpersonal) and a specific distribution of knowledge (such as memory, perspectives, facts, beliefs) can be found among participants. Hence, failures will result from crises coming either from one of these dimensions, or from their conflicts. Invention of new coordination schemes is limited by our ability to conceive new forms of relations, and to adapt these relations to the various *forms of knowledge* used in the course of action.

Using this approach, Hatchuel and Weil (1995) showed how, in usual industrial life, three main forms of knowledge can be identified, calling for three basic coordination models: (1) coordination by prescription of procedures; (2) coordination by plan and promises; and (3) coordination by actor building. If we leave out the first one, the other two models do not match the Mintzberg classification, as relational and cognitive variables are mixed in each case. Let us examine briefly the three coordination models through elementary situations of industrial life.

Coordination by prescription of procedures

This first example is about coordination between a prescriber, say a technician, and an operator having to do some task according to the technician's prescriptions. Usually, knowledge is transferred from the first agent to the second through a list of procedures designed like a cooking recipe and the relation between them is often hierachical. Good coordination here lies in the progressive sharing of a common 'context model' by the two actors: despite their different knowledge and positions they have to reach a simplified but common view of the work to be done and of its contexts. Problems arise from the fact that the operator's knowledge gives necessarily greater importance to details that the technician ignores or cannot take fully into account. Their relational model (including communication channels, frequency of meetings and comprehensive or technocratic attitudes from the technician) will play an important role in the acceptability and control of this 'common context'. In some cases, the relational model is absent or very loose, and writers about cooking have to hypothesize at least about the type of kitchen and equipment that serves as a common context between the author and the reader.

Coordination by plan and promises

Coordination is now supposed to take place between a repairman and an operator using some equipment that cannot always be repaired without the intervention of the repairman. In industrial contexts, the relation between these two professionals is difficult to stabilize; it stands somewhere between hierarchy and informal trade-offs, even if client–supplier philosophy is advocated by managers. The main reason for this fuzzy relational model is found in the nature of the knowledge to be exchanged. This knowledge goes beyond a checklist: it is a set of causal links between the machine design and the story of failures and repairs. Hence, it is a complex chain of inferences (about machine behaviour) created by events (failures), and of actions (repairs) creating events (machine behaviour), a chain which cannot be fully described and shared equally by the two actors. Here, a common context model is still necessary but no more sufficient, as the two players also have to share, for example, a definition of events signalling that something is going wrong: that is, if certain events occur, the operator promises to call the technician, and the latter is supposed to intervene. This is precisely what has been called an *interactive plan* (Ponssard and Tanguy 1993), as warning variables and commitments to revise the first agreements are included in the plan. In such a case, participants must at least share some reasoning procedures and some principles of efficiency in order to discuss their perceptions and causal interpretations. This coordination model can easily be extended to situations where functional managers or experts from different fields have to cooperate.

Coordination by actor building

In this third case let us consider a planning agent and the department manager who requires planning. This situation presents many peculiarities. The relation is hierarchical, but the manager can hardly prescribe precise work procedures or assign permanent priorities to the planning agent. The knowledge of the planning agent is also specific. With few recipes and no stable inferences, the agent tries to find combinations between conflicting and evolving constraints and goals. Hence, the nature of his knowledge is very difficult to define: it is memory, skill and trade-offs of a strong 'political' nature. The basic entrepreneurial dimensions of the department are often affected by the choices of the planning agent. Good coordination does not rely here on a particular set of rules, but rests on an unstable process of delegation and legitimation: a process of actor building. The planning agent by his action must convince that he has some talent to do the job, and he will experiment in situations where he is a powerful actor in the department, as well as moments where his work seems of poor utility. Here, coordination directly concerns goal setting, as goals are permanently being revised according to possible and feasible arrangements. Such actor building processes may be external to organizations and rely on professional assessments, yet in many situations it is left to internal mechanisms: project leaders, divisional executives, strategic committees are all built on a model that is no different to that of the more humble planning agent.

In all these cases, recognizing the double nature of coordination is a departure point for more complete approaches where distribution of knowledge and relational models have to be studied in detail.

4 Towards a dynamic view of coordination: projects, collective design and managerial innovation

Keeping in mind the preceding framework, how can we analyse change and the dynamics of coordination schemes? What happens, for example, when new rules are settled or when some events lead to knowledge renewal (technological innovation is only a particular example of this kind of renewal)? Two practical situations of organizational life face such dynamic contexts: coordination during innovative projects involving collective design activities and implementation of new coordination schemes.

Adam Smith's needle factory impressed the great economist and his readers, but the image of continuous order coming from the shop is not adequate to characterize the process by which such a factory was designed and erected. The actors of this process are numerous and we can at least usually distinguish between the manufacturer willing to build a new plant for some production purposes, the engineers and architects contracted to design and plan for the project, the different sub-contractors and craftsmen in charge of building or supplying equipments, etc., but what are the coordination mechanisms that lead to an efficient plant?

The complexity of this kind of project is such that all types of coordination mechanisms will be required, but it is of the utmost importance to note that adequate coordination mechanisms will necessarily change during the life of the project as people concerned and available knowledge both evolve during the project. In other words, coordination will be reshaped at each phase or at each significant event of the project.

During the first steps of the project, stakeholders have to reach a broad consensus on the planned output: interests, values, beliefs and estimates are all matters of controversy. Thus, information, expert opinions, tests, prototypes and manager's decisions can be called upon to reach agreements and commitments. Afterwards there comes a phase of complex cooperation. This second phase calls for coordination models of a different kind according to the level of the actors involved in the project (Moisdon and Weil 1991). At the manager's level, we find simplified plans and promises based on rough functional borders and usual control variables (costs, quality, delay). At the technician's level, it is a process of 'hypercommunication': intense and numerous exchanges crossing all the functional borders. This coordination flow is driven by the need to find creative compromises between the functional components of the product and the very fine knowledge regulations that interplay at this level: technical cultures, economic estimations, interpersonal agreements, time or resource pressures on problem solving.

Facing fierce competition and rapid renewal of markets, all manufacturers are seeking to reduce the lead-time of these design phases (Clark and Wheelwright 1992). One way to realize this reduction is by accelerating the speed of knowledge exchange so that production requirements and market tests could be integrated before a precise product design is reached. Such trends increase the burden of hypercommunication and the performance obtained will be limited by knowledge shortages or knowledge sharing problems, and by the ability of managers to foster team cooperation.

For these reasons, collective design activities will receive increasing interest from management and research, and will be a place for strong organizational innovation. The resulting new forms of coordination will greatly influence the frontiers and domains of the firms (Hatchuel and Weil 1999).

Implementing coordination: innovation and rationality

To implement new coordination mechanisms one must face the old question of the relation between theory and action in managemen. According to the preceding conceptual framework, introducing new coordination models means accepting new knowledge regulations and new relational rationalities. In some cases, it also means introducing new actors as well as changing the relations between existing ones. Hence, one can never be sure that a coordination model will work as expected. It depends on the agreement and commitment of other people (relation-based rationality), and will have to face complex learning processes and knowledge shortages (knowledge-based rationality).

Despite such uncertainties and limitations, a coordination scheme always presents some seducing rationality to those who try to implement it. Rationality appears in the alleged causal links between this coordination scheme and some desirable results. Mixing rationality and beliefs is the paradox of any innovation, but managerial principles or models present some specific features which increase the paradox. A new coordination scheme has both to be accepted by the actors concerned and to produce some expected improvements. An efficient factory is not only a factory where people appreciate and adopt some coordination schemes, but also where these schemes are convincingly associated with some progress. Therefore, coordination models, like any management technology, must combine the motivating attributes of mythologies and the consistency of rational thought (Hatchuel 1993). Due to this internal tension, implementation requires the development of a collective learning process where initial myths are progressively tempered and rational patterns used without dogmatism. Managerial models may be useful references but only if the necessary adaptations to real individuals and real contexts are understood and allowed.

By combining relational and cognitive approaches to coordination, by looking at static models and dynamic processes, by identifying the part of mythology and of rationality in any coordination model, a better understanding of coordination can be reached and past research usefully revisited. Future research can also find in this framework a departure point for empirical investigations and conceptual development, while providing increased usefulness for managers.

Further reading

(References cited in the text marked *)

* Barnard, C.L. (1938) *The Functions of the Executive*, Cambridge, MA: Harvard University Press. (A classical view of managers and organizations.)
* Chandler, A.D., Jr (1977) *The Visible Hand*, Cambridge, MA: Belknap/Harvard. (A history of the coordination and managerial mechanisms of US enterprises.)
* Clark, K.B. and Wheelwright, S.C. (1992) *Revolutionizing Product Development*, New York: The Free Press. (An overall methodology for the management of product innovation and development.)
* Crozier, M. and Friedberg, E. (1977) *L'acteur et le système*, Paris: Seuil. (A sociological analysis of the political games in bureaucracies.)
* Cyert, R.M. and March, J.G. (1963) *A Behavioural Theory of the Firm*, Englewood Cliffs, NJ: Prentice Hall. (A model of the firm describing how existing 'slacks' absorb tensions and contradictions between different coordination mechanisms.)

* Dalton, M. (1950) 'Conflict between staff and line managerial officers', *American Sociological Review* 15: 342–51. (A description of classical conflicts between hierarchical and functional structures.)

* Fayol, H. (1925) *Industrial and General Administration*, Geneva: International Management Institute. (Henri Fayol's pioneering work, which helped lay the foundations of modern administration science.)

* Gide, C. (1911) *Cours d'économie politique*, Paris: Sirey. (Charles Gide, a great French economist of the early twentieth century, sets out his views on cooperation.)

* Hatchuel, A. (1993) 'The nature of managerial knowledge: birth and life of rational myths', paper presented at the EGOS Conference, July. (A theory of managerial techniques, of their developments and complex impacts in enterprises.)

Hatchuel, A. and Weil, B. (1992) *L'expert et le système*, Paris: Economica. (An approach to organizational life through the study of the various types of knowledge existing in industries; and an analysis of their evolution and crises in innovative contexts.)

* Hatchuel, A. and Weil, B. (1995) *Experts in Organizations*, Berlin–New York: Walter de Gruyter. (An approach to organizational life through the study of the various types of knowledge existing in industries; and an analysis of their evolution and crises in innovative contexts.)

* Hatchuel A. and Weil B. (1999), 'Design oriented organizations', working paper, Proceedings of the European conference on Product development, Cambridge July 1999. (A presentation of new organizing principles for innovative collective design processes.)

* Mintzberg, H. (1979) *The Structuring of Organizations*, Englewood Cliffs, NJ: Prentice Hall. (A typology of organizations based on different design parameters, particularly on coordination principles.)

* Moisdon, J.C. and Weil, B. (1994) 'Collective design. Lack of communication or shortage of expertise? Analysis of coordination in the development of new vehicles', in MacLean, D., Saviotti, P. and Vinck, D. (eds) *Designs, Networks and Strategies*, proceedings from COSTA3, Brussels: European Commission Directorate General. Science Research and Development. (A study of horizontal coordination between different technicians and experts in new car design.)

* Peters, T.J. and Waterman, R.H. (1982) *In Search of Excellence*, New York: Harper & Row. (A comparative study of managerial methods in different type of firms.)

* Ponssard, J.P. and Tanguy, H. (1993) 'Planning in firms as an interactive process', *Theory and Decision* 34: 139–59. (An approach to the role of common knowledge in decentralized parallel decision process.)

* Selznick, P. (1948) 'Foundations of the theory of organization', *American Sociological Review* 13: 25–35. (A sociological view of cooperation in organizations.)

* Shingo, S. (1987) *Non stock Seisan hoshiki Eno Tenkai*, Tokyo: Japan Management Association. (The Japanese model of process coordination in factories.)

Shingo, S. (1990) *La production sans stock*, Paris: Les Éditions d'organisation. (A French translation of his 1987 work.)

* Taylor, F.W. (1895) 'A piece-rate system. Some steps towards partial solution of the labour problem', *Transactions of the American Society of Mechanical Engineers* 16: 24–33. (Taylor's first paper, a detailed analysis of shop coordination problems in relation to worker's and manager's type of knowledge.)

* Williamson, O. (1975) *Markets and Hierarchies*, New York: The Free Press. (An economic theory of organizations and markets through the concept of transaction costs.)

* Woodward, J. (1965) *Industrial Organization: Theory and Practice*, Oxford: Oxford University Press. (A typology of industries and its implication on managerial principles and models.)

Technology and organizations

Ray Loveridge

1 **Defining technology**
2 **The social construction of technology**
3 **Technology as social control**
4 **Technology as information**
5 **Technology and innovation**
6 **Post-Fordism, post-industrialism and post-modernism**
7 **Balkanization or synergy in approaches to technology?**

Overview

In the study of organizations, 'technology' is often defined as an operational tool, the design of which is dictated by the demands of efficiency within given market conditions. In the past technology has been treated as an independent or exogenous causal factor shaping organizational design. It is evidently the case that machines designed to transform materials, information or people (through means such as medicine or transport) can incorporate design principles that are not readily understood outside an engineering discipline and are therefore not easily challenged. However, organizational theorists have questioned the immutability of engineering design along a number of dimensions.

Taken more broadly, technology can be interpreted as all the means used by humans to control their environment, including bureaucracy or organization itself. Thus, like organizational structure, technological configurations can be regarded as modes of control or of means of reducing uncertainty in the exercise of managerial power. As such, they can provide more or less ability to monitor and meter their performance by central management. Communications and information technology (CIT) can be seen to be rapidly taking the place of bureaucratic modes of operational metering and monitoring within contemporary society.

As well as contributing to the value-adding functions of the organization, technology has always been incorporated into the service provided by many consumer products. Competitions or contests between rival corporations are now increasingly based on product innovation rather than price; hence the study of the management of innovation and of means of creating conditions conducive to creativity among organizational members has recently experienced an enormous revival. Nevertheless it remains true that the speed of technological innovation is presently accompanied by enormous social costs. Without adjustment in national and international infrastructures designed to cope with technological change, long-term effects on wider society may ultimately be described as destabilizing.

1 Defining technology

At its simplest, technology is defined as a tool. It is commonplace among historians to see the use of increasingly sophisticated tools as providing a convenient means to divide the evolution of society into epochs or periods of civilization. We even speak of pre-history as Stone, Iron or Bronze Ages. At this higher level of generality we can speak of all organized knowledge as the tool by which humans attempt to control their social and material environment. In other words, all modes of organizing people for the purposes of controlling or coordinating their activities can be considered a form of technology.

This ambiguity in definition is more than a semantic issue. It is difficult to escape the endogenous influences of technology within modern thinking and acting. However, it could be useful to consider these structuring technological influences in descending levels of abstract conceptualization. First, they are contained in *ideologies* of industrialization or modernization in which technological (or administrative) innovation is regarded as 'progress', and resistance from whatever source is labelled 'conservative' and viewed with approbation. It has underpinned the spirit of modern nationalism and perspectives on comparative national development for much of the last 150 years. Today it infuses almost all managerial and organizational literature.

Second, bodies of *disciplined knowledge* have emerged in which causal and systemic relations between material and/or social elements in specified situations are postulated and related to empirical observations (empirical positivism). Their origins can be traced to the European Renaissance, through what is often described as the Age of Reason or the eighteenth century Enlightenment. Observation, categorization and the related conceptual explanation can be seen as constituting more or less scientific knowledge in terms of its reproducibility and generalizability.

Third, there are *techniques* or procedures to be adopted in processing information relating to data on social or material operations. This knowledge may gain its explanatory and predictive value from scientific observation or from the accumulation of experience in the operations themselves (the so-called 'learning curve'). Techniques may be more or less codified in the form of texts and manuals or embodied in tacit routines. In the latter mode they often relate to the specific organizational system in which they arise and can be regarded as contributing to its unique competence (Nelson and Winter 1982).

Finally, these techniques can be incorporated in the mechanical, material or electronic *design and programming* of hardware and software, in other words in machines and capital equipment. This is the most articulated form of technology.

Technological innovation is often described as moving through these layers of abstraction from scientific discovery or invention to the design of new operational techniques, tools and consumer devices. In fact, it appears that the reverse is often the case. Improvements in design can result from user experience in operating with existing tools, and bottlenecks or 'reverse salients' in the development of new operational systems can shape the direction of research done in so-called 'pure' science. The influence exercised respectively by the customer-user or by the scientist or technologist is often described as providing either a pull or a push in bringing about innovation (Rothwell 1977).

A further definitional distinction to be made is that between product and process (or production) technology. At the level of the firm or sector it is evidently important to distinguish between the importation of technological resources and the exportation (to other firms, sectors or to final consumers) of the value added product. Studies of technology often reflect this dichotomy in their author's preoccupation, either with the installation and implementation of 'imported' process technology or with the invention and design of new products. Over the last two decades there has been a growing emphasis in the management literature on the relationship that each type of innovation has for the other, particularly in designer–user inter-firm transactions within the value chain (Womack *et al.* 1990).

2 The social construction of technology

The most prevalent critique of an autonomous and objective technological logic stems from its use as a device to control the actions of others. Contemporary studies highlight the social shaping of the range of options that usually exist in most critical decision making on technology. Choices often appear to be determined by implicit or explicit conspiracy on the part of one group to control the future actions of another. For example, Noble's (1985) account of the manner in which computer numerically controlled (CNC) machines were introduced in the GE and Lockheed Corporations emphasizes the importance that management and their US Government customers attached to removing control over the programming of their machines from the existing shop floor operatives.

Other studies emphasize the importance of the socio-emotive needs of actors reflected in their responses to technology rather than from any direct concern for its mechanical effectiveness. The early work of Rogers (1983) on the diffusion of new technology suggested the existence of layered networks through which new ideas were channelled, filtered and reconstructed in socially compatible terms by opinion leaders. More recently, Callon (1992) has demonstrated the manner in which technological knowledge is constantly reconstructed in interpersonal transactions as it traverses social networks.

Perhaps the most controversial and, at the same time, most influential exploration of innovation in knowledge creation is that put forward by Kuhn (1962), in his explanation of changes in scientific modelling and research. At any one time the scientific community is seen to give precedence to a dominant explanatory model or *conceptual paradigm*. Its influence in shaping scientific work is not simply based on its efficacy in providing solutions to intellectual 'puzzles'. This is because the technical procedures prescribed by the model have acquired a normative significance within the moral order of a specialized group of scientists. Paradigmatic change is, therefore, a long drawn out process in which social, as well as intellectual, provision must be made for the retention of group solidarity within the profession. In recent years the Kuhnian concept of the paradigmatic interpretation of technological possibilities in both product and process applications has been applied to various managerial situations.

National culture has also been found to provide significantly different bases for the meaning given to technology and to technological innovation at all levels of organizational hierarchy. Qualitative micro studies of attitudes among operatives in the 1970s contributed a qualitative dimension to the broader societal comparisons of Maurice *et al.* (1982). In the latter work, the widely different organizational structures used in conjunction with similar plant and equipment by German and French employers are explained in terms of the institutional context of business, and most particularly in the occupational qualifying processes deployed in each country. Similar findings have emerged from Sorge *et al.*'s (1983) study of computerized manufacturing systems in Germany and the UK, and in a larger six-nation comparison of the utilization of information technology (IT) in retailing, banking and healthcare delivery (Child and Loveridge 1990).

3 Technology as social control

The most fundamental of the social constructionist critiques is possibly that of feminists. The history of the emergence of the concept of scientific 'objectivity' is seen to have provided a bridge to pre-industrial religious belief in at least one important respect. This was the discounting of personality characteristics perceived to be inextricably linked with the female gender. By alienating the intellect from emotive and affective sources of social action the 'mechanical' philosophers of the eighteenth century legitimated the continued closure of knowledge work to women. By the same token the historical contributions of women to the 'advance of science' have been effectively written out until recently. More insidiously, women have been socialized into an acceptance of an ancillary role within this 'advance' and as a consequence have lost status in each succeeding wave of innovation (Faulkner and Arnold 1985).

Beyond this powerful critique, organizational writers are often divided somewhat crudely into neo-Marxian or neo-Weberian, called after these German founding fathers of social science. Weber (1924) saw the pursuit of mechanical and bureaucratic efficiency as providing an essentially neutral arena in which groups could compete for market or status advantages. In the neo-Marxian interpretation of history the process of standardization, routinization and specialization in the design of organizational tasks is seen as representing the steady and relentless expropriation of operational knowledge by owners of capital. Moreover, the relations of production present in the workplace, or labour process, are usually seen as the primary influence shaping the institutions of modern (civil) society. The history of the development of the principles and procedures embodied in production management and epitomized in the work of F.W. Taylor (for example, *The Principles of Scientific Management*, published in 1911) was used as the basis for the most influential of recent analyses in this genre, that of Braverman (1974).

Neo-Weberians vary in the importance attached to the pursuit of status advantage among interest groups. Those who elevate it to a central role in the creation of societal institutions, as for example in the formation of new occupations around particular modes of technology, are often conjoined with Marxian authors, under the label of 'conflict theorists'. Many other analysts see the managerial pursuit of control as being solely related to the survival of the organization and to the satisfaction of a diversity of stakeholders. Conflict is viewed as explicable and soluble within this more limited frame. Hence, much of the organizational literature on process innovation is concerned with overcoming resistance to technological change among existing operative staff (Wilkinson 1983).

These strategies usually involve the alignment of the localized task commitments of the operative with those compatible with the aims of strategic management. They differ in the degree and type of involvement allowed to, or required of, recipients of management communications. They also vary in the extent to which organizational designers accept the design parameters embodied in pre-existing machines and their configuration in the workflow. Over much of the last century a debate has been carried on between behavioural scientists and those whom Taylor described as 'scientific managers'. 'Behaviouralists', for the most part social psychologists, have argued that the rationalization and fragmentation of labour services recommended by Taylorist systems have led to the demoralization, and ultimately to the alienation, of labour. Perhaps the most radical among social science approaches to job design was that arising out of the so-called 'action research' conducted during the 1950s in the UK and India by the Tavistock Institute, and in the USA by the Institute of Social Research at Ann Arbor, Michigan. These researchers advocated the design of workflow and accompanying activities in a manner that 'optimized' its match with the sentient needs of operatives.

Contained within all levels of this debate there exists a tension between the managerial need for control over a stable ordering of activities and an accompanying need for entrepreneurial flexibility and creativity. A second strand in the job redesign argument advocates the devolution of responsibility as a means of encouraging 'bottom up' innovation rather than simply attempting the self-development of individual employees. The most important contemporary development in this approach to line management is to be found in the concept of total quality management (TQM). Originating from the work of production engineers, it recognizes the impossibility of metering and monitoring even relatively simple line tasks as advocated in old-style scientific management. Instead, it advocates operator or group self-monitoring of their own performance.

Unlike earlier human relations approaches, the TQM approach attempts an alignment of work group goals with those of the corporation, rather than shaping the latter around operative needs. Group membership is formally prescribed rather than spontaneously entered into and, through the operation of IT, group performance can often be more easily monitored centrally than under bureaucratically administered Taylorist systems (Pollert 1988). For all of these reasons some observers prefer to describe TQM as 'top-down' innovation.

4 Technology as information

In the 1950s the emergence of organizational behaviour as a management discipline was heavily shaped by prescriptive approaches to the control–commitment debate. Another school of researchers sought to describe influences acting on contemporary organizational structures before arriving at their design prescriptions. Among the most significant of the exogenous influences, or contingencies, to be investigated was seen to be the mode of operational technology employed by the organization. A small study of 100 British engineering firms in the mid-1950s provided one of the most important empirical bases for this approach. Woodward's findings (1958) suggested that organizational structure could be related fairly closely to the size of the batches produced and to the operational exigencies resulting. Later, Bright (1988) produced a detailed typology of operations technology based on a larger sample of US manufacturers. This emphasized the degree of integration between stages of materials process and provided a taxonomy not unlike that of Woodward, although not claiming the same causal importance in shaping the overall organizational configuration.

Woodward's typology gained, and retains, credibility both from its conceptual proximity to the axioms of batch engineering disciplines and from its rich case history description. During the 1950s and 1960s the findings of social anthropologists and industrial sociologists demonstrated differences in operator behaviours and commitments associated with the particular configurations of process technology.

Other writers interpreted operational processes at a higher level of abstraction, seeing organizational structures as attempts by managers to reduce their level of uncertainty or risk. This approach contained within it the possibility of moving away from the problems entailed in arriving at an agreed objective measure of technology. Instead, observers defined strategically important contingencies as those subjectively adjudged to be so by senior executives. In practice Perrow (1986) chose to see executive uncertainty as arising from: (1) variability in information flows including their scope and regularity (roughly equating with Woodward's linkage between batch size and variations in market demand); and (2) with the ability of the executive to comprehend and analyse the operational processes (that is, to embody operational knowledge in codified techniques or machines). Along these dimensions Perrow plotted the levels of discretion allowed to operatives in the different modes of organization arising from these higher order contingencies (Figure 1).

Stated in another way, executives were seen to attempt to guard against dependency upon others in the interpretation of information on strategically important operational matters. This more abstract definition of contingency surfaces in many more recent approaches to organizational analysis, most notably that of Williamson (1980). The latter author suggests that executive desire to absorb uncertainty is reflected in the type of contractual linkage established between suppliers of services, for example employees, and the organization's management (see Figure 2).

Figure 1 An informational typology of operational processes
Source: Adapted from Perrow (1986)

Figure 2 Internally segmented market
Source: Williamson (1980)

Previously, in the 1960s, a group of researchers at what is now the Aston Business School had attempted to measure the extent of commonality required in the administration of organizations. Taking technology as comprising both its material and knowledge components, but placing emphasis on integration between stages of the workflow, they concluded that as the size of the organization grew, the influence that the structure of shop floor operations had in shaping administrative structures diminished. Control passed to 'procedures dictated by standardization of the new specialists who devise the procedures' (Pugh *et al.* 1969: 124).

Although subject to methodological criticism, the Aston studies contributed *inter alia* to an understanding of two evident problems for Western management at that time. The first was that the coordination and control of the segmented activities of large-scale organizations was itself a significant cause of cognitive complexity and uncertainty for strategic managers. The second was the association of formal bureaucratic control with grievance-related conflict and unionization among employees. The two-way nature of control within bureaucracies had been illustrated by the studies of shop floor employees described earlier. One carried out among auto components manufacturers in Ohio and Michigan in the 1950s (Sayles 1958) suggested that work groups reacted differently to attempts at control (see Figure 3).

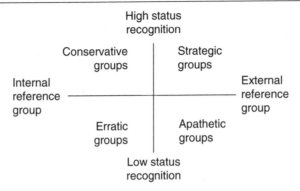

Figure 3 Patterns of grievance among shop-floor operatives
Source: Adapted from Sayles (1958)

5 Technology and innovation

The grievance-related behaviour described by Sayles and others might be seen as typical of post-Second World War industrial relations in Anglo-Saxon countries. Often it was triggered by attempts at 'top down' or imposed innovation. Groups defended their vested interest in prevailing bodies of technological knowledge or sought greater recognition in both status and market terms.

Equally, descriptions of the prevailing managerial model of 'bottom-up' technological innovation were rooted in pluralistic conflict. In most Anglo-American histories of innovation, whether brought about by the adoption of external inventions or through internal design, the process was, and is, presented as one full of conflict. Wilkinson (1983) and others suggest that junctures between the stages that mark the passage of implementation and use of innovation within routine operations can each become the locus of contestation. The propose–dispose dialogue that takes place represents a segmentation of interests within organizations.

Almost all case histories make use of Schon's (1963) concept of the need for innovators to acquire a sponsor or product champion in the higher echelons, or 'clan'. Burgelman and Sayles (1988) go so far as to suggest that a system of sponsorship or patronage should be built into the formal structures of 'hi-tech' firms in a manner that enables innovation to diffuse across departmental, divisional or other functional, intellectual or cost/profit centre boundaries within the organization (see Figure 4). These latter have grown out of a need to establish predictable order but, by the same token, have become institutionalized barriers to the absorption of technological change.

In a much earlier study, Sayles and Chandler (1971) had suggested that the management of intellectually complex projects, such as that facing the moon landing planned by the National Aeronautics and Space Administration of the US Government (NASA), could be too complex to be controlled through a centralized bureaucracy. It was accomplished by delegating and devolving responsibility through market-based contracts, combined with continuous open dialogue around problem definition and design solutions. This market-led dialogue

Levels \ Key activities	CORE PROCESSES		OVERLYING PROCESSES	
	Definition	Impetus	Strategic context	Structural context
Corporate management	Monitoring	Authorizing	Rationalizing	Structuring
		Organizational championship		Selecting
New ventures management	Coaching stewardship	Strategic building	Delineating	Negotiating
		Product championship		
Department leader/venture manager	Technical and need linking	Strategic forcing	Gatekeeping Idea generating Bootlegging	Questioning

Figure 4 The stepped process of bottom-up innovating

produced a culturally normative commitment to project goals while keeping boundaries fluid.

This network model of inter-organizational collaboration in the development and design of new technology has grown both in prescriptive, as well as descriptive, significance since the 1970s. The notion of conjoining the chain of linked production stages present within the organization in sequence with those outside its boundaries, in a vertical collaboration along the value-adding chain, is central to the concept of 'lean production' seen by Womack *et al.* (1990) to be the dominant new mode of organization in the automobile industry.

The more unlikely condition of horizontal collaboration across competing organizations in the development of technology (as opposed to defensive cartels) has also become the widely accepted basis for joint ventures. A more Utopian concept is that of 'flexible specialization', in which small artisanal enterprises are seen to collaborate in the provision of an external, regionally based, infrastructure. This allows them to attain the economies of scale and scope necessary to compete on equal terms with large multinational corporations (MNCs). In spite of its aspirational nature, the notion of inter-firm collaboration on a regional, or 'industrial district', basis has received policy recognition by the European Commission and some states in the USA.

The influence of information technology

Underlying many accounts of these collaborative ventures is the importance of IT in enabling, and even creating, the means by which organizational boundaries have been pierced, and organizational hierarchies flattened. Responsibility for carrying out the required tasks can be devolved to operational staff or to sub-contractors, who can be offered a measure of autonomy in their performance within parameters set or agreed centrally.

IT has effectively provided the means whereby many of the metering and co-ordinating activities of the bureaucracy can be automated, thus enabling the electronic monitoring of materials or people processing activities from the centre. The ultimate deployment of IT is seen to constitute a form of 'systemofacture' (Kaplinsky 1984) or total business system that fully integrates all of the functional activities of the organization and enables them to be related to centrally set series of strategic goals and related benchmarks.

Systems integration in this manner is likely to become increasingly technically practicable over the first decade of the twentieth-first century. For rationally deterministic theorists such as Perez (1985), the simple availability of a 'virtually unlimited' cheap supply of the new information technology will, as in previous historical epochs, result in the proliferation of a new managerial paradigm of organizational 'best practice'. This will entail the adoption of a much more flexible approach to the division of labour within the firm, both across tasks, and contractually, in the employment of 'spot' labour (see Figure 2).

A similar segmentalism can be seen to have evolved in the manner that corporations choose 'preferred' suppliers and users or distributors of their products, as described by Womack *et al.* (1990). In the USA, strategic theorists have adopted the term 'switchboard corporation' to describe the skeletal administration of managerial/service workers (clan) required to maintain short-term contracts with (loose teams of) professional and spot workers.

6 Post-Fordism, post-industrialism and post-modernism

Perez's description of the new 'techno-economic' paradigm currently utilized by managers is not entirely technologically driven. Emphasis is placed on a shift in consumer tastes that is seen to have taken place towards a greater individualization within social habits and, therefore, in diversity in consumption (1985: 449). She, like other writers, has been influenced by the description of the historical disjuncture seen to have occurred both in patterns of trade and in technology over the last quarter of the twentieth century. Over this period academic debate has increasingly focused on 'world view' or over-arching explanations of this change.

Of particular importance for neo-Marxian writers has been the analysis of the French *regulation* school (Aglietta 1975). The symptoms of bureaucratic sclerosis described earlier are seen to have been a by-product of the increased ability of the large firm to create a mass market for its standardized goods in the urbanized setting of industrialized countries. Since Henry Ford recognized and articulated the principles of this 'regime' in 1922, it has been described by these Marxian analysts as 'Fordist'. By the same token, changes in consumer tastes, accompanied by technological innovation, are seen to have led to the new organizational modes referred to as *post-Fordist*.

Throughout the 1960s the movement from manufacturing to service work was the subject of governmental concern in all industrialized societies. Daniel Bell (1973) was one of the early commentators on a so-called *post-industrial* society in which ultimate value in exchange would derive from knowledge inputs rather than from manual effort. His was a generally optimistic view on the outcomes, from the application of automation to manufacture, and the resultant deployment of labour in the provision of direct services. One such mode to have gained prominence in projections of the future is that of 'teleworking' or working from an IT link to the individual service provider's home. The merging of work with leisure is sometimes seen to be part of a 'professionalizing' of society.

At a still more abstract level the term post-industrialism has been extended to mean the relinquishment of the modernist basis of intellectual disciplines. Influenced by the work of French linguistic sociologists many recent management writers have gone further in predicting an abandonment of systems-rational modes of managing. Paradoxically, the onset of *post-modernism*, as this position is often described by its advocates, is seen as having been heralded and shaped by the algorithmic reasoning embodied in IT software.

All three holistic views on the societal outcomes of technological innovation have framed much of the academic debate around the current crisis in Western manufacturing over the past decade. Others adopt a more contingently open view. Some industrial economists see the present disjuncture in organizational forms as merely the latest adjustment to business 'climacterics' coinciding with so-called long waves of technological development. Each of these waves has contributed to a movement over two centuries of industrialization, from the use of manual energy and primitive machines to the current development of IT. Shifts in generic technologies, such as new energy sources, can bring about convergent market developments which destroy sectoral boundaries. Freeman *et al.* (1982) and others see these movements as giving rise to new sources of sectoral or industry specialization. Thus IT is seen as having brought about an erosion and revision of these boundaries since 1970.

At sector level, the familiar life cycle metaphor is often used to describe the diffusion of a standardized 'best practice' across firms providing similar products. The four phases of the historical process of standardization of 'best practice' (shown in Figure 5) is that derived from the history of the automobile sector by Abernathy *et al.* (1983). Their separation of the social basis of trading relationships from the technological bases of operational competences, upon which

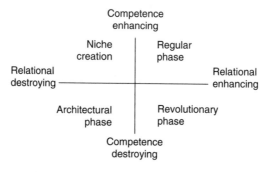

Figure 5 Phases in sectoral or corporate learning

the corporate reputation is based within the sector, provides important analytical scope for explanation of technological development along socially differentiated trajectories across different regional and organizational communities. Tushman and Anderson (1986) adopt a similar bifurcated approach to their analysis of the disruptive effects of innovation within the strategic context of the corporate portfolio.

In effect, these contingent analyses of technological innovation see emergent organizational forms as relating the continued success of corporate responses to the opportunities and threats present within phases in sector formation – and reformation. The analysis of Williamson quoted earlier sees these responses as being shaped by the overhead costs of corporate governance. Others emphasize the *scope* of the firm's diversified usage of its core technological capability. Yet others weigh the achievement of *synergy* across all such activities more heavily. These benefits are enhanced within the MNC by its ability to transfer technology across national boundaries by virtue of its internal jurisdiction over information flows (Teece 1987).

7 Balkanization or synergy in approaches to technology?

Given the permeation of technology into all areas of social activity, and the manner in which social aspirations shape technology, it is hardly surprising that Nelson and Winter (1982) should speak of the 'Balkanization' of technology studies. Yet since the 1980s there has been a growing acknowledgement of the existence of differing theoretical perspectives within the academic community itself. This awareness has been brought home by the strategic position taken up by operational management in the design of new organizational forms. In addition, the former distinction between Marxian and Weberian approaches to innovation has also been blurred by the new significance attached to growing consumer influences by post-modernist theorists. However, there is a clear distinction between optimists and pessimists in the interpretation of present trends in technological development: this often coincides with a division between those interested in modelling successful technology management for prescriptive purposes and those more concerned with its wider social effects.

The movement in research has been towards the establishment of contextual configurations of institutional settings within which innovation takes place. This may be exemplified by the significance attached to occupational qualification structures in shaping changes in the workplace division of labour in the already quoted studies by Sorge *et al.* (1983). Such cross-national comparisons have been extended to the effectiveness of other societal institutions, such as the family and financial sources, in providing infrastructural contexts, or national innovation systems (Kogut 1993).

Success in national industrial policy can be seen to be related to the extent to which existing institutions channel the development of new knowledge streams in a productive or non-productive manner. For this to occur there has, of course, to be some agreement around a complementarity in purpose between strategic goals and institutional bases. It appears possible that this occurs within the more successful social orders of certain nations such as Germany and Japan (Altmann *et al.* 1992). The trusting or clan-like nature of inter-organizational and intra-organizational relationships within these national systems are not easily reproduced in the contexts of Western liberal societies.

As in other areas of organizational analysis, the effects of culture have come to be seen as critical in shaping more or less innovative stances towards the adoption or rejection of new process or product technologies. Unfortunately there is little detailed evidence in recent case research to provide strong anthropological foundations for claims in either direction. Many of the workplace changes described earlier as involving devolved modes of responsibility are regarded sceptically by some industrial sociologists, who describe the effects of exposure to recessionary market forces as being as coercive as those experienced under overt bureaucratic regulation. Furthermore, the emergence of new forms of strategic networking can result in a systemic rationalization whose effects lie outside of the influence of either local management or employee representatives (Altmann *et al.* 1992).

If, as some suggest, the modernization project is bringing about a convergence between the institutions and ideals of those nation-states, it is evidently not complete. Indeed, the differentiated nature of the institutions of industrializing countries appear to make them more or less effective vehicles for the implementation of new technology. It remains with the citizens of those countries to determine the ultimate costs and benefits of allowing regional institutions to be shaped by a technological contest between MNCs.

Further reading

(References cited in the text marked *)

* Abernathy, W.J., Clark, K.B. and Kantow, A.M. (1983) *Industrial Renaissance*, New York: Basic Books. (An attempt to diagnose the structural failure of US manufacturing by modelling the historical development of the automobile industry.)
* Aglietta, M. (1975) *A Theory of Capitalist Regulation*, trans. D. Sernbach, London: New Left Books, 1979. (A description of a general theory of modern capitalism in which the regulation of civil society through the creation of consumer markets is seen as complementing that of the prevailing mode of control over the labour process.)
* Altmann, N., Kohler, C. and Meil, P. (1992) *Technology and Work in German Industry*, London: Routledge. (A collection of essays by members and associates of Institut Für Sozialwissenschaftliche Forschung, Munich on current debates around developments in German process technology and their impacts on skill formation and job structures.)
* Bell, D. (1973) *The Coming of Post-industrial Society*, New York: Basic Books. (One of the earliest prognostications on the effects of the decline of employment in the manufacturing sectors of Western economies. Still one of the most prescient, although heavily criticized at the time for neglect of analysis of social class implications.)
* Braverman, H. (1974) *Labor and Monopoly Capitalism*, New York: Monthly Review Press. (A study of Taylorian influences on workplace regulation. Led to a revival of Marxian analysis of workplace relations particularly among European sociologists.)
* Bright, J.R. (1988) *Automation and Management*, Cambridge, MA: Harvard Business School Press. (Bright continued the work of Woodward (1958). In her later work she responded to

critics by moving away from the closely determinate significance attributed to process technology.)

* Burgelman, R.A. and Sayles, L.R. (1988) *Inside Corporate Innovation: Strategy, Structure and Managerial Skills*, New York: The Free Press. (The authors suggest an analysis of the design–innovation process based on product champions within a large US hi-tech firm.)

* Callon, M. (1992) 'The dynamics of techno-economic networks', in R. Coombs, P. Saviotti and V. Walsh (eds), *Technological Change and Company Strategies*, London: Academic Press. (An overview of the approach taken by French anthropologists to the social shaping of innovations through transactions along 'filiere' or networks.)

* Child, J. and Loveridge, R. (1990) *Information Technology in European Services*, Oxford: Blackwell. (Study of the use of IT in the European service industry.)

* Faulkner, W. and Arnold, E. (1985) *Smothered by Invention*, London: Pluto Publishing. (An example of the feminist reinterpretation of the male-dominated record of technological invention and the effects of its implementation on women's role in the process.)

* Freeman, C., Clark, J. and Soete, L. (1982) *Unemployment and Technical Innovation: A Study of Long Waves and Economic Development*, London: Frances Pinter. (An interesting re-interpretation of the work of Kontratiev (1925), Schumpeter (1934) and Mensch (1979) on the historical existence of long waves of technological development.)

* Kaplinsky, R. (1984) *Automation: The Technology and Society*, London: Longman. (This might be considered as the most significant of a long series of government-inspired reports dating back to the 1950s which attempted to predict the effects of automation. Kaplinsky maps the stages of development through which machine control has moved and extrapolates to what is now familiarly known as total 'business systems'.)

* Kogut, B. (ed.) (1993) *Country Competitiveness*, New York: Oxford University Press. (An interesting collection of papers on how national institutions have encouraged or inhibited technological innovation with analytical contributions from the editor.)

* Kuhn, S.T. (1962) *The Structure of Scientific Revolutions*, Chicago, IL: University of Chicago Press. (Since the publication of this work the debate between so-called relativists and positivists among both natural and social scientists has gained in strength. Subsequently the debate has been extended to challenging the Kuhnian notion of the incommensurability of paradigms.)

* Maurice, M., Sellier, F. and Silvestre, J.-J. (1982) *Politique d'éducation et organisation industrielle en France et en Allemagne: essai d'analyse sociétal*, Paris: Presses Universitaires de France. (When this comparative study of workplace hierarchies within France and Germany was first published in the early 1970s, it provided a pioneering attempt at explanation of the labour process through wider societal institutions.)

* Nelson, R. and Winter, S. (1982) *An Evolutionary Theory of Economic Change*, Cambridge, MA: Harvard University Press. (Regarded by many industrial economists as providing a new bridge to organizational analysis; describes organizations as moving along path-dependent innovation trajectories. These represent incremental learning curves in the adaptation of knowledge 'routines'.)

* Noble, D. (1985) 'Social choice in machine design', in D. MacKenzie and J. Wajcman (eds), *The Social Shaping of Technology*, Milton Keynes: Open University Press. (A study of the political process of decision making leading to the introduction of CNC machines into the craft-dominated areas of aerospace manufacture.)

* Perez, C. (1985) 'Microelectronics, long waves and world structural change', *World Development* 15 (4): 441–63. (Part of a series of works from the Science Policy Research Unit at the University of Sussex. It offers one of the most explicit definitions of the new organizational paradigm emerging from scholarly debates in the 1980s.)

* Perrow, C. (1986) *Complex Organisations: A Critical Essay*, New York: McGraw-Hill. (Examines the degree of indeterminacy created by process technology, along with other elements in the managerial environment, as shaping organizational responses.)

* Pollert, A. (1988) 'Dismantling flexibility', *Capital and Class* 2 (3): 42–75. (Describes the devolved modes of organization as being exploitative, so long as TQM and other modes of diffusing responsibility are not complemented by decentralized authority. Suggests that terms such as 'flexibility' and 'empowerment' are often used to cover socially coercive modes of management better defined as neo-Fordist.)

* Pugh, D.S., Hickson, D.J. and Hinings, C.R. (1969) 'An empirical taxonomy of structures of work organization', *Administrative Science Quarterly* 14: 115–26. (This paper is one of a series published by the Aston School at the end of the 1960s and through the 1970s. The work of the School possibly represents the high point of structural positivism in the study of organizations.)

* Rogers, E.M. (1983) *Diffusion of Innovations*, 3rd edn, New York: The Free Press. (First published in 1970, this overview of research on technological diffusion relied heavily on the so-called two-stage model of communication popular in market research in the 1940s and 1950s. It remains, in this updated version, one of the most insightful social-psychological texts on the subject.)

Rose, M. (1988) *Industrial Behaviour*, 2nd edn, Harmondsworth: Penguin. (A comprehensive and insightful account of the development of behavioural science in Europe and North America with respect to developing management needs. This edition contains an extensive review of the comparative national systems approach.)

* Rothwell, R. (1977) 'The characteristics of successful innovations and technically progressive firms', *R&D Management* 7 (3): 258–91. (This paper has been a significant contributor to the development of the concept of product champion in case histories of product innovation within British companies.)

* Sayles, L.R. (1958) *Behaviour of Industrial Work Groups: Production and Control*, New York: Wiley. (One of a number of US and British participant observer studies of the workplace undertaken in the 1950s. Most illuminating in the discussion of the interaction between technological configurations and patterns of shop floor relationships.)

* Sayles, L.R. and Chandler, M. (1971) *Managing Large Systems: Organizations of the Future*, New York: Harper & Row. (An early case study of inter-organizational networking, focusing on the birth and development of NASA.)

* Schon, D. (1963) *Displacement of Concepts*, London: Tavistock. (Possibly the most quoted source of the concept of product champion, deriving from a staged series of British case studies carried out by SPRU and collectively known as the SAPPHO Project.)

* Sorge, A., Hartmann, G., Warner, M. and Nicholas, I. (1983) *Microelectronics and Manpower in Manufacturing, Applications of Computer Numerical Control in Great Britain and West Germany*, Aldershot: Gower. (Useful comparison of computerized manufacturing systems in Germany and the UK.)

* Teece, D.J. (1987) 'Profiting from technological innovation: implications for integration, collaboration, licensing and public policy', in D. Teece (ed.), *The Competitive Challenge*, Cambridge, MA: Ballinger. (One of the most original exponents of the concept of transaction costs in the analysis of the appropriation of technological knowledge and skills.)

* Tushman, M. and Anderson, P. (1986) 'Technological discontinuities and organizational environments', *Administrative Sciences Quarterly* 31 (2): 439–65. (The authors analyse the corporate responses to technological and market discontinuity in their environment.)

* Weber, M. (1924) *The Theory of Social and Economic Organization*, trans. T. Parsons, New York: Oxford University Press. (In this work Weber defines the organizational dimensions making up the ideal type of bureaucracy.)

* Wilkinson, B. (1983) *The Shopfloor Politics of New Technology*, London: Heinemann. (One of the earliest and best of the many workplace studies carried out in Europe during the 1980s, largely directed at discovering obstacles to the adoption of what was generically labelled 'new technology'.)

* Williamson, O.E. (1980) 'The economics of organization: the transaction cost approach', *American Journal of Sociology* 87 (November): 548–77. (This paper has inspired a range

of studies using transactional cost approaches to technological knowledge as an appropriable asset.)

* Womack, J.P., Jones, D.T. and Roos, D. (1990) *The Machine that Changed the World*, London: Macmillan. (One of a series of reports on the automobile industry from this MIT-based team. Gained worldwide popularity from its case comparisons of production modes in the USA, Germany, Japan, France and the UK, coining the term 'lean production' to describe Western adaptations of Japanese organizational procedures.)

* Woodward, J. (1958) *Industrial Organization: Theory and Practice*, Oxford: Oxford University Press. (Woodward's original typology spanned eleven categories of process technology and took in a range of organizational variables such as span of control and the number of hierarchical levels.)

Organizational information and knowledge

Kenneth Laudon and William H. Starbuck

Overview

Throughout the world, economies have been putting more and more emphasis on service industries, and especially on information work. The explosive growth of the Internet, and related World Wide Web technologies, has significantly quickened the transformation of economies into 'information economies'. This article surveys the types of information work, of information workers, and of computer systems to support information work. It then examines knowledge-intensive firms (KIFs) – the organizations that depend most strongly on knowledge and information work. KIFs try to convert knowledge into capital, but they generally have precarious bases for success.

1 Organizations as information processors

The idea that organizations process information is rather recent. Before 1950, neither academics nor practising managers regarded organizations as decision makers or information processors. Theories of leadership did not discuss decision-making skills or communication skills. Although economists portrayed firms as choosing prices or output quantities, they assumed that firms had perfect information and unlimited analytic abilities. Some economists even argued that the decision making and information processing within firms could not matter because any firm that took suboptimal actions would go bankrupt. Thus, the decisions of surviving firms would have to conform to economists' theories about optimal behaviour.

An information-processing perspective began to appear around 1950. Some management writers described managers as decision makers with limited capabilities. Some social psychologists studied problem solving by small groups, and implicitly treated groups as information processors in which different group members played different roles. Groups processed different kinds of information at the beginnings, middles, and ends of problem-solving sessions. Some psychologists began to use computer programs as models of human problem solving. Some economists began to talk about possible limitations on economists' theories. In 1958, Forrester and March and Simon described organizations as information processors. In 1963, Cyert and March portrayed organizations as systems that learn and they described some organizational decision processes in detail.

The 1970s brought many studies of organizations as decision-making and information-processing systems. Observers came to see organizations as flexible activity systems as well as stable structures, and the focus gradually shifted from physical activities to mental ones. In the late 1980s, theories about business strategies began to focus on core competencies – firms' domains of expertise. Also, there came renewed interest in professional service firms. By the 1990s, theories about organizations began to consider how the new Web-based technologies change organizations' relationships with vendors, customers and employees. These theoretical developments reflect a long-term evolution in the work that organizations do.

2 The rise of information work

Since the turn of the twentieth century, the more affluent countries have been moving toward service and information economies and away from agricultural and manufacturing economies (Machlup 1962; Rubin and Huber 1986). The fraction of workers using information to produce economic value has been rising, and the fraction working with their hands in factories or on farms has been declining. In the USA, the percentage of jobs in manufacturing fell from 27 per cent in 1920 to 13 per cent in 1999. In the USA and Canada, manufacturing employment was growing at an average annual rate of 2.0 per cent during the 1960s, but it declined at an average annual rate of 0.4 per cent during the 1980s and 1990s. In Japan, manufacturing employment was growing at an average annual rate of 4.1 per cent during the 1960s, but it declined at an average annual rate of 1.1 per cent during the 1990s. In western Europe, manufacturing employment was growing at an average annual rate of 0.5 per cent during the 1960s, but it declined at an average annual rate of 1.5 per cent during the 1980s and 1990s. Among white-collar workers, the fastest-growing occupations have been clerical, professional and technical workers, and managers and administrators.

Six factors have been involved in this shift. First, Third-World and developing societies have become centres of manufacturing, while the so-called advanced societies have shifted toward services. In Europe, the telecommunications sector has been growing just under 14 per cent annually, and the software and computing services sector has been growing 15 to 20 per cent annually. In the USA, the telecommunications sector has been growing about 19 per cent annually, largely due to investments in fibre-optic infrastructure. Second, knowledge-intense and information-intense products and services have grown rapidly, and the production of traditional products has also been using knowledge more intensively. Third, business has invested heavily in equipment to support information work.

In the USA, computing and telecommunications equipment accounted for 20 per cent of capital investment in 1990; this figure had increased to 30 per cent of capital investment by 1999. Fourth, knowledge workers and information workers have replaced manual production workers within the manufacturing sectors. Technicians who monitor computer-controlled machine tools, for instance, have often replaced machine-tool operators. Fifth, workers have increased education and information-processing skills. Sixth, new kinds of knowledge-intense and information-intense organizations have emerged that are devoted entirely to the production, processing and distribution of information. These new kinds of organizations already employ many millions of people, and the Internet seems to be opening up vast new opportunities for such work.

As early as 1976, the value of information-sector products and services had already exceeded that of the manufacturing sector in the USA. By 1999, the information sector (including services) accounted for 78 per cent of GNP, and 62 per cent of the US workers were doing some type of information work. The USA, however, represents an extreme case. For instance, the USA has about 60 per cent of the world market in computing and telecommunications equipment, followed by Ireland, India and Israel. In the software and computing services sector, Japan has about 8 per cent, the European Community has about 25 per cent, and the USA has about 55 per cent of the world market, although it does appear that software development is rapidly moving out of the USA. The USA has been benefiting financially from this situation: its returns on invested capital have been 58 per cent for investments in information technology as compared with 14 per cent for other investments. Moreover, about 94 per cent of the gains in productivity due to information technology have translated into lower prices for buyers and only 6 per cent of the gains have translated into higher profits for sellers.

This entry surveys information work, information workers, and the computer systems that support such work. It then examines the organizations that are most dependent on knowledge and information work – knowledge-intensive firms.

3 Information, knowledge, and information work

Information is a flow of data that has meaning, and knowledge is a stock (or inventory) of information. In one sense, knowledge is to information as assets are to income. However, knowledge is more than an accumulation of information: it is an organized collection that reflects the intentions of the humans who create and interpret it. Thus, knowledge resembles an organized portfolio of assets.

Some activities draw on extensive knowledge without processing large amounts of current information. Management consulting would be one example. Conversely, an organization can process much information without using much knowledge. For instance, Automatic Data Processing (ADP) produces payroll cheques. ADP processes vast amounts of information, but it is probably more capital-intensive than knowledge-intensive. Producing a payroll cheque requires little expertise, and many people have this expertise.

Distinctions between data, information and knowledge are often difficult to apply. From one perspective, ADP merely processes information for other firms, using mainly capital in the form of computers and software. From another perspective, ADP succeeds because it does its specialized task better than its customers can do it themselves. This superior performance likely comes from both expertise and returns to scale, so knowledge and large scale reinforce each other.

Economists use the term 'information workers' to denote everyone who primarily creates, works with, or disseminates information (Machlup 1962). They include in the information-worker category: (a) clerical workers who mainly process data or preserve it without attempting to understand it, (b) clerical workers, librarians and sales personnel who interpret information and act upon it, (c) detectives, journalists and researchers who mainly generate new information, and (d) experts such as consultants, lawyers and certified accountants who mainly apply accumulated knowledge.

Information workers can be distinguished by their formal educations and cognitive skills. Some information workers – such as sales personnel, estate agents and secretaries – typically do not have advanced educational degrees. On the other hand, experts – such as engineers, judges, scientists, writers and architects – usually must obtain advanced degrees or professional certifications because they exercise independent judgement and creativity based on their mastery of specialized knowledge.

Workers often draw distinctions that an outside observer cannot. For instance, experts gather information through interviews or reading; they analyse and interpret this information; and they make written and oral reports to clients and colleagues. There are strong similarities across people, sites and projects. Nevertheless, some experts say that they are applying old knowledge to new problems, others that they are creating new knowledge, and still others that they are preserving knowledge that already exists.

The experts who see themselves as producing new knowledge emphasize the recency or originality of their information and the differences between their findings and those of predecessors. They may classify such work either as basic scientific research or as applied research on markets, products or processes. Other experts see their work mainly as applying existing knowledge to current problems. For instance, when most lawyers do research, they analyse and interpret previous cases and they emphasize the continuity over time of knowledge and its meaning. To gain acceptance of their rulings, most judges de-emphasize the innovative quality of their reasoning. Distinguishing between creating knowledge and applying it can be difficult. Lawyers may be more successful if they reinterpret precedent cases imaginatively, or if they conceive original strategies. Basic research may have direct applicability, and applied research may contribute fundamental knowledge. When it comes to systems as complex as a human body or an economy, people may only be able to create valid knowledge by trying to apply it.

Some experts describe themselves as memory cells. They say their jobs are to preserve information that their clients have difficulty preserving. Because the

US military services rotate assignments frequently, military personnel lack job experience and cannot manage long-term projects. Also, military wage scales are too low to attract and retain highly educated experts. To compensate, the military services sign contracts with firms that provide long-term continuity of management and expertise. These firms employ civilian experts who do not rotate assignments frequently and who either manage long-term projects directly or advise military managers.

Creating, applying and preserving complement each other. At least over long periods, merely storing knowledge does not preserve it. For old knowledge to have meaning, people must relate it to their current problems and activities. They have to translate it into contemporary language and frame it within current issues. Effective preserving looks much like applying. As time passes and social and technological changes add up, the needed translations grow larger, and applying knowledge comes to look more like creating knowledge. Conversely, for new knowledge to have meaning, people must fit it into their current beliefs and perspectives, and familiarity with existing knowledge signals expertise. Evaluators assess completed research partly by its applicability, and they judge research proposals partly by the researchers' mastery of past research. Thus, Rand Corporation, which derives some income from research grants, makes elaborate literature searches before writing grant proposals. Rand also employs public-information staff, who highlight the relevance of research findings.

When describing *The Knowledge-Creating Company*, Nonaka and Takeuchi (1995) asserted that Japanese companies show greater ability to create new knowledge than do American companies. Since creating, applying and preserving often substitute for each other, this assertion implicitly raises the question as to whether Japanese people may define 'creation' differently than Americans do. Might the apparent differences in knowledge processing occur mainly in the ways people categorize their activities?

In the USA, capital investment in information-work machinery – primarily computers and systems – surpassed investment in traditional capital goods in the 1980s. However, firms have found it difficult to make capital-budgeting decisions about information technology because it is so difficult to measure the productivity of information work. It appears that information-technology investments in US factories did raise productivity during the 1980s. On the other hand, in industries like finance, insurance and real estate, huge investments in information technology did not increase productivity. However, by the 1990s, researchers were finding evidence that information technology was yielding much higher returns on investment than traditional forms of capital in diverse industries. Stock-market valuations of companies – the final measure of firms' effectiveness – were higher the more they invested in information technology. Nevertheless, investment results differed from one firm to another, suggesting that management and organizational design were key contingencies.

4 Office automation

Information work concentrates in offices, and office automation systems facilitate the processing, distribution and coordination of information. No longer a mundane clerical pool or a bureaucratic nightmare, the office is one of the most important work sites. Offices today integrate diverse arrays of professional, managerial, sales and clerical employees. Office work is complex and cooperative, and yet highly individualistic. It resembles an orchestra of highly trained individuals who collaborate more than a factory of workers who perform preplanned tasks (Laudon and Laudon 2000).

Indeed, telecommuting has made it more common for the participants in an office to be physically apart. In 1998, about one-eighth of the US workforce was spending at least one day a week working at home. Telework cultures promote different values, norms, behaviours and symbols than do the cultures in on-site offices. Specifically, telework cultures emphasize work performance rather than stable social relations and shared identities. Norms of interaction become topics for continuing negotiation between employees and employers, and employees gain freedom to exhibit more diversity (Dunbar and Garud 2001).

Offices perform three critical organizational roles: They coordinate and manage the work of professional and information workers. They link the work being performed across all levels and functions throughout an organization. They couple an organization to its environments, including clients and suppliers (Laudon and Laudon 2000).

To fulfil these roles, nearly all offices perform five major activities: creating documents, filing information, managing projects, coordinating individuals and groups, and scheduling individuals and groups. Document management typically consumes about 40 per cent of the total effort, with the other activities splitting the remaining 60 per cent in roughly equal shares. Further, many offices include specialized experts who perform creative tasks such as calculating, drawing and simulating.

The first wave of office automation supported only clerical activities such as word processing and simple task coordination, but new software supports a diverse range of office activities. Dhar and Stein (1997) have described a variety of software tools that support decision making by knowledge workers.

Document-management technologies support word processing, desktop publishing, document imaging and workflow management. Document-imaging systems store, retrieve and manipulate digitized images of documents. The documents themselves can be discarded. Two or more people can work simultaneously on the same document; work need not be delayed because a file is out or a document is in transit. Workflow systems automate processes such as routeing documents to different locations, securing approvals, scheduling, and generating reports. With effective indexing, users can retrieve files based upon their contents.

Groupware is software that supports collaboration within work groups. It seeks to improve groups' effectiveness by providing electronic links that help them to schedule meetings, to meet, to communicate with each other, to develop ideas collaboratively, to share the preparation of documents, to share knowledge, and to exchange information on the work of members. Groupware usually provides electronic group calendars, electronic mail, and software that permits members in remote locations to have video conferences. These functions presuppose powerful electronic networks. Corporate intranets are providing standard platforms on which to build collaborative work tools. Products such as Lotus Notes and Microsoft's Workgroup permit workers to share information and to create information-sharing applications.

Personal information managers: Firms have traditionally maintained huge corporate databases on mainframe computers, but microcomputers offer office workers the opportunity to develop their own personal databases for clients, customers, suppliers or vendors. Few office workers have created such databases because database languages have been difficult to use. Some software firms are producing personal information managers, which are database systems customized for the needs of salespersons, managers, estate agents or stockbrokers. Other software firms are developing more user-friendly methods for creating personal databases. By the late 1990s, information workers were using small palm-sized database and communication devices – such as the PalmPilot and Hewlett-Packard Jornada – to coordinate their daily schedules and to store business contacts.

Project-management software portrays a complex project as an assembly of simpler subtasks, each with its own completion time and resource requirements. Once a user specifies what each subtask requires, the software can produce delivery schedules and resources allocations. Two project-management techniques are Critical Path Method (CPM) and Program Evaluation and Review Technique (PERT). Project managers use graphical user interfaces and they have access to high-quality presentation graphics, permitting photographic slide and overhead transparency output. Whereas older project-management software focused on single users, contemporary packages offer access to many members of a work group.

Specialized workstations: Chancellor Capital Management, Inc., developed specialized investment workstations to help it manage funds for 300 clients. Chancellor's former systems were mainframe-based, incompatible, error-prone and difficult to use; they stored data separately in accounting, trading, research and analytical systems. That arrangement compromised data integrity, and it impeded searches for information. Thus, Chancellor wanted to reduce drudgery and to give traders and asset managers more time to make decisions and to develop strategies. They wanted to integrate their front and back offices so that dataintegrity issues would disappear and all systems would report identical information.

Chancellor built a network of powerful workstations that integrate data from the firm's investment-management systems and its portfolio-accounting systems. Chancellor also installed a user interface with a number of windows; instead of having to switch from one database to another, a user can easily switch from one window to another. Some formerly time-consuming calculations have become automatic. Trading within the firm has become paperless, as have communications with brokers.

Computer-aided design (CAD) automates the creation and revision of designs. For instance, Alan R. Burns, a mining engineer from Perth, Australia, used CAD to turn an innovative idea into reality. The tyres of off-road vehicles take a terrible beating that produces frequent tyre replacements and costly downtime. Mr Burns conceived a tyre with independent tread segments that could be replaced individually. The segments are not pneumatic so they are not subject to punctures; and people can replace them quickly, without removing the wheel from the vehicle. Burns used a CAD workstation to develop a visual representation of a segment, and he modified thickness, tread shape, and other factors until he achieved an acceptable design. The CAD software enabled him to simulate operational characteristics for each visual model and to calculate the tyre's stresses and strains under specified loading and usage conditions. Once Burns approved a design, he used the same software and the same model data to design a mould for the tyre segments. The software could perform flow analysis to locate potential problems such as uneven cooling or shrinkage. One output was instructions for the milling machines that cut the mould from tool steel.

Virtual-reality systems offer visualization, rendering and simulation capabilities far beyond those of conventional CAD systems. They use interactive graphics software to create computer-generated simulations that are so close to reality that users believe they are in a real situation. Virtual reality is interactive in such a way that the user actually feels immersed in a world that exists only in a computer. To enter that world, a user dons special clothing, headgear and equipment. The clothing contains sensors that record the user's movements and immediately transmit that information back to the computer.

For example, Japan's Matsushita Electric Works developed a virtual-reality application it calls Virtual Kitchen to help stores sell kitchen appliances and cabinets. Prospective buyers bring their kitchen layouts to a department store, where staff enter the design into a computer. The customers then don the appropriate equipment and suddenly find themselves in the kitchen they designed. They can try the appliances in various sizes, colours and locations. They can open and close cabinet doors and drawers. They can walk around and discover the feel and ambiance of the new kitchen.

Although virtual reality may appear fantastic, its benefits may turn out to be very concrete. The architecture and engineering industries are using visualization systems to help clients visualize their future buildings and to help designers place equipment, doors and walls in optimal locations. Visualization systems permit managers to share screen content over the Web when making plans. Technology descended from Web-based games can enable physicians to direct surgical instruments remotely, and remote surgery techniques may prove useful for remote sites such as oilrig platforms, distant scientific observatories and mineral-exploration camps.

Intranets are firm-wide networks that use standard Web technologies such as HTML, TCP/IP and client/server hardware and software. In the late 1990s, most large firms aggressively moved their myriad office applications onto intranets. A single network and networking standard could unify the hundreds of disparate software applications found in modern offices. Intranets have greatly expanded the scope, speed and accuracy of corporate information and decision making.

5 Knowledge-intensive firms

Knowledge has great importance for knowledge-intensive firms (KIFs). KIFs are firms that derive substantial revenues from products or services that incorporate expertise, and most KIFs employ many experts – such as auditors, computer programmers, consultants, researchers, lawyers, market researchers and medical doctors (Starbuck 1992).

If one defines the KIF category more broadly, many more firms fit into it but they have fewer similarities; if one defines the KIF category more narrowly, KIFs look more alike but there are fewer of them. Sveiby and Lloyd (1987) perceived 'knowhow companies' as a very broad range of firms that can be categorized on the basis of their managerial or technical expertise. They said law firms have high technical expertise but low managerial expertise, whereas the McDonald's fast-food chain has high managerial expertise and low technical expertise. On the other hand, Ekstedt (1988) said 'knowledge companies' should be distinguished from industrial companies, high-technology companies and service companies 'such as hamburger chains'. In his schema, both high-technology companies and knowledge companies have high knowledge intensity, but high-technology companies have higher intensity of real capital than do knowledge companies.

Although KIFs may be professional firms, many KIFs are not professional firms because not all experts belong to recognized professions. A profession has at least four properties besides expertise: an ethical code, cohesion, collegial enforcement of standards, and autonomy (Schriesheim *et al.* 1977). Professionals' ethical codes require them to serve clients unemotionally and impersonally, without self-interest. Professionals identify strongly with their professions, more strongly than with their clients or their employers. They not only observe professional standards, they believe that only members of their professions have the competence and ethics to enforce these standards. Similarly, professionals insist that outsiders cannot properly supervise their activities. Management consulting and software engineering, for example, do not qualify as recognized professions even though the people who do these jobs well have rare expertise. They are not professionals because the ultimate judges of their expertise are their clients or their supervisors, and because their employers set and enforce their ethical codes and performance standards.

KIFs form a broader category, in which many issues reflect labour markets, interpersonal networks, and experts' individuality, self-interest and social standing. Yet, most KIFs have nearly all the properties that observers have assigned to professional firms. For instance, many experts design their own roles, divide work to suit their interests, compete for resources, and emphasize autonomy, collegiality, informality and flexible structures.

Sveiby and Risling (1986) argued that KIFs call for new definitions of ownership and new ways of controlling the uses of capital. Traditional notions of ownership, they said, assume that financial or physical capital dominates labour, whereas human capital dominates in KIFs. Sveiby (1994) observed that a publishing firm operated in distinct markets: an information market and a knowledge market. Whereas sellers offered products to buyers in the information market, the knowledge market required interactions between buyers and sellers.

One should not, however, assume that knowledge resides only in people. Besides the knowledge held by individual people, one can find knowledge in: (a) capital such as plant, equipment or financial instruments; (b) firms' routines and cultures; and (c) professional cultures. People convert their knowledge to physical forms when they write books or computer programs, design buildings or machines, produce violins or hybrid corn, or create financial instruments such as mutual-fund shares (Ekstedt 1988). Organizations seek to capture the knowledge and expertise of their workers in various knowledge-based systems – decision support systems, databases and case files, some of which are automated (Laudon and Laudon 2000). Conversely, people may gain knowledge by reading books, studying buildings, buying shares or running computer programs. People also translate their knowledge into firms' routines, job descriptions, plans, strategies and cultures. Nelson and Winter (1982) treated behavioural routines as the very essence of organizations – the means by which firms can produce predictable results while adapting to social and technological changes. Simultaneously, Deal and Kennedy (1982) were saying it is cultures that perform these functions.

Both KIFs and individuals can gain new expertise by buying capital goods. Computer software affords obvious examples. Not long ago, expertise was uneven across accountants who handled income taxes. Now, every accountant has low-cost access to software that makes no arithmetical errors, omits nothing, incorporates the latest changes in tax codes, and warns of conditions that might trigger audits by tax authorities. Many law firms have begun to use automated knowledge-creation systems. These systems use various techniques (rule-based or neural-network pattern recognition) and Web-based search engines to characterize the content of document databases. For instance, Autonomy Inc. (*http://www.autonomy.com*) has created a system that automatically places tags in the large databases used by law firms. Once the data have been tagged, lawyers can search for specific cases that meet their criteria – for instance, all the murder cases since 1900 where a knife was used in self-defence.

Describing McDonald's as a firm with low technical expertise overlooks the expertise in McDonald's technology and organization. McDonald's success stems from its ability to deliver consistent quality across diverse environments and despite high turnover of low-skilled workers. To get such results, the firm operates extensive training programmes and conducts research about production techniques and customers' tastes. Although training at Hamburger University may give McDonald's managers more skill than those at most restaurants, McDonald's managers likely have no more skill than those in most production firms. Also, McDonald's uses technology and routines to control workers' activities.

6 Converting knowledge into capital

KIFs convert individual expertise into organizational property. These conversion processes produce at least three types of organizational property: physical capital, routines, and organizational culture.

Physical capital: KIFs may be able to turn expertise into concrete capital. For instance, decades of experience enabled the large public accounting firms to create systematic auditing procedures. The firms then turned these procedures into checklists that novice accountants and clerical staff can complete. Similarly, research occasionally produces databases that have value beyond the projects that created them. KIFs exploit these databases by proposing new projects that would draw upon them. So-called 'knowledge work systems' are investments in information technology that are designed to increase a firm's knowledge base (Laudon and Laudon 2000).

Converting a KIF's knowledge into capital can fundamentally alter the nature of the firm, turning it into an ordinary production firm and losing its knowledge base while strengthening its financial base. For instance, Orlikowski (1988: 179–267) detailed a consulting firm's efforts to capture its experience as software. Over ten years and many projects, consultants built various software tools that helped them plan projects and carry them out efficiently. The tools originated separately when consultants saw needs or opportunities, but the firm's general production philosophy implicitly guided these developments and rendered the tools mutually compatible. Also, at first, isolated people used these tools voluntarily, but informal norms gradually made their use widespread and mandatory. Thus, the tools both expressed the firm's culture in tangible form, and reinforced the culture by clarifying its content and generalizing its application. Generalization made the differences among clients' problems less and less important, and it weakened the contributions that clients could make to problem solving. Generalization also reduced the influence of more-technical consultants and increased the influence of less-technical consultants. In their interviews, the consultants stressed the tools' strong influence on their perceptions of problems and their methods of solving them. Eventually, the firm started to sell the tools to other firms. At that point, the firm's culture, methods and experience became products that other firms could buy.

Routines: Like all other firms, KIFs develop routines to handle familiar situations efficiently (Nelson and Winter 1982; Starbuck 1983). Routines are a form of social capital – assets that, once learned and honed, become bases for success in the marketplace. However, formalized routines look bureaucratic, and highly educated experts dislike bureaucracy. Much research has pointed to conflicts between professions and bureaucracies, and some of these conflicts apply to expertise in general (Schriesheim *et al.* 1977). Most experts want autonomy, they want recognition of their individuality, and they want their firms to have egalitarian structures. Among the service KIFs, only those having long-term contracts with a very few clients seem able to bureaucratize. Even such KIFs must bureaucratize cautiously, for their expert employees have external job opportunities.

Organizational culture: Cultures must be built gradually because they are delicate and poorly understood. Building a special organizational culture takes much effort as well as imagination. Imitating another firm's culture is usually impossible because every culture involves distinctive traditions.

Maister (1985: 4) wrote admiringly of 'one-firm firms', which stress 'institutional loyalty and group effort'. In contrast to many of their (often successful) competitors who emphasize individual entrepreneurship, autonomous profit centres, internal competition or highly decentralized independent activities, one-firm firms place great emphasis on firm-wide coordination of decision making, group identity, cooperative teamwork and institutional commitment. Maister also warned that one-firm firms might become complacent, lacking in entrepreneurship, entrenched in their ways of doing things, and inbred.

Orlikowski (1988: 152–60) studied a consulting firm in which the overtly technical training programme functioned as a culture incubator. Most consultants seem to agree with the one who said: 'The biggest advantage of the school is the networking and socializing it allows. It really is not that important as an educational experience.' Alvesson (1992) too described a consulting firm that spent much effort on formal socialization. The top managers ran a 'project philosophy course'. They also sought 'to sell the metaphor *the company as a home* to the employees'. Designed to foster informal interaction, the building has a kitchen, sauna, pool, piano bar and large lounge area. The firm supports a chorus, art club and navigation course. All personnel in each department meet together every second week. Every third month, each department undertakes a major social activity such as a hike or a sailing trip. The firm celebrated its tenth anniversary by flying all 500 employees to Rhodes for three days of group activities.

It appears that many KIFs attempt to build cultures by selecting experts carefully, using teams extensively, developing very serious mission orientations, managing growth cautiously, and encouraging open talk. However, very few KIFs discourage internal competition, emphasize group work, disclose information and elicit loyalty to the firm. Most KIFs seem to deviate from the one-firm model in having multiple profit centres, assessing the productivities of individual experts, revealing only the financial information that laws require, decentralizing activities, encouraging entrepreneurship, and not involving everyone in decision making.

Along with Maister (1985) and Orlikowski (1988), we observed firms in North America, where the societal cultures encourage individualism. Since organizational cultures interact with societal cultures, KIFs may use cultures differently in other contexts.

7 Precarious monopolies

Stinchcombe and Heimer (1988) described successful software firms as 'precarious monopolies'. They are monopolies insofar as they exhibit unusual abilities. Niches evolve naturally as individuals and small groups concentrate on specific streams of innovation. The firms also strive explicitly to develop and maintain unusual abilities. Unusual abilities help the firms to market their services and to avoid head-on competition.

This may be a common feature of many KIFs. Many KIFs have unstable knowledge monopolies. Stinchcombe and Heimer pointed out that the partial monopolies enjoyed by software firms are constantly at risk, both because technological changes may make unusual abilities obsolete and because key experts may depart. Computer technology has been changing especially rapidly, and the software firms' relations with clients and computer manufacturers repeatedly expose their experts to job offers. To sell their services to clients, software firms have to publicize the talents of their key experts, and this publicity creates job opportunities for the touted experts.

Professional firms may have more difficulty sustaining monopolistic positions than other KIFs do. Because the recognized professions try to control knowledge and to preserve their members' autonomy, firms that employ many professionals run into opposition if they seek to convert professional expertise to organizational property. Moreover, many products of professional firms are easy to imitate. For example, Martin Lipton invented the 'poison pill' defence against unfriendly corporate takeovers; but, after other law firms saw examples, Wachtell, Lipton was no longer the sole source for poison pills.

8 Organizations as knowledge and information producers

Most of the theories about organizations derive from pre-computer-era understandings and technologies. The reigning views of how organizations organize work, develop values and manage themselves derive from the 1960s and 1970s. Although the idea that organizations process information is a fairly recent one (1960s), the new reality is that organizations do increasingly depend upon knowledge and information. This new reality lies far beyond the limits of contemporary theory. We need new theories of organizational culture, structure and management process.

For instance, VeriFone Corporation is the world's largest producer of transaction-automation systems. It manufactures credit-card-verification hardware and systems that are used throughout the world. Since 1988, the company's revenues have been growing 25 per cent per year. VeriFone is a KIF whose primary task is processing transaction information; its success comes from explicit and tacit knowledge of the credit and cheque-authorization processes. Its knowledge routines – the core competencies of the organization – are highly distributed across manufacturing and administration nodes located around the globe. VeriFone has no headquarters but instead has created a highly decentralized, hydra-headed organization. VeriFone's culture is not based on face-to-face interaction, but on intensive use of electronic mail and other electronic forms of communication. Its management processes also differ from accepted practice: key senior managers have no single offices but instead manage through electronic communications.

Baumard (1999) has contributed to a theory about organizational knowledge generation. He studied four organizations that were facing challenging situations and attempted to explain how they developed knowledge appropriate to these challenges. His explanation emphasized the importance of tacit knowledge in providing, or impeding, sense-making frameworks. He observed that senior managers tend not to appreciate tacit knowledge and therefore fail to exploit it well.

No current theories adequately explain firms such as VeriFone, and such firms' ultimate success remains to be seen. However, these KIFs do suggest the future of organizations, as managers shape new organizational forms for the information age.

9 Converting information into knowledge and organizational assets

Converting information into knowledge and then into organizational assets is especially important for KIFs. KIFs that do this more effectively than other KIFs in the same industry will probably survive longer.

Just like individual people in the Internet Age, KIFs face the problem of coping with exponentially increasing message traffic produced by ever more efficient transaction and messaging systems. Customers may contact an organization physically at an office site, or through the telephone, the Web, or a mobile device. How is an organization supposed to keep all this straight? As organizations install powerful sense-and-response systems – like point-of-sale systems, inventory-monitoring systems, extranets that connect vendors to their production systems, and customer-relationship-monitoring systems – their ability to sense can easily overwhelm their ability to make sense (make knowledge) and then to respond – to turn the information stream into an organizational asset through one of the avenues described above, e.g. a new routine, a new cultural element or a new revenue stream.

Information technology offers five partial solutions to this problem of organizational sense making (knowledge creation): expert systems, case-based reasoning systems, neural networks, data mining, and filtering. Expert systems develop classification systems that classify new information into established categories or rules that can be acted upon. Case-based reasoning systems collect and categorize stories (often in the form of digital video files) and then provide human users a natural-language interface to the database of stories. Neural networks recognize patterns in the incoming data stream, and then humans can prescribe actions for each pattern recognized. Data mining uses a brute-force technique in which huge transaction databases are analysed for associations in the data. For example, after purchasing a dress, what is the customer's next most likely purchase? Filtering systems automatically tag information in message streams and in complex, unstructured databases (for instance, a database of court cases and testimony) on the basis of criteria supplied by users.

The Web has exacerbated the challenge facing KIFs with respect to sense making while offering extraordinary opportunities for knowledge creation and sharing. The Web now encompasses about 800 billion pages, most of them containing text. All firms rely on the Web as a source of information and knowledge. Corporations are converting nearly all their internal documents to HTML formats for use on their internal intranets, and converting most of their daily transactions to Web formats.

Unfortunately, there are no standards for classifying all these documents, or even a language to describe the contents of rich documents like spreadsheets and databases. Indeed, the underlying HTML format is incapable of solving these problems. A new markup language, XML, offers some hope. XML will permit organizations, and entire industries, to define new types of objects, rich text documents like databases and spreadsheets, and other objects like videos, audio tracks, invoices, and so forth. Software programs have been created that will automatically classify the contents of text documents into industry-standard knowledge categories. For instance, Expertez is an automatic tagging program that can quickly filter all the information in the Security and Exchange Commission's database and pull out the documents that a user is seeking. The publishing industry, along with the US Department of Defense, is moving to create standardized XML tags for distance learning, publishing, legal and medical databases. These auto-tagging programs can help organizations understand a very wide range of documents – including video and audio objects – and share this knowledge with millions of users. Through industry agreements, industries will be able to communicate, classify, and understand the myriad documents and forms required to do business in the Web era.

These developments are very important. What could be involved here is the potential codification of the entire collection of learning objects in a specified language. At some point, it will become possible to use a Web browser to scan the entire inventory of learning modules in, say, the English language, and to select only those that fit particular needs in terms of subject, length and modality (video, audio or text). If this potential becomes real, its impact will be analogous to the development of organized libraries in Alexandria around 500 BCE, except on a much grander scale.

Further reading

(References cited in the text marked *)

* Alvesson, M. (1992) 'Leadership as social integrative action. A study of a computer consultancy company', *Organization Studies* 13: 185–209. (This is one of several studies in which Alvesson discusses ways a consulting company creates and uses its culture.)
* Baumard, P. (1999) *Tacit Knowledge in Organizations*, London: Sage. (This book reports the author's research and summarizes writings about the development of knowledge by organizations.)

* Cyert, R.M. and March, J.G. (1963) *A Behavioral Theory of the Firm*, Englewood Cliffs, NJ: Prentice-Hall. (This book outlines a processual theory about how firms make decisions regarding prices and outputs.)

* Deal, T. and Kennedy, A. (1982) *Corporate Cultures*, Reading, MA: Addison-Wesley. (This book reviews evidence about the effects of organizational culture on performance.)

* Dhar, V. and Stein, R. (1997) *Intelligent Decision Support Methods: The Science of Knowledge Work*, Upper Saddle River, NJ: Prentice-Hall. (This book describes diverse software techniques for applying knowledge to problems in organizations.)

* Dunbar, R.L.M. and Garud, R. (2001) 'Culture in-the-making in telework settings', in C. Cooper and C. Earley (eds), *Handbook of Organizational Culture and Climate*, Wiley. (This chapter discusses the effects of telework on organizational cultures.)

* Ekstedt, E. (1988) *Human Capital in an Age of Transition: Knowledge Development and Corporate Renewal*, Stockholm: Allmänna Förlaget. (Ekstedt relates the organizational patterns in different industries to their knowledge-development practices.)

* Forrester, J. W. (1958) 'Industrial dynamics – A major breakthrough for decision makers', *Harvard Business Review* 36 (4): 37–66. (This article describes organizations' decision making as complex processes in which the consequences of earlier decisions feedback and influence later decisions.)

  Harvard Business School (1994) 'VeriFone: The Transaction Automation Company', Boston MA: Harvard Business School, case 195-088. (This teaching case describes the history of the Verifone Company and its situation in 1994.)

* Laudon, K.C. and Laudon, J.P. (2000) *Management Information Systems: Organization and Technology in the Networked Enterprise*, 6th edn, Upper Saddle River, NJ: Prentice-Hall. (This well-known text describes the roles of information systems in support of knowledge-intensive organizations and work; it is one of the first efforts to define a class of information systems called 'knowledge work systems'.)

* Machlup, F. (1962) *The Production and Distribution of Knowledge in the United States*, Princeton University Press. (Machlup treats knowledge as a form of economic capital.)

* Maister, D.H. (1985) 'The one-firm firm: what makes it successful', *Sloan Management Review* 27 (1): 3–13. (Maister defines and describes 'the one-firm firm'.)

* March, J.G. and Simon, H. A. (1958) *Organizations*, New York: Wiley. (The first comprehensive review of theories about organizations, this book innovated by describing how organizations process information.)

* Nelson, R.R. and Winter, S.G. (1982) *An Evolutionary Theory of Economic Change*, Cambridge, MA: Harvard University Press. (Nelson and Winter portray firms as evolving systems of routines.)

* Nonaka, I. and Takeuchi, H. (1995) *The Knowledge-Creating Company*, Oxford: Oxford University Press. (Nonaka and Takeuchi say that the success of Japanese companies arises from their ability to convert tacit knowledge to explicit form.)

* Orlikowski, W.J. (1988) 'Information technology in post-industrial organizations: an exploration of the computer mediation of production work', Doctoral dissertation, New York University. (Orlikowski describes the effects of computer technology on work practices in a consulting firm.)

* Rubin, M.R. and Huber, M.T. (1986) *The Knowledge Industry in the United States, 1960–1980*, Princeton: Princeton University Press. (This work updates the original book by Machlup (1962); it develops the same themes with more recent data.)

* Schriesheim [Fulk], J., Von Glinow, M.A. and Kerr, S. (1977) 'Professionals in bureaucracies: a structural alternative', in P.C. Nystrom and W.H. Starbuck (eds), *Prescriptive Models of Organizations*, Amsterdam: North-Holland: 55–69. (This article concisely and clearly summarizes the literature about how professional values conflict with bureaucracies.)

* Starbuck, W.H. (1983) 'Organizations as action generators', *American Sociological Review* 48: 91–102. (Starbuck argues that organizations often act non-reflectively and not in response to external stimuli.)

* Starbuck, W.H. (1992) 'Learning by knowledge-intensive firms', *Journal of Management Studies* 29 (6): 713–40. (Starbuck defines knowledge-intensive firms and surveys the practices that enable them to learn.)

* Stinchcombe, A.L. and Heimer, C.A. (1988) 'Interorganizational relations and careers in computer software firms', in I.H. Simpson and R.L. Simpson (eds), *Research in the Sociology of Work, Volume 4: High Tech Work*, Greenwich, CT: JAI Press: 179–204. (This study explains the precariousness of success by software firms.)

* Sveiby, K.E. (1994) 'Towards a Knowledge Perspective on Organisation', Doctoral dissertation, University of Stockholm. (Sveiby compares information-based firms with knowledge-based firms.)

* Sveiby, K.E. and Lloyd, T. (1987) *Managing Knowhow*, London: Bloomsbury. (This book was the first one in English to discuss the knowledge firm.)

* Sveiby, K.E. and Risling, A. (1986) *Kunskapsföretaget – Seklets viktigaste ledarutmaning?* (The Knowledge Firm – This Century's Most Important Managerial Challenge?), Malmö: Liber AB. (This book was the first to put forth the concept of a knowledge firm; it was widely read in Sweden.)

Humanistic perspectives on organizational functioning

Power

Stewart R. Clegg

Overview

In small organizations power operates principally through direct control premised on surveillance. The proprietor knows the work intimately. Others can be overseen easily by virtue of this knowledge. Power equates with command. The right to command is granted by ownership of the means of production and is typically vested in distinct proprietorial knowledge. This is not always the case, however: there may be delegation from the principal to an agency.

Irrespective of the principal–agent relation as either personal or impersonal, one may say that command is discursive. One does as one is told or shown. Hence, prototypically, when one wants a brief, rough and ready definition of power, it is usually offered in terms that stress strategies for achieving conformance with superordinate preferences. However, power may involve somewhat more than merely getting others to do what one wants them to, even against their will (the most usual definition). Such a definition stresses only the negative, not the positive, aspects of power.

1 Power, disciplinary practices and organization design

Modern organizations, those that dominated the twentieth century, are thought of as being typically large in scale rather than small businesses. There is no single universe of organization-appropriate knowledge. Tasks were fragmented, skills diverse and knowledge differentially codified, held and valued in these organizations. Strategies for the construction of centralized loci of power tried to steer a common path for the organization. Typically, knowledge would be divided between that which was more valued – generally more esoteric, abstract intellectual work – and that which was less valued – generally more mundane knowledge principally related to manual rather than mental labour. Some jobs were designed as essentially supervisory while others were designed primarily in terms of the execution of orders derived from supervisors and their superordinates. Hence power was structured into the organization design. Organizations were designed as if they had an organic common function, as if they were a unitary organism, in spite of the evident fact that they are not. To produce organic functioning only occurs when obedience is assured. For this to occur, uniqueness has to be rendered as routine; training, drill and discipline, known collectively as 'disciplinary practices' (Foucault 1977), have to produce organ(ic)ization if this unity is to prevail.

At the core of disciplinary practices is 'surveillance'. Surveillance may be to a greater or lesser extent mediated by instrumentation. Historically we may note that the tendency is for a greater instrumental mediation of surveillance as it moves from a literal supervisory gaze to more complex forms of observation, reckoning and comparison, whether personal, technical, bureaucratic or legal. Certain forms of technique, being already available, had a certain legitimacy which enabled them to be more widely dispersed than they might otherwise have been within similar institutional 'niche spaces'. Environmental pressures served to structure system integration into a limited range of organizational forms.

Surveillance practices and a limited range of organization forms rarely if ever eradicate the differences between people: they merely contain them within organization cognition and design. Organization members formed in different identities, working in and from distinct discursive locales, use competing calculations to struggle for scarce resources. They do so within the space of a privileged notion of how, organically, they are designed to relate to each other within the formal organization and the identities that this organization bestows. Where some notions are privileged then, by definition, some are not: they are marginalized or discriminated against.

Some discussion of the way in which power is structured in a privileged organization design is composed in terms of class structure (see Clegg and Dunkerley 1980 for a discussion of some of the key literature). Class models are usually constructed around a series of binary oppositions. Different models have different ways of generating middle-class positions from the capitalist/worker polarities upon which these models were premised. Such models assume that class is the most salient base for identity. Empirical research in this tradition suggests that this is not the case (Baxter *et al.* 1991). Instead, aspects of civil society, such as personal support for sports clubs, seem more important.

Marx argued that class interests are structurally pre-given, irrespective of other bases of identity. Few scholars accept that this is the case today. Instead, they argue that interests are variable, and depend on whatever organizational mechanisms of representation and outflanking can be constructed. Weber differed from Marx in seeing command as something that could be premised on knowledge of operations as much as ownership. Indeed, in certain circumstances of remote ownership, operational command would be more strategic. From Weber's perspective, organizations could be differentiated in terms of people's variable control of methods of production, as well as through Marx's dichotomous categories of ownership and non-ownership of means of production. While the latter have inscribed the key social relations of capitalist modernity – those of production, of property, of ownership and control – the former constitute the technical relations of production, embedded in diverse occupational identities, from which the subjective life-world of the organization, its culture, will grow.

2 Power and contract

The central institution governing social relations in organizations is contract, broadly conceived in terms of the non-contractual elements of trust and power vested by employers, as well as in terms of the discretion and autonomy gained by employees (Fox 1974). The social relationships that are established through contract embed power in three specific ways. First, the positions are defined in terms of differential skills and knowledge. Technical knowledge of an esoteric, central and unsubstitutable type becomes a locus of power that many researchers have focused on. Second, length of office has 'the tendency to increase ... power still further by the knowledge growing out of experience in the service' (Weber 1978: 225). Third, the mandators of the contracts that hire labour power typically can impose their interests on the exchange through an unequal access to organizational resources such as capital, networks or knowledge.

Normally contracts secure the terms of membership. From the employer's point of view, or that of their agents, an employee represents a capacity to labour hired from the market, yet employees always retain discretion over the application of their labour power. The knack of successful management and supervision involves translating into actual labour power the hours of the day that the person hired rents to the employing agent. Always, because of embodiment, the people hired as labour power retain ultimate discretion over themselves, what they do, how they do it. It is, after all, the hire of their bodily capacities that the hirers seek to use. A potential source of resistance resides in this inescapable and irreducible embodiment of labour power.

Management manages discretion most effectively and economically by substituting self-discipline for the discipline of an external manager. Less effective but historically more prolific have been the attempts of organizations to close the discretionary gap through the use of rule systems, the mainstay of analysis of organizations as bureaucracies. Such rule systems seek to regulate meaning in order to control relations in organizations through the structure of formal organization design. A hierarchy is prescribed within which legitimate power is circumscribed.

3 Hierarchy, power and legitimacy

Power in organizations necessarily concerns the hierarchical structure of offices and their relation to each other. Implicitly, this concerns 'legitimate power'. Social scientists have rarely felt it necessary to explain why it is that power should be hierarchical. The closest attempts to do so are the work of scholars concerned with issues of organization democracy, who have explored the limits of direct democracy in organizations. By extension, one can argue that these provide 'functional' arguments as to why we have hierarchy (Abrahamsson 1993).

Much of the literature has highlighted what Thompson (1956: 290) termed 'illegitimate power'. Legitimate power may be said to be that distribution of power that is warranted by the formal design of the organization. Hence, by this reckoning, power is illegitimate when it is unprescribed; that is, when it is not an expression of formally authorized design. Thompson researched two US Air Force Bomber wings. The work of the personnel was characterized by highly developed technical requirements in the operational sphere, for both aircrew and groundcrew. While the aircrew were formally more authoritative than were the groundcrew, the latter were in a more highly centralized position within the workflow of the base. The aircrew depended upon the groundcrew for their survival and safety. Effective communication with the groundcrew was a prerequisite of the aircrew's peace of mind. Consequently, the groundcrew had a degree of power that one would not have anticipated from the formal organization design, due to their technical competency *vis-à-vis* the flight security of the planes and the position of organizationally strategic communication that this placed them in, safety concerns being central for aircrews.

Other writers confirm Thompson's view that it is the technical design of tasks and their interdependencies that best explain the operational distribution of power, rather than the formal prescriptions of the organization design. Some tasks will be more essential to the functional interdependence of a system than will others and some of these may be the exclusive function of a specific party. Weber's (1978) analysis of the role of permanent bureaucratic officials *vis-à-vis* politically elected representatives noted that such officials can frequently exercise power over the representatives because they have esoteric knowledge, due to their permanency, that representatives elected for the life of a parliament do not have. It was such technically based but formally unprescribed power that Thompson focused on when he termed power that was prescribed by structural design 'actual power'. Thompson (1956: 290), writing as a pioneer of organization studies of power, remarked that 'research workers have seldom regarded actual power … [but] … have stressed the rational aspects of organization to the neglect of unauthorized or illegitimate power'. Other researchers were to echo this distinction as they followed in Thompson's footsteps in studying power.

Some landmark research may be noted. Gouldner (1954) termed formal organization design a 'mock bureaucracy' where the actual practice of power routinely breached the formal design of rules for its comportment. Crozier (1964) linked the exercise of power by personnel to control over sources of organizational uncertainty, focusing on maintenance workers in a French state-owned tobacco monopoly whose job was to fix machine breakdowns referred to them by production workers. The production workers, at the technical core of the organization, were highly central to the workflow-centred bureaucracy that characterized the organization. The maintenance workers were marginal, at least in the formal representation of the organization design. In practice, however, the story was very different.

The production workers were paid on a piece-rate system in a bureaucracy designed on scientific management principles. Most workers were effectively de-skilled. The bureaucracy was a highly formal, highly prescribed organization, except for the propensity of the machines to break down. The effect of them doing so was to diminish the bonus that the production workers could earn. To maintain earnings the production workers needed functional machines. Stoppages made them extraordinarily dependent on the maintenance workers, without whose expertise breakdowns could not be rectified. Consequently, the maintenance workers had a high degree of power over the other workers in the bureaucracy because they controlled the remaining source of uncertainty in the system. Management and the production workers were aware of this. Attempts had been made to try to remedy the situation. Planned preventive maintenance by the production workers had been tried but manuals disappeared and sabotage occurred. Maintenance workers were indefatigable in defence of their relative autonomy, privilege and power. Through their technical knowledge they could render the uncertain certain and the non-routine routine. The price of normality was a degree of autonomy and relative power in excess of that formally designed for them.

Crozier's (1964) study was a major landmark. He had taken an underexplicated concept, power, and had attached it to the central concept of the emergent theory of the firm – uncertainty. After this work by Crozier the field developed rapidly. A theory emerged, called the 'strategic contingencies theory of intra-organizational power' (Hickson *et al.* 1971). It sought to build a theory from existing ideas, particularly that power was related to the control of uncertainty and that, following Tannenbaum (1968), it could be measured.

Tannenbaum developed a measurement of power, the 'control graph'. The graph maps the means of the 'perceived' power of each level in the formal hierarchy of an organization. It does so by looking at the average of the sum of the perceptions by people in the organization of the amount of power that is vested at various levels within it. In this way, it is suggested, reasonably objective, or at least intersubjective, measures of power may be achieved. It became apparent that power was not something that was fixed: it could be increased. Organizations quite similar structurally could design power quite differently.

One of the theoretical innovations of Hickson *et al.* (1971) in measuring power in organizations was their use of a formal functionalist model. The organization was conceptualized as comprising four functional sub-systems or sub-units. The sub-units are interdependent. Some are more or less dependent and produce more or less uncertainty for other sub-units. What connects them in the model is the major task element of the organization, conceptualized as 'coping with uncertainty'. The theory ascribes the differing power of sub-units to imbalances in the way in which these interdependent sub-units cope with and handle uncertainty. Sub-units are open to environmental inputs, the initial source of uncertainty internally resolved into more or less certainty in transactions between the sub-units. Sub-units are more or less specialized, differentiated by the functional division of organization labour and related by a need to reduce uncertainty and maintain the overall system; 'to use differential power to function within the system rather than to destroy it' (Hickson *et al.* 1971: 217). Reducing uncertainty is the goal achieved by sub-unit exchanges. The capacity of sub-units to cope with changing sources of uncertainty determines power defined in terms of 'strategic contingency'. The most powerful are the least dependent sub-units that cope with the greatest systemic uncertainty, although there are certain qualifications: namely, that the sub-unit will not be easily substitutable by any other sub-unit and that it will be central to the organization system.

A conceptual slippage accompanies this analysis. Those sub-units that are least dependent are regarded as most powerful. To conceptualize an organization as composed of sub-units is to flatten out the normal hierarchical representation of it as a 'structure of dominancy' in Weber's (1978) terms. It is to view it on a horizontal rather than vertical axis. According to strategic contingency theory, a number of assumptions are made about the unitary and functionally cohesive nature of sub-units, not as a precondition for analysis of power but instead as one of its accomplishments, tacitly assumed. Organizationally, each sub-unit typically will be a hierarchy with a more or less problematic culture of consent or dissent. For it to be unitary there must exist some internal mechanisms of power that allow it to be treated as if it corresponded to such a representation. The theory elides this question by assuming that management will have unitary definitions and that these will prevail. Sometimes they may. When they do, management has exercised power. When they do not, management may be said to have been out-manoeuvred. An implication of this conceptualization is that it assumes the phenomenon that it seeks to explain. The strategic contingencies theory of power unfortunately explains very little that is important in an understanding of power. Indeed, it refrains from such an explanation, given the tacit assumptions. Nonetheless, it has been influential, not least on the development of the resource dependency model. Pfeffer (1981) developed a view of power premised on a resource dependency model. In such models, information, uncertainty, expertise, credibility, stature and prestige, access and contacts with higher echelon members, and the control of money, rewards and sanctions, have all been identified as bases of power. However, possessing scarce resources is not enough in itself: contextual pertinence, control and appropriate use will also be required.

In principle, all resource lists are infinite. Different phenomena are possible resources in different contexts. Without a total theory of contexts, which is impossible, one could never achieve closure on what the bases of power are. In the trial and conviction of the murderers of the South African ANC member and leader, Chris Hani, during the Apartheid regime, the 'invisibility' of a black maid to the white members of a household was a central plank in the convictions gained. Her invisibility was premised on both her race and gender. In a household arranged along racist and sexist lines, within the legal framework of an apartheid system that sustained such definitions of reality with the force of law, these were invisible organizational attributes. Her 'resource' was her marginality, her downtroddenness, her organizational role as a servant of power: organizationally taken for granted in the domestic household, she could see yet not be seen. Thus, her testimony secured convictions against the denials of those more powerful than her, in the context of a court of law which was itself relatively autonomous from the original organizational context of resources and dependencies.

To summarize, one may say that the mainstream of literature on organization power developed around the relationship of power, legitimacy and formal structure. It was the dichotomous relation of power and authority to the axis of legitimacy that became constitutive of the 'contingencies' and 'resource dependence' approaches. The concept of power has been reserved for exercises of discretion by organization members unsanctioned by position in the formal structure, premised on illegitimate or informal resource control effected by the organizational division of labour.

4 Power and gender in organizations

Feminists agree that gender relations are characterized by power relations. There is no similar agreement as to how this might translate into social theory, let alone into organization theory (see Hearn *et al.* 1989). Early contributions conceptualized gender in terms of the numbers, power and opportunities open to men and women and the supporting roles women frequently were expected to play outside organizations. Women were systematically subjected to power that was frequently implicit, tacit and non-conscious, a classic case of two- and three-dimensional power: the hegemony of the way things are (Lukes 1974). Women's positions in organizations were analysed as inseparable from their broader social role. Sex roles associated with the demographically dominant gender spilled over into the workplace, becoming incorporated into the work roles: the armed forces compared with nursing are probably the best polar opposite examples of this. Both have a highly authoritative modern organizational lineage but with very differently gendered members and practices.

By the 1970s scholars were increasingly aware of the gender-blindness of organization studies. Major contributions were reassessed in terms of how their contribution to the literature was often premised on unspoken assumptions about gender or unobserved and unremarked sampling decisions or anomalies in gender terms. For example, in Crozier's study (1964) the maintenance men were all men while the production workers were women. As Hearn and Parkin (1983) were to demonstrate, this blindness was symptomatic of the field as a whole, not of any specific paradigm within it. A peculiar irony attaches to this. Gender and sexuality are extremely pervasive aspects of organizational life. In some major occupational areas they are integral to the definition of the organization: secretaries, receptionists and flight attendants – 'the Singapore Girl' – are invariably defined in their organization identity through their gender and the projection of forms of emotionality and sexuality that are implicated in this. The mediation of, and resistance to, the routine rule enactments of organizations are inextricably tied in with gender. Moreover, organization studies are themselves gendered: how else could identity have been so long privileged as something seen from the vantage point of white males?

Functionality attaches to dominant ideologies, and is presumably the reason why they dominate (Abercrombie *et al.* 1980). Yet, it is not always a function of repression of the subordinated. A dominant ideology maximizes an organization's ability to act. Consensus and strong adherence to one ideology are not merely results of people's analytical and perceptual deficiencies; they are necessary conditions for organizational survival. The decisions that characterize organizational action will be a result, not a cause, of the actions of those organizations, flowing from ideology rather than rationality. Organizations do not produce actions that are masculinist so much as masculinism produces organizations that take masculinist action without even being explicitly aware that this is what they are doing, because of the nature of ideology. The relevance of Lukes' (1974) three-dimensional view, with its stress on power operating through routine actions that work against the real interests of some categories of subject, is evident. Masculinist organizations work against the interests of those women who are involved with them. Certain male identities constituted in socially and economically privileged contexts will be routinely more strategically contingent for organizational decision making, access and success in hierarchically arranged careers (see the excellent discussion in Wilson, 1999).

5 Power, strategy, rules and resistance

Organizations are uncertain political locales in which negotiation, contestation and struggle between organizationally divided and linked agencies is a routine occurrence. To achieve strategic agency requires disciplining the discretion of other agencies: at best, from the strategist's point of view, such other agencies will become authoritative relays and extensions of strategic agency, perhaps with a capacity for creativity that runs in organizationally goal-focused tracks. (A totally disciplined army squad in the field of battle, obediently subject to higher authority and its commands, would be an extreme example. The actual agents, in this case the army squad, remain literally non-actors in this process: the only action which is formally allowed is for them to obey unquestioningly, sometimes on penalty of death for mutiny, desertion or insubordination in the field of battle. Ideally, they become agents without interests other than obedience to others' commands. Practically, they rarely are, especially in highly autonomous field situations.) In this respect the army, as Weber was well aware, represents only the most condensed and concentrated form of much of the moral content of 'normal' organizational power and discipline, at least as it applies to low-trust, low-discretion positions submitting to authority.

For maximum retained discretion, authority should be delegated, but not power. Obedience cannot be guaranteed when authority is delegated, if only because of the complexity and contingency of human agency. Hence, a storehouse of disciplinary techniques has become available to help organizations achieve strategic aims through the production of disciplined personnel. Not only are there many consultancy, advisory or sub-contracting agencies and their recipes, there are also the enduring sediments of previous practice and precedents, 'the files', the repository of all that is formally recorded and known, the span of control, divisional and departmental cleavage and so on. These practices endorse and enable obedient wills and constitute organizationally approved forms of creativity and productivity through a process of authoritative externalities such as rules, superiors, etc. and through the acquisition of organizationally proper conduct by the member.

In practice, authoritative structures rarely, if ever, conform to their depiction in the organizational programme. Things change imperceptibly over time in ways which are not captured by a static idealization. Organizational memberships change; particularly competent 'power-players' may make more of a position than a less competent predecessor, and so on. It is because of the existence of these potential sources of destabilization of formal order that the mainstream literature on power in organizations has focused on 'illegitimate' or undesigned power.

There is a more fundamental reason why the focus on illegitimate power has preoccupied researchers. The inadequacy of formal designs and their depictions of the structure of the organization is premised on more than just the drift that unforeseen contingencies bring to the control of events. Any superordinate member of a complex organization will be just one relay in a complex flow of authority up, down and across organization hierarchies. Yet, resistance will tend to be pervasive. Authorities created organizationally are rarely resistance-free and presumably passive relays in their extensions of power may exercise discretion. Notions like 'choice' and 'discretion' are intrinsic to power relations, suggests Lukes (1974). It is the ability to exercise discretion, to have chosen this rather than that course of action, which characterizes power.

Power will always be inscribed within contextual 'rules of the game' which both enable and constrain action. Action can only ever be designated as such-and-such an action by reference to rules which identify it as such. Rules can never be free of surplus or ambiguous meaning: they always index the context of interpreters and interpretation. Rules can never provide for their own interpretation. Both rules and games tend to be the subject of contested interpretation, with some players having not only play-moves but also the refereeing of these as power resources. Consequently, rules imply discretion. Here we confront the central paradox of power: the power of an agency is increased in principle by that agency delegating authority; the delegation of authority can only proceed by rules; rules necessarily entail discretion and discretion potentially empowers delegates. From this arises the tacitly understood basis of organizationally negotiated order, and on occasion, its fragility and instability.

Resistance to discipline will be irremediable because of indexicality. It can never be wholly controlled in terms of the stabilization of membership categories across space and time. Total control is impossible, in part because of agency. Agency implies choices: choices necessarily entail matters of moral being. What one takes to be sacred and what one takes to be profane depends utterly on relations of meaning. Such relations of meaning are as resistant to total control as are relations of production. Resistance to any attempt that seeks to freeze meaning in any specific regulation of it will always be intrinsic to the nature of language as a moral framework. At its most successful, resistance outflanks power.

6 Power and outflanking

The notion of 'organizational outflanking' explains why it is that the dominated so frequently consent to their subordination and subordinators. Frequently, it is because they lack collective organization to do otherwise, because they are embedded within collective and distributive power organizations controlled by others. Organizational outflanking can be thought of in at least two related ways. One of these concerns the absence of knowledge on the part of the outflanked. The other concerns precisely what it is that the organizationally outflanked may know only too well. First, let us consider the most evident absence of knowledge: ignorance. Frequently those who are relatively powerless remain so because they are ignorant of the ways of power: ignorant, that is, of matters of strategy such as assessing the resources of the antagonist, of routine procedures, rules, agenda setting, access, informal conduits as well as formal protocols, the style and substance of power. It is not that they do not know the rules of the game so much as that they might not recognize the game, let alone know the rules. Of course, this is a particular problem where an overwhelmingly technologically superior form of life meets one which is by contrast less developed in technical terms. Historically the vast majority of cross-cultural contact has occurred on this basis: consequently it has been the force of arms and the soundness of strategy which has settled the outcomes. However, it should not be assumed that overwhelming resources will necessarily ensure success. To do this means that they must be deployed on a battlefield suited to their deployment: strategically minded opponents will flee rather than fight until they have enticed the opposition into a match with a timing, duration and a terrain more of their own choosing.

Ignorance often extends to a simple lack of knowledge of other similar powerless agencies with whom one might construct an alliance. Thus, an absence of knowledge may also be premised on isolation: one would resist or could do so more effectively if one were not isolated. One step further from isolation is division. Time and space may be ordered and arranged to minimize the interaction and mutual awareness of subordinates, or even to render one group of subordinates invisible to another. Complex divisions of labour may achieve this, as may the extreme experience of competition. An example of the latter might be the arrangement of concerted action within an organization in such a way that it is experienced in individuated rather than collective terms, through mechanisms that construct an egocentric environment.

With organizational outflanking premised on ignorance the costs of action are unknown, the probability of the outcome unclear, the benefits uncertain, the risks evident. However, organizational outflanking can also take place under conditions which render the possession of such knowledge useless. Dull compulsion, busy work, arduous exertion and ceaseless activity are a routinely deadening discipline for the blithest of 'theoretically' free spirits. The most resistant of wills may bend in time without recourse to some alternative. Time is double-edged here: both using up the time of an agent on the performance of routine tasks as well as reinforcing the habituation that such a performance produces over time.

Despite this numbing effect, ritual routines may also be employed as bulwarks against encroaching meaninglessness.

7 Managing with power

'Power corrupts ...' One does not have to complete the aphorism to realize ambivalence. Things that are thought illegitimate are often kept under wraps, shrouded in secrecy and not acknowledged as such. In the past, power has been consigned to a conceptual closet. Not every theorist thought it belonged there, however. Parsons (1963) defined power as functional for social systems such as organizations, and hence as legitimate by definition. Foucault, another theorist of positive power, provides a detailed history of some power practices and techniques that have characterized modernity in a way that is non-reductive and complements Weber (Dandekker 1991), although he understate the importance of Max Weber's (1978) argument concerning discipline. Different emphases on power occur through the course of Foucault's work. First, there is his work on genealogy as the natural history of specific practices. Second, the work on the 'care of the self', where histories are used to critique the present, by uncovering the constituted nature of what have been taken as the here-and-now; third, the discussion of government or 'governmentality'.

In Foucault's (1977) most influential genealogical model of 'surveillance and discipline' power is constituted in an intimate relationship with liberty. Because the exercise of power presumes a free subject, in a well-known formula, there will always be resistance. Where liberty is extremely limited, because power is stable and hierarchical, then Foucault terms it domination. (The parallelism of this account with that of Weber's (1978) discussion of *herrschaft* is evident.) Two models of power are compared and contrasted: the repressive and the positive. (Foucault's (1977) concern with the facilitative and productive aspects of power relates to the kind of arguments made most clearly by Parsons (1963).) In general Foucault does not offer a critique of power: it would be impossible to do so because, to coin a phrase, power has no other: it is inescapable. Liberation from power is only a dream (or a nightmare). However, specific forms of power may and do change. The 'punitive' power of corporal excess may be contrasted with the 'positive' power of bureaucracy. However, Foucault is adamant that there can be no space outside of power, no knowledge that is pure truth. (In this way are utopia and dystopia avoided.) In reading Foucault it is necessary to uncouple a sociological from a philosophical question concerning truth. The former deals with what passes for truth rather than asking what is truth – with how truth-effects are produced, in the Foucauldian vernacular. It is the latter that concerns Foucault, rather than the former.

In Foucault's model of power relationships through government – the structuring of action through conduct – which he defines as the capacity of people to regulate their own behavior through various rationalities – his treatment of liberalism suggests that it is conditions of relative autonomy that define the nature of political community. Foucault suggests that democracy is neither an ideal with which to measure actual practice nor a method for producing utopias. It is the messy and politically expeditious ways of making sense of politics its participants routinely use. It is this fundamental approach that Flyvberg (1998) takes from Foucault. He provides a deeply documented, rich, narrative of one complex set of issues and processes associated with the many ways in which political communities were constructed and de-constructed in the laborious pursuit of local interests and issues surrounding a proposed traffic-plan for the city of Aalborg in Denmark.

Aalborg was not unusual in respect of its power relations: they were sufficiently asymmetric as to verge on domination. Here, the authority of technical rationality was a weapon of the politically weak – those without other resources at their disposal. Hence, not surprisingly, technically rational plans were constantly undercut and attempts at democracy secured on that technically rational basis proved weak. Neither a normative emphasis on democracy nor rationality proved sufficient to avoid domination by those with superior power. Such power defined reality and, not surprisingly, the rationality it accepted depended on power rather than legality. One of the main strategies of the dominant group was to use techniques of rationalization as power: indeed, the greater the power the lesser the rationality. Thus, we might conclude that power is more ordinarily stable than conflictual and that its relations are constantly being produced and reproduced in the process. Where power relations are stable then power relations are more characteristically rational.

In stable situations that display a characteristic rationality, Pfeffer (1992) notes there are seven steps to the effective use of power:

1 Decide what your goals are; what you are trying to accomplish.
2 Diagnose patterns of dependence and interdependence; what individuals are influential and important in your achieving your goal?
3 What are their points of view likely to be? How will they feel about what you are trying to do?
4 What are their power bases? Which of them is more influential in the decision?
5 What are your bases of power and influence? What bases of influence can you develop to gain more control over the situation?
6 Which of the various strategies and tactics for exercising power seem most appropriate and are likely to be effective, given the situation you confront?
7 Based on the above, choose a course of action to get something done.

There is no guarantee that organizationally disparate tactics, strategies and actions will cohere across diverse scenes and actions. Crucially, managing with power means achieving a common definition, a genuine accord, on which to base strategies, tactics and actions. Organization showdowns are only one of the ways that strategies, tactics and actions get done. More positive uses of power involve less machismo and more listening, working with rather than against others.

Power seeks to impose a specific meaning on an uncertain context. Crozier's male maintenance workers sought to exclude the female production workers. By contrast, those who advocate bottom-up decision making seek to listen to what others in the organization have to say. From empowerment, the giving of voice to those frequently unheard, they seek to enhance the overall systemic powers of the organization; to mobilize resources and get things done. This use of power frequently means giving way in the organization conversation, not claiming a special privilege because of title or experience, not being selectively inattentive to others but using power through exploring context and then listening and attending to it. Organization context involves the identities of the people involved in it – not just those of the systems programmer, accounting or equal employment opportunity officer, but also black or white, straight or gay, male or female. Organizations may listen or may not, be homophobic rather than relaxed about the range of potential identities their members may embrace, be a boy's club rather than an arena equally open to people whatever their gender, or they may work with the creativity and diversity of people's identities rather than against them. Politics of power will accordingly be different, premised on active listening rather than assertive denial through the instrumentality and ritual of established power. To build such organizations, ones that seek to extend the organization conversation rather than to exploit its lapses, would seem to be one of the more pressing aspects of the future organization agenda for post-modern times.

The challenge for future power theory is, as Pfeffer (1992: 340) suggests, 'to manage with power'; to recognize, diagnose and respect the diversity of interests and seek to translate and enrol them within one's course of action, while at the same time listening to what these others are saying, modifying one's position accordingly and choosing the appropriate strategies and tactics to get done whatever is chosen. Sometimes, after all that, it will still mean getting others to do what they would not otherwise have done, even against their resistance. Power can be like that. Yet, it does not have to be so. Coercive power should be the refuge of last resort for the diplomatically challenged and structurally secure, not the hallmark of management's right to manage.

Further reading

(References cited in the text marked *)

* Abercrombie, N., Hill, S. and Turner, B.S. (1980) *The Dominant Ideology Thesis*, London: Allen & Unwin. (This text, as much as any, orientated social scientists to the limits often implicit in the use of categories of 'dominant ideology' to explain why things that theoretically might have been predicted did not occur empirically, thus saving the theory against the data.)
* Abrahamsson, B. (1993) *Why Organizations? How and Why People Organize*, Newbury Park, CA: Sage Publications. (Explains why organizations exist in preference to markets and examines the conditions of existence for the emergence of hierarchy, bureaucracy and democracy in organizations.)
* Baxter, J., Emmison, M. and Western, J.S. (1991) *The Class Structure*, Sydney: Macmillan. (A detailed look at class and stratification at work, at home and at play in Australia. Identity emerges as far more contingently related to play and home than work.)
  Clegg, S.R. (1989) *Frameworks of Power*, London: Sage Publications. (Probably as comprehensive a coverage of the many approaches across diverse disciplinary perspectives as one

will find on the topic of power. Develops a perspective on power framed through a model of 'circuits of power'.)

* Clegg, S.R. and Dunkerley, D. (1980) *Organization, Class and Control*, London: Routledge & Kegan Paul. (This text argues that the history of organizations may be seen from a 'power, control and resistance' perspective. Covers organization theories quite comprehensively from the beginning to the end of the 1970s although some of its assumptions and arguments seem somewhat outdated today.)

* Crozier, M. (1964) *The Bureaucratic Phenomenon*, London: Tavistock Publications. (This is one of the classics of organization theory and probably the first book that was translated from French into English to have such a widespread impact. Enormously influential in its linking of 'power' with 'uncertainty'.)

* Dandekker, C. (1991) *Surveillance, Power and Modernity*, Cambridge: Polity. (A useful historical survey of the military roots of much of modern factory management in Taylorism and the importance of these for modern bureaucracy.)

* Flyvberg, B. (1998) *Rationality & Power: Democracy in Practice*, Chicago: Chicago University Press. (A magnificent ethnography of the rationalities of power over a ten-year cycle of town-planning in the Danish city of Aalborg.)

* Foucault, M. (1977) *Discipline and Punish: The Birth of the Prison*, Harmondsworth: Penguin. (An extremely influential translation of a French text on power, spelling the intellectual end of the strong 'labour process' thesis and showing instead how forms of power were predated in bureaucratic institutions. Affinities with Weber's work on 'discipline' present themselves.)

* Fox, A. (1974) *Beyond Contract: Work, Power and Trust Relations*, London: Faber & Faber. (A classic text on power that is greatly underutilized. Demonstrates how assumptions about the level of 'trustworthiness' that organization designers make about their members structure the types of power that they deploy and the forms of resistance that they encourage.)

* Gouldner, A.W. (1954) *Patterns of Industrial Bureaucracy*, New York: The Free Press. (The classic text of functionalist industrial sociology, best read today for the way in which it shows that no objectivity attaches to the bureaucratic nature of a given organization structure of rules: it depends on the contexts of interpretation and the strategies of the different actors.)

Hardy, C. and Clegg, S.R. (1996) 'Some dare call it power', in S.R. Clegg, C. Hardy and W. Nord (eds), *Handbook of Organization Studies*, London: Sage Publications. (An overview of theories of power in organizations in the context of broader social theories.)

* Hearn, J. and Parkin, P.W. (1983) 'Gender and organizations: a selective review and a critique of a neglected area', *Organization Studies* 4 (3): 219–42. (A review article that notes, with respect to some of the classics of the literature, the relative neglect and the degree of gender-blindness of some of the major contributions. Argues for the centrality of gender to all organization studies.)

* Hearn, J., Sheppard, D.L., Tancred-Sheriff, P. and Burrell, G. (1989) *The Sexuality of Organization*, London: Sage Publications. (This book develops the claims of the previous article in a series of studies that demonstrate its implications in various areas of organization life.)

* Hickson, D.J., Hinings, C.R., Lee, C.A., Schneck, R.E. and Pennings, J.M. (1971) 'A strategic contingencies theory of intra-organizational power', *Administrative Science Quarterly* 16: 216–29. (The first attempt to pull together the scattered insights of the literatures of organizations, political science and decision making, in order to create a unified theory of intra-organizational power.)

* Lukes, S. (1974) *Power: A Radical View*, London: Macmillan. (The most influential, shortest and most elegant book ever written on power. Introduced the idea that there has been a progressive opening up of a one-dimensional view of power to a two-dimensional view, focused on 'non-decisions', which in turn is capable of critique from a third dimension, that of hegemony.)

* Parsons, T. (1963) 'On the concept of political power', in T. Parsons (ed.), *Sociological Theory and Modern Society*, New York: The Free Press. (Parsons demonstrates long before Foucault that power has a positive side, that it may be conceptualized as a circulatory medium, similar to money, and capable of enhancing system value.)

* Pfeffer, J. (1981) *Power in Organizations*, Boston, MA: Pitman. (A standard, if somewhat pedestrian, organization theory text which discusses power from the resource dependence perspective without acknowledging the debate around the concept effected by works from Lukes and Foucault: in this respect rather misleading and ethnocentric.)

* Pfeffer, J. (1992) *Managing with Power*, Boston, MA: Harvard Business School Press. (Further developments of the arguments of his 1981 text, this time more orientated towards executive and MBA teaching requirements. More punchy in its style, although somewhat restricted in its intellectual concerns.)

Scott, J. (ed.) (1993) *Power*, 3 vols, London: Routledge. (An enormously expensive three volume set that your library should have, if only because it contains almost every article that you will ever need to refer to, from the existing range, if you wish to follow up some classic references to 'power'.)

* Tannenbaum, A. (1968) *Control in Organizations*, New York: McGraw-Hill. (Introduced the notion of 'control graphs', a concept that was influential in work that sought to establish the extent of hierarchical 'power distance' in organizations.)

* Thompson, J.D. (1956) 'Authority and power in identical organizations', *American Journal of Sociology* 62: 290–301. (One of the earliest functionalist accounts of power in organizations couched in terms that subsequently would have been called 'resistance'; unfortunately, it does not use this concept and begins an identification of the concept of power with its 'illegitimate' expression in otherwise tacitly unquestioned and thus 'legitimate' hierarchical structures.)

* Weber, M. (1978) *Economy and Society: An Outline of Interpretive Sociology*, G. Roth and C. Wittich (eds), 2 vols, Berkeley: University of California Press. (The classic text of all organization theory, and much else besides. There is far more in this text on 'power' than the index would suggest: the sections on domination and rule should be read, as well as those on power.)

* Wilson, F. (1999) 'Genderquake? Did you feel the Earth move?', *Organization* 6 (3): 529–41. (An excellent account of the importance of gender in power and society and its continuing marginalization by mainstream scholars.)

Organizing, process of

Barbara Czarniawska

Overview

The process of organizing can be considered either as an effect of organizations (organizing is what happens within organizations) or as a cause of organizations (organization is a result of organizing). The latter conception leads to a change in the approach to organizational analysis and in ways of understanding organizational life. Instead of searching for final and universal definitions, one looks for the definitions created and used by people engaged in organizing. Attention is focused not on structures but on processes.

The most clear and succinct formulation of the process view is undoubtedly that of the US organization theorist Karl E. Weick. His work is closely related historically – both forwards and backwards in time – to a number of other approaches, despite his views on many matters differing from these. The earliest process approach to organization theory was that of Taylorism, which treated organizing as a kind of exercise in logistics, an exercise crucial to effective production. Quite a different position was taken by social constructionist approaches, both those regarding social construction as involving efforts directed outwardly – at creating and influencing the world by organizing it – and those emphasizing the fact that such efforts invariably mean organizing also being directed at acquiring both individual and organizational identity.

Empirical studies of how organizing occurs in actual practice reveal the emergence of patterns of organizing that seem indicative of the future: organizing in terms of networking. Networking is communicative activity, often on a large scale and symbolic in character, in which the establishing of connections is frequently facilitated by complex technological means.

This entry begins by focusing on the process of organizing as a way of conceiving of organization and organizations as a whole. It then contrasts processual and structural approaches to organization before dealing with various ways in which organizing has been conceived.

1 Organizing as being and as doing

In most modern languages the term 'organization' is rather ambiguous, despite differences from one language to another in the nuances of meaning involved. This ambiguity can be illustrated by four definitions of 'organization' which Webster's dictionary (1981: 802) provides:

> 1a: the act or process of organizing or of being organized ... b: the condition or manner of being organized ... 2a: ASSOCIATION, SOCIETY b: an administrative and functional structure (as a business or a political party) ...

Besides representing alternative uses of the term, these four definitions can also be seen as dynamically related. The process of organizing leads to a state of being organized; such a state, if prolonged, becomes reified linguistically, being regarded as an entity, an object, a structure, one that assumes a quasi-independent existence. The process of organizing can thus be seen as a cause that results initially in organization, conceived as a state and, upon prolongation of this, in an organization having an existence of its own.

Organization theory deals most commonly with organization in this latter sense. Emphasizing the process of organizing instead, however, serves both to highlight the relative instability of organizations, a frequently neglected matter, and to provide fresh insight into organizations generally.

2 Performative versus ostensive definitions of organization

Useful insights into differences between an organizing process approach and other approaches to organizations can be achieved if the distinction is made in organization theory between ostensive and performative definitions, analogous to Latour's (1986) use of the term in his discussion of the definitions of society.

One way of acquiring an understanding of a concept, as illustrated above, is to consult definitions found in dictionaries or encyclopedias. Such definitions are often useful due to the consensus regarding them being high. They can be termed *ostensive* in the sense that they assume that the concepts which they define are possible to demonstrate; that they can be made visible. Ostensive definitions of social phenomena such as organizations assume that, like physical objects, they possess a limited number of clearly determinable properties which can be discovered and described by an outside observer, who can present them in a simple and a clear-cut way to others.. In this sense one can 'demonstrate' an organization much as nineteenth-century naturalists demonstrated their specimens: 'Here is organization X; it is tightly controlled, highly centralized, and relatively open to innovation.'

The naturalists of the nineteenth century quarrelled a lot about such matters as the anatomical characteristics of a given species (to what extent the characteristics of the specimen at hand were typical?), its physiology, its habits and its history. Social sciences, including organization studies, moved by an ambition to emulate natural sciences, inherited such difficulties and augmented them. It can indeed be much easier to measure the length of an insect than the effectiveness of an organization. In addition, whereas insects cannot protest the definitions associated with them, people engaged in organizing can and often do.

Thus, for arriving at definitions and understanding concerning what organizing embodies, one can go into the field to see what people actually do when they organize. This provides the basis for *performative* definitions. Performative definitions, unlike ostensive ones, do not aim to avoid the linguistic complexities (an ideal borrowed from natural sciences, which suggests that demonstration should replace description and that what is described is silent). Performative definitions stem directly from discursive practices found in the field.

Ostensive definitions of organizations assume that discovering the properties typical of a given organization is possible in principle, even if doing so in practice may be difficult. Performative definitions, on the other hand, which consider an organization as a temporary product of organizing, assume that whereas it is impossible in principle to describe any given organization (partly because an organization changes while investigation of it is taking place), it is nevertheless quite possible in practice to do so. One can say, for example: 'In 1993, while studying a major organizational reform which took place in company X in the years 1991–1993, I noticed that the actors involved tended to supervise each other's actions closely, carefully following instructions from top management, but that they were curious and positive towards new ideas.' Another observer, entering the field in 1994, might perceive quite a different situation. Yet another researcher, doing a parallel study but concentrating on changes in the use of computer technology, could, ignoring the aspects just mentioned, have achieved a different description, quite satisfactory for understanding technological changes during the period under study. Thus, with performative definitions, organizations are ascribed neither a nature nor an essence in any absolute sense; rather, organizations are considered to be what the people producing them made them at the time when those who were observers conducted their observations.

A statement by an observer such as that cited above could not be incorporated into an ostensive definition. Such definitions assume that organizations and their properties are durable and constant over time and space, quite independently of being observed or not. When organizations are defined ostensively they are easily equated with the buildings in which organizing takes place. One often speaks of actors entering and leaving an organization, inhabiting it, moving from one organization to another, crossing the organizational borders, engaging in 'gate-keeping'. Yet despite such physical, object-like metaphors, one speaks again and again of what people are doing, and of how different actions relate to one another. Also, in discussing organizations, one often refers to nets of actions people perform. Although many different people may be involved in creating and recreating a given net of actions, once no one is doing so any longer, the net ceases to exist. A factory in which no one produces anything any more is not an organization and may well be referred to simply as 'that old factory building'. It is organizing that makes organizations, not the other way around.

In this sense, although performative definitions indeed assume there to be certain durability over time (otherwise social institutions would be precluded), this is a durability based on repetition and artefacts, not on the existence of an object-like structure. In a stable organization, people do essentially the same things again and again in organizing. The similarity from one such performance to the next is nevertheless only approximate; actors forget, make errors, innovate, and deviate from norms and rules.

The difference between the two types of definitions has consequences – for practitioners, consultants and researchers alike – with regard to the ways in which organizations can be studied, explained and understood. Whereas ostensive definitions are attempts to explain principles, performative definitions are attempts to explore practices. The emphasis on organizing in connection with the latter amounts to the postulate that in organizational analysis attention should be shifted from principles to practices and, consequently, from structures to processes.

3 Processes versus structures

One of the most significant works in organization theory during the 1970s was *The Social Psychology of Organizations* by Daniel Katz and Robert L. Kahn (1966). The authors advocated a powerful version of organization theory in which organizations were considered as open systems, the *raison d'être* of which involved the transformation of inputs from the environment into outputs directed likewise at the environment. This conception represented a clear critique of those images of the firm upheld in neo-classical economics. It regarded functionalism as the basic mode for interpreting organizations. Karl Weick's book *The Social Psychology of Organizing*, first published in 1969, was obviously intended both as a continuation and as a challenge to this work that was on its way to becoming a classic.

The challenge in Weick's book, however, remained virtually unanswered, the book provoking largely puzzlement and few substantial reactions. Only when its second edition appeared in 1979 did the public show itself prepared to absorb its message. The remainder of this entry sketches out developments in organizational thinking which, although not always stemming directly from Weick, are nevertheless related to the view of organizations that he promulgated.

To understand Weick's message it is important that one considers two influences central to his book. One of these, coming from social psychology, is perhaps best expressed in Floyd H. Allport's (1962) article 'A structuronomic conception of behavior', which criticized the idea of a group as a social entity being distinctly separate from the individuals forming it, and argued against the kind of social psychology that took 'relationships' between these two types of identities as its basic subject. Taking certain earlier sociological work as his point of departure, Allport suggested that all collectivities are created by the actions performed by individuals. He regarded an 'organization' as a set of actions chosen for observation among a myriad of such actions. He reasoned that if one insisted on studying 'structures', then the only structures there were to study were structures of events. His conclusion was that 'we live in and through structuring at all levels' (Allport 1962: 18).

This line of thought, radical at the time, was taken up again some twenty to thirty years later: in Giddens' structuration theory (Giddens 1979); in new institutionalism (March and Olsen 1989; Powell and DiMaggio 1991; and in constructivist sociology of knowledge (Latour 1986).

Another crucial influence on Weick's work was that of Maruyama (1974), a bacteriologist who in the early 1970s propagated ideas of the kind which later brought fame to biologists Humberto Maturana and Francisco Varela, popularized in the social sciences through the writings of Niklas Luhmann (1990). Maruyama's conception of social systems was based on that of a closed, or self-reproducing (self-referential), system which constantly attempts to re-create itself according to its own definition of identity and which changes largely by error and default.

The consequences of this idea for many were too radical to accept. What Karl Weick accomplished in exploiting it, however, was to convince students of organizations that the proper focus of attention is not structures but processes, and not organizations but organizing. He argued that events must be endowed with meaning and that this meaning must be constantly negotiated between the people engaged in the events – and this was the sum and substance of organizing.

Although Weick's re-conceptualization of organizing is of crucial importance in the history of organization theory, one should bear in mind that the history of ideas can perhaps more fruitfully be presented as a spiral moving up and down than as a linear process. Robert Merton (1965), claiming that all ideas exist at all times, has shown that seemingly epochal discoveries can be traced back to earlier ideas and that ideas undergo never-ending transformations at each turn of their popularity. In accordance with this, the notion of organizing can be traced back not only to Allport but also to Plato and Machiavelli. Thus, even if Weick's work is presented here as a milestone to understanding how organizations function in society, earlier forerunners of this perspective on organization and management theory do exist. Taylorism can be seen as belonging to those, although its relevance lies not so much in the historical value as in the fact that in the 1980s this line of thought acquired a novel meaning, directly relevant for organizational practice. Various ways of understanding organizing are presented below, with Weick's ideas as a main point of reference.

4 Organizing as logistics: Taylorism and time management

Organizing can perhaps most simply be seen as the art of causing people and things to be in the right place at the right time. This manner of understanding the process has a long tradition in military circles. In the context of production and service organizations, on the other hand, the tradition is much shorter. There it can be said to have started in the UK during the time of the industrial revolution. The work of the Cambridge mathematician Charles Babbage (1791–1871), inventor of the Analytical Engine, which was intended to replace the work of computers (people whose job it was to compute), is of special relevance here. It was with the development of this machine that the notion of a system was developed and was applied to the human body, to machines and to the workshop. Implicit here was the idea that it is not connections between physical parts that matter, but rather connections between various operations. The types of connections viewed as most important were those of coordination and control (Schaffer 1994).

Organization theory is most commonly linked with Babbage's follower in the USA, the mechanical engineer Frederick Taylor (1856–1915), who proposed the theory of *scientific management*. The core of both Babbage's and Taylor's thought was to transfer the notion of the effective functioning of machines to that of the effective functioning of those who operated the machines. Scientific management is often called a 'machine theory of organizations' (Katz and Kahn 1966), but the metaphor tends to evoke the association of people being cogs and of organizations being metal structures. Taylor, in fact, did not analyse organizational structures; he analysed organizational action taking machine action as a model. He advocated specializing, breaking tasks down into small fragments, and coordinating and controlling with the aid of a time standard.

The advantages of scientific management and of its extension, operational research, were first examined in organizational analysis of the production process. Organizing was conceived here as producing, other functions being geared to serve this main process. However, when marketing became important in the 1960s, and service organizations began to dominate the organizational landscape in the early 1980s, Taylorism seemed to have become obsolete. The 'Japanese challenge' brought it back soon thereafter in a new form, that of *time management*.

The Japanese challenge materialized mostly on the production front in certain industries in which the USA and Europe had been dominant earlier (the automotive and electronics industries). Attempts to determine the forces behind Japanese success brought two factors to the fore: organizational culture and time management. *California Management Review*, well situated geographically for following developments on both sides of the Pacific closely, published a series of articles on these topics in the 1980s, those on time management being of relevance in the present context.

Much of what has been written about time management is linked to military logistics and Taylorism in that it emphasizes organizing as aiming to get people and things to the right place at the right time. However, time management is more than that: it advances Taylor's analogy between the production process and the functioning of the machine one step further, since it also concerns the time management of management itself. Time management analysts such as Stalk and Hout (1990) were interested in the logistics not only of production but also of management. In their terms, there is a right and a wrong time to introduce innovations, to yield to fashion, to change and to resist change. Time adds a new value aspect to all managerial activities, machine-like solutions being applicable here. Organizing is viewed as an allocation in time and space that can be performed at any level of abstraction. Thanks to computerized information systems, not only industrial production but also services and management itself can be broken into manageable parts, be subjected to specialization and be coordinated. The argument that machines are too simple to support the complexity of social systems tends to be contradicted by the increasing complexity of machines, which makes them more and more indispensable for the operation of social systems.

There is yet another way of regarding organizing as time-and-space management, a way closely related to the linguistic aspects of organizing discussed below. This involves the notion of a *dispatcher*, a term applied within both production and semiotics. In joining the latter two areas, the term highlights the often overlooked proximity between machine analogies and those approaches to the organizing process that emphasize the role of language. Organizing is viewed in the latter context as involving the creation of scripts and plans of action, these specifying who is supposed to do what by what means at what time and in what place (Latour 1994). Such scripts need not have the form of a depersonalized production plan as in early Taylorism; they can be in the form of a ritualistic saga of the past or an idealized vision of the future. They fulfil the function of a dispatcher in that, when endorsed, they send people and things across expanses of time and space.

Although one might suppose such dispatchers to be the core around which all organizing takes place, there must also be some agreement regarding identities of people, things and places, as well as a common way of measuring time, if the right people and things are to arrive where they should on time. Thus, the notion of organizing as dispatching needs to be complemented by consideration of those aspects of organizing necessary for dispatching to take place. Whereas viewing organizing as involving logistics assumes the ordering of a pre-ordered reality (in which persons and things have names), the two approaches described below assume that the process of organizing begins much earlier; reality, if it is to be ordered, must first be manufactured.

5　Organizing as enactment

Enactment is a concept difficult to translate to other languages from English. In other languages it tends to be understood either in legal terms, such as 'making something valid by decree', or in dramatistic ones, such as in denoting the 'setting on a stage'. Both chains of associations, however, should be activated at once. Enactment can be understood as the creation of reality by linguistic means. The dramatistic aspect is important for preventing, as Weick (1979) says, its confusion with 'enthinking', or the idea that if people can think something up it will become true. Enactment is a linguistic operation, but a highly social one (if others fail to cooperate the enactment has not worked). Also, it has a strong material underpinning: it is not a mere play on words. Through enactment, mountains are moved, money is spent or wasted and people are made rich or made to suffer.

Several aspects of enactment are important within the context of organizing. One of these is *bracketing*. This relates to an observation first formulated in social psychology by William James; namely, that the world is accessible as a buzzing, pulsating, formless mass of signals and that one's task is to try to make sense of them. One needs to select some portion of the signals to scrutinize more closely: this is what bracketing is about. Experience leads to the development of 'blueprints', 'interpretation schemes', 'patterns', 'templates' and 'theories' which make bracketing easier. In imposing these on the world, one completes the first stage of enactment, limiting the variety of stimuli to be made sense of.

There is a paradoxical aspect to the use of all kinds of schemata: that much as they facilitate life in general and organizing in particular, they also act as blinders; the more successfully they are used, the more resistance they create when the attempt is made to dispose of them. This paradoxical property pertains to all routines, schemes and simplifications employed in trying to deal with the overwhelming complexity of the world. Thus the notion of bracketing itself, while illuminating some aspects of organizing, obscures certain others. It suggests that bracketing is performed on what is already there, a suggestion that is open to question when other aspects of enactment are brought to the fore.

Another important aspect of enactment is its active character. Things are put in the world as we know it by one's looking at them; they are created by human attention. This aspect of enactment is very obvious in the context of organizing: in introducing order one creates something that was not there from the beginning and which can be 'seen' because it has been thus created. In the study of economic phenomena, *self-fulfilling prophecies* (Merton 1948) have attracted much interest. If people are told that banks can become insolvent, they will rush to the banks to withdraw their savings, making the banks insolvent, as was observed during the Great Depression.

The concept of enactment is sometimes considered subordinate to organizing conceived in the broader sense of reality construction and sometimes not. Here enactment represents that part of reality construction in which primarily cognitive processes are involved (thus the emphasis on bracketing). In contrast, various versions of social constructivism that emerged some time after Weick's book appear to go beyond the purely cognitive. The strong cognitive emphasis, although limiting the applicability of the enactment metaphor generally, enhances its applicability in one particular context: that of conceptualizing *organizational environment*.

There are three major ways of conceptualizing the environment in organization theory (Smircich and Stubbart 1985). The most common of these is in terms of an 'objective environment' that exists 'outside' the organization and influences it – either deterministically or in a two-sided process in which the organization attempts to influence the environment, which in turn 'reacts'. The environment is usually seen as having the upper hand: rewarding and punishing and thus 'selecting' those organizations that are skilful in 'adapting'.

Another way of viewing the environment is to regard it as 'perceived'. Emphasis is placed here on the actors involved and their cognitive activities, organizational actors being assumed to research the environment and to attempt to formulate strategies for dealing with it which are subsequently put to the test. In such a 'scientistic' view, the environment is seen as being objective, real and 'out there', just as in the 'objective' approach. The focus of attention here, however, is more on issues of correctness or faultiness of perceptions and on improving their accuracy.

A third conception of the environment, that of its being enacted, takes quite a different stand, assuming, in line with Allport (1962), that what one should study are actual patterns of events. In this view, 'environment' and 'organization' are labels that denote such patterns. Indeed, as Charles Perrow (1991) pointed out, in contemporary society the environment of an organization consists of other organizations. The 'borders' of an organization are seen as arbitrary, the actors deciding what should be counted as being inside or outside and the observer examining chains of events and deciding to cut them at certain arbitrary points. Thus, in studying an organization engaged in trade, one could ask whether the customers belong to 'the organization' or to 'the environment', since without actors occupied with buying there can be no one involved in selling. Both actors and observers focus on those segments within chains of events that appear useful and feasible for gaining the understanding they seek.

During the early period of industrialization when a limited number of formal organizations were readily distinguishable from other forms of social order such as the family, the feudal order and the church, the separation between 'organizations' and their 'environments' was more clear-cut. Nowadays, service organizations tend to attract greater attention than industrial ones and non-organized society has nearly vanished, even the enemies of formal organizations tending to be organized in opposition. Such conditions make the concept of the enacted environment a particularly timely one. It is the organizational actors themselves who, through a process of bracketing, decide what belongs to their organization and what does not, as well as what entities or events outside their organization are relevant and thus to be classed as environment. In marketing, for example, new customer groups are constructed through the creation of new lifestyles produced by the linking of a particular combination of products with an appropriate ideology.

It would be folly, however, to suppose that people could create reality in any way they wished. In part this is because there are countless organizations and innumerable people who are trying to enact environments to their liking all the time. Some of them are more successful in enacting an environment that matches their visions than others. Some engage in power games and in lobbying activities so as to gain adherents to their particular conception of the environment. All of them have to cajole material realities, which sometimes cooperate and sometimes do not. Nevertheless, when thinking of the planet as we know it and trying to imagine how it was, say, 10,000 years ago, one sees that it perhaps cooperated all too well; that human beings were all too successful in enacting their ideas of how the environment should be. If human beings had simply reacted to the environment as it was and adapted to it, they might conceivably have earned an extra pair of hands – if evolution had been sufficiently kind to them.

Weick illustrated the usefulness of the idea of enacted environments for organizational analysis in highly dramatic settings – those of societal crises. He showed how, in the context of events such as the Bhopal, Chernobyl and Challenger catastrophes, 'action precedes cognition and focuses cognition' (1988: 307). Although enactment is certainly not the major causal force in the material world, it can be seen as a central mechanism governing human participation in the world. The ambiguous notion of 'crisis management', traditionally conceived as reactive action in the face of escalating problems, can thus be revamped to that of 'organizing in the face of crisis'. Here the active aspect of making sense of things when confronted with pressing events is emphasized.

The notion of enactment provides many new insights into the puzzles of organizing, but it fails to solve one type of problem well known in organization theory. This is the problem of formal versus informal organizations; of the irrationality lurking behind the rational surface in organizations; of subconscious processes undermining what conscious patterns of organizing accomplish; and of the fact that behind cognition lie emotions. Although the concept of enactment provides a reinterpretation of organizational cognition, it does not capture emotions or values (see for example, Daft and Weick 1984). One way of dealing with this is to postulate the existence of some other form of organizing, some kind of 'counter-organizing': a sort of 'de-construction' to complement reality construction. Another is to look for concepts that defy the cognition–emotion dualism.

Some theories that treat organizing as social construction endeavour to reach beyond this traditional dualism, claiming that there is no distinction between the cognitive and the emotional, that emotions are socially constructed in the sense that one would not know what feelings to have if socialization had not taught one that (Harré 1986), and that putting emotions aside in an act of pure reason is pure fantasy, sometimes achievable by machines but not by humans. Similarly, it is argued that there is an emotional element in expectations one has regarding machines, in dreaming up machines which are able to do what people cannot.

Such limitations in the applicability of the concept of the enacted environment may be reflected in two ways: in the fact that this concept is closely connected with theories of cognition and that the exclusion of emotions and to some extent of values is a heritage of that tradition; and in the fact that organizing through enactment is orientated outwards. Under the latter view, it is the collective efforts of organizational actors to project their subjectivities outwards that create an organizational world. The next approach to be considered complements this by regarding organizing as being proactive and reactive in one and the same act, with people and organizations creating themselves while attempting to create the world.

6 Organizing as identity construction

In the search for ostensive definitions many 'thing' metaphors have been applied to organizations, which have been described as machines, organisms or even psychic prisons (Morgan 1986). Although there are comparatively few metaphors capturing the process character of organizing, their number is growing. They have in common the vision of a socially constructed reality (made popular by Berger and Luckmann 1966) in which organizing represents one type of construction (Salaman and Thompson 1980). Such metaphors are often accompanied by reflection directed at the role of language in the process of organizing and the fact that the vocabulary employed by organizing need not be one of rationality. The reflective use of metaphors reveals that both labelling and metaphoric descriptions, those important tools of reality construction, are applied not only to that which is thus constructed, but also to those who carry out such construction.

Organizing creates worlds, but it also provides the people and organizations involved in the process with names, roles and identities. Through the use of language, people endow their actions with meaning and themselves with identities as actors. To understand a given organizing process, one must understand the meanings and identities the process produces. This perspective makes possible the redefinition of such organizational realities as leadership, gender, budgeting and accounting, the latter two aspects not often examined in this context.

The best known redefinition based on constructionist perspective is that of leadership. Whereas the latter was once perceived as a property of individuals or as an organizational function, it has been re-conceptualized in the idea of leadership as a symbolic act (Pfeffer 1978). In line with this, leadership has been suggested to involve a complex process of specific identity allocation, a process of the *management of meaning*, in which leaders and followers alike participate (Smircich and Morgan 1982). Borrowing images from *gestalt* psychology, Smircich and Morgan argued that in formal organizations the sensemaking aspect of organizing is linked with one special role, that of the leaders. This argument is especially salient when applied to the example of large, complex organizations: if sensemaking was the activity done separately by everyone at once, this in itself would produce not order but rather a high degree of complexity. In the latter case there is not only the 'buzzing and pulsating world' to bracket and make sense of, but there also are hundreds of sense-makers with their own schemata and preferences. Negotiations in an effort to make common sense of this would prove unrealistic if all were to negotiate with all. Leaders are persons given a special prerogative: that of organizing the organizing. In some cases, leaders interpret this prerogative as the right to impose their frame of meaning on their subordinates, resulting in autocratic leadership. In democratic institutions, in contrast, the leaders or managers negotiate with subordinates how things are to be interpreted. Instead of everyone negotiating with everyone else, a dialogue is established in what is basically a dyadic relationship. Such a negotiation process has its complexities, dealt with in detail by traditional leadership theory. In the present context of leadership being conceptualized as the management of meaning, sensemaking, (or 'world-making' in the case of enacted environments), however much it may be the task of everyone in the organization, is the special prerogative and responsibility of the leader.

Although this prerogative of sensemaking for the whole group can in principle be given to someone, it is in practice created by how the group acts towards the individual in question. Also, an individual can initiate it, disregarding the formal structure of positions. The notion of 'informal leadership' alludes to the well-known organizational phenomenon that, regardless of what an organizational chart may say concerning who is in charge, it is easy to identify the actual leader. This is a person who takes initiative in managing meaning for others. Titles and formal positions, although stabilizing the process of organizing, do so only temporarily. Identities are constantly renegotiated. A person in the position of a leader who continually fails to negotiate convincing interpretations of reality with the group is no longer the leader, but is rather 'an incompetent leader', quite a different identity.

Some of the most far-reaching consequences of conceiving organizations in terms of an ongoing process of organizing are in relation to issues of gender. The latter is a relative newcomer in the organization and management area, having come into focus in connection with questions of organizational structure. There was found to be a gendered structure within organizations, with differences in many dimensions such as those of wages, access to managerial positions, work-task character and the like being shown to vary with the gender dimension.

The notion of gendered organizing processes (Acker 1992) took a different perspective. It opposed the idea both that people enter an organization as accomplished men and women who end up in the appropriate gender group and that the only way of decreasing discrimination is to diminish or change other properties which seem associated with gender. In the gendered process view all organizing is gendered, the creation of sense and order being accomplished 'through and in terms of a distinction between male and female, masculine and feminine' (Acker 1992: 252). In these terms, organizing creates gender, or at least re-confirms it, by assuming a world in which the two sexes are treated differently, even if they have the same jobs, competencies or qualifications. Gendered processes mean that sex discrimination is not something that happens aside from, and possibly despite, the basic process of organizing. Rather, it means that sex discrimination is built into the very process of organizing, male and female identities being constructed in the process of organizing itself. Through the distribution of tasks, so that nurturing and care activities are given to women, the idea is enacted that women have a 'natural' preference for nurturing and caring. Achieving equality in organizations becomes more complex but also more feasible when organizing is conceived as gendered.

The notion of gendered organizing has another important function: it refocuses attention on the physical reality that is an inseparable part of organizing, and one which may be easily lost sight of in cognitive and constructionist views on organizing. Human bodies are part of organizing, and so is the physical reality of the machine. Increasingly, analysts are recognizing the need to re-introduce materiality into language-focused approaches. Also, the relation between symbols and what they claim to represent is being questioned more and more. What are perhaps the most surprising results of such questioning concern the role of budgeting and accounting in the process of organizing.

Traditional interpretations of budgeting and accounting practices involved two fundamental assumptions: that budgets and accounts are but a reflection of objectively existing reality (a report on reality composed of numbers rather than of words) and that they function as the basis for decision making. Although such interpretations are frequently valid, they have been complemented by others, which conceive budgets and accounts as conversation devices or means of communication, which are part and parcel of the process of sensemaking in organizing.

In a highly proclaimed study Olsen (1970) found budgeting to be a ritual act, the main function of which is to express the norms and values shared by the people engaged in the organizational activities in question. The field research he conducted showed budgeting to represent less a means of translating needs into policies than a process in which such needs and the corresponding values and beliefs are formed, negotiated and confirmed in an organizational setting. This study led to many other investigations in which it was found that budgeting can be the preferred mode of conversation about difficult issues of wishes and preferences, a matter facilitated by the rationalizing and objectivizing effects of using numbers (Czarniawska-Joerges and Jacobsson 1989). The actors involved in the organizing process decide not so much on the next action to be taken – something that depends on many situational factors – as on the collective identity of the organization. For example, a local authority may place great value on care of the elderly or on organizing the leisure time of young people. Such identity decisions, constantly renegotiated, are of enormous importance. Action here is governed mainly by the *logic of appropriateness* (March and Olsen 1989). This consists of matching a given type of identity with a given type of situation and an accessible repertoire of actions. Each choice of action confirms a particular type of identity, yet each new situation requires the reassertion of such an identity. A 'green organization' does things that a polluter does not do, but the characteristic of 'being green' is not acquired once and for all; it has to be re-acquired with every action. Budgeting is thus regarded here as a process of constructing future identities.

Looking at budgeting as a part of active organizing rather than as an artefact used to support decisions helps to avoid the frustration experienced in many studies that have regarded budgeting as an instrument of planning and control. Rather than being a faulty instrument of control, it becomes an effective means of expression, negotiation and dialogue.

A similar change in perspective has taken place in accounting studies. One study exemplifying this trend is entitled 'Financial accounting: in communicating reality, we construct reality' (Hines 1988). Accounting is seen in these terms not as the reporting of past events but as a powerful instrument for creating organizations and their environments, for creating order out of chaos and for organizing in general. Much of this power lies in the fact that financial accounts speak the language of numbers rather than words and can thus reduce conversation to categories that are easier to grasp than are statements in the rich and ambiguous language of words.

Similarly, Boland (1993), in detailed studies of accounting practices, has shown that, as well as the construction of information systems and the like, accounting is not an activity performed parallel to that of organizing: it is part of organizing itself. For the people involved it means moving through and being located within the organizational space (which is an important part of organizational identity), as well as creating (expanding, shrinking or redefining) this space; it also means interacting with other people and thus forming one's identity by the position one takes towards others – such as users of the accounts provided by information systems, as well as other constructors; it means making moral choices such as those involved in any other act of organizing.

Studying budgets and accounts as representing the process of organizing calls for an interest in matters which are less central in studies of leadership, such as the questions of which information systems should be used in producing budgets and accounts and which technology is required. Increasing attention is being directed at such matters in studies of organizing as practised in the field.

7 Organizing as hybrid networking

Performative definitions of organizations imply that, for understanding what organizing is and what it can be, it does not suffice simply to turn to the literature. One must go to the field and see what is happening, what people do when they organize. Performative definitions, unlike ostensive ones, do not become imperishable when 'dried' between the pages of a volume. They exist in doing, in those who organize defining what organizing is. Studies of organizing processes conducted in the 1990s provide a surprisingly homogenous picture of organizing as *networking*, even if networking itself is characterized by a high degree of variety and plurality.

Classic network theory (Tichy *et al.* 1979) stems from sociometry as it appeared in social psychology. Although it focuses attention on actors rather than structures, it nevertheless stops short of capturing what is actually taking place in organization fields as these are conceived in the new institutionalist theory (Powell and DiMaggio 1991). Network theory concerns who interacts with whom, how repetitive interactions are and what contents are conveyed. Institutionalists emphasize the fact that interactions last longer than actors and that, once a certain pattern of interactions has been institutionalized, it persists, even when the actors have been changed. Even if interactions change every time they are reproduced and new actors contribute to change either by default (wrongly reproducing the interaction pattern) or by design (planned change), repetitiveness gives identity to the actors who participate in interactions and who perform organizing.

Although both the institutional and the network perspective have a long tradition in the social sciences, advances in communication technology have recalled attention to them, suggested new perspectives on networking and emphasized the understanding of the organizing process they can provide. Using periodization as a sensemaking device, one can view such technological advances as proceeding from the industrial revolution to an information revolution of sorts and, finally and more significantly, to a revolution in communication.

Communication has conventionally been treated as one aspect of organizing, no doubt important, but not central. There is a growing awareness that communication may well be the central aspect of all organizing. Influences from outside organization theory and current trends in societal debate have contributed to this change. Two prominent German philosophers, Jürgen Habermas (1984) and Niklas Luhmann (1990), for example, attempted to arrive at a general theory of communication, albeit from different perspectives. The strong interest shown in this area reflects the need to capture what is observed but what still needs an appropriate vocabulary to be described, explained and interpreted.

In technological terms the 'communication revolution' is often described as involving historically three stages. The first was the invention of printing, celebrated by many as the true beginning of the modern era. The second was the development of the whole array of reproduction and communication techniques that marked the beginning of the mass communication so typical of the twentieth century. The third was the advent of electronic communication media, heralding the 'global village' (McLuhan 1964), a necessary prerequisite for a global economy (Wallerstein 1974).

Networking is both a metaphor for and a literal description of the organizing processes which are emerging. The term is used in the sense of interconnections being established between actors, and also between actors and various technologies and social institutions (Callon 1992). It is also used in the narrower sense of people being connected via computers and by the media of electronic mail, teleconferencing, television and all kinds of telecommunication with others who have similar interests. Such connections have led to the terms communication and transportation being treated as virtually identical within the context of the increasingly popular notion of *information highways*, launched in 1993 by US Vice President Gore to denote the social infrastructure of organized society.

New trends such as these cannot be interpreted adequately when they first appear. Also, the more revolutionary the changes that occur, the more difficult it is to predict what future form they will take. Nevertheless, certain aspects of the phenomenon of organizing as networking and its various consequences appear crucial.

One of these is the ongoing *disembedding* and *re-embedding* of many social phenomena, including events of an economic or political character (Giddens 1990). No invention that is useful remains local; it is immediately translated into a form suitable for the media. It is copied, changed, transformed, translated and propagated globally. Every time a translation, imitation, or application takes place, it occurs at some concrete point in time and space. Nothing remains where and when it originated; everything must be re-embedded in one form or another to even be said to exist at all.

An obvious example of disembedding is one found in financial markets, where abstract economics has replaced concrete economics. This has resulted in the earlier idea of money having an equivalent in gold or goods becoming obsolete, it no longer being possible to determine any fixed connections between such highly mobile symbols and their referents. Yet discerning students of stock markets' ups and downs cannot but note that this highly symbolic, disembedded communicative activity has very concrete, localized consequences at every turn of events (Abolafia 1996). In this sense organizing becomes a flux and a transformation (Morgan 1986); structures are temporary and dissipate before the eyes of the observer; the organizing of production processes turns into organizing virtual realities and cyberspaces in which the concrete and the abstract, and quantitative and qualitative aspects intermingle so that none of the dualisms that provided order to the world as it was traditionally comprehended seem relevant any more (Downey and Dumit 1997). Yet it is only the observers, those who stop to reflect, who are struck by the complexity and paradoxicality of this process. The actors involved go about their networking in everyday organizational life with ease. Doing so is taken for granted by the new generation, raised and educated as it is with the help of computers.

Another aspect of organizing as networking is the role of technology and machines. The increasing dependence of human beings on machines is a topic as old as technology itself. Both technology studies and science fiction lead readily to a demonizing or a glorification of this process (Joerges 1989). More accurately, one should speak of a *hybridization* of social action taking place, in which persons and machines create actors together. 'Consider … the case of a nuclear power station. This is a hybrid, a monstrous group which regulates interaction between graphite rods, turbines, atoms, operators, control board, flashing lights, concrete slabs and engineers' (Callon 1992: 141). Latour (1992) speaks here of *actants*, or collectivities of actions, human beings, machines and knowledge, all of them necessary to make something happen. Networking connects actants with one another, enhancing their total effect. Simply analysing separately the various elements involved does not suffice for understanding their synergetic capacity.

At the same time that actors go about networking in various networks with which they become familiar, there exist countless other networks of such complexity that they remain incomprehensible. It is claimed that no one, for example, can understand the entire complexity of operations carried out by transnational companies – neither the actors nor the observers (Brown 1987). Trust in abstract expert systems replaces concrete understanding (Giddens 1990).

Conceptualizing organizing as networking not only reflects emerging features of the field, but also combines in a unique way two disparate traditions of organizational theorizing: the material and the symbolic traditions, or those emphasizing technology and those emphasizing language. It permits one to tackle both the economic and the political aspects of organizing simultaneously, showing that taking account of costs is as important for understanding networking as is consideration of the new sort of power distribution it produces. In such a perspective, structures and hierarchies lose much of their traditional significance. Nothing else is lost, however. The idea of organizing serving to create order out of chaos remains intact, its meaning enhanced by the insight that organization represents a temporary state, something achieved anew in organizational life on a daily basis.

8 Peering into the future: organizing organizing

Although networking can become an apt metaphor for organizing as it occurs in the twenty-first century, electronic networking is also faced with an urgent need for organizing. Cyberspace can lead to an information chaos of unparalleled proportions. One may need to shift the metaphor here to a higher level and speak of managing meaning within the untamed landscapes of virtual reality.

Such need for higher-order metaphors stems in part from the feeling that inherited imagery does not allow one to grasp the current level of complexity found in organizing. The earlier conception of organizing as involving physical objects, including human bodies, has shifted to one involving more abstract levels of the symbolic analysis in which thoughts too are subjected to organizing. As more and more physical tasks are delegated to machines and the variety of abstract activities increases, direct supervision gives way to control on the basis of technical and professional norms. This leads to the meta-level of organizing increasing in prominence. Computer networks, for example, have organizers who teach newcomers the rules and exclude those participants who disobey. Language has increasingly become the crucial medium of organizing. Language machines develop with increasing rapidity to keep pace with the requirements it entails.

It may well be characteristic of organizing at the outset of the twenty-first century that the production of organization will become more important than the organization of production (Cooper and Burrell 1988). There is a widespread feeling that dramatic changes are taking place, the term 'postmodern' being used to suggest that tomorrow's organized society will be different from today's. That an era in which the process of organizing has been seen as paramount is approaching its end.

At the same time such predictions constitute a well-known rhetorical technique used in periodization, a form of sensemaking involving the supposed opening and closing of epochs by giving them names. This is a process of organizing deeply entrenched in history. A typical tendency here is to dramatize, predicting that all that is known will vanish in the epoch to come. One can thus safely suppose that in the future the form and content, but not necessarily the centrality, of organizing will change.

In considering the different waves of conceptualization that have occurred in connection with organizing from the time of the industrial revolution to that of the revolution in communication, one can discern three major trends. The first was a tendency to treat humans as machine-like. The second was to protest and to emphasize the human side of organizing, neglecting the role of the machines. The third was to humanize machines, in the many meanings of the verb. The latter opens up fascinating possibilities for action and reflection alike, for both organizing and organizational analysis.

Further reading

(References cited in the text marked *)

* Abolafia, M.V. (1996) *Making Markets. Opportunism and restraint on Wall Street*, Cambridge, MA: Harvard University Press. (A unique in its kind, participant observation study of New York Stock Exchange.)

* Acker, J. (1992) 'Gendering organizational theory', in A.J. Mills and P. Tancred (eds), *Gendering Organizational Analysis*, London: Sage Publications, 248–60. (Shows how gender is a part of modern organization rather than a deviation from the rational ideal.)

* Allport, F.H. (1962) 'A structuronomic conception of behavior: individual and collective', *Journal of Abnormal and Social Psychology* 64 (1): 3–30. (A conceptual treatise. Specialized.)

* Berger, P. and Luckmann, T. (1966) *The Social Construction of Reality*, Harmondsworth: Penguin. (A classic of the social constructivist approach to the sociology of knowledge; much used in organization studies to provide a methodological perspective.)

* Boland, R.J., Jr (1993) 'Accounting and the interpretive act', *Accounting, Organizations and Society* 18 (2/3): 125–46. (An unusual and innovative way of viewing management accounting systems.)

* Brown, R.H. (1987) *Society as Text: Essays on Rhetoric, Reason and Reality*, Chicago, IL: University of Chicago Press. (A difficult but important collection of essays on modern society and its organizations.)

* Callon, M. (1992) 'Techno-economic networks and irreversibility', in J. Law (ed.), *A Sociology of Monsters: Essays on Power, Technology and Domination*, London: Routledge, 132–61. (Affirms the crucial role of an understanding of technology in the shaping of society.)

* Cooper, D. and Burrell, G. (1988) 'Modernism, postmodernism and organisational analysis', *Organization Studies*, 9 (1): 91–112. (A review article on the impact of postmodern philosophy on organization theory.)

* Czarniawska-Joerges, B. and Jacobsson, B. (1989) 'Budget in a cold climate', *Accounting, Organizations and Society* 14 (1/2): 29–39. (Analyses multiple functions of budgeting and sets them in the context of a national culture.)

* Daft, R.L. and Weick, K.E. (1984) 'Toward a model of organizations as interpretation systems', *Academy of Management Review* 9 (2): 284–95. (A conceptual treatise on cognitive organization theory.)

Downey, G.L. and Dumit, J. (eds) (1997) *Cyborgs & Citadels. Anthropological Interventions in Emerging Sciences and Technologies*, Santa Fe, NM: School of American Research Press. (Famous anthropologists share their insights about cyborg society.)

Gibson, W. and Sterling, B. (1991) *Difference Engine*, London: Bantam Books. (A historical thriller speculating on what would have happened to England if Babbage had used steam energy to operate his computers. An excellent if fictitious study of organizing, emphasizing the role of language and technology in the process.)

* Giddens, A. (1979) *Central Problems in Social Theory*, Berkeley, CA: University of California Press. (A theoretical work in sociology.)

* Giddens, A. (1990) *The Consequences of Modernity*, Oxford: Polity Press. (Although not written within the tradition of organization and management theory, the book provides comprehensible and valuable insight into the nature of modern society.)

* Habermas, J. (1984) *The Theory of Communicative Action*, Boston: Beacon Press. (A philosophical treatise, highly valued by organization communication consultants.)

* Harré, R. (ed.) (1986) *The Social Construction of Emotions*, Oxford: Blackwell. (A scholastic but readable introduction to constructivist thought in psychology and the resulting changes in the understanding of individual identity.)

Hassard, J. and Parker, M. (eds) (1993) *Postmodernism and Organizations*, London: Sage Publications. (An unpretentious collection of papers applying a postmodern perspective to organization theory and describing typical reactions to attempts to apply it.)

* Hines, R.D. (1988) 'Financial accounting: in communicating reality, we construct reality' *Accounting, Organizations and Society*, 13 (3): 251–61. (A constructionist view of accounting.)

* Joerges, B. (1989) 'Romancing the machine – reflections on the social scientific construction of computer reality', *International Studies of Management and Organization* 19 (4): 24–50. (Analyses the metaphors of computers invented and applied by their users and theoreticians alike.)

* Katz, D. and Kahn, R.L. (1966) *The Social Psychology of Organizations*, New York: Wiley. (A classic in the field; several editions exist.)

* Latour, B. (1986) 'The powers of association', in J. Law (ed.), *Power, Action and Belief*, London: Routledge & Kegan Paul, 261–77. (Redefines the notion of power by challenging the use of the law of inertia as a metaphor for the diffusion of ideas.)

* Latour, B. (1992) 'Technology is society made durable', in J. Law (ed.), *A Sociology of Monsters: Essays on Power, Technology and Domination*, London: Routledge, pp. 103–31. (Affirms the crucial role of an understanding of technology in the shaping of society.)

* Latour, B. (1994) 'On technical mediation', *Common Knowledge* 3 (2): 29–64. (A fascinating re-contextualization of the role of technology in society and in organizations.)

* Luhmann, N. (1990) *Essays on Self-reference*, New York: Columbia University Press. (Explains the concept of self-perpetuating systems in the context of social systems.)

* March, J.G. and Olsen, J.P. (1989) *Rediscovering institutions*, New York: The Free Press. (A rewarding and instructive example of the new institutionalist perspective as used in combining political science and organization theory.)

* Maruyama, M. (1974) 'Paradigms and communication', *Technological Forecasting and Social Change* 6: 3–32. (Explains the notion of communication systems in cybernetics.)

McCall, M.W., Jr and Lombardo, M.W. (eds) (1978) *Leadership: Where Else Can We Go?*, Durham, NC: Duke University Press. (A collection of articles by prominent writers in the field who turn the notion of leadership on its head.)

* McLuhan, M. (1964) *Understanding Media*, New York: McGraw-Hill. (A classic in providing an understanding of the role of mass media in society. The expression 'global village' stems from this work.)

* Merton, R.K. (1948) 'The self-fulfilling prophecy', *Antioch Review* 8: 193–210. (A classic article showing how collective beliefs can turn into reality.)

* Merton, R.K. (1965) *On the Shoulders of Giants*, New York: The Free Press. (A provocative and insightful rendition of the history of ideas.)

Mills, A.J. and Tancred, P. (eds) (1992) *Gendering Organizational Analysis*, London: Sage Publications. (A collection of readings for those who believe that having women in managerial positions is not the only solution to the problem of sex discrimination in organizations.)

* Morgan, G. (1986) *The Images of Organization*, London: Sage Publications. (A rich, imaginative book presenting organization theory as a series of differing perspectives on the world and on life.)

* Olsen, J.P. (1970) 'Local budgeting, decision-making or a ritual act?' *Scandinavian Political Studies* 5 (5): 85–118. (A study showing the symbolic function of budgeting processes.)

* Perrow, C. (1991) 'A society of organizations', *Theory and Society* 20: 725–62. (A view of modern society as completely organized.)

* Pfeffer, J. (1978) 'The ambiguity of leadership', in M.W. McCall, Jr and M.W. Lombardo (eds), *Leadership: Where Else Can We Go?* Durham, NC: Duke University Press. (A revolutionary article showing that the role of leaders is to symbolize a possibility of control.)

* Powell, W.W. and DiMaggio, P. (eds) (1991) *The New Institutionalism in Organizational Analysis*, Chicago, IL: University of Chicago Press. (An anthology of highly representa-

tive works on the new institutionalist organization theory. Intended for a scholarly audience.)

* Rosen, M. (1990) 'Crashing in '87: power and symbolism in the Dow', in B.A. Turner (ed.), *Organizational Symbolism*, Berlin: Walter de Gruyter. (Illustrates the notion that symbolic activity can have concrete results.)

* Salaman, G. and Thompson, K. (1980) *Control and Ideology in Organizations*, Milton Keynes: Open University Press. (One of the earliest works in constructivist tradition, employing a critical perspective towards organizing.)

* Schaffer, S. (1994) 'Babbage's intelligence: calculating engines and the factory system', in J. Uglow and F. Spufford (eds), *Cultural Babbage*, London: Faber. (A historical analysis of Charles Babbage's life and work in the context of contemporary and modern cultures.)

Schultz, M., Hatch, M.J. and Larsen, M.H. (eds) (2000) *The Expressive Organization: Connecting Identity, Reputation and the Corporate Brand*, Oxford: Oxford University Press. (A processual approach to organizational identity.)

Sims, D., Fineman, S. and Yiannis, G. (1993) *Organizing and Organizations*, London: Sage Publications. (An engaging, readable book addressed to students and practitioners and applying the process perspective to practical examples taken from British organizations.)

* Smircich, L. and Morgan, G. (1982) 'Leadership: the management of meaning', *Journal of Applied Behavioral Science*, 18 (3): 257–73. (A field study demonstrating the use of the concept of the management of meaning in interpreting organizational life.)

* Smircich, L. and Stubbart, C. (1985) 'Strategic management in an enacted world', *Academy of Management Review* 10 (4): 724–36. (Takes up and develops Weick's concept of enactment.)

* Stalk, G., Jr and Hout, T.M. (1990) *Competing Against Time. How Time-based Competition is Reshaping Global Markets*, New York: The Free Press. (A normative, non-problematizing introduction to time management.)

* Tichy, N.M., Tushman, M.L. and Fombrun, C. (1979) 'Social network analysis for organizations', *Academy of Management Review* 4 (4): 507–19. (Focuses on classic network theory.)

* Wallerstein, I. (1974) *The Modern World System*, New York: Academic Press. (A historical treatment of the emergence of a global economy.)

* Weick, K.E. (1979) *The Social Psychology of Organizing*, 2nd edn, New York: Addison-Wesley. (A classic for those interested in the concept of organizing.)

Weick, K.E. (2000) *Making Sense of the Organization*. Oxford: Blackwell. (This volume brings together the best-known and most influential articles on sensemaking by Karl Weick. It claims that the effective organization is one that understands this process of sensemaking and learns to manage it with wisdom.)

Cognition

Jacques Girin and Benoit Journé

1 **Cognitive sciences and management theory**
2 **Individual rationality**
3 **Cognition and collective action**
4 **Distributed cognition**

Overview

How do managers perceive the situations and the problems they face? How do they build mental representations of these situations? Indeed, how do they reason about these situations and problems? Understanding how managers – and other actors – reach conclusions about the organizational world in which they work has been, from the start, a key question in management science. A deeper understanding of managers' cognitive processes can give us a better grasp of their decision making, and, more broadly, of organizational action in general.

Recent developments in cognitive sciences provide valuable insight on these matters. Drawn from a very wide range of scientific fields, cognitive science studies highlight cognitive processes at three distinct levels: individuals, groups and more complex sets which combine people, offices, objects, texts and so forth. At the level of the individual, Herbert Simon's idea of bounded rationality has been the cornerstone of management science thinking since it was introduced in 1955 – as well as being probably the most influential contribution since Max Weber's discussion of rationality types. The technique of cognitive mapping has been increasingly adopted as a tool to capture mental processes. On the experimental front, developments in experimental psychology have vigorously challenged many traditional hypotheses. For instance, they have disproved the notion that decisions and actions flow 'naturally' from reasoning and have demonstrated the complexity of the relationship between reason and action.

Such advances have led to fresh approaches to the analysis of collective cognition and the development of 'knowledge management'. Among the many theories being developed, we mostly find questions regarding interactive rationality, organizational learning, organizational memory and collective intelligence.

Finally, extensive work on group cognition has led to one of the most outstanding contributions of the cognitive sciences to management science: the concept of distributed cognition. In this perspective, complex systems created from mixed components such as people, offices, objects, publications, etc. have been identified as the locus of cognitive activity. Memory, intelligence and reason can thus be seen as properties of such systems rather than just limited to individuals.

1 Cognitive sciences and management theory

Since the late 1960s, social science researchers have increasingly focused on the issue of cognition. A number of studies on similar subjects have contributed to create a scientific trend called the cognitive sciences. The cognitive sciences do not represent a 'discipline' as such, but a body of works originating from various 'classical' scientific disciplines such as philosophy, psychology, linguistics, computer science or neurobiology. Consequently, the cognitive sciences label covers a very wide scientific field of research that can be hard to define. In effect, the boundaries of this scientific domain are both vague and moving, and the main common element to the works in cognitive sciences is that they deal with the notion of cognition in one way or another.

In fact, the very concept of cognition is equally hard to define. In its primary sense, cognition stands for the workings of the human mind. Mental operations such as perception, categorization, reasoning, memorizing and verbalizing are all part of the broader notion of cognition. Several of these issues have been at the heart of philosophical inquiries for centuries and they have generated several research works in modern psychology and philosophy. The specificity of the cognitive approach is that it asserts – as does behaviourism – that mental events can be studied without relying exclusively on introspection. However, it differs from behaviourist psychology inasmuch as it uses 'subjective' concepts such as beliefs, desires, intentions or meaning as descriptive of mental activity (Suchman 1988). In psychology, the cognitive approach was developed by Jean Piaget (see Piaget 1951) whose works remain an important reference in this field.

The notion of cognition takes a different meaning in the context of the technical achievements of computer and information sciences. In this context, an implicit comparison is made between human reasoning capacities and those of mechanical devices which can perform better on specific problems than the human brain. Intelligence is then seen as a faculty attributable to machines as well as to human minds. In a series of texts prepared for the Stilliman conferences at Yale University, John von Neumann (1958) gives a fascinating overview of the possibilities and limits of a 'mathematization' of the human mind. These texts stand as a testimony to the days when researchers were gradually discovering the potential of such an approach to cognition, and, as it happens, von Neumann's estimates turned out to be remarkably accurate.

Carried away by the enthusiasm of these early days, people believed that problems such as automated translation or object recognition would be easily solved. As things turned out, researchers came to the apparently paradoxical conclusion that it is easier to build very effective 'expert systems' in highly specialized fields than to model adequately the knowledge acquisition processes of a five-year-old child.

Over the years, computer modelling of cognitive capabilities followed several distinct directions. For instance, von Neumann – one of the inventors of the first computer – opened the way for an approach which considers that intelligence must proceed by sequential calculations operated on the basis of symbolic representations. On the social sciences front, this approach could be supported by developments within highly formalized disciplines, such as generativist linguistics.

Yet, as computers and modelling techniques improved, research on the mechanical workings of the brain progressed from breakthrough to breakthrough. A host of new techniques enabled researchers to focus their study of chemical and physiological processes which underlie the activity of neurones in the brain. These studies generated an alternative to symbolic computation for the understanding of intelligent systems. From a biological perspective, the issue no longer rests on each individual element's computation capability but on the array of interrelationships between a multitude of simple elements: *networks*. At this stage, 'connectionist' approaches that had hitherto been eclipsed by the successes of their computational counterparts regained favour. This, in turn, led to rapid developments in 'neural networks' mathematical models.

In the present day, the concept of cognition has progressively spread from human brains and computing machines to much broader fields. Questions arise about the cognitive capabilities of groups of people, but also of complex systems including people, machines, texts, objects and so on. Traditional social sciences such as sociology, anthropology and social psychology each contribute to the issues of cognition from their own specific perspectives. In due course, management science has also come to focus on a number of practical management issues which arise from cognitive research, and has brought its own particular perspective to bear on these subjects.

This entry will concentrate on three main areas: individual rationality, cooperation between organizational actors in working situations and collective cognitive capabilities. Our first concern will be to give an overview of the question of individual rationality, which lies at the core of many classic works in the management field. Second, we will broaden the question of individual rationality to study collective rationality and the dynamics of cooperation within groups of organizational actors. Finally, we will concentrate on how the presence or absence of objects affects group capabilities and on the proprieties of composite systems.

2 Individual rationality

Classical analysis

Max Weber's classical analysis (1956) distinguishes four types of rationality: by finality, value, tradition and affectivity. In the case of rationality by finality individuals choose through *reasoning* the means they consider best adapted to the ends they pursue. Rationality by value appears when individual behaviour is a result of an individual determination to conform to certain moral values, as opposed to traditional rationality, where the individual simply conforms to tradition and other inherited habits. Finally, affective rationality covers all the instances where, in the face of overwhelming events, people's reactions are determined by their feelings at the time.

Of these various forms of rationality, only the finality type is directly depend-ent on reasoning. In all the other cases of 'rationality' actors can justify their be-haviour by comments such as: 'this is how things must be done'; 'we've always done it like this'; or 'I couldn't do anything else'. Some authors have tried to in-vestigate further the depth of the cognitive field by examining how the behaviour of managers can be affected by their moods or feelings (see Sims and Gioia 1986). However, we will limit ourselves to a more restrictive understanding of cognition which mainly relates to the relationship between reasoning and action.

In truth, Weber gave a special place to the finality form of rationality. It was to become the primary principle in the construction of his ideal types which attempted to describe and explain complex realities such as bureaucracy. The other forms of rationality were only supposed to come into play if the ideal type built on this basis was insufficient to provide a satisfactory understanding of the observations.

The assumption of the actor's rationality is also that which classically pre-vailed in economics. To be more precise, it was thought that economic actors based their behaviour on a notion of maximization of expected utility, as put for-ward by von Neumann and Morgenstern (1947). For example, if the consumer wants to purchase a product, he will choose the one that, for the least cost, does what he wants it to do for him, or else he will choose the product that, for a given price, does the most things for him; in other words he will choose the best combi-nation of price and utility.

This is where the work of Herbert Simon, precursor and founder of the cogni-tive sciences and a specialist both in organization theory and artificial intelli-gence, has an important role to play. According to Simon (1955; March and Simon 1958), the conditions according to which the economic agent could maxi-mize their expected use of a product are never brought together. Indeed, maximi-zation of expected utility implies collecting and analysing a large amount of data, something the agent is not able to do in practice, first because it would require a lot of effort to go and look for this data, and second because even if it could be found, it would not be possible to analyse it all. These ideas can be demonstrated by a simple example. If I want to make sure that I am paying the lowest price for a common consumer product, I will have to visit all the shops likely to be selling the product, noting and comparing all the prices, maybe even trying to get them to lower the price, before making an ultimate informed choice. We can see that the 'price' of this information can quite quickly become very expensive, given that it requires me to devote time, effort and money to go from one shop to the next. The issue, according to Stigler, is to know at which point the cost of search-ing for new data is likely to be greater than the gain I hope to make from it.

Simon's notion of *bounded rationality* is somewhat more complex because it also brings into play the cognitive capability of the individual. A choice is not made according to data which is objectively present in a given situation, but ac-cording to a 'definition of the situation' which is actually a simplified, bounded, approximate 'model' of the real situation. Apart from those situations to which there are routinized responses, the individual will start a search which is somewhat random. They do not search for the best possible choice, but will stop at the first opportunity which seems satisfactory. They will not go all over town looking for the best price for the sweater they want to buy, but will visit a few shops until they find one that they like which is about the right price.

This notion of the first satisfying opportunity is decisive, since the choice resulting from this form of rationality will largely depend on the path taken. If the individual starts shopping for the sweater going from the east end of town to the west end, the results will probably not be the same as if they had started in the west end. In order to understand better this essential aspect of the phenomenon, the term *procedural rationality* is more easily used today than bounded rationality.

Centred around Simon's ideas is another debate, that of knowing whether the plans for action made by actors have a role to play in the outcome. Lucy Suchman (1987), who represents the thought on *situated action*, believes that plans are only a springboard for actual action and that they in no way determine the action itself. For instance, she gives the example of the sportsperson who wants to canoe down the rapids of a river. In order to choose the best itinerary, they will take the time beforehand to study the river, the currents, the rocks, etc. in order to plan the route. However, when it comes to doing it, the actual action will most likely have little to do with those plans. Numerous instantaneous adjustments will be made, by resorting to embodied *skills*, skills which will allow the person to feel the current, the movement of the canoe, and to respond skilfully to any changes. All of this would indicate that the actual action plans have been abandoned. Vera and Simon (1993) strongly disagree with this view, claiming that on the contrary, the success of stunts or such sportive exploits is directly linked to the capacity of the stuntsperson or the sportspeople to stick very rigorously to strict action plans.

Cognitive maps

An attempt to systematically account for the forms of reasoning used by managers has been made in the field of cognitive mapping. Cognitive maps are a technique used to graphically represent human reasoning. The maps show a number of concepts or variables linked up by positive or negative ties. For example, we could have a positive relationship between product advertising and product sales, and a negative relationship between product price and product sales. These relationships, and dozens more, are shown by a diagram drawn on a sheet of paper, which can be studied and interpreted. The study of cognitive maps has allowed us to come to several conclusions:

1 Some variables can appear as more important than others, for example, if they have an influence on several other variables.
2 Loops can appear, when arrows linking variable A to variable B come back to A by another path. In this case, does the reciprocal influence of B on A and of A on B have a stabilizing effect or a destabilizing one?
3 Where two variables are linked by more than one path, which of the paths will be the one favoured in the reasoning of the actors?

An interesting example of the use of cognitive maps is proposed by Hall (1984) in his analysis of the decline of the *Saturday Evening Post*. Hall shows that in times of crisis, the paths used in reasoning are the simplest ones, and that the effects of feedback via the loops are ignored. For example, after a period during which a rise in subscription prices was followed by a seemingly lasting increase in sales, it was concluded that the cost of subscription had had no effect on the number of readers. Faced later with a sudden fall in sales, it was therefore decided that the editors were to blame and action was taken accordingly, without of course halting the downward trend in sales. Other measures were then taken which also turned out to be equally inappropriate. Thus, the causal reasoning used after the initial experience was too simplistic. Indeed, Hall's study shows that the rise in subscription costs had in fact resulted in a reduction of its faithful readership, compensated by an increase in occasional readers. Only by making the difference between the paths distinguishing faithful and occasional readers, could they have responded favourably to the fall in sales, by realizing that they did actually have to do something about the cost of subscription.

The limitations of cognitive maps fall mainly into three categories:

1 The graphic representation itself can soon become extremely complex and difficult to master.
2 The actual nature of the relationships between the variables is difficult to determine, and even harder to quantify. Thus, it is often impossible to calculate the real influence, or combined influences, of paths or loops.
3 Nothing can ensure that the graphic representations on the maps, inasmuch as they are the results of series of interviews, really represent the actual reasoning used in real action.

Cognitive maps can be drawn up at an individual level or at a collective level; for example, a department, a section or even a whole organization. They are usually based on open or semi-open interviews, or very occasionally on more spontaneous expression from people *in situ*. When establishing a collective cognitive map, there is a lot of toing and froing and some confrontation to ensure consensus and agreement on variables and on the relationships between them.

This process not only serves to visually demonstrate something that already exists, but also creates something new: an awareness on the part of the individuals of their reasoning and thought processes, and where a group of people is concerned, an explication of the reasons of agreement or disagreement. From this angle, the cognitive map technique can also be seen as an interesting method of intervention within a group (see Eden 1992).

Reasoning and action: a complex relationship

It is fairly normal to believe that individuals act according to how they think. Most people use this hypothesis when they are trying to work out what someone else is going to do. This hypothesis also underlies the technique of drawing up a cognitive map: if we think we know, after having drawn up such a map, how someone else reasons, and if we assume that they are going to behave rationally to the end, then we think that we can predict how this person will behave in certain conditions. However, as we have seen in the debate between symbolic computation and situated rationality, the latter have a slightly different hypothesis. They consider that the rationality which is present in action is not quite the same as that which is present symbolically, particularly in plans, and that action is something other than just following plans.

Several experimental psychology tests carried out by Festinger (1957) have clarified this point well. Festinger was fascinated by situations in which people had to adopt behaviour that went against their beliefs. For example, asking a student who disapproved of racial prejudices to put forward the arguments defending such prejudice, and vice versa. In these situations, the individual feels what Festinger has described as a cognitive dissonance. Tests have shown that people tend to try and reduce the dissonance they are experiencing. This means that when a person is forced to behave in a way that contradicts their beliefs, they will often try to adjust their beliefs to their behaviour. This process, called *rationalization* (Beauvois *et al.* 1993), in fact directly contradicts the preceding idea that behaviour would conform to the way of thinking.

Another way to interpret these tests is to say that the process does not actually consist of a change in the way of thinking, but is rather a form of discovery of that person's true way of thinking. Their actual behaviour would enable the person to infer their way of thinking from their behaviour. This theory is called *self-perception* (Bem 1967). In this case, we could affirm that we cannot hope to establish an individual's way of thinking through interviews or questioning, but only if we can see them confronted with different choices of action.

In the same line of thought as Festinger and Bem, Beauvois *et al.* (1993) have focused more specifically on the way in which people's actions follow on from one another. The *commitment theory* that they have developed shows how people can find themselves drawn into a series of actions going in a particular direction, without having had any intention to do so at the beginning. The first step, taken willingly, does not usually cost the individual very much, but subsequent steps can cost more and more, and seem to follow on, one from the other, in a kind of fatal snowball of events. An example of this is to ask students that smoke to be part of an experiment which involves asking them to refrain from smoking for a few hours, then to involve them further and ask them to stop smoking for a few days, etc. Getting them to commit themselves to such a sequence of events successfully is more likely to work if you leave them with very little time to think between the successive steps: this is what Beauvois *et al.* call *act rationalization*. The idea is that, without time to think about the act they have just accomplished, people will be more likely to commit themselves to a subsequent action along the same lines as the first because it in some way makes more sense of the previous act. Act rationalization or the rational reducing of the cognitive dissonance, could thus be two different elements of an alternative where time and urgency play a crucial role.

Although there have been few studies in this area in the management sciences, it is clear that their potential value is extremely important. In the many cases where a manager's behaviour appears, with hindsight, to be characterized by an unfortunate obstinacy to persist in error, commitment theory and act rationalization could probably provide the best explanation for such behaviours.

The cognitive approaches to management must not neglect these tests and theories which deeply question, at least at an individual level, the nature of the relationship between thought and action, and particularly the hypothesis that action/behaviour results from thought. The relationship between thought and action is certainly complex, and appears even more so when we go from the individual level to collective level, as we shall see.

3 Cognition and collective action

As soon as several people get together to cooperate on a task, the issue of the nature of the relationship between individual ability and collective capacity is raised. More and more studies suggest that the group is the basic unit of the creation and transfer of knowledge. Brown and Duguid (1991) speak of 'communities of practice'; others like Boland and Tenkasi (1995) suggested the term 'communities of knowing'. The term 'communities' stresses the importance of the tacit side of organizational cognition (like shared experience and know-how). In this section, we shall be looking at the question of whether or not the relationship between thought and action is the same at the group level as at the individual level.

Interpersonal coordination and interactive rationality

The issue of coordination has constituted a major contribution to the study of organizations. When we look at organizations, it is not surprising that we wonder how independent individuals, who are required to coordinate their actions, actually manage to do so.

Thomas Schellings's theory of focus points (1960), provides us with an interesting framework for analysis with which to look at this question. This theory can be easily demonstrated by a simple and classic example, that of the appointment. Take for example two people who have set a precise date for an appointment in Paris, but who, for whatever reason, have not fixed a precise time or location. The idea suggested by the theory of focus points is that, in such circumstances, each person is going to try to find a time and a place that have certain characteristics that will distinguish them from all other possible times and places, hoping that by a similar sort of reasoning, the other person will have reached the same conclusion. Midday, for example is a time that is distinguishable from other times, and most people will try to find their partner at this time. The issue of where is something more of a problem as people's perceptions of distinguishable places differ enormously. Preliminary tests indicate that in the case of the appointment in Paris, most French people will choose the Eiffel Tower, whereas Americans tend to choose the American Embassy.

It is possible to see a cultural variable emerging here: what makes one place, within the same geographical area, distinguishable from the rest? What makes it a focus point? This largely depends on the cultural background of each individual. The Eiffel Tower would be more prominent in the mind of a French person, while in the same city, the American Embassy would be more prominent for an American. The meeting seems more likely to take place if the people involved have more things in common, reason in the same way and belong to the same culture. So what happens when people who are brought together to coordinate have very different ways of thinking? This is often the case, within companies, between finance people and production people, between production and sales, etc. Can we apply Schelling's ideas to these situations? This is the issue raised by Ponssard and Tanguy (1993). The conclusions they draw are based on the notion of looking, not at the supposed common cultural background of the actors, but at the capacity a group has to build, in action, joint perceptions that can be used as focus points.

In order to clarify this line of reasoning, let us return to our appointment in Paris. Instead of taking the example of an appointment which must take place just once between several people, let us explore what might happen if this appointment is supposed to take place within the context of a past and ongoing relationship between two persons. For instance, two people who are visiting Paris together suddenly find themselves separated. They will try to find their partner, not in the focus points of the city, but more likely at one of the places they have recently visited together. Rather than the Eiffel Tower or the American Embassy, it could be simply a small local café in the *cinquième arrondissement*, where they happened to have a coffee together the day before. In this instance, we can see that a joint past, even a very recent joint past, involving shared events, can make focus points emerge that have no link to the cultural background of the people involved. Culture here is meant in the sense of 'national culture' or 'ways of perceiving, feeling and thinking', that would be common to both of the parties concerned. In this example, the success of the appointment no longer depends on there being a shared cultural background, but on the immediate history of previous interaction between the people concerned. In such circumstances, even a very heterogeneous group of people of different backgrounds, nationalities, etc. can manage to find each other again in this way.

This line of reasoning has been applied in a more subtle fashion by Ponssard and Tanguy in their work on forecasting and planning in companies. The role of the recent shared history of interaction and relationships is played by economic analysis techniques, whose job is not to provide simple, objective answers to questions, but rather to be used as part of an interactive process that establishes a shared knowledge base. Quantitative methods of this sort are not seen as a means to objectively analyse problems, but as a means to encourage interaction between people, which creates the shared focus points.

Sensemaking in organizations

Making sense of what is going on appears to be one of the main activities of every member of an organization, whatever their level in the hierarchy. This is especially true when the organization faces complex situations. On the one hand, the quality of sensemaking could explain part of the high reliability reached by some organizations in charge of very complex and dangerous technologies (Weick and Roberts 1993); on the other hand, the collapse of sensemaking might explain some dramatic organizational accidents (Weick 1993).

Sensemaking is not only a matter of the interpretation or understanding of an *existing* meaning. It deals rather with the ways people create (enact) what is to be interpreted. 'The act of interpreting implies that something is there, a text in the world, waiting to be discovered or approximated (see Daft and Weick 1984). Sensemaking, however, is less about discovery than it is about invention' (Weick 1995: 13).

According to Karl Weick (1995) seven characteristics distinguish sensemaking from more classical concepts of understanding, interpretation or attribution. They also shape a process much wider than the decision making process. Sensemaking is a reaction to the ambiguity resulting from too many plausible interpretations or uncertainty caused by lack of information.

1 Sensemaking is grounded in identity construction (i.e. sensemaking is committing and there must be a sensemaker, whether it be an individual or a group, who discovers how and what they think).
2 Sensemaking is retrospective. It starts when you look back on unexpected events that have just occurred, interrupting your projects.
3 Sensemaking has to do with the way managers enact sensible environments as legislators enact laws: they act and create new features that did not exist before and which become the constraints and opportunities they face.
4 Sensemaking is social (i.e. sensemaking is arguing. It is produced by interaction between the sensemaker and his audience). Thus coordination of interpretations is at stake.
5 Sensemaking is an ongoing process. This is one of the main difficulties for managers to cope with:

Sensemaking never starts. The reason it never starts is that pure duration never stops. People are always in the middle of things, which become things, only when those same people focus on the past from some point beyond it ... To understand sensemaking is to be sensitive to the ways in which people chop moments out of continuous flows and extract clues from those moments.

(Weick 1995: 43)

6 Sensemaking is focused on and by extracting cues, enacted in the context of the continuous flows of situations.
7 Sensemaking is driven by plausibility rather than accuracy.

These seven characteristics show that sensemaking is no only cognitive but also social and political. Indeed, minorities have to invest great efforts in sensemaking to make themselves heard by a majority.

In the same way, Gioia and Chittipeddi (1991) stressed the social and political sides of organizational cognition. Using an ethnographic study of a strategic change initiation, they showed that the concept of 'sense-making' is linked with the concept of 'sensegiving':

> Sensemaking has to do with meaning construction and reconstruction by the involved parties as they attempted to develop a meaningful framework for understanding the nature of the intended strategic change. Sensegiving is concerned with the process of attempting to influence the sensemaking and meaning construction of others toward a preferred redefinition of organizational reality.
>
> (Gioia and Chittipeddi 1991: 442)

Sensemaking and sensegiving are two phases of a cycle that also includes understanding/influence and cognition/action processes. All three are intertwined. They overlap or occur more or less simultaneously in an organizational learning process.

Organizational learning

An organization is capable of achieving today that which it could not achieve yesterday, or it can improve today on what it did yesterday. For instance, it can learn to make a product that it previously was unable to produce, or even learn to produce it in larger quantities with the same amount of resources. This ability to increase organizational capacity is partly due to increased individual capacity. In the classic example of Adam Smith's pin factory (Smith 1937), the individual skill of each worker increases because workers become better and faster at their task the more times they do it. This is one of the main strengths of the production system as opposed to the cottage industry system that preceded it. However, individual skill is not the only important factor when looking at the overall capacity of an organization. An organization can increase its capacity through many other means; a better distribution of resources and tasks, better coordination between individual workers, new procedures, etc.

The observation that an increase of organizational capacity does not only depend on an increase of individual capacity, has led to the idea of organizational learning. Argyris and Schön (1978) apply a distinction to organizations regarding theories of action, that they had previously only applied to individuals. They make a distinction between 'theories in use' and 'espoused theories'. Theories in use are those that actually govern our actions and behaviour, whereas the espoused theories are those that we express if we are asked about the whys and wherefores of our action or behaviour. At an organizational level, the espoused theories can be found in formal documents, such as organigrams, job descriptions or rules and regulations. However, the theories in use in the organization will be different and, according to Argyris and Schön, can be 'mapped' as shared descriptions of theory in use. These shared descriptions can thus be seen to constitute the memory of the organization.

Learning starts when there is a gap between the results that are obtained and the results that were expected according to the theory in use. In trying to find an explanation for this gap, learning agents will propose ways to correct the errors of the theory in use: but learning only becomes effective if the results of this investigation can become part of the organizational memory, and not just part of the individual's memory.

Just how the organization is supposed to remember what it learns is not really explored by Argyris and Schön. Levitt and March (1988) have made an interesting contribution on this point with their work on routines, identifying a number of ways of thinking and behaving that can be directly linked to the shared past experience of the members of the organization. Routines can be implicit in procedures, but can also be passed on informally from one person to another. Routines are not only brought into question by a process of trial and error, but also by the interpretation given by individuals to each new experience. From this point of view, we get a more subtle picture of the issue of organizational learning, which can be both a source of rigidification or progress.

Organizational learning has had a great success in managerial literature since the 1990s. This issue became central in the new concepts of 'knowledge management' and 'intelligent enterprise'. Creating new knowledge in order to feed a continuous process of innovation would give a new competitive advantage (Senge 1990). Therefore, each firm should try to develop those organizational learning skills.

Ikujiro Nonaka (1994) proposed one of the most complete explanations of the process of organizational learning. According to him, new organizational knowledge is created through the interaction between tacit and explicit knowledge. Four modes of knowledge conversion interact together, generating a spiral of knowledge creation. Such a spiral establishes a link between several levels of knowing: individual, collective (groups of projects) organizational and even interorganizational levels. 'Socialization' is the first step of the spiral. It is a process of sharing experiences that creates tacit knowledge between the group members. The second step is the 'externalization' process that transforms tacit knowledge into explicit knowledge, using mostly stories, metaphors and analogies. 'Combination' is the third stage of the spiral. It is described as the process of systemizing concepts into a knowledge system (i.e. databases or written rules). Then comes the 'internalization' process, the last stage, embodying explicit knowledge in tacit knowledge (know-how) via a 'learning by doing' process. The importance of each step and its place in the spiral varies with the project and the firm. According to Nonaka the role of the managers would be to run the spiral of knowledge creation.

Empirical studies on organizational learning are few and far between because they require lengthy periods of observation. Thus, the work of Charue and Midler (1993), which is based on the accumulation of several long periods of *action research*, is exemplary. In particular, Charue and Midler show that the learning process usually only concerns one section of an organization – a factory or a workshop for example – and that the real issue is that of how to transfer what has been learnt to the rest of the organization.

Organizational memory

The question of organizational memory has remained in the background in the preceding theories on organizational learning, but was later the focus of specific study. It is clearly difficult to imagine human life, or even that of a superior living being, without the use of memory. Similarly, all technical systems capable of accomplishing a sequence of tasks have some form of memory, even a simple barrel-organ, whose strip of perforated paper can be considered as an elementary form of memory. Modern technical data-processing systems all have at least one memory bank, in fact they usually have different levels and types of memory banks. Take, for instance, a simple microcomputer; it has several different registers of microprocessing, weak capacity but fast access memory, the random access memory which is constantly changing, read only memory, with a fixed content, and memory banks such as hard disks, floppies and CD-ROMs.

Thus, the notion that an organization has a memory is a must if we admit that the organization can act, respond suitably to outside stimulation and even learn. Similarly, as we have seen, this memory is more than the sum of the memories of the individuals that make up the organization. This is demonstrated by the experience of several large bureaucracies – such as the army or some public services – which have conserved the knowledge of their past over the spans of several lifetimes.

In addition to this empirical observation, there are also cases where managers have to pay particular attention to the question of organizational memory. For instance, the nuclear industry has to keep records of its operations, for periods of time that can reach tens of years, in order to ensure the safe running of a nuclear power station. Indeed, if a defect is found, on a major water pump for instance, they need to be able to identify whether or not the defect is likely to affect other similar pumps, or if it is reasonable to assume that only this particular pump is damaged. Similarly, if a problem occurs with a pharmaceutical product, it has to be possible to establish whether the problem is linked to a particular production run – which would mean withdrawing the whole lot from circulation – or whether the problem potentially concerns all production. In both cases, the question of organizational memory appears to be directly linked with safety issues. In fact, the attention paid to such record-keeping is often subject to legal regulation.

In order to do more than just draw a simple analogy, and to avoid giving a somewhat anthropomorphic vision of the organization, we shall look more closely at the notion of organizational memory. This is what Walsh and Ungson (1991) try to do. They defend the idea that organizational memory is founded on various elements that can be found throughout the organization. They identify five different sorts of memory retention facilities:

1 *Individual memory*, that is, an individual's memories of experiences within the organization, is in fact the most obvious part of organizational memory. Each person remembers his own personal experience, and particularly crucial moments. Very often, when a problem occurs, the most obvious first move is to check with the older employees to see if it has happened before, and what was done about it.

2 *Corporate culture* is made up of ways of perceiving, thinking and feeling which are handed down throughout the organization's lifetime.

3 *Transformations*, according to Walsh and Ungson, encompass both the way in which raw materials are transformed into finished products and also the way in which a newcomer to the organization becomes a veteran.

4 The *structures* of the organization are the ways in which the organization itself influences the roles given to its members. These structures ensure that the benefit of past experience is passed on into the daily running of the organization.

5 The *ecology*, which concerns the physical elements of the organization. For example, the way that workspaces are organized can reflect past experience in the same way as the structures.

To this list of locations of organizational memory, Walsh and Ungson add an equally important element: external memory. This includes former employees, competitors, bankers, state institutions, etc.

Such a categorization of organizational memory is, of course, open to discussion and improvement. It is clearly obvious that the network of interpersonal relations constitutes in itself a considerable element of the memory. It is not because one person in the organization remembers an important detail that the person who needs that information today is going to be able to find it: they have to know where to find the right person, which is not always easy, especially given the increasing mobility of people within organizations today. In other words, it is as important to remember who remembers what, as to remember something oneself.

Action and collective intelligence

In an organization, the completion of a complex task is generally the result of cooperation of several individuals. A complex task requires the use of mental resources such as attention, discernment, knowledge, willpower, etc. The question here is, should these qualities, and others, be attributed to the individuals, or can they be considered as the result of interaction between more than one individual?

It is clear that the ability of a number of individuals to satisfactorily complete a specific task cannot be assimilated to the sum of their joint abilities. Recent findings in the field of artificial intelligence show that large groups of individually stupid elements can be more efficient than a smaller group of more sophisticated elements. The example of colonies of insects – termites, bees, ants, etc. – also demonstrates the remarkable potential capacity of a large group of otherwise limited individuals. Yet, it goes without saying that these insect colonies are not examples to be imitated by humans, but simple examples to illustrate the difference between artificial intelligence and collective intelligence.

Using the analogy of neural net models in neuroscience, which have been simulated on computers, it is tempting to put forward the idea that if collective mental processes do exist, they must reside in the relations between the various individuals, and not in the individuals themselves. This is the assumption that underlies the work of Weick and Roberts (1993), applied to the control of aircraft movements on board aircraft carriers. The authors add that collective intelligence does not only reside in shared attitudes, shared knowledge, exchanges of ideas or coordination of mental activity. According to them, the source of collective intelligence lies more in the actual coordination of the activities themselves. Collective intelligence is thus more a result of the careful attention paid by each individual to what the others are doing, than of the direct cognitive exchanges.

In that case, the question is to know just how this collective intelligence (*collective mind*) emerges. One of the major conditions identified by Weick and Roberts is that the individuals presuppose the existence of the collectivity. From then on they will behave as if the collectivity existed, and see their individual actions as existing within the context of a system as opposed to being isolated elements. The fact that they do this means that the system does in itself exist, emerging as something bigger and grander than each of its individual members. No individual has a precise idea of what this system looks like, and not everybody has the same mental model of what it actually is. In some cases, it may be that it just takes the mental models of the individual members to be structurally similar enough for the structure of their relations to have the same effect.

The quality of the collective mind resulting from these coordinated actions emerges as being directly linked to the individual qualities of attention and heedfulness in the interrelations. *Heedful performance* differs from *habitual action* in that it adjusts over time according to preceding actions and their consequences. This means actual training and not just a simple drill. Thus, contrary to neural networks, where the characteristics of the system emerge according to the intensification of the relationships between different elements, here it is more the strength and type of these relationships, heedful or heedless, which counts. However, a broader spectrum of the interrelationships, both deeper in time and in space, is another feature of collective intelligence.

This analysis of the way in which the collective mind emerges from heedful interrelations reveals that the system is continually being rebuilt, and that a drop in the mutual heedfulness in behaviour results in an immediate drop in the quality of the collective mind. In other systems such as aero-naval ones, where the speed of response to changes in circumstances is a crucial element of security, accidents can happen due to a slight drop in attention from one participant to another.

The way that newcomers are socialized and taken charge of by the other members is an excellent example of the quality of the interrelations system. Weick and Roberts also insist on the fact that the actual process of induction, for example, when older members answer questions from the newcomers, or when they tell them stories, has a resocialization effect on the members themselves. Thus, successful integration of newcomers has a positive effect on the quality of the system as a whole.

The viewpoint explored by Weick and Roberts is very exciting. On a practical level, this kind of reflection appears particularly useful, not just in the case of systems that have to face up to issues of safety and trustworthiness, but also for those that have to face issues of quality or rapidly changing environments. We should point out however, that in organizations where these variables are not crucial, but where others (for example, productivity) are, the question of collective mind is probably of a somewhat different nature.

4 Distributed cognition

The preceding questions mainly concern people in relation to other people. A broader viewpoint is possible if we take into consideration all of the resources available to these people for completion of their joint tasks, and look at whether or not they bring any cognitive ability to their users. Language and objects are the resources most frequently under observation.

Language

Language itself holds a very important place in the functioning of organizations. At the beginning of the twentieth century, Max Weber observed that the written word was one of the fundamental characteristics of the bureaucratic organization. It is easy to appreciate that this phenomenon has increased enormously since then, and that modern organizations produce and use huge quantities of written documents. On the other hand, in a study on the work of managers, Henry Mintzberg (1973) shows that managers spend most of their time talking, whether face-to-face, in meetings or on the phone.

People usually think that using language corresponds to activities that store and circulate information. This understanding has been deeply shaken in the light of recent developments in the field of linguistics. It would appear that there are many different uses for language, and that they are vastly more complex than just that of a simple vehicle for information. Although there are different points of view to be found in the literature on the different fundamental uses of language, linguists agree on the fact that there are functions other than just communication. For instance, Sapir (1993) identifies three principal language functions – thought, communication and expression – as well as several secondary functions. More recently, Sperber and Wilson (1986) have focused on the cognitive function of language, claiming that it is the most important one.

Even if we do not wholly agree with Sperber and Wilson's point of view, we cannot deny that the cognitive function of language is essential. It is clearly at work within organizations in many cases. For example, look at written procedures or technical instructions. A clearly written procedure must detail precisely what needs to done by one or more people. It is evident that although we sometimes know how to do something very well, setting out in writing exactly how to do it can be a lot harder. In certain trade manuals, for instance, it can be very difficult to describe the skill of an operator in words. For example, how do you describe how to solder well? You can say that the metal must be heated to a certain temperature, as must the two pieces to be joined, and that a strip of another metal must be placed in between. However, we know that such a description can be interpreted in many different ways, for example, when we explain that the desired temperature is reached when the metal turns a certain shade of red. The skill of the worker is impossible to capture in words. On the other hand, it could be claimed that such attempts to describe a skill can be seen as an opportunity to improve on it by making the weak spots in the procedure more obvious.

Thus, just trying to write down, in words, what we do, can constitute a cognitive operation with far-reaching consequences. There are many examples of this with the interviews that are conducted with people in organizations: just by asking simple questions like 'what does your job involve?' or 'how do you do this?' involves real cognitive thinking on the part of the people being questioned. They often say afterwards that it was useful for them, because it made them understand their own role better, or helped them to take a step back from their daily work.

Linguists have also shown that language not only serves to say things, but also to do things. The theory of *speech acts* developed by Austin (1962), enables it to be understood that in organizations, language is not just a vehicle for information. Language is also used to give orders, to threaten, to maintain good relations or to insult, etc.

Finally, recent research on language in organizations (Girin 1990) focuses on the question of interpretation. A message, verbal or written, does not only have a 'content', it also assumes that the receiver of the message is able to put it into context with a whole lot of things that are not specified, but which are none the less essential for the message to be understood. In other words, the receiver must put into use the background knowledge which will give the message its significance. The actual nature of this background knowledge is difficult to describe because it contains both explicit and non-explicit elements.

For example, how do we interpret a request such as 'can you type this letter up for me by this evening'? To all intents and purposes, we know this to be an order and not a question. It activates a whole set of resources such as: the explicit function of the person asking and that of the person receiving it; regulations that are explicit in the company, or in employment law, etc.; usual practice in a particular department or company, which might mean that one does not ask one's secretary to do work that might mean they have to work late. Thus, there is the issue of knowing what is common to ways of acting and thinking, and what is not entirely explicit, or even possible to explicate. The usual answer to this problem is a cultural one, which is not the focus of this entry.

Objects and cognition

The world of companies and organizations is not populated solely by people in relationships with one another. It also contains a certain number of material objects: the buildings which contain the different parts of the organization (offices, factories, warehouses, etc.); the pens and pencils that most people use at some time or another in their work; the machinery, etc.

The fascination for social science theoreticians of man-made objects, which has traditionally been strong in some branches of anthropology, is a relatively recent phenomenon in the study of modern organizations. The idea of linking the question of cognition to that of objects is even more so. What is at stake in these discussions can be understood from three converging points of view.

First, the relationship between humans and objects can be examined. A good example of this is the article by Norman (1991) on cognitive artefacts. The framework for this thinking is that of the relationship between an individual and the world, via an artefact. A simple example of a cognitive artefact is the checklist used by aeroplane pilots. Depending on whether we consider the system from the point of view of an outsider, or that of the user, the transformation caused by the use of the artefact is not the same. From an outsider's point of view, the outcome expected from the use of the artefact is an increase in the performance of the system for an identical task: the checklist is supposed to reduce the risk of errors or forgetfulness, but does not change the fact that what they are trying to do is land without forgetting to lower the landing gear. From the user's point of view however, the artefact changes the nature of the task being undertaken. They do not just have to lower the landing gear, they also have to read the notes that say 'lower landing gear', check that they have completed the preceding item on the list, and say out loud that it has been done, etc. One of the functions of the checklist could be to interrupt the automatic mental processes and avoid undertaking these crucial tasks without full awareness. Once again, we find the issue of heedfulness seen above.

In addition, artefacts play the role of intermediaries between the user and the world, in both directions: action on the world and evaluation of the consequences of that action. Some simple artefacts combine both characteristics, like a basic door bolt, which allows us both to use it, and to see at a glance whether it is open or closed. Such can be called 'symbol-objects'. However, this is not generally the case for a lock that works with a key, and even less for many modern artefacts, particularly computers. The interior of a computer, its *representation* of the world, is one thing, and the way in which it organizes this representation, *vis-à-vis* the user, is another.

The second viewpoint is illustrated by the developments in the sociology of science and techniques. The focus of some researchers has been directed towards the properties of what Johnson (1988) calls the non-humans, a simple example of which would be door hinges, or a door closer. Johnson's idea is that humans can delegate the responsibilities of certain tasks to the non-humans. His method for evaluating the nature of this delegation is to imagine what humans would have to do if the non-human elements did not exist. For example, door hinges mean that humans do not have to make an opening in the wall every time they want to go through it, then fill it up after them. Similarly, the door closer means that there is no need for a doorman to close the door after every forgetful visitor. This substitution of the non-human for the human is not identical however, and the door closer does not do exactly the same thing as the doorman. Although the door closer is less subject to mood swings, or absences, or distractions, it does mean that the people going through the door need to be strong enough to push the spring open, which can be a problem for small children or the elderly. In other words, the door closer prescribes new conditions: it makes the door too difficult for a child or an old person to open. In this respect, it is acting like a human. In the same way, it might not be suitable to treat a policeman like a human being – that is, someone we can talk to person to person – it might be better to treat him as a kind of mechanism, or part of a machinery that is not sensitive to the relationships between humans. Johnson's point of view leads us to envisage a form of sociology where the characters observed could be human or non-human, with role expectations, behaviours, social relationships, etc.

Distributed cognition

The preceding comments have dealt with approaches where the question of cognition is not only looked at at the individual or the group level, but also at the level of systems combining individuals, groups, language and objects. This point of view is that of distributed cognition.

This is a viewpoint shared by many current researchers, as is shown by Hutchins' (1995) article on the landing procedure of a transport plane. During this operation, the strict control of speed is a crucial task. Speed must be gradually decreased until reaching 'reference speed', which is very close to the 'manoeuvring speed', and beneath which the plane might crash. Manoeuvring speed and reference speed depend on several factors, such as the weight of the plane, which can vary during the flight according to fuel levels, and the position of the wing, which also varies during landing, coordinated with the drop in speed.

Hutchins' approach is to take, as one unit of analysis, a system which includes the two pilots, the documents they use and their technical instruments, which he calls 'the cockpit'. In the cockpit, as opposed to the brain, we can observe the cognitive process. We can hear what the pilots are saying, observe what their actions are on the orders and on the other objects, and also observe how the objects themselves influence the pilots. We can observe that, due to the physical positioning of the objects and the documents, the verbal exchanges, etc., several representations of the plane's speed are possible, making it possible to correct any mistakes. Thus, it is possible to speak of the 'cockpit's memory', which is something other than the pilot's memory, seeing as it is the result of both the actions of the men, their cooperation and the properties of the objects. It is therefore a feature of the system itself.

The technologies for cooperation over distance

The developments in information and communication techniques have enabled us to create radically different physical environments for group work. These days it is possible to achieve new kinds of cooperation both time-wise and distance-wise. For a start, the technique of audio conferences has enabled us to 'meet' other people working on joint projects, usually for short periods of time, without being actually physically together in the same place. Additionally, the increasing level of interconnections between computers has given birth to a new world of possibilities, such as electronic mail, long-distance access to data banks, downloading of files, and finally, joint work, asynchronic or synchronic, between users miles apart.

The combination of several of these techniques has led to the creation of services called 'groupware' which has invited further study of a new field called 'computer supported cooperative work'. These studies have the advantage of analysing situations where the phenomenon is usually linked naturally to people working together, who find themselves technically divorced. For instance, the audio relationship between individuals becomes independent of their visual relationship; the boundaries of private and public working space at work is no longer defined by physical barriers; the perceived distances between two people talking and working together bear no relation to the real distances.

The example described by Abel (1990) of the cooperation at a distance between two members of the same laboratory is quite incredible, and provides us with a number of useful observations. The experimental arrangement used by the laboratory that Abel studied put a number of researchers in Palo Alto into contact with others in Portland, 600 miles away. Some of the research projects are undertaken by teams with some members in Palo Alto and others in Portland. The workplaces, for all intents and purposes are identical, with individual offices opening, on three out of four sides, onto a large rectangular common room. Originally, these common rooms were equipped for the audio-visual reunions. Then the system was extended to the individual offices, enabling individuals to establish contact with the other offices and common rooms from their own offices. In this way anybody in the two sites could be contacted.

Among the many observations made by Abel, the following focus on the question of the cognitive ability of groups. First, it would appear that the system that was set up does actually reinforce the cooperation between people in the two sites. However, the fact that the people involved had a prior face-to-face relationship seems to have had a considerably favourable effect on the success of the system. Second, successful cooperation between researchers sometimes requires them both to disconnect. *Disconnection* is where each person temporarily suspends his own analysis of the problem to listen to the arguments and analysis of the other. It seems that in the delicate stages, the 'distance meetings' of the teams is not sufficient, and a 'physical meeting' is necessary. Third, the quality of cooperation is vulnerable to problems of politeness and courtesy, and to problems of the protection of privacy. The groupware techniques raise a whole set of new problems concerning these kinds of phenomena. It was necessary for example, for members of the laboratories to learn new ways of showing that they had finished speaking, or that they wanted to speak, or even ways to limit the length of time that another person could spend 'in' someone else's office.

353

The main lesson to be drawn from these observations is that there is a close link between the collective ability of the group and the social relations between the members of the group.

Distributed cognition should radically change the design of information technology. Boland, Tenkasi and Te'eni (1994: 456) noticed that traditional designs 'have tended to focus either on the individual as an isolated decision maker, or on the group as a producer of [a] decision or policy statement in common', whereas a design based on distributed cognition principles should assist individuals 'in making interpretations of their situation, reflecting on them, and engaging in dialogue about them with others.' Finally, the three objectives of such a design are to enable everyone to improve his own understanding, to better appreciate the understandings of others, and to take into account the network of interdependencies in which they act and think.

6 Conclusion

The cognitive approach of organizations seen above has contributed to the development of some knowledge management methods and tools. A recent study (Ruggles 1998) showed that the three main organizational supports of knowledge management are (1) Creating knowledge repositories (data warehousing); (2) Implementing decision-support tools by codifying best practices, designing experience bases and collecting feedback and recommendations from the field; (3) Implementing groupware to support collaboration (using software such as Lotus Notes). In addition, when asking CEOs about what is still to be done, their answers are first, mapping knowledge (to locate the sources of internal expertise), second, creating networks of knowledge workers and third, establishing new knowledge roles (such as Chief Knowledge Officers).

Note

I would like to thank the participants of the 'Cognition and Management' Seminar held at the Centre de Recherche en Gestion in 1993, for their helpful contributions to this text. In particular, many thanks to Denis Bayart, Anni Borzeix, Florence Charue, Hervé Dumez, Christophe Midler, Nathalie Raulet, Jean-Baptiste Stuchlik and Béatrice Vacher.

Further reading

(References cited in the text marked *)

* Abel, M. (1990) 'Experiences in an exploratory distributed organization', in J.E. Galegher, R. Kraut and C. Egido (eds), *Intellectual Teamwork: Social and Technological Foundations of Cooperative Work*, Hillsdale, NJ: Lawrence Erlbaum, 489–510. (This excellent study – representative of the computer supported cooperative work (CSCW) current – highlights the issues surrounding delocalized cooperation through communication technology interfaces.)

* Argyris, C. and Schön, D.A. (1978) *Organizational Learning: A Theory of Action Perspective*, Reading, MA: Addison-Wesley. (A classic work in the organizational learning area: a necessary starting point.)

* Austin, J.L. (1962) *How to do Things with Words*, Oxford: Oxford University Press. (A philosophical outlook on 'speech acts' from the founder of the current of thought that considers speech as a component of action.)

* Beauvois, J.L., Joulé, R.V. and Brunetti, F. (1993) 'Cognitive rationalization and act rationalization in an escalation of commitment', *Basic and Applied Social Psychology* 14 (1): 1–17. (A rather technical paper presenting recent results in the field of experimental psychology on the issue of behavioural post-rationalization.)

* Bem, D.J. (1967) 'Self-perception: an alternative interpretation of cognitive dissonance phenomena', *Psychological Review* 74 (1): 183–200. (In contrast to its popular success, cognitive dissonance theory has been consistently questioned by experimental psychologists; the author proposes an alternative interpretation.)

* Boland, R., Tenkasi, V. and Te'eni, D. (1994) 'Designing information technology to support distributed cognition', *Organization Science* 5 (3): 456–73. (Article linking the theoretical approach of distributed cognition with the design of information technology.)

* Boland, R, and Tenkasi, V. (1995) 'Perspective making and perspective taking in communities of knowing', *Organization Science* 6 (4): 350–72. (Efficient electronic communication systems designed for communities of knowing.)

* Brown, J.S. and Duguid, P. (1991) 'Organizational learning and communities-of-practice: toward a unified view of working, learning and innovation,' *Organization Science* 2 (1): 40–57. (Ethnographic studies of workplace practices showing significant learning and innovation generated in the informal communities-of-practice.)

* Charue, F. and Midler, C. (1993) 'A French sociotechnical learning process', in B. Kogut (ed.), *Country Competitiveness, Technology and the Organizing of Work*, New York: Oxford University Press. (A theory of organizational learning based on several case studies developed in the French context.)

* Eden, C. (ed.) (1992) *On the Nature of Cognitive Maps*, special issue of *Journal of Management Studies* 29 (3). (A selection of articles that explore the uses of cognitives maps or cause maps for research and intervention in organization.)

* Festinger, L. (1957) *A Theory of Cognitive Dissonance*, Stanford, CA: Stanford University Press. (The starting point of the experimental field of research on cognitive dissonance.)

* Gioia, D.A. and Chittipeddi, K. (1991) 'Sensemaking and sensegiving in startegic change initiation', *Strategic Management Journal* 12: 433–48. (A major contribution to the study of organizational cognition. Very interesting ethnographic method.)

* Girin, J. (1990) 'Problèmes du langage dans l'organisation' (Problems of language in the organization), in J.F. Chanlat (ed.), *L'individu dans l'organization: les dimensions oubliées* (*The Individual in the Organization: The Forgotten Dimensions*) Québec: Presses universitaires de Laval. (The implications for organizational theory of recent developments in language science research.)

* Hall, R.I. (1984) 'The natural logic of management policy making: its implications for the survival of an organization', *Management Science* 30 (4): 905–27. (Cognitive mapping in action: an illustration and analysis of the death of the *Saturday Evening Post*.)

* Hutchins, E. (1995) 'How a cockpit remembers its speed', *Cognitive Science*. (A clear illustration of the notion of distributed cognition.)

* Johnson, J. (alias Bruno Latour) (1988) 'Mixing humans and nonhumans together: the sociology of a door-closer', *Social Problems* 35 (3). (A tongue-in-cheek paper which highlights the predominant role of objects as actors in social life.)

* Levitt, B. and March, J.G. (1988) 'Organizational learning', *Annual Review of Sociology* 14: 319–40. (Routines as a component of organizational memory. An insightful paper at the forefront of organizational learning research.)

* March, J. and Simon, H.A. (1958) *Organizations*, New York: Wiley. (The foundation stone of modern organizational theory. A necessary read.)

* Mintzberg, H. (1973) *The Nature of Management Work*, New York: Harper & Row. (Mintzberg's field research on how managers spend their time which acquired semi-mythical status.)

* Neumann, J., von (1958) *The Computer and the Brain*, New Haven, CT and London: Yale University Press. (A visionary book on the interrelationships between mind and computers. Of historical interest.)

* Neumann, J., von and Morgenstern, O. (1947) *Theory of Games and Economic Behaviour*, 2nd edn, Princeton, NJ: Princeton University Press. (One of the most important works of the century, introducing game theory. Highly technical and arduous to read.)

* Nonaka, I. (1994) 'A dynamic theory of organizational knowledge creation', *Organization Science* 5 (1): 14–37. (One of the more complete models of organizational learning.)

* Nonaka, I. And Takeuchi, H. (1995) *The Knowledge-creating Company*, New York, Oxford: Oxfpord University Press. (Clear illustrations of Nonaka's theory. Useful for knowledge practitioners.)

* Norman, D. (1991) 'Cognitive artefacts', in J.M. Carroll (ed.), *Designing Interaction: Psychology at the Human–Computer Interface*, Cambridge: Cambridge University Press. (An essay on distributed cognition by one of the founders of the field.)

* Piaget, J. (1951) *Play Dreams and Imitation in Childhood*, London: Routledge & Kegan Paul. (A particularly thought-provoking work from the great Swiss psychologist.)

* Ponssard, J.P. and Tanguy, H. (1993) 'Planning in firms as an interactive process', *Theory and Decision* 34 (1): 139–59. (A brilliant explorative work on the notion of interactive rationality.)

* Ruggles, R. (1998) 'The state of the notion: knowledge management in practice', *California Management Review* 40 (3): 81–9. (Empirical study made by Ernst & Young Center for Business Innovation in 1997, revealing the main practices used by firms.)

* Sapir, E. (1993) 'Language', in *Encyclopedia of Social Sciences*, New York: Macmillan. (An anthropological outlook on language. A fundamental contribution which discusses the influence of the structure of language on thought processes.)

* Schelling, T. (1960) *The Strategy of Conflict*, Oxford: Oxford University Press. (A very well-written book which presents how game theory patterns can be applied to social and political situations.)

* Senge, P. (1990) *The Fifth Discipline: the Age and Practice of the Learning Organization*, London: Century Business. (One of the first books making knowledge a valuable asset used by firms to compete in the new information society.)

* Simon, H.A. (1955) 'A behavioural model of rational choice', *Quarterly Journal of Economics* 69 (1): 99–118. (Simon's first discussion of the notion of bounded rationality applied to organizational behaviour. Actually much clearer than most later descriptions of his concepts by other academics.)

* Sims, H.P., Jr and Gioia, D.A. (eds) (1986) *The Thinking Organization. Dynamics of Organizational Social Cognition*, San Francisco, CA: Jossey Bass. (An overview of cognitive outlooks on organizations.)

* Smith, A. (1937) *An Inquiry into the Nature and Causes of the Wealth of Nations*, Modern Library Edition, New York: Random House. (A classic in economics, first published in 1776.)

* Sperber, D. and Wilson, D. (1986) *Relevance, Communication and Cognition*, Oxford: Blackwell. (An innovative discussion of the role of language: a communication tool or a thinking medium?)

* Suchman, L. (1987) *Plans and Situated Actions, the Problem of Human Machine Communication*, Cambridge: Cambridge University Press. (A good example of the work in the field of situated cognition.)

* Suchman, L. (1988) 'Representing practice in cognitive science', *Human Studies* 11 (2–3): 305–25. (A theoretical discussion of the issues surrounding the representing practice in cognitive science.)

* Vera, A. and Simon, H. (1993) 'Situated action: a symbolic interpretation', *Cognitive Science* 17 (1): 1–48. (An answer from the computational cognition movement to the situated cognition position.)

* Walsh, J.P. and Ungson, G.R. (1991) 'Organizational memory', *Academy of Management Review* 16 (1): 57–91. (An important contribution that synthesizes the little-researched area of organizational memory.)

* Weber, M. (1956) *Wirtschaft und Gesellschaft* (*Economy and Society*), Tübingen: Mohr. (The definitive presentation of Max Weber's work, originally written in 1921.)

* Weick, K. (1993) 'The collapse of sensemaking in organizations: the Mann Gulch disaster', *Administrative Science Quarterly*, 38: 628–52. (This in-depth case study shows that most industrial accidents occur when the people involved in the situation were not able to make sense of what was going on.)

* Weick, K. (1995) *Sensemaking in Organizations*, Thousand Oaks, CA: Sage Publications. (A theoretical presentation of the concept of sensemaking and a discussion on the way it shapes the organizational structure and behaviour.)

* Weick, K. and Roberts, K. (1993) 'Collective mind in organizations: heedful interrelating on flight decks', *ASQ* 38 (3): 357–81. (A major contribution to the concept of 'collective mind', illustrated by several thought-provoking case studies.)

Organizational symbolism

David M. Boje

1 **The founding story of organizational symbolism**
2 **Organizational symbolism: a Disney example**
3 **Conclusions**

Overview

On the one hand, organizations produce and distribute symbols with a commercial purpose in mind: they sell them. On the other hand, organizations produce and use symbols for the purpose of legitimation and control of individual and organization behaviour. In the first instance, a corporation's name, products, past and current executives, logo, slogan, labour practices, and ads become symbols in popular culture. Several corporate executives who have become symbols include Lee Iacocca, Michael Eisner, Philip Knight, and Bill Gates. Products that are symbols include the Nike trainer, Mickey Mouse watch, and the IBM computer. The second use of symbols for motivation, leadership, legitimation, and control, as we shall see, can have an impact on the selling of organizational symbols. Corporate stories that are symbolic include the founding of General Motors, the break-up of the telephone company, the rise of Sony Corporation and the rebirth of Harley Davidson. Within a firm various events and actions get symbolized differently by management and labour; and whose symbols and stories hold currency is a matter of relative power. The key problem then in organization symbolism is symbols have multiple meanings (polysemous) – those meanings change over time, and that change is affected by power. In early studies, organization symbols (people, objects, stories, or gestures) were defined as signs that map some other meaning onto them than their literal interpretation. There was not much attention to issues of relative power or to the relation between symbol for sale and symbols for control. The current research trend is towards providing multiple interpretations and multiple paradigms for assessing the heroic and tragic aspects of organizational symbolism.

1 The founding story of organizational symbolism

A bit of history will set the stage for an example I will work through. It is not often that a field of study is founded in a small informal conference in someone's living room, but on 4–6 May 1979 a group of organization theorists gathered at the home of Lou Pondy in Urbana, Illinois decided to meet and explore the implications of symbolism for the study of organization (Pondy *et al.* 1983: xv–xvii). A story is told that symbolizes the beginning. Tom Dandridge, Peter Frost, Gareth Morgan, Bob Hogner and others heard Lou tell his 'bird's egg' story on 6 May (Morgan, Frost and Pondy 1983: 6):

At a closing session of the Illinois conference on 'Organizational Symbolism' Lou Pondy sought to focus the attention of those present upon a bird's egg found in his garden earlier that week. The egg was hollow, and open at one end, revealing the exit through which a young fledgling had made its entrance into the world. The egg was presented by Lou as a symbol of the conference, illustrating the 'hatching of a new field of inquiry' – that of organizational symbolism.

The hatching of this field of inquiry was new and has lived up to three promises. First, the new field was to journey beyond the simple duality of organizations symbolized as either simple machines (frameworks, clockworks) or adaptive organisms (blueprinted growth) metaphors. They sought a new metaphor focused on 'human systems manifesting complex patterns of cultural activity' (Morgan, Frost and Pondy 1983: 4). They referred to their new metaphor for understanding organization as 'level 7 symbol processing system' and 'level 8 multicephalous' or 'multi-brain'. This was the core argument of a paper by Pondy and Mitroff (1979), to move beyond 'open systems theory' to inquiry into the symbolic capacity of formal organizations.

Second, the new field began with a definition of symbol that disrupted any simplistic relation between sign and signified. The definition began with the premise that 'a sign achieves the status of a symbol when it is interpreted, not in terms of strict resemblance with what is signified, but when other patterns of suggestion and meaning are "thrown upon" or "put together" with the sign to interpret it as part of a much wider symbolic whole' (Morgan, Frost and Pondy 1983: 5). What Morgan, Frost and Pondy (1983) do is make sign, symbol, and context loosely coupled. While corporations may advertise and promote a meaning to be attached to their symbols, others can come along and define them for their own purposes. They point out that 'while all symbols are signs, not all signs are symbols' and once signs are 'vested with particular meaning they become symbols'. Lou's 'bird's egg', for example, symbolized the 'hatching of a new field of inquiry' and the story of the egg was invested with a subjective significance that was, for the participants and those who joined in the inquiry, 'woven into complex cultural patterns'.

Third, the initial conference attendees and the writers in the first book on organizational symbolism vested the new field in a variety of interdisciplinary orientations. They did this by turning Burrell and Morgan's (1979) now infamous four paradigm model on its side, and drawing in connections that cut across the four paradigms of the functionalist, interpretive, radical humanist, and radical structuralist. Tipping it on its side, to me, symbolizes the rhizomatic (interconnected) and more critical aspects of the field that have emerged. The tipped model posits eight inquiry approaches to organizational symbolism, four pointing directly to the four paradigms, but four more pointing in-between. Rather than get lost in inter-paradigm issues, I will turn to examples of organizational symbolism that illustrate multiple paradigms and the interplay between organization symbols for sale and for control.

2 Organizational symbolism: a Disney example

Who is better known: Jesus Christ or Mickey Mouse? At issue is how symbols are sold and disseminated for commercial ventures, as well as how organizations use symbols to legitimate and control employee behaviour. The Disney case we will explore can be turned both ways and it illustrates the problems that result from projecting images that conflict with the image-in-use. Given the multiplicity of meanings in any setting, it is no surprise that there are contrary analyses of the organizational symbolism of the Walt Disney corporate enterprises, its theme parks, movie studios, apparel, toys, books, and TV stations. The official meaning of the Mickey Mouse icon, the personalities of Walt Disney or the character of the studios and theme parks has been disputed in various organizational studies.

Pre, modern and postmodern symbolism

I take the position that Disney can be studied as a mix of premodern, modern, and postmodern symbolism and from a variety of paradigms. The premodern symbolism focus is on the transition from craft to modern factory animation methods of administration. The modern analysis looks at shifts in symbolism as the technology of Disney shifted and as new modes of symbolizing, for example, employment became more efficient and fashionable. Finally postmodern studies of Disney symbolism reveal a darker side and more multifaceted construction of symbols and their indexes to reality and fantasy. A postmodern analysis of organizational symbolism gives attention to the plurality and economic context of how symbols are constructed, distributed, and consumed. Postmodernists, according to Rosenau, 'question the attribution of privilege or special status to any voice, authors, or a specific person or perspectives' (1992: xiv). Postmodern analyses reveal the collective and historical dynamics of organizational symbolism, including its multiplicity and contentiousness.

Plurality and symbolism

While Disney executives would prefer we all believe in the magic of Disney, and simply take the 'happy stories' and characterizations of corporate practices at face value, postmodern studies have revealed some darker tales. There is a focus on the plurality of voices and linguistic realities and how some interpretations have more power and persuasion than others do. Deleuze and Guattari (1987) analyse organizations with their 'rhizome' metaphor that assumes less hierarchy and less linear-causal structures than the traditional symbolism of machine and organism, so prevalent in early organization studies. And it was these metaphors that Pondy *et al.* wanted to move away from. Their alternative metaphor and symbol seeks to extricate roots and foundations, to thwart unities and break dichotomies (such as mechanistic-organic) and to spread out roots and branches, thereby pluralizing and disseminating differences and multiplicities, and making new connections among paradigms (Boje 1995: 999–1000).

The meaning of symbols depends upon the locality in a social network and the prior utterances of various intersecting discourses. In a rhizomatic metaphor of organization, symbols (stories, characters, objects, etc.) are the medium of interpretative exchange, and the meaning one experiences depends upon the roots and strands of participation.

A story of Walt Disney, for example, can symbolize to those who know the history and context, a multiplicity of events, sites, encounters, and outcomes. Such symbols are plurivocal (have more than one meaning), and a specific interpretation is dependent upon contextual understanding. Because of the opportunity for multiple interpretation, a good deal of management activity goes into constructing, attaching, and enforcing particular meanings, when a network of alternative interpretations coexist.

Symbols sell products

Disney, for example, has a significant monetary investment in the ways in which Mickey Mouse, Walt Disney, Michael Eisner and other symbols (and icons) get interpreted. Framing corporate symbols in 'bad news' stories in the media, for example, can have an impact on stock prices. From a postmodern perspective, organizations cannot be registered as one symbol, but instead are a multiplicity, a plurality of symbols and a network of interpretations in struggle with one another. There is a dominant interpretation at any one point in time, but that symbolism is subject to change. A good deal of the manager and staff of every public relations department's time is devoted to chasing down symbols and storylines, to spin new meanings from the ones that are about to emerge.

In 1932, Walt learned that a merchandiser was licensed to sell images of Mickey and Minnie on items for children and had done quite well. At the end of the year, Disney had jumped into the merchandising market, and more than eighty major US companies, including General Foods, RCA, and National Dairy, were selling millions of dollars of merchandise with Disney symbols on them. The Disney symbols were manufactured for all manner of products and services for consumers of every age. In the first two years 2.5 million Mickey Mouse watches were sold and Disney symbols appeared on everything from tooth brushes to kitchen sinks. Today, being trained and given credentials by Disney customer service and management training (Disney University) is a symbol that can be exchanged in the market place. 'Going to Disneyland' is a slogan of advertising synonymous with athletic success.

Symbols (and indexed meanings) and stories I grew up accepting about Walt Disney and his Happy Magic Kingdom mask more marginal accounts from former script writers and animators. There are symbolic acts that are only recently being analysed. For example, what is the symbolism of a corporate name? In early official accounts, Walt and no one else created Disney Enterprises and Mickey Mouse. Prior to 1925, Walt Disney and Ub Iwerks were once partners (this one 50–50 ownership) in an enterprise named Iwerks–Disney Commercial Artists Company and another named Disney Brothers Partnership (with Roy

Disney) in which Iwerks held a 20 per cent share. The question of who (Ub or Walt) created Mickey Mouse has been the subject of much study. The early versions of the official story state that on the way back from New York on a train, Walt drew the mouse that would change the cartoon industry. Another version is that Walt's wife, Lillian, suggested that Walt change the mouse's name from Mortimer to Mickey. In 1948, Walt recalled how Mickey Mouse 'popped out of his mind onto a drawing pad at a time when disaster seemed just around the corner' (Holliss and Sibley 1988). Or that a mouse would climb up onto Walt's drawing board to be fed food scraps. But Dave Iwerks, Ub's son, recalls a quite different version of the origin of the Mickey Mouse symbol: 'It's pretty clear now that Mickey was Ub's character'. Ub had taken a sketch of Oswald the Rabbit and rounded the eyes and ears to steal Oswald back from Charles Mintz (a film distributor who hired away Iwerks–Disney animators).

A more complex question is what is the symbolism of Mickey Mouse? Mickey Mouse was preceded and over-shadowed in popularity by Felix the Cat, and before Mickey the Iwerks–Disney partnership turned out cartoons featuring 'Oswald the Rabbit'. Oswald the Rabbit, and later Mickey Mouse, was, by many accounts, an imitation of Felix the Cat and the personality of one of Walt's idols, Charlie Chaplin.

How is Mickey Mouse produced? Originally, Ub, a prodigious artist, simply drew 700 sketches a day and inked them. Walt however, took up the management of the production process: infatuated, like most other animation houses, with Taylorism, he hired less-skilled artists (mostly women) to do the inking work at lower wages. When Walt insisted that Ub specialize his work tasks on just doing key drawings (where movements changed) so that lesser-skilled and less expensive worker/artists could do all the in-between drawings, Ub left on 21 January 1930. Walt was treating Ub in ways symbolic of how managers and owners treat employees by routinizing his job tasks, breaking up his artistic routines, and distributing them to other workers. Mickey Mouse and other symbols were created on an assembly line involving many people. Yet everything went out as skillfully and scientifically crafted images. Walt is symbolized in official corporate history as the founder of modern factory practices of animation. However, historians have documented that Walt copied his administrative procedures from a 1920 book by Edwin Lutz that summarized the applications of Taylor's Scientific Management to animation. Contrary to the spin of official Disney stories, John Randolph Bray, not Walt Disney, was the Henry Ford of animation. Walt, like other animators of his day, imitated Bray's administrative methods in order to Taylorize animation and employ a hierarchy of gang bosses, speed bosses, and repair bosses in order to exploit less skilled women and children as a source of cheap labour. Ub, in my view, symbolizes the end of premodern craftsmanship and skilled apprenticeship training and the rise of modern systems of rational factory production in the animation industry. At this stage in history, the corporate symbolism of 'progress,' 'scientific,' and 'efficiency' legitimated the deskilling and gender-specialities of what was formerly artists' craftwork. Males did skilled work and women and children less skilled tasks.

Symbolism and corporate control

During the 1930s and 1940s the corporate symbolism revolved around 'family' metaphors. Walt considered himself as father to his 'boys' – his term for the male animators, storymen, and gag writers – and 'girls' – his term for the women doing the inking and repetitive drawing work. Disney sold their employees the symbolism of being 'one big happy family', He reinforced the family metaphor by encouraging his boys and girls to bring in their relatives to work for the 'Disney family'. Boys were strongly reprimanded (even fired) for cursing in front of the girls. Families required loyalty to the father figure and to his personally selected staff. Family members worked all hours of the day or night for their paternalistic hero. While Walt could drink on the job, curse, and have facial hair, these freedoms were not extended to his 'family members'. But on 29 May 1941, the family symbolism was dealt a blow when 293 employees went on strike over parochial codes of work behaviour (e.g. having to punch a time clock to get a drink of water) and salary.

The official Disney writers symbolized the strikers as 'militant activists' or 'misguided boys and girls'. Walt, believing his 'family members' had betrayed him, took pictures of the strikers on the picket lines and taped them to his office wall. He then fired each and every one, 25 immediately and others over the next decade. He also gave testimony to the House Un-American Activities Committee to stall the career of Babbitt (along with Hilberman and Sorrell) and to repay them for attempting to unionize Disney Studios. When the National Labour Relations Board required Walt to reinstate Babbitt, Walt fired him again. And when this did not work, Walt demanded that no member of the studio speak to Babbitt. Walt Disney, it is said, had the historical record altered by seeing to it that references to a striking manager named Arthur Babbitt were purged from the Disney historical archives (Boje, 1995: 1008, 1015).

Organizational symbolism at Disney shifted from the metaphor of the family to the 'theatre' with the opening of the first theme park in the 1950s. Disney employees ceased being 'family members' and became 'members of the cast' who wore 'costumes' instead of 'uniforms' and played 'roles' instead of doing 'jobs'. And customers became 'guests'. 'When Disneyland employees went on strike in the mid-1980s, it was as much over the two conflicting contexts of interpretation – whether work was to be seen as drama or family – as anything else' (Eisenberg and Goodall 1993: 39). The family symbolism is still popular among many corporations.

Global and local symbols

As Disney Enterprises established theme parks in France and Japan, organizational symbolism once again became a problem. For example, in Europe, 'Snow White and the Seven Dwarfs' and 'Pinocchio' were seen as over-simplified stories taken from well known German and other European countries' writers. Walt's vision of Middle America as expressed in Fantasyland, Frontierland, and Adventureland, and posthumously, Toontown, had to be adapted to European and Asian consumers. The Japanese have intensified the efficiency, cleanliness, and safety aspects of Disneyland because it fits their preference for order and harmony. The Main Street USA exhibit at Disneyland and Disney World (US) has been replaced by a World Bazaar and the robot President Lincoln has been replaced by a robot crane. Even Mickey Mouse is a bit more stylish and non-Japanese employees are not allowed to wear nametags, so that the *gaijin* can be distinguished from the Japanese.

The name tag marginalization of others, especially Koreans, is not unlike the ways blacks are marginalized to non-show positions in US Disney theme parks (Van Maanen 1992: 23). EuroDisney, on the other hand, had to make some French twists to its organizational symbolism, for example, admitting the national origins of various theme park stories. And Europeans did not take to chairs being bolted to the floor in fast-food style restaurants at EuroDisney. One French intellectual referred to EuroDisney as a 'cultural Chernobyl' and to Disney employment as 'gum-chewing jobs'. French women employed by Disney were infuriated by the dress code stating that 'appropriate undergarments be worn at all times, without transparent, wild colors, or fancy designs', and that 'skirts must be 4 cm above the knee' (Van Maanen 1992: 27). The Tayloristic queuing, automated movements of masses of people, and batched rides and assembly line processes are much less fun at EuroDisney than in Japan, where moving through the machine symbolizes a good time.

Postmodernist interpretations of Disney symbolism

For the radical Baudrillard (1983, 1987), Disney symbols bear no relation to any reality or the structural relationship between 'sign' (subject) and 'signified' (object). Baudrillard (1983) saw in Disneyland the manifestation of hyperreality, 'which like a helium-filled Mickey Mouse balloon, lets us go into the hyperreal' (Fjellman 1992: 301). Baudrillard (1988: 55) sees the US as becoming more and more like Disneyland and Disneyland is 'a parody of the world of the imagination'. Baudrillard presents the most radical position, the implosion of meaning, so that symbols float in hyperreality (i.e. simulations piled upon simulations that substitute symbolism for reality). For example, symbols (characters) from movies, cartoons, concert and other events are sold on T-shirts and become themes for TV series, books, and theme parks that continue the commodification cycle.

Lyotard posits the end of grand narratives, preferring local stories and symbols fixed in local webs and networks of signification. Others take a more affirmative position, elevating values of equality, democracy and ecology to sort out organizational behaviour. Or they are sceptical (e.g. Debord) without surrendering the possibility of grand narrative and the study of meaning (See Rosenau 1992 and Best and Kellner 1997 for good discussions on this point).

Jameson (1983) looks at the 'creeping surrealism' of Disney that has invaded the modern world. The symbols of Disney, like many other corporations, are being mass-produced with no attention to origin or uniqueness. Denzin argues 'the industrial age produces the mirror of production, in which men are induced to believe that their labor (use value) defines their worth (exchange value)'. And many people relate to Mickey and the Magic Kingdom as if they were real, suspending assessment of reality in order to enjoy the shock of the Disney experience. Fjellman (1992: 301) suggests that 'Disneyland functions as an "imaginary effect" concealing that reality no more exists outside than inside the bounds of the artificial perimeter'. For me, Disney is as Baudrillard argues an instance of hyperreality, but one still I think rooted in the modernist story machine. However, the employees who developed the rides and perform in the shows for a minimum wage see a postmodern hyperreality of simulation where the reality of Disney work is 'smile or be fired'.

Interplay of premodern, modern and postmodern symbolism

The point of this section has been to show that symbolism can be approached from structuralist, functionalist, and other paradigms pointed out by Burrell and Morgan (1979). Yet the important insights, I think, come from what falls between the various paradigms and their rhizomatic relationships. Thus, for example, Disney is a mix of modern Tayloristic theme park and story machine along with some symbolic features that can be characterized as postmodern. Hopefully, this brief account of organizational symbolism at Disney has been sufficient to demonstrate an intermingling of premodern, modern, and postmodern discourses and to show that organizational symbolism has done some dynamic shifts over time, such as in the switch from 'family' to 'theatre' symbolism. Not only has the Magic Kingdom symbolism changed over time, but the symbolism recipe is slightly altered to fit cultural tastes around the world.

3 Conclusions

When Pondy, Frost, Morgan, Dandridge and others met in 1979 to define the field of 'organizational symbolism', they established a visionary programme of multi-paradigm inquiry. Their pioneering work planted organizational symbolism as a diverse field with many paradigms and even anticipated the kinds of interplay between modern and postmodern interpretation that I summarized in my example of Disney. The field has a healthy controversy between the functional managerialists seeking symbolic control and more recent, radical critical postmodern positions resisting such control. In this overview I have sought to draw attention to postmodern paradigms that were under-theorized in the Burrell and Morgan (1979) model, which has served to somewhat constrain what gets recognized in organizational symbolism work. One limitation of the pioneers is that the four-paradigm model has become a symbolic icon defining organization symbolism, limiting initial work to less 'radical' cells. Nevertheless as Boyce (1995, 1996) artfully shows, organizational symbolism research can be organized to fit within the four cells.

Early corporate culture research did not address either deeper psychodynamic or political dynamic or hegemonic and ideological contexts of symbolism (Van Buskirk and McGrath (1999: 85). Structural functionalist studies of symbolism in *synchronic* (one time shot) analyses continue to ignore historicity and process dynamics. Pettigrew (1979) argued early on that symbols develop their meaning over (*diachronic)* time as they are used in social interaction and Van Maanen (1977) asserts that symbols are maintained in ongoing social interaction (see also Feldman 1996: 116).

It is only recently that Pfeffer's (1981) bifurcation of 'substantive action' and 'symbolic action' has been called into question (Feldman 1996: 115–17; Fulop and Linstead 1999: 103–4). The debate is framed as symbolism-as-cause in objective reality versus symbolism-as-context in social reality. As Weick (1983: 27) summarizes 'despite repeated appeals for contextual inquiry and sensitivity to context … no one is exactly sure what is being requested or how to produce it'.

And so, given its ongoing contests, research on organizational symbolism will continue.

Further reading

(References cited in the text marked *)

* Baudrillard, J. (1983) *Simulations*, New York: Semiotext(e), Inc. (Essays about where nothing is real, where everything is a simulation. Even the real and our illusion of real aren't possible.)
* Baudrillard, J. (1987) *Forget Foucault*, New York: Semiotext(e), Inc. (Baudrillard's reading of Foucault's writings about power. Power uses spectacle and symbol to seduce and make us complicit in forms of desire.)
* Baudrillard, J. (1988) *America*, London: Verso. (Series of essays on postmodern and simulated aspects of America e.g. 'Caution: objects in mirror may be closer than they appear', (1).)
* Best, S. and Kellner, D. (1997) *The Postmodern Turn*, New York/London: The Guilford Press. (A review of how the postmodern turn has taken place in a variety of fields including organization studies. Good starting point on Debord's work on spectacle.)
* Boje, David M. (1995) 'Stories of the storytelling organization: A postmodern analysis of Disney as 'Tamara-land', *Academy of Management Journal* 38 (4): 997–1035. (Research article that shows the postmodern interplay of dominant and marginal stories and symbols in the history of the Disney enterprise.)
* Boyce, M. (1995) 'Collective centering and collective sense-making in the stories and storytelling of one organization', *Organization Studies* 16 (1): 107–37. (Applies storytelling organizational theory and symbolism to a case study.)
* Boyce, M. (1996) 'Organizational story and storytelling: A critical review', *Journal of Organizational Change Management* 9 (5). (Review of key studies of organization storytelling and symbolism are examined and challenges to the application of story work in organizations are presented.)
* Burrell, G. and Morgan, G. (1979) *Sociological Paradigms and Organizational Analysis*, London: Heinemann. (Applies four paradigms of radical humanist, radical structuralist, interpretive, and functionalist to organization theory.)
Dandridge, T.C., Mitroff, T. and Joyce, W. (1980) 'Organizational symbolism: a topic to expand organizational analysis,' *Academy of Management Review* 5: 77–82. (Early review of symbolism application to management.)
* Deleuze, G. and Guattari, F. (1987) *A Thousand Plateaus: Capitalism and Schizophrenia*, trans. B. Massumi. Minneapolis, MN: University of Minnesota Press. (Advanced treatment of symbolism to postmodern condition.)

* Eisenberg, E.M. and Goodall, H.L., Jr. (1993) *Organizational Communication: Balancing Creativity and Constraint*, New York: St. Martin's Press. (Among other treatments of symbolism are examples of Disney's use of symbols.)

* Feldman, S.P. (1996) 'Management in context: culture and organizational change.' In S. Linstead, R. Grafton Small and P. Jeffcutt (eds) *Understanding Management*, London: Sage. (Feldman rethinks assumptions about symbolism, such as looking at symbols in context, in an organization study of a telephone company.)

* Fjellman, S.M. (1992) *Vinyl Leaves: Walt Disney World and America*, Boulder, CO: Westview Press. (A postmodern look at symbolism at Disney.)

* Fulop, L. and Linstead, S. (1999) *Management: A Critical Text*, Australia: Macmillan Education Australia Pty Ltd. (Provides a critique of Pfeffer's dualism of symbolic and substantive management.)

* Holliss, R. and Sibley, B. (1988) *The Disney Story*, London: Octopus Books. (Gives a look at the history and symbolism of Disney that is beyond the official side of the story.)

* Jameson, F. (1983) 'Postmodernism and consumer society', in H. Foster (ed.) *The Anti-aesthetic: Essays on Postmodern Culture*, Port Townsend, WN: Bay Press. (A wide-ranging essay on, among other things, symbols in postmodern consumption and culture.)

Lutz, E.G. (1920) *Animated Cartoons: How they are made, their origin and development*. New York: Scribers. (A seminal example of the Taylorism applied to animation.)

* Morgan, G., Frost, P.J. and Pondy, L.R. (1983) 'Organizational symbolism', in L.R. Pondy, P.J. Frost, G. Morgan and T.C. Dandridge (eds) *Organizational Symbolism,* Greenwich, CN: JAI Press Inc. (The founding fathers' review of organizational symbolism using a variation on the Burrell and Morgan framework.)

* Pettigrew, A.M. (1979) 'On studying organizational culture', *Administrative Science Quarterly* 24: 570–81. (An early call to study symbolism as well as organizational culture over time instead of as a snapshot.)

* Pfeffer, J. (1991) 'Organization theory and structural perspectives on management', *Journal of Management* 17 (4): 789–904. (Argued for differentiating symbolic management from substantive management.)

Pfeffer, J. and Salancik, G.R. (1978) *The External Control of Organizations: A Resource Dependence Perspective*, New York: Harper and Row.

Pondy, L.R., Frost, P.J., Morgan, G. and Dandridge, T.C. (eds) (1983) *Organizational Symbolism*, Greenwich, CT: JAI Press. (A collection of original essays on the possibilities of organizational symbolsim).

* Pondy, L.R. and Mitroff, I. (1979) 'Beyond open system models of organization', in B.M. Staw (ed.) *Research in Organizational Behaviour*, vol. 1. Greenwich, CT: JAI Press. (An application of Bouldings' levels of systems that included recognition of levels that involved symbolic action.)

* Rosenau, P. (1992) *Post-modernism and the Social Sciences: Insights, Inroads, and Intrusions*, Princeton, NJ: Princeton University Press. (Reviews the trends in postmodern theory ranging from affirmative to more sceptical approaches.)

* Van Buskirk, W. and McGrath, D. (1999) 'Organizational cultures as holding environments: a psychodynamic look at organizational symbolism', *Human Relations* 52 (6): 805–32. (Offers a rare look at the hegemonic and ideological aspects of organizational symbolism.)

* Van Maanen, J. (1977) *Organizational Careers: Some New Perspectives*, New York: John Wiley and Sons. (Demonstrates that developing symbol meaning is a part of on-going interaction.)

* Van Maanen, J. (1992) 'Displacing Disney: Some notes on the flow of culture,' *Qualitative Sociology* 15 (1): 5–35. (Good examples of the use of Disney symbols to marginalize careers on the basis of ethnicity and race.)

* Weick, K. (1983) 'Managerial thought in the context of action', in S. Srivastava (ed.) *The Executive Mind*, San Francisco: Jossey-Bass. (Calls for context-based inquiry into symbolism in organization studies.)

The working of the microcosm

Motivation and satisfaction

André Büssing

1 **Introduction**
2 **Work motivation: past research and future developments**
3 **Work satisfaction: its level, causes and consequences**
4 **A dynamic view of work satisfaction**
5 **Future directions in work motivation and work satisfaction**

Overview

Work motivation and work satisfaction continue to be major topics in organizational sciences because it is assumed that they exert important influence on action and behaviour in organizations. However, as opposed to so-called *hard factors* like hardware, costs and benefits etc., motivation and satisfaction are often called *soft factors*. These soft factors constitute hidden realities in organizations which can not be measured in a direct, objective way. Research results concerning these soft factors do not provide much evidence for a relationship between motivation/ satisfaction and action respectively behaviour. Despite these not very encouraging results, work motivation and satisfaction are regarded as important contributions to human resources in organizations; one should not only take these contributions seriously with respect to organizational culture and identity but also take them into account in managing effectiveness and quality. The chapter gives a short description of well-known work motivation theories which can roughly be divided into process and content-oriented types. Theories of both types show considerable limitations, especially with respect to the prediction of action from motivation. Therefore, several modern theories of motivation, volition and action are introduced. Some of them are distant ('distal'), others are close ('proximal') to action, and some of them allow for a link between the content, process and action perspective of motivation. It appears that these integrative approaches to motivation and volition of goal-directed action may substantially contribute to a better prediction of work satisfaction, employee withdrawal or job performance. Work satisfaction is the most prominent result of work motivation. Its research continues to produce a large number of results relevant to organizational behaviour. However, while work satisfaction is one of the most frequently studied concepts in industrial and organizational psychology, it also suffers from critical shortcomings, especially its mostly theory-free concepts and the very large proportions of satisfied workers and employees in almost all studies undertaken in recent decades, up to the point that more and more researchers speak of these results as having an artificial character. To overcome these problems, a new dynamic view of work satisfaction is presented by introducing a model of different forms of work satisfaction. This model distinguishes forms ('qualities') and not quantities of work satisfaction and allows the processes behind these forms to be explained. By differentiating forms of satisfaction (e.g. resigned, stabilized, progressive) this model permits us to understand the high percentages of satisfied employees in earlier studies. Finally, the chapter points to future directions and discusses the implications of work motivation and work satisfaction with regard to work design and organizational development.

1 Introduction

Motivation continues to be a major topic of industrial and organizational psychology as well as of organizational behaviour. Motivational concepts, such as expectancy, valence, goal setting, self-efficacy, self-regulation, are often used to analyse and to predict a wide range of individual expressions relevant to organizations such as attitudes, perceptions, emotions and behaviour, as expressed in work satisfaction, stress and burnout, withdrawal, turnover, absenteeism, performance etc. Progress in work motivation research has led to a wide scope of results about both the factors and the processes of behaviour and performance in the workplace. This growth of new ideas and concepts from allied fields of psychology is accompanied by increasing concern that influential theories and concepts of work motivation are not sufficient for addressing relevant problems in organizations. For example, to date, prevailing theories of work motivation cannot predict why knowledge is not transformed into action in many areas of organizations, neither have they substantially contributed to distinguishing the effects of motivational processes in simple and complex jobs, the effects of motivation in the interrelationship between work and non-work, or how motivation operates in work groups and teams, etc. Therefore, the aim of this chapter is not only to summarize past research. Rather, new developments that show promising advances in work motivation theory will be briefly presented.

2 Work motivation: past research and future developments

Work motivation theories are commonly categorized into two groups: content- and process-oriented types of theories (Campbell and Pritchard 1976). The first group of theories (see Figure 1) concerns central human needs and motives such as basic or higher order needs, human needs for existence, relatedness and growth, motivational and hygiene factors, intrinsic or extrinsic motivation respectively for particular aspects of work such as feedback or autonomy that are supposed to relate to motivation. On the other hand, the second group of theories (see Figure 1) deals with process variables that are posited to determine cognitive choices for action. Theories of the process type (e.g. the Value–Instrumentality–Expectancy (VIE) model or achievement motivation theories) concentrate on the process of choice for behaviour and emphasize two determinants of choice: the individual's expectation and the individual's subjective valuation of expected consequences associated with alternative actions at the workplace (for more detailed overviews on work motivation theories see e.g. Kanfer 1994; Kleinbeck *et al.* 1990; Leonard, Beauvais and Scholl 1999; Locke 1997; Locke and Henne 1986).

Both content- and process-oriented theories of work motivation show considerable limitations. With respect to content theories, it seems impossible to identify needs and motives that are universal, i.e. important and effective for everybody independent of time and space. Moreover, the impact of constructs from content theories on behaviour and performance is frequently spurious and indirect. What is lacking is a clarification of the mechanisms by which specific needs and motives lead to specific behaviour. However, while one should assume that these mechanisms are subject to process theories, these theories actually focus almost exclusively on the cognitive processes underlying choice, rather than any other part of the motivational process, for example by calculating the expectancy (subjective probability) of various possible outcomes (e.g. good or bad quality of a certain work behaviour), the instrumentality (subjective correlation) of these outcomes for subsequent outcomes (e.g. reduction of income because of slower but high quality work or positive feedback from supervisors for fewer inaccuracies and errors), and finally the valence (subjective value) of these second order outcomes in terms of Vroom's VIE model. One cannot expect to predict actual behaviour from the VIE model because it is only able to determine motivational states for certain behaviour or the most probable choice for a certain effort. Hence, the process theories that dominated the published industrial/organizational literature during the 1960s and 1970s posit almost entirely cognitive choice or cognitive evaluation models based on the expectancy or the equity–inequity theory.

Since it is common to evaluate and compare theories of work motivation by the extent to which they are able to predict job behaviour and job performance correctly, we should be concerned by the fact that the content as well as most of the process theories of work motivation are more or less 'distal', i.e. distant from action. Therefore, we have clustered (work) motivation theories and their associated constructs by their 'proximity' (i.e. closeness) to action according to Kanfer (1994) and by the traditional distinction into content with regard to process theories. The taxonomy in Figure 1 reveals that modern (work) motivation theories are proximal to action as well as typically process oriented. They comprise goals and self-regulation as dominant constructs.

Among these theories the goal-setting paradigm, established by Locke and Latham and their colleagues, has dominated work motivation research during the past two decades (for an integrated model see Locke, 1997). According to this theory, goals influence task behaviour through four mechanisms: directing attention, mobilizing on-task effort, encouraging task persistence, and facilitating strategy development. The theory states two important goal attributes: intensity and content. While goal intensity refers to the strength of goals in terms of importance and commitment, goal content is directed towards aspects such as difficulty, specificity and complexity. Most research has focused on the effects of goal content in the sense of difficulty and specificity by comparing a non-specific goal assignment condition such as 'do your best' with a specific and difficult assigned goal condition such as 'process x orders this week without any mistakes'. Because numerous studies show support for the positive impact of moderately difficult and specific goal assignment on work performance, goal-setting techniques enjoy widespread use in industry. However, studies examining an assignment of goals and feedback cycles indicate that the combination of moderately difficult and specific goals along with performance feedback and, therefore, an enhancement of self regulation resulted in higher levels of performance than either goal assignment or feedback alone.

Self-regulation and control theories relevant to work motivation have been posited, for example by Bandura (1997), Carver and Scheier (1998) or Kuhl (1992). Even though these theories are rooted in different traditions of psychology they have some basic theoretical and methodological positions in common, e.g. goal orientation or (cybernetic) self-regulation modelling. Altogether, these different theories provide complementary, rather than contradictory, perspectives. Empirical research testing the predictions of work behaviour and work performance derived from these models has generally been supportive. Nevertheless, none of these theories takes an integrative perspective in linking distal constructs such as needs, motives, dispositions, flow, affect etc. and proximal constructs of work motivation such as goal setting and self-regulation (for an overview of self-regulation and control theories see Gollwitzer and Bargh 1996).

Recent developments in (work) motivation theory try to establish this link. An important attempt is the Rubicon model by Heckhausen and Gollwitzer (see Gollwitzer and Bargh 1996) and the associated theory of self-regulation by Kuhl (e.g. 1992). The Rubicon model considers the motivational/volitional phases of

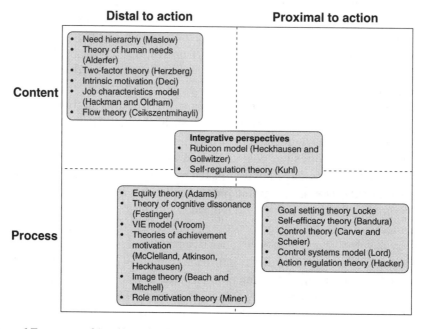

Figure 1 Taxonomy of (work) motivation theories

(work) behaviour while the models mentioned earlier (see Figure 1) are restricted to one or two specific phases. The Rubicon model connects motivation with volition and distinguishes between four phases of motivation/volition with respect to action: weighing (first motivational or choice phase), planning (volitional phase), acting (volitional phase) and evaluating (second motivational phase). Crossing the Rubicon means bridging the gap between weighing and willing, between motivation and intention (see Figure 2). The model combines distal aspects of motivation as well as proximal constructs of goal setting and self-regulation. Therefore, despite the fact that little is known so far about the validity of the Rubicon model for predicting job behaviour and performance, it appears that this integrative approach, or rather 'frame', to motivation and volition of goal-directed action may substantially contribute to better prediction of work satisfaction, employee withdrawal or job performance (see Kanfer 1994).

3 Work satisfaction: its level, causes and consequences

Departing from the common use of terminology, we prefer the term *work* satisfaction over job satisfaction because subjective views of people at work are influenced not only by aspects of the job such as task characteristic, colleagues, pay etc., for example, but they also reflect the larger context of a job's organizational, work and political environment; this anchors work satisfaction as a concept in organizational socialization.

Already 25 years ago Locke (1976) identified over 3,000 studies dealing with different aspects of work satisfaction. There are several reasons for this strong interest in work satisfaction, including the presumed ease of measurement with paper-and-pencil devices and the common-sense linkages between satisfaction and other mainstream concepts such as leadership, performance, reward systems, group processes, and so forth. Even though in recent years there has been a cutback in the total number of papers, research activities dealing with work satisfac-

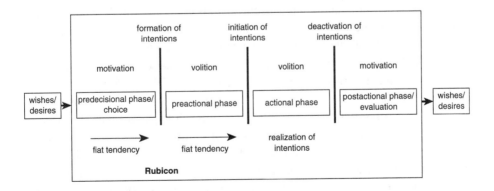

Figure 2 Rubicon model of action releasing by Heckhausen and Gollwitzer (according to Gollwitzer 1996)

tion are still quite alive. Work satisfaction continues to be a major area of interest in the study of industrial and organizational psychology. Indeed, a large proportion of the empirically oriented articles published in this field include work satisfaction as an independent, dependent and/or moderating variable (e.g. Cranny, Smith and Stone 1992; Spector 1997).

Although a large body of research has been accumulated there are still major shortcomings in work satisfaction research. One of these is the loose coupling between its few theories and its measurement. It is a paradoxical situation that while work satisfaction is one of the most frequently studied concepts in industrial and organizational psychology, it is also one of the most theory-free concepts in the field. That is, a 'pleasurable or positive emotional state resulting from the appraisal of one's job or job experience' (Locke 1976: 1300) or 'the achievement of one's job values in the work situation results in the pleasurable emotional state known as *job satisfaction*' (Locke and Henne 1986: 21) is understood as work satisfaction to this day. Most of the definitions of work satisfaction are quite similar, although they may differ in the conceptualization of what they conceive as 'achievement of one's job values'.

Work satisfaction research can be grouped into three major categories: causes and moderators of (dis)satisfaction, consequences of (dis)satisfaction, and surveys of satisfaction levels. Some of the *causes and moderators* related to work satisfaction have included conditions such as job quality, union membership, autonomy, job tension and flexible working hours as well as personal variables such as realistic expectations, self-esteem, value importance or sex differences (see Locke and Henne 1986). With respect to the *consequences* of work satisfaction, research has focused on some commonly presumed forms of job behaviour such as turnover, absenteeism and on-job performance. Meta-analytic studies on turnover and absenteeism clarify that one cannot expect a strong relationship between work satisfaction and turnover as well as absenteeism because correlations with work satisfaction do not reach beyond −.40 for both absenteeism and turnover (e.g. Hackett and Guion 1985). Apart from this overall result, the relationship between satisfaction and absenteeism is generally much less consistent than that reported between satisfaction and turnover, and research on both turnover and absenteeism with respect to work satisfaction is affected by some severe methodological problems related to the conceptualization and measurement of absenteeism and turnover (e.g. Hackett and Guion 1985). Moreover, various meta-analyses confirm a rather weak relationship between attitude-based measurement of work satisfaction and different kinds of job performance such as supervisor ratings, quality, new accounts etc. Correlations from these studies range between .15 and .40 (e.g. Iaffaldano and Muchinsky 1985). Although Katzell, Thompson and Guzzo (1992) could show that intervention studies imply a comparably stronger link between work satisfaction and job performance, the results from work satisfaction research in total have so far provided only a little support for the solution of practical problems such as work redesign or other kinds of interventions in organizations.

Most studies apparently continue to use a relatively a-theoretical, attitude-based measurement via questionnaires to estimate work satisfaction. The wide acceptance of this method of work satisfaction measurement and its abundant use in research – almost to the extent that some researchers see aspects of a 'throw-away' variable (Staw 1984: 630) – is one side of the problem. The other is the high rate of survey studies on satisfaction levels which find a large proportion of satisfied employees. These results seem to be widespread, which means that they seem to be especially independent of population and culture. For example, in the USA, Weaver (1980) found 88 per cent satisfied among 4,709 persons between 1972 and 1978. Similar results can be found independent of country and the specific type of attitude measurement. In Germany, for example, several studies found more than 80 per cent or even 90 per cent satisfied among full-time employed blue- and white-collar workers. Our inspection of a large number of work satisfaction studies since 1980 does not indicate a decrease in these large proportions of satisfied employees in recent studies.

What are the reasons for this impressive proportion of satisfied persons? In recent years, quite a few researchers have become more and more critical and talk about traditional work satisfaction results having an artificial character. Taking into account the diverse negative conditions stated in many studies, for example accidents, insufficient work conditions and work environment, high division of labour, absenteeism and turnover, the positive work satisfaction results in these studies seem somehow superficial. This is not only true for industry, trade and administration. Similar high percentages of satisfied personnel were also found in healthcare settings such as hospitals (see Büssing 1992).

4 A dynamic view of work satisfaction

Work satisfaction research traditionally uses attitude-based measurements, as mentioned above. This method of conceptualization and measurement is criticized for several reasons. Three of these reasons will be outlined. First, despite the large number of studies, we do not find many reliable results for determinants and consequences of work satisfaction (see above). Second, attitude-based measurement of work satisfaction is prone to distortion by several well-known effects, e.g. social desirability or cognitive dissonance. Third, attitude-based measurement of work satisfaction does not consider situational factors such as controllability of work conditions. However, from work satisfaction results gained by attitude measurement it is hard to glean much information about the amount of variance explained by the person or by the situation at work. Therefore, critics point to the important validity problems of traditional attitude measurement of work satisfaction that supposedly supports the artificially high work satisfaction rating patterns mentioned before. With respect to these critics, it seems not to be sufficient to measure work satisfaction in quantitative terms, for example the amount of satisfaction. Instead, work satisfaction should also be looked at in terms of quality, which seems to be an important perspective.

One basic point in this debate is, among others, that traditional concepts of work satisfaction and related methods of measurement are not dynamic. Another point touches on the person–environment perspective. Work satisfaction has to be interpreted as a product of an interaction process between a person and his or her work situation. Variables such as control or power to regulate this interaction and, therefore, the possibilities to influence the work situation play an important role. Therefore, we should see work satisfaction in a different, qualitative perspective. In this light, work satisfaction is not merely a product but rather part of a complex process. Thus, we have to consider at least changes in the work situation by a person depending upon his or her situational control and motives/aspirations on the one hand, as well as changes in the person and his or her motives/aspirations etc. on the other.

In recent studies by Büssing and his group (e.g. Büssing and Bissels 1998; Büssing *et al.* 1999a), a dynamic concept of work satisfaction was analysed. The model was originally proposed by Bruggemann in 1974 (e.g. Bruggemann, Groskurth and Ulich 1975) and introduced to the English-speaking community by Büssing (1992). It explains under which conditions and by which psychological processes qualitatively different forms of work satisfaction evolve, and what the respective consequences for those forms are. This model depends on an interaction view of work satisfaction as shown in Figure 3. It incorporates the widely used understanding of work satisfaction as the degree of fit between the *actual work situation* and *personal aspirations*, as for example in equity theory, VIE modelling of work satisfaction and P–E fit models. Individuals are said to be comparing characteristics of the work situation with a set of personal expectations, motives or needs. The personal component in this comparison is closely linked to the central motivational variable of the model, namely the *level of aspiration* which is conceptualized as an action-related goal in an individual's structure of personal goals. Moreover, the original model by Bruggemann was extended on theoretical grounds by *perceived controllability at work* as a further variable to the original model (see Büssing 1992), arguing that motivation for control ontogenetically precedes and regulates any human activity and that control is a 'cross-cultural and historical universal' (Heckhausen and Schulz 1995); furthermore, perceived controllability of one's work situation serves as a primary means to regulate the person–work interaction and contributes significantly to processes of well-being (e.g. Terry and Jimmieson 1999).

According to this basic understanding, the model distinguishes between six different forms of work satisfaction. The following four variables are central to the model: (1) differences between actual value of the work situation and personal aspirations, (2) perceived controllability, (3) changes in the level of aspiration and (4) problem-solving behaviour (coping). According to this model, work satisfaction is developed in a four-step process which leads to six forms of work satisfaction or dissatisfaction (see Figure 3).

In a first step, a comparison between personal aspirations on the one hand and the work situation on the other leads to congruent or discrepant outcomes, and

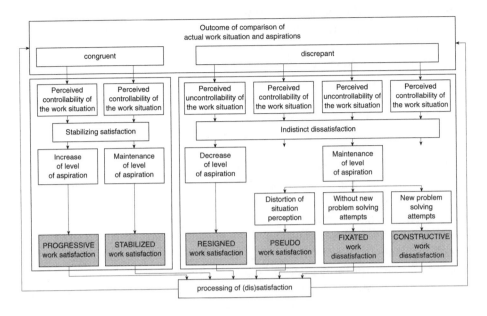

Figure 3 Different forms of work satisfaction according to the extended model
Source: Bruggeman *et al.* (1975); Büssing (1992)

dependent upon the perceived controllability and/or uncontrollability of the work situation, stabilizing satisfaction or indistinct dissatisfaction is the result.

If a person at this second step is on the whole satisfied with his or her work, two forms of work satisfaction may develop at the third step dependent on changes in the level of aspiration (i.e. progressive and stabilized satisfaction). In case of an increase in the level of aspiration, *progressive satisfaction* would follow, whereas *stabilized satisfaction* would be the consequence of a maintained level of aspiration (see Figure 3).

The remaining four forms of work (dis)satisfaction develop on the grounds of a feeling of indistinct dissatisfaction with one's work. In the case of diffuse dissatisfaction at the second step, the model suggests two different outcomes for the level of aspiration according to the third step: decrease or maintenance.

A decrease in the level of aspiration should lead to what is called *resigned work satisfaction*. This form of work satisfaction is supported by results from qualitative interviews which find quite a number of people adjusting themselves to work situations either by decreasing or by shifting their motivation and aspirations to non-work activities. The high percentage of satisfied workers – as often found in the studies presented above – can be claimed to be caused by a more or less large proportion of workers who have passively resigned from their work situation. Therefore, according to this model, resigned satisfaction is only one out of three forms of work satisfaction and must be distinguished from these other forms.

Maintaining one's level of aspiration in the case of diffuse work dissatisfaction can result in three forms, of which the *pseudo-work satisfaction* received the least empirical confirmation. For further research this form was disregarded as the authors doubted the possibility of finding valid operationalizations. The model suggests that the two other forms, *fixated* and *constructive work dissatisfaction*, are closely connected to the coping options, coping resources and problem-solving behaviour a person can mobilize. These coping options, coping resources and problem-solving behaviour patterns of a person are relevant variables at the fourth step, on the way of developing different forms of work satisfaction. Both fixated and constructive work dissatisfaction seem to depend largely upon the well-known coping options in organizations, such as social support at work in one respect and what is called in its abbreviated form 'coping resources' – abilities to use these options – in another respect. However, in contrast to the fixated dissatisfied, the constructive dissatisfied try to master the situation by problem-solving attempts.

Comparing the six different forms of satisfaction and dissatisfaction, constructive dissatisfaction obviously takes a counterpart to resigned work satisfaction (see Table 1 for further description of all forms).

The model of different forms of work satisfaction points to the insufficiency of a merely quantitative view, even if this view is complex and comprises several facets such as colleagues, work conditions, work content, promotion, and so on.

Table 1 Different forms of work satisfaction

Progressive work satisfaction: A person feels satisfied with the work. By increasing the level of aspiration a person tries to achieve an even higher level of satisfaction. Therefore, a 'creative dissatisfaction' with respect to some aspects of the work situation can be an integral part of this form.

Stabilized work satisfaction: A person feels satisfied with the job, but is motivated to maintain the level of aspiration and the pleasurable state of satisfaction. An increase of the level of aspiration is concentrated on other areas of life because of few work incentives.

Resigned work satisfaction: A person feels indistinct work satisfaction and decreases the level of aspiration in order to adapt to negative aspects of the work situation on a lower level. By decreasing the level of aspiration a person is able to achieve a positive state of satisfaction again.

Constructive work dissatisfaction: A person feels dissatisfied with the job. While maintaining the level of aspiration a person tries to master the situation by problem-solving attempts on the basis of sufficient frustration tolerance. Moreover, available action concepts supply goal orientation and motivation for altering the work situation.

Fixated work dissatisfaction: A person feels dissatisfied with the job. Maintaining the level of aspiration, a person does not try to master the situation by problem-solving attempts. Frustration tolerance makes defence mechanisms necessary, efforts at problem solving seem beyond any possibility. Therefore, the individual gets stuck with his or her problems and pathological developments cannot be excluded.

Pseudo-work satisfaction: A person feels dissatisfied with the job. Facing unsolvable problems or frustrating conditions at work and maintaining one's level of aspiration, for example because of a specific achievement motivation or because of strong social norms, a distorted perception or a denial of the negative work situation may result in pseudo-work satisfaction.

Therefore, the work satisfaction we usually think of and that we traditionally measure has to be reconsidered and differentiated. Represented by the forms of stabilized, progressive and resigned work satisfaction on the one hand, and by fixated and constructive dissatisfaction on the other, work (dis)satisfaction cannot merely be regarded and used as a product; rather, it has to be seen as a process-oriented outcome of a person–work interaction.

Thus, our approach to work satisfaction emphasizes four key aspects: (a) the model incorporates the breadth of subjective views of people in the sense that forms of work satisfaction result from processing information and individual experiences at work; (b) the posited processes involving the model's constituent variables imply that forms of work satisfaction are essentially dynamic states of varying stability mainly induced by the individual's goals/level of aspiration; (c) these processes are affected by both person and situation variables interacting with each other, i.e. the actual work situation affects personal aspirations just as the realization of personal goals may influence an individual's work situation; and (d) the model provides the rationale for a differentiation of results in traditional job satisfaction studies, allowing one to segregate the persistently high proportions of satisfied employees into qualitatively different forms of work satisfaction.

So far, studies employing the model of different forms of work satisfaction have led to three important results. First, forms of work satisfaction can be validly differentiated according to the model; for example, the proportion of resigned satisfied persons ranges up to 45 per cent while the ratio of constructive dissatisfied reaches 30 per cent in some studies (e.g. Büssing 1992). Second, forms of work satisfaction depend more on situational factors such as perceived controllability at the workplace by the workers than on dispositional factors. Third, forms of work satisfaction do not function like psychological types, i.e. they are not stable over a longer period of time. Even though this model is an important advancement in work satisfaction research, little is known about antecedents and consequences connected with the different forms of work satisfaction. Moreover, so far there has been a lack of substantial research comparing this model with other prevailing concepts of work satisfaction (see Büssing *et al.* 1999a).

5 Future directions in work motivation and work satisfaction

Work motivation research is giving way to new, more complex theories that are proximal to action and that incorporate elements of older theories, especially distal approaches to motivation. Therefore, the sharp distinction between various theories is reduced. The recent advances in work motivation have been more theoretical, however (e.g. Locke 1997). Even though they clearly aid our understanding of behaviour and performance at the workplace, we lack unique and specific applications of modern motivation and volition theory to the workplace. These applications are urgently needed and they will be a promising start to obtaining a better understanding and prediction of work attitudes (e.g. satisfaction), job and organizational behaviour (e.g. turnover, absenteeism, commitment, stress reactions, burnout) and job performance constructs.

It seems that, since expectancy, equity and goal-setting theory had their important impacts on work satisfaction in the 1960s, 1970s and 1980s, we find only limited influence of new developments in work motivation theory on work satisfaction. However, progress in the area of work satisfaction is dependent on advances in work motivation research. This is especially true for the dynamic model of different forms of work satisfaction presented in this entry. It is a person–environment model which assumes a close interdependence between motivational and dispositional variables on the one hand and situational determinants at the workplace on the other. Although models of human need, intrinsic motivation or motivators and dissatisfiers may provide relatively poor prediction of job behaviour and job performance, few researchers would argue that dispositions play no role in sophisticated models of motivation and volition, especially if one takes into account an estimated distribution of explained variance of work satisfaction according to Arvey, Carter and Buerkley (1991): 40 to 60 per cent of work satisfaction variance is associated with situational factors, 10 to 30 per cent account for person factors and about 10 to 20 per cent of the variance is explained by interactive elements. To gain a better understanding of the interdependence between dispositional variables and situational determinants with respect to work satisfaction, one needs a clarification and better (theoretical) understanding of these variables and their interrelation. Some research in this direction has been performed in recent years; for example, Judge *et al.* (1998) proposed the concept of core evaluations (comprised of self-esteem, self-efficacy, locus of control, non-neuroticism) which show direct effects on work and life satisfaction.

The dynamic view provided by the model of different forms of work satisfaction is of special importance to work in complex organizations which offer many possibilities for rapid sociotechnical changes, and therefore demand a high level of adaptability and dynamic behaviour from the structural and technical system as well as from the personnel. That is, differentiation of forms of work satisfaction could have a considerable impact on organizational studies and their consequences. Workers and employees could not just be divided into a large group of satisfied and a small group of dissatisfied as we have done so far; therefore, comfortable work satisfaction figures could not easily underline and justify organizational structures, internal selection and promotion procedures, production processes, and so on. Taking the idea of different forms of work satisfaction seriously, new perspectives for processes in organizational behaviour and conflict should be discussed. First of all, the large group of resigned satisfied identified so far in all studies should be regarded as strong evidence for a failed person–work interaction, and therefore they should be considered necessary reasons to doubt and not to justify, among other things, aspects of organizational structures, internal selection and promotion procedures as well as production processes. According to the results of various studies and especially the ones of our longitudinal study (see Büssing *et al.* 1999a), we must take into account that resigned work satisfaction is related to reduced well-being, performance and effort as well as resistance to change on the person side and – at least – less adaptability and performance on the organization side. Moreover, another remarkable aspect on the person side of resigned satisfaction seems to be reduced goal-setting activities and, closely connected, restricted professional development and job socialization.

Resigned work satisfaction is one variable of influence noteworthy with respect to studies in organizations. Constructive work dissatisfaction is another. Turnover and absenteeism appear to be only one side of this form of work dissatisfaction, and probably not even the most important one. Another side seems to be activities and engagement in organizational change as well as a higher potential for differential goal setting of the constructive dissatisfied. Therefore, this group should not be – in a one-sided perspective – considered a danger for organizational conflict; instead the critical potential of this group should be emphasized with regard to organizational change, adaptability and improvement. A transformation of this potential into organizational change on one side and personal development on the other requires new strategies of conflict management in organizations and a willingness to broaden control at work as well as participation in decision making for the personnel.

More than the other forms of work satisfaction or dissatisfaction, resigned work satisfaction and constructive work dissatisfaction might have remarkable influence on performance and intervention efficiency in organizations. We know by now that resigned satisfaction is closely connected with reduced effort and willingness to adapt to new and complex demands; however, such demands are typical of the daily work in complex and dynamic organizations in global markets. Resigned work satisfaction seems to be an obstruction to change inside the organization and its adaptability to external challenges. Hence, resigned work satisfaction is thought to be accompanied by growing rates of absenteeism, notification of illness, and a reduced quality of work. Therefore, management and other responsible groups in organizations should take a close look at the group of resigned satisfied personnel to prevent negative effects on performance and quality. Managing resigned work satisfaction seems to be a difficult task, as resignation is not a matter of short periods of time. It seems to be much more a consequence of a longer-lasting conflict between individual aspirations on the one hand and organizational structures as well as specific working conditions on the other. Therefore, the cost-effectiveness of strategies regarding resigned work satisfaction should not be questioned: prevention seems to be far more cost-effective than subsequent changes or correction for it.

In the case of constructive dissatisfaction, organizations are faced with a quite different situation. As mentioned earlier, constructive work dissatisfaction might become an impetus to growth in organizations, because constructive dissatisfied personnel mostly show sufficient frustration tolerance and action concepts for new problem-solving attempts. For this reason, their goal orientation and motivation for altering the negative work situation have to become an integral part of an organizational change planned or at least supported by the management. Offering this group of personnel an opportunity to discuss critical issues in quality circles or autonomous teams might give them an even higher feeling of control over the situation and might meet their high motivation for job control and their willingness to change. Aside from intrinsic task-related aspects such as job control, organizations are also faced with corresponding and growing aspirations with respect to extrinsic features of the job such as pay, promotion or flexible as well as reduced working time. Meeting constructive work dissatisfaction is not free. There are structural, task-related and extrinsic, monetary expenses. But by meeting and regulating these problems an organization prepares itself for better outcomes and higher quality. As a result, organizations should basically look at constructive work dissatisfaction in a positive manner. This form of dissatisfaction demands new and intelligent problem-solving attempts by the personnel as well as by the organization. Organizations need highly motivated and qualified personnel to deal with the growing standards of work processes and technology. Organizations that fail to meet these increasing challenges are prone to fail in meeting other challenges of their socio-technical system as well.

Most of the applications of work satisfaction research in business and management (implicitly) rely on the idea that there is a valid satisfaction–performance relationship and that a happy worker is a productive worker. However, as mentioned above, decades ago, well-known reviews of the literature seemed to establish firmly that worker happiness did not necessarily lead to productivity. Recent research, for example by Wright and Staw (1999), tries to resolve the shortcomings of unsuccessful studies in this field by introducing dispositions. The results point to directional as well as to moderating effects, particularly of affective dispositions with regard to performance. That is, according to these results, state and trait variables, such as positive and negative mood and affectivity of employees, seem to have a marked prediction of performance or an influence on the relationship between satisfaction and performance. Not surprisingly, however, these results are criticized for several reasons. The comment by Ledford (1999) on the prediction of mood and affectivity of performance is not only an attempt to place the findings by Wright and Staw (1999) in a larger theoretical context and a critique of the design, methodology and operationalization of key variables. A major concern of Ledford (1999) is associated with the implications which can be drawn from the results on affective dispositions: 'If only trait-based happiness leads to performance, it is pointless to try to make employees happier as a way of improving performance. … This eliminates the arguments for pay levels, workings conditions, job designs, leadership styles, and so on …' (1999: 27). Another way of approaching the complex matter was chosen by Büssing *et al.* (1999b). In a laboratory study, they looked at differences in performance of different forms of work satisfaction; while controlling for a variety of dispositional factors, on the whole the results did reveal a higher rate in performance, particularly for the constructive dissatisfied who did not lower their level of aspiration and who perceived controllability. Although being one of the basic and crucial questions of applied psychology and a concern in many areas of application, the happy productive worker thesis seems still unresolved.

Neither work motivation nor work satisfaction can be restricted to the workplace. When leaving their office or plant, employees and workers do not leave their work experiences, their thoughts, motivation and feelings behind. Indeed, we find a strong interrelationship between life at work and life outside work with respect to work motivation and work satisfaction. And this interrelationship between the two areas of life and its influences on motivation, satisfaction and quality of life in general is rapidly growing, considering decentralized forms of work organization such as telework and telecommuting. This interrelationship includes constructs that are central to motivation and satisfaction, such as changes in level of aspiration or goal-setting. From this viewpoint work satisfaction is not only part of a broader framework including life satisfaction; it also overlaps with roles and their mutual influence in the different areas of life and with the important relationship between work, family and leisure (e.g. Barnett 1998). Not only for purposes of analysis but especially for valid strategies of intervention and organizational design, the work–non-work interdependence should be integrated into work motivation and work satisfaction research.

Further reading

(References cited in the text marked *)

* Arvey, R.D., Carter, G.W. and Buerkley, D.K. (1991) 'Job satisfaction: Dispositional and situational influences', in C.L. Cooper and I.T. Robertson (eds), *International Review of Industrial and Organizational Psychology*, vol. 6: 359–84, Chichester: Wiley. (This review article provides competing explanations for antecedent conditions of job satisfaction by dispositions or situations.)
* Bandura, A. (1997) *Self-efficacy: The Exercise of Control*, New York: Freeman. (This book gives an impressive presentation of Bandura's work on social cognitive theory and self-efficacy which is most important for work motivation theorizing and experimentation.)
* Barnett, R.C. (1998) 'Toward a review and reconceptualization of the work/family literature', *Genetic, Social, and General Psychology Monographs* 124: 125–82. (This article is a thoughtful contribution to the complex interrelation between work and non-work, particularly with regard to work and family.)
* Bruggemann, A., Groskurth, P. and Ulich, E. (1975) *Arbeitszufriedenheit* (Job satisfaction), Bern: Huber. (This book is what can be called a classic on work satisfaction in the German language.)
* Büssing, A. (1992) 'A dynamic view of job satisfaction', *Work & Stress* 6: 239–59. (This article summarizes research on the extended model of different forms of work satisfaction.)
* Büssing, A. and Bissels, T. (1998) 'Different forms of work satisfaction: concept and qualitative research', *European Psychologist* 3: 209–18. (This article provides a qualitative research approach for studying different forms of work satisfaction.)
* Büssing, A., Bissels, T., Fuchs, V. and Perrar, K.-M. (1999a) 'A dynamic model of work satisfaction: qualitative approaches', *Human Relations* 52: 999–1028. (This article comprises quantitative and qualitative results for a validation of different forms of work satisfaction.)
* Büssing, A., Bissels, T., Herbig, B. and Krüsken, J. (1999b) 'Motivation in different forms of job satisfaction: when nursing knowledge is transferred into action and when it is not', in P.M. Le Blanc, M.C.W. Peeters, A. Büssing and W.B. Schaufeli (eds), *Organizational*

Psychology and Health Care: European contributions, pp. 45–64, Munich: Hampp. (The satisfaction and performance relationship is experimentally revisited in this article by using different forms of work satisfaction.)

* Campbell, J.P. and Pritchard, R.D. (1976) 'Motivation theory in industrial and organizational psychology', in M.D. Dunnette (ed.), *Handbook of Industrial and Organizational Psychology*, pp. 63–130, New York: Wiley. (This handbook article is what can be called a classic of work motivation theory in industrial and organizational psychology.)

* Carver, C.S. and Scheier, M.F. (1998) *On the Self-Regulation of Behaviour*, New York: Cambridge University Press. (This book gives a comprehensive insight into the principles of selfregulation with regard to emotion, motivation and action.)

* Cranny, C.J., Smith, P.C. and Stone, E.F. (eds) (1992) *Job Satisfaction – How People Feel About Their Jobs and How It Affects Their Performance*, New York: Lexington. (One of the few readers of recent years providing an overview of job satisfaction concepts and research.)

* Gollwitzer, P.M. and Bargh, J.A. (eds) (1996) *The Psychology of Action: Linking Cognition and Motivation to Behaviour*, New York: Guilford Press. (This book collects important contributions from the psychology of action with respect to self-regulation and control theories.)

* Hackett, R.D. and Guion, R.M. (1985) 'A reevaluation of the absenteeism–job satisfaction relationship', *Organizational Behaviour and Human Decision Processes* 35: 340–81. (This article presents a meta-analytic sight of the absenteeism–job satisfaction relationship.)

* Heckhausen, J. and Schulz, R. (1995) 'A life-span theory of control', *Psychological Review* 102: 284–304. (This article posits a life-span theory of control which is relevant to processes in work motivation and work satisfaction in particular.)

* Iaffaldano, M.T. and Muchinsky, P.M. (1985) 'Job satisfaction and job performance: a meta analysis', *Psychological Bulletin* 97: 251–73. (This article gives a meta-analytic view of the job satisfaction and job performance relationship; it can be regarded as still being representative today.)

* Judge, T.A., Locke, E.A., Durham, C.C. and Kluger, A.N. (1998) 'Dispositional effects on job and life satisfaction: the role of core evaluations', *Journal of Applied Psychology* 83: 17–34. (This article focuses on the effects of dispositional core evaluations on job and life satisfaction.)

* Kanfer, R. (1994) 'Work motivation: new directions in theory and research', in C.L. Cooper and I.T. Robertson (eds), *Key Reviews in Managerial Psychology: Concepts and Research for Practice*, pp. 1–53, Chichester: Wiley. (This review article provides a sophisticated and integral view of work motivation theory and its application in industrial and organizational psychology.)

* Katzell, R.A., Thompson, D.E. and Guzzo, R.A. (1992) 'How job satisfaction and job performance are and are not linked', in C.J. Cranny, P.C. Smith and E.F. Stone (eds), *Job Satisfaction – How People Feel About Their Jobs and How It Affects Their Performance*, pp. 195–217, New York: Lexington. (This article resumés results of the research on the relation between job satisfaction and job performance and points to implications for intervention and policy in organizations.)

* Kleinbeck, U., Quast, H.-H., Thierry, H. and Haecker, H. (1990) *Work Motivation*, Hillsdale, NJ: Erlbaum. (One of the few books of recent years containing articles that provide an advanced treatment of central concepts in work motivation and satisfaction.)

* Kuhl, J. (1992) 'A theory of self-regulation: action versus state orientation, self-discrimination, and some applications', *Applied Psychology* 41: 97–129. (This lead article gives a comprehensive overview of Kuhl's action and state orientation theory of motivation, volition and action, including examples for application.)

* Ledford, G.E. (1999) 'Happiness and productivity revisited. Comment', *Journal of Organizational Behaviour* 20: 25–30. (This is a thought-provoking comment to place the research on the happy productive worker thesis and its findings in a larger theoretical context.)

* Leonard, N.H., Beauvais, L.L. and Scholl, R.W. (1999) 'Work motivation. The incorporation of self-concept-based processes', *Human Relations* 52: 969–98. (This article reviews traditional theories of work motivation and proposes a meta-theory of work motivation incorporating theories of self-concept.)

* Locke, E.A. (1976) 'The nature and causes of job satisfaction', in M.D. Dunnette (ed.), *Handbook of Industrial and Organizational Psychology*, pp. 1297–351, New York: Wiley. (This handbook article is what can be called a classic of job satisfaction theory and method.)

* Locke, E.A. (1997) 'The motivation to work: what we know', *Advances in Motivation and Achievement* 10: 375–412. (This article presents an integration of empirical research on work motivation and selected elements of eight work motivation theories into a model of work motivation.)

* Locke, E.A. and Henne, D. (1986) 'Work motivation theories', in C.L. Cooper and I.T. Robertson (eds), *International Review of Industrial and Organizational Psychology*, vol. 1, pp. 1–35, Chichester: Wiley. (This review article provides a thorough overview of work motivation theories, including information on job satisfaction.)

* Spector, P.E. (1997) *Job Satisfaction – Application, Assessment, Causes and Consequences*, Thousand Oaks, CA: Sage. (One of the few books of recent years providing a concise and informative overview of job satisfaction research.)

* Staw, B.W. (1984) 'Organizational behaviour: a review and reformulation of the field's outcome variables', *Annual Review of Psychology* 35: 627–66. (This review article is a critical summary of organizational behaviour research with strong relations to work motivation and work satisfaction research.)

* Terry, D.J. and Jimmieson, N.L. (1999) 'Work control and employee well-being: a decade review', in C.L. Cooper and I.T. Robertson (eds), *International Review of Industrial and Organizational Psychology*, vol. 14, pp. 95–148, Chichester: Wiley. (This article offers a comprehensive review of results from research on work control and its influence on well-being and health.)

* Weaver, C.V. (1980) 'Job satisfaction in the United States in the 1970s', *Journal of Applied Psychology* 65: 364–7. (This article gives an overview of the state of job satisfaction in the US; it can be regarded as still representative today.)

* Wright, T.A. and Staw, B.M. (1999) 'Affect and favourable work outcomes. Two longitudinal tests of the happy-productive worker thesis', *Journal of Organizational Behaviour* 20: 1–23. (This article tries to shed additional light on the unresolved happy productive worker thesis.)

Leadership

Frank Heller

1 **Universalist approaches**
2 **Situational leadership**
3 **Limits to free choice**
4 **Leadership and strategy**
5 **Further facilitators and constraints**
6 **Conclusion**

Overview

It has been claimed that in 1896 in the USA the Library of Congress had no book on leadership, but within one person's lifetime, over 5,000 entries on leadership were reviewed by Bass in1981. This explosion of interest has included an enormous diversity of activity by people we call 'leaders'. Fiedler and Garcia in 1987 listed as examples of leadership: Henry V's victory at Agincourt against overwhelming odds; George Washington, who defeated better-equipped English forces; and Lee Iacocca, who produced the dramatic turnaround of the Chrysler Corporation. They then went on to show the macabre side of leadership by including Hitler and the Reverend Jim Jones, who induced 800 of his followers to commit suicide. Looking at more recent events, one could add successful business tycoons like Robert Maxwell in Britain, Alan Bond in Australia and Ivan Boësky in the USA, all of whom defrauded millions of people who had fallen under their leadership spell.

With such a wide range of examples to illustrate a phenomenon described in a single word, one has to ask oneself whether the leadership concept has practical utility for understanding organizational behaviour. The answer is a qualified 'yes'. The qualification implies that some usefulness can be extracted from the available evidence, but great care has to be taken not to overstate the explanatory thrust of a term which has given rise to thousands of different definitions and a variety of *post-hoc* explanations covering both good and evil.

The literature will be divided into two main streams: universalist approaches and situational approaches. The former include great person theories, personality theories, psychoanalytic theories, charismatic, transformational and transactional theories, and great company theory. Situational approaches are, in general, of more recent origin and are based on the assumption that different styles of behaviour, including leadership, are appropriate for contrasting varieties of real-life situations. These are sometimes called contingency theories because they attempt to specify the effect of contingent situations on different behavioural responses. Psychologically oriented theories tend to concentrate on intra-organizational contingencies, like the nature of the task, while sociological theories tend to stress factors external to the organization, like turbulence of the environment.

The contrast between generalistic and contingency approaches is important and it will be argued that the thrust of evidence in support of the latter produces a more realistic analytic as well as prescriptive approach to leadership. At the same time it must be recognized that there is often a degree of overlap between the two schemata.

Finally, we will briefly indicate the growing importance of some organizational theories which do not specifically mention leadership but subsume it.

I Universalist approaches

Perhaps the oldest and best-known literature on leadership uses examples of great persons. It extracts from the description of their personality and behaviour some alleged essential characteristics which are assumed to have universal validity. Using Field Marshal Sir William Slim, one early writer extracts five hallmarks of leadership: courage, willpower, flexibility of mind, knowledge and integrity. The terms vary from analyst to analyst although some, like integrity, have a hallowed place in most historic-descriptive lists.

One of several problems with this approach is that the lists do not critically distinguish between good and evil, between, say, George Washington and Benito Mussolini. Integrity, for instance, can be defined as 'soundness of moral principle, sinlessness, uprightness, etc.' (*Shorter Oxford Dictionary*) and these, like all the conditions listed earlier, would, at the time, have been applied to all the people we have mentioned so far as well as to many people all around us who do not fall into the 'great person' category.

Even if these personal attributes could be validly applied to all leaders, the theory would have limited utility for management because, with few exceptions, they are not easily assessable for selection nor can an individual be trained in them. Moreover, personality theories of leadership have shown no consistent or valid identification with specific traits. This does not mean that personality is unimportant, only that in most cases it is a peripheral rather than a major explanatory factor (Smith and Peterson 1988).

Psychoanalytic explanations of leadership also examine personality using a number of universal concepts. There is a long tradition of applying psychoanalytic theories of personality development and categories of adjustment or maladjustment to biographical data of famous people. Freud, for instance, enquired into the life of Leonardo da Vinci to trace his variations in artistic output and his later interests in biology and engineering to the inhibitions of his sexual drive. More recently the use of psychoanalytic theory has been applied to assess leader motivation and preoccupations. The 'royal road' to understanding senior managers' preoccupations is thought to be through the mechanism called transference, which describes the:

> interface between therapist and patient and ... derive from the kind of relationships which develop between parents and children ... It can be described

as the projection or displacement upon another person of unconscious wishes and feelings originally directed towards important individuals in childhood.

(de Vries *et al.* 1993: 10)

In the de Vries *et al.* schema, 'transference is the determining factor in understanding an individual's style' and is therefore presumably invariant with situations.

Sociological theories have also used broad classifications, for instance Max Weber's famous categorization of charismatic leadership, which has developed into a description of leaders who are able to change the needs and aspirations of their followers to agree with the leader's own requirements. This type is similar to transformational leadership and can be contrasted with the less dynamic, more traditional transactional leader who uses rewards and disciplinary methods to achieve organizational effectiveness more or less around the status quo. In terms of organizational change, the transactional leader will favour incrementalism while the transformational leader is characterized by fairly fundamental and substantial leaps into new domains without necessarily achieving success, but nevertheless imprinting his or her personality on the process (Bass 1992).

Bass used and developed the charismatic transformational concept by relating it to stress. For instance, it is held that under conditions when a charismatic leader's life is threatened, s/he tends to remain cool and composed while non-charismatic leaders suffer the effects of stress. Bass gives the examples of Mahatma Gandhi, F.D. Roosevelt, Benito Mussolini and Ronald Reagan. He produces evidence to suggest that 'to be effective under stress, the leader must be transformational – able to rise above what the group sees as its immediate needs … ' (Bass 1992: 144–5).

The problem with the typologies described so far is that when internal organizational needs or external pressures change, a given leadership type may suddenly become dysfunctional. Since environmental and competitive pressures, changes in technology and other factors often follow distinct cyclical patterns, it would be necessary to change managers very frequently. While, as we shall see, this happens occasionally at the top level, it is not a very practical option that can be applied in general and at all levels.

An alternative approach, but still within the universalist framework, is to discover a leadership style which is superior in all situations. A popular approach used in consultancy and management training postulates a two-dimensional grid: (1) concern for production; and (2) concern for people (Blake and Mouton 1964). Maximizing both gives the best leadership style and this is assumed to apply in more or less all situations.

The idea that the best leader is one who pays equal attention to efficient production and human resources appeals to commonsense and to people who want a simple prescription. This explains why the grid approach is still used in organizational training, but its validity can be seriously questioned (Yukl 1994).

All 'one best style' prescriptions and attempts to reduce the complexity of real-life situations by asking managers to mould themselves on the image of a particular successful person fail to explain the variability and unpredictability of success and failure. We have already given some examples. The case of the tycoon Robert Maxwell is another. He was one of the most successful entrepreneurs of the twentieth century. Awarded the Military Cross for bravery in the Second World War, he became a member of Parliament for a short time and he gradually acquired a disparate range of 800 companies, including several newspapers: the very successful, large circulation *Daily Mirror* in the UK, the *New York Daily News* and *The European*. His empire featured cable TV, a helicopter company, market research organizations and two football clubs. Then suddenly in 1995, this empire collapsed with enormous debts and the discovery that he had illegally used company pension funds.

Economists also lean towards a universalist theory of leadership without using that term. They have a very clear, but untested, view about human nature which they build into their theoretical models about agency. Managers, even chief executives, are agents on behalf of owners, that is to say shareholders, who are called principals. As the term implies, agents are supposed to perform services on behalf of principals who have delegated decision-making authority to the agent. However, agents, (we would call them senior managers or leaders of organizations) are said to have their own self-interests and cannot be trusted to maximize the interests of shareholders. In fact, these leaders are assumed to use guile, to cheat and deceive in order to maximize their own returns. Microeconomic agency theory then devotes attention to this conflict based on a clash of egoisms between owners and hired leaders of organizations and the consequential built-in distrust between them. To minimize the proclivity of leaders to cheat, they have to be given special incentives, like bonus shares.

In transaction cost economics there is a simple explanation for leadership. A leader (entrepreneur or agent) operates at the apex of a hierarchy, that is to say an organization or firm, because within such an organization the costs of transaction are lower than they would be in the market, that is to say, without the organization. The costs are lower because the leader makes a single contract with his employees instead of needing to negotiate a large number of individual contracts in the amorphous market. The two main characteristics or limitations of this leadership theory are negative: one is 'bounded rationality' and the other is 'opportunism' (the motivation to cheat).

It is obvious that the microeconomic theory of leadership motivation is quite different from the empirical evidence and theoretical assumptions of other social science disciplines and we will come back to this later in relation to trust.

There is a superficial resemblance between this economic model of man and McGregor's Theory X, which describes the hard-headed, autocratic, egotistic, self-serving manager. However, it is important to be aware that McGregor counterposed Theory X with Theory Y, which has a positive, humanistic message about people's sense of responsibility and their willingness to work purposefully in groups towards common ends (McGregor 1967). Management theories, in contrast to organizational economics, tend to support McGregor's Theory Y and have accumulated empirical evidence in its support. To stress the difference between these two opposing sets of assumptions, a stewardship theory about corporate governance, that is to say leadership, has been proposed. Under stewardship theory 'there is no conflict of interest between managers and owners ... managers are team players ... that will act in the best interest of owners. Managers are not opportunistic agents ... but good stewards' (Donaldson 1990). Both models start off in a generalistic format but can also be cast into a situational framework.

Every now and again a category called entrepreneurship emphasizes innovation and risk taking and complements the leadership literature or seeks to replace it. Psychometric attempts to measure a personality trait to assess entrepreneurship have been unsuccesful but Chell (2000) argues that this is due to narrow focus and single discipline methodology. Entrepreneurial leadership has to be treated as a process over time, embedded in a range of contexts. We will elaborate on this in the section on situational leadership.

An extension of the universalist 'great person theory' is the universalist 'great company theory' of leadership which has produced a large literature, but is subject to limitations similar to the great person theories.

A particularly well-known example of this approach is the series of books starting with *In Search of Excellence: A Lesson from America's Best Run Companies* by Peters and Waterman (1982). The book was an outstanding success; it was translated into most major languages and is thought to have sold over five million copies. The authors' eight attributes of excellence are:

- managing ambiguity and paradox
- a bias for action
- close to the customer
- autonomy and entrepreneurship
- productivity through people
- hands-on, value-driven
- 'stick to the knitting'
- simple form, lean staff

However, some of the companies used to construct the authors' eight attributes of excellence have failed the test of time. The most telling example is of a company which the authors described as passing 'all hurdles for excellent performance 1961–1980'. This was International Business Machines or IBM, which nearly collapsed under the weight of enormous debts in the early 1990s, though under different leadership it has subsequently recovered. A similar success–failure cycle can be traced in many other attempts to extract universal wisdom from descriptions of case examples.

The retail firm Marks and Spencer, in the UK popularly abbreviated to M&S, was the darling of economic and management analysts for a number of decades. The firm was widely used in Business School case studies as an example of an outstandingly successful company. Its store managers had an enviable reputation for humanistic leadership as well as economic efficiency. The top leadership had built up long-term and close relationships built on mutual trust with British manufacturers. This was used by the government as an example of how to improve the balance of trade by reducing foreign imports. Then suddenly, in the last year of the twentieth century, it lost its magic touch and was heavily criticized for various failures to adapt to changing conditions, and was even discussed as a target for takeover by another company.

2 Situational leadership

McGregor's (1967) Theory X and Y, already mentioned, developed a situational approach by describing a number of situational constraints which can be described by a simple formula: $P = f(I, a, b, c, ... E, m, n, o)$. A person's leadership behaviour (P) is a function specified by certain characteristics of the Individual (I, a, b, c,), for instance, knowledge, skill, motivation and attitudes as well as certain aspects of the environment (E, m, n ,o) which can include the nature of the person's job and reward system. Situational theories spurn simplistic generalization and instead attempt to identify certain leadership characteristics or behaviour that match the complexities of real life. Fiedler (1965) pioneered this approach by showing that effectiveness depends on the interaction between a leader's personality or motivation on the one hand, and the favourable or unfavourable conditions in which he or she is expected to operate. Favourable conditions apply, for instance, when a leader is supported by followers, knows how to carry out specific tasks, and is given sufficient power to handle subordinates. Vroom (1977) and others have developed situational leadership models which take account of different contingencies which determine which decision procedure (from autocratic to participative) will be most effective in the specified conditions. Such models have been found useful for training managers to think and act flexibly and to recognize that leaders have choices which they can use in diverse situations. Most writing on leadership favours participative methods to increase flexibility and competitiveness in modern industry (Lawler 1986; Rooney 1993). However, although most popular and academic literature advocates participative leadership, a wide-ranging review of the research and practice of organizational participation comes to quite pessimistic conclusions. The genuine extent of influence-sharing practices is quite limited in spite of the rhetoric. The systemic requirements that are associated with successful democratic leadership are demanding and rarely implemented (Heller 2000).

One can think of leadership–subordinate interaction as a range of behaviour or styles of leadership describing different degrees of influence-sharing between people or levels. One widely used categorization is called the Influence–Power–Continuum (IPC), which has five or six positions: from no influence, via prior consultation, joint decision making (or consensus) to semi-autonomy and delegation. Each position has to be carefully defined and leaders and subordinates are asked to describe which style is used in relation to a variety of different tasks and situations. The findings from a number of investigations in different countries presents very clear evidence of the impact of situation on behaviour. The same leaders use different styles for different purposes, demonstrating that there is no one best method. The differences in influence-sharing behaviour are found to be functional in the sense that they are relevant to the task and take account of the experience and competence of the people with whom the leader interacts (Heller 2000). The terms participation and, more recently, empowering are widely used to describe some leadership behaviour within the IPC and this extends to the literature on team working and structures like Quality Circles and Total Quality Management. It is often assumed that participative leadership methods are associated with job satisfaction, are more effective, and perhaps more productive than other styles of behaviour, and therefore increase the competitive position of the organization. Findings from seven European countries and the USA show that the main reason for using influence-sharing methods by senior executives is that it increases the quality of the decision. Closely related is the finding that participation leadership releases the existing but often hidden resources of employee competence. (Heller 1992).

Another way of looking at the importance of situational differences is to ask why the same leader is successful in some contingencies but not in others. Little systematic research has been done on this, but anybody who reads the business pages of a quality newspaper regularly will find many examples. The example of IBM has already been mentioned as an illustration of the fallibility of the great company theory, but because the case is so well known, it can also illustrate the importance of situational leadership: John Akers, IBM's chief executive since 1958 and only 58 years old, was fired on 26 January 1993 after a spectacularly successful business career.

Heinz Schimmelbush, the charismatic 49-year-old Chief Executive of the German Metallgesellschaft, was ousted on 17 December 1993. He had been described as the darling of German management circles and had in 1991 been elected German Manager of the Year. He had been with his company for twenty years and rose rapidly through the ranks to become Chief Executive in 1988. He was fired for alleged mismanagement and for not keeping his Board properly informed of serious financial problems which he attempted to cover up with creative accounting.

These two examples illustrate the problem with certain theories of leadership. They point to the weakness of the 'great man' theory mentioned earlier, but in this section we use it to show that unless the quality of leadership is very flexible and can rapidly adjust to changes in technology, or market conditions, or economic climate, it becomes a liability.

3 Limits to free choice

Even in small, face-to-face groups, leaders have been shown to be influenced by the composition of the group, their values and skills. Smith and Peterson (1988) review the very extensive field of group processes and leadership and come to the conclusion that the leader does not usually have the power to determine the culture of the group without the support of historical, economic and structural circumstances.

Leadership, almost by definition, is a voluntary activity, but there are limits to free choice. Many companies run executive development programmes which, like the teaching based on Blake and Mouton's grid (1964) mentioned earlier, train employees to use or conform with the organization's 'house style' rather than with their own leadership inclination. This limitation of choice also applies to situational theories like Vroom's which are normative, by specifying the 'best method' that corresponds to a clearly identified set of situations. Consultancy-based managerial training methods are usually not based on published research, but prescribe preferred leadership styles nonetheless.

Furthermore, west European countries, with few exceptions, have industrial relations legislation which requires organizations to establish certain representative committees to consult their employees on specified issues like changes of ownership and large-scale redundancies. These legal requirements started in West Germany in 1951 with a co-determination law giving workers or their chosen representatives half the places on the supervisory board of the coal, iron and steel industries. Later legislation extended similar provision to the rest of Germany industry (now also in the former East Germany) and to other European countries. The harmonization aims of the European Union will provide minimum legislative support for a variety of social charter measures which limit managerial decision influence. In the USA, collective bargaining agreements often incorporate provisions which constrain managerial decision making for the duration of the contract and can be enforced through legal action. The law or its interpretation is also important in deciding the leadership objectives of senior management and the role of Boards of Directors. Company law in many countries supports the conventional assumption that it is the objective of private enterprise companies to maximize the returns to shareholders. More recently, some commentators have argued that, in the long term, prosperity can more easily be achieved by having regard to a wider constituency of stakeholders. The German co-determination model, which has influenced most company legislation in Continental Europe, gives employees a limited stake in some aspects of organizational decision making. There is now much discussion of extending the stakeholder model to include customers, suppliers and perhaps banks. Such a dispersal of influence complicates the role of leadership by converting it into something like trusteeship. However, creating the conditions for trust (as we argue in the next section) has always been seen as a central responsibility for leaders in all walks of life, although it may reduce the scope for centralized leadership.

Outdated theories and fads and fashions also act as constraints on managers at any given time. With all disciplines, including medicine, the leading edge of knowledge changes over time, and so with leadership. The 'great person' and the 'great company' theories were interesting and useful in their time and will continue to have some popular support, but are unlikely to constitute the leading edge of managerial wisdom in the twenty-first century. Some scientific evidence and the corresponding theories based on them have a longer life than others. What we have called contingency theories are based on extensive research over decades and are more flexible than those they replaced; they are therefore likely to last longer. So, for example, the findings on participative leadership in the 1950s and 1960s became generalized and almost took on the form of a cult. What was called 'system 4' (joint decision making) was taught in business schools all over the world. A colleague reports on a conversation over dinner with Rensis Likert, the founder of system 4 theory, who was asked whether this method would work equally well in all cultures. Likert, pointing to his attaché case plastered with hotel stickers, replied: 'I've been to dozens of countries throughout the world. System 4 works everywhere I have been. Some time I may find a Hottentot tribe where it isn't appropriate. But I haven't found it yet!' A few decades later such a claim is refuted by much evidence (Heller *et al.* 1998). In particular, we are now fairly confident in asserting that the effective use of the participative leadership method depends on a number of characteristics of the system in which it is intended to operate, for instance on the experience and skill of the staff.

The evidence in this section adds to the complexity by giving examples of constraints on the choices available to leadership. It seems that the climate of leadership is to some extent predetermined through training or through the adoption of a managerial fashion within a given organization. An organizational climate creates powerful expectations, thus, for example, trust or distrust is usually associated with past leadership behaviour but affects employee attitudes over a long period of time. The issue of trust, its moral dimension and its role in the development of capitalism and organizational effectiveness has been carefully examined by Fukuyama (1995).

We conclude that leadership is not fully predetermined nor fully free from constraints. One review of the literature (Leavy and Wilson 1994) argues that it is prudent to avoid deterministic theories, which virtually eliminate the role of leadership, as well as the opposite voluntaristic view, which pays no attention to constraints on leadership. They believe that these two views can be reconciled. This will be dealt with in the section on strategy below.

4 Leadership and strategy

Since the 1950s, the literature on leadership has covered three phases. It started with an analysis of individual characteristics of skill and performance and expanded to include wider considerations of followers and groups, as well as the necessary antecedent conditions that helped or hindered the emergence of leaders. More recently, as management has become more firmly established as an intellectual discipline in its own right, the leadership role is seen as a central aspect of the formation of organizational policy and strategy. This trend links leadership to the decision process of the top layers of the power structure and consequently reduces the attention given to the role of lower levels.

Three examples of this approach will be given. The first is the fourfold strategy classification of Miles and Snow (1978). They use the term 'defenders' to describe organizations that devise and, as far as possible, maintain an environment which favours a stable form of organization. Such organizations concentrate on high-quality engineering to produce and distribute goods using mechanistic cost-control structures. By contrast, 'prospectors' favour a dynamic environment where they can discover and work with new, preferably innovative products for which risks and failure rates are high. This type of organization requires flexibility in its administration and technology, and consequently invests in human resources by favouring decentralized unit operations within an organic structure. Third, 'analyser' organizations combine characteristics of defenders and prospectors by minimizing risks and maximizing entrepreneurial profit objectives. Their technology has to contain a stable as well as flexible orientation and their administrations favour a matrix-type human resources system. Finally, Miles and Snow have observed unstable organizations that react inconsistently to their environment and consequently have an erratic and poor performance record; these are called 'reactors'.

In describing these four organizational strategies in terms of structures and administrative processes, they also describe, though indirectly, the leadership behaviour at senior levels which characterize firms pursuing the three viable strategies. The names they have chosen to describe these typologies – defenders, prospectors, and analysers – characterize a set of leadership adaptations to environmental conditions.

A different leadership–strategy connection is developed by Dunphy and Stace (1990), but one which is not inconsistent with Miles and Snow. Their point of departure is a critique of the prevalent organization development (OD) view of leadership, in particular in relation to achieving change. The OD model favours slow, incremental change achieved through leadership that involves employees in the process of building up an organic, flexible and cohesive organization.

Dunphy and Stace have produced evidence to suggest that the OD method is suitable only in a limited number of circumstances. They argue that strategic considerations derived from an assessment of the socioeconomic and political environment may require different strategies. More autocratic and radical alternatives are in part a consequence of the rapidity of external changes or the emergence of new competition. Coercive measures may become necessary if employees are unwilling to respond to the external signals so that the viability of the enterprise is put at risk. Structural changes, like diversification or mergers, may have a similar effect.

These considerations produce a 2×2 typology; vertically it differentiates between (1) collaborative versus (2) coercive modes; and horizontally (3) incremental versus (4) transformative change strategies. Testing the model in a sample of Australian industry which they grouped into high, medium and low performers, Dunphy and Stace report that none of the managers interviewed rated their executives as using a collaborative change style. High and medium-high performers used a variety of approaches, but the directive, tough method was predominant. Low performers preferred careful, timid fine tuning.

They conclude that the OD tender-minded, participative, incremental approach is not a universal or even a preferred solution for Australian industry at the time of their research, though several companies used variants of the 'soft' style in earlier years. They conclude that businesses should, and usually do, select the most situationally valid business strategy to fit environmental circumstances. A policy based on a tough, fast-moving leadership style received support from an advocacy which owes more to consultancy experience than research; it is called 're-engineering' from a book with that name by Hammer and Champy. The authors argue that salvation for modern business does not lie in adaptation or incremental change, but in grasping the nettle of revolution by redesigning and 'starting all over, starting from scratch'.

These strategic management models relate to leadership indirectly and assign it a peripheral or subsidiary role. Leavy and Wilson (1994), however, attempt to integrate technology–environmental determinism with psychological approaches that give primary consideration to human agency and leadership. Their bridge-building is based on an extensive review of the literature and longitudinal field research in a small number of firms in Ireland. Their description of leaders as 'tenants of time and context' stresses the interaction between leadership competence, historic circumstances and specific contextual elements, like technology. Historic circumstances include the national–political climate, which is capable of influencing the ideology and behaviour of leaders and enterprises. Levy and Wilson single out the post-1979 period during which leaders were subject to a more constraining context based on economic–political circumstances which made them more reactive and defensive than in the previous two decades. Even so, during the same period and subject to similar contextual pressures, some firms grew while others failed, and this could be traced back to aggressive or imaginative leadership.

5 Further facilitators and constraints

Leavy and Wilson conclude that the industrial environment is not an adequate explanation of organizational strategy, though it acts as a significant constraint. What other factors should be considered as constraints or facilitators? There is a very large literature on national/cultural differences relevant for leadership. There is evidence that managers in different parts of the world, in northern compared to southern Europe for instance, differ on individualism versus collectivism and on the inclination to share or not to share power. If these differences exist in the population at large, the leadership practices, for instance in collectivist southern Europe or Asia will, presumably, differ from leadership in the more individualistically inclined northern Europe or the USA. However, many companies transcend regions and managers are increasingly expected to be mobile and exercise leadership globally. National/cultural difference theories have become popular, but they are generalistic and this means that they assume that the identified attitudinal or behavioural characteristics are given and cannot be changed contingently to suit different regional or other needs. As with all generalistic theories, the role of training is reduced or eliminated.

Then there is the impact on leadership of two major political–economic changes in the last decade of the twentieth century which are likely to influence the thinking and practice in the twenty-first century. One is the sudden and unexpected financial collapse of major Far Eastern economies in the 1990s and the related vulnerability of Japanese enterprises. This has led to a re-assessment of the previously much-lauded Asian model of leadership with its emphasis on secure employment and benevolent–humanistic human resource management. American and European social scientists and Business School teaching had urged the West to copy several aspects of the Asian model, for instance participative leadership, in order to compete effectively with Japan. Now this model has to be given up or amended.

There is also the trigger for change derived from the collapse of autocratic communism in eastern Europe. Some commentators see this as a triumph of market capitalism, while others are stimulated to search for a 'third way' or 'capitalism with a human face'. One outcome of the tensions created by these alternative models is a re-assessment of the legal as well as moral leadership responsibility of senior management and boards of directors and their relationship with shareholders. Should business leaders seek to balance their concerns in a stakeholder model which could include employees, customers and suppliers? The concept has been debated by managers, economists, politicians and social scientists and adopted by some groups as a useful heuristic device.

These recent trends, as well as others we have reviewed in the literature, suggest that leadership will not be left to one academic discipline like psychology, sociology or economics, but will be researched and analysed within a multidisciplinary framework (Northouse 1997).

6 Conclusion

The complexity of our subject and its undoubted importance in the political economy has led to many interpretations. Some commentators have attempted to eliminate leadership as a significant explanatory force and substitute impersonal explanations, like competition and survival of the fittest; others continue to find charisma and personal attributes to override the situational environmental context. However, situational or contingency leadership theories tend to account for more of the available evidence than 'one best style' theories, though consultants and popular books are still beguiled by their simplicity. One way of reducing the excessive randomness in the field of leadership theories is to concentrate attention on certain core activities and characteristics, for instance by singling out decision making and/or the distribution of power as major attributes of leadership.

It is clear that no paradigm of leadership has emerged in the diverse constituencies of social science. This could mean that the jury is still out, but with more time and effort, an acceptable evidence-based role for organizational leadership will emerge. Alternatively, it is possible that organizational behaviour and, in particular, changes in organizations over time, require a multifaceted explanation in which personal leadership will remain a constituent in a much broader concept that has yet to evolve.

Further reading

(References cited in the text marked *)

* Bass, B.M. (1981) *Stogdill's Handbook of Leadership*, New York: The Free Press. (A classic early book of reference on leadership.)
* Bass, B.M. (1992) 'Stress and leadership', in Frank Heller (ed.), *Decision-making and Leadership,* Cambridge: Cambridge University Press. (Describes the literature which links the theory of transformational leadership with stress.)
* Blake, R. and Mouton, J. (1964) *The Managerial Grid*, Houston, TX: Gulf Publishing Company. (An old classic describing the consultancy package which attempts to train the ideal leader. Still used but now overtaken by events.)
* Chell, E. (2000) 'Towards researching the "opportunistic entrepreneur": a social constructionist approach and research agenda', *European Journal of Work and Organizational Psychology* 9 (1): 63–80. (Chell heads a centre for the study of entrepreneurship and uses a theoretical model called 'social constructionism' to argue for a broad holistic approach.)
* Donaldson, L. (1990) 'The ethereal hand: organizational economics and management theory', *Academy of Management Review*, 15 (3): 369–81
* Dunphy, D. and Stace, D. (1990) *Under New Management*, Sydney: McGraw Hill. (An important theoretical analysis of different approaches to organizational change, including coercive strategies.)
* Fiedler, F. (1965) 'Engineer the job to fit the manager', *Harvard Business Review*, 43: 115–22. (Describes the first research on leadership behaviour within a contingency framework.)
* Fiedler, F. and Garcia, J. (1987) *New Approaches to Effective Leadership*, New York: John Wiley & Sons. (A substantial expansion of Fiedler's early evidence of the situationally determined nature of leadership.)
* Fukuyama, Francis (1995) *Trust:The Social Virtues and the Creation of Prosperity*, New York: The Free Press. (A wide ranging assessment of the multifaceted role of trust in all aspects of our lives.)
* Hammer, M. and Champy, J. (1993) *Reengineering the Corporation: A Manifesto for Business Revolution,* London: Nicholas Brealey. (A typical late-twentieth-century consultancy book addressed to top business leaders in an attempt to influence their strategy.)
* Heller, F. (2000) *Managing Democratic Organizations*, vols I and II, Aldershot: Ashgate Publishing Ltd. (These two volumes present the extensive literature of four research programmes on power and its distribution in organizations at all levels among leaders and subordinates.)
* Heller, F. (ed.) (1992) *Decision Making and Leadership*, Cambridge: Cambridge University Press. (Heller's chapter reviews evidence and builds up a model of human resources based on the need for competence allied to participation.)
* Heller, F., Pusic, E., Strauss, G. and Wilpert, B. (eds) (1998) *Organizational Participation: Myth and Reality*, Oxford: Oxford University Press. (A very extensive review and analysis of participation and other influence-sharing practices, especially in the USA and Europe, at all levels. It describes an important aspect of leadership and its handling of power.)
* Lawler, E. (1986) *High Involvement Management: Participative Strategies for Improving Organizational Performance*, San Francisco: Jossey-Bass. (Puts forward strong arguments for participative leadership now necessary for US companies in order to compete with the Far East.)
* Leavy, B. and Wilson, D. (1994) *Strategy and Leadership*, London: Routledge. (Extensive review of the literature and research evidence in support of a strategic leader model.)
Likert, R. (1967) *The Human Organization*, New York: McGraw-Hill. (Classic book summarizing a decade of important leadership-relevant research.)
* McGregor, D. (1967) *The Professional Manager*, New York: McGraw Hill. (A classic exposition of Theories X and Y as well as a contingency approach to leadership.)

* Miles, R. and Snow, C. (1978*) Organization Strategy, Structure And Process*, New York: McGraw-Hill. (Research-based typology of organizations with leadership implications.)

* Northouse, P.G. (1997) *Leadership – Theory and Practice*, Thousand Oaks, CA: Sage. (Covers a considerable range of different approaches both theoretical and practical; designed for graduate students.)

* Peters, T. and Waterman, R., Jr. (1982) *In Search of Excellence: Lessons from America's Best Run Companies*, New York: Harper and Row. (A best-seller because of its smooth style and broad, easily memorable generalizations, but poor on methodology, and hence unreliable.)

* Rooney, P.M. (1993) 'Effects of worker participation in the USA: managers' perceptions vs. empirical measures', in W. Lafferty and E. Rosenstein (eds), *International Handbook of Participation in Organizations,* vol. III, Oxford: Oxford University Press. (Summarizes data from a large-scale survey of employee-owned firms in the USA where leaders share power with other employees.)

* Smith, P. and Peterson, M. (1988) *Leadership, Organizations and Culture*, London: Sage Publications. (An authoritative review of evidence and theories on leadership with attempted synthesis.)

* de Vries, M.F.R., Miller, D. and Noël, A. (1993) 'Understanding the leader–strategy–interface: application of the strategic relationship interview method', *Human Relations* 46 (1): 1–120. (Describes a psychoanalytic approach to leadership.)

* Vroom, V. (1977) 'Leadership revisited', in B. Staw (ed.), *Psychological Foundation of Organizational Behavior*, Santa Monica, CA: Goodyear Publishing Co. (Vroom and colleagues have built up an important contingency model of leadership useful for management development.)

* Yukl, G. (1994) *Leadership in Organizations*, 3rd edn, Englewood Cliffs, NJ: Prentice-Hall. (The standard comprehensive review of all major research data and theory on the psychology of leadership.)

Groups and teams

Friso den Hertog and Thera Tolner

1 **Definitions**
2 **Teamwork as a cure for bureaucracy**
3 **Organization design**
4 **Group development**
5 **Conclusions**

Overview

Many organizations are involved with the introduction of teamwork. A team can be considered as a number of people (a group) organized around a set of objectives. Teamwork can be regarded as a remedy for the dysfunctions of bureaucratic structures which are still dominant in organizations. The main characteristic of bureaucracy in organizations is segmentation: large problems are being cut into sub-problems and sub-sub-problems. These sub- and sub-sub-problems are allocated to sub-units and sub-sub-units. In the end the solutions offered by these units must be assembled again to form a meaningful whole. Today, bureaucracies must operate in a far more complex and uncertain environment than ever before. They threaten to be destroyed by the burden of activities created by themselves to control and coordinate the segmented organization. In order to survive they must invest in new control strategies. Two of these strategies imply the introduction of team concepts in the design of the organization. One strategy involves the introduction of 'lateral linkages'. These are groups that horizontally cut across the existing boundaries of functions. A special form of this is the management team. The creation of self-contained units is the second team-based strategy. With this alternative the functions are integrated around a certain order flow; complete little firms are created within the walls of a bigger firm. The autonomous production team is an important example of this.

The creation of a teamwork organization is to be approached from a double perspective. The team is both the result of organization design choices and of a development process by which the team members learn from their experiences. Organization design and organization development are to be viewed as two sides of the same coin. The introduction of teamwork in organizations is a matter of careful design. The team is an organization in itself, but at the same time is part of a larger system. Tasks must be allocated between and within teams. Systems must be introduced to control the work process. A number of important structural criteria apply to both the lateral and the production teams: a complete task to be carried out independently; a good link with other groups in the organization; sufficient instruments to steer the group's own process; and a good internal organization.

A sound structure does not necessarily imply an effective organization. Managers and workers alike must learn to work in such a new structure. Important in this respect is that a balance exists between task-orientated activities and the maintenance activities focused on the group atmosphere, that is, keeping good social relationships and a general state of well-being in the group. An effective team is a result of group development.

I Definitions

Groups and teams are key subjects both in modern management literature and in management practice. The words 'groups' and 'teams' are often used as substitutes. In other cases we attach quite different meanings to them. Theorists tend to use the word 'group' predominantly in a descriptive sense, and use a variety of definitions according to their own theoretical perspective. A well-accepted broad definition of a group is: 'two or more individuals in face-to-face interaction, each aware of his or her membership in the group, each aware of the others who belong to the group, and each aware of their positive interdependence as they strive to achieve mutual goals' (Johnson and Johnson 1991). Such groups can be found almost anywhere: in families, schools, sports clubs and work organizations. This entry focuses on groups in work organizations.

In everyday language the word 'team' is often used in a normative sense as a special sort of group with positive traits. Like a sports team, it is associated in daily life with 'cooperation', 'cohesion' and 'teamwork'. 'This group is not a team yet' is a frequently used sentence which expresses the difference in meaning in everyday language. A set of individuals has to be tied together for a certain purpose. The word 'team' is used here as an instrument to fulfil a set of objectives. This is reflected in the following definition: 'a team is a small number of people with complementary skills who are committed to a common purpose, performance goals, and approach for which they hold themselves mutually accountable' (Katzenbach and Smith 1998). However, this formal definition is not so very different from that of a group. This might be the reason why both words are often used as synonyms in the literature. Here we stay closer to the meaning of the terms 'groups' and 'teams' as they are used in daily life and everyday language: the group and the team are regarded as poles of a continuum (Tyson 1989). Any team is to be regarded as a group. The group turns into a team once it gets organized well enough to fulfil a purpose. This implies a process of *organization design* by which effective patterns of task allocation, decision making and communication emerge. The transition of groups into teams is in this respect the result of a learning process or, in other words, the result of *organization development*. The group becomes an effective team by using its experience in following and improving organizational patterns. This represents the double perspective.

2 Teamwork as a cure for bureaucracy

Whereas groups as social entities is probably as old as mankind, organizational interest in groups and teams is more recent. One of the main reasons is that up until now teamwork has often been viewed as a cure for bureaucracy. The main characteristic of bureaucracy is 'segmentation' (Kanter 1983). Large problems are being cut into sub-problems and sub-sub-problems. These sub- and sub-sub-problems are allocated to sub-units and sub-sub-units. In the end the solutions offered by these units must be assembled again to form a meaningful whole. Segmentation is based on the concentration of functions in the firm; tasks, skills and processes of the same kind are allocated to specialized units. This functional concentration takes place at all levels in the organization. At the top level, the traditional main functions are marketing, research and development, production and finance. The main functions are in their turn divided into partial functions. In a marketing department one usually finds groups such as product planning, sales planning, sales, sales promotion and customer services. Finally, one finds functional concentration as an organizing principle on the shop floor. For example, in a traditional tool workshop one finds drillers working with drillers and turners with turners. On the 'shop floor' of an insurance company (see Example 1), tasks are frequently split up according to both the type of insurance and the type of operational task, such as the processing of a policy and the assessment of claims. A characteristic of bureaucracy is the distinction between 'doing' and 'thinking'. The operational or production tasks carried out on the shop floor are carefully stripped from 'indirect' tasks by which the production process is controlled and improved. These tasks (planning, work preparation, maintenance, quality control) are allocated to staff departments, which are functionally concentrated. In this way the functions all become part of a complex machine. Mintzberg (1979) refers in this respect to organizations as 'machine bureaucracies'. Such machine bureaucracies must carry a heavy control load because the strong division of parts requires extensive coordination. Within the bureaucracy coordination demands a steep hierarchy and a complex system of rules and procedures. In this set-up there is no place for teams. Teams are even regarded as a negative element of the organization. Their initiatives might disturb the functioning of the fine-tuned machinery and groups might hide themselves from management control. Frederick Winslow Taylor (Braverman 1974), the father of scientific management, even regarded the group (especially the informal group) as a threat to productivity. In his view workers only want to do as little work as possible for the highest possible pay. He referred to this attitude as 'soldiering'. In a group individuals are given the chance to hide themselves from organizational controls. To him group development was synonymous with 'systematic soldiering'. In a traditional bureaucracy one might make an exception in this respect for groups which are outside the organization and in highly unpredictable situations, like the service or installation unit, the crew of a submarine or a sales group in Africa.

Machine bureaucracy has been very effective for decades. It was the 'era of mass production' in which economy of scale was the leading and compelling guideline: a product was produced for as long as possible in batches as large as possible. However, the dysfunctions of bureaucracy became manifest the moment the organization had to act in a flexible and adaptable way. This was the case when: life cycles of products and services were drastically shortened; smaller batches of customized products had to be delivered; the pace of technological innovation was accelerating and technologies were increasingly melting and integrating into hybrids and systems; competition was taking place in global rather than local markets; and quality requirements of customers became increasingly strict.

At this point the bureaucracy threatens to be destroyed by its own control burden and must invest in new strategies. Galbraith (1973) distinguishes four main strategies. First, the organization simply accepts that it is not effective; for example, it accepts 'slack' in the form of overcapacity or stock. As a second strategy the control system is reinforced by the introduction of 'vertical control systems'. The third and the fourth strategies imply an introduction of team concepts in the design of the organization; the third involves the introduction of *lateral linkages*, or groups that horizontally cut across the existing boundaries of functions (a special form of this is the *management team*); the fourth is the creation of self-contained units in which the functions are integrated around a certain underflow and complete little firms are created within the walls of a bigger firm (the autonomous *production team* is an important example).

Management teams

A characteristic of 'machine bureaucracy' is that the functions which make up the organization do not come together until the top of the firm. Management solves the problems between the functions of the organization; the classic problems between productions and sales and between product development and process development. The management of a factory, division or corporation is confronted with a large variety of interface problems which cannot be solved at a lower level in classic bureaucracy simply because of the lack of horizontal and lateral linkages. It is no surprise that the communication and decision-making channels to the top can be heavily clogged up. In the 1970s such interface problems became increasingly frequent because more and more subjects came into existence that could not be demarcated within the boundaries of the organizational functions: logistics, quality, innovation. Thus, there was a manifest need to act together as a team in the top echelon of the firm, the division or the plant, rather than as representatives of functional sub-interests in the firm. For this purpose 'team-building programmes' were set up, focused on promoting trust and open communication within teams. This was subsequently extended to the lower echelons of the organization. Each manager can be considered in this view as the chairman of his own team. This process is referred to as organization development.

Recent research suggests that it is relevant to make a distinction between teams at the top and other management teams, as well as between team and non-team – also called single leader – opportunities. It is argued that team opportunities are often overlooked, especially at the top of organizations, where implicit leadership theories and soloistic habits easily rule out real team performance. However, not every business situation calls for real team efforts at the top, or in other management teams for that matter. Three tradeoffs are important in considering a team versus a non-team approach to achieve desired organization goals: speed versus performance, leadership clarity versus leadership capacity, and skill versus influence. The acid test for a real team opportunity is formed by (1) the potential value of a team's collective work products; (2) the sharing or shifting of the leadership role among the members, and (3) the common levels of committment and mutual accountability for results (Katzenbach and Smith 1998).

Lateral teams

The establishment of a task force or project group is frequently used when a problem arises that cannot be solved within the normal organization. In cases like these a temporary group is created, composed of the different organizational functions, with the task of solving such a problem. The problem may be related to the development of a product, a new system for job classification or a sales campaign in a new market. Such groups may vary greatly as regards life span, degree of organization, degree of participation, influence and resources. Sometimes such a group has a very short life; for example, members of an *ad hoc* group charged with the internal relocation within an office will cooperate intensively with one another for a limited number of weeks in order to finish a concrete job. A group that must prepare a merger with another firm is similar, but possesses substantially more power. Some groups have a permanent character; for example, the users' councils representing information technology users from various plants. These meet on a regular basis to communicate about different subjects. They often have a representative and advisory character. The time invested in such a team by the members is mostly limited.

In innovation projects the time invested by team members may be the larger part of their working time. The project group may be important to the extent that it becomes the core of the work organization. The functional departments then become suppliers of manpower to a multifunctional or multidisciplinary team. The project manager is really the boss, or a 'heavyweight project manager' (Clark and Wheelwright 1992), who controls the resources and is responsible for the result. The managers of the functional departments are responsible for updating the functional know-how and clearly play an inferior role. In groups with a 'lightweight project manager' the functional managers are the ones that possess most power. This leads to the classic field of tension of the matrix organization: the members of the project team are pushed back and forth by both their functional and their project managers.

Production teams

The team concept is also frequently applied in the primary process of production of service organizations. These groups are labelled semi-autonomous groups, self-managing groups or production cells. By introducing these groups organizations distance themselves from the Taylorist production organization. The teams are given the responsibility for a whole product or a whole service package, or for a meaningful part of the product or service package. Team members learn to perform all tasks or an important part of the tasks. Jobs are being integrated and/or there is a possibility of job rotation. Teams are also given the responsibility for indirect tasks, for example, work scheduling, quality control, maintenance and ordering supplies. Sometimes they even hire new members. Example 1, taken from den Hertog (1994), gives an example of such a group.

Example 1: a large Dutch general insurance company redesigned one its major divisions. In the old situation the work was organized in product units (fire, cars, and so on). Within the product groups the work was split into two main domains: acceptance of risk (processing policies) and assessment of damage claims. The market called for an integration and improvement of services towards the customers. Product units were replaced by regional units responsible for the service of a set of customers (in this case, independent insurance intermediaries). Within each unit insurance teams were introduced which handled the whole range of insurances, both in acceptance and assessment. In the following phase acceptance and assessment will also be integrated in the insurance.

Such groups have a number of advantages (Agurén and Edgren 1980; Roberts 1993). First, the control burden can be strongly reduced. A great number of operations can be taken care of close to their execution, which means that problems can be solved directly where they arise without the intervention of a staff department. The size of the staff services thus can be strongly reduced. Flexibility has increased because it is much easier to introduce a new product variant in a single team than to rebuild a whole production line. The waiting times between functions and operations can also be strongly reduced, so that the throughput time of an order is also decreased. In addition, small batches can be run more rapidly. Thus, not only is the client served quicker, but the stock can also be reduced. Finally, the process is more motivating because the simple jobs that are fragmented in the machine bureaucracy can be combined into meaningful and more complex tasks. The shift of responsibilities to the shop floor and the integration of thinking and doing offers a perspective on a more participative style of decision making within the organization, which better matches the democratic values outside the organization.

Virtual teams

In recent years advances in information and communication technology have offered new options for the development of teamwork. Traditionally we associate teams with face-to-face interactions, being somewhere together at same time, in the same place. The new technologies (intranets and the Internet) make it possible to work as a team, while the members never meet in the same room at the same time. *Virtual teams*, as they are called (Lipnack and Stamps 1997) link people with a common purpose. Virtual teams are becoming increasingly important as building elements for network organizations which have become crucial in the knowledge economy. Technology plays an enabling role here, but building virtual teams remains essentially a process of organizational learning.

3 Organization design

The introduction of teamwork in organizations is a matter of careful design. When looking for an alternative to an assembly line, it does not suffice to take a pair of scissors and cut the larger system into pieces before pasting them together. A number of important structural criteria apply both to the lateral and the production teams:

1 a complete task to be carried out independently;
2 a good link with other groups in the organization;
3 sufficient instruments to steer the group's own process;
4 a good internal organization.

The team is an organization in itself, but at the same time it is also part of a larger system. If one does not take this into account sooner or later the team threatens to be rejected by the surrounding organization as an alien body. This is one of the most essential lessons learned from the introduction of semi-autonomous groups in the 1960s and 1970s (van Eijnatten 1993). In this respect the introduction of team concepts into an organization is a matter of organization design. Tasks must be allocated between and within teams. Systems must be introduced to control the work process. Since 1980 the development of such design strategies for teamwork has made much progress, not only on paper but in the design practice as well (for example, Agurén and Edgren 1980; van Eijnatten 1993; Roberts 1993; Warnecke 1993). The approaches described in this literature share the following similarities:

1 the organization is approached as an entity;
2 the design focuses on production flows;
3 responsibilities are pushed down in the organization as low as possible;
4 formal design rules and design instruments are used in a clear sequence of design steps.

The basic logic on which these approaches are based becomes visible in three main design stages. These stages are outlined using the terminology of the Dutch version of the sociotechnical systems approach (van Eijnatten 1993).

Stage 1: functional requirements

The redesign must enable the organization to better meet the external demands, both current and future, which are placed upon the firm or institution. A strategic analysis of strengths and weaknesses, opportunities and threats is the basis for a

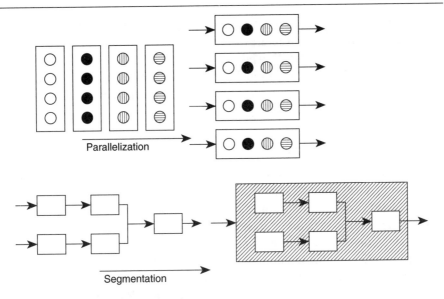

Figure 1 Parallelization and segmentation

list of functional requirements. In design practice this analysis involves a large group of managers and workers, with the purpose of obtaining both a better starting point and support in the organization for the redesign process. Functional requirements may be related to all facets of business, for example: it must be possible to deliver an order within three weeks; stocks cannot constitute more than 10 per cent of total capital; the call rate from the market must be reduced to less than 1 per cent; the quality of work must be matched with the qualifications of the workforce.

Stage 2: the production structure

The focus of the redesign is on the production process: the chain of activities by which material and information is transformed into a product or service. This is also referred to as the production structure. The redesign concentrates on creating parallel production flows – a coherent flow of more or less similar orders. In a machine plant this may concern orders for machine parts that undergo a similar pattern of operations and that are of similar size. In an insurance company (see Example 1) this may be the flow of services performed for a certain part of its clients. When formulating the parallel flows it is important that there exist as few interfaces between the flows as possible. It must be possible to solve the larger part of the problems within the parallel flows. The effect of parallelization is that it radically decreases internal variance of possible operation patterns. The large complex system is rebuilt into a set of smaller, orderly production units that are responsible for a part of the order flow (Figure 1). Production teams are accountable for a whole product or a meaningful, completed part of it. In the case of a highly complex product, such as an automobile or a large information system, it is often necessary to form modules or segments. Segmentation here does not mean the splitting up of tasks but the assembling of meaningful parts of the whole process. The production structure is designed from the top down: the global structures are filled in first, followed by the task structure at group and individual level (Figure 1). This is quite logical because the global structures (main flows and segments) determine the degrees of freedom for the design at detail level rather than the other way around.

Stage 3: the control structure

In this approach the control structure is derived from the production structure. One must first establish what must be controlled before one can determine how the production system can be controlled. If the production structure can be simplified, the control structure can be simplified also. The control structure is designed the opposite way around from the production structure: from the bottom up. As a basic rule, everything that can be controlled locally on the shop floor, within and between teams, must be controlled there. The decisions that remain to be made are subsequently controlled at the following level. In this way only the most essential (strategic) matters are left for the management team. In the design of the control structure the greatest part of staff activities (planning, maintenance, quality control) are brought to the production flows as closely as possible. These activities are performed for the most part within the production teams themselves.

Thus, more or less complete firms come into existence that are able to control a maximum set of operations and decisions within the greater whole. The same organizational logic is followed at each level of the firm. Warnecke (1993) speaks of the 'fractal company' in this respect, because the properties of the whole can be found at each system level. This type of approach has been applied in a large variety of firms: automobile assembly, insurance companies, machine plants, maintenance workshops of air carriers, banks, post offices, chemical plants and oil refineries. Following a sound design strategy with a clear design sequence is crucial to prevent design faults from being ingrained, which are difficult to repair later.

4 Group development

A sound structure does not necessarily imply an effective organization. Managers and workers alike must learn to work in such a new structure. For many people the step from the old to the new situation is a big one. One has often unlearned to carry responsibility and work together in a tightly knit group. This is illustrated by Example 2. The example shows that tasks are broadened. The team members are about to perform the most important operations for all types of insurance. They have much closer contact with clients and must also use a new computer system. The group must be given time to get used to and deal with this much broader task, but equally important is that they must learn what it is like to work closely together in a team. This often becomes clear as soon as a teamwork organization is implemented.

Example 2: On 1st September, the insurance company relocates to a brand new building. This is also the date of the implementation of the new teamwork organization. Anne goes to work with mixed feelings combining curiosity, uneasiness and eagerness. She has to find her way in the new building. Last weekend Anne had a goodbye dinner with her old room-mates. She now shares a room with two new colleagues whom she hardly knows. She feels uncomfortable about the whole situation. She only knows three of the twelve colleagues in the team and decides to make a fresh start and be nice to everyone, not knowing what to expect from them. After some time she begins to feel more secure as a member of the group. Everybody is trying to make the best of the given situation. Only Johan, one of her room-mates, has been irritating her from the start. He is always late for work and to the group meetings and he always has an excuse. Some of Anne's colleagues remain strangers in her eyes. Avoiding them seems to be the practical solution. They are just colleagues and have no authority over her. This goes on for some time.

Suddenly, during a team meeting one day, there is an outburst of anger. The group leader is irritated that more and more people are late for the group meeting. Other members mention the heavy workload and complain about the rather authoritarian way the group leader reacts. Two other team members complain about the way work is divided over group members and about the way the information system functions; they have to ask their colleagues for missing information again and again. Too much client-related information is still not covered by the system. A special meeting is convened after this one, to discuss the work process, make new appointments and discuss responsibilities and procedures. The meeting goes fine, and Anne is quite relieved. Irritations are finally expressed. All agree on the goals they want to achieve as a team. During the meetings following this one the atmosphere has really changed. At last Anne and her colleagues can get their jobs properly done. Missing information is not such a problem any more. There is always a colleague who can help out. Anne begins to like the new working conditions and her colleagues. When someone is late the group deals with this with lots of humour but with a clear message. Sometimes somebody is grouchy or there is a chaotic discussion about procedures. Some people have more know-how than others and have more to say sometimes during meetings. But in general, Anne, as well as her colleagues, seems to have found a balance between the group goals and the way they work together.

Looking at the group described in Example 2, several observations can be made of what working in groups is all about. First, it may be clear that group work is not automatically a pleasure, or at least is not always a pleasure. Negative feelings may rise, but, fortunately, positive feelings may arise as well. The question is: what keeps groups together, despite the negative feelings? Second, the changes obviously take place over time. One might wonder whether there is some sort of basic pattern for groups to develop into effective teams.

What keeps groups together?

Basically, the processes that underlie group development fall into two realms that constantly seek to co-exist. A group engages in goal-oriented or task activities as well as maintenance-oriented activities. The first activities (task roles) are aimed at achieving goals, getting the job done. The maintenance roles focus on the group atmosphere, keeping good social relationships and a general state of well-being within the group. Over-emphasis on one realm at the expense of the other leads to frustration, discontent or withdrawal. In order to be an effective team there must be a reasonable balance between both realms. A structure will evolve out of the task realm that is appropriate to the task group, while out of the maintenance realm a structure will develop appropriate to the emotional needs of group members. Combining the two realms results in group development, in which compromises are sought to balance task and maintenance needs and behaviours (Crawley 1978).

Is there some sort of standard pattern for group development?

In the research on group behaviour, the life-cycle metaphor is often used to describe group development as a 'biological' process, starting with birth and ending with old age or death (departure). A good example is Tuckman's five-stage model – forming, storming, norming, performing and adjourning – which has proved its value in training and consultancy (Tuckman and Jensen 1977). In Tuckman's theory group structure is the result of simultaneous task activities and group-relating (maintenance or social–emotional) activities. The assumption is that a group must go through one stage before being able to go to the next, and every transition holds the risk of regression to an earlier stage.

Forming. As group members come together for the first time they are all looking for reasons to be there. There is insecurity about tasks and about personal interest in the group. Normally group members are polite and somewhat distant, waiting for what is to come. Social contacts per group member are mostly limited to one or two others. There is a great need for clarity and the group leader is expected to offer this. Dependency is high at this stage.

Storming. In this phase individual search takes place. Personal conflicts about roles and responsibilities are common. Often group members compete over positions and status within the group. The atmosphere can be very hostile, not accepting individual differences. A group leader can be heavily attacked at this stage. However, the group still depends on this person – while showing counter-dependency. Facilitating group conflict, leading/coaching the group to dialogue and understanding, should be the leader's major concern in order to reach the next stage.

Norming. Contrasts and differences between group members facilitate them to become more understanding. Acceptance of differences of opinions and views arises. Information is shared with group members, and a sense of shared responsibility grows. Cooperation is central to the group and cooperative patterns emerge that are broadly accepted. Decisions are made on a basis of consensus.

Group cohesion grows and the group is enchanted, being freed from previous tensions. At the end of this stage a feeling of disenchantment may occur, as a reaction to the enchantment and as a reaction toward authority. The group needs the fight with the group leader, to become independent and to set its own norms. A group leader should not go into counter-attack, but should stimulate the group to set standards (within reasonable limits), facilitating the group to the transition to the next stage.

Performing. High performance can be reached at this stage of group development. Group performance is continuously brought up in discussions. The group is looking for improvement to increase performance. We might speak of consensual validation in the sense that group members are positively valued for their own specific talents and limits. Group members are honest in their feedback and accountable for their own behaviour. They have settled for the role each member has, including the group leader.

Adjourning. The existence of groups is limited by time. Over time group members leave and are replaced by others. Changing group composition often implies regression to an earlier stage. The rate of transition will depend on the extent of change. Group departure is often accompanied by rituals, such as having a drink or a last conversation. Some group members tend to look back, others to look forward. Change in group composition enables a group to remain open-minded. New group members can be very 'refreshing' as they do not stick to the norms and routines developed by the former group. They offer the group the opportunity to reconsider its unquestioned, old routines and thus give the group a chance to keep learning.

In the practice of organization redesign there are a number of strategies by which group development can be effectively supported:

Participative design. Members of the future teamwork organization are given an active role in the redesign of their own organization. They become committed at an early stage to the new way of working. Furthermore, they can express their own preferences and the problems they foresee.

Training team leaders. Team leaders are prepared for their new roles as coach, stimulator and decision maker. They exchange experiences during the start-up phase and learn from their colleagues.

Group feedback. At regular intervals the teams reflect on their progress in becoming a 'real team'. In meetings they do not discuss only task-related issues but also maintenance issues.

Introduction of new members. A relative stability of group membership is important, but from time to time 'new blood' must be brought in to avoid the team from becoming rooted in its own behavioural patterns.

5 Conclusions

The main conclusion one can draw from the arguments presented here is that organization design and organization development are two sides of the same coin. New structures will not help when the members of the team stick to old behavioural patterns and when they do not make any progress in the development of satisfying social relationships. The effectiveness and efficiency of a team are dependent on the learning process the team undergoes by passing through successive developmental stages. These stages or phases are facilitated by group leaders, adopting a style contingent on the stage the group is in. The group can then develop its own task and maintenance structure. The group should be autonomous enough to develop itself toward effective and efficient routines and norms, with feedback from group members as the dominant learning vehicle.

However, the design of effective structures is also vital. The group can only develop itself as a self-managing team when it is given a self-contained and meaningful task. Furthermore, the team must be embedded in an organizational environment with enough degrees of freedom to realize its own potential. When the surrounding functions remain untouched and act along the same centralistic and bureaucratic patterns sooner or later the team will relapse into frustration, rebellion or apathy. The team cannot develop itself without the right amount of capacity to control its own processes. The design and development of teams must always be an integrated part of the redesign and development of the organization as a whole.

Further reading

(References cited in the text marked *)

* Agurén, S. and Edgren, J. (1980) *New Factories: Job Design through Factory Planning in Sweden*, Stockholm: Swedish Employers' Confederation (SAF). (A compilation of practical experiences from the Swedish programme for job reform.)
* Braverman, H. (1974) *Labor and Monopoly Capital: The Degradation of Work in the Twentieth Century*, New York: Review Press. (A Marxist interpretation of the development of work organization from the rise of mass production until the present revolution in information technologies.)
* Clark, K.B. and Wheelwright, S.C. (1992) *Revolutionizing Product Development: Quantum Leaps in Speed, Efficiency and Quality*, New York: The Free Press. (This influential book provides a good insight into the different strategies to improve the organization of product design process in practice.)
* Crawley, J. (1978) 'The lifecycle of the group', *Small Groups Newsletter* 1 (2): 39–44. (A brief but illuminating article on goal orientation and maintenance tasks needed to fulfil group needs.)
* Eijnatten, F.M. van (1993) *The Paradigm that Changed the Work Place*, Assen: Van Gorcum. (A historical sketch of the development of human-centred strategies for job design: 'sociotechnical systems design'.)
* Galbraith, J.R. (1973) *Designing Complex Organisations*, Reading: Addison-Wesley. (This small and very readable book is a classic introduction to organization design and still relevant today.)
* Hertog, J.F. den (1994) 'Entrepreneurship at the shopfloor: Nationale Nederlanden', in L.E. Andreasen, B. Coriat, J.F. den Hertog and R. Kaplinsky (eds), *Europe's Next Step: Organisational Innovation, Competition and Employment*, London: Frank Cass Publishers. (A case description which illustrates the introduction of a teamwork organization in a large Dutch insurance firm.)

* Johnson, D.W. and Johnson, F.P. (1991) *Joining Together: Group Theory and Group Skills*, Englewood Cliffs, NJ: Prentice Hall. (A US textbook on group theory. Uses experiential learning throughout the book as a learning tool to students.)

* Kanter, R.M. (1983) *The Change Masters: Innovation for Productivity in the American Corporation*, New York: Simon & Schuster. (This book reports on a research project in which the strategies of successfully innovating US firms are compared with those of less successful firms.)

  Katzenbach, J.R. (ed.) (1998) *The Work of Teams*, Boston, MA: Harvard Business Press. (A book containing 14 *Harvard Business Review* articles first published between 1987 and 1998, discussing topics around creating and managing teams).

* Katzenbach, J.R. and Smith, D.K. (1998) *The Wisdom of Teams*, London: McGraw-Hill International. (A bestseller which describes different issues that are important to team performance, including how to overcome obstacles. Easy to read and peppered with case descriptions).

* Lipnack, J. and Stamps, J. (1997) *Virtual Teams: Reaching across Space, Time, and Organizations with Technology*, New York: John Wiley. (Very practical guide for design and development of teams in the age of the intra- and Internet, bestseller.)

* Mintzberg, H. (1979) *The Structuring of Organisations: A Synthesis of Research*, Englewood Cliffs, NJ: Prentice Hall. (In this book the author presents a typology of organizational structures, dividing them into simple structure, machine bureaucracy, professional bureaucracy and adhocracy. This book is a must for the interested reader.)

* Roberts, H.J.E. (1993) *Accountability and Responsibility; The Influence of Organisation Design on Management Accounting*, Maastricht: Datawyse/University of Maastricht. (The report of a research project in three medium-sized Dutch firms. The study shows how the management accounting systems could be simplified and made more effective after the introduction of teamwork.)

  Tjosfold, D. (1991) *Team Organisation: An Enduring Competitive Advantage*, Chichester: Wiley. (An accessible book with a strong belief in the power of teams and teamwork to gain competitive advantage. Each theme starts with a short case illustrating everyday organizational experience.)

* Tuckman, B.W. and Jensen, M.A. (1977) 'Stages of small group development revisited', *Group and Organisation Studies* 2 (4): 419–27. (One of the many articles providing a model for group development. Its main distinction from other models is the focus on increased efficiency as an outcome of group development.)

* Tyson, B.T. (1989) *Working with Groups*, South Melbourne: Macmillan. (A comprehensive booklet primarily orientated towards bringing theory into practice. Very handy to look up themes, theories and authors.)

* Warnecke, H.J. (1993) *The Fractal Company: A Revolution in Corporate Culture*, Berlin: Springer. (This rather practical book offers an organization design theory for the future firm, with teamwork being one of the main issues.)

Entries into
organizational dynamics

Organizational learning

Silvia Gherardi

Overview

Organizational learning is a relatively recent metaphor for the organization which stands alongside other metaphors, both old and new, such as organizational culture, the open system, the machine or the organism. Metaphorical language is one of the most important devices by which knowledge is generated, and it is based essentially on an analogic process which sets A (the already-known term) in relation to B (the term that one wishes to know). In this way cognitive transpositions come into operation which make it possible to imagine and to talk about the object in question (for example, the organization) as if it were another already-known object. A metaphor works by matching what is distant with what is close, similar features with dissimilar ones, and it is a cognitive tool which develops creativity and social imagination and reveals the importance of language and symbols in the construction of reality and in the formulation of theory. Organizational learning is a metaphor which matches two concepts – learning and organization – and enables exploration of the organization as if it were a subject which learns, which processes information, which reflects on experiences, and which is endowed with a stock of knowledge, skills and expertise. It is a metaphor which problematizes the relationship between organization and knowledge, between organization and the social and cognitive processing of knowledge, between organizational action and organizational thought.

Knowledge is today a vital problem for all organizations because the production of goods and services increasingly involves knowledge; because new information technologies are 'knowledge intensive', and such knowledge has an extremely short life-span and is highly innovative; because flexibility is today the most valued of competences. In the post-industrial age, knowledge is a resource just as important as raw materials, economic and human resources, and may give an organization competitive advantage. Study of organizations as if they were systems which learn may be of assistance in the design of organizations which act according to principles of experimentation, of trial and error, of success and failure, of discovery and invention.

The following sections trace the development of the concept of organizational learning within organizational studies. The aim will be to show the variety of interpretations that have been given to both the term 'organization' and the term 'learning', and to demonstrate how different definitions can be given to the notion of 'organizational learning'. Then, what is entailed by studying organizational learning at the level of individuals, of the organization and of networks of organizations is illustrated.

1 A brief history of the concept of organizational learning

The metaphor of organizational learning is constructed on the basis of analogies with two different entities: the cybernetic system and the human mind.

Fundamental to the former conception is the notion of information. Like other natural or social systems, the organization can be conceived as an evolving information model whose most interesting aspect is its capacity for self-design. The thermostat provides an example: the organization-as-thermostat is able to learn in the sense that it is able to identify and adjust deviations from the standard. This is the 'single-loop' learning that cybernetics bases on four principles (Morgan 1986):

1 Systems must be able to perceive, monitor and seek out significant features of their environment.
2 Systems must be able to connect the information thus acquired with the operational norms that guide systemic behaviour.
3 Systems must be able to identify significant deviations from these norms.
4 Systems must be able to take corrective action when these deviations are detected.

However important the organizational processes which establish norms, standards of variability, information systems with which to adapt to a variable environment, and control and regulation actions may be, the crucial factor is the adequacy of these norms, and therefore the ability of systems to learn how to learn – that is, to develop 'double-loop' learning routines – and thereby acquire the capacity to self-organize themselves. Common to all the literature on organizational learning is a basic assumption – recursiveness – although this is rarely employed except in the ritual homage paid by almost all authors to Bateson (1972) and his concept of deutero-learning; a concept very close to that of the double loop.

The second analogy underlying the metaphor of the organization as a learning system compares it with the human mind. The analogy between organization and mind shifts the metaphor of organizational learning from the organization to the individuals within it, since this kind of learning is no longer the learning objectified in norms, procedures, routines and standards. Rather, it is the cognitive activity which produces images, representations, causal links, and which is sensitive not only to human passions but to the social and organizational conditioning of thought as well.

The relationship between learning individuals and the social systems that benefit from this learning requires a brief historical excursus into the literature on organizational learning, bearing in mind the above two analogies – with the cybernetic system and the mind – because they underpin two radically different conceptualizations.

The works generally recognized as pioneering in this field are those by Argyris and Schön (1974, 1978) and Argyris (1982). Mention should also be made of an author who has always alluded to learning and to the link between learning and decision-making processes, although only few of his works are specifically devoted to this topic. I refer to March and in particular to his inclusion of the concept of learning in the behavioural decision model (Cyert and March 1963), and also to his subsequent jointly authored works (Herriot, Levinthal and March 1988; March, Sproull and Tamuz 1991).

Researchers interested in knowledge have examined specific organizational phenomena in terms of learning defined in a variety of ways:

- As learning curves (Yelle 1979), a concept which probably stands at the basis of the most long-standing interest in learning. Learning curves rest on the principle that the person-hours required to produce a unit of output decrease in proportion to the experience accumulated. Productive processes display characteristic learning curves in relation to a set of organizational factors. Hence derives the idea that there is something more than mere individual learning and that experience constitutes a transferable body of knowledge which may become institutionalized and incorporated into situations different from the original ones.

- As behavioural change through trial and error. Learning is a self-regulating process which detects errors and corrects them or, if preferred, which checks actions against their outcomes and makes appropriate adjustments to subsequent actions. This conception may be applied to the organization as an information processor (Galbraith 1973) or as a producer of knowledge on the nexuses between input, output and their reception by the environment.

- As adaptation to the environment, and therefore as the capacity to 'fit in', to adjust to external stimuli which must be opportunely and rapidly discovered. Learning is therefore synonymous with structural change and acts as a signal of successful evolution. Moreover, learning as systemic wisdom does not come about solely within organizations or within competitive relationships among organizations. It also appears in the networks of informal learning (Trist 1983) established among numerous organizations by means of collaborative exchanges.

- As economy of search. The economizing of cognitive energies in problem solving has been demonstrated by Newell and Simon (1972). New solutions are first looked for in familiar settings and then, because the costs of the search increase proportionately, in progressively more unfamilar ones. Those solutions that have proved valid in the past are more likely to be the ones adopted in the future. They are learnt and retained as long as they continue to function. Learning takes place through the incorporation of experience into search rules, into attention rules, and into organizational goals (Levitt and March 1988).

- As the modification of mental maps. Since Argyris and Schön (1974) pointed out the gap between what organizations say they do (espoused theory) and what they actually do (theory-in-use), learning resides in the ability to bring explanations and the ideas guiding what is done into alignment with the organizational changes introduced. These authors make explicit reference to the cybernetic analogy; but at the same time they stress that organizational change requires modification of the way in which organizations represent reality to themselves. In this connection Ansoff (1980) has developed a version of action-learning research in which organizational change and learning proceed in parallel because one of the cornerstones of action research has always been learning (learning by doing or learning by experience).

The diverse knowledge interests of researchers have located learning at various positions along a continuum with adaptation to the environment at one extreme (together with the analogy of the cybernetic system), and the autonomous elaboration of thought at the other (together with the analogy of the organization as a mind). Note that it is not necessary to choose one of these two extreme conceptions and to elevate it to the status of 'true learning'. It is more interesting to preserve the complexity of learning by bearing in mind that elements of quasi-automatic alignment, exigencies of cognitive economy and knowledge capitalization, adaptation and proaction may all be co-present in the relationship between organization and knowledge.

In order to show the polysemy of the term 'learning', I shall make explicit reference to four systematic surveys of studies on organizational learning (Argyris and Schön 1978; Shrivastava 1983; Fiol and Lyles 1985; Huber 1991) which comprise approximately 200 titles.

Argyris and Schön identify six conceptualizations of learning, according to how the organization is conceived:

- If it is a group, then learning takes place at the level of the interactions among individuals performing a task.
- If it is a collective actor, it learns from the experience stored in organizational maps and action-plans.
- If it is a structure, it learns by changing in accordance with the external and internal environment.
- If it is a system, it learns through error-regulating mechanisms.
- If it is a cultural system, learning is a process of socialization, of transformation of cognitive and judgemental patterns, as well as deliberate transformation of reality.

If it is a political arena, the subject-matter of learning is the strategies – competitive and cooperative – employed to control organizational dynamics.

Shrivastava identifies four conceptualizations of organizational learning: as institutionalized experience, as adaptation, as knowledge of action–outcome relationships, as assumption sharing. In the first conception, by organizational learning is meant only that learning embedded in standard operating procedures, methods of communication and coordination, and shared understanding about tasks that have a persistent effect. In the adaptive approach, organizational learning is a complex process of mutual intraorganizational regulation triggered by the combination of different kinds of perceived stress. From the perspective of organizations as systems of knowledge of action–outcome relationships, organizations are purposeful systems or information processors relying on available inputs to confront the turbulence of their environment. From the assumption-sharing perspective, organizations are artefacts based on the cognitive maps that their members use to orient themselves in their interactions, and organizational learning consists of the process whereby these maps are modified.

The third typology (Fiol and Lyles 1985) seeks to prescribe what can be legitimately defined as organizational learning. Fiol and Lyles distinguish between the development of behaviour and the development of cognition, so that changes of behaviour constitute adaptation while learning only takes place within cognition, where it is hierarchized into low-level (single-loop) and high-level (double-loop) learning. For Fiol and Lyles organizational learning consists in the improvement of actions through better knowledge and understanding, while cognition is the development of reflections, knowledge and associations between past actions, their efficacy and future actions. But if we examine the definitions of learning and cognition more closely we discern the profound embarrassment, shared by all enquiries in the field, over a too-sharp distinction drawn between thinking and doing, over the difficulty of establishing a logical priority between thought and action, between the self-constitution of the subject (individual or organization) and its self-relationing to the environment.

The most interesting aspect of Fiol and Lyles's work is that they distinguish three areas of agreement among studies on learning:

- acknowledgement of the importance of adjustment to the environment;
- a distinction drawn between learning by individuals and learning by organizations;
- identification of four contextual factors which create and reinforce learning, and which are created by learning in turn: culture, strategy, structure and environment.

The most recent survey of the literature is by Huber (1991), who proposes closer integration among studies of organizational learning. Huber identifies four constructs correlated with learning: knowledge acquisition, information distribution, the interpretation of information, and organizational memory. There is an abundant and diversified literature on the first two constructs, but the last two have been relatively ignored and require a great deal of further empirical research.

Huber concentrates on knowledge acquisition, which he divides into five sub-processes by which an organization acquires knowledge. It should be stressed, in fact, that Huber views learning as a process which he defines as follows: 'An entity learns if, through its processing of information, the range of its potential behaviours is changed' (Huber 1991: 89).

Unlike other authors, therefore, Huber does not assume that learning immediately translates into either change or increased learning, or into competitive advantage. The translation of learning into subsequent action is a different matter.

2 Learning as a social phenomenon

Knowledge, interaction and mutual comprehension are based on reflexivity and recursiveness. A mirroring process takes place between the intrapsychic level and the level of social cognition whereby one may say that cognition is the product of social interaction (Gherardi and Nicolini 2000). Learning is a more complex process than simple adjustment of behaviour, because it requires the subject to be able recursively to articulate and organize the reality in which he or she moves.

Almost every community that works, which collectively manages work processes, and the processes of problem solving and the institutionalization of the solutions that have proved effective, is a community that learns. In other words, occupational communities weave together those social relationships that enable the individual to learn and to become a member of that community by acquiring the technical knowledge required by its work, the knowledge necessary to behave in a way appropriate to work situations, and the deontology of that community. In this case these are individuals who learn within a context of social relations, using an existing knowledge base, enriching it, experimenting with it, and passing it on to new members. Learning is still fluid, scarcely formalized and sparsely codified.

The term 'community of practice' used by Lave and Wenger (1991), Brown and Duguid (1991) and Wenger (1998) has the merit of highlighting a situated view of knowing and learning. Brown and Duguid propose the concept of learning-in-working to stress the fluid evolution of learning within the work process, i.e. in practice. Since it is work practice that contains the potential to develop skills, there are certain conditions that facilitate the learning of skills and render the process more agreeable. The concept of participation highlights the fact that learning does not take place solely or principally in the minds of individuals but rather stems from the participation of individuals in social activities. Working and organizing are social practices engaged in through a set of activities situated in specific contexts of interaction. Organizational learning is learning-in-organizing, because working, learning and organizing are not distinct activities within a practice. The concept of participation, therefore, gives access to a practice-based theorizing of learning that takes place in action and through action.

As in other areas of other activity, subjects (whether individuals or groups) develop skills more easily if they:

- are motivated to do so, i.e. if they are prepared, informed, anxiety-free, etc.;
- have a sufficiently comprehensible task to perform and know what is expected of them;
- are able to play an active role; i.e. are able to participate in the process;

- are able to experiment;
- receive cognitive reinforcement, i.e. information on action accomplished, and whatever else may constitute a subjective reward;
- can establish relatively stable trust relations with co-decision-makers, thereby developing collective decision structures which incorporate reflexivity;
- can derive pleasure from decision-making activity.

An organizational structure which creates these operational conditions implicitly provides better conditions for learning by the individuals and groups internally to it. However, this does not necessarily imply that individual and collective learning will be transferred to the organization and become organizational learning. People learn while they work, but they do not necessarily learn things that are useful for the organization; nor are they necessarily willing to transfer useful knowledge to the organization and to codify it in a manner that renders it usable by others. Knowledge is produced and transmitted in a context structured by the power relations that render learning by individuals a local and social phenomenon, one difficult to single out and study because there may be legitimate reasons for concealing it. However, it is a phenomenon that is produced when people are engaged in developing a collective mode of doing something (a practice). The social dimension of learning has suggested the existence of a group mind taking the form of cognitive interdependence focused around memory processes. People working together give life to a single transactive memory system, complete with differentiated responsibility for remembering their experience. In similar manner to the neuron connections in the brain, the behaviours of people in organizations may be spontaneously and tacitly activated, and interconnect so that they coordinate an intelligent action. Social learning may thus be seen as a network of collective behaviours based on distributed knowledge (Tsoukas 1996).

3 Learning as an organizational phenomenon

Discussion of learning as an organizational phenomenon must begin by clarifying the relationship between individuals who learn and organizational processes, thereby avoiding the risk of anthropomorphizing the organization (Nicolini and Meznar 1995). I shall therefore assume that learning and cognition are situated human activities. They are psychological and social processes which find in the organizational context not only a container for action but also organizational processes of support or inhibition, structures which incorporate the results of those human activities and operational routines which embody the knowledge produced by a plurality of group minds. It is assumed that it is important for the subject reflecting on the conduct of the organization to be aware that knowledge is an organizational resource, and that it is therefore necessary to monitor the quantity, quality, distribution, ownership and vintage of the stock of organizational knowledge.

Starting from the latter assumption, we may say that the knowledge available to an organization is more or less fluid, more or less consolidated, more or less objectified in artefacts, more or less localized in the mind of a few, and so on. Knowledge is acquired in a variety of ways: by relying on the knowledge available at the moment of the organization's birth; by learning from experience; by learning from the experience of other organizations; by recruiting bearers of knowledge necessary to the organization but which it does not possess; by searching for information about the environment and about the organization's performance; by improvisation. Much of the knowledge utilized by an organization lies in the public domain. It is widely available and not protected by particular constraints, and may have been directly acquired from incoming material. This is the case of the knowledge incorporated in raw materials, in machinery and in equipment. Other knowledge may be less accessible because it is protected by patents or property rights, or because it is generated within a system of interests intent on limiting undifferentiated access to it, or because it is too specialized to be publicly available. Yet other knowledge may prove even more difficult to acquire because it is less codified, more fluid, and more internal to its bearers/producers: these are the representation schemata, the codes used to interpret events, the abilities and skills that have been developed through experience and which are jealously guarded by the community that has produced them; they are habits and everything that for brevity's sake is called organizational culture and tacit knowledge.

Alongside the knowledge incorporated in more or less material products, there are two further types: the knowledge incorporated in standard operational procedures, and the knowledge incorporated in individual and collective professional expertise (communities of practice, work groups, teams, etc.). In both cases part of such knowledge is available externally to the organization that uses it (scientific or professional knowledge), while another part is internally produced and is highly specific, that is, largely untransferable. Organizations devote a great deal of time and resources to codifying and diffusing the knowledge they use. To do this they establish routines understood in the broad sense as manuals, job descriptions, circulars, memos and forms, as well as personnel selection, socialization and training procedures.

Codification is the principal way to incorporate knowledge; but not all knowledge is equally incorporable, either because it is the nascent state or because it is difficult to codify, or because its codification takes time and money. Organizations also differ in the extent to which knowledge is incorporated into routines: artisan activity relies more on diffused 'craft-specific' knowledge than do bureaucracies. Organizations that change rapidly and deal with problems that resist immediate analysis rely more on informally diffused knowledge than do organizations operating in simpler and stabler environments.

Knowledge is a strategic resource, but awareness of its potential as an organizational resource may be highly diversified. For example, a routine is the objectification of knowledge of how something should be done; but everyday practice may alter, even considerably, the habitual manner of doing that 'something' because, from an abstract norm, the routine becomes praxis by the incorporation into action of knowledge produced locally by a 'community of practice'. A routine, moreover, has limited capacity for specification because it cannot incorporate expertise to do with tacit knowledge, ability and skill; and nor does it codify what is presumed to be so well known as to be taken for granted.

Classic organization theory conceptualized this problematic in terms of an opposition between formal and informal organization. It thus evidenced the gap between planning and execution that lay at the basis of this concept of organization. By reducing the distance between planning work and its execution, by considering organizations with, so to speak, high knowledge density, by socially building the knowledge required by productive processes and therefore viewing the organization as a set of occupational and professional communities, or communities of practice, the problem of managing knowledge is formulated in different terms. Attention thus focuses on the gap between knowledge codified into routines – abstract knowledge – and practical knowledge or knowledge in action.

However, knowledge in action may modify routines; that is, it becomes codified knowledge and an organizational asset.

For most of the time and in most of their activities, individuals and organizations rely on mental habits, on what is taken for granted, on thinking-as-usual, on automatic functioning and on quasi-automatic decisions. This allows considerable energy-saving and usually works well in familiar situations. In situations that are unfamiliar, new, uncertain or ambiguous, however, it may prove disastrous. These other situations require a different level of attention, active thought, reflexive activity, conscious control of behaviour, a more systematic search for solutions and analysis of the situation. From quasi-automatic decisions one passes to decisions on the validity of decision-making premises or to innovative decisions.

Nonaka and Takeuchi (1995) have advanced the idea of organization as hypertext, in which the interaction between tacit and explicit knowledge is a key factor in fostering learning and producing new knowledge in organizations. This process, which they call 'knowledge conversion', is a social process which is not restricted to individuals. Using the two dimensions of tacit and explicit, four modes of knowledge conversion are singled out. Each form of conversion creates several occasions for learning and acquiring new knowledge. However, tacit and explicit knowledge are not, of course, separate kinds of knowledge, and their interplay is fundamental to the process of learning. Learning in organizations can be portrayed as a spiral of knowledge acquisition whereby individual tacit knowledge is 'organizationally' amplified through the four modes of knowledge conversion, crystallized into routines, institutionalized by those in charge, and then circulated through the organization. This in turn has a backwash effect on the milieu of action of individuals and of communities of practice, starting the process all over again. This never-ending process is based on individual learning, but its characteristic pattern depends on the specific characteristics of the organization. It is consequently possible to talk both of learning in organizations and of organizational learning.

For organizational learning to take place, a number of conditions are necessary: the presence of reflexivity, willingness to monitor actions, motivation to transfer knowledge and the ability to translate knowledge-in-action into organizational change. People and communities of practice are those that learn; organizations change and their change is sometimes brought about by the incorporation of learning, but it may also occur in other forms, for example through contagion, through variation and selection, through conflict, through problem solving, or through turnover in their members.

4 Knowing and learning in networks

It is widely recognized that the styles of management and the interpersonal skills that individuals need when working on a collaborative project are quite different from those required in a traditional functional area. Studies on groupware technologies, the diffusion of complex innovations, collaborative industrial projects in fields like biotechnology, and R&D networking have shown that organizational learning is not only – or simply – an internal learning process. It instead involves and evolves in a network of organizations and organizational levels. Learning as networking is an appealing concept (Araujo 1998) and network technologies are always implied even when not directly addressed.

Firms delay the in-house adoption of complex technology until they obtain sufficient technical know-how in order to operate it successfully (Attewell 1996). In response to this knowledge barrier, new institutions (service bureaux, consultants, and simplification of the technology) come into existence to lower those barriers. The diffusion process is facilitated (or otherwise) by organizational learning processes and competence development, as well as by institutional practices.

When the knowledge base of an industry is both complex and expanding and the sources of expertise are widely dispersed, the locus of innovation will be found in networks of learning: a variety of firms, research institutions and universities combine their efforts in interorganizational collaborations. Norms of liberally sharing information on the frontier of research, in the biotech industry, give rise to a barter economy – as Kreiner and Schultz (1993) call the interactional infrastructure that fosters the emergence of collaborative R&D venues. Minor favours and services are exchanged within the biotech community. This non-canonical practice of information exchange is implicitly condoned by a hierarchy aware of their existence and unmanageable character. A barter economy is by its nature an informal knowledge economy based on personal relationships and operating with a certain amount of tact. Non-canonical practices of information exchange between rival organizations on a routine basis also occur in more mature industries.

Knowledge networking is a prominent feature of innovating and problem solving. The information and capabilities needed to solve a problem must be brought together physically or virtually in a single place. When the information can be shifted at little or no cost, the need to transfer information from its point of origin to the problem-solving site will not influence the locus of problem solving. Von Hippel (1994: 430) labels as 'sticky' the information that is costly to acquire, transfer and use. When the information is sticky the patterns of distribution of problem solving are affected in several ways. Von Hippel considers the stickiness of information in mainly economic terms (as the incremental expenditure required to transfer a unit of information to a specified locus in a form usable by a given information seeker), but the causes have to do with the nature of the information itself, with the amount of information that must be transferred, and with attributes of the seekers and providers of information. Tacit knowledge in human expertise is widely used in technical problem solving and – as Polanyi (1958: 52) noted – even in modern industries indefinable knowledge is still an essential part of technology. Tacit knowledge and aesthetic understanding (Strati 1999) are what render knowledge a skill and what make skills stickily human.

In sum, knowing and learning as networking (Araujo 1998: 330) 'depend on a range of factors that are outside the control of any organization and are associated with the network of relationships conducted both through canonical, institutionalized links between organizations and non-canonical, informal links established between individuals in organizational fields.'

5 Conclusions

The metaphor is an instrument for thinking and producing knowledge. And the metaphor of organizational learning stands as a valid alternative to the image of the rational organization because it depicts an organization grappling not only with trial and error but also with the ambiguity of interpretative processes, of experience, of history, of conflict, and of power. Learning suggests that a sequence of experiences – and not the abstract processes of rational thought – is the basis of action, and that the organization possesses a further resource – knowledge – which is an asset, an investment and a good that must be maintained. In this case one may say that the organization is a place of learning; it comprises processes of organizational learning. However, one can also say that the organization is learning because the activity of organizing is a form of practical knowledge. Therefore the concept of organizational learning cannot be confined within the boundaries of a single organization when an organization is a set of interlocking, differentiated and shifting relationships among communities of knowing which extend beyond the contracts and property rights that define the formal boundary of the organization.

The intimate relationships between knowing and doing suggest the indeterminate and emergent nature of collective competency that cannot be controlled centrally. Therefore organizations can be analysed as distributed, emergent, and decentred knowledge systems.

Further reading

(References cited in the text marked *)

* Ansoff, H.I. (1980) *Managing the Process of Discontinuous Change*, Brussels: Institute for Advanced Studies in Management. (A good methodological reference text for combining learning and action research.)

* Araujo, L. (1998) 'Knowing and learning as networking', *Management Learning* 3: 317–36. (The paper conceives learning as residing in heterogeneous networks of relationships between the social and material world.)

* Argyris, C. (1982) *Reasoning, Learning, and Action*, San Francisco: Jossey-Bass. (A constructivist analysis of the links between thought, learning and action, and in particular of the barriers against learning at the individual and organizational levels.)

* Argyris, C. and Schön, D. (1974) *Theory in Practice*, San Francisco: Jossey-Bass. (The reference text for those wishing to distinguish between espoused theories of action (the theories that people report as the basis for their action) and the theories of action inferred from how people behave (theories-in-use).)

* Argyris, C. and Schön, D. (eds) (1978) *Organizational Learning*, Cambridge: Addison-Wesley. (Sets out a typology of the various definitions provided of organizational learning according to how the organization is conceived.)

Attewell, P. (1996) 'Technology diffusion and organizational learning: the case of business computing', in M. Cohen and L. Sproull (eds), *Organizational Learning*, Thousand Oaks: Sage, 203–29. (An empirical study of the diffusion of business computing in USA reporting on the spread of it, on the learning processes and skills required, and on the changing institutional practices associated.)

* Bateson, G. (1972) *Steps to an Ecology of Mind*, New York: Chandler. (The essential text on the logical categories of learning and their hierarchy.)

* Brown, J.S. and Duguid, P. (1991) 'Organizational learning and communities of practice: toward a unified view of working, learning and innovation', *Organization Science* 2 (1): 40–57. (An article of fundamental importance which identifies communities of practice as emerging organizational entities which aggregate around the knowledge required to implement a work practice.)

* Cyert, R.M. and March, J.G. (1963) *A Behavioural Theory of the Firm*, Englewood Cliffs: Prentice-Hall. (The first text on organization to set learning in relation to decision making, adaptation and change.)

* Fiol, C.M. and Lyles, M.A. (1985) 'Organizational learning', *Academy of Management Review* 10 (4): 803–13. (A survey of the literature which sets the levels of organizational learning in relation to the strategic management of the firm.)

* Galbraith, J.R. (1973) *Designing Complex Organizations*, Cambridge: Addison Wesley. (The reference text for a conception of the organization as an information-processing system.)

* Gherardi, S. and Nicolini, D. (2000) 'The sociological foundation of organizational learning', in A. Berthoin Antal, M. Dierkes, J. Child and I. Nonaka (eds), *Handbook of Organizational Learning*, Oxford: Oxford University Press (forthcoming). (A sociological approach to organizational learning which singles out eleven narratives on learning and identifies in the concepts of participation and reflexivity the main contribution to the field.)

Hedberg, B. (1981) 'How organizations learn and unlearn', in P. Nystrom and W. Starbuck (eds), *Handbook of Organizational Design*, Oxford: Oxford University Press. (The most systematic treatment of the processes of unlearning and of the reasons why organizations do not learn.)

* Herriot, S., Levinthal, D. and March, J.G. (1988) 'Learning from experience in organization', *American Economic Review* 75 (3): 298–302. (The essay analyses learning from experience in decision processes with reference to the manner in which learning is produced within an ecology of learning.)

* Huber, G. (1991) 'Organizational learning: the contributing processes and the literatures', *Organization Science* 2 (1): 88–117. (A review of the literature along four constructs related to organizational learning: knowledge acquisition, information distribution, the interpretation of information and organizational memory.)

* Kreiner, K. and Schulz, M. (1993) 'Informal collaboration in research and development – the formation of networks across organizations', *Organization Studies* 14(2): 189–209.

(Non-canonical practice of information exchange is studied within the biotech community and barter is described as an informal knowledge economy.)

* Lave, J. and Wenger, E. (1991) *Situated Learning. Legitimate Peripheral Participation*, Cambridge, MA: University Press. (A number of ethnographic studies of apprenticeship where the notion of community of practice appears for the first time.)

* Levitt, B. and March, J.G. (1988) 'Organizational learning', *Annual Review of Sociology* 14: 319–40. (Organizational learning is a form of intelligence, viewed as routine-based, history-dependent and target-oriented, despite the turnover of personnel and the passage of time.)

* March, J.G., Sproull, L. and Tamuz, H. (1991) 'Learning from samples of one or fewer', *Organization Science* 2 (1): 1–13. (Organizations learn from experience but sometimes experience is infrequent. Some methods for dealing with this difficulty are suggested.)

* Morgan, G. (1986) *Images of Organizations*, Beverly Hills: Sage. (The reference text for those wishing to explore the role of metaphor in the development of organizational theories.)

* Newell, A. and Simon, H. (1972) *Human Problem Solving*, Englewood Cliffs: Prentice-Hall. (This path-breaking book focuses on the rules of cognition in problem solving.)

* Nicolini, D. and Meznar, M. (1995) 'The social construction of organizational learning', *Human Relation* 48 (7): 727–46. (This article suggests a social-constructionist approach in which organizational learning transforms acquired cognition into accountable abstract knowledge.)

* Nonaka, I and Takeuchi, H. (1995*) The Knowledge-Creating Company: How Japanese Companies Create the Dynamics of Innovation*, Oxford: Oxford University Press. (Using the two dimensions of tacit and explicit knowledge, the book singles out the four modes of knowledge conversion.)

* Polanyi, M. (1958) *Personal Knowledge. Towards a Post-Critical Philosophy*, London: Routledge and Kegan Paul. (The Hungarian philosopher who initiated the debate on tacit and explicit knowledge.)

* Shrivastava, P. (1983) 'A typology of organizational learning systems', *Journal of Management Studies* 20 (1): 7–28. (This review of the literature is organized around four concepts of learning: as institutionalized experience, as adaptation, as knowledge of action–outcome processes, as assumption sharing.)

* Strati, A. (1999) *Organization and Aesthetics*, London, Sage. (The relevance of the relationship between aesthetic understanding of organizational life and tacit knowledge problematizes the cognitivist dominance in organization studies.)

* Trist, E. (1983) 'Referent organizations and the development of inter-organizational domains', *Human Relations* 36 (3): 269–84. (Organizational learning is not a phenomenon which can be enclosed within the walls of a single organization; exchanges among organizations provide further occasions for learning.)

* Tsoukas, H. (1996) 'The firm as a distributed knowledge system: a constructionist approach', *Strategic Management Journal* 17: 11–25. (Organizations as distributed knowledge systems contrasts the topographic view of organizations which regards the organization as a container of knowledge and a locale of learning.)

* von Hippel, E. (1994) 'Sticky information and the locus of problem solving: implication for innovation', *Management Science* 40 (4): 429–39. (In this paper the concept of 'sticky' information is introduced and discussed in relation to the locus of innovation.)

* Wenger, E. (1998) *Communities of Practice*, Cambridge: Cambridge University Press. (A social theory of learning is developed through the concepts of practice, meaning and identity.)

* Yelle, L. (1979) 'The learning curve: historical review and comprehensive survey', *Decision Science* 10: 302–78. (The article clearly and thoroughly reviews the use of learning curves in the study and representation of learning.)

Organization development

Diether Gebert

1 **Definition, objectives and reasons**
2 **Criteria for planned change – antecedents and present thrusts**
3 **Types of intervention**
4 **Outcomes of organization development**
5 **Present currents and trends**

Overview

Organization development (OD) is understood to mean planned change based on the paradigm of action research. OD can thus be described as a learning process. The active development of an organization towards its desired corporate identity succeeds only if this change process is undertaken holistically. From a behavioural perspective this means, for example, that the behavioural conditions that lie within the person (qualifications, motivation) as well as those lying outside the person (organizational structure, technology) must be modified. The process of change is also described as a political process. That is, in which phases of change and for which reasons is the mobilization of power salient? Lastly, the change process is often examined in terms of whether, and how, basic assumptions within an organization can be decoded through analysis of symbols.

Starting at the action level, this entry first examines the person-centred approach, which addresses the question of how to develop both the social competence that fosters cooperation and the general intellectual competence that promotes innovation. Second, the structural approach is investigated to show which OD measures have been and are increasingly being taken. Moves to reintegrate hitherto segregated work sequences and attempts to decentralize decision making play a main part. Third, attention turns to interventions bearing directly on the analysis and change of interpersonal relationships. Team development, role negotiation and survey-feedback methods are explored, and prerequisites for their success are pointed out.

Overall, evaluations of OD bear out the potential fruitfulness of its key approaches. But follow-up studies have thus far shown the outcomes to be widely variable, meaning that the degree of success or failure cannot be precisely forecast in each case. Accordingly, conditions on which OD measures depend for their success are discussed in the latter part of the text.

This entry concludes by showing that a new approach called organizational transformation (OT) is beginning to gain acceptance in the literature. The difference between OT and traditional OD is pointed out, and the opportunities and risks of organizational transformation are considered.

I Definition, objectives and reasons

In contrast to spontaneous, unintended changes within a company, organization development (OD) is understood to mean planned change (the meaning of 'planned' is discussed later). The concept of OD encompasses all endeavours (usually lasting several years) to develop an organization (for example, factory, school, hospital) as a whole from state one to state two, whereby the nature of state two when the OD commences is only vaguely known, not already operationalized. Substantively, it concerns itself with the alteration of organizational structures and processes, as well as with the specific conditions under which activities are carried out and the characteristic features of social interaction (communication, management, cooperation) in the various subsystems of the organization.

The primary reasons for embarking on OD are environmental shifts in the economic, technological and social sectors. Growing competitive pressure compels, for example, leaner structures and management's concentration on the processes crucial for the organization's added value. Typically, if the actual state of the organization in this sense does not conform to the demands made upon the organization, this mismatch signals the need for OD. OD is also warranted by the introduction of new information and production technologies, because of the elemental changes they imply in organizational structure, the conditions under which activities are executed and social interaction. Motivation for undertaking OD can emanate from shifts in social values and norms. An example of the former is the transition to postmaterialist values that has been observed in many Western countries. It has manifested itself in the call for greater democracy, transparency and workers' participation as well as in the demand for greater openness in communication. Social changes of this kind are often juxtaposed with rigid corporate structures, giving rise, in turn, to a mismatch between the organization and the demands made upon it. Changes in norms have put forward the problem of incorporating women into professional life, for example, and the pressure to integrate ecological and ethical issues.

Modern efforts to shape corporate identity likewise lead to OD. In this realm, the firm's perceptions, values and behavioural patterns (Who were we? Who are we compared to others? Who do we want to be?) are not the only questions. Corporate identity also has structural dimensions. Which changes in organizational structures and processes are needed in order to achieve and vitalize the new identity? Which changes in task content, in job conditions and social interactions should be undertaken?

In summary, the objective of OD is to overcome the often self-mediating mismatches between the current characteristics of an organization and the environmentally mediated demands upon it. Flexibility and innovative capacity thereby become pivotal objectives of OD. Moreover, the accelerating rate of economic, technological, and social change means that OD also aims to enhance the learning ability of the organization and help it master the management of change *per se.* Against this background, it is not surprising that OD is becoming an ever more important subject in university study and the further training of managers.

2 Criteria for planned change – antecedents and present thrusts

Learning through action research

Reconstructing the historical roots of OD, one repeatedly comes across the German psychologist Kurt Lewin, who emigrated to the USA in 1945 and founded the Research Center for Group Dynamics at the Massachusetts Institute of Technology. At this research centre, which after Lewin's death in the 1950s was directed by David Bowers, Rensis Likert, and others at the Institute for Social Research at the University of Michigan, Lewin worked out the theoretical and pragmatic foundations for what he called action research. At the pragmatic level, action research means in part that data are collected with conventional methods of empirical social research (surveys) but are then not fed back exclusively, if at all, to experts but to the people involved, who themselves try to modify their situation according to the information they receive in this way. Integrating the participants into the change process is thus a core feature of action research (Argyris and Schön 1996). At the theoretical level, the necessity of integrating members of the organization into the change process follows from the fact that science faces fundamental obstacles when seeking to capture all the special features of the individual case that an organization represents, and then trying to propose solutions tailored to those features. The resulting gaps in knowledge must therefore be compensated for by tapping into the insider knowledge possessed by the members of the organization. The principal objective of action research is not to confirm scientific theory but to solve problems that surface in day-to-day practice.

In addition to practical relevance, action research has a research dimension. The members of the organization who receive the results of the analysis of the organization's actual state develop hypotheses about which changes in, say, co-operation and coordination could serve as vehicles for overcoming certain mismatches identified at the outset. They then test these hypotheses in their own areas of responsibility. In the optimal case, they thereby not only solve their own problems but also generate data and experience which, in turn, are available to science as heuristic aids for the formulation of theory. Because the members of the organization will not normally discover an optimal solution at their first attempt, it is assumed that the development of such heuristics occurs through iterative loops of participative learning.

This specific understanding of action research, in which the traditional antithesis of 'theory versus practice' is replaced by the collaborative alternative of 'theory through practice', which fundamentally changes the relation between the scientific and non-scientific communities. No longer do enlightened and informed scientists (as the subject) confront a nescient factory (as the object) that is sometimes artificially kept unaware of the true nature of the treatment being administered or assessed. Instead, scientists and practitioners confer even on the early issues of selecting an appropriate method of data collection, not just later on the matter of using the survey results. This design transforms the subject–object relation into a subject–subject relation.

In this sense the organization's internal or external change agent (the scientist or practitioner) is not supposed to advise the company as a doctor would a patient. In action research the salient feature is process consultation, in which the change agent promotes change by helping the company help itself. The change agent does so by participating as an observer of OD processes and episodes, and aids group diagnosis of them chiefly by making 'meta-communication' possible. The main assistance offered by the process consultant is not specific substantive input about the advantages and disadvantages of, say, a certain organizational principle being considered. The process consultant tries instead to help by feeding back to the group members the manner in which they are communicating about this problem. The consultant examines the way they deal with dissent, the means by which pressure to conform is exerted, the modes for handling imbalances in power relationships, etc., in order to increase the validity of communication.

Process consulting contrasts with the traditional kind of expertise-based consulting, which is orientated to the engineering sciences. The model of consulting in that field – the doctor–patient model by which the sick organization is administered a certain medicine – is convenient in many apparent respects. It is no wonder, then, that the procedural consulting practised in OD is usually accompanied by varieties of expertise-based consulting. The critical point is to ensure that input by experts does not violate the spirit of action research. Action research is intended to ensure that necessary insider knowledge comes to bear on the development of viable solutions; it is supposed to provide a learning forum in which to acquire skills for managing change.

Holistic approach to change

A holistic approach to planned change accentuates the necessity of changing not only the external conditions (the situation) that are partially responsible for behaviour, but also the internal conditions (the attitudes) of the person. Strategies for changing attitudes, or the person, have been developed primarily in the USA; strategies for changing the situation have more clearly been developed in Europe as well. Both thrusts, and the need to combine them, are explained in this section.

With an eye to changing attitudes, Kurt Lewin helped develop the method of group-dynamic training that has become known as sensitivity training, laboratory training or the T(raining)-Group. Lewin initially spelled out the method with an example, the gradual reduction of racist and religious prejudices and the building of democratic attitudes.

Like many efforts at OD in general, group-dynamic training thus has a recognizably normative orientation characteristic, namely, the conscious endeavour to overcome authoritarian structures in favour of a cooperative partnership. Lewin's experiments with group-dynamic training led, in 1947, to the founding of the National Training Laboratories (NTL) in Bethel, Maine, which is occasionally regarded as the birth of OD. The classic form of this training consists of having approximately ten managers retire to a hotel for one to two weeks and observe themselves as a group under the direction of a leader trained in this method. In doing this, the members of the group, who have no common past and will have no common future, learn in effect that they do not study group dynamics in a textbook but directly through their own personal experience. The group is told to concentrate not on the 'there and then', that is, the experiences in the professional world, but on the 'here and now', or what is happening specifically in this training group. This highly unusual task and the trainer's refusal to contribute substantially to mastering the unstructured initial situation sets the group searching, a process usually accompanied by some degree of anxiety. By trying to come to grips with this generally threatening predicament on its own, the group reproduces the socio-psychological process (the group's finding itself) as though in a laboratory. Characteristic features of situations and processes that are encountered in reality and described in relevant textbooks are 'experienced' by the group directly in a time-lapse effect, magnified under a microscope so to speak.

Optimally, this theme-specific sensitization to general processes of group dynamics leads to sensitization of the individual (and a change in attitude). The attitudinal change occurs by having the participants give each other feedback on what has been observed and experienced here and now, so that a mirror is held up to each participant in order to prompt discussion of past (for example, authoritarian) behavioural patterns and to reinforce and stabilize newly tried out behavioural patterns (of a cooperative nature) that depart from the previous ones.

This strategy had its limitations, however, for it quickly became clear that training isolated individuals changes little within an organization. Patterns of communication and cooperation are altered only when that person's various role partners also adjust their expectations in the same direction. Holistically speaking, it was only consistent for OD to include all members of the social system, beginning at the top, in an analogous process of gathering experience right from the start.

A later expansion of these approaches centred on the individual emphasized that the four variables of task, people, technology and structure (communication and authority structure) were intermeshed, and that OD could succeed only if it took this interdependence into account. This holistic way of thinking still applies in one variation or another today.

In Europe, this aspect of situational development is a further independent historical source of OD and has been the foremost interest at London's Tavistock Institute of Human Relations. The trail was blazed by field studies on the impact of technologically induced restructuring of work groups in coal mining. The research noted that the number of psychosomatic disorders soared with the disintegration of previous group structures. The Tavistock Institute stressed the necessity of interpreting the corporate entity as a socio-technical system, with the focus of analysis being on the linkage between processes of production technology, work organization, and social interaction. In more modern parlance, this means that if flexible manufacturing systems (technology) require greater decentralized self-regulation among skilled workers (job enlargement), the foreman must alter his or her leadership style (social processes, different authority structure), a change that chiefly encourages processes of outcome-related self-description and self-assessment within the work group. Since it is necessary for the leader to be prepared to allow this self-regulation and for the workers to be willing and able to exercise the wider scope of responsibility in a self-regulating manner, due motivation and qualification of the actors must be ensured.

The Tavistock Institute has also done much to foster the implementation of semi-autonomous work groups, which are familiar from field studies in Scandinavia as well.

The holistic line of thinking within OD is also formally rooted in behavioural theory, according to which every behaviour (R, response) is a function of the person (O, organism), the situational characteristics preceding the behaviour (S, stimulus), and the behaviour's after-effects (C, consequence). For example, assume that the aim of decentralization policy is for managers to transfer certain tasks and the attendant rights and responsibilities to subordinate levels in the hierarchy and that the subordinate levels are to accommodate this change rather than constantly delegate back responsibility. The S-O-R-C paradigm suggests what various strategies must contribute in a holistic approach.

To achieve the behavioural change desired, sufficient motivation and qualification of the persons concerned must be ensured. This is achieved through the 'person-centred approach', which consists essentially of persuasion through enlightenment, information, etc., in specially designed seminars and proper follow-up practice using certain leadership tools.

However, being willing and able to do this is not enough (the O component). It is important to facilitate the intended behaviour (R) among all participants in each situation (the S component). With the specific case of promoting delegative leadership, this can mean buffering the risks of decentralization by equipping the employees with an efficient information technology that enables them to analyse and decide matters on their own. Providing the employees with this sort of information technology also promotes their emotional willingness to assume responsibility, not just the willingness of the leaders to cede responsibility.

In addition, moves to decentralize must avoid the common mistake of trying to limit risk by decreeing an elaborate set of norms and directives that simultaneously standardizes and formalizes task accomplishment. Pursuing these kinds of bureaucratic control strategies would only offset the effects of flexibilization, increases in innovation and motivation, improved utilization of human resources, and other results sought from decentralization policy. The danger of decentralization expanding bureaucratic control in this way cannot be overestimated. Thinking holistically about the issue of decentralization, one would also have to contemplate revising the lines of authority so as to minimize bureaucracy.

Shaping the situation so as to elicit the target behaviour is one component of the structural approach. In keeping with the S-O-R-C paradigm described above, the other component to discuss is the consequence (C). With this component it is not a matter of whether a person is fundamentally willing and able to behave as intended. Nor is it about whether the situation is such that it makes that behaviour possible (by affording relief and eliminating obstacles). The issue surrounding the C component is that the target behaviour must also be normatively permitted and positively reinforced. For instance, the exercise of the intended behaviour must be followed not only by official approval but, say, by praise, never by punishment.

Rules of this type are actually self-evident, but OD practice shows how frequently they are ignored. When middle management applies the principles of management by delegation, it is not unusual for senior management to become impatient, testy and aggressive when mid-level executives can no longer give immediate information about every detail of a particular procedure, as inevitably happens when responsibilities are transferred down the hierarchy.

More abstractly formulated in terms of the logic of the C component: if a certain intended behaviour embodies the company's desired new corporate identity in an especially typical way, then the gratification sought by the employees must be made more and more contingent on, not disassociated from, manifestation of that very behaviour. This also means that the intended behaviour must be taken into consideration in the criteria for work assessment and promotion. In the holistic approach, the C component calls attention to the fact that the repertoire of personnel policies must be analysed and shaped with an eye to its ability to elicit the intended behaviour consistently.

It follows from this S-O-R-C paradigm that the only promising combination is that between the person-centred approach (the O component) and the structural approach (the S and C components). No one strategy is sufficient by itself. On the contrary, an imbalanced strategy is bound to cause disappointment with OD results and often even makes the situation worse than it was originally (Gebert 1976).

Nevertheless, imbalances in strategy are not rare, in part because the person-centred approach (the O component) and situational management (the S component) are separate purviews at the board level. The former falls to the personnel department; the latter, to the department responsible for organization, which usually also handles data-processing and information technology. Institutionally and organizationally, then, procedures that belong together are segregated. The chances of pursuing a holistic approach are further curtailed by the fact that the board members representing these two spheres of responsibility have different professional backgrounds and styles of thinking, complicating communication and cooperation between them from the start. Unfortunately, these circumstances are sometimes reflected in the empirical literature as an 'either-or' viewpoint (depending on the relative power of the board members) rather than as a perspective embracing more than one approach.

The political dimension

In modern organizational theory the structures of organization and interaction are interpreted much less as a reflection of inherent constraints than as a reified manifestation of specific interests. Historically speaking, this idea, too, was anticipated by Kurt Lewin in his 'force field analysis', according to which given structures mirror a temporary equilibrium between driving forces and restraining forces. OD implies changes in power relations and therefore proves to be a political process in essence. Kurt Lewin distinguished between three phases of change processes: unfreezing, moving and refreezing.

Unfreezing

Unfreezing takes place at the organizational level basically when the driving forces are ascendent and the restraining forces are weakened. In practice, this process requires the visibility of senior management support for OD and, hence, the mobilization of power. The necessary shift of power favouring driving forces over restraining forces can be effected by reference power, whereby senior managers persuade members of the organization that the corporate praxis needs to be changed and can be changed. To unleash motivation for change, these two cognitions must be combined. Either one alone will not suffice. If this persuasion succeeds, relative power shifts in favour of the driving forces.

To achieve unfreezing, power is used not only gently but often toughly as well. Typical of the latter form is the strategy of removing opponents of change from their positions of power and transferring them elsewhere.

Moving

The process of moving likewise requires the use of power. Here, too, reference power can be mobilized, as when key senior managers model behavioural patterns vital to the new corporate identity being sought. Imitative learning can thereby be prompted at subordinate managerial levels (Gebert 1976).

In the phase of moving, it is important for certain measures (for example, attendance at seminars or specific workshops) to begin with senior management itself. Experience shows that top-down strategies usually have a greater chance of succeeding than bottom-up strategies do. The shift toward a new equilibrium thus necessitates consistency and explicit commitment. Management clearly and openly throws its weight behind the driving forces.

The counterpart to consistency and explicit commitment – the use of power as moderated by patience and tolerance – is critical in this phase, too, however. Patience is a salient factor because the learning process, mediated through action research, takes time. Tolerance is necessary because learning through action research sometimes means making mistakes. Lastly, tolerance toward burgeoning interactional diversity and plurality is warranted because particular guiding ideas favoured by senior management are expounded in quite different ways in the various subsystems of a large organization. Indeed, it must be so since all contingency theories of leadership and organization maintain that there is no one correct way of leading, organizing, or cooperating. Because it is essential for the special features of the personnel and task organization to be taken into account, the outcome of OD consists of actually living certain visions and making them tangible across the various sub-systems of an organization. As such a plurality is functional for the success of the company as a whole, senior management must show both consistency and tolerance for deviation in the phase of moving.

Refreezing

The process of refreezing requires the power of reward to be used to synchronize the normative and structural alignment of the C component in the S-O-R-C paradigm. Sanctioning of the altered interactional and organizational structures and consistent positive reinforcement of the desired behaviour through the power of reward is crucial to establishing the new equilibrium.

Another major aspect in the refreezing phase is to halt the change process. The management of innovation in the phase of moving must be followed by management of acceptance in the refreezing phase. There are many indications that the spirit of the phase of moving is qualitatively different from the mind-set that is helpful in the stabilization phase. These two mind-sets cannot be simply taken for granted. Some companies perform well in the phase of moving but have trouble when the mood for change must be dampened. Conversely, there are other companies whose strengths have lain in stabilizing a previous change but whose mentality precludes any new departure. If OD is conceived of as a long-term process in which refreezing must at some point be followed again by an unfreezing, can the course of change in the underlying mind-sets be planned at all? If so, how? This problem has not been sufficiently thought through.

The political character of OD also makes it necessary at the outset of the unfreezing phase to install a steering committee that includes representatives of senior management and the members of the organization, experts for details, the internal and/or external change agents, and representatives of special interest groups (for example, labour). In addition to guiding the substantive and temporal dimensions of the change process, the steering committee has the function of buffering the resistance inevitably spawned by a shift in power. This kind of steering committee is already mandated in Germany and some other countries because issues of personnel policy usually surface in the course of OD.

If the forces restraining a process of organizational change are seated primarily in senior management, many consultants advise against launching an OD process. Instead of resignation, however, an opposing power base can be actively built from the bottom up. The danger is that senior management perceives this strategy as threatening, so the process of organizational change is thwarted by overt sabotage or the familiar strategy of appointing project groups.

The symbolic dimension

Members of the organization share certain basic assumptions that guide their actions but that have become so ingrained that the actors are no longer aware of them. These collective assumptions are what Schein (1985) sees as organizational culture. If the prevailing basic assumption is that 'truth' in the scientific sense means something to be discovered, an organization will prefer to have *ad hoc* committees of experts address even those questions that require no special expertise. If, however, the assumption is that 'truth' is ultimately arrived at through discussion (in the constructivist tradition of science), then the operant structures will be those of discursive and participative leadership even when the issue at hand is one that only special experts are qualified to judge. Over time basic assumptions can become dysfunctional and ill-matched to the demands of the environment. In that case, OD calls for diagnosis of, and, if necessary, change in shared attitudes.

Basic assumptions are not directly observable, but often they can be analysed at the symbolic level. The personal computer, for example, is not only a useful tool, it also symbolizes the principle of rationality. When representatives of vested interests ostentatiously shake hands at a press conference, it symbolizes high regard for consensus and harmony. The German Railroad's ubiquitous clock is not only an instrument for measuring time; it symbolizes the principles of absolute reliability. Uniforms worn by civil servants underscore principles like the necessity for integration and hierarchy. As the German Democratic Republic's brand of socialism collapsed and the ruling Socialist Unity Party (SED) was forced to relinquish its virtually exclusive role in governing the country, the 'roundtable' – a conference or discussion involving *several* participants – came to symbolize the principles of equality and openness. To put it generally, then, many of the day-to-day things around us, and many of the things each of us does (for example, what we do and do not control in a company), have an additional symbolic dimension. They not only stand for themselves but are also signs of something. Orientation is conveyed at this symbolic level, and the members of an organization are scarcely aware of it.

Because of these interrelations, the analysis of what is symbolically represented in a corporate entity will be helpful in the diagnosis of basic assumptions. In principle, the analysis is a decoding process. Because every symbol has more than one meaning, only cautious interpretation can link the sign back to its reference point (the basic assumption). Hence, the analysis of specific symbols has only a heuristic function. After specific hypotheses about the structure of the basic assumptions have been developed through symbol analysis, it is important to seek additional symbols and ask whether the basic assumptions in these cases, too, are encoded with similar meaning. One must beware of interpreting symbols too mechanistically. Symbols have more than one dimension *vis-à-vis* what they stand for. Indeed, mechanistic interpretation must be resisted because symbols characteristically distil – as in company insider jokes – the fragilities, contradictions, ambiguities, and seeming irrationalities of corporate reality. For all the difficulties with the analysis of symbols, however, decoding is an extraordinarily intriguing and fruitful field that can aid a change agent's diagnosis immensely.

If interpretations of symbols are provided, the members of the organization must act with due caution to promote self-reflection; the gesture may be gratefully accepted, thereby offering an interesting opportunity to bring out the organization's hitherto partly subliminal corporate identity and make it accessible to contemplation.

This application represents a process of unfreezing throughout the organization. The literature also discusses the possibility of utilizing changed symbols specifically to further the phase of moving or refreezing. Although such a tack is possible in principle, one must be careful to guard against manipulation and the danger of reducing the symbol to a superficial marketing device.

3 Types of intervention

The person-centred approach

As we have seen, the structural approach changes the behavioural conditions outside the person, whereas the person-centred approach changes those residing within the person. As far as OD is concerned, the processes of attitudinal change and qualification underlying the person-centred approach focus primarily on promoting the social competence needed for cooperation and the basic competence needed for flexibility and innovation.

When it comes to nurturing social competence, two aspects are differentiated, social sensitivity and action flexibility. Among other things, social sensitivity requires the mechanism of role taking. The person must be willing and able to visualize the world and their own behaviour from the standpoint of others. Drawing on the I–me distinction going back to G.H. Mead, the idea is that the possibility of fostering increased behavioural sensitivity tends to be greater when a person learns to distinguish between the looking-glass self (how do I appear to others?) and the conception of self (how do I appear to myself?). Feedback in classic group-dynamic training serves the function of informing the person via the reflected self.

The ability and willingness to develop flexibility in taking action is a main aspect of social competence partly because all recent contingency theories of leadership underline the need to lead in different ways, depending on the situation and set of people involved. As it is grounded in leadership theories centred on situational considerations, the training for social competence therefore aims at enhancing the ability of a manager to arrive at a valid diagnosis of the given leadership situation and at augmenting that person's ability and willingness to respond flexibly as required by the particular circumstances at hand. Participants practise diagnosing situations by analysing a wide variety of case studies. Action flexibility is taught through role playing and similar techniques in which managers are trained in different patterns of action. Classic group-dynamic training seeks to engender this flexibility by using laboratory conditions to create latitude for the participants to try out new behaviours and explore different facets of their habitual behaviour as encouraged by the trainer.

Because the desired behavioural changes necessitate attitudinal changes as well, and because attitudes have to do with both the cognitive and affective dimensions, the learning process must incorporate the emotional level before attitudes can change. This is one of the basic assumptions of classic group-dynamic training as described earlier. But experience-based learning like this entails the risk that the integration of the emotional level in the learning process will trigger a group dynamic that the trainer can no longer control. Emotionally loaded feedback can quickly offend the person at which it is directed – with incalculable consequences. In terms of chaos theory, the integration of the affective level in the process of attitudinal change implies the risk of instability in which the dynamics of the social system will take their own, rather unpredictable direction and will defy external intervention by the trainer. This higher chance that attitudes will change if the emotional level is integrated thus comes at the price of incalculable risks for the individual.

By contrast, classically orientated human-relations training, which traditionally tends to stress the cognitive dimension, has a major advantage in making the learning process highly controllable and the risks minimal. The danger is that such undertakings are less effective in that they do not bring about the attitudinal change necessary for the desired change in behaviour. This is the dilemma that must be carefully kept in mind with OD processes. A wide variety of compromises are being tested to overcome it. Intensive role playing combined with corresponding feedback to the role players is one approach being tried; others are various modern forms of outdoor training.

There are solid arguments for not confining the learning process to the cognitive level. A socially incompetent behaviour (for example, always smiling instead of telling the boss the critical things one feels) can be interpreted as avoidance behaviour serving to ward off anxiety. Since avoidance behaviour is always reinforced by a decrease in anxiety, the corrective experience, that it is indeed possible to speak one's mind to the boss under certain other circumstances and in a certain other way, will be systematically circumvented. The objective of 'self-assertiveness training' is to facilitate this corrective experience by confronting the person with the situation he or she always runs from. Through this exercise, the person learns that anxiety is not generally justified, that it really is possible to cope with such potentially threatening situations, depending on the situational context and the nature of one's behaviour.

Confident leaders are freer of anxiety and therefore demonstrate greater social competence. That is why facilitating corrective experiences by improving social competence is a priority, though the risks must always be borne in mind.

The second key problem with building social competence is the issue of transfer. If the person-centred approach succeeds in forging the willingness to adopt certain behaviours, how can this willingness be transported from the place of learning to the place at which it is to be applied (the company)? In general, the transfer problem can be solved only by proceeding holistically with the S-O-R-C paradigm. Change in the behavioural conditions residing within the person must be complemented by change in the behavioural conditions lying outside the person.

In the context of the person-centred approach, attempts were made at one time to solve the transfer problem by conducting group-dynamic training in the actual work group. Instead of a 'stranger lab', 'family labs' were run. The concept of family labs is attractive in that the place of learning and the place of application are identical. But because group-dynamic training in the real work setting wreaks havoc on long-term prospects for cooperation, this strategy proved to be rather inappropriate.

Today, the transfer problem is being tackled largely in other ways. To work through the learning process and training experiences purposefully, one approach has the participating manager meet beforehand with their own supervisor to discuss the kind of questions or issues for which the manager in training actually wishes to find an answer or resolution. While training is in progress, the trainer must make it as clear as possible in which sense the training experiences reflect corporate reality and, hence, to what degree they can be transferred to the actual work setting. The relation to work must constantly be recalled and discussed systematically. After training, the participating manager is to speak with his or her supervisor about which of the experiences or possible solutions seem promising and set a date by which to report back about them. Lastly, transfer vitally depends on having the participant sit down afterwards with their colleagues and discuss with them which specific conclusions for future collaboration are to be drawn from this training. This step makes the transition to team development.

Increasingly, the aforementioned thrust of the person-centred approach is on the development of general intellectual competence relating to flexibility and innovation. In contrast to the diversification of specialized knowledge, general intellectual competence has to do with expanding the horizons and outlooks of the employees. The intention is to raise the number of functions they can perform and, hence, the flexibility of their deployment. They will then be intellectually equipped to cope with the trend toward the reintegration of functions previously segregated in the division of labour and with the ever faster pace of change in manufacturing and information technology. Cultivation of general intellectual competence therefore also requires the acquisition of abstract solution schemata and methodological expertise that make it possible to transfer experience from one activity to another. For innovation it is important to train employees to be able and willing to examine critically the way they go about things, to try out new things, and to experiment with the experiences of colleagues when dealing with their own problems.

Two things must be remembered when developing general intellectual competence. Unlike the process of deepening specialized knowledge, which is best handled primarily by thinking through and practising what is demanded by the present activity in one's particular company, the cultivation of future-orientated basic competence must have the person confront problems that go beyond his or her current activity. The person is also expected to discuss potential solutions with peers from other companies, not only in order to acquire general, abstract schemata for flexibility but also to learn to discriminate between certain solutions and see them in perspective.

Experience shows that further training of this sort is anything but natural, at least in small companies. One reason is that this very form of training is classified as too theoretical and academic by those who arrange for it – although empirical studies show how salient it is for innovation and, hence, for the economic success of small businesses, too. What proves to have eminent practical relevance in the long run risks belittlement because it is branded as irrelevant from a short-term viewpoint (Gebert and Steinkamp 1990).

The second aspect to emphasize about the cultivation of general intellectual competence is that it has a chance of paying off for the company at each echelon of management only if it is actually tapped or needed. The potential for innovation abides in basic competence. To free innovative behaviour it is necessary, but not sufficient, to develop that competence. The cultivation of general intellectual competence must go hand in hand with the development of social competence at all relevant levels of management so that the responsible supervisor is willing and able, through proper dialogue, to activate the potential for innovation among the employees. In times of crisis it is imperative to maximize the use of the employees' potential for flexibility and innovation. Those periods call for sensitive and encouraging – not discouraging – leadership that invites discussion, and that requires enormous social competence. Understood in this way, the strategy of human resources development calls for a holistic concept of further training in order to achieve the decisive effect of building general intellectual competence and social competence together.

The structural approach

The structural side of OD encompasses a variety of strategies. In German-speaking regions, analysis of the structure and regulation of the formal organization is foremost. OD processes have often been initiated by a switch to a divisionalization, matrix organization or profit-centre organization.

All efforts to lay down written, process-orientated guidelines for management and collaboration are categorized under the structural approach. These types of principles were worked out in the Federal Republic of Germany in the 1970s, partly to accommodate the value change that took place in society (accentuation of autonomy, participation, openness and transparency). They also represent an attempt to ensure a common normative fundamental understanding that avails the integration of the organization's subsystems. Because of the aforementioned necessity to apply the rules of management, cooperation and organization differently from situation to situation and to place them all in perspective, such broadly formulated principles remain pallid, and risk coming across as empty words that have little practical relevance and inspire no commitment. But joint elaboration of management guidelines like these prompts within an organization a process of discussion and reflection that in itself serves the objective of OD.

A third course of action within the structural approach is to change specific job content and the conditions under which members of the organization carry out their activities. In industry, improvements in ergonomic conditions of work (for example, occupational safety and health, noise abatement and protection from heat) have been the main changes (in Germany known as 'improvement in the quality of work life'). To change the content of work, job enlargement and job rotation are frequently used strategies (again, mostly in industry). Job enlargement is understood as a strategy that essentially makes for a quantitative expansion of the work activity, in that the person holding a particular position executes not only one but several, usually similar, parts of a production task. The principle of job rotation is that employees exchange their activities regularly for what are normally similarly structured ones of colleagues.

Whereas job enlargement and job rotation in effect counteract monotony, job enrichment is a more demanding strategy in that the employee is offered both a broader quantitative scope of work and specific discretionary and control functions. The strategy of forming semi-autonomous work groups goes a step further still. They decide their own modes of operation in keeping with their objective, doing tasks that have been broadened by job enrichment. This strategy not only intensifies content-related work motivation but also expands the opportunity for social cooperation.

Endeavours to introduce semi-autonomous work groups in particular have reverberated to widely varying degrees in different European countries. Whereas the acceptance of this strategy is relatively high in Scandinavian countries, which helped to develop it, the installation of semi-autonomous work groups is still very rare in Germany. Although performance, work satisfaction and (as a learning outcome) the level of qualification and product quality have improved in Germany, many of the observed effects have only been temporary, the costs of setting up semi-autonomous work groups have been high, and political resistance has often appeared. Substantial scepticism has been voiced not only by foremen and master craftsmen but by employers as well, for in their eyes the granting of semi-autonomy heralds undesired extensions of industrial democracy.

In the wake of the Japanese challenge in the 1980s, interest within the structural approach shifted to the establishment of 'quality circles'. Although it has been repeatedly stressed that this procedure might produce other results if imitated outside the Japanese culture, where it is highly popular, the concept of quality circles has spread significantly in the USA and many European countries. It is often reported that the work of quality circles strengthens job commitment and, especially, the workforce's inclination to innovate. Experience shows that installing quality circles has the decisive effect of breaking through the notorious barrier between senior management and the organization's rank and file. The work of quality circles thrives on the fact that suggestions for improvement prepared by each group and under the direction of a facilitator have a much higher chance of even coming to the attention of the corporate leadership through institutionalized bottom-up communication. In terms of action theory, corporate reality thereby tends to be perceived as mutable, a vital outcome if the motivation to change is to be inspired.

Within the structural approach greater and more consistent efforts are now being made to reintegrate, that is, to overcome the separation of tasks and move away from over-specialization (Elden and Chisholm 1993). This is particularly true in industry, where these kinds of changes are part of the move toward more flexible production technologies and smaller lot sizes. At the same time, there are broader attempts to invest employees with the discretionary authority necessary to handle their widened scope of activities. This trend can also be interpreted as a logical extension of classic job enrichment. Economic benefits are anticipated, too, because this decentralization and the support of self-regulation will probably promote lean management. Simultaneously, the increased motivation of employees is likely to improve the quality of products and services, while the new organization of workflow should save time.

This process is unprecedented. What psychologists and sociologists have long recommended for motivational and normative reasons often failed to take hold in corporate reality because the ideas did not seem technologically or economically profitable. Now, for the first time ever, a wide range of specialists – production technologists, cost-conscious economists, psychologists and sociologists – are recommending much the same thing. It is still too early to judge, however, whether this is the historic moment that will defuse OD's intrinsic tension between the goal to improve the quality of work life and the goal to raise efficiency.

The fact remains that many companies have a segregated internal labour market. The core workforce performs a qualified activity that really can be considered enriched in the sense that it combines reintegration of previously discrete parts of a work sequence and decentralization. More and more often, for example, skilled workers operating numerically controlled machines now not only set up the devices and clamp and remove the work-pieces, they also carry out reprogramming, quality control and simple maintenance. In some industries, however, this core workforce is complemented by a peripheral workforce still dominated by a Taylorist division of labour. Sparked principally by the Japanese challenge, the structural approach has gained momentum and opened new, previously less distinct alternatives as part of OD. Conservative currents have been noted again in recent years. A study by Adler and Borys (1996) in a Californian car factory has shown that detailed, cost-related standardization (regimentation) of work processes is no longer worked out by specialists in top-down fashion but rather by the employees themselves in certain cases. As strategies, an enabling bureaucracy and democratic Taylorism seem to be serving well for the time being, but it remains to be seen how well they fare in the long run (Adler and Borys 1996).

Occasionally, euphoric words are heard today about nurturing entrepreneurship in the enterprise and extending it even to the industrial sector. It should not be overlooked, however, that information technology, too, is a source of new options not always consistent with the structural approach's goal of fostering enterprising initiatives through a suitable form of work organization. Administrative employees often report that the range of things they do has grown as a result of new information technologies in banks and insurance companies, but they sometimes complain that they have less freedom to make decisions. Given the transparency and greater controllability that information technology has brought to all work cycles, there is an undeniable risk that today's proclivity to decentralization is paralleled by recentralization. In other words, perhaps the trend away from external regulation and towards self-regulation is being counteracted. Holistically speaking, the chief concern is to ensure that production technology, organizational structure and information technology are harmonized in a way that advances the goal of OD.

The relationship approach

Unlike the person-centred and structural approaches, the relationship approach addresses the social relations between the members of the organization. The key vehicle herein is team development. After management training, the task of team development in aiding transfer is to ascertain specifically what the various concepts and experiences discussed at a seminar or training course mean for the actual work group. In team development the supervisor meets with their employees in a work group (usually in the presence of a facilitator), analyses weaknesses in rules of conduct up to that point, and begins negotiating with the employees a change in those rules so as to improve the efficiency of their cooperation. The primary focus is not the personality structure of the individual but reciprocal role behaviour.

One way to proceed can be to have every group member engaged in team development (including the supervisor) first define his or her role expectation of the other members by responding to three items.

1 It would help me increase my own efficiency if you would make the following clearer: (for example, 'stand up for us more vigorously on the Board when we delegate our own responsibilities to subordinates in order to gain time to speak to customers', 'please explain the Board's business plans in more detail so that we have a better orientation' or 'fight more to have the Board take account of our proposals for change, and inform us where things stand with the various management discussions').
2 It would help me increase my own efficiency if you would cut down or stop doing the following: (for example, 'do not prescribe towards which clients we must be stricter or more lenient, when granting special conditions. Leave these individual decisions to us and measure us only on the overall outcome at the end of the planning period').
3 You have helped me increase my efficiency by... and I hope you will continue to do so: (for example, 'you have not looked for a scapegoat when a client's credit has had to be taken away and the bad debt written off. That has really boosted our motivation and team spirit,' or 'the way you involved us in establishing management by objectives was helpful because it means we do not feel we are being terrorized by imaginary numbers').

The role expectations that all group members have of the focal person are then written onto a large flip chart and thereby visualized. Controversial role expectations are debated among the participants with the help of the facilitator, the results are noted in writing as changes in the rules, and this record is signed by all the participants as an informal agreement.

Given the undeniable corporate reality of the difference between the supervisor's power and that of the employees, the presence of a facilitator or process consultant is usually unavoidable. When one party attempts to monopolize discussion, for example, the facilitator can moderate this well-known abuse of power by giving the other side an opportunity to speak. When misunderstandings arise, the facilitator can expose problems in communication by requesting one side to restate what the other has just said. He or she can support the verbally weaker party by offering germane interpretations of that person's stance. In mediating the communication between the partners in the negotiation, the facilitator's paramount and most difficult function is to achieve a measure of openness great enough to tackle recognized shortcomings, but not so great that it becomes offensive and thereby inimical to long-term cooperation. It is therefore justified to require that facilitators have long and varied experience with group dynamics and demonstrable social competence.

Besides assistance from a competent consultant, two additional prerequisites must be fulfilled if team development is to proceed successfully. First, it is essential that the altered rules of the game are formulated in an observable and verifiable way, for only rules recorded in this manner can be tested for their efficiency and learned from. This point must be stressed because 'established' operationalizations of rules of conduct are frequently circumvented to prevent change for political reasons. (A variety of management principles, some of which have even been dealt with in management seminars, owe their attractiveness precisely to the fact that they are ultimately unverifiable and, hence, arbitrary.) Action research and corresponding organizational learning would thereby be systematically blocked.

Second, the action research model is based on the assumption that it is necessary to tap insider knowledge in order to compensate for gaps in the knowledge of the scientists and other consultants participating in the process. But even insider knowledge does not preclude errors, and this is one more reason why team development must be understood as an iterative process. Systematic analyses show that team development leads to a viable structure for cooperation within the work group especially if the process is conducted frequently, that is, if the new rules of conduct are arrived at in a joint learning process (Gebert 1976).

Of course, conducting team development in the framework of the relationship approach is made easier if the group members have already acquired concepts and experiences of the person-centred approach, which make them aware of what can be discussed in the first place. Similarly, it is helpful if the team-development exercise can be preceded by a phase of survey feedback. Questionnaires for ascertaining management behaviour or the climate of the organization are abundant enough to permit one to survey the status quo of cooperation as seen by the participants before team development is undertaken. The results can then be summarized and presented to the group (for example, by comparing them with trends in other groups). This kind of feedback to the participants has several effects. One is that the group emerges with an agenda and therefore knows what needs to be talked about as part of team development. A second effect is that the need for action becomes graphic. Third, the fact that there is data feedback, which is never without risk for supervisors, signals that management endorses the change process. This enables the participants in the team to recognize that their current way of working together must, and can, change. That perception is seminal in generating the motivation for change. The spark provided by the survey–feedback strategy is empirically well documented (Gebert 1976; Bowers and Hausser 1977).

In practice, however, it often happens that comparatively detailed data collection is not followed up by feedback. The information is kept strictly secret in a vault rather than summarized and made available to the respondents. To the employees this mechanism indicates lack of support by senior management, and the motivation for change is nipped in the bud (Gebert 1976). That is precisely why it is imperative for management to decide *before* information is gathered how much it is willing to bear the consequences that could result from data feedback. Data collection without feedback can worsen the status quo.

With respect to today's underlying objective of intensifying the integration of all functional areas within the company, it is important in the relationship approach to improve the quality of cooperation not only within work groups but also between them, for example, between production and marketing. Such problems can usually not be treated satisfactorily through the structural approach alone; failings in cooperation between certain departments also reflect the social psychology of sustained mutual prejudice.

To treat these troublesome problems, many consultants recommend 'feedback meetings'. They are conducted in various ways. For example, the members of department A gather as a group to answer the questions 'how do we see the other group?' and 'what is our impression of how we are, presumably, seen by the other group?' In a separate meeting the members of department B do the same. Respondents can complete the task fairly efficiently by selecting what they judge to be the appropriate word from a range of semantic alternatives. The key step is then to exchange these categorizations so that each department is made aware of the other's view. Not until the third step does a feedback meeting take place in the strict sense. At that point the causes and effects of the prejudices are discussed in the presence of a facilitator, and an attempt is made to unfreeze self-perceptions and the perceptions of others by critically exploring the way they have been characterized semantically.

4 Outcomes of organization development

At various points above, reference has been made to effects of individual OD measures. In terms of quality control, 'meta-analyses', in which evaluations of up to 100 original studies have been compiled from secondary sources, have become available for assessment of at least OD's classic repertoire (Neuman *et al.* 1989; Beekun 1989). In turn, these meta-analyses can be summarized for the trends they discern.

One expected finding on 'soft' criteria for success, such as commitment and improvements in cooperation, communication and the climate of the organization, is that team development and the survey–feedback strategy (the relationship approach) have positive effects, as does the installation of semi-autonomous work groups. Improvements in soft criteria have also been observed to result from group-dynamic training, provided its main purpose is to illuminate work-related interpersonal processes and not to afford psychotherapeutically based self-experience.

The same is substantially true for 'hard' (performance-referenced) criteria of success if, for instance, the quantity and quality of work outcomes is defined at the group level. Under those circumstances the measures just cited in connection with the person-centred approach, the relationship approach and, most particularly, the structural approach tend to enhance performance.

Lest this summary spawn exaggerated optimism, the fact is that all the meta-analyses known to date show that the results of these measures vary widely across the original studies. The mean is positive, but this trend must not obscure the fact that the measures are inefficient in some cases and may even worsen the situation in others. There is no general answer to the crucial practical question of why the same measures have different effects under different conditions. The special conditions upon which success depends differ from measure to measure. The effectiveness of rather classic group-dynamic training declines with people who tend to be anxious. The installation of semi-autonomous work groups has proven fruitless when the employees are interested almost solely in earning money, that is, if they have an instrumental attitude toward work. The strategy of action research will have little chance of succeeding in highly centralized, bureaucratic organizations.

The paradox is that the individuals, groups and organizations most in need of these measures profit less from them than those with less need. For the most part, classic OD benefits comparatively mature companies – those that have already gone through a process of unfreezing, regardless of what prompted it.

On the other hand, these comments are not intended to convey too pessimistic a picture, either. If deterioration of the initial situation has been reported in empirical studies, it does not mean in any way that the OD concept itself is faulty. Failures are often due to mistakes in the application of the concept, not to flaws in it. If self-regulating semi-autonomous work groups are created but then given little additional work content and decision-making authority, it is no wonder that the results are disappointing, for the workers are disillusioned as well.

An analysis of OD efforts in the Federal Republic of Germany in the 1970s showed, for example, that the dominant strategy can be characterized as 'wash me, but don't get me wet' (Gebert 1976). A half-hearted procedure revealed itself, for example, in one-sided reliance on the structural approach, lack of consistency in combining its measures holistically with those of the person-centred approach, and the organization's renunciation of responsibility by manoeuvering external and internal consultants into the classic doctor–patient model. The OD concept should not be rashly blamed for blatant, if understandable, shortcomings in its application.

5 Present currents and trends

For some time now, the literature has distinguished between organization development and organization transformation (Porras and Silvers 1991). The principal thesis is that OD is a comparatively soft method that lends itself well to overcoming past types of problems. It is asserted, however, that the present is a time of radical upheaval that will require radical methods of change. They are subsumed in the characteristic term 're-engineering' and constitute what is understood today as organizational transformation (OT). In this rather strong-arm approach to change, drastic external intervention combined with coercive measures and the scientific standards of perfection regain an earlier attraction.

Three aspects of this current are notable. First, it is welcome in that it breaks with OD literature's customary predilection for grandiloquent, illusionary assumptions that humans are good, and does not share the distinctly normative argumentation of its objectives. The OT approach brings fresh air into the debate; it actually does fit the strategy to the situation, an idea that had long since become a truism in general management and organizational theory. Just as there is no one correct style of leadership or organizational structure, so there is obviously no one correct style of change. Indeed, a systematic effort to provide the empirical and theoretical underpinnings for a contingency approach to the management of change can only be welcomed.

Second, the timing of OT's entry into the debate makes one ponder. The approach was not born in the 1960s but in the 1980s. There are fairly good indications that the hardships of the open society, with its key characteristics of democracy and pluralism, were being experienced ever more keenly at exactly that time not only in Germany but in the USA as well. A general loss of orientation seemed to unfold, making the antithetical model, the closed society, more attractive again. The nostalgic look backwards, neo-conservativism, the spread of sects, and similar developments stood as eloquent testimony of the macro-social crisis of the open society. At exactly the same time in the 1980s, visionary and charismatic – transformational – leadership was propagated within companies to establish meaning and orientation where society seemed to have lost them.

Is the OT approach therefore essentially an anxious reflex to the headaches of the open society? Is this the deeper reason for the striking reception given to this concept in recent literature? The naive adoption of the parallel concept of visionary leadership in major companies in Germany and elsewhere arouses suspicion, even embarrassment, because neither the macrosocial background nor the specific way of linking this corporate practice back to society at large is being discussed, much less understood. Hence, there are mixed feelings about the OT approach. There is the danger that OT will not be used to complement OD as a contingency approach but to replace it in general. OT will then not only serve op-

erational efficiency under specific conditions but will ride toward tacit legitimation on the wave of macrosocial closure.

Third, the OT concept is associated with an affinity for coercion but also with
positive concepts such as courage, strength and power. These three aspects make
the concept particularly attractive emotionally. It is a grotesque fact that present
discussion, inspired primarily by certain theoretical models in the natural sciences, simultaneously revolves around the construct of 'autopoiesis', in which
the inherent dynamic of self-regulating social systems is elaborated in a way that
accords external regulatory interventions little chance. As a reflection of macro-
social currents of thought, this new branch of literature discusses the logic of the
limits on the controllability of social systems. It is the logic of the change agent's
impotence. Later resignation is already programmed into the power-based
approach of the OT formula.

Because international competition has intensified in recent years in terms of
both innovativeness and cost structures, organizations must promote
innovativeness by creating structures that open space for initiative within the
workforce. At the same time, efficiency requires closed, regimented, limiting
structures. Against this background, discussion in the latter half of the 1990s has
focused more and more on the question of whether, and how, these contradictions and dilemmas can be held in balance (Gebert and Boerner 1999).

In addition, ever keener competition and successful management of economic
crises increasingly require not only the activation of human capital but also the
fostering of mutual trust, that is, the building of social capital. Paradoxically,
trust as social capital is especially in demand at this time but is shaken particularly by organizational technology, strategies for turning troubled companies
around, and programmes for eliminating hierarchies (Sitkin *et al.* 1998). Such
contradictions and paradoxes will demand more attention in organization development than they have received thus far.

For all the plausibility of its core concepts and all the empirical evidence for
the effectiveness of many of its measures, the discipline of change management
still stands on shifting ground. Susceptibility to fashion is always a conspicuous
signal. The appeal of the discipline (its comparatively great practical relevance)
lies in its main origins – consulting practice. However, so do its weaknesses: its
continuing lack of comprehensive outlines for a theory of social change. Only
solid theoretical foundations will ensure the composure that will withstand the
wide swings of the pendulum, set in motion by whatever discussion happens to
be current.

Further reading

(References cited in the text marked *)

* Adler, P.S. and Borys, B. (1996) 'Two types of bureaucracy: enabling and coercive', *Administrative Science Quarterly*, 41: 61–89. (Discussion of new forms of work organization.)
* Argyris, C. and Schön, D.A. (1996) *Organizational Learning II: Theory, Methods, and Practice*, Reading, MA: Addison-Wesley. (Introduction to organizational learning.)

Baldwin, T.T. and Padgett, M.Y. (1993) 'Management development: a review and commentary', in C.L. Cooper and I.T. Robertson (eds), *International Review of Industrial and Organizational Psychology 1993*, vol. 8, New York: Wiley. (A compilation and evaluation of the literature on management development.)

* Beekun, R.J. (1989) 'Assessing the effectiveness of sociotechnical interventions', *Human Relations* 42: 877–97. (A meta-analysis of the empirical effects of sociotechnologically based structural measures.)

Bouchikhi, H. (1998) 'Living with and building on complexity: a constructivist perspective on organizations', *Organization* 5, S. 217–31. (Theoretial reflections to the structure of organization.)

* Bowers, D.G. and Hausser, D.L. (1977) 'Work group types and intervention effects in organizational development', *Administrative Science Quarterly* 2: 76–95. (Empirical evaluation of survey feedback, team development and other approaches.)

Eden, C. and Huxham, C. (1996) 'Action research for the study of organizations', in S.R. Clegg, C. Hardy and W.R. Nord (eds), *Handbook of Organization Studies* 1996, London: Sage Publications. (Discussion of theory, methods and results of action research.)

* Elden, M. and Chisholm, R.F. (1993) *Special Action Research Issue*, special issue of *Human Relations* 46 (2): 121–298. (Special issue that informs about the concept of action research and its further developments today in various fields of application.)

* Gebert, D. (1976) *Zur Erarbeitung und Einführung einer neuen Führungskonzeption* (Towards elaboration and introduction of a new management concept), Berlin: Duncker and Humblot. (Describes and evaluates factor-analytic strategies of organization development in the Federal Republic of Germany.)

Gebert, D. (2000) 'Zwischen Freiheit und Ordnung. Widersprüchlichkeit als Motor inkrementalen und transformationalen Wandels in Organisationen – eine Kritik des punctuated equilibrium-Modells', in G. Schreyögg and P. Conrad (eds), *Organisatorischer Wandel und Transformation, Managementforschung Bd. 10*, Frankfurt/ Main: Gabler, 1–32. (Discussion of the dynamics of orgnizational change.)

* Gebert, D. and Boerner, S. (1999) 'The open and the closed corporation as conflicting forms of organization', *The Journal of Applied Behavioral Science* 35 (3): 341–59. (Introduction to theory and practice of change management and paradoxical interventions.)

* Gebert, D. and Steinkamp, T. (1990) *Innovativität und Produktivität durch betriebliche Weiterbildung* (Innovativeness and productivity in companies through further training), Stuttgart: Poeschel. (Empirical description and evaluation of strategies for further training in small businesses in the manufacturing sector.)

Guzzo, R.J., Jetta, R.D. and Katzell, R.A. (1985) 'The effects of psychologically based intervention programs on worker productivity', *Personnel Psychology* 38: 275–91. (Meta-analysis of the empirical effects of the structural approach.)

Hill, R.L. (1990) *Building More Effective Work Teams through Role Negotiation*, London: Orion. (An introduction to the technique of role negotiation as part of team development.)

Marrow, A.J., Bowers, D.G. and Seashore, S.E. (1967) *Management by Participation*, New York: Harper & Row. (Detailed longitudinal description of an organization development programme in a production firm.)

* Neuman, G.A., Edwards, J.E. and Raju, N.S. (1989) 'Organizational development interventions', *Personnel Psychology* 42: 461–89. (A meta-analysis of the empirical effects of classic measures of the person-centred, structural and relationship approaches.)

Pasmore, W.A. and Woodman, R.W. (eds) (1991) *Research in Organizational Change and Development*, vol. 5, London: JAI Press Inc. (Discussion of organizational culture, transformational leadership, organizational learning and recent methods of organization development.)

Pasmore, W.A. and Woodman, R.W. (eds) (1992) *Research in Organizational Change and Development*, vol. 6, London: JAI Press Inc. (Discussion of organizational culture, transformational leadership, organizational learning and recent methods of organization development.)

* Porras, J.I. and Silvers, R.C. (1991) 'Organization development and transformation', *Annual Review of Psychology* 42: 51–78. (Scientific summary and comparison of the theory and methodology of organization development and organizational transformation.)

* Schein, E.H. (1985) *Organizational Culture and Leadership*, San Francisco, CA: Jossey Bass. (Discussion of how to explain, diagnose and possibly change organizational culture.)

Sitkin, S.B., Rousseau, D.M., Burt, R.S. and Camerer, C. (eds) (1998) 'Special topic forum on trust in and between organizations', special issue of *The Academy of Management Review* 23 (3): 393–620. (Discussion of important problems in respect to the nature, conditions and effects of trust.)

Stajkovic, A.D. and Luthans, F. (1997) 'A Meta-Analytic Review of the Effects of Organizational Behavior Modification on Task Performance: 1975–1995', *Academy of Management Journal* 40 (5): 1122–49. (Systematic and comprehensive evaluation of the Organizational Behavior Modification Programs.)

Organizational performance

Peter Clark

1 **Key interface**
2 **Structural contingency perspective**
3 **Nations: 'hidden' influence of context**
4 **Audits: costs, performativity and interpretation**
5 **Surveillance: the electronic gaze?**
6 **Capabilities and organizational learning**

Overview

Organizational performance is significantly shaped by the national context. Domestic firms experience endowed factors, use their domestic market as a major context for learning, and tend to become shaped to its characteristics. This process is referred to as 'entrainment' and its influence affects the ability of firms to cross the borders from their nation of origin. There are zones within which firms can choose to manoeuvre, and to some degree firms can reconstitute features which might be unfavourable in the longer run. The ability of firms to extend their zone of manoeuvre is influenced by how they learn from their performance (Penrose 1959). Consequently organizational performance occupies a key interface between organization behaviour, strategy and international management.

In organization behaviour the position of performance in the structural contingency theories (Galbraith 1977) and research studies was dealt with extensively in the seminal *Handbook of Organization Design* (Nystrom and Starbuck 1981), but more recently, *The Handbook of Organization Studies* (Clegg *et al.* 1996) treated performance only in terms of metaphor.

The structural contingency theory of performance requires extensive revision. There are two major areas of revision. First, to account for the hidden impacts on performance of the national context of the firm. The hidden aspects include the roles of factor endowments (for example, raw materials), the institutions and the market characteristics (for example, size, homogeneity and speed of saturation). These hidden aspects impact on the performance of firms by creating an envelope of opportunity. Firms have to be aware of the envelope, yet can enrol elements in the context which reshape the envelope. Second, it is important to be aware of the differences in approach between the practices of auditing performance within firms and the concepts and theories used in organization behaviour. Within firms of all kinds – public and private, commercial and custodial – there are extensive arrays of performance data covering very diverse aspects. The financial dimensions of the array are highly influential in constituting the recipe knowledge about strategic directions. The influence of accountancy on the everyday understanding of performance is significant, but should be closely scrutinized. The aim is to develop a theory which links organizational learning to the selective usage of performance measures, in particular, to explain the role of intangible assets. Organization behaviour is at the leading edge in developing a more substantial understanding of performance. Undertaking these developments is a major challenge.

I Key interface

There are six reasons why performance is a key interface. First, there has been a significant shift in the definition of best practice organization away from mass standardization into knowledge creation and innovation. The international success of firms from the USA, the Pacific Rim and Germany suggests that definitions of best practice should include features which are found in those nations. Second, political elites and corporate leaders are giving increasing attention to the use of quasi-market mechanisms. This stimulates the auditing of performance for the parent organization and its sub-units. The latter are placed in quasi-market situations. This reflects the shift from a producer-anchored capitalism to one in which consumerism and information are central. Third, information technology enables the collection of data about performance. Also computer modelling of perfect futures and the application of virtual displays reveals the complex ways in which various processes contribute to performance. Systems such as Enterprise Resource Planning (ERP) seem to promise an integrative view of action. Fourth, the professional associations connected to accounting and to information services gain high fees and rents from developing and diffusing measures of performance for a wide range of organizations. Fifth, firms wish to develop their own recipe knowledge about the dynamics of performance. Finally, external stakeholders monitor selected dimensions of performance. Ecological interests monitor the level of pollutants and the use of scarce resources.

2 Structural contingency perspective

Organization behaviour is influenced by the forms of law-like knowledge constituted in economics. Industrial economics concentrated upon the strategic relationship of the firm to its economic context (Rumelt 1974), especially in the choice of sector and in the positioning of the firm within the sector (Porter 1985). Economics treated the organization structure, key processes and the transactions with the context as a black box. Opening the black box began in the late 1950s (Penrose 1959; Burns and Stalker 1994). Organization behaviour was founded on the claim that its structural contingency theories of organization design provided a highly effective approach to achieving high performance (Nystrom and Starbuck 1981).

In the late 1950s there were two contending theories to explain the differences between successful and unsuccessful performance as assessed by survival and profitability. One theory emphasized universal solutions to be applied everywhere. The autonomous work group was widely promoted for every kind of

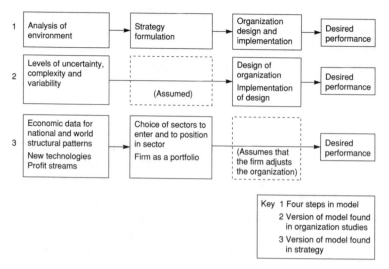

Figure 1 Neo-rational, linear model of performance

organization and social movement (for example, kibbutz). The alternative theory was derived from systems thinking. The theory of equifinality shows that high performance is achieved by different routes. Some firms might decentralize decisions while also increasing the degree to which procedures were formalized. Other firms could transfer control to professional specialists.

Organization behaviour established a third approach by selectively adapting systems thinking. The contingency and congruence fit perspective specified the conditions under which given structural solutions led to varying performance. Burns and Stalker (1994) connected the viability of any organization to its ability to match the degree of variety in its environment with internal mechanisms for encoding the variety and activating solutions from its repertoire. Their theory of performance is evolutionary. Firms that chose strategies and structures without congruence to their environment will underperform.

After the 1970s the connection between organization behaviour and strategy was established. This connection is still unfolding and is shown in stylized format in Figure 1. The linear, four-step and quasi-rational approach is an outside-in approach. From the organization behaviour perspective (see version 2) the environment is analysed to ascertain the degree of complexity and ambiguity and their stability or otherwise in the future. This information guides the design of organization structure. The design of an organization is also shaped by strategic decisions, because those will influence features such as the economies of scale and scope. In the strategy version (version 3) the environment is analysed by searching for those sectors which are expected to provide the most favourable sources of profits in the future. The pharmaceutical sector was desirable in the 1980s, but less so in the 1990s. Within any sector there are wide variations in profitability. The aim is to select a position. Key choices are whether to be a firm which provides low-cost commodities or provides items which are differentiated from one another. Currently the strategic approach is being challenged by organization studies.

Six problems arose with the assumptions underpinning Figure 1 and its usage of the structural contingency approach to performance. First, the approach assumes that firms can move from sector to sector without friction, in a manner similar to the economists' theory of frictionless adjustments of the markets. In practice most firms can only alter their finite capabilities rather slowly: television producers cannot easily move into tourism. Second, the approach assumes that knowledge about the best positioning to achieve high performance will be acceptable to the political groupings. Yet, firms are milieus of political bargaining and are set in contexts where external stakeholders may exert influence. For example, the credibility of a firm to its financial community is crucial. Third, performance is treated as end-variable with only small feedback inputs into the state of the firm. Past performance is and should be a source of scrutiny and interpretation. Past performance is the foundation for developing new strategies. Fourth, the four sequential steps are too rigid and do not allow for iterations, abortions and variations in the decision process. Fifth, the treatment of the external context is too narrow (Nohria and Eccles 1992) and too close to the immediate context of the firm (see Figure 2). There is a neglect of impact of societal forces (Powell and DiMaggio 1991; Scott 1995) and of the hidden influence of the national context (Maurice and Sorge 2000). Sixth, the measurement of performance in research studies intended to support the structural contingency perspective is mainly based upon financial data (for example, profits) measured as a cross-sectional slice describing the past. Reviews typically conclude that research studies relied upon inconsistent operational definitions and simplistic measurements (Pennings 1975).

The limits of the structural contingency theory of performance are handled in two major revisions. First, to include the national context. Second, to develop a processual, learning theory of performance.

3 Nations: 'hidden' influence of context

Until recently the explanation of the performance of firms largely excluded features within the national context. However, contemporary theories claim that the national context provides an envelope of opportunities and constraints (Clark 2000). The context contains zones of manoeuvre. So, Clark (2000) contends that Henry Ford could not have achieved such large sales for the Ford T between 1908 and 1926 if he had started from the UK or France. Also, it is unlikely that the performance of the Italian firm Benetton could have been achieved after 1965 if they had started up in the UK because of the existing structure of the market for clothing. To survive and grow all firms require an envelope of opportunity within which there are the necessary resources and markets for the outputs. These envelopes tend to influence clusters of firms at the level of the sector. There are two theories which illustrate the shaping role of contextual factors in the nation of origin: the theory of societal institutions and elective affinities (Sorge and

	Past definitions	Current definitions
1 Focus	(a) End variable (b) With narrow focus upon tangible financial features (c) Objective, opaque, measurable, single form and relatively stable (d) With focus upon tangible assets	(a) Output and input variable (b) Focus is multiple, layered and hybrid with extended attention to adaptive capabilities, symbolic reputation and political nesting (c) Socially constructed, potentially transparent, many alternatives, highly interpreted, potentially contingent and subject to revision (d) Treatment of intangible assets. The progressive attention to the firm's ownership of propositional learning and licensed ownership (for example, patents)
2 Scope	(a) Inside the firm (b) The firm taken as an aggregate	(a) Includes overall value chain and related networks. How the context can shape the propositional learning. Examining the position within a network. Competition between contexts. Looking for changes in performance to arise from changes made earlier and later in the value chain which runs from suppliers to the final consumer (b) The calculation of scores for every sub-unit within a virtual trading model
3 Timeframe	(a) Here and now, yesterday and last year	(a) Future survival five years ahead and consequences of trends
4 Modelling performance	(a) Linear, end variable (see Figure 1) (b) Neo-rational, knowledgeable about cause and effect relationships	(a) Interactive. A starting point for future planning (b) Uncertain, obscure connections subject to conjuncture, contingency, discontinuity and chance. Economics of ignorance
5 Political nesting	Taken for granted and therefore not part of calculus	Explicit consideration, considering the possibilities of lobbying to have issues put off the political agenda or put on the agenda
6 Symbolic–reputational	Regarded as an intangible asset too difficult to calculate	Seriously examined and weighted with precise calculations. Increasingly recognized as an essential facet of performance
7 Propositional learning	Complete neglect	Serious concern with the capacity of firms to learn and articulate propositions and a recipe knowledge about the ways to high performance
8 Sustainable performance	Slight interest	Concern with continuous innovation and of exnovation as well as adaptation and experimentation

Figure 2 Performance: past and current definitions

Maurice 2000); the six-factor theory of competitive advantage (Porter 1990, 1998).

International comparisons reveal that some sectors do better in certain societies. For example, the German automobile sector has performed better than the British automobile sector. The question is: how important are the institutions within a nation through which knowledge is brought into play within firms? The theory of elective affinities (Clark 2000) seeks to demonstrate that the German success and the British failure is explained by the interaction between the institutions of knowledge management and the strategic directions chosen by a nation's firms (Maurice and Sorge 2000). In the German case there is a positive elective affinity because the management of knowledge creates highly competent mechanical engineers, a connected hierarchy of skill within the firm and the strategic choice of producing cars that are distinctive rather than produced as commodities. The theory of elective affinities redefines the role of the structural contingency theory. The theory of elective affinities is not deterministic in the relationship between institutions and firms, because institutions change slowly. Corporate leaders often choose strategic directions which have a poor affinity with the societal institutions.

The theory of the competitive advantage of nations (Porter 1990, 1998) locates the societal institutions of knowledge management (just discussed) in the context of six interacting factors: the endowed factors, the degree of rivalry between firms, the role of government, chance, the role of support sectors (for example, design, marketing) and the influence of the national market. The role of the endowed factors deserves cautious attention because their absence or presence exerts an influence. Endowed factors include: raw materials, soil, rivers and climatic features. For example, the USA has a historical abundance of endowed factors for agriculture, and there were many kinds of hard and soft wood which could be used for many purposes: making fires, building houses, fences, making equipment. One of the early developments in the USA was the fast running saw-milling machines which wasted vast quantities of wood and substituted technology inputs for labour inputs. These early developments of technology became cumulative and defined a trajectory or path of development. Equally important is the influence of the national market (Clark 1987, 2000). National tastes differ significantly. For example, the Japanese prefer household consumer goods which are small, multi-functional, portable, possess fine surfaces, are packaged delightfully and are accompanied by extensive information (Porter 1990). The Japanese market for consumer goods tends to be homogeneous, very conscious about newness and quickly saturated. To survive, the Japanese firms have created many variants of products (for example, Sony Walkman) through short design cycles.

4 Audits: costs, performativity and interpretation

Inside firms there has been a very significant transformation and expansion in the ways in which performance is audited, assessed, explained and utilized as the basis of action (Power 1994). It is essential to compare the situation now with that which existed when organization behaviour emerged as a discipline.

Figure 2 shows that in the 1960s the performance of firms was primarily assessed in terms of simple financial criteria: profits, rate of return on investment, the tangible assets (for example, buildings, equipment), the total sales value, the market value of the firm and the number of employees. The assessment criteria are essentially financial except for the number of employees. The performance of the firm was normally assessed by a detailed examination of the documents and records. The timeframe of the assessment was a cross-sectional slice, narrowly focused upon profits and with a short timeframe that was heavily orientated towards the recent past (Johnson and Kaplan 1987). There was little statistical analysis and only the rare use of linear models applied in very slow running computer programs. The share price was the one item which assessed future potential. This narrow focus of the criteria, the timeframe and the exclusive preoccupation with events within the firm was often regarded as an objective assessment which was largely beyond contention. It was assumed that explaining performance to the various interested parties – later known as stakeholders – was a matter of detached, rational interpretation. Explanations of performance were quite brief.

Today, the assessment of performance is extensive, intensive and the subject of debate and struggles over the interpretation and the implications. Every type of organization and its sub-units undertake an intensive and extensive collection of performance data about themselves. The data are stored electronically and statistically analysed at frequent intervals. Retail outlets enter data into electronic point of sale equipment by category of sale and that data will be used by regional centres and by corporate headquarters for immediate operating decisions and as an input to strategic planning. Public sector organizations such as libraries and schools are equally affected. Performance measures are applied at all levels in the organization. Small sub-units are expected to provide detailed statements. Units are placed in league tables visible to those inside and outside. The performance of units influences their retention in the portfolio of the organization.

Organizations collect an increasing amount of data about the other organizations among which they are clustered (see Nohria and Eccles 1992). Firms routinely obtain data on the performance of their suppliers. The data cover twenty or thirty major aspects plus hundreds of minor aspects. Suppliers are scored for actual performance against a scale that is benchmarked against global standards. Scoring includes attitudes to quality, speed of response, customer service and continuously reducing costs. Electronic data interchanges imposed by major firms provide the foundation for performance ratios which are not known to the supplier.

The arrays of data are very extensive. The result is hybrid collections of data about performance, but their interpretation is complex. Statistical analysis of a descriptive type is extended to forms of factor analyses and there is increasing use of computer models based on interactive equations. One aim is to order the hybrid data into new clusters. There are sophisticated attempts to audit intangible assets (for example, reputation, the appropriability and durability of corporate knowledge). For example, the value of reputation includes the public image of the firm – how it cares for its environment – and the extent to which its logo is widely known. There is increasing attention to the symbolic performance of the firm, to the semiotics of the firm's position in the economy of symbols.

It is relevant to highlight the extent to which the social construction of performance is becoming transparent. The dominant players in constructing definitions of performance have been and are still the professions of accountability. Accountants are sometimes described as the paper prophets (Tinker 1987). The construction of a heuristic knowledge about performance by accountants is directed towards enabling features of capitalism such as system integration, property ownership and the return on investment. There is an extensive array of software packages that claim to promote system integration (e.g. Enterprise Resource Planning). Practising accountants often imply that their knowledge is detached and objective. However, social constructionist perspectives observe that accountability is shaped by competing interests. So, there is extensive shaping of the data in terms of certain interests. Radical perspectives emphasize the imprecision of performance measurement and in the labour process perspective, alternative criteria are proposed. Even orthodox perspectives increasingly recognize the massaging of data, sufficiently so for the 'massaging of performance' statistics to be a variable in research studies.

5 Surveillance: the electronic gaze?

The socially defined performance of individuals and units within the organization is highly visible by their representation in both hard (e.g. production monitoring systems) and soft (e.g. auditing tools) technological systems, potentially subjecting them to the gaze of surveillance. Is there a new kind of electronic surveillance in organizations? This issue has aroused considerable interest (see *Journal of Accounting, Organizations and Society*).

The concept of the gaze arises from Foucault's (1977) observation of changes in the dominant mode of social governance since the 1700s. There has been a shift from overt displays of the state's control over physical violence (e.g. torture, execution), to more private forms of incarceration. These are based on the dividing and surveillance of inmates and are taken to represent a long-term trend in governance which rests upon the power of technologies (both hard and soft) to control at a distance. Central to the concept of surveillance is the concept that it disciplines those subject to it. Modern organizations are part of that long-term trend and also central sites for innovation as in human resource technologies for control. Information technology enables the performance of individuals and units to be monitored at a distance because of the plentiful information that is generated about performance and the underlying processes. This information is highly mobile and often easy to transfer. Information technology is a disciplinary mechanism forming a web through which the intense surveillance of actors could potentially occur.

Translating the concept of gaze into the modern era draws attention to the ways in which performance is embedded in software systems. The new information technology is a web of power which is a potential disciplinary mechanism. There are performance data on minute aspects of organizational life (for example, the key strokes of the secretary, e-mails, conversations). The measurements of performance are finely graded and categorized. The rationality of efficiency and productivity is utilitarian, self-contained and non-theoretical. Every unit is the object of information about performance. The use of abstract rules of comparisons (for example, costs of time) means that the performances of different units are immediately comparable. Scores can be distributed and normalized. The supermarket manager can show the checkout operators the computer printout on which their speed of shifting merchandise is compared with all the others who work there in the same week. At the level of the firm, there are international comparisons based on benchmarking each major dimension against the best in the world.

This electronic process has analogies with the concepts of the panoptic ('overseeing all') control of performance, incorporated within which is Foucault's (1977) concept of the disciplinary gaze. Panoptic control is less visible than direct supervision because it operates through hard and soft technologies, techniques and tools, but is more intense, continuous, lighter, more rapid, more economical in time and is hierarchical from the lower-level units up to higher level units. Today the employee is subject to the gaze of the electronic recording of performance and this creates an awareness about performance. The panoptic potentials of performance systems are attractive to certain management styles. An authoritarian style will find that the data present numerous opportunities. Within organizations there is the potential for the totalizing, panoptic surveillance of all actors, but the extent to which this is realized is largely contingent upon management style and organizational context. Modes of response vary between situations. One important feature is that superiors are judged on the performance of their subordinates.

The gaze is known to those who are observed and this feature leads to the development of counter-strategies at all levels of the organization. There is a dialectic of control, that is to say, even powerful strata can be presented with contextual interpretations which create uncertainties about performance data among those most able to define the scope of the gaze and who have access to its findings.

6 Capabilities and organizational learning

The performance of firms has been shown to vary over short periods and over longer periods, such as the decade. Even major firms face exit. These variations in performance undermine claims about best practice based solely on the structural contingency theory. The search for better concepts, theories and guidelines is stimulated by the availability of extensive measurement and more interactive forms of computer modelling. Information technologies inscribe vast amounts of data giving them durability and visibility. The data provide managements who invest in categories with the opportunity to develop a managerial knowledge which potentially relates variations in performance to the dynamics of the context. Those firms which succeed will be at an advantage.

Theories of performance and organizational learning have and are being developed. They are more eclectic than theories supplied by a single discipline or function. Performance is analysed as a multi-dimensional reconstruction of cause–effect relationships in the past and as a foundation for developing several scenarios of how finite capacities will match future situations. Constructing a theory of performance and organizational learning renews interest in the original contributions of the economist Penrose (1959), especially her emphasis upon how the growth of managerial knowledge is the foundation of corporate success. The problem is how to use performance data as a foundation for growing conjectural, propositional learning and the distinctive capabilities of the firm.

When examined from the perspective of a single management function – especially the finance function – the arrays of performance data are viewed as hybrids. First, the varied character of the data does not pose a problem for interpreting performance scores in relation to inter-firm and international comparisons known as benchmarking. The use of benchmarking requires increasing attention to the hidden international influences discussed in the previous section. Learning theories of performance need to recognize the extent to which the national and regional context enables or hinders the performance of an organization. Second, the role of the hybrids of performance data in guiding future performance is much more serious and difficult to interpret within existing analytic frameworks in organization studies. The hybrid character of performance data challenges their usage as the basis for developing better firm-based heuristic knowledge.

Consequently, there is a strong trend for the detailed analysis of the relationship between activities and future performance to take a qualitatively new direction, because of its potential for reducing major areas of cost in society, especially in those expensive activities employing professionals (for example, education, welfare, health, custodial and public services). In all nations, firms have been exploring the relationship between performance scores and activities. Activity-based costing is one collection of practices for this task. The principles of activity-based analysis of performance are increasingly being used in all types of setting, including the running of orchestras and the operation of the custodial services. The availability of performance data about existing practices is being compared to theoretical alternatives modelled on the computer. For example, in education the development of multimedia forms of the delivery of knowledge is being compared with existing practices.

In order to develop a core framework around which developments can be arranged, it is necessary to emphasize and clarify the role of the time dimension and to make greater use of the concept of capabilities. Performance measures are loaded with estimates of time. Anglo-American interpretations of performance are mistakenly criticized for their tendency to short-termism. Unpacking the time and learning dynamics of performance is central and underway (Gell 1992; Clark and Staunton 1993). Time as a resource and timing as a strategic capability are central to successful performance. The injunction to 'compete on time' exemplifies the development of the new best practice. Leading firms routinely audit their capability at just-in-time (reducing inventory and inducing attention to all disruptions) and time-to-market (the pace at which the firm can deliver new services and new products to customers). Organization studies is developing methods of auditing the responsiveness of the firm towards the future.

The concepts of capabilities and business processes are of increasing interest (Grant 1998). Performance is an interactive and driving factor in the new thinking. The previous attention to the vertical dimensions of hierarchy and structure in the structural contingency theory are being replaced by the analysis of horizontal processes through the concept of corporate capabilities. One major development is the analysis of corporate knowledge, especially its durability and its ease of appropriability by other firms. The theory of business process re-engineering does provide a wide and useful starting point for thinking about performance, but makes many untested assumptions about organization behaviour.

Performance is viewed more and more as a processual state of becoming in the future (Clark 2000). The processual dynamics contain two different cycles which should be connected. One cycle is the shorter term of the operating cycle for the factory and office. The other is the medium-term cycle of innovation and renewal in the design of products and services. Performance data should be part of a theory of the unfolding of the cycles in the future. Measures applied to the operating cycle should examine the ratio of productive time to total time. Retrospective scrutiny reveals that there is much non-productive time. The problem has been recognized. Computer-based analytic techniques can model the recurring flows of stocks, finance, labour and other dimensions in order to locate the key dependencies and bottlenecks. The serial character of the operating cycle is a formative context for organizational learning. Computer-based modelling is used to teach members of the firm how they currently perform and to provide a reflexive understanding as the basis for developing superior alternatives. The longer cycles pose many challenges to understanding performance, especially in sectors such as pharmaceuticals and genetic engineering, where long-term cycles are fifteen to twenty years. Interpreting performance data can be deceptive because of the high fixed costs at the start of the cycle for a new product (for example, drugs). There are increasing attempts to calibrate performance at an early stage in the long-term cycle of activities, in order to anticipate future consequences. There are many sources of uncertainty and ignorance.

A key problem in developing a learning framework for performance is how the centre gains and interprets relevant performance data from remote, distant units, within both the firm and its network of customers and suppliers (Nohria and Eccles 1992). How does the centre add value and enable the understanding of the costs of alternative opportunities? The centre has to articulate visible signs and records which meaningfully represent key features of distant locations, as defined by the categories in the firm's stock of knowledge (codified and tacit), and connect these inscriptions to the strategic choices. The relevance of the inscriptions is increased when they are strong, mobile, readily understood and can be manipulated. Their role is to represent distant locations. Inscriptions in the form of numbers (for example, budget evaluations), maps, blueprints and schematics fit the requirements of the centre. Inscriptions permit the centre to be informed and analytical and to learn from performance. Reflexive learning at several levels is possible. In this way performance can be transformed into a key element in testing the firm's stock of knowledge about high performance. There is clear evidence to show that the role of the centre in constituting propositional learning requires considerable development.

Figure 3 sets out the problem. The firm is shown as having three major clusters of processes: propositional learning, capabilities and strategic directions. First, propositional learning refers to the various knowledges which members of the firm have institutionalized from past experiences as ways of recognizing how events in the external environment create opportunities and also dangers to the survival of the firm. Propositional learning provides the categories through which the environment is enacted. Firms differ in their propositional language and hence in their definition of what the present means and of what may happen in the future. The propositions will be part of the everyday language of organizational members. We should assume that those close to the apex of the firm use a language which has very significant consequences for the direction of the firm. Their capacity to develop that language is central to high performance. The propositions about the causes of high and low performance are open to a double interpretation. There is the issue of their application to the future environment. Also, there is the political issue of how the interpretation of the future is related to the capabilities of the firm.

Second, the capabilities of the firm can be viewed as a repertoire only part of which is actively in use at any one period of time. Other parts will be dormant, yet ready to be activated. For example, military organizations are expected to be able to activate different capabilities when in a zone of conflict, compared to being outside the conflict zones for periods of training and in peacetime. The performance of these capabilities requires the development of methods of monitoring, especially when capabilities are used infrequently. Finally, the propositional learning and the capabilities will influence the strategic choices of direction by the organization.

A learning framework (as in Figure 3) connects the whole temporal frame of the firm to how its inputs and throughputs interact in the marketplace. The firm's stock of propositional knowledge has to develop new concepts of temporality including the problem of how performance is interpreted and activated by those actors which undertake strategic time reckoning (Clark 1985). Failure to grow the stock of propositional knowledge will lead to exit (Clark 2000).

Much of the environment is defined after the event and this is shown in Figure 3. Firms will vary widely in their handling of this feedback linkage. As shown in Figure 3, the future environment can be different to previous experiences. These

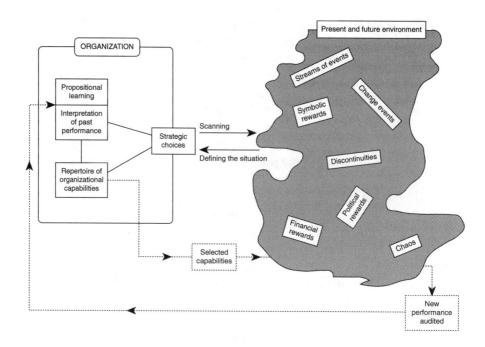

Figure 3 Performance and propositional learning

differences challenge the viability of the existing propositions linking performance to actions. For example, it is likely that successful learning contains a significant element of recognizing that high performance contains elements which are unintended and emergent from interaction with the context. Recognizing and institutionalizing these emergent potentials in a new propositional language typically confronts the political coalitions and truces in the organization. The outcome may be internal conflicts. Under those conditions the population ecology theories postulate that firms will experience great difficulty in altering their propositional learning and in reconfiguring their repertoire of capabilities. However, organization theory, while explicitly recognizing the problem, seeks to identify the requirements for adaptation and provide a body of understanding by which the capabilities of firms to achieve different kinds of performance can be undertaken. Zuboff (1988) demonstrates that this learning requires much more than the simple automation of past sources of performance information through information technology. So, although performance data can be the basis for a deeper understanding of the processes by which success can be separated from failure, firms face the real danger that they will merely use the potentials of information technology to automate past data. The growing availability of data could lead to more effective theories of performance as process. So, the development of a learning theory of performance is *the* challenge in organization behaviour.

Further reading

(References cited in the text marked *)

* Burns, T. and Stalker, G.M. (1994) *Management of Innovation*, London: Tavistock Publications. (Key source for the structural contingency approach to performance, originally published in 1961. See revised preface for problem of process.)
* Clark, P.A. (1985) 'A review of the theories of time and structure for organizational sociology', in S.M. Bachrach and S. Mitchell (eds), *Research in the Sociology of Organizations*, vol. 4, New York: JAI Press Inc. (Examines the treatment of time as a resource, temporal inventories and strategic time-reckoning.)
* Clark, P.A. (2000) *Organisations in Action. Competition Between Contexts*, London: Routledge. (Connects the temporal and spatial dynamics of performance and national contexts.)
* Clark, P.A. and Staunton, N. (1993) *Innovation in Technology and Organization*, London: Routledge. (Examines the role of organizational knowledge and capabilities in strategic innovation and sustainable performance.)
* Foucault, M. (1977) *Discipline and Punish: The Birth of the Prison*, Harmondsworth: Penguin. (Explains panoptic control over performance. Applied to the formalized templates and best practice in French society.)
* Galbraith, J.R. (1977) *Organizational Design*, Reading, MA: Addison-Wesley. (Information costs theory of designing to incorporate high performance.)
* Gell, A. (1992) *The Anthropology of Time: Cultural Constructions of Temporal Maps and Images*, Oxford: Berg. (An extensive survey of cultural constructions of the time dynamics of performance.)
* Grant, R.M. (1998) *Contemporary Strategy Analysis*, Oxford: Blackwell. (Intangible assets, corporate routines and their relation to strategic performance.)
* Johnson, H.T. and Kaplan, R.S. (1987) *Relevance Lost: The Rise and Fall of Management Accounting*, Cambridge, MA: Harvard Business School Press. (Analysis of the rise, fall and potential rise again in the use of analytic procedures of relating cost performance to activities.)
  Journal of Accounting, Organizations and Society, Oxford: Pergamon Press. (Useful starting point for specific articles and citations on accountability, accounting, performance and critical perspectives.)
* Maurice, M. and Sorge, A. (2000) *Embedding Organizations*. Amsterdam: John Benjamin.
* Nohria, N. and Eccles, R.G. (1992) *Networks and Organizations: Structure, Form and Action*, Cambridge, MA: Harvard Business School Press. (Extensive examination of the role of network ties in performance.)
* Nonaka, I. and Takeuchi, H. (1995) *The Knowledge Creating Company*, New York: Oxford University Press. (A discussion of the differences between Japanese and Western firms in their creation of knowledge of performance situated in time.)
* Nystrom, P.C. and Starbuck, W.H. (1981) *Handbook of Organizational Design*, 2 vols, Oxford: Oxford University Press. (An extensive and revealing review which introduces the role of organizational learning. Contains an excellent index.)
* Pennings, J.M. (1975) 'The relevance of the structural-contingency model for organizational effectiveness', *Administrative Science Quarterly* 20(3): 393–410. (Incisive critique of the structural contingency theory of performance, its conceptual consistency and research findings.)
* Penrose, E. (1959) *The Theory of the Growth of the Firm*, Oxford: Blackwell. (Limits in neo-classical economic theories and implicit usage of recipe knowledge.)
* Porter, M.E. (1985) *Competitive Advantage: Creating and Sustaining Superior Performance*, New York: The Free Press. (Seminal statement of the strategic economic theory of performance.)

* Porter, M.E. (1990) *The Competitive Advantage of Nations*, London: Macmillan. (The hidden influence of six national determinants on long-term corporate performance. Clear, simple, open to revision.)

* Porter, M.E. (1998) *On Competition*, Cambridge, MA: Harvard Business Review.

* Powell, W.W. and DiMaggio, P.J. (1991) *The New Institutional Analysis in Organizational Analysis*, Chicago, IL: Chicago University Press. (Excellent contributions treating the symbolic dimensions of performance.)

* Power, M. (1994) *The Audit Explosion*, London: Demos. (The importance of separating auditing from the explanation of performance.)

* Rumelt, R.P. (1974) *Strategy, Structure and Economic Performance*, Cambridge, MA: Harvard Business School Press. (The relationship between economic performance and the extent to which the portfolio of the firm is related to core capabilities.)

* Scott, W.R. (1995) *Institutions and Organization*, London: Sage.

* Tinker, A. (1987) *Paper Prophets*, New York: Praeger. (Radical, critical analysis of accounting approaches to performance.)

* Zuboff, S. (1988) *In the Age of the Smart Machine: The Future of Work and Power*, New York: Basic Books. (Distinguishes firms using information technology to automate existing practices, from redesigning practices to inform decisions.)